NOV   2011

THE SPORT OF KINGS AND THE KINGS OF CRIME

Sports and Entertainment
Steven A. Riess, *Series Editor*

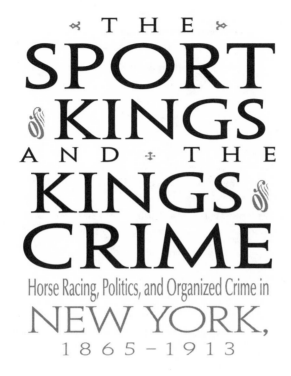

THE SPORT of KINGS AND THE KINGS of CRIME

Horse Racing, Politics, and Organized Crime in
NEW YORK,
1865–1913

STEVEN A. RIESS

SYRACUSE UNIVERSITY PRESS

SKOKIE PUBLIC LIBRARY

For a listing of books published and distributed by Syracuse University Press,
visit our Web site at SyracuseUniversityPress.syr.edu.

ISBN: 978-0-8156-0985-8

Library of Congress Cataloging-in-Publication Data
Riess, Steven A.
The sport of kings and the kings of crime : horse racing, politics, and organized crime
in New York, 1865–1913 / Steven A. Riess. — 1st ed.
p. cm. — (Sports and entertainment)
Includes bibliographical references and index.
ISBN 978-0-8156-0985-8 (cloth : alk. paper)
1. Horse racing—New York (State)—New York—History.   2. Horse racing—Political aspects—
New York (State)—New York—History.   3. Organized crime—New York (State)—New York—
History.   4. Political corruption—New York (State)—New York—History.   I. Title.
SF335.U6N747 2011
798.4009747—dc23   2011011114

Manufactured in the United States of America

*In honor of my uncle Theodor Finder (1920–2000),
Holocaust survivor and refugee, war hero (MIA,
POW), husband, father, businessman, mensch.*

STEVEN A. RIESS is the Bernard Brommel Distinguished Research Professor in the Department of History, Northeastern Illinois University, where he has taught for thirty-five years. He is the author of several books on the history of sport, including *Touching Base: Professional Baseball and American Culture in the Progressive Era* (1980, 1999) and *City Games: The Evolution of American Urban Society and the Rise of Sports* (1989), and editor of several volumes, including *Sports in America from Colonial Times to the Twenty-First Century: An Encyclopedia* (2011), *The Encyclopedia of Major League Baseball Teams* (2006), and *Sports and the American Jew* (Syracuse University Press, 1999). Riess has received several grants for research and teaching from the National Endowment for the Humanities.

Contents

Illustrations and Tables

Photographs and Drawings

Map

Tables

ix

Preface

I t has only been since the late 1970s that historians finally recognized the importance of sport in American history, and they subsequently produced excellent books on the subject.[1] However, they barely recognized the prominent role of horse racing in the nation's history. Thoroughbred racing was the first major sport in early America and, following the Civil War, was one of the three great American spectator sports, along with baseball and boxing, long before people cared one whit about professional basketball, hockey, or football. Thoroughbred racing remained very popular for much of the twentieth century and was the best-attended spectator sport in the United States in the 1950s and 1960s. Great stallions like Nashua, Swaps, Bold Ruler, and Secretariat captured the public's eye. However, racing thereafter declined, struggling to compete with public interest in other sports, notably professional football, automobile racing, Major League Baseball, and college and professional basketball, and lost its monopoly over legalized sports betting. Racing still gets occasional attention, especially each spring during the Triple Crown racing season, and particularly the Kentucky Derby. There was a brief flurry of renewed fascination with the turf following the publication of Laura Hillenbrand's *Seabiscuit* (2001) and the production of the outstanding motion picture *Seabiscuit* (2003) and compelling documentaries.[2]

Horse racing in North America dates back to the colonial era, when it was one of the first organized sports, completely under the control of the upper class. The sport struggled in the North after the Revolution because of its aristocratic associations, which made it inappropriate in a democratic Republic, and its connections to gambling, which made it a vile amusement in the eyes of evangelical moral reformers. By the 1840s, pressure from northern reformers resulted in widespread criminalization of gambling, although in the South it remained a popular pastime, enjoyed by slaveholders and other lovers of horseflesh and friendly wagering.[3]

Racing in post–Civil War America underwent an amazing renaissance. The rebirth of the sport relied in part on the status conferred to men who bred and raced horses and operated jockey clubs and racetracks, but its popularity mainly came from the opportunities it provided for gambling, legally at racecourses and illegally off the tracks. A sport that had been virtually moribund in the North became an expansive national industry, based at first in New York State and New Jersey, with major racing centers in New York City and the resort towns of Saratoga, New York, and Long Branch, New Jersey. The New York metropolitan area continued to dominate the sport in the 1880s, but several other new racing centers emerged, including Cincinnati, St. Louis, Chicago, Louisville, New Orleans, and San Francisco. By 1897, there were 314 American tracks and another 43 in Canada.[4]

Sports gambling flourished in the late nineteenth century, including betting on professional and amateur sporting events, which led to several states passing laws to regulate or eliminate wagering. New York, where gambling at the tracks was legitimized, remained the national capital of the turf with the most outstanding racecourses, the largest purses, and the finest thoroughbreds, as well as the creation in 1894 of The Jockey Club (TJC), an elite association created to set national standards for the sport and of the State Racing Commission (SRC) one year later, to supervise turf sports in New York.[5]

Thoroughbred racing was the rare sport that was trendy with both the social and economic elites and the lower classes. The elites constituted the leadership and membership of the prestigious jockey clubs that were the backbone of the sport. The elite tracks intended to advance the breed, enhance the social status of members, and promote sociability among the upper crust. They made some money for stockholders but mainly reinvested profits back into the tracks. Upper-class racing fans enjoyed the excitement of the race, the wagering that accompanied the contests, the ambience of the extravagant clubhouses, and the status that went along with racing horses, belonging to restricted social clubs, and making big bets. They were conspicuous consumers who were accustomed to high-risk business deals, like Jay Gould and Jim Fisk's effort to corner the gold market in 1869.

Racing's popularity led to the creation of proprietary tracks by entrepreneurs of modest social backgrounds. These tracks were commercial ventures that tried to make money by selling admission tickets, leasing concession privileges, and getting fees from legitimized bookmakers who took bets on the track and telegraph services that reported race results to interested parties off the track that included newspapers, poolrooms (betting parlors), and handbooks (off-track bookmakers). The profit-oriented tracks relied heavily on the patronage of the masses rather than upper-class racing fans. Those fans also enjoyed the excitement of the race, enhanced by the thrill of the wager. These bettors sought a quick score by using their expertise as racing handicappers (or clients at bucket shops) to make an astute speculation, just as wealthy investors did in the stock market.[6] Gambling in America was a product of a competitive and materialistic society that respected risk takers ranging from colonial Virginia planters to industrial capitalists like Cyrus McCormick and John D. Rockefeller and merchants like Marshall Field.

This book focuses on New York, the largest US city, which was the national capital of commerce, finance, communication, and culture. It was the center of American racing in the late nineteenth and early twentieth centuries with the most important racecourses and most prestigious races and the preeminent source of racing information through Western Union, sporting weeklies, and the daily press. New York was also the unsurpassed center of legal and illegal gambling on horse races.

This book examines three major topics: first, how and why New York became the national center of horse racing after the Civil War; second, how and why it maintained that status until the state government briefly halted horse racing in the early 1910s; and third, how and why legal and illegal gambling flourished in that era.

Horse racing thrived because it was a high-status sport that attracted the interest of the rich and well-born, as well as men of new money, who relished the thrill of the race and the wagers placed on its outcome. Thoroughbred racing flourished because spectators enjoyed the pageantry, the exciting races, and most of all the gambling, without which there would have been no racing. The betting made the racing more exhilarating and interesting to watch and then discuss with fellow spectators. Betting was a means for spectators (primarily men) as well as off-track bettors to demonstrate confidence in their expertise. Gambling was, in general, a popular activity among the male bachelor subculture, along with drinking, fighting, and chasing women. The men who participated in the "sporting life" personified manliness. Many of the men who bet on the races were undoubtedly single men who could afford to splurge a few dollars on a horse. In New York in 1890, 51.8 percent of men ages twenty-five to twenty-nine were single, more than in Chicago, Cincinnati, and New Orleans but less than in San Francisco and Denver.[7]

What kept the sport operating, despite considerable public opposition on moral grounds to the gambling, fixed races, and abuse of animals, was that the turf provided a key nexus between machine politicians and organized crime. The post–Civil War revival of racing in New York started with rich men who owned and bred thoroughbreds and established prestigious jockey clubs like the American Jockey Club (AJC) to certify and enhance their social status and, ostensibly, to improve the breed of horses. The success of elite tracks like Jerome Park in New York, Sheepshead Bay in Brooklyn, and Monmouth Park in Long Branch encouraged entrepreneurs to establish proprietary racetracks, not for prestige or concern for the breeding stock but to make money.

Virtually all track operators, be they elite sportsmen or money-hungry businessmen, were politically well connected, which enabled them to protect their
investments, just like many other businessmen at the turn of the century. Racing's
success required the political influence of Democratic elite jockey club leaders like
August Belmont, as well as proprietary track owners like Phil Dwyer of Brooklyn,
who, despite their different social backgrounds, were both allied with Tammany
Hall boss Richard Croker, himself a prominent breeder and racer. Political connections were essential for success in a sport that generated enormous moral criticism
because of the gambling connection. Track operators needed a lot of clout in the
state legislature and the governor's mansion to secure laws permitting betting at
the tracks and then needed influence to block reformers' efforts to criminalize
racetrack gambling that was taking place in other states, including New Jersey
in late 1893. One year later, the New York State Constitutional Convention gave
upstate Republican critics a chance to revise the constitution, which seemed sure
to terminate racing. However, racing interests used their influence to circumvent
the new document by creating a state racing commission to supervise the turf in
conjunction with The Jockey Club, a small, extremely elite voluntary organization
set up to regulate American thoroughbred racing. This marked the first state effort
to ever regulate and supervise sport. The tracks that operated under this system
needed political influence to protect their operations and secure the best possible
racing dates.

The powerful alliance between urban machine politicians and racetrack
owners enabled thoroughbred racing in New York to flourish for about forty-five
years without interruption. They used whatever means they had at their disposal,
including bribing state legislators. Nationally, however, racing was in difficult
straits, and by the late 1900s, only twenty tracks were still in operation. There
was a nationwide effort by moral reformers in the late nineteenth century to end
gambling, which was adopted by the Progressive movement. Chicago's important
racecourses were closed in 1905 by Mayor Carter Harrison II, who tried to use that
accomplishment to gain national office. The well-known St. Louis tracks were also
closed that year by progressive Republican governor Joseph Folk, who secured
laws banning horse racing and making gambling on horse racing a felony.[8]

The New York racing interests came under ever-greater attack, especially
under a barrage of attacks by progressive governor Charles Evans Hughes, who
in 1908 passed laws that barred gambling at the racetracks. The tracks managed
for two years to find loopholes to circumvent the intent of the bans and stay in
business. However, the Agnew-Perkins Acts of 1910 closed the loopholes, making
track operators liable for any gambling violations. They were now forced to close,
and there was a blackout at the New York racetracks. There seemed to be a chink

in the armor of the seemingly omnipotent Tammany Hall. Three years later, however, thoroughbred racing resumed, although it was not because of Tammany's clout, or the repeal of the Agnew-Perkins Acts, but because of a court ruling that created a means to circumvent the gambling bans by permitting oral wagering. As a result, several area courses reopened, including the outstanding Belmont Race Course, built in 1905, but three Brooklyn tracks, Sheepshead Bay, Brighton Beach, and Gravesend, never reopened.

New York was the center of illegal horse race betting. There were some years in the late 1870s and early 1880s when racetrack gambling was banned but went on surreptitiously. But for the most part, illicit horse race wagering meant off-track betting, which was always against the law. Off-track betting was a well-organized, illegal enterprise that reformers in the late nineteenth and early twentieth centuries went after, with limited success. Historian Mark Haller, the dean of criminal historians, defines such ventures as businesses that sell "illegal goods and services to customers who know that the goods or services are illegal." These illicit undertakings were typically "victimless" crimes. In the late nineteenth century, gambling syndicates, often heavily Irish, provided such illegal services as prostitution, loan sharking, and especially gambling. More recently, other illegal goods included bootleg liquor, pornography, banned drugs, quack medicines, exotic animals, and unlicensed weapons. Haller characterizes illegal enterprises as having three main features: the systematic corruption of police and politicians, overlapping connections among illegal businessmen, and internal economic business factors such as specialization and diversification. Prostitution, loan sharking, and gambling existed long before the rise of "organized crime," usually identified with the emergence of Italian American crime families. The illegal enterprises commonly operated as crime syndicates. Haller defines a crime syndicate as "a system of cooperation so that many retailers are backed by the same group of entrepreneurs." This system enabled bookmakers, madams, and loan sharks to limit the financial risk and problems they might encounter with the justice system.[9]

Off-track bookmaking was mainly an important enterprise in larger cities, especially Chicago and New York, as well as some wide-open smaller towns like Covington, Kentucky, and East St. Louis, Illinois, which were suburbs of major racing centers. There were two main formats for off-track betting: poolrooms, which were betting parlors mainly located downtown or midtown and occasionally in suburbs outside the jurisdiction of local authorities, and handbooks (bookmakers), mainly located in working-class residential neighborhoods. This gambling was a cornerstone for the rise of syndicate crime, and ultimately organized crime, and one of the main sources of its income. Horse racing was a crucial element in the alliance between the underworld and urban political machines as big-city crime syndicates worked in close cooperation with machine politicians and local police to protect this illegal business.

Haller points out that there were three patterns for gambling syndicates to emerge in the late nineteenth century under the oversight of Irish politicians. Sometimes a local gambler became a neighborhood party leader. For example, in Chicago Mike McDonald, a professional gambler, who became a ward committeeman and powerful figure in the local Democratic Party, formed a crime syndicate in the 1870s to protect the local gambling business. Its control of track betting provided an important cornerstone for the rise of organized crime. The most notable professional gambler in New York to become a prominent Democratic politician was John Morrissey, who was previously the American boxing champion (1853–58). However, his gambling career was much more independent of his political career, highlighted by election to the US Congress in 1866.[10] A second pattern, according to Haller, was for a notable gambler to become closely associated with prominent ward politicians and the local police. His example in Chicago was South Sider Jim O'Leary, who dominated off-track gambling through his connections to ward politicians and Police Inspector Nicholas Hunt, who ran the Stockyards precinct. This model was also very common in New York City, but the difference was that Chicago's gamblers were tied to ward machines, whereas in New York it was the citywide Tammany Hall machine.[11]

The third pattern Haller describes was for prominent politicians (usually local ward leaders) to take charge and supervise gambling activities by their allies. His examples were alderman Michael "Hinky Dink" Kenna and "Bathhouse" John Coughlin of the First Ward that encompassed the city's segregated vice district (the "Levee"). Similarly, in New York at the turn of the century, Big Tim Sullivan, the number-two man in Tammany Hall and a well-known sportsman, became the head of the Gambling Trust that controlled the poolroom business in New York. His organization operated successfully because it had access to capital, the means to collect debts, excellent communication networks that provided accurate and speedy racing news, and protection from the penal codes through its allies in political machines and the paid-off police who provided advance warning about raids and lenient justice if arrested. Horse race gambling was one of the main victimless crimes that helped crime syndicates get under way.[12]

As I first pointed out in my book *City Games: The Evolution of American Urban Society and the Rise of Sports,* baseball, boxing, and the turf all had close ties to urban politics, reflecting the dominant role of urban machine politicians in many cities like New York. These commercialized sports employed clout to secure the best possible sites for their semipublic sporting sites, provide protection against governmental interference, and obtain special treatment from local municipalities.[13]

The New York Giants baseball team, widely recognized as "the Tammany team," was owned from 1895 to 1902 by Andrew Freedman, a real estate agent who was Boss Croker's best friend and chairman of Tammany's Finance Committee. Manhattan's other team, the New York Highlanders, founded in 1903 (and renamed the Yankees in 1913), was owned by Tammanyites Police Chief William Devery and gambling kingpin Frank Farrell, who sold the team in late 1914 to Jacob Ruppert, the wealthy beer magnate and a four-term Tammany congressman. The Brooklyn Dodgers' main stockholder, Charley Ebbets, served four years on the Brooklyn City Council and a term in the state assembly. These executives used political clout to advance their business interests by deterring possible interlopers, gaining inside information about potential ballpark sites, maintaining low license fees, getting the city police to patrol outside and inside the grounds for free, and fighting for baseball on Sundays.[14]

In the case of prizefighting, which was illegal until 1896, Democratic politicians used their clout to stage "exhibition" bouts to circumvent the laws. Coney Island in the early 1890s became an important site for illegal boxing matches under the protection of local political chieftain John Y. McKane, whose allies, including Kings County Democratic boss Hugh McLaughlin, held fights at the Coney Island Athletic Club. Then, in 1896, New York became the second state to legalize pugilism after Louisiana. State Senator Big Tim Sullivan took the lead in passing the Horton Act, which permitted sparring matches in buildings owned by athletic clubs, and then soon became the leading boxing promoter in New York City. Upstate Republicans repealed the Horton Act in 1900 because of the sport's brutality, unruly crowds, the importance of gambling in the sport, and the influence of Tammany Hall. However, a "boxing trust" led by Sullivan and other leading Democrats kept the sport alive at "membership clubs," where fights were limited to a few rounds and were not heavily advertised. In 1911, the Democrats gained control of the state government and enacted the Frawley Act, which legalized bouts under a state athletic commission. The Republicans overturned the boxing law in 1917, but the sport gained a lot of respect during World War I because of its use in training soldiers for combat. In 1920, the Walker Act permanently legalized prizefighting. Tammanyite James J. Walker, the future mayor of New York, sponsored the legislation, and Governor Al Smith, another loyal son of Tammany, signed the bill into law.[15]

Besides the connection between commercialized professional sport and urban politics, the sporting enterprise was also heavily involved, in varying degrees, with organized crime, primarily because of its interest in gambling. There was considerable illegal gambling on professional baseball in its early years, culminating with the Black Sox Scandal of 1919 and the public image of New York gambler

Arnold Rothstein as the man who supposedly fixed the World Series. In the case of boxing, a sport where gambling was rife, mobsters took over the sport after World War I and regularly fixed fights. However, the connection between organized crime and sport was most important in horse racing, an enormously valuable venue for wagering. The crime syndicates used their connections with machine politicians to protect their illegal betting. In addition, as historian Mark Haller points out, by the 1920s and 1930s, underworld figures drawn from the bootlegging world also often operated the racetracks themselves.[16]

From the public point of view, off-track gambling seemed to be monopolized by one all-powerful syndicate. However, in New York, Sullivan's "Gambling Trust" shared the business with other syndicates. In Chicago, Mike McDonald dominated the gambling scene in the 1870s and 1880s, with the friendly acquiescence of his peers. Then, for nearly twenty years, the business was divided into four main syndicates, until Mont Tennes achieved a virtual monopoly by employing his control of the racing wire, political connections, and violence.

The organization of this book is chronological and topical. The first chapter provides a brief history of the American turf, with particular attention to the ups and downs of racing in antebellum New York. The next chapter examines the rebirth of racing in New York with the rise of the elite American Jockey Club in 1865 and its creation of Jerome Park Race Track a year later. Belonging to the AJC, especially as a life member, certified a person's social status. The AJC provided a model for other first-class elite American tracks, whose jockey club members supported racing to promote competition, the breed, and their own social status. Jerome Park's elite management was in the forefront of racing reform, employing dash races and experimenting with pari-mutuel betting. The track had a lot of political clout yet constantly struggled with the state regarding the sport's legitimacy. In 1877, the legislature passed an important antipool law to fight rampant gambling that led the AJC to replace auction pools with bookmaking, which became the main form of horse race betting in the United States.

The third chapter looks at the rise of thoroughbred racing in Brooklyn, the nation's third-largest city in 1880, with a population of 566,663. Between 1879 and 1886, three major tracks opened: the prestigious Sheepshead Bay course, operated by several AJC members, and the proprietary Brighton Beach and Gravesend tracks. They all had political clout to prevent interference with gambling at the tracks. Social activists in the early 1880s, like Anthony Comstock, worked feverishly to enforce the antipool laws and halt gambling at the tracks, but the close ties between Brooklyn politicians and gamblers blocked their efforts. The cooperative criminal justice system seldom arrested, and nearly never convicted, bookmakers.

Chapter 4 scrutinizes the creation and impact of the Ives Act in 1887, a major new racing law that barred horse race gambling in New York State, except at racetracks and only on races contested on-site. The Ives Act legalized on-track bookmaking and created in theory a monopoly for them over horse race gambling. This law helped thoroughbred racing flourish, attracting large crowds and earning big profits. In 1890, the new elite Morris Park Racetrack opened in Westchester County, supplanting Jerome Park, which eventually became the site of a reservoir.

Chapter 5 examines thoroughbred racing next door in New Jersey, which catered to New York and Brooklyn racing fans, especially since Brooklynites owned some of its tracks, which were located closer to Manhattan than the Brooklyn courses. The most important Jersey course was the elite Monmouth Park track, but by the early 1890s, there were also five proprietary tracks, all run by men with powerful political connections. The most notorious were the outlaw tracks at Guttenberg and Gloucester, operated by machine politicians tied to illegal bookmakers and poolrooms. Democratic politicians tied to the tracks took over the state legislature in 1893 and promptly legalized horse race gambling to protect their racing investments and the interests of their associates. However, there was such uproar by moral reformers that the machine politicians were defeated in the next election. The horse racing ban lasted nearly fifty years.

Chapter 6 focuses on the bureaucratization and regulation of New York horse racing. In 1891, the elite metropolitan tracks tried to deal with such problems as fraud, corruption, and winter racing and established the Board of Control to supervise eastern racing. However, the board proved ineffective, which worried racing men that the sport's failure to police itself was leading to growing public opposition to the turf. Consequently, the leading figures in New York racing, like August Belmont II, replaced the board in 1894 with a more vigorous supervising agency, modeled on the elite English Jockey Club, known simply as The Jockey Club, whose fifty members were the crème de la crème of New York society. The Jockey Club established uniform rules for racecourses that accepted its direction; set up a racing calendar; licensed all participants, including trainers, jockeys, and owners; and strictly punished code violators. Tracks that did not adhere to its rules were declared outlaw tracks, and anyone working or racing there was barred from TJC's tracks.

The fears of racing men were well founded because in 1894, racing was halted not only in New Jersey but also in Chicago, where the outstanding Washington Park was forced to close. The legality of horse racing was a big issue at the 1894 state constitutional convention. The revised document, ratified by the electorate that fall, included an article that prohibited all horse race gambling, which apparently ensured the end of racing in New York State. Chapter 8 examines how the clout of leading track owners, racers, and breeders, in alliance with Tammany Democrats, saved the sport one year later through the Percy-Gray Act, which permitted racing at one-mile tracks managed by incorporated racing associations. Horse racing was placed under the joint control of TJC and the new State Racing Commission, which collected 5 percent of each track's gross revenues to distribute to state agricultural societies. The new law left the door ajar for unobtrusive betting that to strict interpreters of the state constitution seemed patently illegal.

Chapters 7 and 10 study the illegal off-track betting parlors. Although there were divided opinions about the acceptability of gambling at racetracks, there was none over the illegitimacy of off-track gambling. Nonetheless, in the 1890s, poolroom betting thrived, with betting parlors in Long Island City, Brooklyn, and especially Lower Manhattan and the Tenderloin District on the West Side, which received their information directly from the tracks via Western Union. The patently illegal poolrooms often operated openly, protected by Tammany Hall and payoffs to the police. Customers preferred off-track betting because their bookmakers were much more accessible and cheaper to reach than racetracks on the outskirts of town and accepted smaller bets than track bookmakers did. In the early 1890s, the tracks began fighting back. They tried to block the rooms from getting racing information, using their own political clout to pass the Saxton Anti-Poolroom Law in 1893, and two years later got support from President Theodore Roosevelt of the Police Board, who promised to close the poolrooms. However, the gamblers belonged to the powerful crime syndicate led by Big Tim Sullivan and several top municipal officials, who controlled most of the poolrooms. Despite state investigations, enormous press coverage, critical essays by muckrakers in prominent periodicals, and the earnest work of reform politicians, the authorities could not (or would not) eradicate off-track gambling. The evil became even more pervasive with the growing popularity of handbooks, who were bookmakers who took bets in saloons, candy stores, cigar shops, and on the street in working-class neighborhoods. The authorities never did eradicate the illegal off-track gambling.

Racing struggled in New York because of the depression of 1893 but flourished thereafter. Chapter 9 analyzes the racing scene from 1897 through 1907 when the New York turf completely dominated thoroughbred racing in North America, with the largest crowds, the leading purses, the finest stables, and the biggest profits. In addition to established tracks in Brooklyn, Westchester, and Saratoga, Queens County, the home of antebellum racing, staged a great revival with three clout-heavy courses. Aqueduct opened as a fleabag facility in 1894 but developed into a decent facility, and another proprietary course, Jamaica Racetrack, opened in 1901. However, the most important new course was the new elite Belmont Race Track, which opened in 1905, replacing Morris Park. It quickly became one of the featured tracks in North America.

The final substantive chapter examines the demise, but also the restoration, of racing. Moral conservatives and progressive reformers formed a strong alliance against horse racing behind Republican governor Charles Evans Hughes, who made the ending of racing a cornerstone of his progressive program. Hughes primarily opposed Percy-Gray on constitutional grounds, although his grassroots support, mainly from rural evangelical Protestant New Yorkers, came on moral grounds. Hughes signed the antiracing Agnew-Hart Act, which passed in the state legislature in 1908 by the narrowest of margins and only after a special session. However, the tracks found a way around that edict and survived for two more years until 1910, when Hughes's old allies rewrote the penal code with penalties aimed at track operators. The Agnew-Perkins Acts killed racing in New York, and the sport was dead in nearly every major racing site outside of Maryland and Kentucky. However, the racing interests did not give up and won a major legal decision that provided a loophole, and racing resumed in 1913, although the Brooklyn tracks never reopened. By the 1920s, New York had largely regained its status as the cornerstone of American racing. However, the reformers were still unable to halt off-track gambling and largely gave up.

Acknowledgments

This project has seemingly taken forever to complete. I would like to thank the National Endowment for the Humanities, which helped the project along with a Summer Research Grant in 1992. Northeastern Illinois University (NEIU) showed unusual patience in granting me three sabbaticals for my work on horse racing. I also received four research grants from the Committee on Organized Research dating back to 1990 to purchase microfilm copies of the *New York Morning Telegraph* and the *Chicago Herald Examiner* and travel funds to research in archives in New York and Springfield, Illinois. I originally intended this project to be part of a comparative history of horse racing and gambling in New York and Chicago, but the vagaries of the publishing game precluded that plan. A companion volume on horse racing, politics, and crime in Chicago is nearing completion. I want to thank a number of institutions for giving me the opportunity to test my ideas in public forums. They include the 2007 Bernard Brommel Research Professor Lecture at Northeastern Illinois University in Chicago and the Seward Staley Address at the annual meeting of the North American Society for Sport History at Texas Tech University. In addition, in 2009 I delivered the keynote address at the Faculty Interdisciplinary Symposium on Leisure at Chowan University in Murfreesboro, North Carolina.

Debra Siegel and her Interlibrary Loan staff at NEIU performed yeoman assistance for my work. They are part of the remarkable Consortium of Academic and Research Libraries in Illinois system that makes it possible for scholars throughout the state to get speedy access to library materials from this fabulous resource. Joe L. Davis did a wonderful job preparing the photographs for the book. Thomas Gilcoyne, volunteer historian at the National Museum of Racing, made available for me autobiographical material on Gottfried Walbaum. I want to thank Kathleen Kornell, the rights and permissions/awards manager at the University of Illinois Press, for permission to reprint a map of New York racetracks from my prior book *City Games: The Evolution of American Urban Society and the Rise of Sports* (1989).

I would like to thank Timothy Gilfoyle of Loyola University and the anonymous readers at Syracuse University Press for their careful reading of the entire manuscript. Thanks to my colleague Patrick Miller for his incisive suggestions. I want to thank the entire staff at Syracuse University Press for their support over the years, including former acquisitions editors Ellen Goodman and Annelise Finegan. I was blessed to have truly outstanding support by my copy editor, Annette Wenda. My wonderful wife, Tobi, provided judicious criticisms, but also much-appreciated pats on the back along the way. I want to thank my youngest daughters, Jamie and Jennifer, for not getting on my case for a project that began before they were playing AYSO soccer and did not get completed until after they graduated college. In addition, thanks to my oldest daughter, Jodi, who kept my computer running and tried to explain business accounting to me. I am, of course, responsible for any errors.

THE SPORT OF KINGS AND THE KINGS OF CRIME

1

The Rise of Horse
Racing in America

Having been present at most of the large gatherings of this country, we do not
hesitate to say this exceeded in number any previous assemblage of the People.
We were at the Ascot races in England last year when London poured forth its
tens of thousands to get a view of Queen Victoria and Prince Albert. . . . How
many people were present . . . we do not pretend to say; but we have no hesitation
in saying that there was a larger number at the Union Course yesterday.

—JAMES W. WEBB, publisher, *New York Courier and
Enquirer,* on the Fashion-Peytona race of 1845

Horse racing was the most important sport in early America, even if not permitted in certain colonies because of concerns about gambling. The sport
provided the emerging upper class with a means to demonstrate prowess, manliness, and self-confidence; display wealth; and certify social status. Racing developed in the last third of the seventeenth century, although there apparently was
a race as early as 1607 when the Jamestown town council banned impromptu
racing in the streets to protect pedestrians.[1] The first formally sponsored race
took place on Long Island in 1665, just one year after the British took over New
Netherlands from the Dutch. Governor Richard Nicolls organized annual races
at the Newmarket Track in Hempstead, a one-mile course, in emulation of the
pleasures of the Restoration Court, naming the course in honor of King Charles
II's favorite track.[2]

Horse racing in the late seventeenth century was a vital aspect of the lifestyle of
"great planters" who employed the sport to emulate the English gentry, gain social
status, and demonstrate their manliness. By the mid–eighteenth century, the sport
was firmly established in the upper-class social calendar in several colonial towns,
including New York, Williamsburg, Annapolis, and Charles Town. Elite jockey
clubs were established to supervise the sport and operate enclosed racetracks
where thoroughbreds competed. After the United States became independent, the

1

turf's aristocratic pretensions, along with the gambling, dampened interest in the Northeast, and racing was widely barred. However, by the 1820s, elite gentlemen revived the sport in New York, the scene of major events from 1823 through 1845. Thereafter, economic problems and moral questions about horse race gambling virtually killed the sport in the Northeast. The sport remained popular in the South, especially among major plantation owners, and New Orleans became the new center of thoroughbred racing.

Racing in the Colonial South

Horse racing was the most popular sport in the southern colonies by the late seventeenth century. Leading Virginia great planters dominated the "sport of kings," imitating the social life of English country squires. Historian T. H. Breen has argued that the pervasive gambling among elite colonial Virginians reflected their individualism, sense of honor, materialism, and even their livelihood. Equestrians risked their future on a tobacco crop, which was hardly a sure thing. Their product was susceptible to poor weather, pestilence, and floods; getting lost on the way to market because of storms or piracy; and ending up in oversaturated markets. Planters were even vulnerable to unscrupulous overseas partners. These men also sought excitement and risk in their leisure pursuits.

At a time when few people owned horses, planters used the sport to demonstrate their courage, brawn, and intelligence, riding their own working horses over short distances on rural roads. They used the contests to win valuable wagers, gain respect, earn peer recognition, and promote a sense of shared values and consciousness among the gentry. These gentlemen employed the rituals of betting and racing to certify their superior social status and encourage fellowship between the landed elite and the community of mass spectators at the races, thereby reinforcing traditional patterns of respect and deference. The elite also used the sport to deflect potential social conflict among themselves by establishing formal agreements and social conventions to facilitate racing and betting. Legal proscriptions barred the common folk from betting with great planters because they were overstepping class boundaries and could not afford to go into debt. Planters relied on the courts to settle betting disputes, providing a role model to the masses.[3]

By 1700, Virginian planters raced at twelve tracks and twenty-four by 1730. In the 1740s, rich planters began importing expensive purebred Arabian horses from England to use exclusively for racing. The offspring of the first thoroughbreds were larger and stronger and had more endurance than American steeds, bred for the English style of long-distance racing, which supplanted the American tradition of sprint events that was losing its social cachet.[4]

Racing was a rural sport, yet colonial cities, despite the primitive stage of urbanization and the small populations of even the largest towns, played a big role in its development. The secularization and cosmopolitanism of cities provided an environment where a positive attitude toward horse racing and gambling flourished, albeit tempered by local values and traditions. Cities became a major locus for sporting pastimes because of their larger populations and because residents had sufficient discretionary income and free time to encourage the rise of sports entrepreneurs, especially tavern keepers, and voluntary athletic organizations, like jockey clubs. These associations helped members of the social and economic elite differentiate themselves from lesser sorts, sustaining the face-to-face relationships developed in commerce and the professions. Local governments entered the sporting scene to protect community norms, maintain order, and prevent the pleasure of a few from interfering with commerce. The evolution of sport and urban society in the colonies foreshadowed many important trends once sport became more popular and better organized and urbanization accelerated.[5]

The principal site of mid-eighteenth-century southern racing was Charles Town, South Carolina, a town of about four thousand in 1740. In 1734, the South Carolina Jockey Club held its first race at the York Course, sixteen years before the formation of the English Jockey Club. The track provided a public venue for racing that enabled wealthy southerners who raced horses to secure honor and for the jockey club to recoup expenses by charging admission. Turf historian John Hervey claims the Williamsburg Jockey Club was even older. In 1739, the Virginia capital of two thousand residents had mile races around a circular track. Four years later, the Annapolis elite formed the Maryland Jockey Club. Races at these colonial capitals were the social events of the year. By the 1760s, several thousand people attended southern meets, including women, welcomed for the moral tone they provided. The crowds included such notables as George Washington, who subscribed to the purses given by the Williamsburg Jockey Club and attended races in Philadelphia and Annapolis.[6]

Racing in the North

Northern communities, especially in Puritan-dominated New England, were less receptive to the sport of kings because they saw gambling as an immoral activity by which people, coveting their neighbors' prosperity, tried to gain wealth without working for it. In 1672, the Essex County Court of Massachusetts Bay barred horse racing within two miles of any town meetinghouse to prevent the betting that accompanied races and protect pedestrians from speeding horses. Two years later, Plymouth punished anyone racing horses in the streets or common roads five shillings or an hour in the stocks.[7]

Philadelphia Quakers also opposed racing because sports, games, and "loose behavior" diverted man from work, God, and the "First Day" (Sabbath). They sought to exercise social control over the non-Quaker half of Pennsylvania. In 1682, the new colony's assembly prohibited rude and riotous sports like bull baiting and cockfighting, discouraged attendance at sports contests for fear that excited crowds would detract from public discipline, and banned running races because they stimulated such sins as the wish to excel (vanity) and gambling (coveting another's property).[8] Nonetheless, there was racing in Philadelphia, causing leading citizens in 1695 to petition the government to curtail the sport.[9]

The rise of a northern urban elite had a crucial impact on eighteenth-century sport, particularly horse racing. Upper-class merchants became increasingly wealthy in the course of the century. In Boston, for instance, the top 10 percent had 46 percent of the taxable wealth in 1687 and 63 percent in 1771, compared to Philadelphia, where the upper class owned, respectively, 46 percent and 72 percent for similar years. Thus, the elite had the time and discretionary income to participate in a leisurely lifestyle, which they increasingly desired. It provided them with a means of conspicuously displaying their inherited status or personal achievements.[10]

Elite colonial urbanites had many of the same aristocratic pretensions as New York patroons and southern planters. Philadelphia, the largest city in 1760 with a population of nineteen thousand, developed an increasingly secular, heterogeneous, and changing social structure typical of larger colonial towns, with a sophisticated social life centered in taverns and coffeehouses. Well-to-do Philadelphia Anglicans and even some orthodox Quakers emulated the English gentry by establishing a wide-ranging club life and copying English country pleasures like hunting, riding, and fishing. The social clubs were voluntary associations established to promote sociability and maintain ethnic and class distinctions. Philadelphia's Schuylkill River Colony, a fishing society founded in 1732, was the first colonial sports club and the city's most exclusive men's club.[11]

Elite Philadelphians remained divided over racing. Nonetheless, in 1766, twenty-one "gentlemen of the turf," led by merchant John Cadwalader, organized the Jockey Club "to Encourage the breeding of good horses and to promote the pleasures of the turf." Its annual meetings drew horses from Virginia to New York and such horse fanciers as George Washington.[12]

Cosmopolitan New York, the third-largest city in the British colonies, had the gayest social life of any colonial city, as an aristocratic British culture superimposed itself on a Dutch heritage, and local religious scruples were less inhibiting than in any other city. New York's elite social life included clubs, the theater, and such sports as horse racing, coaching, yachting, hunting, and sleighing, some of which were sponsored by royal governors.[13]

New York was the main center of northern racing and vied with southern cities as a racing center. The New York Subscription Plate, a two-mile, best two-out-of-three-heat race first took place in 1725 at the Church Farm Course (the current site of Columbia University). In the late 1730s, a new style of racing became very popular there following a race around a circular track in April 1735, near the DeLancey Arms Tavern in the Bowery. One year later, Francis Child charged six pence to spectators, marking the first admission fee to an American sporting event. By 1750, high-stakes races at the Newmarket Track drew about a thousand horse-mounted spectators. Owners of the best horses, such as the Morrises and DeLanceys, were members of the mercantile and landed elite and invested heavily in their racing stock, some of which they raced at southern tracks. James DeLancey, son of a former chief justice and lieutenant governor of New York, was a noted horseman. A member of the Jockey Club of Philadelphia, he owned a private course and stables at Bowery Lane (present-day First and Second streets) at the southern end of Manhattan Island. He also belonged to the prestigious Macaroni Club, whose members in the late 1760s were young rakes who enjoyed turf sports and donated purses of one hundred pounds and more to both the Newmarket track and the Powles Hook track (in New Jersey). In 1775, he sold his stud and moved the family to England.[14]

Metropolitan New York had at least seven courses in the city and vicinity in the early 1760s. In 1762, there were races at the DeLancey Arms and in Harlem. One year later, the Beaver Pond Course and another on Staten Island opened, both sponsored by Freemasons, offering modest purses. These tracks lacked the stature of Newmarket. Between 1757 and 1763, innkeepers primarily ran them, intent on profiting from thirsty customers. But the recession that followed the French and Indian War cut down on crowds. These promoters mostly relied on local horses rather than English imports and offered modest purses.[15]

The Revolution and After

The coming of the Revolution and the accompanying social upheaval largely halted the turf. In 1774, Philadelphia radicals in the provincial assembly passed a bill to discourage racing and other gambling sports in an effort to impose their value system upon the entire community. The Continental Congress convened on 5 September and subsequently passed a similar resolution against aristocratic social pretensions. Congress established the Continental Association six weeks later to boycott English products, and the association called for an end to cock-fighting, horse racing, and other elite pastimes. Once war broke out, racing in Charles Town stopped, as many owners used their horses for the cavalry and others hid their mounts in the swamps. Segments of the elite still enjoyed their exclusive pleasures, abetted by the British presence in Philadelphia in the winter of 1777–78, which confirmed for many patriots that the colonial upper class was deficient in republican virtue. The Continental Congress returned there in 1778, and it approved a resolution on 12 October encouraging each colony to suppress the theater, racing, "and such other diversions as are productive of idleness and dissipation." Pennsylvania banned Sunday activities and all gambling sports.[16]

Racing still went on during the war in Loyalist New York, where there were contests at Long Island at Hempstead Plains and Beaver Pond and especially Brooklyn's Ascot Heath (at Flat Land Plains, south of Flatbush). In 1779, tavern keepers at the Kings' Arms sponsored racing. There was a meet on 13–15 November 1780, at distances of one to two miles, and even a contest for women. On 16–19 April 1781, there was another meet at Ascot Heath, attended by hundreds. The top prize was one hundred pounds for the "Noblemen and Gentlemen's Subscription Purse," a goodly sum for officers living beyond their means. Then, after the Revolution, a new track opened at Maidenhead, behind the old DeLancey mansion.[17]

Racing in the Early Nineteenth Century

The post-Revolutionary racing scene did not fare well in the North, where the public opposed a sport that reflected the materialism of the old Loyalist elite, encouraged lazy behavior among spectators, and based its popularity on the sin of gambling. Philadelphia turfmen arranged races for a few years, despite various legal barriers. Consequently, fifteen hundred mechanics and twelve hundred manufacturers petitioned the legislature in 1802 to halt racing as deleterious to their interests. They decried it as more appropriate to the lifestyle of idle English gentry than to hardworking, moral republican citizens.[18]

New York's Harlem Course had races through 1801, but one year later the state outlawed the sport. The new law attacked the turf in no uncertain terms: "Horse racing is a growing evil, productive of dissipation, idleness, and many other vices, ruinous to individuals, and detrimental to the good people of the state." The reformers were concerned about the gambling, rising debts, drinking, and disorderly conduct. However, sporadic matches still occurred, and a report to the assembly in 1804 found that public sentiment was so strong against the law that the authorities could not enforce it. This report encouraged contempt among racing fans (who included wealthy spectators as well as artisans) for government authority and for social reformers, forward-looking mechanics, and religious revivalists promoting moral reform. Racing occurred at eighteen locations in the state between 1785 and 1810.[19]

The status of the turf was quite different in southern and western cities, where horses were essential for transportation and as work animals.[20] Charleston was the capital of the turf, but nearly all southern cities had racing at the turn of the century. Charlestonian Charles C. Pinckney, Federalist vice presidential candidate in 1800, was the president of the city's Washington Racecourse, the most prestigious track in the South. The track featured weeklong meets every February that marked the highlight of the social season and drew people from far away.[21]

The most famous western equestrian in the early Republic was Andrew Jackson, a self-made man and former Tennessee congressman, senator, and judge, who acquired the Heritage plantation in 1804. One year later he became a partner in the Clover Bottom Race Course in Nashville. Jackson wagered heavily and spent extravagantly to secure top horses like Truxton, who eventually earned him more than twenty thousand dollars in purses and wagers, plus stud fees. In 1806, Jackson got into an argument with Charles Dickinson about a debt owed him by Capt. Joseph Erwin, Dickinson's father-in-law. The hostilities were exacerbated by remarks made impugning the honor of Rachel Jackson. The outcome was a challenge and a duel. Dickinson was the most outstanding duelist of the era, but, surprisingly, Jackson managed to kill his rival after taking the first bullet to the chest. Jackson sold off most of his stock in 1816, figuring it was unfitting for someone with higher political ambitions. However, two years after he was elected president, Jackson got back into racing in partnership with Rev. Hardy M. Cryer. Following his reelection, he brought several of his thoroughbreds to the White House and raced them in the name of his nephew Andrew Jackson Donelson.[22]

The Rise of the New York Turf

Antiracing opinions in New York State began to weaken around 1815, following the end of the War of 1812, as supporters claimed that racing promoted agricultural development by improving the breed. Racing aficionados, notably Long Island gentry, organized the Society for the Promotion of the Useful Arts to demonstrate the qualities of racehorses at agricultural fairs. They were Knickerbockers, elite Anglo-Dutch, and Huguenots, typically Episcopalians, who enjoyed a good time, unlike the more devout Yankees, whose families came from New England. In 1821, the legislature approved a bill by a vote of fifty-three to fifty, legalizing two racing seasons in Queens County, while requiring the sheriff to keep order and remove any gaming tables. New York City provided the strongest support for the bill with seven votes, plus four from Queens and Suffolk counties. The measure was approved because the public believed that the breed was improved through competition and expected that respectable folk would run the sport, instead of "sharps." However, the support for racing was tenuous, since a companion bill to legalize racing in Kings County was overwhelmingly defeated.[23]

The New York Association for the Improvement of the Breed (NYAIB) abetted the sport's rebirth. Popularly known as "the jockey club," its members included such wealthy gentlemen as Assemblyman Walter Livingston and industrialist John Cox Stevens. The organization built the Union Course in Jamaica and established purses of one thousand to nineteen hundred dollars per meet, much higher than anywhere else. The course quickly became the center of northern racing. The press supported the NYAIB, expecting it would keep order and prevent gambling. The events were still long-distance heat races that ranged from one to four miles, perceived as a test of speed and bottom (perseverance and courage). The meets ran only three days, with just one event per day.[24]

The racing scene benefited enormously from the presence of a star racehorse and the development of great intersectional contests between northern and southern steeds. The outstanding northern horse was Cornelius Van Ranst's undefeated American Eclipse, retired to stud as a six-year-old in 1820. However, he was brought him out of retirement to promote the new Union Course. In 1822, the eight-year-old easily defeated Sir Charles, a noted southern horse, at Washington's National Course. The victory convinced William R. Johnson of Virginia, the "Napoleon of the turf" and the leading American horseman of his day, to propose a match at the Union Course between Eclipse and a top southern steed at twenty thousand dollars a side. A group of New Yorkers, led by Hoboken industrialist John C. Stevens, accepted the challenge.[25]

On 27 May 1823, a huge crowd estimated at twenty thousand ventured to Long Island to attend the match race between Eclipse and the four-year-old southern stallion Sir Henry, where they bet one million dollars. The audience included Andrew Jackson, back in the US Senate, Vice President Daniel Tompkins, and former vice president Aaron Burr. Sir Henry took the first heat in 7:37, a record time. This was the first heat that Eclipse, ridden by William Crafts, instead of his regular rider, Samuel Purdy, had *ever* lost. Purdy was back on board for the next heat, which Eclipse won in 7:49, a record for the second heat of a four-mile race. In the decisive third heat, with both stallions tired, Eclipse won in a slow 8:24. Local press reports glowed with pride of the northern horse's triumph. Press coverage noted the audience's decorum, the large crowd at the ladies' stand, and the presence of men of wealth and taste. The southern press reported the outcome less favorably, feeling that the better horse had lost.[26]

The race occurred just three years after the important Missouri Compromise, when sectionalism was becoming an important political and social issue, and just before the rancorous presidential election of 1824. The Eclipse–Sir Henry race provided a safe, nonaggressive outlet for mounting regional rivalries. As historian Melvin Adelman argues, "Northerners . . . identified with the horses' courage, confidence and success, and felt they had demonstrated their own manliness by supporting the aged but tested hero against considerable odds. Moreover, they realized that they had defeated the South at its own game, just a few years after the revival of the sport in the North." It represented a victory of the northern way of life over southern civilization.[27]

There were four more "great" intersectional races over the next two decades (along with other lesser events) that captured the national imagination because of the quality of the horses, publicity, size of the audiences, and symbolic importance of the matches. The second great intersectional race occurred in 1825 when New York's Ariel raced Flirtilla of Virginia. Ariel won the first heat, but the southern horse took the next two, providing a measure of revenge for the prior Great Race. Interest in New York racing cooled off after this match because of the Union Course's poor condition. The clubhouse needed repairs, the stands were decaying, and security was insufficient. Furthermore, the NYAIB was in heavy debt, and its purses no longer drew the best southern horses.[28]

Former congressman and New York mayor Cadwallader R. Colden, a Knickerbocker who belonged to the NYAIB, tried to restore the sport in the late 1820s. He could not convince his fellow members to invest heavily in racing but got the NYAIB to give up its interest in the track, and he assumed full control. Colden became responsible for its upkeep, scheduled meets, and made all the necessary arrangements with horsemen who raced there. His goals were to run excellent meets and make money.

In 1829, Colden introduced three innovations to make his investment profitable. Colden reduced the number of racing days, originally five, to three, but offered two races a day. Then he added a second meet two weeks later, to make it more economical to keep top horses there. Finally, he enclosed the entire track and charged admission, ranging from twenty-five cents for general admission to three dollars for a four-horse carriage. Beforehand, American and English tracks had charged only for choice locations or grandstand seats. Sandown Park was the first English track to charge all racegoers, but it did not occur until 1875.[29]

Colden's best-laid plans came to naught, however, and business never reached his expectations. Adelman's careful analysis of Colden's venture indicated that he spent twenty thousand dollars a year to run the track, which meant that with a ten-day racing schedule, the promoter needed to sell two thousand admissions at an average price of one dollar a ticket to break even, which he evidently did not do. Then on 20 October 1830, there was a riot at the Union Course because Colden had insufficient money to pay a purse. He resigned his rights as track owner, and the NYAIB again took over racing operations. In 1833, Virginian Alexander L. Botts gained control of the Union Course and two years later brought in fellow Virginian David H. Branch as his partner. They were experienced, well-connected racing hands who had previously owned tracks in Virginia.[30]

The third great intersectional race took place in 1836 between the North's Post Boy and the South's John Bascome. It was not a matter of assessing (Post Boy was sired by Sir Henry and was a half brother of Eclipse) but a test of the preparation and riding techniques of the regions. Bascome's victory was attributed to superior training and ridership.[31]

The Botts-Branch partnership brought horse racing in metropolitan New York to its antebellum peak. Prizes rose, membership in the jockey club increased, and high-quality horse racing began in 1837 across the Hudson River in Hoboken, New Jersey, where the state legislature had three years earlier modified the turf laws to permit horse race gambling. Botts and Branch leased a site in Hoboken for six thousand dollars a year and built the sixty-thousand-dollar Beacon Race Course, the most lavish track of its day. However, this was not a good year to open such an ambitious venture because of the panic of 1837 and the ensuing five-year depression. The Beacon track was conveniently located and of high quality, but it did not draw much interest from thoroughbred racers and instead mainly staged trotting and pedestrian contests. Adelman asserts that the collapse of the "beacon of the future . . . [was] the symbol of the demise of horse racing in New York."[32]

The Decline of Racing in New York

The depression badly hurt New York racing, contributing to poor attendance at the fall meet and often pushing the price of horses below the cost of breeding them. It was a big setback to breeders, who in the early 1830s had purchased expensive English horses. There were also internal causes for the sport's decline, such as mismanagement of the rundown Union Course, the weak leadership of the New York Jockey Club (NYJC), the high cost of attending racing, and the sport's inability to secure the level of support it enjoyed among the southern elite. Finally, there was the moral question of gambling. Many New York horsemen sold off their thoroughbreds, and the industry moved west to Kentucky and New Orleans. The bad conditions caused the Virginia crowd to drop out by 1841.[33]

The expense of attending came down to high admission fees and the cost of transportation. The *Spirit of the Times,* a weekly aimed at upper-class readers that was the most popular sporting journal in the nation, estimated the cost of travel-ing the eight miles from South Ferry, Brooklyn, to the Union Course by ferry and railroad was one dollar. However, since service was so bad, anyone who could afford it went by private conveyance, which cost nearly five dollars. Admission costs fluctuated. The average ticket cost between one and two dollars, and stand-ing room along the track was usually fifty cents, though often there were twenty-five-cent tickets. These combined costs made attendance expensive for anyone below the prosperous middle class. Working-class fans could attend but had to save up, especially if they intended to bet. Attendance was also limited by the brief racing seasons that lasted about a week in the spring and fall. Adelman concludes that these factors made it certain that the press exaggerated the size of the huge crowds attending the intersectional races, since otherwise promoters should have made a go of racing.[34]

The gambling at racetracks put off many New Yorkers who believed that the betting that accompanied racing was sinful and immoral. Most New Yorkers in the metropolitan area, as well as statewide, were Protestants who abhorred the expansion of such a vile pastime. People were supposed to follow the Ten Com-mandments, not covet their neighbors' wealth, and embody the Protestant work ethic, earning their money by working (unless they were capitalists whose invest-ments worked for them). Such beliefs were vigorously reinforced during the Sec-ond Great Awakening of the 1830s, which was especially strong in western New York State's "burned-over district." Evangelical Protestants sought to clean up society to prepare for the Second Coming of Christ, and gambling was high on their list of immoral activities. At this time, wagering opportunities were rapidly increasing, facilitated by the rise of professional gambling and, some would add, the stock market. As historian David Johnson points out, gamblers in the mid-nineteenth century "created complex and subtle connections among themselves, their customers, politicians, and the police which redefined the context in which law enforcement occurred. By creating conditions that severely restricted the abil-ity of the police to suppress them, gamblers not only assured their own fortunes, but they also laid the foundations for modern 'organized crime.'"[35]

In 1842, Henry K. Toler of New Jersey, a former NYJC steward, took over the Union Course as a business proposition. The economy was recovering, the press had again become more supportive of racing as a means to improve the breed, and the North and South each had an outstanding horse to vie for national honors. Toler scheduled the fourth great intersectional race between the leading northern horse, Fashion, "queen of the turf," and the southern stallion Boston, for twenty thousand dollars. Fashion's owner, William Gibbons, did not believe in personal wagers and would not directly participate, but instead he lent the horse to Toler and his syndicate. This event was the most publicized race in the United States in nearly twenty years, and New York turfmen hoped it would help restore popular interest in flat racing, but it did not. Boston was a slight favorite, but Fashion won the first four miles in 7:32.5, a new world's record by 2.5 seconds, and took the second heat as well in 7:45.[36]

This was a grand sporting event, but it did not go on without some problems. Transportation was a serious issue, as transit firms gouged their patrons. The Long Island Railroad sold enough tickets by eleven in the morning to fill all its trains but continued to sell tickets anyhow. The *American Turf Register* decried the LIRR's arrangements as "an imposition!" charging extravagant prices and providing poor service. One train with more than two thousand passengers arrived *after* the first heat was completed. Hundreds walked to the course, and "some people paid $10 to stand in a charcoal cart to get to the track." An extraordinary variety of vehicles filled the roads to the track, including elegant carriages, stylish cabs, "lumbering omnibuses and thousands of fancy go-carts, wagons, and hackney coaches."[37]

The seating area, with six thousand spaces, included a ladies' stand and an enclosed "privileged space" in front of the stands, reserved for New York Jockey Club members and "strangers," who were charged ten dollars. William T. Porter, owner and editor of the *Spirit of the Times*, took umbrage at that high fee and accused Toler of greed. The fee included admission to the track for the entire year, which was of no value to out-of-towners.[38]

Insufficient preparations were made for the huge throng in attendance. The press, which had little experience in estimating large crowds, reported some 50,000–70,000 people present overall. This figure seems very unlikely, as New York and Brooklyn combined had a population of 348,943.[39] Still, it was a large and unruly audience:

> At one o'clock . . . , owing to the want of an efficient police, and their inability to see the race, more than a thousand persons climbed over the pickets, from the field into the enclosed space while a mob on the outside tore down a length of fence, and stove through a door in the stand, and swarmed into the cleared space. For a time it seemed impossible for the match to take place at all! A crowd of loafers made a rush up the stairs leading to the Club Stand, but they were summarily ejected. At length Yankee Sullivan, Jeroloman, and several other distinguished members of the Fancy, undertook to clear the course, which they did in an incredibly short time, by organizing a party of their friends, who formed in line, with clasped hands, quite across the space, and marched from one end to the other, thereby driving outside of the gate every person without a badge. Of course there were among this mob several ugly customers, but Yankee Sullivan had only to "let fly with his right," or Jeroloman give any one of them "a teaser on his smeller," to fix his business! On the

whole, the mob conducted themselves very well under the circumstances; the great majority were in perfectly good humor, and had the proprietors taken the precaution to paint the tops of the pickets with a thick coat of tar, and engage a strong body of police, no such disgraceful scene would have occurred.[40]

The final great intersectional race was in 1845 between the fillies Fashion and Peytona, who, at age six, was two years younger than her rival. William Porter promoted the ten-thousand-dollar purse event at the Union Course. Racing by this time, according to Adelman, was starting to assume a modern structure. It was a national sport with sports journals, studbooks, and publicized national racing schedules. Furthermore, turf leaders were standardizing the rules, and promoters were operating enclosed racing grounds.[41]

The event received enormous press attention, including front-page coverage from the popular *New York Herald*, one of the nation's first penny papers. The *Herald*'s lengthy report captured in detail the ambience of the grand spectacle, including the trip to the track, crowd behavior, the rituals of the event, and the race itself. Most spectators got to the course by a forty-minute ride on an overloaded train from Brooklyn that cost forty cents. When they got to the track, they discovered a carnival-like atmosphere, with concessionaires selling food and drink. The mile track had one section enclosed with space for horsemen, carriages, and a grandstand.[42]

A key problem that day was maintaining order among impatient fans who ran onto the course, sneaked into the stands, picked pockets, or participated in other mischief. About twenty-five constables provided security, bolstered by several noted shoulder hitters, including the infamous Butcher Bill Harrington and future boxing champion Yankee Sullivan, all under the direction of Capt. Isaiah Rynders, Tammany boss of the Sixth Ward (home of the notorious Five Points slum) and head of the Empire Club, a clearinghouse for politicized gang activities. The race drew a crowd estimated at seventy to one hundred thousand, far in excess of the track's normal capacity. Even if only a small proportion of spectators had paid for their admission, the management would have made a huge profit, which could have encouraged them to arrange another great intersectional race. Peytona, carrying 116 pounds, won two straight four-mile heats in 7:39.75 and 7:45.25 to defeat Fashion, carrying 123 pounds. The victory was seen by southerners as affirmation of their way of life. Peytona eventually won a record $62,500 in prize money during her career, winning thirty-two of thirty-six races.[43]

The race proved to be the last hurrah for New York racing, and national attention turned south, particularly to New Orleans. The New York turf was done in by several factors, some old and some new. They included modest crowds at most

1. The race between Fashion and Peytona at the Union Course on Long Island on 13 May 1845 was the fifth and final great intersectional race between northern and southern horses. *Source: Peytona and Fashion,* a Currier and Ives sketch in the author's possession.

events; competition from harness racing, a more American and middle-class sport; the shift westward of the breeding industry; the jockey clubs' inability to finance racing; limited commercialization; and widespread religious and social criticism because of the turf's connection to gambling. These circumstances put racing on the defensive and alienated many rich New Yorkers. By the 1840s, the sport was entirely in the hands of elderly Knickerbockers, who were declining in numbers.[44]

A Failed Comeback

Racing barely continued in New York in the late 1840s and then totally collapsed by the end of the decade. There was no spring meet in 1849, the fall meet was a failure, and there were no races at all from 1850 to 1853. In 1854, S. J. Carter of New Orleans secured a state charter to build a track in Queens and incorporated the National Jockey Club (NJC) with the support of William W. Boyden of Tennessee and Lovell Purdy, son of the great jockey Sam Purdy. Their ambitious syndicate purchased a 141-acre farm in Newton, Long Island (present-day Corona, Queens), where they built the $165,000 National Course that included a twelve-thousand-seat grandstand, with additional space for around thirty-eight-thousand spectators. The

NJC's two meets in 1854 each lasted six days. The inaugural meet in June was the most extensive ever held in the United States at the time, with $6,000 in prizes, more than double the purses of meets back in the mid-1830s. The track was generally highly regarded, but the *Clipper,* an important one-year-old sporting weekly published in New York, complained about the cost of admission and believed the track was really just for the elite. The National Course suffered a significant drop in attendance in the fall, tied to high ticket prices, the failure to run announced races, and general mismanagement, resulting in little interest from local horse owners. The corporation was in such serious financial distress that the track was foreclosed in February 1855.[45]

In 1856, several members of the NJC reorganized themselves as the Fashion Jockey Club and raced at the Fashion Course (the renamed National Course) in Newtown, but it was a terrible meet. One year later, the legislature granted a new charter to Lovell Purdy's syndicate. However, he lost the lease that summer to a higher bid from John Cassady, whose venture also failed after a single meet. The much-beloved Samuel Purdy tried a comeback with the purchase of the old Centerville, Long Island, trotting track that dated to 1825, but it held only one meet, in the spring of 1859. Following the virtual demise of racing, the Fashion Course was sometimes used for baseball, including a best two-out-of-three-game all-star match between baseball teams from Brooklyn and New York in 1858.[46]

2

The American Jockey Club and the Rebirth of the New York Turf

The recreation . . . has every accessory which can render it attractive and invigorating. The drive though the Summer beauties of Central Park, and the fresh green
lanes of Westchester in the perfect June weather, is alone a sufficient delight. In
the surroundings and incidents of the course itself, the gaiety and animation of
the crowd, the shifting kaleidoscope of bright colors and pretty faces, the inspiration of happiness from the sight of thousands of happy people, the music, the
fresh air and the sunshine, the excitement of the brief contests—all these are elements of a rare and varied enjoyment, such as sends the jaded worker back with
a fresher heart to his labors.

—"Spring Meeting at Jerome Park," *New York Times*, 10 June 1871

Northern racing was virtually moribund from the mid-1840s through 1861, even though an 1854 New York State law permitted the formation of turf organizations "to improve the breed of horses." In 1861, for instance, a one-day meet at the Fashion Course was the only race in the entire Northeast. However, one year later, though the Civil War was in full swing, there were twenty-four days of racing in the Northeast. Racing at Long Island's Union Course and at Philadelphia and Boston tracks helped Northerners temporarily forget about the carnage of the day. In 1863, there were five-day meets in New Jersey and Philadelphia, a three-day meet at the Centerville trotting track, and, most important, a four-day meet at Saratoga Springs, an upstate resort popular with New York's affluent.[1]

Saratoga was the scene of trotting starting on 14 August 1847, when the renowned Lady Suffolk won the first race at the Saratoga Trotting Course, and one month later, the track hosted a thoroughbred race. There were occasional races there over the next few years, including even some steeplechase events, but thoroughbred racing did not take hold there until the early 1860s, mainly owing to John Morrissey, the former American boxing champion and New York City's

leading gambler. The success of flat racing at Saratoga directly led to the organization of the American Jockey Club (AJC) after the Civil War by financier Leonard
Jerome and his friends, who reestablished thoroughbred racing in New York City
as a high-prestige sport.[2]

Historian Melvin Adelman, the preeminent student of nineteenth-century
New York sport, argues that the resurgence of New York horsing was owing to
a variety of factors. Wealthy New Yorkers were creating racing stables because of
personal satisfaction with their horses' accomplishments and a desire to enhance
and certify their elite status. They continued to claim that racing was essential
to promote the improvement of the breed that benefited the stock needed for the
military and other uses. The wartime decline of the southern breeding industry
provided new opportunities for northern breeders who could test their stock at
nearby New York tracks. Local turfmen made important innovations in the competition, most notably the abandonment of heat racing and the adoption of the
English dash system that New York's antebellum courses had used sparingly.
Thereafter, shorter contests became the principal form of thoroughbred racing in
the United States after New York adopted it because it enabled more races each
day, often accompanied by larger purses. The result was more betting and less
harm to horses that competed in longer races.[3]

Other developments internal to the sport included the start of two-year-old
racing; the emergence of permanent stakes races, most notably the Belmont Stakes
in 1867; handicap events (making favorite horses carry heavier loads); and claiming races (contests in which all competitors can be purchased, usually at a set price
up to post time). The purpose of claiming races was to discourage an owner or
trainer from entering an obviously superior horse in a race against inferior competition to secure an easy win since another owner could "claim," or buy, that horse
at below market value.[4]

There were also external factors that encouraged the rebirth of racing, which
was an integral part of the postwar boom in sports. These causes included urbanization; the rise of industrial capitalism; technological innovations, particularly the
telegraph, which facilitated communication; and the expansion of railroads to carry
horses and fans to distant racetracks. The rise of sport in general was also indebted
to the emergence of a positive sports creed in the 1830s and 1840s that justified
wholesome and uplifting sports for the middle class, but that ideology did not benefit horse racing. Finally, after years of horrific carnage, people wanted fun and
were prepared to spend money to enjoy commercialized sports and other entertainments.[5] American tracks rapidly emulated the AJC model because promoters, horse
owners, and gamblers saw the benefit from enlarged programs. Yet while racing
styles changed after the Civil War, the sport's main justification remained the belief

that it existed to improve the breed. Journalists claimed the turf promoted honor and public spirit and boosted the local economy by attracting tourists. Supporters also claimed that racing provided healthful recreation, enabling fans to escape urban congestion and pollution and leave their problems behind them.

John Morrissey and the Rise of Saratoga

In 1862, John Morrissey opened the first upscale casino at Saratoga Springs, which became an immediate success. One year later, "Old Smoke," a former boxing champion, gambler, and Tammanyite, led a syndicate of New Yorkers in organizing a race meet there to cater to summer residents and attract other tourists. They staged two races a day for four days, charged $1 for admission, and spent $2,700 on purses and extra funding for stakes events. The experimental meet drew fifteen thousand people and turned a profit.[6]

A key figure in the betting at Saratoga was Dr. Robert Underwood of Lexington, Kentucky, a Jewish veterinarian born and reared in Dublin, Ireland, a breeder and seller, who revived organized betting in the North in the basement of the United States Hotel. Considered the "founding father of modern bookies," Underwood introduced the auction pool system, a betting format started in Europe, to the United States. Underwood purportedly sold the first pools on running races in New Orleans in the winter of 1855 on the race between Lexington and LeCompte, and remained a prominent pool seller into the 1870s. He operated auction pools exclusively for high rollers and kept 3 percent of the pool for his services. The *Horseman* described him as "a Jew" who "had the magnetism of the Israelites to draw the scrip out of the pockets of the 'innocents abroad' who were anxious to get rich quick on other people's money." The auction pool system was introduced because too many bettors were no longer settling their bets and stakeholders too often absconded with the stakes.[7]

The "auctioneer" paid a fee to the track for the right to operate an auction in which the highest bidder got to pick the horse of his choice, usually the favorite. Then there was bidding for the right to make the next selection, and so on down the line. The pooled money from the auction went to the person who had bid on the winning horse, minus the auctioneer's standard percentage fee for facilitating the wager, normally 3–5 percent. Pool sellers could arrange multiple pools on a particular race. They themselves were not gambling but providing a service.[8]

The successful venture encouraged the organizers to sponsor racing on a permanent basis. Morrissey secured just over $20,000 from metropolitan New York "gentlemen of high social position" to set up the Saratoga Association for the Improvement of the Breed (SAIB) and build a permanent new track. His backers included Cornelius Vanderbilt, the richest man in America, who put up $3,000. The Commodore was one of the few elite New Yorkers who befriended Morrissey, raced trotters with him in Central Park, and gave Old Smoke valuable business advice. Morrissey kept a one-third share in the track, making him the largest stockholder, a fact not widely publicized. He also ran auction pools and, as chief betting commissioner, arranged person-to-person bets for elite high rollers.[9]

Morrissey's associates in the SAIB included president William R. Travers, a stockbroker, who belonged to twenty-seven men's clubs, and vice presidents John Purdy, a wine dealer and gentleman jockey; financier Leonard Jerome; and John R. Hunter, owner of the leading stud farm in the Northeast. Hunter also served as a judge during the meet and on the track's Executive Committee, along with Erastus Corning, president of the New York Central Railroad.[10]

Morrissey was a self-made man, born in Ireland in 1831. Three years later, his family immigrated to Canada and from there to Troy, New York. John was a tough youth involved in street gangs, who left home at age seventeen for New York City to make his name. He immediately made his way to Rynders's Empire Club, where he challenged the roughest men there to a fight. They pulverized him, but the members admired his pluck. Morrissey became an emigrant runner who enticed new immigrants to move into certain boardinghouses. He subsequently joined the Dead Rabbits, a renowned Irish American street gang whose members worked elections as "shoulder hitters" (intimidators) for Tammany Hall. In 1852, the twenty-one-year-old moved to California, seeking instant wealth in the gold fields and an opportunity to challenge Tom Hyer, the preeminent western brawler. He did not fight Hyer but did box his trainer, George Thompson. One year later, Morrissey returned east and took on champion Yankee Sullivan at Boston Four Corners, New York, for a $2,000 purse. After round 36, Sullivan got into an argument with a Morrissey second, never made it to scratch for the next round, and thereby lost his title.[11]

Morrissey used his newly won fame to become increasingly prominent in Tammany Hall, where he commanded the organization's intimidators and repeat voters. In 1854, he led a faction that backed the successful mayoral candidacy of Fernando Wood. One year later, Morrissey got into a street fight with Butcher Bill Poole, leader of the Bowery Boys, a Protestant Know-Nothing street gang that detested the Irish Catholics, who beat him up. Morrissey subsequently sought revenge against Poole, and he and some Empire Club friends confronted Poole in a saloon. During the contretemps, Poole was shot and killed. The authorities arrested Morrissey for the murder but released him. His last professional fight occurred in 1858 when he successfully defended his title against John C. Heenan, the Benecia Boy, in eleven rounds at Long Point, Canada, for a bet of $2,500. Morrissey thereafter retired from the ring but remained a well-liked figure among the sporting crowd.[12]

Morrissey's personal popularity and political prominence helped him become a prominent figure in gambling circles, worth $500,000 in 1864. Old Smoke had dabbled in gambling during his sojourn in California and then at his own New York saloon. He was a partner in sixteen faro banks and the city's leading gambling hall and was heavily into "policy," a poor man's gambling format in which bettors tried to predict a three-digit number selected by a daily lottery drawing. Policy was legal in some states, but not New York, where C. H. Murray and Company dominated the business. By 1870, Morrissey was the firm's largest shareholder and helped provide its political protection.[13]

Morrissey was also involved in one of the first notorious betting episodes in baseball history. He owned the Troy Haymakers, an outstanding nine, who in August 1869 defeated the Brooklyn Atlantics and later that month played the all-salaried Cincinnati Red Stockings during their triumphant eastern tour. In the seventh inning of a surprisingly tied game, the Haymakers started a riot. The game was summarily canceled, saving Morrissey and his friends from losing a wager of $17,000. The tie marked the only blemish in the Red Stockings'

2. Built in 1863, the Saratoga Racetrack in upstate New York is the oldest formal sports facility still operating in the United States. *Source:* "A Finish on the Celebrated Saratoga Course," *Harper's Weekly* 50 (25 Aug. 1906): 1218.

undefeated season (57–0–1). Morrissey was involved in other sporting promotions. In 1877, for instance, he contributed $500 to the purse for the American championship-sculling race at Lake Saratoga, won by Charles E. Courtney. Ten thousand people attended the event, and there was a lot of pool betting on the outcome.[14]

Morrissey served two terms in Congress (1867–71), but broke with Boss William M. Tweed in 1870. He joined the Mozart Hall wing of the Democratic Party and survived the boss's fall in 1871. John was later welcomed back to Tammany Hall, but in 1875, Boss "Honest John" Kelly, expelled him, fearing his growing power. Morrissey had the last laugh, however, when elected, over Kelly's opposition, to the state senate from Tweed's old district. Two years later, he shifted to a silk-stocking district, where he defeated Tammany grand sachem Augustus Schell. Senator Morrissey died in 1878, very rich (he owned three-eighths of the Saratoga Casino) and very popular, renowned as a defender of the working man and a generous contributor to charities. Some fifteen thousand admirers accompanied his body to the cemetery in the rain. However, "Old Smoke" never won the recognition he craved from the elite.[15]

Saratoga's Second Season

In the summer of 1864, horse racing was hardly foremost in the minds of most Americans with the outcome of the Civil War and the future of President Abraham Lincoln's regime both in doubt. The racing season began with a seven-day meet at St. Louis and then three days at Paterson, New Jersey, where the Passaic County Agricultural Association sponsored the Jersey Derby, the first derby in the United States. Saratoga reopened on August 2, employing a 125-acre site near the original track, purchased for $12,500. The proprietors laid out a one-mile course and a grandstand that still exists. Standing room cost fifty cents, with $1 for the grandstand, $1 for viewing from a carriage, and $10 for a five-day pass. The opening event was the Travers Stakes, the second-oldest ongoing major spectator sporting event in North America, exceeded only by the Queen's Plate at Toronto's Woodbine Racecourse that started in 1860. Twenty thousand attended the opening, described by the *Herald* as "brilliantly successful." However, the *Tribune* was very critical of the meet, concerned about the gambling nexus, the alleged mistreatment of horses, and the jockeys' integrity: "Anybody who supposes that this species of amusement has anything to do with the improvement of the breed of horses is capable of believing that prizefighting has for its object the improvement of the breed of man."[16]

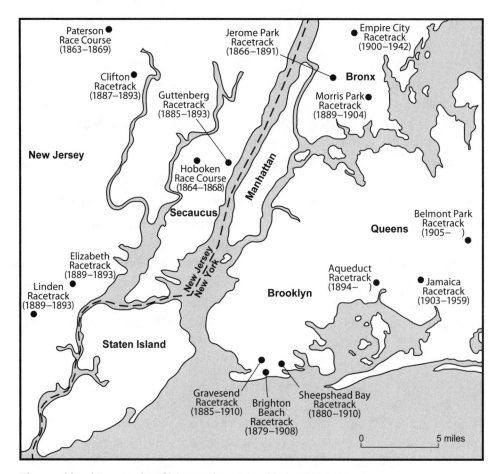

Thoroughbred Racetracks of Metropolitan New York, 1863–1910.

In 1865, with the Civil War just concluded, the track held its third meet over six days. Opening day was a joyous occasion, drawing a reported forty thousand spectators. Management improved the plant with a separate ladies' stand, two thousand cushioned seats in the roofed grandstand, and two thousand seats in an uncovered stand. Saratoga barred African Americans from the seating era, even though half of the jockeys were African American. Blacks could entertain whites, but it did not entitle them to sit with whites.[17]

The success of the racing experiment drew two noted gamblers to join Morrissey's faro business in 1864, Henry Price McGrath, originally of Lexington, Kentucky, who had made his name in New Orleans, and John Chamberlain, of St. Louis, a noted blackleg (that is, a cardsharp or riverboat gambler). They joined Morrissey's syndicate and invested $50,000 in a luxurious facility at 5 West Twenty-fourth Street. After an argument with Morrissey in 1867, they formed their own establishment down the street. Two years later, McGrath returned to Kentucky, with a profit of at least $200,000, to become a top breeder, winning the first Kentucky Derby with Aristides in 1875. Chamberlain moved to Long Branch, New Jersey, where he invested in a big gambling hall and helped establish the Monmouth Park racecourse in 1870.[18]

The American Jockey Club

The success of upstate racing encouraged elite New Yorkers to resume thoroughbred racing in the metropolitan area but not at the old Union Course or Fashion Course, which, according to historians Edward Burrows and Michael Wallace, had "been taken over by the *hoi polloi*." The primary mover was SAIB vice president Leonard Jerome, who late in 1865 decided to develop a great racetrack patterned after the famous and elaborate European facilities. Jerome himself pledged $25,000 to the project, but his main contribution was bringing men of wealth and integrity back into control of the sport. The aim was to make the facility the grand national course, a focal point for New York society, and certify New York's status as the leading American city.[19]

Jerome was originally a Rochester attorney, publisher, and Whig politician, who raced harness horses as a hobby. In 1850, he moved to New York City to become a Wall Street speculator in partnership with Travers and emerged a millionaire by selling short during the panic of 1857. His other investments included a one-fourth interest in the *New York Times* and railroad deals with Cornelius Vanderbilt. Jerome became a prominent figure in New York society and a member of such prestigious men's clubs as the New York Yacht Club. His daughter Jennie married Lord Randolph Churchill, and they had a son named Winston.[20]

The American Jockey Club was capitalized at $750,000. Its officers included financier August Belmont, treasurer of the National Democratic Party (1860–72), who served as unpaid track president for twenty-one years; vice president Jerome; treasurer William Butler Duncan; and secretary Dr. John B. Irving. The AJC's Villa Park Site and Improvement Association purchased the 250-acre Bathgate Farm for $250,000 in Fordham, Westchester County, less than five miles from New York City (today's Knightsbridge Road and Jerome Avenue in the East Bronx) at a site long renowned for horse breeding. Local equestrians applauded the location because they were uninterested in returning to the distant Long Island racetracks. The AJC built and operated the $280,000 Jerome Park racetrack there, named in honor of its founder. Charles Wheatley, who had planned the Saratoga course, designed Jerome Park and in 1867 became track secretary and manager. The *New York Times* anticipated the opening would be "an era of note in the history, not alone of racing in America, but in the annals of New York Social life."[21]

Jerome Park opened to the public on 25 September 1866, featuring dashes and heat races. Despite its odd oval shape, critics immediately recognized it as the finest turf facility in the United States. There was a two-story eight-thousand-seat grandstand, a twenty-five-hundred-seat stand for club members and guests, and a luxurious clubhouse that included an outstanding hotel with a dining room, ballroom, and sleeping accommodations. Management barred gambling, the sale of liquor, or any booths from the grounds. Carriages or saddle horses were charged $1 for entering the track, while all spectators except for club members, their guests (minors and two women), and servants in livery paid $1. A grandstand seat, where ushers seated the patrons, was another $1, but ladies unaccompanied by a gentleman were barred from the grandstand. The clubhouse would be used year-round, with facilities for skating, sleighing, trap shooting, and other sports.[22]

The opening-day crowd, with Gen. Ulysses S. Grant as the guest of honor, was estimated at twenty-five thousand, including nine thousand men and women packed into the grandstand. In addition, many wagonloads and thousands of spectators beyond the fences had an unimpeded view. The presence of large numbers of colorfully dressed women was a welcomed big change, which certified the stature of the event. The sporting crowd was there, naturally, including John

3. The Fordham Stakes on 10 June inaugurated the 1868 program at Jerome Park, New York, won by General Jackson, a five-year-old, carrying one hundred pounds, owned by Captain Moore of the Kentucky Stable. His other steed in the race set the pace for the victorious horse, a maneuver known as the English system. *Source: Harper's Weekly* 12 (27 June 1868): 408–9.

Morrissey and Boss Tweed, himself a member of the AJC, wearing white hats and gloves, as was beautiful Josie Wood, owner of the leading sporting establishment in the city. Although the management barred liquor sales, beer and bourbon were readily available.[23]

The track's inaugural became the social event of the year, and the press reported in detail about the fashions worn by elite women spectators. According to W. S. Vosburgh, the leading racing historian of the early twentieth century, "The opening of Jerome Park was marked by a display of female beauty, wealth and fashion that amazed the country." Women were meant to be seen at the track, adding their loveliness to the splendor of Jerome Park, but not as serious fans. The track was still a male bastion. They were the connoisseurs of horseflesh who made wagers based on their "expertise."[24]

The new track received great press notices. The *Times* noted that "never before has a meeting been inaugurated under such admirable management. Money, with the directors, is a matter of secondary import" compared to integrity, fairness, and honor. The writer claimed that opening day surpassed any prior event in American turf history. The only criticisms were that the betting was limited to a single auctioneer and that the railroad back to New York City was located more than a mile from the track. Another journalist applauded the event as marking the revitalization of the turf in the United States and pointed out to his readers the significance of thoroughbred racing in England, France, Germany, and Russia. Some editors were originally shocked that "ladies of Gotham's leading families should be seen at a public horse race," but soon recognized they were wrong. These women felt perfectly comfortable and protected at the track's elegant clubhouse. In fact, the press quickly recognized that their presence added stature and respectability to the sport. Newspapers and magazines subsequently gave considerable coverage to the fashionable female spectators.[25]

Looking back in 1881, the *Spirit of the Times* wrote, "The inauguration of Jerome Park witnessed the attendance of the most reputable citizens of the Union, accompanied by their families. . . . Jerome became the favored shrine, the Mecca of all that was cultured, refined, and fashionable in New York society. It inaugurated a new era . . . , and to this day the most esteemed lady in the land can attend the contests of the turf, without any departure from those proprieties of life which render her sex estimable."[26]

Although the track received widespread recognition as a fashionable and respectable site managed by prominent New Yorkers, the AJC had a rough row to hoe. Right after the Civil War, people were only beginning to recover from the crisis and give attention to sports, which, the *Spirit* claimed, "are the symbols of peace and prosperity." There was still some prejudice against aristocratic racing compared to the more democratic sports of trotting and baseball.[27]

Horse racing and the new AJC did not beguile everyone. The *Nation,* a noted reform periodical, begrudgingly acknowledged the club's efforts to elevate the American turf, which had been "abandoned to as thorough a set of sharpers as ever disgraced a moral and religious community," but considered the effort misguided:

> An attempt has been made within the last fortnight to make horse racing a "genteel" amusement in this country—something which people belonging to what is called "good society" will go to see, and seeing, grow fond of. . . . A good course has been laid out, a "grandstand" provided, the sale of liquors prohibited, and everything done that money or zeal can do to surround the enterprise with an air of respectability, and above all, to make the course a "place fit for ladies." Good horses, too, were entered for the opening races; a very fair running was made; the weather was fine, the proceedings were marked by the utmost order, and General Grant was there. And yet we have no hesitation in saying that, regarded as an attempt to naturalize horse-racing amongst us . . . it was a complete failure, and will prove a failure no matter how often repeated.

The *Nation* thought that the basic problem was that Americans were not equestrians. Virtually no easterners rode horses, including Jerome and Belmont, the main men behind the AJC.[28]

Turf, Field, and Farm also pointed out the high cost of going to the track: a dollar for each horse pulling the wagon, a dollar for the driver, a dollar for each rider, and then another dollar for each person to get into the grandstand. "The whole financial part of the arrangements," the writer claimed, "suggested that the thing was not got up in the interest of horse culture, but like a traveling circus, *to pay*."[29]

An 1871 *Times* editorial recognized that harness racing, rather than flat racing, fitted in better with "our utilitarian convictions. In a country where riding is so infrequent and driving so universal, the racer must necessarily be regarded only as a costly and useless luxury, while the trotting horse receives all care and cultivation." However, it did admit that the sport under the AJC's exceptional management encouraged riding: "If more and better riders are to be seen in our streets today than years ago, the improvement may be traced, in no slight degree, to the stimulus given by the meetings of the Jockey Club."[30]

"Racing Is for the Rich": August Belmont and the AJC

August Belmont, the longtime AJC president and one of the prime movers in American elite racing, was born in 1813 in Alzey, a German Rhineland village annexed by France in 1798. It became part of the Duchy of Hesse in 1816. His father, Simon Belmont, was a prominent landowner and a leader in the Jewish community. August went to work for a local branch of his distant cousins, the Rothschilds, at eleven, and worked his way up to the job of confidential clerk. In 1837, he was sent to Havana to protect Rothschild interests there. August first landed in New York, where his employers decided he should remain to watch over the firm's local investments, as their local agent had declared bankruptcy in the panic of 1837. He soon organized his own firm, August Belmont and Company, that worked closely with the Rothschilds. As his firm prospered, Belmont ardently tried to fit in with New York society, despite his Jewish origins, and largely divorced himself from his family in Europe. He encountered a lot of anti-Semitism, yet in 1849, he married the daughter of Commodore Matthew C. Perry. They raised their children as Episcopalians, although August himself never converted. Belmont became very active in Democratic politics, earning an appointment as minister to The Hague (1853–57). Three years later he became chairman of the National Democratic Party and ran Stephen A. Douglas's unsuccessful campaign for the White House. He remained party chairman until 1872.[31]

In 1865, when the AJC was organized, Belmont owned only a few horses but went into breeding heavily one year later. He established the Nursery Stud at Babylon, Long Island, employing the sage advice of renowned trainer Jacob Pincus. The farm was more than eleven hundred acres, which included a one-mile track and a grandstand. Belmont's first big triumph came in 1869, when Fenian won the third Belmont Stakes. Belmont had moderate success racing in the 1870s but dropped out of competition in 1882 because of ill health. He returned to breeding in 1885 and reestablished his stable in Lexington, Kentucky. By the time he resigned as AJC president two years later, his stable was one of the finest in the United States. His horses led in prize money in 1889 ($125,635) and set a record in 1890 by winning $171,350. Belmont's contributions to the turf were recognized by an honorary membership in the English Jockey Club, one of the most exclusive sports clubs in the world.[32]

The AJC Membership

Power in the AJC resided in its 9 directors, who represented the track's 50 life members, the crème de la crème of New York society. Only 17 of them owned thoroughbreds, yet all shared a passion for the turf and helped finance the club. They tried to secure favorable press treatment to bolster the AJC's public image, relying on the 6 newspaper publishers who were life members, including horseman James G. Bennett Jr. of the *New York Herald*, Henry J. Raymond of the *New York Times*, and Mason Marble of the *New York World*.[33]

In 1866 and 1867, the AJC had some 862 members who paid a $75 initiation fee and $25 in annual dues, entitling them entry to the grounds and the clubhouse. Members entered the track by a private entrance, parking their carriages close to the fence overlooking the course, where they picnicked, waited upon by liveried servants. There was a big gap between the classes of membership since regular members had little say in the club and were reportedly treated contemptuously by the life members.[34]

The clubhouse, open just to club members, was a unique feature of Jerome Park. According to Vosburgh, "The club-house was always open; an excellent *chef* was in occupation, and it soon became the great society rendezvous." There were many bedrooms, "and it became quite the thing for an owner to take a party of friends to dinner, stop overnight and be up . . . [to] see the morning gallops."[35]

Adelman found that 70 percent of the members lived in New York City and an additional 19.2 percent in the metropolitan area. Two-thirds (65 percent) made their living in finance and commerce, but there were also politicians, hotel managers, clerks, and craftsmen. Life members were slightly less involved in finance or commerce (58.3 percent), but much more likely to be in transportation or a profession. Eight percent of life members were in agriculture (including some southern horsemen), compared to merely 0.3 percent of all club members. Life members had an average income of nearly $60,000, significantly greater than the entire cohort's, which was less than $27,000. Three-fifths of all members were rich, and nearly all others were well-to-do. Four-fifths (83 percent) had incomes of more than $3,000, compared to 2 percent of all New York household heads. They were predominantly Protestant, but there were Catholic and Jewish members. Membership definitely provided status, but not necessarily enough to serve as a jumping-off point into more prestigious metropolitan men's clubs. By the 1880s, membership surpassed 3,000 and was less exclusive.[36]

The Development of Racing at Jerome Park

The AJC in 1867, its first full year of operation, held meets in spring, summer, and fall. Most spectators took the Harlem Railroad to the track, but since the nearest station was more than a mile away, they hired a two- or four-wheeled vehicle to finish the journey. Dr. Underwood operated all the auction pools, while vendors sold wine, beer, and liquor. Nonetheless, decorum was maintained. There were just three races on opening day, but other dates usually had four to six races, with as many as eight horses in an event. The AJC offered the largest purses in the country, financed by entrance fees and subscriptions by the club and other contributors. By 1871, prizes reached about $40,000, which helped make Jerome Park the preeminent American track.[37]

By the 1868 season, dash racing prevailed, giving fans more chances to bet. The *Herald* and several other dailies opposed shorter races, which they believed ruined the breed. However, the *Times* supported the new system, which it claimed produced horses with more stamina and speed and resulted in fewer breakdowns from the strain of multiple long-distance heats.[38]

Club members reserved the center of the main public stand for themselves, which the *Spirit* felt was unjustifiable. It criticized this elitism that "was undoubtedly conceived by members who had got into society by accident. . . . The idea of those persons probably was, that the American Jockey Club might be made a convenient vehicle for the foundation of an aristocracy . . . built upon the backs of the People. . . . The public always acts well when it is well treated; and high prices would be just as reliable a security for good conduct on a race-course, as at the grand opera. . . . An entertainment cannot be popular and select at the same time."[39]

The AJC took a step toward bolstering racing interest by opening a betting room for wagering and the exchange of intelligence in June 1868 at its committee rooms at Twenty-first and Broadway. Membership cost $10 a year. There was no intention of ending the popular auction pools, but merely to provide a convenient location where members could get the latest turf news, make bets, and settle their wagers, like at Tattersall's in London.[40]

Most metropolitan newspapers, regardless of first impressions, became strong supporters of Jerome Park. The most detailed coverage was for opening day because it marked the start of the racing season and, increasingly, the start of the social season as well. Opening-day reports typically included a lot more than just the outcome of the races. Articles described the journey from New York to the track; the character of the crowd by gender, occupation, and social status; the quality of track management; and the betting.

The *Times* consistently saluted the organization, noting in 1871 that the AJC had encouraged horseback riding and healthy outdoor recreation and was free of the problems normally associated with thoroughbred racing. Local interest in racing was on an upswing when it seemed to be dropping in England because of corruption and recent "scandalous 'jockeying.'" "In every respect," the *Times* noted, "Jerome Park may compare more than favorably with the most famous English race-tracks, and indeed, bids fair before long to be the sold heir of their vanished glories."[41]

The *Times* believed that the public had many reasons to thank the AJC: "If only because they have given excuse for a few additional holidays to a community overworked and sadly in need of them, they have merited thanks and substantial support." It found the drive there through Central Park and Westchester in June to be delightful, possibly the finest in America. An editor recommended the pleasant atmosphere at the course, along with "the gaiety and animation of the crowd, the shifting kaleidoscope of bright colors and pretty faces, the inspiration of happiness from the sight of thousands of happy people, the music, the fresh air and the sunshine, the excitement of the brief contests." Jerome Park comprised all the "elements of a rare and varied enjoyment, such as sends the jaded worker back with a fresher heart to his labors." The *Times* suggested that busy businessmen who took time off from work would enjoy an afternoon at the track with its wonderful ambience, security provided from offensive characters and gambling outside the betting area, and the integrity of the races:

> From most of the evil associations that usually hedge round a race-track, Jerome Park is singularly free. Disreputable persons are to be met there, as they are to be met in any place of public resort. But they are kept within proper and rigid limits—one must, indeed, look for them to find them. From the Grand Stand and the Club-house such persons are carefully excluded, and ladies may, and do, go to the track with even greater security than to opera or ball. Betting may go on, but betting there is everywhere, and this, too, at the Park is mostly confined to the mystic circle that gathers about the quarter-stretch and the pool-stand.[42]

The press also applauded the AJC for leading the reform of racing. In 1875, for instance, the AJC raised the minimum weights carried by two-year-olds from 100 to 110 pounds and for three-year-olds from 110 to 118. The purpose was to displace lightweight boy jockeys whose competition "had done so much to prevent the development of an intelligent race of adult jockeys."[43]

Racing Audiences

Jerome Park never intended to be a democratic institution, instead granting special privileges to its members and charging high admission prices that, along with the cost of carfare, hindered working-class spectatorship. The metropolitan dailies and the sporting press frequently criticized the cost of tickets, comparing the system unfavorably to the English tracks, where the courses were open to the masses for free, with special fees for the grandstand. *Turf, Field, and Farm,* a leading national sports periodical, supported high admission prices in 1866 to keep out the lower sorts and to give wealthy men the freedom to protect the sport: "The prestige of Jerome Park only can be preserved by a strict enforcement of the rules which necessitate a grading of classes. Throw the course open to the rabble and in a very brief time it will degenerate and become a synonym for all that is rude and licentious. Unfortunately . . . classes *do* exist, and upon the racecourse, as elsewhere, we have to deal with the stubborn fact. . . . We do not hope to effect a social reform through the medium of racing." After all, as Belmont himself said, "Racing is for the Rich." However, by 1871, *Turf, Field, and Farm* changed its opinion, claiming that all classes were interested in racing and that cheaper, graduated admission prices would produce larger crowds and more profits from increased concession sales and make racing a national sport.[44]

Jerome Park was not intended to be accessible to the working class, but Jerome did lay out the course so the masses could watch races from a public hill overlooking the park. "Dead Head Hill," so nicknamed because there was no admission fee, was across the road from the main entrance and provided a very good view. Spectators could see the starts of half-mile races better than fans in the grandstand but could not make out a close finish. The audience was heavily Irish but included African Americans and other lower-class groups. Entrepreneurs on the hill sold sandwiches, lemonade, beer, and bourbon.[45]

The working-class *Herald* wanted to make flat racing more democratic, and in 1869 the paper suggested adopting the English system of free admission to the course but keeping a fee for the grandstand. The *Spirit* believed that although the scheme worked well in England, and might popularize the turf in the United States, this policy would not fit American racing conditions, which lacked the enormous space of English tracks. The *Spirit* recommended cutting ticket prices in half, which would draw twice as many spectators and thereby maintain the same total gate. Racing scholar Melvin Adelman argues that the unwillingness of the AJC to countenance free admissions or sharply reduced rates reflected insecurities among the American upper class, more open to talent and less limited to family background than the English aristocracy. In Great Britain, the elite were sufficiently confident in their status that they mingled and even participated in sports like cricket with their social inferiors, hardly the case in the United States.[46]

Jerome Park's middle-class support was not very strong and seemed to be declining. J. Wilson, a letter writer to *Turf, Field, and Farm*, warned in 1871 that Jerome Park was losing the support of middle-class families because of the cost and discomfort of the experience. A typical family of four spent fifteen to twenty-five dollars for the carriage ride to the track, plus a one-dollar tip, five dollars for entrance at the gate for them and the driver, and four dollars to get into the grandstand. Another option for getting to the track was to be "jammed into a dirty car, with half a hundred tobacco-chewing pool buyers." Wilson recommended increasing audiences and producing "a holiday for the middle classes" by lowering field tickets to twenty-five cents and the grandstand to fifty cents. He also encouraged railroads to provide cheaper fares, as well as better and more frequent service. Wilson also recommended reducing round-trip coach fares from the train station to the track to twenty-five cents.[47]

The *Times* also recommended going after the respectable middle class as sound business and, it could have added, a means to gain more respect for a sport constantly beleaguered by critics for its gambling. The paper reported that at opening day in 1875, the middle and lower classes were underrepresented among the twelve thousand spectators, who mainly consisted of the elite and some of the more unsavory segments of the male bachelor subculture: "The American Jockey Club should remember that for one who uses the magnificent approach by Central Park and Central Avenue, there are a hundred plebeian patrons who reach the course by railroad and through the by-lanes of Westchester. After all, in this and other enterprises, the dollars of the middle-class thousands count for more than the subscription tickets of the wealthy few."[48]

In England, the more respectable elements did not go to races, which they believed was not a reputable sport, though certainly middle-class people did go to mix with the aristocracy and landed gentry and enjoy the ambience of the racegoing experience. Only a small number of spectators were aristocrats, except among the four hundred or so spectators who saw the races at Newcastle. Betting was widespread at men's clubs, like Tattersall's, which were open only to members who bet with each other. Tracks near London drew well on Saturday afternoons because they were accessible to the working class. Most attendees were lower class, especially on holidays, like major bank holidays that drew more than seventy thousand spectators. These events, particularly the Epsom Derby, were characterized by a carnivalesque experience.[49]

Women at Jerome Park

The press gave a lot of attention to women spectators. In the antebellum era, respectable northern women did not regularly attend races because the poorly managed tracks drew a raucous crowd. This custom changed after the Civil War, widely attributed to Jerome Park, which drew large numbers of women on fashionable social outings.[50] The *New York Times* claimed that the most notable feature of the opening of Jerome Park in 1866 "was the encouragement given it by the ladies of our City." They had largely stayed away in the past because of disorder: "The crowds were always more or less rough and reckless, and no comfort or pleasure could be derived which in the least compensated for the risks run in the getting out and back." However, "All this is changed—there were at least a thousand ladies at the Park yesterday, and in time it will become as marked an event among the gentler classes of the Metropolis, as we believe it has already among the turf men and their encouragers of the masculine persuasion."[51]

The *Times* believed the presence of "ladies of fashion, ladies domestic, ladies professionally literary, ladies of birth and culture, ladies of dress, and ladies of more quiet tastes" would quickly help elevate thoroughbred racing: "The ladies have given the club and the course their indorsement and no doubt each day's racing will be marked by the same good order and quiet that characterized that of yesterday—a feature in very large degree attributable to the presence of so many ladies. The brilliant costumes of the fair witnesses upon the stand lent an air of graceful beauty to the scene which would have been intensely sombre in its tone without them."[52]

Turf, Field, and Farm commended Jerome Park for catering to women by promoting the social aspects of race day and recommended trotting tracks copy it

4. The annual (1886) spring meeting of the American Jockey Club at Jerome Park afforded great entertainment to lovers of sport, even though the state banned betting on the course. These stylish spectators enjoyed the coach ride to the track and the opportunity to see and be seen by others, admire their social set's fashionable new spring clothing, and watch good racing. Drawn from photographs by Bidwell. *Source:* "Coaches at Jerome Park on a Race Day," *Harper's Weekly* 30 (19 June 1886): 389.

to elevate "the moral surroundings of the sport." "Wherever pure woman goes," noted the magazine, "she carries an air of refinement with her, and by her very presence enriches and ennobles." Their quality was infectious, and if rough sorts went to the track (which *Turf, Field, and Farm* denied), these rascals would be so abashed that they would behave properly. *Turf, Field, and Farm* thought the track should not charge women $2 for admission because their presence made Jerome Park a "seat of elegance, the home of fashion, and the resort of health-giving, ennobling pleasure," and they brought male spectators with them. The magazine criticized the track's paternalistic policy of not allowing women to walk from the grandstand to the clubhouse without an escort.[53]

Women were always an important element of the Jerome crowd because they added glamour and status to the sport. In 1886, for instance, a Detroit reporter noted, "It is no unusual sight to see well-known actresses, bucolic visitors, book-makers, sweethearts and highly respectable young girls jumble together in a row on the grand stand with all social lines and distinctions swept away." However, the journalist further pointed out the "special and separate accommodations for ladies who are 'in society.' At Jerome there is usually a magnificent show of lovely women but the every day mob cannot get within 1,000 feet of them and must content itself with gazing at the beauties from afar." They arrived in their own coaches, employed a separate entrance, "and are in every way aloof of bonbons and gloves and no end of jollity." The reporter disingenuously claimed that "the ladies do not bet, of course."[54]

Gambling at Jerome Park

The Auction Pool

The primary method of betting at Jerome Park was the auction pool system, a betting format started in Europe. It was common for pools at Jerome Park to reach $2,000 to $5,000. The auction pool system was open and public but had obvious disadvantages. The biggest was that it was heavily stacked in favor of wealthier bettors, who could outbid others for the favorite horses. Small bettors had little chance to participate, much less bet on their preferred horse. A second problem was that bettors had no odds on which to base their decisions and could figure out the betting percentages only after the pool was completed. Bettors also complained about exorbitant, if not extortionate, commissions and unscrupulous sellers trying to confuse them. One advantage of this system was that money wagered on a scratched horse was refunded (which bookmakers did not do),

5. The auction pool was the first organized betting system on American racetracks. It favored wealthier bettors, who could consistently outbid rivals for the favorite horse, which won more than 40 percent of the time. Drawn by Frederick Barnard. *Source:* "Selling 'Auction Pools' on a Horse Race," *Harper's Weekly* 32 (11 Aug. 1888): 589.

although there were cases when odds in auction pools were subverted by the scratching of a horse.[55]

The Pari-Mutuel

In 1871, Jerome introduced the pari-mutuel system, which he had observed at Parisian racetracks. The betting scheme was invented in 1865 by Parisian perfumer Pierre Oller to supplant what he believed were bookmakers' unfair odds. He started out selling tickets at a *fixed price* for any horse in the race. The wagered funds were pooled together, and bettors holding winning tickets split the pool, less 5 percent for Oller. The approximate odds were determined by dividing the pool, less the commission, by the amount bet on each horse. Oller had simple totalizers built for the French racetracks that automatically figured the odds, which constantly changed as more money was bet. The accuracy of the calculations was problematic until 1930, when the American Totalisator Company invented an electromechanical device that displayed results on an electronic board at Pimlico Racetrack. Oller's first machine was set up in the field of the Paris course facing the grandstand and enabled the poor to gamble. A bettor paid 30 francs and received a card with the name of his chosen horse. Oller's innovation was so popular that he opened a betting parlor in a large Parisian building where he operated several machines that took bets on French and English races. In 1870, he operated a pari-mutuel on the Bourse, and men began to take mutuels on the rise and fall of favorite stocks. However, the government suppressed the system after brokers complained of the competition, and reformers argued that the proliferation of betting with those machines "led to embezzlements . . . and an increase in suicides." The apparatus gained popularity outside France. In Russia, where racing was the nation's first national pastime, the state introduced the totalizator in 1876, and there were more than fifty in use by 1910. The government took 10 percent of the take, using profits to support the breeding industry for military purposes, and set aside another 1 percent for charity.[56]

The AJC originally managed its pari-mutuel system with a minimum $5 wager. Jerome found it very difficult to get people to properly operate the apparatus, which issued betting slips that automatically recorded the number of bets placed on each horse, so one day he even worked the machine himself. The track also had a problem with counterfeit tickets, sometimes cashed as late as two weeks after a race. Following the spring Jerome Park meet, the pari-mutuel business was leased to Morrissey's old associate John F. Chamberlain for a large percentage of the action. The new system seemed to be a popular innovation. According to the *Spirit of the Times*, "At Jerome Park there was such a rush to buy tickets that not half of those who wanted them could be supplied." Betting with the machines was certainly a savvy choice. For example, in 1872, long shot Nackajack at 234–1, paid nearly $1,200 for a $5 bet with the machine, whereas bookmakers offered odds that ranged only from 5–1 to 20–1.[57]

Publisher George Wilkes of the *Spirit of the Times* originally supported pari-mutuels to promote democracy on the turf. He found it "somewhat astonishing to see how rapidly these pools are increasing in public favor." This proved that "a much larger part of the community is interested in horse racing." The system gave people "outside the ring of large speculators a chance of making their investments on favorable terms."[58]

However, by the end of 1873, the *Spirit* was losing its confidence in the pari-mutuel system and instead recommended something along the line of London's Tattersall's, "by which betting among gentlemen can be regulated though a system of booking the odds at various periods of the year; and the integrity of these proceedings protected and in some sort guaranteed by a quasi jurisdiction of the Jockey Club." The *Spirit* preferred the English system of bookmaking to pari-mutuels, which was barred in England, "because it is always under wholesome and responsible control, while the Paris Mutuel machine, though an honest enough system in itself, can be easily perverted by a roguish operation so as to steal nearly every dollar invested through it." The *Spirit* took to task "that incorrigible rascal Chamberlain," who, when he noticed a lightly bet horse coming up the homestretch with a lead, supposedly dropped two or three cards on that equine in the pool box in the name of a confederate.[59]

In 1874, Chamberlain lost the pari-mutuel privilege to Morrissey, who paid $12,000 to run the betting. Morrissey added a dozen new machines and enlarged them so every horse in a large field could be bet. Morrissey purportedly made $25,000 for a six-day spring meeting at Jerome Park in 1874, more than two-thirds the amount of all the purses and stakes combined. On the first day of the fall meeting, which featured five races, 12,496 $5 pari-mutuel tickets were sold for $62,480, providing a 5 percent commission of $3,124. The machines were so profitable that Morrissey had ten or twelve similar machines made for Saratoga.[60]

However, the French betting scheme had serious problems. Heavy plungers disliked it because their large wagers depressed odds on their horses. Then, since the odds shifted during the betting, the exact odds were unknown until all bets were totalized. Once bookmaking came into vogue, pikers preferred using their friendly bookmaker, who would take smaller bets and even provide credit.[61]

There were also suspicions that pari-mutuel managers fixed races by bribing jockeys or altering the reported number of transactions to lower payout odds. A Brooklyn butcher and his friend caught Morrissey's agents swindling patrons by watching the machines after a pool was closed. They noticed that when the bettors' attention turned to the race in progress, "a secret spring was put in motion by which the register of the winning horse was increased, the added number being taken from one or more of the losing horses." In a $1,000 pool with 10 tickets sold on the winning horse, the pool operator would get $50 as his fee, and each winning ticket would be worth $95. However, if the register reported 15 winning tickets, each receipt was worth $63.33, and the operator would pocket an additional $316.67.[62]

The very accessibility of the relatively inexpensive pari-mutuels was problematic, because it encouraged people who could not afford to gamble to place bets. The *Times* claimed that the pari-mutuel's "introduction to this country has done more to foster and encourage the spirit of gambling than any other one thing. Only men who could afford to lose were able to take a share in the auction pools, where the price of a horse rose into the hundreds, and often into the thousands, but the Paris Mutual [*sic*] reaches down into the pockets of the poor man, and while taking his last cent, perhaps, spurs him on to the passion for gambling which usually results in his utter ruin and degradation."[63]

Jerome Park used pari-mutuels for just a few years before dropping it because the machines were unpopular with its patrons. However, other prominent jockey clubs adopted the apparatus, including nearby Monmouth Park. Baltimore's Pimlico track in 1873 used pari-mutuels for the Preakness, and in 1878, the Louisville Jockey Club, sponsor of the Kentucky Derby, also introduced the French betting format. In the mid-1880s, tracks in Washington, DC, and Chicago's Washington Park also adopted the new form of wagering. However, it did not supplant the more popular betting options of auction pools and bookmaking.[64]

Bookmaking

Bookmaking began in England around 1840, when bets were recorded in a ledger. Bets were made with bookmakers in the plebeian "outer betting ring" unless one paid a fee to be admitted into the elite "inner ring." The roofed rings were located next to the grandstand and near the finish line. Each bookmaker had his own stall with a big blackboard that posted odds. The bookmaker stood on a raised platform so his clients could see him and he could see his competitors' odds. The bookmakers attracted bettors who could not afford to bid for their favorite horses in an auction pool. The Philadelphia firm of Sanford, Sykes, and Eves was purportedly the first American bookmakers, taking bets shortly after the end of the Civil War on cricket, regattas, and trotting. In 1871, James B. Kelly, the first New York bookmaker, opened a book on the Belmont Stakes and was soon followed by English bookmakers. Jerome Park introduced bookmaking at the track in 1872 with little success. The bookmaker levied a 1 percent commission charge on winning bets, and the track got 5 percent of all the money bet. Afterward, the AJC sold the betting privilege to an individual who in turn charged bookmakers to operate. Each bookmaker advertised his odds on a slate, and bets were recorded in a notebook. The new betting system was unpopular at Jerome Park because the fixed odds were less attractive than the pools. Consequently, the AJC dropped bookmaking and returned to auction pools.[65]

Morrissey and Kelly were the main backers of the bookmaking system. Historian David Johnson surmises that they supported it because some of their wealthy clients liked it, the system could be used to influence betting odds, and it was a new source of revenue for them. Kelly was a partner of Chauncey Bliss. He secured the gambling privileges in various locales while Bliss handled the financial affairs. Kelly's appearance belied his occupation. When he appeared before a legislative committee in 1887 investigating pool selling, Kelly was described as a man "whose benevolent countenance, silver-gray hair and beard, quiet manner, and subdued style of clothing made him look much like a financial magnate, gave his occupation as that of 'speculator,' and it was only when he described his important connections with Coney Island gambling that the audience could divest itself of the idea that they were about to listen to a Wall-street veteran."[66]

Kelly was one of the first bookmakers to take bets on future events. The concept came to him at a Baltimore racing meet in the fall of 1869, when Kentucky breeder John Coffee was so sure his horse Foster would win the Dinner Stakes that he decided to make a book and take all the bets he could get. Kelly was influenced by Coffee's enterprise:

> Coffee's book set me thinking, and it occurred to me that bookmaking would not be a bad business for a man who had not a great deal to do and plenty of money to carry it out. Therefore, at this same meeting at Baltimore in 1871 I went to . . . other owners and asked them if they would care to back their entries in some of the future events. They mostly all did so, and I opened an office at 1134 Broadway. . . . That Winter I opened a $10,000 book on each of the closed events at Long Branch, Saratoga, and Jerome. I sent out circulars all over the country and especially to horsemen. I put Harry Bassett favorite, as he deserved to be, at 5 to 1, and Marie Louise at 8 to 1, and the others at prices ranging from 15 to 1 to 50 to 1. The public, and especially some rich horse owners, took to the new system very kindly, and I got in a great deal of money, so much in fact that I had $10,000 in ready cash in some of my books long before the events were to come off. Mr. August Belmont and Mr. Pierre Lorillard were among my best customers.[67]

In 1872, when the directors of Jerome Park insisted that Morrissey make a future book on closed events, Bliss joined up with Morrissey. Kelly made a future book in 1873 on races at Jerome, Monmouth, and Saratoga. Morrissey continued for the next few years to take bets during the winter for future stakes races. The future books were great for his cash flow, putting money into his pocket for several months that he might employ for other uses. It also gave Morrissey insight into how money was flowing for big stakes races, enabling him to reset odds more favorably for himself when the season actually began. There was speculation that Morrissey intended to become a national oddsmaker, but he had more than sufficient business in New York.[68]

Kelly's partners included William Lovell and the venerable Dr. Underwood, who retired just before his death. Shortly afterward, the firm was compelled to move to Hoboken. In 1875, Jerome sent Charles Bathgate to Kelly and asked him to make post books at Jerome Park. Seven or eight men opened books at the track, including Mike Cridge of the firm Cridge and Murray. They took up the end front row in the grandstand and carried small cardboards on which odds were posted. There was not a lot of competition, and very short odds were laid. At the next meet, several more bookmakers appeared, and booths were built for them near the end of the grandstand. Business was so good that management built a betting ring.[69]

The Antipool Bill

Betting on horses was considered a legitimate endeavor in New York State, based on the revised statutes of 1830 that allowed the loser of a bet to sue for, and recover, his stake. Nonetheless, there was always a lot of moral opposition to gambling, mainly based on religious grounds. Reformers believed that the selling of pools was "iniquitous and demoralizing," as exemplified by one prominent firm's advertisement that "in order to give working men a chance," they had reduced the minimum price of a pool ticket to $1.[70]

Hostility peaked after the 1876 Tilden-Hayes presidential election on which huge sums were staked. John Morrissey alone was the stakeholder for pools worth an estimated $350,000. As returns came in, it became apparent that the winner would not be determined for weeks, if not months, because of fraudulent voting in South Carolina, Florida, and Louisiana. Morrissey announced that all bets were off and returned the wagers, less a 2 percent commission. Local and national pool sellers followed his lead.[71]

In response to the wagering on the presidential election, and the ensuing chicanery that led to widespread complaints by clients who felt ripped off, legislators introduced several bills to forestall pool selling on future political campaigns. The first proposals recommended banning pools inside buildings, with the intent of allowing pool selling at racetracks. However, rural legislators demanded a total prohibition on pools. They submitted a bill prohibiting the keeping of any room anywhere to record bets, register wagers, or sell pools on human feats, animals, or elections with the maximum penalty of a $200 fine and a year in jail.[72]

The *Times* supported a stringent bill, "because it is demanded by considerations of public morals and public decency," since every year foolish people lost money to pools and sharpsters swindled them. The editors pointed out, "Even if fairly conducted, the pool-sellers' business is a form of gambling, which is recognized in law as a forbidden occupation, and . . . it is notoriously used by swindlers to cheat the public, as was largely done by Morrissey and others in the pools on the Presidential election." The paper had limited sympathy with simple and greedy people who dealt with professional gamblers and asserted that "the toleration of pool-selling in public is a scandal and a nuisance."[73]

Turf supporters lobbied in Albany against the legislation. Representatives from the AJC and the Saratoga Racing Association (SRA), along with prominent breeders and horse owners, spoke before the state assembly's Judiciary Committee. Saratogans were very concerned about the antipool bill because racing had become a big part of their tourist trade. The SRA began holding two summer meetings in 1870, backed by local hoteliers who made so much money during the racing season that they gave the track $10,000 to support the extra meeting in mid-July. However, the lobbying was to no avail, and the bill to ban pool selling passed the assembly on 7 March by a resounding vote of ninety to ten.[74]

The *Times* applauded the vote, noting that "wherever the practice of betting has attained large proportions, it has had a demoralizing influence on horse-racing, and legislative efforts in England to place it under summary restrictions have had a very healthy effect both on the morals of, and the healthy interest in, the sports of the turf." It urged the AJC to recognize that the character of horse owners, jockeys, and fans "has not improved since the practice of public betting grew to its present dimensions."[75]

Belmont, Jerome, Hunter, and other members of the AJC petitioned the state senate's Committee on Internal Affairs for an exemption from the antipool law during its racing season, arguing they should not be held accountable because of abuses by other betting operations. The AJC spokesmen claimed the club had been formed to improve the breed by testing speed in races and was offering prizes worth $80,000 to attract the best horses. The track needed a large attendance to pay for its expenses, which meant it needed gambling under "a well ordered and well-conducted system, under which all persons who attend these exhibitions, and take an intelligent interest in them, may safely and fairly stake such sums of money . . . upon the accuracy of their judgment in regard to the qualities and merits of the animals which contend for the prizes and rewards."[76]

Senator Morrissey criticized the bill, reminding his colleagues that no senator had as great an interest in the proposal bill as he did, since "Old Smoke" was the biggest stockholder in the $250,000 Saratoga racetrack and had multiple other gambling interests. Morrissey argued that passage would hurt the state's $10 million breeding industry while benefiting the competition in New Jersey, Ohio, Maryland, and Pennsylvania. His oration and other opposition to the bill fell on deaf ears. The Senate approved the antipool bill on 24 April by a vote of twenty-one to zero, with Morrissey abstaining. Democratic governor Lucius Robinson signed the bill three days later, and it went into effect on 15 May. Gamblers, pool-room men, and track proprietors allegedly spent $30,000 to protect their interests, but to no avail.[77]

The Impact of the Antipool Law

The *Times* was pleased with the new law that promised to kill pool betting, freeing hundreds of young men from the gambling vortex and people of all classes from a passion for gambling without ruining thoroughbred racing or the breeding industry as widely feared. Fans were expected to keep going to the races and owners to continue breeding fine horses. The editors claimed, incorrectly, that nearly all the eminent owners and breeders favored the new law and that the main opposition was just from gamblers, who "would as readily buy a pool on the jumping frog as on the finest horse that ever ran." The *Times* did not want to see a decline in thoroughbred racing, which needed to be maintained because of its popularity with the affluent, who otherwise would be going to Europe for diversion. New York had to compete with Paris, which spent millions to promote tourism, getting "dollars that should be aiding to restore the prostrate business of America."[78]

Turf supporters maintained there was a need for racing to promote the breed, but that argument did not impress segments of the local press who believed that thoroughbreds were good only for racing. The *Spirit*, not surprisingly, claimed that the continued excellence of American horses depended on thoroughbreds to continue improving such intermediate strains as trotters and steeplechasers. Charles J. Foster, publisher of the *Sportsman*, rated the finest turf journalist of the day, considered the new law, passed by a "vicious and hypocritical gang" at Albany, "tyrannical." He applauded Saratogans who stood up for their rights and liberties.[79]

The AJC warned that if betting at the tracks ended, the result would ruin horse racing and severely damage the breeding industry. As one letter writer to the *Times* noted, "From time immemorial horseracing and betting thereon have been so associated that it is not an easy matter to separate them, and a horse-race [sic] without betting is something like the play of 'Hamlet' with *Hamlet* left out." The AJC criticized the antipool law as tyrannical and absurd and claimed "a great mistake is made when anything is done to distract from a place of amusement such as Jerome Park is."[80]

The jockey club attacked critics who questioned the turf's morality, claiming with flowery rhetoric that it "exercised a civilizing and ameliorating effect upon the characters of the lower order of sporting men by their stringent rules and the respectable manner in which they have managed to run four meetings." The AJC went on to ridiculously claim that "these men, finding that no rowdyism would be tolerated, and discovering that good behavior secured respectful treatment, took pattern after the gentlemen in whose company they happened to be for the time being, and gradually the influence exerted has been to shape their general conduct for the better." Management denied any misconduct on its grounds. Wires previously strung above the picket fence between the lawn and track, "lest the rowdy element would make a rush over the fence during a race and tamper with the horses," were not needed and were coming down. Of course, the AJC would not have strung up the wire in the first place unless someone thought it was needed.[81]

The AJC did not allow pool selling at the track, discontinued pari-mutuels, and focused on bookmaking, which seemed the only sports betting system the new law considered legal. Management permitted a bookmaker to operate at Jerome Park if he could prove his dependability and paid a $10 fee. The track reserved the northern enclosure of the grandstand and about four hundred feet of the lawn for bookmaking, which it divided into an "inner ring" for major bookmakers catering to high rollers and an "outer ring" where smaller bets were taken.[82]

Racing fans accustomed to auction pools stayed home on opening day (2 June), leaving the grandstand half empty. Fans paid a $1 fee to enter the betting ring on top of the $2 admission to the grandstand. A reporter noted the "absence of enthusiasm, excitement, and deep interest in the races" and found that the small bettors did not understand the new bookmaking system. The bookmakers did not draw a lot of interest, and most betting was between private individuals. The *Times* was not concerned that attendance was down for the first four racing dates, since "a large proportion of the old habitués either betake themselves to the pool-rooms at Hoboken or stay at home, because they fail to take any pleasure in the sport for its own sake, and because the rather vulgar kind of betting with which they are familiar is no longer possible." They would not be missed, and lovers of sport "will find in their absence a fresh reason for including the race-track among those places which can be resorted to without contamination, and be made the source of healthy and sustained pleasure." The *New York Times* was upbeat about the future of Jerome Park, because it anticipated that without gamblers (forgetting about the bookmakers) and their deleterious influence, racing would be more enjoyable for people who wanted a few hours of pleasure, healthful excitement, and outstanding equine competition.[83]

The *Times* was comfortable with the English bookmaker and gave him his due: "The bookmaker must not only exercise keen judgment, but he must be very industrious as well. It is important that once started, his book should be filled, as every horse untaken means so many more dollars risk to him. He has to balance his bets, so that whichever horse wins, the amount he will have to pay will not break him, and if possible, so as to make a profit in any but the most extreme event." The advantage of bookmaking was that "a man will always know the odds against him, a thing that was impossible in the French pools, every bet made up to the moment of starting changing the odds." However, bettors did have problems with bookmakers who accepted only bets that were "play or pay" (bets stood even if the horse scratched) and offered odds about one-half fair value.[84]

Fan interest did not pick up during the seven-day fall season, which began with just 2,000 present, one-fourth the usual audience and including just 150 women. The races were excellent, but attendance was the worst in Jerome Park's history, and the meet was a financial disaster. The *Times* was disappointed with the crowds, though it rated the sport as "healthier, manlier, and more interesting" than in England. Public interest was hurt by the absence of auction pools, the higher cost of attending and betting, and the club's fencing off the best sections open to the public, including the quarter stretch, discouraging the mixing of fans with hard-core bettors.[85]

Even Dead Head Hill was just about deserted, with only about 100 spectators making bets as small as $0.25 with bookmakers. The AJC had recently built a tall painted-board fence to obstruct the free vantage point and erected a plain grandstand there, where seats cost just $0.25. But it was more trouble than it was worth and was torn down one year later.[86]

Overall, the immediate impact of the antipool law was very negative for Jerome Park and the breeding industry. Jerome Park's receipts fell off by two-thirds between 1876 and 1877, from $71,061 to $26,487, its first decline ever. The *Spirit of the Times* attributed the first decline in yearling sales in many years to the new law, which led several local breeders to export horses to Europe. Outside of metropolitan New York, the authorities did not interfere with pools sold at racetracks, reflecting widespread public opposition to the antipool law. Saratoga not only ignored the new law but even extended its meet to a record forty-two days, while the Grand Circuit of trotting, which included Buffalo, Utica, Rochester, Elmira, and Poughkeepsie, still sold pools. Consequently, the AJC believed it was being picked on unfairly.[87]

The problems at Jerome Park led to speculation in 1878 that the AJC would move its operations to Monmouth Park, recently purchased by David Withers and several other AJC members, including Jerome and Belmont. When the season began on Memorial Day, the AJC cut general admission tickets by half to $0.50, though prices were back to $1.00 for the Belmont Stakes. The *Times* hoped that the holiday, the cheap prices, and the excellent competition would restore attendance even "without the incentive of betting." The meet had terrible weather, starting with a storm on opening day that kept attendance down to about 1,000. Continuing downpours kept attendance light for the other four days, with just 500 people at the Juvenile Stakes and 3,000 at the Belmont Stakes. However, the *Brooklyn Eagle* blamed the poor turnout less on the weather than on the public's lack of faith in the English system of bookmaking and the occasional welshing by bookmakers.[88]

Attendance picked up at the fall meet. More than 10,000 people attended opening day, and another 2,000 economical fans watched from Dead Head Hill. The crowd hoped to bet with pool sellers, but 200 policemen at the track kept them away. The 20 or so bookmakers present monopolized the betting and did a solid business.[89]

Conclusion

The creation of Jerome Park was a landmark in the history of the American turf. Organized by the prestigious American Jockey Club, Jerome Park rapidly surpassed Saratoga as the most important elite racetrack in the United States and provided a model for the many first-rate tracks built in the next twenty years, like Monmouth Park, Churchill Downs, the Bay Course in San Francisco, Sheepshead Bay in Brooklyn, and Washington Park in Chicago. Its ambience helped make thoroughbred racing an immensely popular sport under the control of the social elite, who employed Jerome Park as a social center. Management was in the forefront of racing reform, with innovations like dash races and pari-mutuel betting. However, its future was clouded by the passage of the antipool law in 1877, which compelled the AJC to discontinue auction pools and replace it with bookmaking, which became the main form of horse race betting for decades to come.

3

The Emergence of the Brooklyn Racetracks, 1879–86

Sheepshead Bay . . . is, as regards beauty of location and surroundings, probably
without equal in the world. . . . Besides the natural attraction of forest, ocean, and
all that, the quality of the track, its form, the fact that the whole of the race can be
seen from all points of view, and the liberality of all arrangement for the public,
make it easily the first place of its kind in the world.
— "The Autumn Meeting of the Coney Island Jockey Club,"
Brooklyn Daily Eagle, 25 August 1881

In 1879, Jerome Park, a snobbish and extremely popular haunt of the "400 Hundred," started the year as the only thoroughbred track in the immediate metropolitan area. However, its monopoly was soon broken with the opening of two thoroughbred tracks in Coney Island, a distant resort in southern Kings County, which, over the next two decades, would become the national playground of America. The Coney Island Jockey Club (CIJC), which established the Sheepshead Bay Racetrack, replicated the AJC as an elite jockey club, while the Brighton Beach Racing Association (BBRA) operated the Brighton Beach Racetrack, which was the first major proprietary (profit-oriented) track in the nation. These two tracks had a huge potential market, since Brooklyn in 1880 was the third-largest city in the United States with a population of 566,663 and was accessible by public transportation from New York City, whose population was 1,206,299. These two new tracks strengthened New York's claim as the national center of thoroughbred racing. Thoroughbred racing in the area became so popular that a second proprietary track opened in 1886 in Coney Island. A lot of gambling accompanied the heightened interest in the turf, despite the recent antipool law. The Brooklyn track operators had no problem at all with the anti-betting laws because of their political clout, which rankled social reformers like Anthony Comstock, who wanted to terminate all gambling on the turf, both on and off the tracks.

Jerome Park in 1879

Management hoped to build on the successful fall 1878 meet by making several improvements in its grandstand, the largest in the United States, to make it more user-friendly. Thus, the track removed the wire fence enclosing the betting grounds at the far northern end of the stand, thereby opening it up to the public for no additional cost. The AJC particularly tried to enhance its popularity with women by putting in comfortable new cushions in the ladies' section of the grandstand. A big effort was made to enhance the concessions operations, where "the eatables and drinkables furnished were poor in quality and scant in quantity, and the prices charged were exasperatingly exorbitant." A new firm gained the concessions privilege "with the intention of selling first-class New York goods at New York prices." When the spring meet began, "purchasers were more astonished as gratified . . . when after recognizing the excellent quality of the goods furnished they received their change and discovered how reasonable the prices were."[1]

The 1879 spring meet opened on Decoration Day with about 12,000, half in the grandstand, with an additional 3,000 fans watching from Dead Head Hill. Profits from the gate, concessions, and betting privileges more than covered the generous $19,000 in purses. Attendance averaged about 4,000 for the rest of the meet. Entrance to the betting enclosure and the quarter stretch cost $2.50, standing room was $0.50, and women paid $1.00 for a grandstand seat. Children got in free when accompanied by an adult.[2]

The bookmaking privilege in 1879 sold for $11,450, 43 percent more than the $8,000 previously paid to run auction pools. However, racegoers were still unhappy with bookmaking and preferred auction pools: "They are slow to learn the ins and outs of book-making. They understand the English turf maxim that 'a bet is never well laid until it is well hedged' thoroughly," but had no idea how to hedge a bet.[3]

The *New York Times* continued to laud the AJC for its high standards and contribution to the city's quality of life. Yet it was concerned that the elite, who provided the backbone of racing's support, were growing lukewarm in their interest: "Very many of our wealthiest residents do little to encourage the sport unless it is on foreign soil. Here, at home, they are hardly ever seen at a race-track; but just as soon as they go to Paris, their first inquiry is 'Where are the races?' and they faithfully attend them every day."[4]

The New York press continued lavishing attention on upper-class female spectators whose presence lent status to the sport. Reporters pointed out that the women enjoyed the excitement, the fresh air, and, for a few, even the betting.

Some were keen students of the various betting guides and skillfully determined betting odds. As one fan pointed out, "Why cannot we make a few dollars in the same way as our husbands and brothers?" The *New York World* encouraged giving them the same kinds of special accommodations like women had at the Melbourne, Australia, grandstand, where there were two immense retiring rooms the size of ballrooms, with a full run of mirrors, cosmetics, and pincushions with threaded needles.[5]

One constant complaint was the transportation. Ideally, the ride by train from downtown was just twenty-five minutes, but that was seldom the case. In 1880, Leonard Jerome's newly incorporated $200,000 Jerome Railway opened, and the Jerome Park Railway Company completed a much-anticipated half-mile semicircular spur from the back of the grandstand to the Harlem Railroad's Jerome Park Station. The round-trip fare was $0.60. Nonetheless, travel was still problematic, especially for big events. For instance, on opening day in the spring of 1884, the Harlem Railroad provided two special twenty-car trains, but it was inadequate for the crowds. The fully packed trains left hundreds at the Grand Central platform. The first train was so overloaded that it could not make the rise of the hill by the station, and the second was so late that it arrived after the first race.[6]

One year later, conditions were still inadequate. One locomotive was too weak to carry its eleven cars and stalled. The Harlem line supplied cars reserved for ladies and their escorts, but many women had to stand in the aisles while ungallant men remained seated. The *Times* took the Harlem Railroad to task for its repeated poor preparation and recommended the AJC build its own rail line to the park if it hoped to attract fans beyond the carriage trade. The paper also criticized the track for its slow-moving lines at the box office. Some fans became so impatient that they bought admission tickets from scalpers at the train station at 25 percent above face value.[7]

The influential *New York World* complained that rail service had barely improved over a decade, with much larger crowds going to the track, and blamed poor transportation for limiting holiday crowds at not only horse races but also baseball games and other entertainments. The *World* hoped that William H. Vanderbilt, owner of the Harlem Railroad, had learned from Epsom Downs, where two railroads ran in competition with each other. The trains there carried about 50,000 people on Derby Day.[8]

The *World* had the largest circulation of any New York newspaper, based on its extensive treatment of popular topics like crime, entertainment, and sports. Its coverage of racing in 1884 included two photographic features about the leading American turfmen. According to Joseph Pulitzer's biographer, "The *World* covered the turf more as a patron than a chronicler of contemporary sports." The daily proudly supported the growth of thoroughbred racing and looked forward to the day when American horses would be superior to British. An editorial questioned how anyone could oppose racing: "The idea of any narrow-minded bigoted crusade being made against horse-racing is absurd. . . . The Turf is getting to be an American institution, and it is one which ought to be encouraged as it is in European countries."[9]

The Rise of the Brighton Beach Racing Association

In 1879, the Brighton Beach Racing Association was established with little fanfare, with plans to operate a proprietary racetrack in Coney Island, a wide-open resort in the town of Gravesend, Kings County. Popularly known as "Sodom-by-the-Sea," Coney Island had the potential to become an outstanding summer resort because of excellent beaches and rapidly improving transportation that cut the time of travel for more than 2 million people in metropolitan New York to one hour. There were steamboats from Lower Manhattan and downtown Brooklyn to Coney Island Point, in addition to nine steam-powered trains and one horsecar line from downtown Brooklyn. Manhattanites relied on ferries to get to Brooklyn until the completion in 1883 of the 1.13-mile Brooklyn Bridge, the longest suspension bridge in the world.[10]

Entrepreneur William A. Engeman, the head of the BBRA, was a self-made New Yorker who first got into racing as the owner of a thoroughbred stable. Engeman, born in 1840, apprenticed as a ship's carpenter and then went west to make his fortune. He got rich in the lumber business and returned in 1868 to open a popular restaurant. In 1871, he began buying Coney Island real estate and helped promote the area as a resort.[11]

Engeman built the eighty-thousand-dollar Brighton Beach Fair Grounds (soon known as the Brighton Beach Racetrack), just behind his old Ocean Hotel, and close to the Brighton Beach Depot in less than thirty days, using 500 workers. A modest facility, especially compared to Jerome Park, it had the advantage of several alternative routes to the course. The track was accessible by six railway routes, including the Brooklyn, Flatbush, and Coney Island Railroad (later known as the Brighton Line and today's D Train); Andrew R. Culver's Prospect Park and Coney Island Railroad (the F Line), which had a "Race Track" station; and the New York and Sea Beach Railroad (the N Route). Fans also arrived by steamboats and carriages via a nearby parkway. By the end of the century, spectators paying twenty cents for an excursion fare got to the track from Brooklyn Bridge in just thirty minutes.[12] However, accessibility did not come without a cost, because by the mid-1880s, roughnecks created havoc on the public transit to Coney Island. The lines responded by trying to segregate the toughs from respectable fans, moving them to the bow of boats and the front of train cars.[13]

The new track had a mile-long course for racing, with wider turns and wider backstretches and homestretches than at Jerome Park. It also had a 2.5-mile course for steeplechasing constructed on a one-foot-thick bog covered by a layer of loam and clay at least six inches thick, making for an elastic surface with good footing expected to be extremely fast. Engeman tried to attract good stables by charging no entrance fees to races, providing one hundred free stables for horses in training and offering generous purses compared to Jerome and Monmouth. There were two two-story grandstands with ocean views; one sat 8,000 at fifty cents and the other 5,000 at twenty-five cents. There was additional space on the quarter stretch for 30,000 standees. However, Engeman was so uncertain about the track's viability that he built the grandstand so it could easily be converted into a row of cottages if his investment failed.[14]

The BBRA sought a large working-class clientele, hoping to draw interested parties who previously bet with neighborhood bookmakers or saved up for an occasional trip to Jerome Park. In England, working-class betting with street bookmakers became very popular in the 1870s, particularly among artisans and youth, who mainly bet what they could afford. Historian Ross McKibbin considers their betting a rational hobby, a sort of poor man's stock market that provided excitement for people employed in boring, repetitive work. Bettors selected their wagers based on careful study of such essential data as the horse's prior record, breeding, track conditions, trainer, and the jockey that were readily available in the press and from tipsters. American racing fans until the late nineteenth century generally considered the jockey as just along for the ride and not a determining factor. The conventional wisdom was that favorites won because they were superior, not because of the rider, especially at a time when so many jockeys were African American, who were considered inferior and unintelligent. Working-class people who gambled were unaccustomed to saving for the future, and, instead, many relied on winning bets to supplement their incomes.[15]

Brighton's inaugural season began on 28 June, with 2,000 in attendance, and featured a heat race, a dash, a steeplechase, and a band to entertain men and women in the grandstand. The meet ran 34 days, with 130 races and $51,100 in added purses. Despite its accessibility and generous purses, the first year was a struggle. Engeman soon added other entertainments, including chariot races, trapeze artists, and walking and running matches. He also used philanthropy to legitimize his business and improve community relations. Engeman staged a benefit to aid the local Catholic church and donated profits from an extra meeting to needy owners and track workers. The next spring he held a rousing benefit to aid St. John's Home, an orphanage recently destroyed by a fire. By the mid-1880s, he had given thousands of dollars to churches, hospitals, and similar institutions.[16]

The *Spirit of the Times* was optimistic about the "crude and homely" course, because its accessibility gave Brighton the potential to become "the most popular racing point in America." Local hotels, bathing pavilions, shops, saloons, restaurants, and transit lines were all interested in the success of the track, which "gives them additional passengers, customers and guests, not upon a scanty scale, but it will draw to the Beach thousands and tens of thousands who would not otherwise think of visiting it except upon holidays." The *Times* was less enthusiastic and welcomed another nearby option, the elite Coney Island Jockey Club, "because there has been enough seen at the Brighton Beach Race-course this summer to demonstrate the necessity of an association to encourage the breeding of thorough-breds [*sic*] freed from the swindling operations which accompany tests of speed without the restraint of respectability."[17]

In 1880, Engeman hired the energetic James McGowan as secretary of the BBRA to supervise a 41-day meet. McGowan worked as a youth for the *New York Herald* and then served with the old fire department. He graduated to membership in Boss William Tweed's Americus Club when it was a controlling influence in New York politics. McGowan first became heavily involved in racing when Saratoga opened, clerking for pool auctioneer Underwood. McGowan's association with politicians like Morrissey helped him make friends with prominent persons, especially actors, who were big racing fans. During his eleven-year tenure with the track, McGowan played a key role in Brighton's success. Brighton ran more events (albeit of average quality) than any other track. The 1881 meet lasted 52 days, doubling to 100 one year later, and topped out at 125 in 1884, when Brighton had 548 races, surpassed only by the previous year's 567 events. Brighton quickly became one of the most profitable tracks in the country, reportedly earning Engeman between $100,000 and $200,000 in 1882 and more than $100,000 in 1883. The BBRA relied heavily on gambling for its profits, earning 5 percent on all the pool money wagered and another $7,000 a day from the sale of privileges connected to the pool business.[18]

Brighton, and the other Brooklyn tracks, advertised regularly in the newspapers, indicating the cost of tickets ($1.00 for grandstand, $0.50 for ladies, and free admission to the infield in 1891), the starting time (2:30 p.m.), the number of events (typically 7), and routes to the site. The track often put out ads together with the transit companies, usually noting the departing times of special race-day trains. The traction lines also had their own ads, like "Sea Beach Route to CI. Excursion tickets 25 cents. Cheapest and most direct route."[19]

William Engeman died in 1884, replaced by brother George, the track's vice president. The following year, after three straight years of more than 100 racing days, the number of racing days declined, to 94 in 1885, and then dropped precipitously to 30 in 1887, where it stabilized for the next several years. There was an average of 174 races from 1887 through 1895, compared to 434 in the prior seven years. The decline reflected competition from the new Brooklyn Jockey Club (BJC), another proprietary track that opened in 1886. The amount annually added to purses was about $51,000 from 1879 through 1881, which doubled in 1882 to $105,950, and maxed out in 1884 at $181,650 ($331 per race). The BBRA topped out on a per capita basis in 1894 when $100,600 was added to its 168 races, or nearly $600 per event.[20]

In 1885, Brighton Beach became the birthplace of winter racing in metropolitan New York when the regularly scheduled meet was prolonged by inclement weather. Engeman had previously experimented with winter racing in December 1882 when he leased the New Orleans Fair Grounds for five years to complement the idle northern turf. The *Spirit of the Times* was skeptical about the move, concerned that heavy winter rains in the poorly draining delta city would flood the track. It also questioned the ability of New Orleans to attract sufficient patronage, even with good conditions, because "there is a decided smack of Brighton Beach in its association in this New Orleans experiment, and, whether justified or not, the public have come to expect something in the hippodroming line in that connection." Engeman quickly decided he had made a mistake after a cold spell hit the Crescent City and relinquished his lease. Thereafter, the New Louisiana Jockey Club started a winter season on 27 January 1883, and several northern stables sent their horses there for the meet.[21]

Brighton filled an important niche in racing as the "people's track." As the *Spirit* pointed out in 1896, before the track opened, "there was no racing for the great army of people who cannot go to the mountains or the seashore in summer, but who wish to enjoy a whiff of the ocean breeze occasionally, and Mr. Engeman decided to fill that want with a crude and homely [structure], but the people took to it at once, and year by year it grew in extant and influence. Mr. Engeman's motto from the outset was: 'Plenty of racing for owners, poor as well as rich, and amplitude of good sport for the people.'"[22]

The *Detroit Journal* in 1886 described the character of the Brighton Beach crowd, including the "rag-tag and riff-raff" of Coney Island who daily went to the track, along with two to three thousand sports from Brooklyn and New York who came to bet their $2.50 on the pools:

> The crowd is composed of extraordinarily heterogeneous elements. Negro stablemen, Irish saloonkeepers, French barbers, German tailors, Scandinavian boarding

TABLE 1. RACING AT THE BRIGHTON BEACH RACING
ASSOCIATION, 1879–95

Year	Racing days	No. races	Amount added ($)
1879	34	130	51,100
1880	41	273	51,250
1881	52	239	51,125
1882	100	471	105,950
1883	106	567	144,900
1884	125	548	181,650
1885	94	509	147,110
1886	74	431	122,250
1887	30	184	46,760
1888	30	159	63,410
1889	26	150	75,000
1890	30	180	93,100
1891	31	210	156,800
1892	24	145	94,600
1893	30	181	112,200
1894	28	168	100,600
1895	31	186	80,860

Source: Spirit of the Times 131 (18 Apr. 1896): 414.

house runners, toughs, plugs, . . . young clerks, policemen off for a day, crooks of every variety from sneak thieves to expert bank cracksmen, canal boatmen, waiters, hackmen, bootblacks, English visitors (who are as likely as not to be men of title), diminutive jockeys, farmers, flashy sports, all elbowing their way in and out, smoking cheap cigars, drinking quantities of beer and betting all they are worth on every race.[23]

The typical spectators did not dine at the clubhouse but purchased food from vendors who sold homemade refreshments, including chocolate coconut candies. One old-timer particularly remembered "the Mammy with those succulent friend chicken parts at 15 cents and a quarter. 'Deelish!'" He also remembered that a few bookies would take bets of as little as $0.25.[24]

The Detroit reporter did not have a high regard for the 300 or so women usually seen at Brighton, who were hardly comparable to the elegant ladies found at Jerome Park:

As may well be expected, the women who accompany these men are not socially lovable. They are a strange lot. . . . Some of these are hard-featured, coarse and repulsive creatures dressed in gorgeous red or blue satin gowns, with their slim fingers loaded with showy rings, and their hair bleached to a sickening shade of yellow. They bet rather heavily, intrusting their money to more or less broken and disappointed young men who attend the women in a shame-faced way. I have heard those creatures swear like pirates at their losses. . . . They are the dregs of the race course. I have never seen them in the light of day except at Brighton Beach.[25]

Brighton Beach was never a favorite among turf writers. The advent of winter racing only further convinced the New York press of its unwholesome qualities. The *Times* described it as a "pesthole of race-track gambling" whose "main purpose . . . is to furnish a basis for pool selling for the miscellaneous crowd that throngs the Coney Island beaches. . . . It is there that the clerks, cashiers, and office boys of the city are drawn into the fever of betting on races, and many a petty theft or serious embezzlement may be traced directly to the demoralizing influence of the track and its evil surroundings."[26]

The *Tribune* also had little regard for Brighton, with its hundred days of racing with "broken-kneed, muscle-bound wheezy hacks" that kept the city's poolrooms busy. The paper had little hope for stamping out the gambling spirit that "will be gratified, if not at the race-course, then in Wall Street or in the grain pit. If men are prevented from backing their fancies in horseflesh they will gamble all the more furiously in stocks or grain, in cotton or pork." On the other hand, the *Tribune* gave high marks for Jerome Park and Sheepshead Bay, where minimum $5 bets limited the wagering to people who could afford them: "The men who lose will generally be losing their own money and not money stolen from employers, and their losses will not hurt them."[27]

Brighton's reputation hardly improved over time. In 1892, the *New York Tribune* pointed out that there were constant accusations in the press about "collusion between certain owners who control the services of jockeys whose skills at abetting the flag and jockeying on the turns, such as cutting off, coming in collision, carrying to the outer rail of their opponents, is superior to any other jockeys on the turf." Three years later, the *Tribune* concluded, "Brighton Beach has been a quagmire in the pathway of racing from its conception" because of too many fixed or questionable races, as well as its introduction of winter racing, emulated by Clifton, Guttenberg, and Gloucester in New Jersey.[28]

Still, Brighton Beach did make some positive contributions. Brighton's lengthy calendar provided many opportunities for younger jockeys to race and gain experience, and it was a training ground for judges, starters, and other racing officials. The BBRA's financial success helped democratize the turf by encouraging entrepreneurs to develop new proprietary tracks to make money, and its lengthy racing season encouraged the creation of modest racing stables that bred cheaper, lower-quality thoroughbreds that otherwise would have been unprofitable. Of course, democratizing the turf was hardly favored by the sporting elite, who believed that tracks like Brighton hindered the improvement of the breed.[29]

The Origins of the Sheepshead Bay Race Track

In late June 1879, the AJC arranged a three-day meet in the Coney Island section of Gravesend at the Prospect Park Fair Ground and Race Course, a very fast track that dated back to 1863, previously used for harness racing. It was located four miles from city hall, and two and three-quarter miles from Prospect Park. The course had several nearby rail lines and was also accessible by a very fine driving road through Prospect Park. The elite were already familiar with the area since several eminent men's clubs, including the Union League, already had their own private rooms at the Brighton Beach and Manhattan Beach hotels.[30]

The meet was such a success that on 4 July, the organizers formed the Coney Island Jockey Club, with annual meets in June and September to fill the gap between the Jerome Park and Monmouth Park meets. Leonard Jerome, whose control of Jerome Park had been weakened, was the moving spirit behind the new club and its first president. The CIJC's blue-blooded founding governors were mainly a younger generation of wealthy horsemen rather than the AJC's life members, who soon became major stable owners. They included financier August Belmont II; stockbroker James R. Keene; club secretary James G. K. Lawrence, sportsman and son of the former governor of Rhode Island; tobacco manufacturers Pierre Lorillard and George L. Lorillard; William K. Vanderbilt, the railroad tycoon; and A. J. Cassatt, vice president of the Pennsylvania Railroad.[31]

While the *Spirit* was optimistic about the opening of Brighton in 1879, it was absolutely giddy about the prospects for a world-class track at Coney Island, where there were perhaps six sites near the beach just as good as the BBRA's. The sports weekly believed that patronage for a well-conducted course there would justify the expense for a first-rate facility. The *Spirit* believed that American tracks, even Jerome Park, the most expensive in the nation, were inferior compared to such foreign tracks as Newmarket and Ascot in England, Longchamps (Paris), or Frendenauer (Vienna), "which all had immense public patronage justifying those expensive and magnificent stands." The *Spirit* advised sending an architect to Europe to learn how to build such splendid courses. It recommended a three-story grandstand commanding a full view of the ocean that would protect spectators from the afternoon sun, with an accessible roof like at Longchamps, and seating sections divided into ordinary apartments and private boxes large enough for entire families who would rent the space by the meet or the year.[32]

The CIJC was concerned about the feasibility of building a track at Coney Island because of the uncertain nature of the soil. At first, the CIJC attempted to purchase the Brighton Beach Racetrack and remodel it, but Engeman backed off at the last moment. Instead, he offered Jerome a ten-year contract at $25,000 a year to become president of the BBRA, which he declined. Thereafter, the CIJC, originally capitalized at $100,000, increased its funding to $250,000 and decided to build its own world-class facility, fulfilling the hopes of the *Spirit*. The stockholders limited their profits to 7 percent and promised to reinvest any excess back in the track. Jerome located a 112-acre site (Ocean Avenue and Haring Street, Avenue V and Avenue X), with fine, sandy loam soil, three-quarters of a mile from the ocean and a short walk from the imposing two-year-old Manhattan Beach Hotel that barred Jewish customers. The Manhattan Beach Railroad had a station two hundred yards away, and the Brooklyn, Flatbush, and Coney Island Railroad was within four hundred yards. Pedestrians and carriage riders could get to the site on Ocean Parkway that ran right between Sheepshead Bay and the Prospect Park Fair Grounds racecourse.[33]

In the summer of 1880, the Sheepshead Bay Racetrack opened and was soon acclaimed as the finest, handsomest, and best-located track in the United States and the one whose races had the highest integrity. The track, the future scene of many memorable contests, originally cost $135,000, but improvements over the next five years brought the price tag to $300,000. The track was one mile long with a three-mile course for steeplechasing. Experts applauded the quality of its stables and the grass (turf) racing surface added in 1886, unlike any of the faster dirt tracks widely used elsewhere. The five-hundred-foot two-story grandstand seated five thousand spectators with an entresol (mezzanine) divided into two reserved boxes. The edifice was laid out to look obliquely toward the ocean, affording a pleasant shade in the afternoon and avoiding glare off the ocean. A $25,000 three-story Queen Anne clubhouse, soon known as the "American Ascot," was built on land donated by the Manhattan Beach Hotel and included a large hall, nine whist rooms, a billiard saloon on the second floor, and bedrooms on the third. By 1890, the average daily attendance was almost eight thousand, and its major stakes events drew some of the largest crowds in North America.[34]

Sheepshead Bay had two ten-day meets in 1880 that averaged ten thousand spectators, who paid an expensive $2.50 for admission, which helped keep out the riffraff. There were 118 bookmakers present on opening day, who paid $100 per day to operate, plus sufficient pari-mutuel machines to take care of the more than $75,000 bet that day.[35] The track's upper- and upper-middle-class audience had the highest social status of any metropolitan track. The picturesque atmosphere at Sheepshead Bay made it very popular with women, including parties of women and daughters, whose presence gave the track an aura of respectability. Women fans were said to appreciate the quality of the accommodations, the noise level, and the order at the track, attributed to Robert Pinkerton, who was in charge of security. As the *New York World* pointed out, "Mr. Robert is quick and perhaps a little rough to those that have felt his power now, but it is that power, backed up by ability, that gives security to all law-abiding citizens present and is a terror to the very few of the criminal class who escape the argus-eyed detectives at the gate and succeed in reaching the crowded stand or betting ring."[36]

The *Spirit* was effusive in its praise of the new course, which it described as a "fairy land" whose "surroundings are charming and enlivening." It expected that within a year, when "the grass shall be green as Ireland's shamrocks, and the soft breath from the seas shall kiss the maiden's cheek in the grand stand . . . the universal judgment will be that no such place as these beautiful grounds at Sheepshead Bay were ever even dreamed of by Ponce De Leon." The *Spirit* lauded the management for its great judgment and prudence, for hiring experienced and polite personnel, and for giving holders of French "mutual" tickets the benefit of the odd cents, which other tracks held back. Its reporter even praised the Kelly and Bliss firm that managed the betting grounds.[37]

One surprising problem at Sheepshead Bay was the lack of courtesy among spectators, a dilemma common to all tracks except Saratoga, where the *Spirit*'s "Albion" observed that "every man in his seat and every parasol and umbrella [are] lowered; that every person obeyed the rule willingly." Racing officials responded to criticisms of crowd control by claiming they could not prevent people from acting as they wished. As the horses sped by, fans would rise and block the view of people behind them. "Albion" saw men at Sheepshead Bay rush to the front of the grandstand set aside by management for ladies, which he regarded as "ungallant, disrespectful, and utterly wanting in decency and a high sense of self-respect." He argued that spectators would behave better if prevailed upon, which was just what happened when the CIJC put out one thousand lawn chairs, and fans complied with its request not to stand there and block the views of seated fans.[38]

Sheepshead Bay became an integral part of the so-called Atlantic Circuit of thoroughbred racing in 1881, which included Jerome Park, Monmouth Park, Saratoga, Brighton, and Pimlico (Baltimore). From 18 May to November, these tracks had 152 days of competition, with about seven hundred races. A spring midwestern season composed of tracks in Louisville, Lexington, Chicago, Cincinnati, and St. Louis complemented it, along with a southern winter circuit that included

Savannah, Charleston, Macon, Augusta, Atlanta, Mobile, and New Orleans. These three circuits attracted 70 percent of all racing spectators.[39]

Sheepshead Bay's development far exceeded expectations. In 1881, the CIJC declared a 27 percent dividend on capital stock, which was increased from $250,000 to $350,000. Its facilities were already overwhelmed by inadequate seating and insufficient stalls for horses. The crowds taxed the capacity of arriving boats and railroads. Fans on opening day had to wait two hours at South Ferry in Manhattan, and hundreds arrived after the feature race was over. The CIJC spent three-fourths of its surplus to secure more land and build new stables and for beautification projects that included fountains, pagodas, statues, and shaded walks. The jockey club was less successful in compelling bookmakers to keep pace. Their odds seemed very short compared to pools, especially with place betting, and unlike English bookmakers, they did not give odds on third-place (show) finishers.[40]

The big crowds were drawn by Sheepshead Bay's stunning facilities, outstanding races, accessibility, lowered admission fees in 1881, and patriotic feelings engendered by the successful invasion of the European turf by American horseman Pierre Lorillard IV, the nation's biggest tobacco manufacturer, whose Iroquois captured the Epsom Derby and the St. Leger Stakes in 1881. Iroquois was the first American-born and -bred horse to win a major European event. In addition, English immigrant James R. Keene's Foxhall won the Grand Prix de Paris (French Derby). Keene made his first fortune in San Francisco as a stockbroker who specialized in mining stocks before moving to Wall Street in 1876. He went into racing in 1879, when his $15,000 stallion Spendthrift won the Belmont Stakes.[41]

Admission fees were cut by half to the field, quarter stretch, and grandstand, which was applauded by the *Spirit,* an advocate of democratizing racing, like in England, where it claimed flat racing was the national sport. The *Spirit* encouraged American tracks to copy the cheap ticket policy of the Louisiana Jockey Club, which operated the New Orleans Fair Grounds. The LJC began in 1872 to seek large crowds by charging $1.00 for general admission and $0.50 for access to the infield. The Fair Grounds course even admitted African Americans to the public stand but barred them from the quarter stretch by the finish line. The LJC further tried to promote itself by introducing pari-mutuels in December 1873. Despite its innovations, the track struggled, and it closed after the spring 1880 meet.[42]

The LJC's successor, the New Louisiana Jockey Club, continued to democratize racing to enhance its commercial appeal and offered free admission to the infield at its first meet. It staged occasional Sunday races and experimented with evening races under electric lights in 1881. However, the illumination was insufficient, and night events were dropped. Six years later, local bookmakers took over the Fair Grounds track and eagerly admitted African Americans and white working-class bettors shunned by more prestigious tracks. In December 1892, the bookmakers formed the Crescent City Jockey Club, which no longer set aside parts of the grandstand for preferred groups. General admission was reduced to $0.50 to make everyone feel welcome, and women were admitted free.[43]

The CIJC enjoyed excellent press relations until the 1881 summer meet when an experienced *New York Times* racing reporter questioned the fairness of a judge's decision. The track president was so irate that the reporter was forcibly ejected from the grounds. The *Times* reassigned him to Jerome Park and instituted a lawsuit against the CIJC. The *Times* complained that "there are some young men with apparently more money than brains who are connected with both tracks, and who seem to think that they can lord it in this free country with more insolent arrogance than they would dare to show in any public place of the most despotic of European States."[44]

Despite this contretemps, the CIJC became more and more popular and outgrew its plant, drawing nearly fifteen thousand spectators to opening day in 1883. The grandstand's five-thousand-seat capacity, barely half of Jerome's or Monmouth's, was inadequate. Half of the spectators that day had to stand to see the races, blocking passageways and creating a safety hazard. Betting was so heavy that season that the increased number of bookmakers and pool sellers were insufficient. In addition, railway facilities were poor, particularly for return trips, and commuters often jostled women in the rush to get on the trains.[45]

In 1884, the CIJC rebuilt the entire facility. The mile oval racing surface was redesigned to a mile and a furlong (one-eighth of a mile), making it the longest in the country. The course's old problem of a sharp turn and short homestretch was remedied by making the turn home more gradual and allowing for a four-hundred-yard straightaway. The old field stand at the north end of the grandstand was replaced by a spacious roofed facility with a concrete floor that protected bettors from the elements. However, there was still insufficient space for the big crowds, who provided plenty of business for the more than forty bookmakers who worked the site. One of the two most prominent bookmakers told a state legislative committee in 1887 that he took in as much as $50,000 in one day of work, while paying the CIJC $4,000 to $5,000 a day to operate.[46]

The 1884 season marked the instigation of the Suburban Handicap, the first of the CIJC's great annual races, which became the nation's most prestigious handicap race. Then one year later, a second major event was added, the Futurity for two-year-olds, although it was not actually raced until 1888. Horsemen in 1885 nominated 752 horses for the inaugural before they were even born at a cost of $25 apiece. Fourteen eventually made it to the starting line in 1888 for the inaugural

6. The favorite, Proctor Knott, won the six-furlong Futurity Race on 3 September 1888. Painted by Louis Maurer and published by Currier and Ives in 1889. *Source: The Futurity Race at Sheepshead Bay,* in possession of the author.

race. The $40,625 first prize, the richest purse in North America, was won by Proctor Knott, owned by George Scoogan and Samuel W. Bryant. The event drew a glamorous crowd, one-fourth of whom were women. The Futurity's average purse (1889–1902) was $54,042, topped by a record $77,000 in 1890 when August Belmont II's Potomac won $60,674, the largest prize in the century. Sheepshead Bay's third classic race was the Realization Stakes, started in 1889 with a lofty $40,000 prize, and it soon became the richest race in North America for three-year-olds. It was renamed the Lawrence Realization Stakes in 1899 in honor of track president James G. K. Lawrence.[47]

Mike Dwyer, Phil Dwyer, and the Brooklyn Jockey Club

The Dwyer Brothers

In 1886, Philip J. and Michael F. Dwyer established the Brooklyn Jockey Club, the third Coney Island track, which became one of the preeminent proprietary racetracks in North America. They were sons of a Cleveland butcher-shop owner, who in the early 1870s expanded the family firm into a highly profitable Brooklyn wholesale meat business. The Dwyers first got into horse racing in 1875, with Phil in charge of buying horses and Mike taking care of the racing and betting. Four years later, they had the leading stable in metropolitan New York. They were not breeders like patrician-horsemen Pierre Lorillard, David Withers, August Belmont, or A. J. Cassatt, but they liberally supported the breeders, paying top prices. By 1893, Dwyer horses had won 78 of 246 starts and placed 83 times. They were the leading money winners in 1881–83, 1886, and 1887, and by 1888 had made about $1 million in purses. Between 1883 and 1888, they won two Kentucky Derbies, one Preakness, and five Belmont Stakes. Their finest horses included Miss Woodford, the first American-bred horse to win more than $100,000 ($118,365), and Kingston, who won 89 of 138 starts, earning $138,891.[48]

Mike Dwyer's success led to a lot of jealousy and resentment, likely enflamed by his humble social origins, as well as his unsavory methods. He employed his position and power to enter horses in selling races well below their capabilities just so they would win bets for him. Sometimes Mike entered top horses in lower-level claiming events when they were out of condition, presumably for training purposes. Normally, such horses would be claimed, but no rival stable would dare put in a claim for a Dwyer horse racing below class for fear of retribution. The betting public, who did not know what was actually going on, generally supported the very successful Dwyer stable and would bet on the horse. However, if Mike entered an unprepared horse, he would bet on another owner's horse. "But otherwise," the *Spirit* noted, "his management is worth studying. If there is a horse capable of going with the best, he goes." That, of course, was a big *otherwise,* and the weekly was wrong to advise their readers that "the shadow of suspicion has never darkened their career."[49]

The brothers had dramatically different betting philosophies. Phil was a modest and cagey bettor, whereas Mike was one of the turf's heaviest plungers. "M. F. Dwyer is the most remarkable man I have ever met," said John A. Morris, founder of Morris Park Racetrack in 1890: "He is the only man who has fought the bookmarks for ten years and beaten them." However, Mike was not infallible and lost about $250,000 in 1892 alone. Mike also spent hours at the gaming tables and was one of gaming king Richard A. Canfield's top clients at his Saratoga gambling house. One summer Mike averaged $5,000 a night in winnings for several weeks at roulette, but then his luck turned and he lost $90,000 in one evening.[50]

In 1893, the crusading *Chicago Daily News* compared Mike Dwyer to Pierre Lorillard, the turf legend, who seven years earlier established the luxurious town of Tuxedo Park in fashionable Westchester County, where he built the finest country club in the United States. When it came to betting, Lorillard loved long shots and distrusted the public's judgment, whereas Dwyer preferred to seek out others in the know before betting and preferred playing favorites. Lorillard trained his horses at the secluded Rancocas farm in New Jersey, while Dwyer always staged final prerace trials in public. Lorillard was a good winner but a terrible loser, while Dwyer accepted his fate calmly. He did not scold jockeys or trainers, complain of foul rides, or criticize judges, starters, or jockeys. Lorillard enjoyed a good time, but Dwyer was as ascetic as a Trappist monk and did not smoke, drink, read, travel, or mix in society.[51]

The Dwyers broke up their racing partnership in 1890 after Mike went to race in England over his brother's opposition. By then they had earned about $1.5 million in purses and stakes. Mike went broke in the late 1890s. He became ill and was often seen at local tracks in an invalid's chair. Mike died in 1906 at the age of sixty. Phil continued his stable with his son and died a millionaire in 1917.[52]

The Brooklyn Jockey Club

The Dwyers organized the Brooklyn Jockey Club on 3 March 1886, with Phil as president. Their other principal partners were William Hyde, vice president of the theatrical firm of Hyde and Behman, and Democratic congressman William Scott of Pennsylvania, whose wealth in coal mines and railroads exceeded $15 million. They bought the site of the old Prospect Park Fair Grounds, whose grandstand had burned down two years earlier, where they intended to construct the $400,000 Gravesend Racetrack. Gravesend was one of the six original Kings County towns that dated from 1645, but it did not become part of Brooklyn proper until annexed in 1894. Its population in 1880 was just 3,674 and a decade later only 6,934. The new track (bounded by Ocean Parkway and Gravesend Avenue, King's Highway and Avenue U) was the most accessible Brooklyn track, less than forty minutes from New York. All rail lines to Coney Island ran close by, including the Prospect Park and Coney Island Railroad, which dropped off passengers at the "Race Track" station, and the Long Island Railroad from New York.[53]

The Dwyers ran into a problem because George Engeman held the lease on their site through November, and there was concern he might create trouble for his new competitor. However, the BJC's powerful political associates warned Engeman that if he interfered with the new track, he would be closed down. He halted his attacks on the BJC and kept his track open only on days when the BJC did not operate.[54]

Gravesend opened on 26 August 1886 with a crowd estimated at fifteen thousand. There was a thirty-piece band to entertain the fans, more than sixty betting commissioners to take their wagers, and Pinkerton agents to guarantee order. The track started out with a fifteen-day meet operating on Mondays, Wednesdays, and Fridays, alternating with the more prestigious Sheepshead Bay that ran on Tuesdays, Thursdays, and Saturdays. So much racing saturated the market (especially since on-track betting was not yet fully legalized) that the CIJC experienced its worst fall meeting to that time, while the BJC earned profits that were smaller than expected.[55]

Gravesend's track was oval, with two very long stretches, and fast, wide turns. The surface was a light loam, apt to get dusty in dry weather. Experts soon considered the course one of the safest, yet fastest, tracks in North America. The eight-thousand-seat grandstand, not completed in time for opening day, was double tiered and sufficiently raised at the top of a sloping lawn to provide a fine view of the races. However, it was closed in the rear and, despite plenty of windows, lacked good air circulation, a problem on hot days. The judges' and timers' stands were ornate pagodas. The judges' stand had a massive parasol on top that obstructed upper-deck views of close finishes. The grandstand had ladies' retiring rooms and the finest barroom and restaurant of any American track. The grandstand, like at Sheepshead Bay, was connected by a bridge to the clubhouse, which had a pleasant dining room overlooking the course and an ample balcony. Overall, the *Spirit* rated Gravesend as one of the most comfortable tracks in the world, although far from the most beautiful.[56]

The Fight to Halt On-Track Gambling in New York

In 1880, before the start of the racing season, the three-year-old Society for the Prevention of Crime (SPC) lobbied Inspector Thomas W. Thorne, who was in charge of police operations at Jerome Park, to enforce the antibookmaking and antipool laws. He warned the Jerome Park stewards prior to opening day that if anyone tried to sell pools or register wagers, there would be arrests. At four o'clock on opening day, Thorne nabbed English bookmaker Mattias Sharp for betting. He had offered to bet $5.00 to $2.50 that a certain horse would not win a race. When a bettor accepted the odds, Sharp entered certain figures and a name twice in his memorandum book, tore off half the sheet, and gave it back to the bettor.[57]

AJC members were indignant at being singled out by the authorities, especially since, as the *Times* recognized, the law "has been a dead letter, so far as the race tracks are concerned, ever since its passage." There had been some arrests of pool sellers in New York State, but outside of New York City, "the auction and mutual pools have been sold as freely since the passage of the law as before." Other thoroughbred tracks in the state amassed hundreds of thousands of dollars from the sale of privileges. The AJC reportedly took in about $90,000 for the betting privileges after the 1877 pool law was passed, but Theodore Moss, an influential AJC member, believed the track had also lost $100,000 a year from potential sales of the betting privileges after it ended the auction system. He complained about the new zealous fight against bookmaking that was overlooking the illegal off-track betting parlors (poolrooms): "Why didn't they make arrests in the City yesterday if they were so anxious to enforce the law. Pools were openly sold on our races in Barclay street, at Hunter's Point, and at other places in the City and Long Island, and no complaint was made against this plain violation of the law."[58]

Club officers got a temporary injunction in June, restraining the police from interfering with its operations. AJC counsel J. Sergeant Cram contended that the track had complied with the 1877 law barring pools and that bookmaking was very different from pool selling, because the bookmaker staked his own money, while the pool seller got a percentage of the money wagered without risking anything. The AJC also claimed that racecourse bookmaking was outside the scope of the law since it did not exist in New York when the law was written. The AJC kept getting adjournments until the summer meeting was over and then discontinued the case. At the start of the fall meeting when police tried to interfere with bookmakers, the AJC's lawyers got a new temporary injunction, asserting that bookmaking was not public betting within the meaning of the law and that the case should be tried before a referee. One year later, on 1 October 1881, Judge Charles Donohue heard a motion to continue another AJC temporary injunction to restrain the Police Board from interfering with bookmaking. Its attorneys claimed that the only betting was between individuals and that no devices registered or recorded them. This policy of securing temporary injunctions continued for several years to keep the gambling going on and the police out.[59]

Bookmaking, the only form of wagering allowed at Jerome Park, was rapidly gaining popularity. Bettors got superior odds on favorites, who then won only about 25 percent of the time, than from other betting formats. Bookmakers organized informal associations to protect themselves. They offered short odds for first- or second-place combination bets, betting formats the public considered illegitimate, unbusinesslike, and fraudulent. A rebellious public overthrew the combination established at Saratoga because it seemed to curtail competition among bookmakers. The *Spirit* rated James Kelly as the wildest oddsmaker among the major bookmakers, while it pointed to Albert H. Cridge as a bookmaker who operated on business principles and seldom offered the best odds. Rival bookies watched his board and emulated his odds.[60]

Bookmaking at Jerome Park's spring 1881 meet operated without interference, and the fans loved it. On 5 June, the *Times* reported, "It was almost impossible to wedge one's way among the packed throng who were excitedly endeavoring to place their money on one or other of the contesting horses."[61]

In late September, a new gambling syndicate was formed that included James E. Kelly, Charles Reed, T. B. Johnson, and Albert H. Cridge, who had secured the betting privilege for $2,500 a day. They built a betting ring (seventy-five by forty feet) for bookmaking near the southern end of the grandstands with twenty-six horseshoe-shaped cages (five by four feet) with a rail in front that each rented for $150. Each cage had a slate or blackboard attached to a pole showing the names of horses and the odds offered. The syndicate rented the spaces to fourteen bookmaking companies and five individuals. The bookmaker would stand on an eighteen-inch block, shouting out the odds, usually with three assistants who filled out tickets, entered bets, and handled the money. Clients included politicians, lawyers, bartenders, and "sharp colored boys."[62]

The *Times* thought the police should have been more diligent in suppressing the gambling and questioned the police commissioners' sincerity in their drive against bookmaking because they always seemed to be looking for an excuse to hold back even though they had the authority to take immediate action. If the police did their duty, "every officer of the AJC would be indicted for licensing gambling on their race-track, just as every book-maker offering bets on horses would be arrested on the spot."[63]

Trotting men then did not favor bookmaking because they were accustomed to pool selling in which public competition fixed the odds. In February 1882, Senator Treanor introduced a bill to allow pool selling at trotting and racing meets, but it quietly died. He explained, "The business of racing horses . . . has long had the tacit sanction of common law, and less rigid ideas have prevailed as to betting on turf events. Such betting has been regarded as an innocent amusement; and the very nature of the business causes it to go hand in hand with wagers, so that when the sweeping Pool Bill was enacted it dealt a serious blow to the prosperity of the turf and breeding interests."[64]

New York bookmakers by the end of 1881 were making their game riskier, more amenable to a mass market, and more profitable than pools. Historian David Johnson argues that the national breakthrough for bookmaking came in 1882 when the Dwyer brothers convinced Col. Lewis Clark to permit their bookmaking friends to work at the Kentucky Derby in return for their racing Runnymede in the race.[65]

Bookmaking was expected to be part of the racing scene at the AJC's 1882 fall meeting, but District Attorney McKeon ordered gambling halted on opening day, 30 September, of the fall meeting. Inspector Dilks and his detectives were at the track and told AJC officials that no betting could occur and that club members would be indicted if there was betting. The leading bookies did no business, but certain lesser bookmakers moved about the crowd, taking a considerable number of wagers on the qui vive. During the second race, bookmakers Harry Telmah and James Jackson were arrested for taking bets. Telmah claimed he was simply entering a memo in an old telegraph book, and Jackson said he was jotting down grocery accounts. Their arrests discouraged further gambling.[66]

The *Times* surprisingly criticized the district attorney's actions at the Westchester track, since it had previously opposed bookmaking and continued to do so in the future, though it applauded his tough stand on policy, lotteries, faro, and some other popular athletic sports. The paper thought he was unfairly going after the AJC, with its excellent leadership and support of "innocent pursuits and pastimes," instead of just the bookies. In the past, the AJC was often victimized by similar police actions, "but public sentiment and Judge Donohue have uniformly sustained it against the Uhlans of the law." The *Times* further pointed out that halting betting would hurt attendance and injure tourism.[67]

On 7 October, Jerome Park sought an injunction to restrain the police commissioners from interfering with the bookmaking. The AJC ostensibly hoped to get a legal decision to resolve the matter before the spring racing season. At this time, Jerome explained to the press that the track site was the property of the AJC's real estate arm, the Villa Park Site and Improvement Association (VPSIA), which rented the site in return for 90 percent of admission fees and the sale of privileges, including bookmaking. Thus, Jerome ingenuously claimed, the AJC was not responsible for the gambling.[68]

Two weeks later, Judge Van Brunt ruled against the track since the legislature had ruled against all betting, which meant any betting on horse races was illegal. He recognized that the bookmaking concession had been annually sold since 1878 to certain persons who had openly employed that privilege until recently, without any municipal interference, and that elsewhere bookmaking had been accepted as lawful and was protected by the police. Van Brunt also recognized that the legislature could not have barred the mere making of a record to help the memory of a bettor since such actions had not existed when the law was enacted.[69]

The AJC circumvented the police with its temporary injunctions, but in the spring of 1886, the police halted bookmaking at the course. Any cash transactions and all open records of wagers were broken up. The police made a number of arrests, including John Stowe, the chief "penciller" for Kelly and Bliss, and bookmaker Ridge Levien. Thereafter, bookmakers bet only with people they knew, jotting down the figures on visiting cards or loose slips of paper and settling up later at their city offices. The suppression of gambling dramatically injured the track's bottom line, but Jerome stepped in with his friends to finance the operation, renewing the obligations racing fans had to him. The track was very dear to Jerome, who saw it as his monument and, according to the *Spirit*, "originally intended that when he died it should pass into the hands of the city as a public pleasure ground."[70]

The *Times* that summer concluded that horse race betting thrived despite the antipool law, even when strictly enforced, as at Jerome Park. The editors were livid that the growing interest in betting at proprietary tracks was surpassing interest in racing, with courses opened daily, rain or shine, for second-rate horses and for bets as low as fifty cents: "Blood and form went for nothing; the races were delayed until the pool boxes were full . . . , and the result was always prearranged, except now and then, when the swindlers broke faith with one another." The audiences were denounced as "nameless women, and known criminals, and youths who had stolen postage stamps to get the 'stake' for a bet." These judgments were unduly harsh on the Coney Island proprietary tracks and more fitting for Guttenberg, the year-old crooked bookmakers' track in New Jersey.[71]

The AJC's Executive Committee expected the authorities would tolerate at their course the betting commission system used at Coney Island and Gravesend in which go-betweens bet money from clients with bookmakers. However, corporation counsel Emile H. Lacombe informed the police commissioners that they had to prevent all betting, and the brass ordered Inspector Thomas F. Byrnes and the detectives at the central office to enforce the law. On the opening day of the fall 1886 meet, high society was absent and the clubhouse deserted. Still, an eager crowd at the betting enclosure surrounded the bookmakers, and the betting went on. However, before the fourth race, police officers arrested two alleged bookmakers. The enforcement of the law put the track's future in doubt. Turfmen agreed that the AJC could not go on more than ten days without betting and the accompanying fees.[72]

The track operated three more dates, but on 2 October, following races without betting, music, or any enthusiasm, the Executive Committee terminated the meet: "We are unwilling longer to submit to the unjust discrimination practiced against the American Jockey Club. . . . We cannot see why private betting is illegal at Jerome Park when public betting is allowed in Harlem and other parts of the city. An army of detectives has attended this meeting and followed and shadowed our visitors. We think that the law has not only been offensively enforced, but enforced beyond its spirit and its letter." The Brooklyn Jockey Club added racing dates to pick up the slack. The AJC did reopen for election day with a combination of amateur and professional racing, accompanied by a band. Jerome tried to sustain elite interest with a luncheon and dance at the clubhouse, but the typical enthusiasm of prior election-day races was absent. The more than thirty police officers present prevented any open gambling.[73]

The *Spirit* supported the AJC's complaints, questioning why more than one hundred off-track betting parlors were open, while the powers that be suppressed wagering at prestigious racetracks that encouraged the improvement of the breed: "The betting rooms in town are of no benefit to racing. They are frequented by idlers and half-grown boys, who seldom attend races, but bet upon horses the same as they would upon a game of cards. The betting rooms are a source of vice and idleness, while betting on the courses is confined to a very different class of people." The weekly asserted that "if the authorities will suppress betting at a well-located race-course, the legitimate sphere of betting, and allow it to go unchecked in the vile dens in town, they cannot complain if people accuse them of interested motives, if not, indeed, of sinister designs upon the Jockey Club."[74]

The Anti–Horse Race Gambling Fight in Kings County

Unlike in New York City, Kings County officials did not make the slightest effort to fight gambling at local tracks. Republican district attorney Isaac Catlin arrested not a single bookmaker from 1879 until 1882 because he claimed there had been no complaints. In 1883, he secured fifty-seven indictments but not a single conviction. The bookmaking business at the Coney Island tracks was very lucrative for men with sufficient political clout to secure immunity. Kelly and Bliss leased the book-making privilege in the early 1880s at Sheepshead Bay for four thousand dollars a day (although on special dates the fee rose to fifty-one hundred dollars). Sheeps-head Bay had twenty-five bookmaking booths in 1883, thirty in 1884, forty-five in 1885, and sixty in 1886. The *New York Times* observed: "It may seem strange to the ordinary reader that a firm of gamblers can guarantee immunity from penalty for openly breaking the laws of this State, but Kelly & Bliss do this, and are so confi-dent in their power to continue the business that they risk $61,000 without hope of regaining it if the venture falls through some streak of virtue in the officers of the law." Kelly and Bliss, of course, denied paying money for protection.[75]

Kelly and Bliss sublet the betting privilege to other bookmakers but kept some betting stalls for themselves. On good days they turned over around fifty thou-sand dollars in bets. Their most famous clients were the firms of Tully and Sim-monds and Cridge and Murray. The latter carried on a longtime keno game in the Fifteenth Ward and ran the most exclusive gambling house in New York City at a brownstone mansion at 13 West Twenty-eighth Street. Detectives had free access there until Detective Dusenbury arrested a thief, for whom there was a warrant, coming out of the building. Cridge and Murray were so mad they forbade thieves and the police from their gambling rooms.[76]

The prevailing permissiveness motivated male reformers to fight horse race gambling just as they were trying to clean up fighting, drinking, pornography, and prostitution. The renowned Reverend T. DeWitt Talmage, pastor of the

Presbyterian Brooklyn Tabernacle and editor of *Frank Leslie's Sunday Magazine* (1879–89), vigorously spoke out against horse racing with gambling. He declared in 1882 that it was morally wrong, events were probably prearranged, and bettors were usually duped: "There ought to be one word written on the brow of every pool-seller, as he sits deducting his 2 or 5 per cent, and slyly running up tickets on his own account on the winning horses, and on the brow of every book-maker, as the owner of the horses by extra inducement has his horses scratched from the race, and on the brow of every jockey who slackens the speed, according to agreement, that another may win, and upon the judges' stand and every board of the surrounding fence, the unmistakable word, 'Swindler.'"[77]

Another prominent gambling critic was public curmudgeon Anthony Comstock, who, together with members of the YMCA, founded the New York Society for the Suppression of Vice in 1873, best known for promoting social purity and investigating obscenity. Comstock was the SSV's chief agent and secretary and helped secure a federal obscenity law in 1873 popularly known as the Comstock Act. He believed Americans had strict, traditional moral values that the government laxly enforced. Comstock went to war against obscenity, blasphemy, free thought, free love, and gambling, evil behaviors that damaged good Christian families.[78]

Comstock first arrested people for lotteries in 1876 and soon thereafter went after policy shops and gaming rooms, making more arrests for gambling than for obscenity. By the end of the century, the SSV had made 710 arrests for gambling and related crimes, including going after lax police officers. Comstock believed that betting on horses was a special snare for young businessmen: "Clerks who cannot get away from business may have the opportunity to gamble brought to them. They bring the demoralization of the race-course into the circles of business, thus setting another devil-trap for young men in the walks of daily life."[79]

The SSV competed with the Society for the Prevention of Crime, organized in 1877 by the Reverend Howard Crosby for the honor of halting gambling. Crosby died in 1891 and was succeeded as president by Charles H. Parkhurst of the Madison Square Presbyterian Church, who served until 1908. Parkhurst was best known for his sojourns into the Tenderloin District, where he investigated saloons, policy shops, gambling dens, and disorderly houses, which he followed by hiring detectives to find evidence of malfeasance by such officers as Captain "Clubber" Williams and Bill Devery. Parkhurst's pressure for inquiries into police methods and Tammany Hall's alleged corruption contributed greatly to the formation of the Lexow Committee's investigation of the New York City Police. Comstock saw the SPC as an inexperienced upstart that benefited from the reputation of the SSV.[80]

In September 1883, Comstock stepped up his attack on racetrack gambling, securing indictments against certain gamblers. His and other reformers' efforts preceded the formation of Great Britain's National Anti-Gambling League in 1890, which became a powerful force seeking tougher legislation and sending agents to tracks to prosecute bookmakers and track managers. Comstock also went after Police Chief John Y. McKane of Gravesend, and several of his subordinates, for aiding and abetting wagering at the Brighton Beach track.[81]

McKane was the influential political boss of Gravesend, whose power base, the John Y. McKane Association, controlled three hundred Democratic votes. Prematurely bald, stout, and middle-aged, McKane did not smoke, drink, or gamble and was superintendent of a Methodist Sunday school. He started out as a constable and by 1879 was the supervisor of Gravesend. By 1883, he was also president of the Police Board, the Town Board, the Board of Health, the Water Board, and the Board of Town Auditors. Chief McKane allowed drunkenness, prostitution, and gambling to flourish at Coney Island. In 1882, he personally bailed out twenty-three men arrested for gambling. McKane was also a contractor who built half of the hotels and two-thirds of the buildings in Gravesend. His company made between $85,000 and $142,000 from racetrack construction projects, including 125 racetrack betting booths, yet claimed ignorance about gambling at the tracks.[82]

By 1884, McKane could no longer claim to be in the dark. Not only did Comstock inform him about the wagering, but he also read about it in the papers. McKane was officially clued into the gambling on 22 April, when the new Democratic Kings County district attorney, James W. Ridgway, ordered the chief to stop pool selling at the tracks.[83]

Ridgway himself claimed only recent knowledge of the gambling when he noticed press advertisements discussing pool selling. The district attorney promised to push every case to the best of his ability but continued the policy of toleration and protection of his predecessor, Republican Isaac Catlin.[84]

In June 1884, Comstock secured grand jury indictments of twenty-three pool sellers who had recently operated at Sheepshead Bay. Eleven of them, including Albert Cridge, Herman Schneider, James E. Kelly, and Dougal McDougall, appeared in the district attorney's office on 30 June and gave $1,000 bail, furnished by Robert Furey, a former lieutenant of Brooklyn's Democratic boss, Hugh McLaughlin. Then they all went to the track. Comstock could not get warrants against the other malefactors. District Attorney Ridgway was uncooperative and did not issue warrants against the gamblers or raid their operations. He simply informed them of the indictments and asked them to appear the next day for a bail hearing. Comstock was livid about the criminal justice system's weak support, complaining that "every obstacle has been thrown in his way by those who should have been most active in rendering him assistance." Comstock complained that there must have been a leak, because the main offenders knew beforehand that formal charges were coming and came prepared with bondsmen. Comstock subsequently secured more information that he sent on to Ridgway, but there was still no action, perhaps because of a rumored $50,000 payoff.[85]

The *Brooklyn Eagle,* which supported gambling at Sheepshead Bay, took Comstock to task for his fight with Ridgway and the CIJC, blasting him for making "all of his performances as spectacular and sensational as the circumstances would allow," and applauded the district attorney, who "has treated the blustering utterances of Comstock with the contemptuous indifference which they deserve." No one had elected Comstock, and if he wanted to play district attorney, the *Eagle* suggested, he should run for the office.[86]

The *Times* regarded the trial of the alleged pool makers as "a roaring farce, with obviously no pretensions of rising to the dignity of a serious scandal," reflective of the government's ineffectiveness in fighting gambling. For example, two of the arrested bookmakers were supposedly Herman Schneider, who had a black mustache and black hair, and Dougal McDougall. As the *Times* pointed out, "Somebody must have mixed the rascals up. . . . Schneider, upon trial, was Snyder, with light hair and eyes . . . and Dougal McDougall turned up as John T. McDougall. The prosecution proved everything except that the prisoners were the individuals who sold the pools."[87]

The turf's opponents, particularly Henry Berghe's American Society for the Prevention of Cruelty to Animals, established in 1866, also criticized the sport for abusing animals. An ASPCA agent on 9 August 1884 tried to stop a race at Jerome Park because he believed, incorrectly, that an entered horse was unfit to run. The *Times* found it implausible that racing owners would mistreat their horses and contended that "thoroughbreds in training are probably of all animals those upon which cruelty is least liable to be practiced. . . . The modern modes of racing, though conclusive tests of speed, are hardly ever cruel tests of endurance and a thoroughbred is apt to lead a life quite as long as that of a horse engaged in a less conspicuous career, and much more luxurious."[88]

In the fall of 1884, the authorities in upstate Buffalo halted the sale of pools at trotting races, resulting in a sharp decline in attendance at the Grand Trotting Circuit. The *Spirit of the Times* responded by calling for a repeal of the antipool law. The weekly acknowledged that gambling should be properly limited but argued it was impossible to stop gambling by legislation. The paper asserted that pools should be sold only at tracks during meets, with accounts open to inspection by track officials, and never off the track, because those gamblers were not interested in racing but simply drawn to the speculative side of the sport.[89]

The press, including the *Spirit,* unanimously opposed bookmaking because it lacked the open character of pool selling and because the bookmakers were

becoming very flashy, openly operated their own stables, and organized themselves to drive out the competition and possibly fix races. As the *Times* pointed
out, "Since the system of bookmaking became established in this country there
has been a conspiracy to systematically rob the public which has grown rapidly
in strength. It is well known that certain bookmakers control the movements of
several racing stables, and a powerful combination has been formed to make the
peculation of 'skinning the lambs' this year much easier and more remunerative
than heretofore." There was a lot of suspicion about fixed races, but proof was
difficult to secure, especially when orchestrated by a wily trainer. As the *Times*
explained, "It is a very easy matter for a jockey to pull his horse, especially in a
large field, without being discovered, but it is much easier to send a horse with
a good reputation to the post unprepared and totally unfit to contest with less
speedy animals."[90]

The *Tribune* was equally dismayed by the increasing numbers of bookmakers,
"faro-bank keepers, roulette riggers and professional swindlers of all sorts to run
horses on our leading racetracks since they were not likely to be any more scrupu-
lous with horses than their own dirty businesses." An editorial titled "Swindling
on the Turf" indicated that bookmakers had enough chances to get the public's
money from betting and were going too far by also running horses. "They should
leave that costly luxury to the men whose motives and plans are not open to suspicion from baseness of character and daily custom of law-breaking."[91]

Chief McKane and the Betting Problem

In 1885, it appeared that reform pressure secured improved enforcement of the
gambling laws at the Brooklyn tracks. On 17 February, two weeks after a raid
against off-track Gravesend poolrooms, District Attorney Ridgway warned local
track owners of prosecution if they tried to sell pools during the racing season.
The *Times* applauded the action but said it was too little, too late, since the district
attorney had long been unresponsive to the *Brooklyn Union* newspaper and other
local reformers' fight against gambling at Coney Island. The *Times* hoped Ridgway was finally taking the necessary actions to ameliorate declining conditions
at Coney Island:

> He seems now to have been aroused from a state of easy acquiescence in the
> daily violation of the law to something like a determination to attend to its
> enforcement. The owners of the hotels on Coney Island ought to have insisted in
> their own interest on the suppression of pool selling. The devotees of that pas-
> time are not themselves of the class who makes big Summer hotels "pay," and

their presence drives more desirable visitors to other resorts. Coney Island has visibly deteriorated in the last three years, and the change is in a large part due to the presence and prominence of the "horsy" element and the cheap gamblers of the racetracks.[92]

Expectations of concerted police action further increased before the racing season when Chief McKane announced his new resolve to fight the gambling. He was originally reluctant to act against the BBRA, noting, "Four hundred persons in this town get their living from the track, and I've been unwilling to interfere with their bread and butter." Now, he explained, "Public sentiment has grown too strong for me, and the pool law has been too clearly construed for me to hold off." He warned George Engeman a week before the opening of the BBRA's season not to allow pool selling at the track, promising to arrest all violators, even Engeman if necessary. The track opened in late May without pool selling, but, as advertised, pool sellers were present on Decoration Day, along with pari-mutuels. There were no police present when Brighton opened, but after winning bettors cashed their tickets for the first race, and bets were sold on the second race, McKane appeared on the scene with about twelve plainclothesmen. They arrested three pool sellers and gathered up tickets, books, entries, and cash boxes. Later on, they also arrested Engeman and track superintendent Charles Hoff, who ran the pools.[93]

The *Eagle* reported that the night before opening day, the BBRA paid McKane one thousand dollars to allow pool selling. McKane's response to the accusation was to take action at the track. He denied any disagreement with Engeman regarding control of patronage at the track, claiming that he was satisfied with the number of jobs he controlled there, which was reportedly more than fifty. The 1887 Bacon State Assembly Committee investigation of Brooklyn politics found the one hundred men working security at the track at five dollars a day had all been sent by McKane. Engeman accepted them because he did not want to offend McKane. Besides, Engeman pointed out, the private guards were all gamblers, and he would make the money back from them anyhow.[94]

Local residents were unhappy with the raid because they believed the tracks were crucial for the local economy. Since racing had begun at Coney Island, local merchants serviced the tracks, which needed feed, hay, horseshoes, and other equipment, and provided fans with food, entertainment, and housing. Hotels catered to the bookmakers and the rest of the racing crowd, who also frequented local restaurants and music halls. Furthermore, about three thousand people worked at the tracks each season, and Avenue U became known as "Trainers' Row" because so many trainers lived there. By 1900, the BJC was Gravesend's biggest employer, with hundreds of workers, mainly first- or second-generation Irishmen, as well as white and black southerners. Many of the transient menial employees working as stable boys, exercise riders, and rubbers lived at the track or in boardinghouses, often in a neighborhood of shanties and cottages called the "Gut."[95]

A Coney Island rally on 5 June, at Edgar's Hotel, protesting the suppression of pool selling, drew about a hundred butchers, grocers, hotel keepers, and real estate holders representing Gravesend, Sheepshead Bay, and the lower part of Coney Island, worried their businesses would collapse without the tracks. Hotelier P. M. McDonald noted a general demoralizing of businessmen since the stopping of pool selling and feared a 50 percent drop in property values and many foreclosures. Speakers blamed the legislature, Comstock, and a few fanatics for the woes of Brooklyn racing. Former judge Watson wondered, "Why was it that Judges and men of high position would go to Jerome Park and bet on the races? The aristocrats up there were allowed to do as they pleased for pleasure, but at Coney Island men who devoted their time exclusively to what was countenanced at Jerome Park were arrested and their business broken up." The consensus was that New Yorkers wanted pool selling.[96]

Speaker after speaker noted that the law had been steadily broken for five years, and "things should go on as they had been." Watson absolved McKane of blame, pointing out, "They make books in Westchester County and they sold all the pools they desired at Cedarhurst in Queens County, but you are prevented at Coney Island. Why, the rich, proud aristocracy of our country can bet with impunity, but the poor man at Brighton Beach has no right, according to the present state of affairs, to buy even a $5 mutuel pool." More than one hundred residents approved one petition favoring pool selling and a second resolution opposing the local authorities from "practically ending racing by stopping selling pools on the track."[97]

Chief McKane met with the Citizens' Committee appointed at that mass meeting and told them he had no personal problem with pool selling. Responding to a complaint that pool selling had brought a rough crowd to Coney Island, McKane argued that there was more rowdyism at Rockaway in a day than at Coney Island in a month. The committee admitted that while pool selling was illegal, other unlawful things also occurred without interference.[98]

The authorities informed Sheepshead Bay before it opened on 11 June that they would halt any betting. A sign on a pillar supporting the pavilion proclaimed that pool selling was illegal and prohibited and that the track would take offenders into custody and hand them over to the police. Nonetheless, on opening day, forty bookmakers were there, ready for business, with blackboards up and odds posted for the first race. However, certain mysterious signals were given, and the bookmakers put away their blackboards, and the mutuel machines "disappeared as if by magic."[99]

The CIJC introduced a new betting scheme known as the "contributions to premiums" to circumvent the gambling laws. The plan was to open up its general racing fund to minimum "gifts" of five dollars to reward horse owners whose equines exhibited the highest qualities of speed and endurance. The intent was to build up a pool of fifty thousand dollars, of which the track would keep 5 percent and the subscribers 5 percent ("dividends"), with the balance going to horse owners.[100]

Bookmakers prepared to adopt the "contributions to premiums" method in expectation of McKane closing them up. If the new system were employed, each booth would become a "Bureau of Control," registering certificates composed of coupons that entitled the holder of a winning horse to a proportionate dividend of the premium on that horse. "Consolation premiums" were offered holders of coupons on horses coming in second. However, after the CIJC got an injunction to prevent the authorities from interfering with the bookmakers, about forty or fifty bookmakers jumped back into action, and the new scheme was dropped.[101]

The Brooklyn Tracks and Bookmaking in 1886

On 17 June, bookmaking at Sheepshead Bay was halted without any apparent explanation. Police Superintendent William Murray was preparing to get the necessary information to make arrests and gain convictions when the bookmakers got wind of his plans and suspended operations. Police magistrates then required direct testimony that races upon which money was wagered actually occurred and also that the horses represented by purchased tickets actually competed. This proof was difficult to come by when bets were on out-of-town races but far easier with local races.[102]

The halting of betting at Sheepshead Bay and Brighton Beach was temporary because the right people presumably received their payoffs, and the pool sellers were back into business.[103] When Brighton closed for the season in mid-November, the *New York Tribune* claimed it was only because the betting public had run out of money: "The human victims have been so thoroughly fleeced that the plucking is no longer profitable." The editor pointed out that "a generous share of the spoils has found its way into the possession of those whose duty it was to enforce the law" and claimed the track had done more harm to honest racing than any track in the country.[104]

In 1886, some new methods were introduced to get around the antibetting rules. Betting commissioners at Sheepshead Bay supposedly served as brokers who enabled people who did not know each other to bet orally among themselves. The commissioners paid their way into the track, and if they received money from anyone to bet on a horse, they were required to give a receipt. They charged a

1 percent commission if they placed the bet. The CIJC employed Robert Pinkerton and four operatives to watch the commissioners and prevent the recording or registration of any bets. Special Agent Oram of the SSV visited the track on 12 June and found no difference in the betting paraphernalia under the commission system compared to the betting over the prior two years. He made a five-dollar bet with Appleby and Johnson at 5–1, which clerks recorded on a card and a long sheet. The public assumed that Comstock was too busy crusading against photographs of cigarette girls playing baseball to spare time contesting the commission business. The SSV arranged a test case of the commission betting system's legality, but the jury could not come to a decision.[105]

Brighton Beach experimented with a new betting scheme devised by William B. Duryea. Ostensibly, a method to improve the breed, Duryea's plan, according to the *Times,* "is the latest manifestation of that mysterious psychic force which produces the mind cure. . . . After buying five-dollar interests in the horses, they concentrate all their will power on a desire to make the horses in which they are interested win. The subtle psychic fluid penetrates the intervening atmosphere and imparts additional strength and speed to the horses, thereby beyond question improving them." The editorial snidely noted that "eminently respectable and intelligent people, including all who patronize churches with more frequency than they do barrooms, are quite sure that it is betting."[106]

In September, the county tried the BBRA for permitting the registering and recording of bets at the track and in a building it owned and operated. The jury deliberated for thirty-six hours but failed to reach a unanimous vote, so the case was dismissed. All these trial results convinced many bookmakers that no jury in Kings County would ever convict them.[107]

That month, Comstock went to war with Ridgway. He wrote a letter to Democratic governor David B. Hill urging Ridgway's removal unless the district attorney followed up on indictments. Comstock's message included many documents reminding Hill that beginning in December 1884, he had been informed about Ridgway's nonenforcement of antigambling laws. Those charges were withdrawn at Hill's request and after the district attorney's pledge to the SSV that he would enforce the law, a vow Comstock thought had been repeatedly broken. The SSV had instigated more than one hundred indictments against Kings County gamblers since Ridgway's election, but none ever went to court.[108]

The pressure on Ridgway from Comstock and an upcoming election led him to clamp down on the BBRA. Enforcement of the antipool laws resulted in small crowds of about five hundred spectators and the loss of $4,000 a day. In mid-October, George Engeman closed up and moved his operations to his track in Clifton, New Jersey.[109]

When the BJC briefly resumed racing on 7 October, with wagering, Ridgway warned that the betting must stop and personally told the sheriff's representative to enforce the law. Consequently, the bookmakers operated without paraphernalia, employing the English oral system, giving odds verbally instead of posting them on a slate. Bettors paid their money and received a blank numbered card as a receipt. When the *Brooklyn Eagle* criticized the gambling situation at Gravesend, the BJC pulled its press passes and withdrew the track's printing business from the paper. Dwyer warned that if the press continued to denounce betting, he would kick its staff off the grounds even if they bought their own tickets.[110]

Racetrack Gambling and the 1886 Election

Racetrack gambling was a primary issue in the fall election for attorney general. Republican and Citizens' Party candidate Gen. Benjamin F. Tracy denounced racetrack gambling, estimating that some $12 million yearly passed through the pool boxes. Tracy supported the sport of racing, but declared, "Using horses as mere instruments of gambling and as a business is no better and no worse than faro, roulette, or three card monte." He did not have a big problem with Sheepshead Bay, where gambling was incidental to its goal to improve the breed, but chastised the proprietary tracks, especially Brighton, which he claimed had netted $350,000 in just one season. The BBRA owned and controlled its own pool-selling privileges, charging 3–5 percent on pools. Tracy pointed out that the presence of racetrack gambling offered a ready opportunity to wager, and "especially among young men and boys it has created a mania for gambling so strong as to impel its victims to obtain money . . . for the purpose of gratifying a passion to gamble." The Democratic *Brooklyn Eagle* came out for Tracy because of his position on gambling and because of the incumbent's inaction and his support by pool sellers and other "sports" (criminals and speculators). The *New York Tribune* called on Brooklynites to rise up against the intolerable evils of gambling and pool selling regardless of party lines.[111] However, despite the media's opposition, Ridgway was easily reelected.

Conclusion

Overall, the *Spirit of the Times* gave American racing an unfavorable rating compared to England, where tracks relied directly on the public for revenue and did not recognize betting, considered only incidental to the sport. Americans preferred the indirect tax of charging bookmakers to operate rather than higher admission fees, which made the clubs too dependent on the professional gamblers. The *Spirit* also pointed out that Americans had less leisure than European racing fans and could not be expected to attend every day in such large numbers as occurred overseas, where racing was staged three times a week.[112]

The *Spirit* identified a marked decline in elite patronage. The upper class, which preferred the high-status courses like Jerome Park, Sheepshead Bay, Saratoga, and Monmouth, appeared to be turned off by racing's becoming too professionalized and attracting an offensive element. The elite's changing vacation patterns also affected attendance. The well-to-do formerly stayed in town until July and returned early in September. However, in the 1880s, they were leaving in June and not returning until October or November, if not later, and were away during the racing season.[113]

New York in the early 1880s was the unquestioned epicenter of American thoroughbred racing. By 1886, the metropolitan area had two of the leading elite courses in North America and two of the most prominent proprietary tracks. In addition, the sport was booming in nearby New Jersey, and the summer meet in upstate Saratoga provided some of the most glamorous weeks of the social calendar. New York tracks had the largest purses and the most eminent races, and they drew the largest crowds. However, the gambling issue cast a heavy pall over the turf, and pressure was mounting for a resolution. Reformers in New York had made some headway against Jerome Park but not in Brooklyn, where they encountered a strong alliance of professional gamblers and local politicians, including the Democratic boss of Coney Island and the Kings County district attorney. Unable to secure redress from the local criminal justice system, the reformers turned to the state legislature for a solution to horse race gambling. At the same time, the jockey clubs also looked to Albany for a resolution in their favor, which was the legalization of betting at the tracks.

4

The Ives Pool Law of 1887

Whether it is wiser for the State to regulate and restrain—by license laws which
can be enforced—and thus apparently tolerate an evil, which cannot be eradicated, or to pass futile prohibitory laws against the evil, is an old question upon
which moralists disagree and upon other sides of which much can be said. The
only practical test of such a question is actual experiment. The Legislature . . . has
chosen to make a trial of the same policy with reference to pool selling which this
State has so long pursued with reference to sales of intoxicating liquors.
—GOVERNOR DAVID B. HILL, quoted in *New York Times,*
26 May 1887

The cornerstone of New York racing was, like everywhere else, the gambling, which in the 1880s was primarily with bookmakers. The 1877 Anti-Pool Law made the keeping of any room to record wagers or sell pools on human feats, animals, or elections illegal and was enforced mainly against the Jerome Park Racetrack, but racing circuits in the rest of the state encountered little interference. In the mid-1880s, reformers like Anthony Comstock tried to halt horse race gambling at the Brooklyn tracks where the authorities, including the police, the district attorney, and local judges politically connected to the track operators, had given the racecourses a pass. The growing difficulties racing operators faced led them to seek a change of the state penal codes so they could operate without interference from the authorities. They wanted a new law that would permit wagering at their tracks, while simultaneously invigorating the bans on off-track gambling that were harming their business. The tracks called upon their political allies to enact the Ives Act in 1887, which they hoped would protect their business and get the reformers off their backs.

The First Efforts to Revoke the Anti–Pool Room Laws

After the Anti-Pool Law passed in 1877, the gambling interests tried to get a reversal but had little chance of success with the Republicans in control of the legislature. Their luck seemed to change in 1882 with the election of Democrat Grover Cleveland as governor; the Democratic Party captured the state legislature as well. At the start of the 1883 legislative session, Col. Michael C. Murphy and former judge Joseph Koch submitted bills to the assembly and the state senate, respectively, to permit pool selling at racetracks. Murphy's ill-advised proposal called for empowering a judge in each county to designate one local track for pool selling. Not surprisingly, the racing magnates in Kings County, where there were already two thoroughbred tracks, opposed that plan. Koch's better-designed bill exempted racetracks from current antigambling laws. Both bills advanced out of committee but not much further, partly for fear that pool selling would occur legally outside the racetracks.[1]

In 1884, Democratic senator Cornelius Van Cott of New York City tried to secure on-course gambling with his innocuously titled bill, "An Act to Enforce the Obligations of Contracts," but it had little support and died. One year later, the AJC and the CIJC had a bill introduced in the assembly by Daniel E. Finn to amend the 1884 act Incorporating Associations for Improving the Breed of Horses, proposing that agricultural and fairground societies, as well as trotting and racing associations, sponsor up to four fifteen-day race meets. The intent was to confine pool selling and betting to events at incorporated associations that would suppress and abolish systematic betting organized by irresponsible folk. Expectations were high that the amendment would pass the assembly. The state's twenty-six racing associations and other groups interested in supporting agricultural fairs backed the bill. Carloads of supportive petitions arrived from New York, Brooklyn, Buffalo, Rochester, and Utica.[2]

Churchgoers, as expected, opposed the bill. In addition, certain New York and Kings County legislators also resisted the plan, under the influence of the Brighton Beach track, which often enjoyed privileges that Jerome Park did not have. According to the *New York World*, "It is hinted that a ring of politicians protect the island course from the effects of the present law and annually receive a big pile for their influence. They are therefore opposed to the passage of a bill, which will relieve them of the influence of their 'pull.'" The assembly did not approve the bill.[3]

The *World* was a strong supporter of racing. An editorial titled "Shall Horse-Racing Be Killed?" noted that prominent people such as Judge Brady, Cornelius Vanderbilt, Leonard Jerome, Pierre Lorillard, and Senator Roscoe Conkling favored modifying the law against betting so the breed would continue to improve. There could be no racing without betting: "Every Jockey Club in the country knows that not two hundred people could be induced to attend a race if they could not have a small stake in the events." The editor favorably compared betting on horses to the stock market:

> If we are willing to give up horse-breeding and the sport of the turf, in which we are rapidly excelling England, then we may try to make everybody believe that it is an offense to bet $20 on a horse, while it is no offense to put up a margin of a thousand dollars on a stock gamble. But if we want to keep up the sport, to improve our magnificent breed of horses, to continue to show English racers the heels of our flyers and to give employment to thousands of trainers, jockeys, stable hands, and other employees, then we must have such a law as is now proposed at Albany and which allows men who go to races to bet on the horses under proper and entirely safe and sufficient restrictions.[4]

Rumors floated that passage of a bill allowing gambling at the tracks could cost up to $300,000. Renowned turf patron Pierre Lorillard balked at supporting any such fund. He preferred to give away his horses "than consent to obtaining legislative relief by other than legitimate means." However, his threat was hollow, since he could easily race at Monmouth Park in New Jersey where his stables were located. Nonetheless, with the limited likelihood of getting on-track gambling passed, there was speculation that the CIJC would move its events to Monmouth and that the AJC might hold its fall meeting at a driving park under construction at North Bergen, New Jersey. However, neither option took place.[5]

The Ives Pool Bill

The issue of racetrack betting came to a head in 1887. Opposition to gambling did not go away, but increasingly people were distinguishing between on-site gambling by true racing fans who could afford to bet and off-track betting by individuals interested only in the wagers and not the sport. There was widespread support for a new law to support racing with on-track betting while simultaneously suppressing off-track wagering. There was once again a lot of talk about possible bribery to pass a racing bill. The AJC's attorney indicated that back in 1885, votes to pass a racing bill were valued at $10,000 apiece, and an assemblyman suggested the current price would be $150,000. The AJC claimed it never had, and never would, spend a cent to secure such legislation.[6]

The AJC and the CIJC asked Assemblyman Eugene S. Ives of Saratoga to draw up legislation permitting gambling exclusively at racetracks. He introduced a bill in February calling for a 5 percent tax on the admissions receipts at racetracks. Thoroughbred tracks within twenty miles of New York City or Brooklyn would be assessed at least $4,000 a year and trotting facilities $1,000 minimum. Meets would be limited to twenty days each year, during which time Section 351 of the penal code that banned gambling would not apply at the tracks. The state could use the revenue for prizes to improve cattle, sheep, and horses at state and county fairs. This bill was perceived as a high-license act that would stamp out poolrooms just as high liquor licenses closed low-class saloons. The proposal garnered considerable support from bettors in New York, Brooklyn, and Buffalo and from agricultural societies and county fairs that would share in the proceeds.[7]

Consideration of the Ives bill became entwined with Assemblyman A. S. Bacon's investigation of Kings County corruption. Witnesses included bookmaker James B. Kelly and Gravesend police chief John Y. McKane. The committee discovered that gamblers loaned or gave money to McKane and the local police, that McKane almost never interfered with gambling when he went to the tracks, and that he made sure the Brooklyn police similarly looked away. McKane arrested no more than twelve people for gambling at local tracks between 1884 and 1886, claiming his department lacked the staff to do the job. According to one gambler, it seemed the police were at the track "only to preserve Order."[8]

The investigation focused on Kings County district attorney James W. Ridgway's ineffective fight against racetrack gambling. The Democrat, elected in 1883, indicted some one hundred alleged perpetrators through early 1887, with just nine convictions. The Bacon Committee concluded that the district attorney carefully delayed action until the racing season was nearly over so he would not hinder the commission of the crime. Then once indictments were procured, he prevented anyone from being punished. Ridgway's raiders never seized any paraphernalia, and his office indicted innocent men to discredit the prosecution of professional gamblers. He refused to support the grand jury's efforts to indict the Brooklyn sheriff for failing to fight the gamblers.[9]

The committee interviewed former Brooklyn sheriff Louis R. Stegman, who admitted an intimate acquaintance with pool operator Paul Bauer, Chief McKane, treasurer Al Battersby of the BBRA, and the Engemans. Stegman claimed he lost his financial records but produced a journal with some fiscal data, including a notation for $2,000 borrowed from William Engeman. The sheriff admitted knowing that pool selling was going on at Coney Island and was aware the law required him to prosecute offenders, but he did not think it was his job "to spy and snoop around and find out things when no complaint was made." Stegman claimed that if his superiors had so ordered him, he would have stopped the gambling.[10]

Sheriff W. C. Farley, who succeeded Stegman, also never tried to enforce the anti–pool selling law, probably because gamblers often loaned or gave him money. Undersheriff "Bub" McLaughlin, nephew of Brooklyn party boss Hugh McLaughlin, reported that George Engeman had loaned Sheriff Farley $4,000 for his reelection campaign.[11]

A track employee who formerly worked in the BBRA poolroom's cash room estimated that about $40,000–$80,000 was wagered each day. He denied money was set aside for bribes, but his boss, Dr. Henry F. Meininger of the Coroner's Office, disagreed, claiming that $1,000 from each day's receipts went to the managers, presumably for bribes to secure immunity. Alanson Tredwell, a New York clothier, said when summering at Sheepshead Bay that he met treasurer Al Battersby of the BBRA and was shown a $1,400 check for bribes.[12]

When the pool act was under consideration, Ives agreed to alter it to avoid charges of special legislation. He deleted the annual tax on the New York, Brooklyn, and Saratoga tracks because it discriminated against them and gradually increased the number of racing days at any single track to sixty days. On 21 April, the assembly, despite its Republican majority, passed the bill by a vote of sixty-nine to forty-eight. Only four Democrats opposed the bill. The senate added more amendments that established a racing season from mid-May to mid-October and made off-track betting a felony instead of a misdemeanor. Religious leaders like Anthony Comstock and Rev. Dr. Thomas D. Talmage tried to block the bill, but on 12 May, the senate approved the Ives bill by a vote of seventeen to fourteen. All twelve Democratic senators supported the bill, along with five Republicans.[13]

Reformers besieged Democratic governor David B. Hill to veto the bill. Talmage, who claimed to represent three thousand ministers, declared the Ives bill sought to make gambling as legitimate as the sales of groceries or dry goods, while Comstock argued that pool selling was equivalent to the illegal lottery. Ives responded that his bill was a regulatory measure against urban poolrooms, the number of which had recently quadrupled. William E. Bowman of the Rochester Driving Association insisted that betting on a horse race was not sinful and was no different from speculating on stocks or on produce and oil exchanges. Gen. Daniel Butterfield, an upstate Republican, said the bill would give reputable racing associations control of their tracks. He asserted that Confederate cavalrymen had superior mounts over their Union foes because of their lifelong interest in horses.[14]

Hill did not return the Ives Act to the legislature within the required ten days, so it became law on 25 May without his signature. He explained that the bill was within the legislature's purview; assemblymen and senators, along with the press, thoroughly discussed it; and it involved no constitutional question. Hill noted that empowering the state to regulate and restrain gambling to certain times and places, and to impose a license fee for the privilege, was similar to how the state controlled the liquor trade.[15] Ultimately, Hill pointed out, "All laws must finally rely for their enforcement upon the support of public opinion. It is conceded that public opinion has not supported and enforced the present law. . . . In most localities, the present law has been practically a dead letter. It is urged, and with much show of reason, that this bill, which presumably keeps pace with public opinion, will be generally enforced and will, in its practical working, actually diminish the total quantity of pool-selling within the State."[16]

The *New York Times* supported the Ives Act, which seemed to ensure the future of the New York tracks. It looked forward to having off-track betting rings broken up and called on jockey clubs to take energetic steps to help close the poolrooms: "What the police apparently refuse to do, the gentlemen managing the race tracks can do easily, as nobody can secure the necessary evidence of guilt more readily than they can."[17]

The sporting press, not surprisingly, supported the new pool law. The *Spirit of the Times* acclaimed Ives as one of "the greatest concessions ever made by the Legislature of the State . . . for it permitted the encouragement of a wholesome sport, which has become the favorite amusement of thousands of people" and initiated taxes to help finance local agricultural fairs.[18] The sports weekly saw passage as strong encouragement for the building of new racetracks. The *Spirit* regarded the current tracks as inadequate for modern demands. New tracks, it recommended, should be located no more than twenty miles from town, have good transportation, not be oval in shape, and not exceed a mile in size because fans wanted courses with half-mile straight finishes so they could see the sprint to the flag. The *Spirit* singled out the Van Cortlandt estate in Upper Manhattan as a potential new site, but the city had already decided to make it into a municipal park.[19]

Racing under the Ives Act

The enactment of the Ives pool bill meant that bookmakers could now ply their vocation at the track without fear of interference. Jockey clubs intended to exclude from their courses anyone convicted of taking off-track bets, but, according to the *Times*, "the gamblers laugh at this and claim that they can evade it by inducing the police, whom they openly assert to be their protectors, to arrest an outsider when an arrest is found necessary for effect."[20]

Legal wagering began on 27 May at Gravesend. Henry Stedeker leased the betting privilege and charged sixty bookmakers $100 a day, which he divided with the Brooklyn Jockey Club. The bookmakers then drew for choice of stalls in the betting area, arranged in the shape of three sides of a square. The best locations were near the upper end of the pavilion, where customers entered and exited. Since the odds were largely the same at each stall, location was very important.[21]

Jerome Park opened three days later, on Decoration Day, highlighted by the Withers Stakes. The crowd was so large that the Harlem Railroad could not cope with the traffic, and some spectators did not get home until after nine o'clock. The

Times suggested that the Ives Act gave Jerome Park a new lease on life, for otherwise it might have closed down.[22]

The highlight of the racing calendar was the Suburban Stakes on opening day at Sheepshead Bay, which reportedly attracted more than $500,000 in prerace wagers. The crowd included men, women, and children of all social classes and was reportedly the largest in New York since the great intersectional races of the 1840s. Estimates ranged from twenty-five thousand by the *Brooklyn Eagle* to forty thousand by the *Times*. Most of the betting, which went as high as $5,000 for the feature race, was with bookmakers, who paid a $60 fee. Penn Railroad executive A. J. Cassatt's Eurus won in a big upset. Just seventy-one people backed him in the mutuel pools, earning $230.65 for a $5.00 bet.[23]

The Metropolitan Turf Alliance

In January 1888, the sixty-member Bookmakers' Association (BA) that controlled and managing the betting privileges on most eastern tracks went out of business after handling an aggregate of some $300 million in bets. The press attributed the breakup to the unexpected discovery of a scheme to repeal the Ives Act and charges that some members were not solvent. However, no member had ever repudiated a bet. The sixty-five-member Metropolitan Turf Alliance (MTA) replaced the association. This new group was actually the BA in a new guise with the same members, including Sol Lichtenstein, "king of the ring," whose odds were generally copied by the other betting men. The only prominent bookmakers not in the MTA were Kelly and Bliss. The MTA sought control of the betting privileges that summer. The BA and the new MTA had excellent political connections that enabled members to often secure exclusive rights to make book at the New York tracks, or at least secure the choice positions in the betting ring. The alliance charged a $500 initiation fee, used to set up a liquidation fund to cover unmet debts. Joseph J. Gleason was elected president, with J. E. McDonald as vice president, Tim J. Sullivan (not to be confused with Tammany leader Big Tim D. Sullivan) as secretary, and Jacob Shipsey as treasurer. The directors included James McCloud, who had allegedly masterminded the Louisville Grays baseball fix of 1877. In the future, memberships cost up to $7,000, as much as a seat on the New York Stock Exchange.[24]

The alliance set a maximum of sixty betting stands at any track where it controlled the betting privileges, with its members having first option. The MTA claimed it would regulate and systematize betting, relieve jockey clubs of managing the betting, and effectively guard against welshing. Rumors abounded that the alliance would organize its own track if it did not get its way.[25]

The jockey clubs rebuffed the new alliance, concerned about the shady reputations of such defiant poolroom operators as Peter De Lacy, James Mahoney, and William Lovell and certain new members responsible for the operation of Guttenberg and Clifton in New Jersey. Such men, the *Times* noted, were "furnishing the money for the purses and running expenses of these bare-faced swindling and gambling concerns, which are run mainly for the benefit of De Lacy's and Lovell's rooms in this city, and similar fifty-cent concerns in Paterson, Hoboken, Jersey City, Newark, Washington, St. Louis, Baltimore, Pittsburgh, Chicago, and New Orleans." The *Tribune* concurred, describing the Turf Alliance as a "band of brigands, including men responsible for some of the most notorious racing frauds of recent times." The jockey clubs announced they would bar any bookmaker who sold off-track pools or opened a future book, which caused considerable consternation among members of the MTA. A. H. Cridge, Ridge Levein, George Lovell, and J. V. Daley all found themselves barred from the prestigious area tracks.[26]

Even more troubling for the jockey clubs was a report that the MTA intended to organize a three-man executive committee to set the same odds on each race for all bookmakers and not allow them any leeway. They found this plan unacceptable and refused to allow the alliance to dictate to them. The BJC and Monmouth went further and refused to recognize the alliance and would deal only with individual bookmakers, though they later changed their minds. The jockey clubs wanted to regulate on-track betting themselves to maximize their own returns. They preferred permitting as many bookmakers at the track as possible to make betting more convenient and encourage better odds through competition. The *Tribune* recommended employing the French and auction pools instead of bookmaking to enhance the tracks' income with more honest forms of betting less amenable to frauds, including fixed races.[27]

Some MTA members also involved with poolrooms sought to repeal Ives because poolrooms were where "the opportunities for fraud are absolutely unlimited, and the illicit profits are larger than honest gains made in fair and open competition on any respectable race track." The poolroom proprietors backed Assemblyman Daniel E. Finn's bill to prohibit selling French and auction pools at the tracks, which would allow only bookmaking on the courses. Finn's political sponsor, the well-known poolroom operator Peter De Lacy, had drawn up the bill. De Lacy had been previously ruled off the New York tracks by the jockey clubs and expelled from the Bookmakers' Association for selling off-track pools, and he wanted revenge. De Lacy was an Irish immigrant who had gone into New York politics as a young man. He affiliated with Tammany Hall, particularly with Richard Croker, before he became Tammany's boss, and also John J. Scannell, a saloon keeper, hotelier, and professional gambler who became fire commissioner in 1893. De Lacy moved from politics to gambling and was on his way to become the poolroom king of New York, clearing $1 million by 1890.[28]

De Lacy partly blamed James E. Kelly, who with his partner, Chauncey Bliss, controlled the French and auction pools at Jerome Park and Sheepshead Bay, for getting thrown off the tracks. Several pool sellers, including De Lacy, Cridge, Murray, Lovell, and James Mahoney, raised $60,000 to repeal the Ives Act and end pool selling at the tracks, or at least enable them to legally sell pools at their off-track sites. The poolrooms enlisted investigator Joseph B. Britton to help create an unusual coalition to fight Ives that included Anthony Comstock and various New York and Brooklyn ministers. "It doesn't seem fair to me," argued Comstock, "to let a man bet at the track and to arrest another for doing the same thing in some-place outside the race-course. The law says in effect that if a man straddles the fence around a race-track he may reach across it with his right hand and give his money to a book-maker. That's legal. If he reaches outside with his left hand and makes the bet with a poolroom keeper that's illegal."[29]

Prior to the formation of the MTA, the BJC controlled its own betting privileges through Henry Stedeker, and Monmouth contracted with the firm of Appleby and Johnson to deal with the bookmakers. Then, in 1888, the MTA secured betting privileges for the BJC meet for $6,250 a day. Its intent, unknown to the Dwyers, was to monopolize the betting ring and keep out bookmakers who were not members. The BJC doubled the added money for races to attract better horses that increased betting interest and benefited the bookmakers. At the end of the summer, the alliance also gained control of betting for the twelve-day CIJC meet and promptly did away with place betting on pari-mutuels, a hostile gesture to its clients. The press worried the sport would soon be in the MTA's clutches.[30]

Bookmaking Versus Pari-Mutuels

Early in 1888, the Louisville Jockey Club (LJC), the senior western racing club, announced the first steps to reform on-track betting when it abandoned bookmaking for auctions and pari-mutuel pools. The AJC reported it would do the same, and the CIJC declared it would give half of its betting ring over to pari-mutuels. The *Spirit* had anticipated such action since 1884, because bookmakers had badly abused their position. There were too many bookmakers making too much money; they had close connections to owners, jockeys, and trainers; and they themselves owned racehorses. The horse owners often entered their animals into events for which they had no chance, just to encourage betting. Substituting French pools would result in more honest races and higher revenues. In France, the authorities permitted bookmaking only in the paddocks, because there such gambling was based on skill and knowledge, but barred it in the cheap seats, where wagering was considered based on chance. Then in 1891, the parliament banned all gambling at the tracks except for the pari-mutuels.[31]

Prior to the start of the spring 1888 meet, the AJC's new president, John Hunter, who replaced the retiring August Belmont, and James E. Kelly, who owned the French mutuel machine at Jerome Park, decided to exclude bookmakers from the track. Kelly decided that only French mutuels and auction pools would operate. Kelly already used the pari-mutuels at the Cedarhurst and Pelham trotting tracks and the CIJC, where bettors could make $5, $25, or $100 wagers. However, Kelly was going against the tide. Racing fans opposed the new scheme. The public preferred book betting, with no 3–5 percentage fees, open odds, and place betting, which was unavailable with the mutuels. Back in 1887, gamblers at Jerome Park and Coney Island bet about ten times as much with bookies as with the machines. As the *Times* pointed out, racing fans felt the fee was exorbitant and an amount "no shark on Wall Street would think of charging." The *Times* blamed this situation in part on the greed of the jockey clubs, not satisfied with their enormous dividends, and warned they might be killing the golden goose. Most AJC executive committeemen favored having some bookies at the spring meeting to let the public bet as they pleased, and they decided to permit twenty bookies that had no financial stake in horses and had not violated the law by keeping betting rooms in New York to operate.[32]

Whereas the *Times* was very critical of pari-mutuels, the *Tribune*, which claimed to print more racing news than nearly any paper, favored the pari-mutuels and proclaimed in a headline: "Abolish the Bookmakers." It applauded the AJC for suppressing bookmakers, "the worst enemies of high-class racing in this country. Most of them have been law-breakers from their youth up, foes of good order, decency and honesty, and combinations among them to defraud owners and the public have been frequent and notorious. What else could be expected from dealers of marked cards, spinners of roulette-wheels . . . , [and] graduates of the lowest groggeries." They were held responsible for most racing scandals and abuses. The *Tribune* considered the small percentages taken out of the mutuel pools by jockey clubs a trivial tax compared to the cut of the bookmakers. Its editors estimated there were one hundred bookmaking firms in the country, averaging more than $10,000 a year in profit, which was probably a big exaggeration.[33]

The *Spirit* agreed with the *Tribune*, noting that pari-mutuels were a tried-and-tested system at Longchamps in Paris, which did away with the need for corrupt bookmakers or middlemen. In this system, the public contributed "directly to the racing fund by paying the club a percentage of the bets on the mutuals." The *Spirit* studied the returns of the five 1887 New York meets at which both book and pari-mutuels operated and reported that the machines paid better odds. If someone bet $5 on each race with the pari-mutuels and a bookie, the payoff for the entire season at Jerome Park, Sheepshead Bay, and Gravesend from the machines was $558.22 more than from the bookmakers. The differential occurred because bookies often rounded out their books by throwing a lot of money into mutuels at the last moment, which reshaped the odds because other bettors would follow their lead. Otherwise, pari-mutuels would have done even better. Nonetheless, the *Spirit* recognized the public preferred the books, although "bookmaking even when honestly conducted, is a losing game for the public. Betting in mutuels the money passes from hand to hand among the public, less the percentage, which they pay the club to give the purses, and thus furnish the amusement. Betting in books, on the other hand, is the work of a score or more of men, arrayed in antagonism to the public; they absorb the money and grow rich as the public grow poor."[34]

The *Spirit* was convinced that "bookmaking was an octopus that was spreading its fangs over the turf," and unless jockey clubs abandoned it, "the time would come when no self-respecting gentleman could afford to have his name identified with racing. Racing cannot exist without speculation, for this is a speculative age; speculation permeates trade and commerce. However, speculation should always be incidental to racing. The tendency is today to make racing incidental to speculation."[35]

The *Spirit* noted that the public previously had little chance to become fond of pari-mutuels because of the 1877 antipool bill but claimed there was renewed interest in the pari-mutuels following the passage of the Ives Act. In 1887, $100,000 daily passed through the machines at Brighton Beach, and there was even heavier betting at Monmouth Racetrack in Long Branch. The *Spirit* speculated that track sponsorship of gambling might promote greater integrity and generate more revenue for higher-stakes races. The *Spirit* claimed such leading horsemen as Lorillard, Astor, and Scott favored pari-mutuels, in part, because "they dislike the conspicuous potentiality of bookmakers."[36]

Pierre Lorillard believed that bookmaking robbed the public and undermined jockeys, trainers, and owners, which was a large part of why he considered severing his close ties to the turf:

> I am very much opposed to the bookmakers, because they rob the public and they rob owners of horses. There is no fairness in their dealings. All bookmaking is against the horses. They are unscrupulous to a degree and in their capacity as middle-men . . . , they manage to appropriate at least $1,000,000 a year. . . .
>
> I fear that the clubs are actually afraid of the bookmakers. These fellows threaten the clubs, or at least they will do so through the legislature if they are

interfered with. They use money at Albany, and they have already tried to use the legislature as a menace to the clubs attempting to have the Ives law repealed. . . .

All bookmaking is against the horses. A bookmaker, of course, could not live unless he bet against the horses, and in the course of plying his trade he steals stable secrets and buys up jockeys and trainers. The bookmaking system is therefore demoralizing to jockeys and trainers, and hurtful to everything and everybody connected with racing. The bookmakers are, with few exceptions, rascals who would be fit subjects for the prison when their more profitable trade of robbing the public on the race courses is at an end. We have outlived the necessity for these fellows.

He estimated there were about one hundred bookmakers, earning from $10,000 to $25,000 a year.[37]

Pari-mutuels seemed to become more popular over the next few months, and by 1893, certain tracks employed electric totalizers to instantly record wagers and adjust odds. However, habits were hard to break, and the bookmakers remained dominant. In Louisville, where manager M. Lewis Clark tried to halt bookmaking at Churchill Downs in favor of pari-mutuels, pressure from racing fans and bookmakers compelled him to reverse his decision, and instead he closed the pari-mutuels in 1889. The New York betting public also stuck with the bookmakers, with their face-to-face presence, even though the pari-mutuels gave the bettor a better shake. Pari-mutuels did not replace bookmakers at the New York tracks until 1940.[38]

The Racing Chart

Betting was strongly promoted by the creation of the racing form in 1888, which provided interested parties with a wide variety of relevant data so bettors and bookmakers wagering on a race could make educated assessments of its outcome. Racing reporter Frank Bryan of the *New York Journal* created the racing form at the Guttenberg track and sold copies for $1 to six or seven subscribers. One client made about $10,000 with the information. The customers suggested to Bryan that he copyright his format, but he saw no business opportunities in it. Then in 1889, the racing chart first appeared in print in the *New York World*.[39]

Racing in Westchester County

The 1888 season was expected to be the AJC's finale because the city had decided in 1887 to buy the site for a reservoir. The *Times* did not give the AJC a positive send-off, complaining about its accessibility, the recent falloff in the quality of management with the retirement of Belmont as president, and a decline in the club's prestige. Newly appointed AJC president John Hunter, who received the enormous salary of $10,000, held views out of line with many members, who wanted a younger and more progressive leadership. The AJC was a shadow of its former self and owned only the clubhouse and a downtown office. The track site was still the property of the Villa Park Site and Improvement Association, a $750,000 firm whose main stockholders were its president, John Hunter, Leonard Jerome, William A. Duer, and James W. Wadsworth (acting for the estate of his late father-in-law, William R. Travers, who had recently died). Yet the *Tribune* applauded the AJC, whose membership encompassed "the wealthy, liberal and public-spirited part of the community that takes an interest in the breeding and development of horses," and said it was still the most prestigious of any jockey club.[40]

On opening day, 29 May, attendance was smaller than normal, which the *Spirit* attributed to a decline in the presence of professional bettors and women. On the other hand, "There was a renaissance of fashion . . . recalling a great day at Newport or Bar Harbor. Many of our leading society families which had not visited Jerome Park in years were present. . . . [T]he usual 'parade' from the club-house to the grand stand took place, and crowds gathered to witness the pleasing pageantry as the belles of Manhattanese society escorted by their cavaliers matched across the track in columns of two—a superb spectacle, typifying the triumph of civilization."[41]

The *Spirit* commended the AJC for sticking by the mutuels over the bookmakers, which it considered "an issue of Honest Racing vs. Rascality." The AJC encountered considerable opposition, including from bookmakers who owned horses refusing to run their horses there and from honorable gentlemen who from self-interest (their heavy bets would lower odds on their favorite horses), pique, or misconception also were disaffected by the new policy. The public and the press seemed more supportive of mutuels as the idea became more familiar to them. The apparatus became so busy that the track needed to get more machines and cashiers.[42]

Experts agreed that the meet was poorly run but disagreed on the financial results of the spring meet. The *Times* considered it a failure, but the *Spirit* reported the first seven days were the AJC's most profitable ever. The AJC sold $776,290 in mutuel tickets, charging a 5 percent commission, and just $11,116 in auction pools for which it took 3 percent, making the track's share of the betting $39,148. Overall, the AJC grossed $43,048 ($6,150 per day) in a week, or a net profit of $37,448 ($5,350 a day after the track's $800 daily expenses). This amount was outstanding, especially since there were three days of inclement weather, competition from Brooklyn tracks, inadequate betting facilities, and many horses withdrawn by their owners (several leading stables did not even send their horses to the meet), resulting in indifferent fields in too many contests; in addition, the meet was mismanaged. Bookmakers zealously fought the AJC during the meet, fanning jealousies between rival racing clubs and canvassing horse owners to ensure their current and future absence. Racing fans were displeased with their betting options, especially $5 bettors who preferred bookmakers even though the parimutuel machines were simple and fair.[43]

The *Spirit*, like other contemporary reports, was very critical of the meet, insisting that successful racing required operating on sound business principles. The sporting weekly pointed out that owners would not enter their horses if unsatisfied with racing conditions, purses, and stakes, nor would the public attend mismanaged meets. The *Spirit* recommended that jockey clubs be flexible regarding betting and provide bookmaking if the big stable owners sought it, mutuels if the $5 and $10 bettors wanted it, and auctions if the big bettors preferred it.[44]

In the fall, the track acceded to the demands of the bookmakers and built a large new twenty-five-thousand-square-foot betting ring that included a brick floor like the BJC's, with accommodations for up to eighty bookmakers. The *Times* rated the meet an artistic failure that failed to meet expenses. The gate for the spring and fall meets combined was $74,480, compared to $167,760 for Coney Island, $127,840 for the BJC, $34,920 at Saratoga, and $11,580 at Yonkers' old half-mile Driving Club, where the new Yonkers Racing Association ran thoroughbreds for the first time. Of course, the AJC also earned revenues from members' fees, sale of the betting privileges, bar and restaurant privileges, paddock tickets, programs, and poolroom correspondents' privileges, which cost $165 a day back in 1887.[45]

The AJC recognized its end was near but wanted to continue sponsoring thoroughbred racing and carry on as an elite social institution. The AJC had never focused on moneymaking, and its governing board was generally satisfied with simply promoting the turf. The stockholders never made as much as 10 percent of their investment during Jerome Park's many years of operation.[46]

In November, several leading eastern jockey clubs, including the AJC, the CIJC, and the Monmouth Park Jockey Club, met with members of the Western Turf Congress, including the Washington Park Jockey Club and the Louisville Jockey Club. They agreed that no bookmaker association could contract for the betting privileges on any of those tracks and decided to bar MTA members from making book at their courses. There were also discussions about standardizing weights and racing rules for the entire United States.[47]

The Rise of the New York Jockey Club and the Morris Park Racetrack

The creation of the New York Jockey Club (NYJC) in October 1888 was a serious challenge to the AJC's supremacy in New York City. The new racing association was organized by John A. Morris, a summa cum laude Harvard man who eventually spent $5 million on his racing property, stables, and horses, with Leonard Jerome as president. The NYJC announced plans to build a new and better racing facility near Jerome Park, where it would pay a 6 percent profit to its investors.

Morris was the son of steamship-line owner and horse breeder Francis Morris, who in 1860, with northern racing moribund, sent his son and noted horseman Richard Ten Broeck to England with some of his finest horses to test the English at their game. After John returned, he went to work for his father's company. In 1868, John invested $100,000 with Charles T. Howard and set up the infamous Louisiana State Lottery, paying the state an annual $40,000 fee for the rights, and they ran a daily lottery in New Orleans. Morris eventually became the majority stockholder.

The lottery had a nationwide clientele and averaged a 48 percent annual return. In 1889 alone, the stockholders made $3.4 million. The lottery became notorious for bribing state legislators, for which it supposedly had a $500,000 reserve fund. However, in 1890, Congress passed a law banning the interstate transport of lottery materials, which constituted 90 percent of the lottery's business. The firm went out of business in 1893 when its charter expired, although Morris organized a new venture, the Honduras Florida Lottery, that operated out of Tampa. The lottery made Morris fabulously wealthy, with a fortune that reached $25–$30 million.[48]

Morris and his racing associates first considered Upper Manhattan for a racetrack, but, as previously mentioned, the municipality was already planning a public park there. Instead, the syndicate selected one mile beyond the city limits in Westchester (annexed to the Bronx in 1895) for the new Morris Park Racetrack that had a rich racing heritage, two miles east of Jerome Park, one mile from the Bronx River, and twelve miles from city hall. The *Spirit* reported that the place was selected "because of its wealth of picturesque beauty, which to a club which has always observed the social side of racing is essential, and because of its superior grasses and water, which are essential to the health of horses," and also because several nearby railway routes were anticipated in the near future.[49]

Charles W. Bathgate, a renowned racing agent, whose father's farm was the site of Jerome Park, secured the necessary land for the NYJC, misleading the property owners, who thought it was for a private training track. Otherwise, they would have hoisted their asking price. Bathgate started out in late 1887 by buying 102 acres from B. G. Bradford for $700 an acre at a time when the NYJC was encouraging rumors of a move to North Bergen to mislead adjoining landowners. In the following spring, Bathgate purchased the adjoining 125-acre Hatfield farm and the 123-acre Dennerlein property.[50]

The Opening Campaigns at Morris Park Racetrack, 1889–90

The 1889 metropolitan racing season started out with another conflict between jockey clubs and bookmakers, charged $100 a day to operate the year before. The bet takers wanted lower fees. President J. J. Gleason of the MTA refused to pay more than $60 a day to work at the BJC, while President Dwyer refused to take less than $75 a day and reserved the right to run French mutuels. Over in New Jersey, Dwyer's Clifton charged $75 a day, while the outlaw Guttenberg track charged $65. Dwyer figured his fees were reasonable and competitive, especially since the BJC's attendance was triple these Jersey tracks, offered $1,000 prizes, and presented at least six races daily. Furthermore, the BJC already had a reputation as one of the best betting meets in the United States. In the end, the tracks wound up charging $75–$100.[51]

The AJC continued in business in 1889, flush with all-time-high profits in 1888. It offered record stakes that attracted the most horses ever to Jerome Park. Despite the anticipated closing of the track, the club made significant improvements in the plant. The AJC built six new stables for six hundred horses, a 100-yard covered brick walkway from the railway station to the grandstand, and a new turntable that made it easier for trains to reverse themselves. Special trains ran on race days with women's cars, drawing-room cars, and a separate entrance at the track and at Grand Central Station.[52]

After the season, the AJC's landlord, the Villa Park Site and Improvement Association, rescinded its lease. The AJC made money in the spring, but the October meet was a failure because of competition from the nearby new Morris Park Racetrack. The AJC was in no condition to fight its rival, especially given weak support from jockey club members who had no share in the profits, and decided to mortgage its property.[53]

The beautiful new million-dollar Morris Park Racetrack opened on 20 August 1889, promising to surpass its rivals with $86,500 in purses. The opulent and palatial facility, a mile beyond the city limits, was situated between the Van Nest and Westchester stations on the Harlem River branch of the New Haven Railroad that ran right by the grounds. Morris used his clout to grab a section of Pelham Parkway that abutted the track. Westchester superintendent of parks John Conover was a close ally, and Morris's son, John Heenan Morris, was on the newly created park commission.[54]

The Morris Park racecourse was very expensive, partly because the 350 acres comprised hills and valleys that required a huge expenditure for grading, draining, and other preparations. The jockey club built a mile-and-three-furlong course, laid out in a horseshoe shape rather than the customary oval. The design made possible races of one and a quarter miles or less with only one turn starting on the backstretch. There was also a three-quarter-mile straight stretch running diagonally across the infield, known as the Eclipse Course. The track had a mile and a half of stables with space for eight hundred horses and freshwater from a 500-foot artesian well. The track employed the latest electric timing apparatus recently introduced in Australia.[55]

Architects William H. Day and Thomas R. Jackson devoted a lot of attention to the beauty of the facility, including the 650-foot iron and brick French-styled grandstand. Its fifteen-thousand-seat stands, said to surpass anything in Europe, had concrete floors and were 100 feet deep, unusual since there was just one tier, open in the rear to provide light and ventilation. Twenty-six arches of pressed brick, topped by a beautiful cornice, supported the roof. The first rows of seats were 12 feet high to ensure visibility. The lawn between the grandstand and the track was sloped to offer all spectators unobstructed views. The 300-by-50-foot betting room was below the stands, very advantageous on rainy days, and the mutuels were located to the right of the betting ring. There were some eighty bookmakers under the supervision of James E. Kelly. There was also a free field for racing fans where they could bet with books or pari-mutuels at a minimum of $2. All fans received free programs, and there was musical entertainment between races, as at Sheepshead Bay. Morris Park had a sumptuous dining room, with bars for wines and mineral waters. The quality of refreshments was very good. Surprisingly, "city prices" prevailed, which meant no gouging of spectators. A notable feature was ice-water fountains, more refreshing than overpriced mineral water.[56]

The *Spirit* gushed with praise of the new track, which introduced a new era in racing: "There is nothing like it in this country. From a primitive wilderness, has been built an exquisite work." The paper applauded Morris, who "has rendered the public indebted to him for the greatest reform in race-course management."[57]

What made Morris Park so special?

It was the magnificence of the buildings at Westchester, the beauty of the grounds, the perfection of detail shown in its management and its liberality toward the public. Extortion in refreshments of inferior quality which for years had been the shame of our racecourses was unknown at Westchester. Ice-water which formerly had been banished that the bar privileges might be enhanced by means of public

7. The New York Jockey Club's magnificent Morris Park Racetrack opened in 1889. Drawn by Hughson Hawley. *Source:* "The Grandstand and Race-Track of the New York Jockey Club Preparing for the Opening," *Harper's Weekly* 33 (17 Aug. 1889): 656–57.

thirst was now abundant, and free toilet rooms fit only for cattle pens were at Westchester worthy of boudoirs. The stables were horse palaces, the dwellings for stablemen fitted with all modern improvements; the sanitary precautions were such as a Board of Health might study with profit.[58]

The fall opening on 2 October was a grand event that included $14,000 in added money, compared to $6,700 at nearby Jerome Park. The only flaw in the meet was transportation glitches, the bane of racing fans. Many elite spectators drove to the track from Central Park through Harlem over the bridge to Southern Boulevard or took a longer route up Jerome Avenue to Fordham Road and then across by the Pelham Avenue Road to the Bear Swamp Road at the rear of the track. Other patrons arrived via the Harlem Railroad and then rode the final mile and a half by stage from Fordham Road. The New York, New Haven, and Hartford Railroad monopolized the most direct route to the track and on race day increased the regular $0.20 round-trip ticket to $0.50. However, it was unprepared for the large racing crowd and provided insufficient cars for the return trip. Many riders were especially rankled by the need to walk over the Harlem Bridge to connect from the el to a branch railroad at 132nd Street.[59]

The NYJC grossed $64,111 (an average of $3,206 per day) for its twenty days of racing, most of the profit (72.9 percent) coming in its ten-day summer meet. The state received 5 percent of the gate ($3,206) in taxes. During the fall meet, the NYJC split dates with the AJC and daily outgrossed it, $1,735 to $1,046. The AJC lost an estimated $85,000 in 1889, including about $30,000 in the spring and $60,000 in its twelve-day fall meet. By then, the Villa Park Site and Improvement Association was ready to move on.[60]

The AJC, with its waning prestige and $100,000 debt, was taken over by the NYJC in December. The new club absorbed all the AJC's eight hundred members, producing a jockey club with twenty-four hundred members, and its stakes races. In 1890, Morris Park staged the Preakness, a fixture in Baltimore until racing was curtailed there. The glamorous race was then suspended until 1894, when it moved to Gravesend, its site for fifteen years.[61]

Despite all the track had going for itself, Morris Park did have some problems. In its second year, management discontinued musical performances to save money. This move seemed to reduce Morris Park to the level of proprietary courses. Morris had to tighten his belt because of the Louisiana Lottery's severe legal problems that led to its ultimate demise.[62]

The Ives Law in Brooklyn

Racing flourished in Brooklyn under the Ives Law. In 1889, twenty thousand attended the Brooklyn Handicap at Gravesend, double the previous year when a morning rain limited the crowd. However, betting was problematic because, as previously mentioned, the Turf Alliance and the BJC could not agree on the proper fee. When the BJC opened, all bookmakers were welcomed to work if they paid the track's fee for the privilege. The MTA boycotted the track, and there were not enough bookies to cover the demand for betting. The bookmakers' most avid clients were saloon keepers, who lost so much at the track that many "who formerly had good credit with the breweries and wholesale liquor houses are now obliged to purchase their stock in small amounts and pay cash."[63]

Sheepshead Bay in 1889 enlarged its track to a mile and a quarter, making it the longest in the country, a furlong longer than Morris Park's course. The CIJC's main event was the sixth Suburban Stakes on 19 June, already acknowledged as the leading handicap event in North America and whose winner was rated the nation's outstanding thoroughbred. The Suburban attracted extensive prerace betting, which reflected national interest in the race. The crowd was about twenty-five thousand, surpassing the grandstand's capacity and exceeding by five thousand the Suburban of 1888. Fans knew from experience they had to leave home early to get to the track on time, yet still the transportation facilities were overwhelmed. The *Spirit* reported:

> As early as eleven o'clock the boats winging out of Whitehall and Thirty-Fourth Streets were crowded, while the Brooklyn trains showed that the tide had set in. By noon the jam was awful, yet those who departed at that hour were fortunate, as an hour later the piers became so crowded that the gatemen were almost carried away, and the boats were dangerously full. At Bay Ridge, the cars were not plenty enough, and one-half of the people had to remain behind for the next trains. The crushing and pushing to get off the boats was frightful, and several ladies came out of the melee with their clothes almost torn off their backs.[64]

8. The Suburban Handicap, first run in 1884, drew a broad audience far beyond gambling and racing fans. Twenty thousand attended the 1892 renewal, won by Montana, ridden by Edward "Snapper" Garrison. Owner Marcus Daley collected the $18,000 purse. Drawn by T. De Thulstrup. *Source:* "The Suburban Handicap," *Harper's Weekly* 36 (18 June 1892): 596–97.

Dollars and Racing

In 1888, the first full year of racing under the Ives Act, the state received more than $21,000 in taxes based just on gate receipts. This intake was based on revenues that included $167,760 at Coney Island, $127,840 at Gravesend, and $74,760 at Jerome Park. One year later, in 1889, there were 130 racing days for the AJC, CIJC, BJC, BBRA, CIJC, NYJC, and New Jersey's Monmouth Park, with a daily average of five thousand spectators. The *Tribune* estimated that the typical paying customer bought a $2 admission ticket. Total expenditures for field, grandstand, and paddock badges came to $600,000. There was a big disparity between attendance and paid admission because one-third to two-fifths of the spectators were "deadheads" who got in free. An 1891 newspaper report claimed that bookmakers and their employees distributed a thousand tickets a day to encourage people to attend and place bets, while owners, trainers, and jockeys gave away even more passes.[65]

Racing in metropolitan New York in the late 1880s involved an enormous cash flow for fans and track operators. Going to the track cost a lot more than buying tickets or getting passes. Fans spent $325,000 just on train fare to get to the races. Then, once inside, an average racegoer spent $0.25 for food, beers, or cigars, which amounted to $130,000. Typically, three thousand fans would bet $5 on all six races, which came to $90,000 a day. In all, $1,055,000 was bet on the metropolitan tracks. Revenues ended up in the hands of the jockey clubs, "all of which pay handsome dividends," with their gross more than covering the daily overhead of about $10,000 a day ($1,144,000 for the year). The *Tribune* estimated that the eighty bookmakers who regularly worked the track earned $10,000 a man, which seems much too high an estimate.[66]

In 1890, the state's five major racetracks grossed $576,917, which, combined with the Hudson River Driving Park Association's and the New York Driving Club's minor meets, produced $29,108 for the state's coffers. The leading jockey club by a wide margin was the CIJC, which grossed $206,667, followed by the NYJC and the BJC, which each took in nearly $137,000. The BBRA pulled in half as much as those tracks, $63,910, and Saratoga just $32,628.[67]

Conclusion

The Ives Pool Act of 1887 had important national implications because it provided a model for other states like Illinois to emulate.[68] The legislation established that there was a legal differentiation between betting on horses at state-recognized racetracks and betting with professional bet takers off the tracks. This distinction enabled "true racing fans" who took the trouble to go out to the tracks to make legal wagers, while people who would not bother to see the races, but gambled anyhow, would not be permitted to bet. There were definite class implications, because working-class folk had less free time and discretionary money to get to the tracks than the more well-to-do fans. The new law gave racetracks special privileges, understandable because they footed the bill for racing and supported a significant industry aimed at producing high-quality animals. Off-track pool-room operators, on the other hand, were considered parasites who took advantage of the public interest in horse racing. They did not help improve the sport, while fleecing people who could not afford their financial losses. The new law also bene-fited bookmakers with sufficient connections or resources to operate at racetracks compared to the small handbook operators who worked out of saloons or cigar stores or on the streets. They were often financed by "backers" or "bankers" who shared in the risks.

Reformers like Anthony Comstock found little satisfaction in the new law, which neither ended gambling on horse races nor eliminated bookmaking at the tracks. Racing experts and reformers wanted to eliminate bookmakers, whom they blamed for a lot of the corruption at the tracks, especially fixed races, but the Ives Act did not accomplish that goal. Instead, the market determined the form of betting employed at the tracks. Racing experts and reformers supported the popularization of pari-mutuel pools that seemed fairer to the bettor and provided a very good return to the tracks that operated them. However, the gambling public preferred bookmakers.

Most important, the Ives Act did not eliminate the core problem of illegal off-track gambling. Although the law clearly barred poolrooms and handbooks, implementation was another matter. The underworld figures who operated pool-rooms with the connivance of legal businesses, including real estate agents and especially Western Union, utilized their political clout to operate with little, if any, interference from the authorities. These wide-open illegal enterprises were a major source of revenue for crime syndicates, promoted a lack of respect for law and order, and took revenue away from the racetracks.

5

Politics and the Turf
in New Jersey, 1870–94

The racecourse managers and the racecourse gamblers in New Jersey fully
deserve the calamity which has befallen upon them. . . . They constantly mani-
fested an insolent contempt for all that honorable and upright citizens hold dear.
The whole racing element in the state was practically responsible for the infamies
which were practiced at Trenton—the briberies, the bullying and browbeating,
the frauds and crimes which were committed there.
     —"The Prospect for Racing," *New York Tribune*, 9 January 1894

The Garden State was a major racing center in the post–Civil War era, highlighted by Monmouth Park, one of the most prestigious courses in the country. By 1890, there were six tracks in operation, five of which were profit-oriented
proprietary facilities. The owners had powerful political connections, just like in
New York City, and used their influence to advance and protect their racing interests, even gaining control of the state legislature following the election of 1892.
A plebeian racing culture emerged, with widespread gambling, both on and off
the tracks, and the turf endured some of the worst conditions of any American
racecourse. Crooked racing was rampant, especially at outlaw tracks that operated
year-round. A strong reform movement emerged to fight the racing crowd, and in
1893, the reformers made horse racing the central issue in the state legislative election. The outcome dramatically recast the course of the turf in the Garden State.

The Rise of Monmouth Park

New Jersey was the first northern state to resume thoroughbred racing on a
permanent basis after it virtually died out in the mid-1840s. In 1861, the Passaic
County Agricultural Society built the Riverside Racetrack outside Paterson by the
Passaic River, but the coming of the Civil War prevented its opening until June
1863, two months before Saratoga. In 1864, the meet was expanded, highlighted

by the Jersey Derby, the first American "derby," a mile-and-a-half stakes race for three-year-olds, modeled after England's Epsom Derby. More than eight thousand attended the inaugural, won by Norfolk. The track closed in 1869 owing to competition from the more accessible and elegant Jerome Park.[1]

Monmouth Park opened the next year, and it soon became one of the great American racecourses. John Chamberlain, a former Morrissey associate, emulated his old mentor's success at Saratoga by making Long Branch, a town founded on the coast of southeastern New Jersey in 1867, an elite resort and gambling center. An "instant" and more democratic resort compared to Saratoga or Newport, Rhode Island, it became a popular haunt for American presidents beginning with Ulysses Grant, who had a summer home there.[2]

Chamberlain opened a major gambling house in Long Branch in 1869 and with J. McB. Davidson bought the 128-acre Hulick farm three miles from town for $32,500, where he planned to build a half-mile trotting course. The plans went awry, but one year later, he organized the $100,000 Long Branch and Seashore Improvement Association, in which he held a 70 percent share, to build a racetrack on his land. The six-thousand-seat $40,000 grandstand, the largest in the United States, had three pavilions ornamented with fancy slate and a steep French-styled roof. Monmouth Park received high marks for its accessibility by rail to New York and Philadelphia, its commodious grandstand, the "princely sums" of its stakes races, and retaining control over concessions and keeping keep down prices. The *New York Times* applauded Chamberlain for "adding another institution of popular enjoyment to those we already possess" and for placing track management under a jockey club "composed of some of our wealthiest and most respected citizens."[3]

The racetrack's president, state senate president Amos Robins, was largely a figurehead, and Chamberlain ran the operation. His partners included Henry P. McGrath, his old gambling associate; Tammany boss William M. Tweed; John M. Davidson, a favorite Tweed Ring contractor; noted horseman and patrician Pierre Lorillard; and robber barons Jim Fisk and Jay Gould of the Erie Railroad, who reputedly "practically owned the legislature." Fisk and Gould stood to make a lot of money transporting fans to the track. Chamberlain, Tweed, and John Hoey, a minor stockholder, were also members of the prestigious American Jockey Club.[4]

The first five-day meet, composed of sixteen races, began on 30 July, with fewer than 4,000 in attendance, described by the *New York Times* as "a brilliant show" with "three capital races." It was highlighted by the Americus Cup Race, also known as the "Tweed Purse" because Tweed donated the prize money, allegedly from purloined city funds. Tweed's political and social club, the Americus,

9. This engraving portrays the first event at Monmouth Park on 30 July 1870. The track was one of the most outstanding in North America. Its 450-foot grandstand had space for seven thousand spectators. Drawn by A. W. Waud. *Source:* "Grand Stand, Monmouth Park: The Hurdles Race," *Harper's Weekly* 14 (13 Aug. 1870): 521–22.

appeared in full uniform, with a marching orchestra. The crowd included various Tammanyites, including New York's fire commissioner and city chamberlain (treasurer) as well as various aldermen, senators, and assemblymen.[5]

The selling of auction pools to rich racegoers (sometimes costing as much as $5,000 to win) was against the law in New Jersey and opposed by local residents. The club members in 1871 tried to convince the community that there could be no racing without gambling and that the track brought in a lot of business to the area. The track lost a lot of political clout that year. Fisk and Gould, who had tried unsuccessfully to corner the gold market in 1869, were otherwise occupied in 1871, trying to stay out of jail for their railroad manipulations, while Boss Tweed was toppled in New York for stealing from the government. The track retained minor county officials as special officers of the track, and company funds were used to help nominate and elect proracing county and state officials. Chamberlain also relied on petty bribery of police officials and judges to prevent any interference with the racing but was less successful in driving out off-track auction pools protected by local township and county officials. His answer was to initiate pari-mutuel betting at Monmouth.[6]

Monmouth Park was at first very successful. On 2 July 1872, opening day attracted nearly forty thousand spectators, drawn from a broader cross-section of the population than Jerome Park. As the *Times* reported, "There was the rough, pure and simple, there was his brother with the tawdry trappings of Tammany, there was the sturdy laborer, there was the intelligent mechanic. . . . There were tradesmen, bankers, brokers, and railway men, oilmen. There were clerks . . . , newspaper boys . . . , tired printers who had worked throughout the night, and jaded editors whose labors had ceased also only with the dawning. In fine there was almost every class and condition." The crowds included women, who from its earliest days bet with the pari-mutuels.[7]

Olive Logan, a British journalist, visited Long Branch in 1876. She described the racing scene as relatively sedate and far less carnivalesque compared to Epsom, where the crowd was raffish and entertained by minstrels, fortune-tellers, and jugglers. Americans going to Monmouth, by contrast, were "grave and sedate," not too different than if they were going to a Methodist camp meeting. The betting scene was far more serious, with the gamblers in a somber temper, as if they were purchasing grain futures or real estate. Logan was very critical of the time between heats, which she described as "inane dullness" and "characteristic[ly] American."[8]

Despite the track's popularity, the *Spirit of the Times* heavily scrutinized Chamberlain. Editor George Wilkes, a Republican, was very critical of Chamberlain's financial backers, including Tweed, who held a $40,000 mortgage on the property. In the fall of 1873, Wilkes accused Tweed and Chamberlain of placing four lamps at the track's entrance that they stole from New York's Department of Public Works. Wilkes further asserted that Tweed let Chamberlain fill his steam yacht with city coal at the municipal dock and that the authorities closed Morrissey's New York gambling house on Chamberlain's behalf.[9]

Wilkes accused Chamberlain of pocketing $100,000 in profits and selling watered stock while paying no dividends to his partners, who had paid $1,000 a share. The *Spirit* claimed the track was merely "an appendage to the cheating gambling-house on the sea shore" and that Chamberlain gave politicians winning tickets for his Jerome Park pools, redeemable at his New York gaming house.[10]

Attendance began to decline by 1876, despite the tourism boom in Philadelphia for the Centennial Exposition. This decrease was precipitated by adverse press publicity exposing Chamberlain's shady financial and gambling operations and growing charges of crooked racing. The result was that Monmouth's creditors foreclosed on the track.[11]

The Elite Take Over Monmouth Park

Appraised at $250,000, Monmouth was sold in a foreclosure sale on 5 April 1878 for a bargain $57,190 to a syndicate headed by businessman David Dunham Withers, a respected member of New York society. Withers was a horse breeder and racer, whose stable twice earned more than $60,000 and a total of more than $500,000 during his twenty-three-year racing career. He was an AJC director who played a major role in drawing up the club's "Rules of Racing" and was considered the "Solon of the track," the preeminent racing authority in America. However, critics considered Withers arbitrary and stubborn and called him the "autocrat of the American turf" in part because he preferred English racing methods and ideas over American customs. Withers's partners in the Monmouth Racing Association (MRA) included such famous AJC members as tobacco magnates Pierre and George Lorillard, August Belmont, James Gordon Bennett Jr., and George P. Wetmore, a future Rhode Island governor and U.S. senator. George Lorillard, the new track president, was a physician by training but did not practice medicine. He was a renowned sportsman who was an excellent oarsman and marksman. Lorillard devoted himself to managing the family yachting and other sporting interests and as a partner in the P. and G. L. Lorillard tobacco business. His stable, started in 1874 with James G. K. Lawrence, was among the finest in North America, leading the nation in 1878 with $67,875 in winnings.[12]

The purchase of Monmouth was tied to New York's 1877 antipool law that made betting at Jerome Park problematic, while auction pools and pari-mutuels could be readily sold at the Jersey track. The antipool law also drove several pool sellers to Hoboken and other New Jersey locations, where the gamblers encountered weak interference by the authorities. The new owners looked to make only 6 percent on their investment and reinvest excess profits back in the track. New York professional gamblers controlled the betting at Monmouth, including "Big Mike" Murray, a former dealer for Morrissey, and Chamberlain, who, with his partners, Cridge and Hackett, paid $6,200 for the privilege and raked in $11,500.[13]

The Monmouth racecourse opened under its new management on 15 April 1878 with all the prominent turfmen in attendance. The *Times* described it as the "finest, fastest, and safest race-course on the continent," yet it struggled at first. Philadelphia sportsmen did not ardently support Monmouth, so the track concentrated on the New York trade, which was hindered by the long travel time, which should have been less than ninety minutes. However, there was just one track to Long Branch, which regularly resulted in a thirty-minute wait for switchovers. This delay made Monmouth less attractive than Jerome Park and, later, Sheepshead Bay, even though its stakes races were among the most lucrative. The Jersey track was also hindered by serious competition in the summer of 1881 between Monmouth and Saratoga, with whose shorter meet it overlapped. Monmouth's attraction to New Yorkers increased once travel time was significantly decreased after the laying of a second track cut the forty-mile ride to a more manageable eighty minutes.[14]

Withers shrewdly cultivated the goodwill of Jerseyites to protect his new investment and reportedly owned or influenced a majority of county officials. Withers and the Lorillards had breeding farms in the state and hired only those workmen for their farms or the track who pledged to vote correctly on election day. They tried to curry favor with local farmers by buying fodder and produce from them. However, Withers was not omnipotent and could not prevent his pari-mutuel manager from being arrested and convicted for carrying out a lottery. As a result, Monmouth abandoned the French betting system in favor of the British system of bookmaking that had not been ruled illegal.[15]

The MRA, like all other jockey clubs, needed substantial political clout, particularly crucial in New Jersey, where the laws were not very supportive of the turf. Until 1880, betting on any race, serving as a stakeholder, advertising a race, or riding in a contest was illegal. The revised penal codes that year exempted bookmaking and pool selling at the racetracks. Seven years later, when New York passed the Ives Act, New Jersey's racing laws were amended, making racetrack betting noncriminal, which meant the authorities could not convict anyone for betting at the track. However, disputes over bets could be resolved in civil court. On-track gambling was considered legal until 1891, when the Court of Errors decided in the *Haring* case that the current law was unconstitutional. In 1888, John L. Haring and John B. Collins were fined $600 and $400, respectively, for keeping a disorderly house where they sold pools on races. They appealed, claiming the amendment in 1887 to the penal codes had legalized poolrooms.[16]

Monmouth Park under Withers's leadership was one of the most important tracks in America. Opening day in the late 1880s typically drew more than twenty thousand fans and at least sixty bookmakers who paid $125 a day for the privilege. Monmouth had a long racing season of twenty-five dates, starting on 4 July and running through the end of August; put on some of the finest and richest races of the century; and led the nation in average daily purses ($9,500). Its major stakes events included the Monmouth Oaks (1871), one of the first stakes events exclusively for fillies, and the Lorillard Stakes (1883), briefly the most lucrative race in the country.[17]

Racing was so popular at Monmouth that in 1890 management built a huge $180,000 track to accommodate the demand. The new 640-acre facility was the nation's largest, featuring a 1.75-mile course and a 700-foot iron grandstand, which made Monmouth the finest course of its day. The track was accessible by both the Pennsylvania and the New Jersey Central railroads and by boat from Brooklyn's Sandy Hook. Fans could buy a round-trip ticket and admission for $1.50. Races began at 2:30, and with trains standing by at the end of the day's events, spectators could easily make it back to New York the same day. Ideally, trains were back in New York by 7:00 p.m., although in the early 1880s, they often did not get back until 10:00 p.m. There were some other problems besides accessibility. Monmouth employed the English style of running clockwise, which was unpopular with trainers and spectators, and events started 1.5 miles from the grandstand, which meant that spectators could not see each horse's relative position until the match was nearly over. Despite a few flaws, operations were so profitable that costs of construction were expected to be paid off by the end of 1891.[18]

The Rise of the Proprietary Tracks

Guttenberg and the Hudson County Ring

Whereas Monmouth Park represented the finest in American racing, the Guttenberg Track exemplified the worst, built in 1885 by Phil Hexamer for the North Hudson Driving Park Association, originally employed for Jersey City–area men who raced their fast trotters there. It was an "outlaw track," unaffiliated with any regional or national association that regulated the turf and abiding by no nationally recognized standards. Located in the town of Guttenberg (now part of Union City), Hudson County, the half-mile track was directly opposite One Hundredth Street in Manhattan. The New York sporting fraternity arrived by the New York and Weehawken ferry from Jay Street or Forty-second Street over the Hudson River and then took a ride, either on a narrow-gauge steam train, a horse-drawn railroad or, according to the *Eagle,* a strong critic of Guttenberg, "a tedious journey in dilapidated hacks." A rickety omnibus ride cost $0.05, and a more stylish ride by landau cost $0.25 to $0.50.[19]

A few months after racing began, former justice of the peace Johnny Carr, best known for having run a gambling dive on a Hoboken barge, leased the course. The operation remained relatively minor, but became infamous for its cruel practice of winter racing. Then in 1888, Carr formed the $110,000 Hudson County Jockey Club (HCJC) with three powerful friends, bookmaker Gottfried "Dutch Fred" Walbaum; Nicholas V. Crusius, a New York wholesale liquor dealer who lived in Hoboken; and County Clerk Dennis McLaughlin, "the moving spirit behind the track." Crusius was responsible for the track's political payoffs, while McLaughlin was the Hudson County Democratic boss and right-hand man of Governor Leon

Abbett, himself a product of the county machine. McLaughlin provided politi-cal protection that went up to the state police chief. The *Spirit* described them as "a few German and Celtic politicians, who openly boast that they are above and beyond the law." The *New York Sun* claimed the "Big Four" ran the county "as absolutely as the Czar dominates Russia."[20]

Walbaum, who became president of the HCJC, previously owned a Bowery gambling house, a poolroom by the Brooklyn Bridge, and a Lower East Side "dis-orderly house." He was politically well connected, a poker partner of President Chester A. Arthur when he was collector of the Port of New York. Walbaum was among the most prominent New York–area bookmakers, running at one time ten different books that did a $4,000 a day business. However, he made most of his money by selling information over the telegraph wires to 320 East Coast pool-rooms that each paid him $10 a day. Walbaum established his own racing stable, which seemed to win only on afternoons when he bet on his horses. Walbaum did so well in the gambling business that in 1890 he bought 90 percent of the Saratoga Race Track for $375,000.[21]

Over the next few years, the "Big Four" reportedly made $4,000–$5,000 a day from the track. The track offered purses of about $2,800 to $3,000 a day, with bet-ting available from twenty to thirty bookmakers who were charged $100 per day. Guttenberg became a mile track in 1889, with the grandstand and new betting ring heated by stoves and protected from the elements by a glass front. The *Tribune* considered "Guttenberg in their hands . . . a thieves' paradise. The felons of New York, Brooklyn, Jersey City, Newark and other cities made the Guttenberg track their place of rendezvous and their headquarters. Never was a more odious and detestable travesty of racing than that which was carried on among the sharpers, the sneak thieves, and the buccaneers of Guttenburg [*sic*]."[22]

The track's superintendent was former assemblyman John Patrick Feeney, a detective attached to the county prosecutor's office and president of the Jersey City Board of Police Commissioners, who was in the liquor business. He was also a chief constable at the Guttenberg Track. In 1890, he led a couple of raids against poolrooms, including one in February against a room operated by a Newarkite trying to muscle in on the Jersey City action and a local poolroom owner who had apparently fallen out with the town's political regime.[23]

Thomas F. Egan ran the betting ring and was in charge of printing tickets, badges, and programs. Crusius reportedly ordered him to print one hundred thousand clubhouse badges and distribute them as widely as possible. Walbaum said they ended up in "every barber shop, delicatessen store, fruit stand," and any other place where men hung out to encourage betting at the track.[24]

The HCJC not just relied on the Big Four's political clout for protection but also bought protection. In 1889, the company increased its capital stock to $600,000 (much of it heavily watered) and gave large blocs to local politicians and leaders in Trenton. Shareholders included three Hudson County assemblymen and county judge E. T. Parton, who briefly served as the club president. The HCJC's political influence enabled the management to operate freely, with little fear of interference from the press, the clergy, or honest citizens. The track especially counted on the county sheriff, who impaneled only men favorable to Guttenberg for grand juries organized to indict track operators for misconduct. This setup typically quashed potential indictments against the Big Four.[25]

The operators rebuilt the course in November 1889, described by the *Times* as first class, bested only by the newly built Morris Park. The one-mile track was as "good as a track as there is in the country," with a drainage system superior to any metropolitan track except Morris Park. The new stove-heated grandstand seated three thousand spectators protected from the elements by a glass front and a new enclosed betting ring. Weekday winter attendance was typically about 3,000, while Saturdays and holidays drew 10,000 to 12,000. Admission was $1. The track also had a clubhouse with four hundred members who enjoyed a two-story well-appointed clubhouse.[26]

During the winter of 1891–92, the Law and Order League made a determined fight against the Big Four that resulted in daily arrests at the track, including Walbaum, who was involved in several bookmaking operations there. Walbaum then decided to vacation at Hot Springs, Arkansas, a popular gambling resort, perhaps to escape the reformers' wrath. His friends arranged a testimonial dinner to see him off with Jersey City mayor Orestes Cleveland presiding. This gala epitomized the cozy relationship between the HCJC and local politicos. Cleveland praised Walbaum as "a most exemplary citizen." Other attendees included Mayor Edwin Stanton of Hoboken, County Clerk McLaughlin, and several state assemblymen, all reputedly Guttenberg stockholders. They came at Walbaum's behest to "show the Law and Order League how the politicians of the county regard their persecutions."[27]

Guttenberg's spring races were at first of good quality and provided a training ground for future winners of the prestigious Brooklyn and Suburban stakes, but for the most part, they were low-quality events where boys and other young jockeys rode second-rate horses. A rare world-class race occurred on 26 September 1893, a one-and-a-quarter-mile match race between Tammany, 1892 horse of the year, owned by copper magnate and Tammany supporter Marcus Daly, and Lamplighter, the other outstanding four-year-old of 1893, recently purchased by

Walbaum from Pierre Lorillard. The race drew fifteen thousand people, including New York City's leading sportsmen. Tammany easily won the race, and Daley took a $2,500 side bet from Walbaum.[28]

Races occurred year-round at Guttenberg, even during blinding snowstorms, below-zero cold, or fog so dense that spectators saw neither the horses running nor the posted results. The weather was so bad that one day in February 1893, Peter De Lacy closed his Manhattan poolroom and refused to take bets. The press was especially agitated by the introduction of two-year-old racing in the winter of 1890 because the horses' bodies were not yet strong enough for the rigors of such events.[29]

Guttenberg's audiences were mainly thugs and other disorderly characters, including Hoboken and Jersey City liquor dealers, ordered by McLaughlin and his friends to bet there instead of the Harrison and Newark betting parlors. The *Times* covered Jersey racing extensively and described patrons as "people who dared not show their faces in New York City during the daytime for fear of police recognition and arrest."[30]

Proprietary Tracks Boom in New Jersey, 1887–89

The liberalization of New Jersey's racing laws in 1887 and the success of prestigious Monmouth Park and the plebeian Guttenberg Track encouraged the establishment of proprietary tracks in the late 1880s in Clifton, Linden, and Elizabeth, all close to New York City and all operated by New Yorkers or Brooklynites. George H. Engeman and his nephew William, proprietors of the Brighton Beach course, were enticed by reports that Guttenberg was making big money, and in 1887, they took over the Passaic County Agricultural Society, which had raced thoroughbreds in Paterson back in 1864. They established the Clifton Racetrack, in which they eventually invested $200,000, and featured winter racing. The Engemans encountered a number of problems with the authorities that might have been resolved through sound politics, but they consistently supported the losing factions in local elections.[31]

In early 1888, Assemblyman McDermitt of Essex introduced a bill in Trenton to prohibit pools at the racetracks in response to "the outrageous swindling performances at Clifton and Guttenberg . . . for the benefit of the city pool rooms," but the measure failed. Poolroom operator Peter De Lacy fought the proposal in cooperation with the MRA and the Pennsylvania, Jersey Central, and Erie railroads that carried racing fans to the track. The legislature later voted to ban winter racing, but Democratic governor Robert S. Green vetoed the bill.[32]

In the following year, Assemblyman O'Neill submitted a bill to limit racing to a season running from 15 June to 15 October and establish a 10 percent tax on gross receipts, but it died in committee. These restrictions would have made it difficult for new tracks to operate, particularly with competition from nearby New York courses. From 1889 through 1898, both party platforms called for banning racetrack gambling, but the actions of state Democrats hardly adhered to that position.[33]

In 1889, two new tracks opened in Union County, but with weaker political connections than Guttenberg or Monmouth. Michael F. Dwyer, the renowned plunger and brother of the BJC president, organized the New Jersey Jockey Club (NJJC), which operated a course in Elizabeth. It was twenty minutes from New York City by ferry and both the Pennsylvania and the New Jersey Central railroads, making it the most accessible legitimate track in the metropolitan area. The other new facility was the Linden Track, situated just outside Newark, located on an old farm site purchased for $15,000 by the Linden Blood Horse Association (LBHA). Its leading stockholders were bookmaker James E. Kelly, whose firm managed the betting rings at Sheepshead Bay, Morris Park, and Monmouth Park, and New York bookmaker and gambling hall proprietor Lucien O. Appleby.

Linden was closer to New York than Clifton, adjacent to a main line of the Pennsylvania Railroad, just thirty minutes from New York and less than twenty-five from Jersey City. Races began at 1:30, an hour earlier than Elizabeth, which was probably too early for New Yorkers to leave from work. The races were mainly of the $500–$600 variety, with a daily overhead of about $1,500 to $1,800. The NJJC paid Elizabeth nearly $3,000 in real estate taxes and $250 for a liquor license, whereas Linden's taxes were about $1,800.[34]

Dwyer, along with Withers, forbade anyone at their courses from telegraphing information. They hoped to bolster attendance by making bettors go to the tracks instead of downtown poolrooms. However, Henry Clay Ditmars of Western Union circumvented the orders by stationing messengers near the tracks in trees or nearby towers. They received signals from confederates inside the courses with the names of starters, betting odds, and the final results, which they transmitted from a nearby telegraph station to New York and, from there, across the country. The Dwyers then hired Pinkertons to prevent people at their tracks from signaling race results to off-track confederates.[35]

Gloucester: The Outlaw Track of Southern New Jersey

The success of the proprietary tracks led to the establishment of a southern counterpart to Guttenberg, the Gloucester Racetrack, that soon had an even-worse reputation. Gloucester opened in 1890 with a 250-acre facility and three-quarter-mile track, thirty minutes from Philadelphia, in suburban Camden County. It had a five-thousand-seat grandstand and staged five races a day for meager $250 purses. The track operated daily, rain, shine, or snow, from 1 September 1890 through 4

April 1891, except for Sundays. The contests were nearly always travesties, raced by horses that could win nowhere else, and fixed races were a matter of course. There were races in which *no* owner instructed his jockey to win because they all sought betting coups by wagering against their own horses. Bookmakers at the track worried that sharpsters would fix a race and wipe them out.[36]

William J. Thompson, the powerful Camden County Democratic boss, elected to the state assembly in 1890, presided over the track. The "Duke of Gloucester" was born in Ireland but grew up in Philadelphia, where he boxed and owned a saloon. He subsequently moved to Gloucester City to run a hotel and developed the town into a low-life resort similar to Coney Island's West End, which one wag described as a model of decency compared to Gloucester. Thompson owned virtually everything in town, including a hotel, a casino, and Fancy Hill, a nearby pleasure ground, as well as a ferry line across the Delaware to Philadelphia and the electric railroad that ran to the track. The infamous racecourse, built on landfill, was his chief source of revenue. Daily profits, estimated at $2,500, helped make Thompson a millionaire.[37]

Thompson paid off Philadelphia journalists who covered Gloucester racing to not report the track's dismal state of affairs or write about public officials at the races. Thompson openly used his political influence to promote the track and prevent interference by county officials or reform-minded law-and-order organizations. Thompson also used his control of Gloucester to further his political ambitions. Employees knew their jobs depended on voting a straight Democratic ticket. In addition, whenever elections were coming up, Thompson gave away many free passes to encourage voters to support his candidates.[38]

Thompson's right-hand man was starter Thomas Flynn, a former lobbyist, saloonkeeper, and bookmaker, whom he paid $5,000 a year. Flynn was also a state assemblyman from Passaic, even though he really lived in Philadelphia. Thompson's influence helped Flynn become Speaker of the state assembly in 1893.[39]

The spectators at Gloucester were the same kinds of people that frequented Guttenberg. The *Tribune* identified them as "murderers, highwaymen, burglars, pickpockets, sneak thieves, bunco-steerers, and petty swindlers of all sorts" who gamble "with the proceeds of their crimes." It recommended that if the New York or Philadelphia authorities were seeking notorious criminals, they could probably find the rascals at Guttenberg or Gloucester.[40]

The 1890 Legislature and Proposals to Legalize Racing in New Jersey

In anticipation of efforts by reformers to go after Jersey racing, Monmouth, Elizabeth, and the Linden tracks went to the legislature for protection. On 27 January

1890, Assemblyman Leonard Kalisch of Newark introduced a bill to regulate horse racing that would ensure the opening of racetracks independent of political influence. Kalisch recommended a 5 percent tax on the gross of any racing association, a thirty-day limit of racing at any track, and the establishment of a racing season from 1 May to 1 September, which would kill winter racing. The state's racing interests formed a coalition with Elizabeth businessmen hoping for a boost in commerce and the major railroads, who had a financial stake in the sport because of the traffic it generated. Monmouth's president then was railroad magnate A. J. Cassatt, future president of the Pennsylvania Railroad and a New Jersey breeder.[41]

The biggest fight of the entire legislative session occurred when the Kalisch bill came up for a second reading on 26 February. Among the opponents was Republican assemblyman Thomas McCran, who denounced the Union County tracks as "Hellish institutions" that were ruining the youth of Paterson, "a city of milk and honey." The strongest resistance was surprisingly from Hudson County assemblymen, who strongly favored the turf but opposed any limits on racing and wanted winter racing at Guttenberg and Clifton. The state house amended the Kalisch horse racing bill to legalize racing and pool selling at the tracks for fifty-five days a year with 5 percent of each track's gross receipts going to the state. The senate then deleted the ban on winter racing, and the revised bill easily passed the legislature.[42]

Observers expected approval to be a formality, but Governor Abbett was in no hurry to sign the bill. Political scientist Richard Hogarty believes that Abbett was concerned about the reaction of conservative Protestant voters in the upcoming election and chose to test public opinion.[43]

The antiracing forces had not marshaled during the legislative debate but got into gear after the Kalisch bill passed. Rev. Everard Kempshall of Elizabeth's First Presbyterian Church led the protest and, with other Protestant leaders, pressured Abbett with sermons and rallies against the turf. Kempshall led a delegation of more than one hundred clergymen, merchants, and businessmen to Trenton on 17 June, where they met in the assembly chamber. Former assemblyman William H. Corbin addressed them, contending the bill was unconstitutional because it legalized gambling and provided for a lottery. He also asserted the state was solvent and did not need a 5 percent tax, especially from gambling. Then the delegates met the governor and presented him with a petition signed by three thousand people opposed to the racing bill. The document claimed that racetrack gambling demoralized the state's youth, caused workers to lose time and money, and would make suburban towns "the reservoir of the scum of the cities."[44]

The *Trenton Daily True American*, no friend of political bossism or loose morals, thought the petitioners were out of line. The paper denied that the bill legalized crime, because bookmaking was not intrinsically a crime and gambling was criminal only when the law declared it so. The editors also believed it was better to regulate gambling than ban it, even if wagering harmed youth. Gambling was pervasive in society, they noted, ranging from Wall Street to church fairs, and keeping it illegal, but unenforceable, led to lack of respect for the law, which was worse than the gambling itself.[45]

Abbett decided not to approve the racing bill by what amounted to a pocket veto, apparently swayed by the court of public opinion. His action came so late in the session that there was no time for reconsideration. The governor was influenced by the very strong feelings against winter racing in northern New Jersey and resentment throughout the state against powerful Hudson County politicians and railroad magnates who seemed to have overstepped their bounds in subsidizing certain racetracks and helping lobby for them. In addition, by opposing the tracks, Abbett was retaliating against David Withers, the only track operator who had not supported his recent unsuccessful run for the U.S. Senate. Furthermore, Abbett's approval of the Kalisch bill might have created undesired competition for his friends who ran Guttenberg and Gloucester and were going to operate regardless of the law.[46]

Abbett still had an eye on a U.S. Senate seat and found the proposed legislation too controversial. He was a professional politician and was always aware of the impact gubernatorial decisions would have upon his career. According to his biographer, Abbett "was a genius at brokering political differences. As much as any politician in the country, Abbett understood the essence of the political game and played it better than most of them. He was shrewdly attuned to the temper of the times." As Hogarty points out, a potentially divisive issue cooled down, and in the fall, the Democrats won both branches of the legislature. However, Abbett failed to secure his much-sought-after Senate seat, which went instead to James Smith Jr. of Newark, a leather manufacturer who had served just one term as alderman. The outcome was partly in retaliation for Abbett's vetoing of Democratic legislation and in gratitude for Smith's generous financial contributions to the party.[47]

De Lacy Takes on the Jersey Tracks

The Jersey racetracks' immunity from criminal prosecution was severely tested in the spring of 1890 by an unusual alliance of convenience between poolroom operators and moral reformers. Peter De Lacy, king of the New York poolroom men, sought revenge against the racetracks who were trying to squeeze him out, even if it meant cooperating with Law and Order Leagues who wanted to eliminate gambling altogether. The reformers portrayed pool sellers as a greater nuisance and more dangerous than saloon keepers yet worked with De Lacy against a mutual enemy.[48]

De Lacy took charge of the fight, focusing on Elizabeth and Monmouth. Two of his sheet writers secured warrants against them under an obsolete state law for "assisting in keeping a disorderly house," meaning anyplace where betting occurred. The press scoffed at a law that made a well-conducted, orderly racecourse into a "disorderly house." Nonetheless, on 3 May, all bookmakers at the Elizabeth track were arrested, and three days later, Judge Van Syckel charged the grand jury to indict them and the track's officials. Van Syckel said that racing was legal, but the tracks discredited the state: "The pernicious effect of these lawless institutions were already demoralizing the youth of the community. The race tracks were pest holes, prolific of vice and crime." The racing men were not worried, since the sheriff had protected them in the past and the jury foreman was a Rahway hotel keeper and fan of racing. However, indictments were returned, and convictions were secured against the Union County tracks for maintaining disorderly houses, which carried a fine of $500.[49]

De Lacy resumed his harassment of racetracks and on-site bookmaking that summer after Monmouth Park opened, with even greater vigor than he had exercised against the bet takers at the spring meets at Elizabeth and Linden. A "pious" De Lacy and Michael Murray, a fellow New York gambler, began raiding Monmouth Park on 4 July when "America's Greatest Race Course" opened for the summer, sending one of his clerks to swear out warrants against sixty-eight bookmakers. The county detective made arrests following the fifth race. Withers anticipated problems and had a justice of the peace on hand who released the detained bookmakers on $100 bail provided by bondsmen Withers furnished, and the bookmakers resumed business. On the following day, seventy-five bookmakers were arrested, as well as MRA president Cassatt, treasurer Withers, and general manager T. M. Croft, accused of running a disorderly house. Thereafter, arrests occurred nearly daily. The Monmouth crowd anticipated no trials because the county's attorney general kept getting continuances to tire out the witnesses and make them give up. However, when the attorney general went on vacation, a judge ordered the cases to trial. Then the bailiff refused to take action, claiming the attorney general had instructed him not to serve the summonses, warning he would not be paid. The trials went on, and the bookmakers all pleaded guilty. They were fined $200 and warned that a second conviction would send them to prison.[50]

De Lacy renewed his efforts against the tracks when Elizabeth and Linden opened for the fall, pledging "to make things warm." He claimed no hostility toward Linden but needed to treat everyone equally. After several bookmakers were arrested, the police and local justices got active, "because many arrests could be made and the yield of fees was bountiful." The track managers, who originally considered the arrests an annoyance, bailed out the bookmakers. Many were convicted and fined $200 to $500, which spread fear and consternation among them. On 7 January 1891, NJJC executives were found guilty of allowing bookmaking on the track. Matthew Corbett, a bookmaker, who had invested $50,000 in the track, pleaded guilty to charges of taking bets. He was fined $1,000.[51]

A lot of suspicion about the cases developed after Judge Van Syckel refused to publish the names of jurors struck from special panels convened to try the bookmakers and track officials. None came from Elizabeth's poorest wards, and just one came from crowded Linden Township. There were no Irishmen and just two Germans. Most impaneled men, including several from Dr. Kempshall's congregation, were rumored to be antiracing.[52]

In mid-January, De Lacy arranged the arrest of Clifton's proprietors and employees for violating rules against disorderly houses. The track responded by closing down. The Clifton crowd believed no jury would convict them and offered no defense witnesses. Engeman figured that since his track provided four hundred jobs in Paterson, he would be safe even if his political allies could not protect him. Deputy Sheriff Matthew Pettigrew gave very incriminating testimony, indicating that his former superior Sheriff Cornelius A. Cadmus, just elected to Congress, had appointed him expressly to support the track managers. Pettigrew and his fellow deputies were to collect $50 to $75 a day from the track's bookmakers and turn the funds over to track treasurer A. H. Battersby. The court convicted George Engeman, his partners, and local bookmakers, despite their admitted political influence, and handed down significant sentences. William Engeman, Battersby, and track secretary C. V. Sass were sentenced to a year in jail and a fine of $500 and George Engeman to two years of hard labor and $1,000.[53]

The *New York Times* and other reform-minded newspapers and magazines ardently supported the fight against horse race gambling in New Jersey because New Yorkers were heavily involved there as breeders, racers, and track owners, plus they wagered at the nearby tracks or in poolrooms that took bets on Jersey races. The *Times* believed that thoroughbred racing was a beautiful sport when run honestly but decried the corruption that characterized the sport in New Jersey, which it feared might spread to New York. The newspaper accepted the need for betting on the tracks to keep the sport alive, but totally opposed off-track betting as purely gambling for its own sake. The *Times* recommended that Trenton bar winter racing, invariably characterized by "jobbery" and cheating. However, "such a bill cannot be passed while corrupt politicians live and they can find a good source for levying blackmail on racetrack managers instead of confining their depredations wholly to luckless owners of liquor saloons, gambling houses, and other disreputable resorts. Jerseymen have learned New York's tricks, and the Jersey politicians are as good 'workers' when a dollar is to be had as are the Tammany's chiefs."[54]

The Politics of Jersey Racing

The convictions of club officials, especially the Clifton operators, had a significant impact on racing. Clifton, Linden, and Elizabeth tracks all closed down after the courts ruled that racetracks could be considered "disorderly houses," and their sites were converted into farmland. Even more important, the ruling meant that Monmouth Park, previously protected by laws permitting betting at its meets, could open only if it chose to violate the law.[55]

The gambling convictions terrified Withers about the future of New Jersey racing, and he secured an option, just in case, to lease for the upcoming season the recently closed Jerome Park. Withers also formed a coalition with the Elizabeth and Linden tracks to amass a $140,000 fund to lobby and buy off state legislators to pass a bill permitting limited on-track betting similar to the Ives Pool Law. A lot of support also came from the Pennsylvania Railroad, which furnished transportation to Linden and Long Branch, and the New Jersey Central, which provided access to Elizabeth and Long Branch and owned the NJJC's racing site. Withers was so confident in the outcome that he advertised a summer meet with $250,000 in added money and purses.[56]

On 23 February, Assemblyman G. W. Ketcham of Essex presented a communication to the state house of representative signed by seventeen thousand New Jersey women urging the legislature not to pass any law legalizing pool selling or Sunday liquor sales. Moments later, acting on Withers's behalf, Monmouth assemblyman William A. Campbell introduced a package of four bills to authorize local governments to license racetracks for up to five years, ban winter racing, and levy a county tax of 5 percent of the gate.[57]

Religious leaders held statewide meetings and petition drives against the bill. Dr. Kempshall organized the Citizens' League of New Jersey to work against all gambling, as well as against the liquor interests. Anthony Comstock was the featured speaker at an antiracing rally in Trenton where he argued that the main beneficiaries of Campbell's bills would be former New York bookmakers, driven into New Jersey to make a living. He also spoke before the House Committee on Revision of the Laws to oppose racing bills. Comstock first reviewed his experiences combating racetrack gambling in New York and Saratoga, where he had been warned to stay away, or else his "body would be sent home in a box," and then decried the financial benefits promised as "blood-money belonging to famished mothers and staving children."[58]

The *Trenton Daily True American* criticized the racing bills, even though it had supported the Kalisch bills during the prior session:

> Theoretically, everybody who wants to bet on a horse race, ought to be allowed to, but practically the presence in this State of sporting tracks and sporting men and sporting methods disorganizes the communities in which they are established; breeds a spirit of gambling among the young and the dependent, and with the chances against the outside betters, creates danger of wrong doing, peculation, and robbery.
>
> The bills before the Legislature turn over to the logical governing boards the power to say that institutions, primarily illegal, shall be allowed to exist and prey on the public. . . . [T]his is a dangerous power to vest in the Common Council or the board of Freeholders because it immediately makes the members of these bodies the object of venal solicitation by interests which need spend only a small percentage of their illicit gains to create a very large corruption fund. . . .
>
> The whole business has degenerated into a public nuisance, which ought no more to be no more licensed than prostitution or house breaking.

The editors pointed to the degeneration of Long Branch, where pool selling, once decently conducted, had fallen under the control of disreputable gambling interests. They explained that the antiracing folk were "the best element of our people—the mothers and wives who see their homes endangered, the business men, who see society disorganized; the clergy who see the moral anguish and misery in their midst."[59]

The Campbell proposals went down, a result of widespread public resistance and the hostility of the politically connected outlaw tracks who wanted to keep open in winter. Guttenberg and Gloucester purportedly controlled at least twelve votes in the legislature, sufficient to kill any measure they opposed.[60]

A compromise was considered on a local option law authorizing counties to license racecourses and thereby effectively repeal the "disorderly house" statute. This trade-off was acceptable to the outlaw tracks, but not Republicans catering to evangelical rural voters. The assembly was thirty-seven to twenty-two Democratic, and probably would have approved a compromise bill, but not the senate, which was eleven to ten Republican. As the *Chicago Tribune* pointed out, Republicans would not favor it "out of deference to the expressed sentiment of the religious people of the State." The local option bill never made it out of committee. Afterward, the legislature passed a bill on behalf of the gambling fraternity that

shifted disorderly house cases from state to local courts, where community sentiment and political pressure were more powerful.[61]

The failure of the racing bills was the last straw for Withers, who closed Monmouth Park. This move supposedly demonstrated that the MRA obeyed and
respected the law, but the track actually shut down to teach county voters how
strict enforcement of the antiracing laws would hurt them. Farmers, merchants,
hotel keepers, and various railroad lines that had all benefited from the racetrack's
presence suffered financially when the track closed. Their losses brought public
opinion over to the track's side, thereby increasing pressure to revise the law in
favor of the turf. Withers shifted his scheduled program at the last moment to
Jerome Park in July but had a disappointing meet.[62]

The closing of Clifton, Linden, Elizabeth, and Monmouth left Guttenberg and
Gloucester with a monopoly. They remained open because their clout protected
them from the disorderly house law that had undone their rivals. In the spring,
Guttenberg, which was already paying Clifton seven hundred dollars a day for
their racing dates following its owners' convictions, purchased the entire thirty-
day meet of the Elizabeth and Linden tracks for forty-five thousand dollars and
held their races, including prestigious stakes events, at its own site.[63]

Guttenberg's monopoly of Northern New Jersey racing was lucrative, netting
about two hundred thousand dollars since the previous fall, or four thousand dollars per racing day. The track started out the winter season with about eighty bookmakers paying seventy-five dollars a day, or six thousand dollars in total. However,
in mid-March 1891, when the New York poolrooms reopened after a brief hiatus,
the number of bookmakers working the track dropped by half. Other sources of
revenue included the gate (three thousand dollars a day), concession fees, and the
fees paid by poolrooms, which were shared with Western Union. City poolrooms
paid fifteen dollars a day for racing news, and rooms elsewhere paid ten. According to the *Times,* Guttenberg in early 1891 grossed seven thousand dollars a day,
with expenses that included twenty-five hundred dollars for purses and five hundred for political payoffs, but did not account for maintenance and other overhead
expenses, which in March, with reduced returns from bookmaking fees, would
have had to be minuscule to provide a profit of four thousand dollars.[64]

Guttenberg was so profitable it could afford to hire respected race starter J. P.
Caldwell for two years at the unheard-of salary of twenty-five thousand dollars
a year, plus ten thousand dollars of stock in Walbaum's Saratoga Racing Association. The *Spirit* thought this hiring represented "the implicit confidence entertained by the Hudson County Ring in their ability to control racing in . . . New
Jersey, and fully believe that the power they wield at the present time will continue indefinitely."[65]

Antiracing Sentiment in New Jersey

Reformers were pleased with their success fighting the turf in New Jersey and expanded their efforts to destroy the outlaw tracks. In early April 1891, Rev. John L. Scudder, of Jersey City's Tabernacle Congregational Church, organized rallies and raids against Guttenberg and sent many witnesses to the grand jury to testify about its gambling. However, Sheriff Bob Davis, Hudson County's Democratic machine boss, protected the HCJC against Scudder's efforts.[66]

Meanwhile, Camden County ministers and other reformers tried to combat the notorious Gloucester Track, pressuring the governor and county officials to take action. Since Thompson first opened Gloucester, there were occasional indictments there for corruption, but little came of them. Presiding magistrate Judge Hugg owed Thompson his job and so always let him off with a small fine. However, in early spring, Governor Abbett warned his political ally that a show of force was forthcoming to demonstrate the integrity of the governor and local authorities. Consequently, Gloucester closed on 5 April, after 176 days of continuous racing, but reopened two weeks later after the grand jury's term expired.[67]

Thompson's difficulties with the law-and-order people became more serious in November following the *Haring* decision that horse racing accompanied by betting was illegal. The ruling revitalized antitrack forces, who resumed their attacks on Thompson, hoping to clean up the Gloucester pesthole. The Duke appeared unflappable, having easily defeated his critics in the past, and was confident the governor would protect him. However, Thompson was indicted, and the racetrack temporarily closed because of the adverse publicity.[68]

Journalists believed the county had a clear-cut case against Thompson. Twelve witnesses vividly described the low-class people who frequented his drinking establishments and the gambling facilities at Gloucester. According to the *Times*, "The fact that Gloucester City was one vast gambling hell, worse than anything that the frontier mining towns of the West could boast, was proved beyond a doubt." Thompson, throughout the proceedings, appeared poised and confident, certain that no Camden court would dare convict him. When he heard the jurors' names announced, Thompson smiled. The "Duke of Gloucester" indicated he would be acquitted and that the racetrack would reopen at the end of December. Thompson was indeed found innocent.[69]

The acquittal did not dissuade the antivice coalition. Early in 1892, the *Times* and the Law and Order Society of Hudson County initiated a crusade against Guttenberg, culminating in a raid on 16 January by Chief Constable John Graham of Jersey City. However, the forewarned track officials were prepared, and when Graham's thirteen Pinkertons entered the track, six on-duty Jersey City policemen, paid by the track to provide security, assaulted the invaders. The Pinkertons persevered and made eleven arrests, including several bookmakers, President Walbaum, and track manager J. C. Carr, who were charged with keeping a disorderly house. They made bond and returned to the track to continue their business.[70]

A few weeks later, on 4 February, an important meeting about upcoming racetrack bills occurred in the governor's private room at the statehouse. Those individuals present included Thompson; his attorney, Alan L. McDermott; Hudson County clerk Dennis McLaughlin; and Republican leader William J. Sewell. McLaughlin did not care about any proposals that would mainly benefit his enemies who controlled Monmouth, Linden, and Elizabeth. Thompson sympathized with him, but the Duke wanted legislation to protect his own interests, and he was willing to work on behalf of Monmouth and the Dwyers, who owned Elizabeth. The consensus was that prestigious Monmouth deserved help in resuming operations because it would enhance the prestige of the turf, benefit all racing interests, and assist local hotel keepers, who had lost heavily when the track closed in 1891.[71]

Elected officials in the next legislative session unsuccessfully introduced bills similar to the measures voted down in 1891. However, in early March, the legislature approved the so-called Guttenberg Race Track Bill, decried by the *Tribune* as "shameless legislation." It was based on McLaughlin's pet measure that originally proposed that anyone arrested at the track could choose the magistrate to arraign him. The amended bill required anyone arrested at the track to have charges made, or bail secured, in a local court. This provision meant a justice could deal with the case right at the track. An assembly critic said it should have been entitled "An act to encourage and facilitate the nefarious business of the race-track gamblers of the state."[72]

The New Regime at Monmouth Park

David Withers passed away on 13 February 1892, a great loss to the turf. There was a lot of concern about the future of Monmouth Park, where his syndicate had invested $1.3 million. At first, the other officers of the MRA were not keen on keeping it going, having paid just $20,000 for an option to lease Jerome Park for another year. Philip J. Dwyer offered to take the entire meet, dividing it between Jerome Park and other New York–area tracks.[73]

A new syndicate was formed that secured control of the track, led by President A. F. Walcott, a businessman and racehorse owner who possessed one-fourth of the renamed Monmouth Park Racing Association's (MPRA) stock (168 out of 600 shares), while 18 percent was held by Pennsylvania Railroad executives. However, the real power, and the principal stockholder, was John A. Morris, proprietor of the Morris Park Racetrack. Other well-heeled partners included MPRA treasurer Phil Dwyer and his brother Mike, Tammany sachem Richard Croker, U.S. Senator James Smith, various lesser Jersey politicians, and bookmaker Lucien O. Appleby, operator of a notorious Broadway faro game, who had made book at Linden and ran the betting ring at Monmouth.[74]

The daily and sporting press at first welcomed the new leadership. The *Times* had high expectations since Walcott's partner in his racing stable was John Campbell, one of the shrewdest and most practical men on the turf: "The track is now in the hands of men that are progressive, up to the times, and more in touch with race goers than are the managers of any of the other tracks." One of the club's first projects was constructing the elegant New Monmouth Park Hotel.[75]

When Monmouth reopened after a year's hiatus for a forty-five-day meet on the Fourth of July, the only tracks operating in New Jersey were Guttenberg and Gloucester. Its 12,500-seat grandstand was full, and the crowd was estimated as high as thirty thousand people. Seventy-four bookmakers were in the betting ring. The holiday event had a gay atmosphere, with beautiful lawns, beds of beautiful flowers, and tubs of semitropical plants. A popular innovation was the construction of a lane of turf from the saddling paddock to the weighing stand, which gave hundreds of people a chance to check out the horses before and after the races.[76]

However, after this excellent beginning, the track encountered serious problems. The MPRA did not get the expected political protection, and the Law and Order League secured several indictments against the management. By the meet's end, the consensus was that Monmouth had ended up in the hands of less reputable individuals, particularly John Morris. During the summer session, he gave away tout sheets to people exiting the track to advertise his infamous Louisiana Lottery.[77]

State Politics and the New Jersey Racing Scene, 1892–93

The fall election of 1892 was a great success for New Jersey Democrats. The ticket was led by presidential nominee Grover Cleveland and gubernatorial aspirant George T. Werts. It was also very profitable for Thompson, who reputedly won eighty thousand dollars by betting on Cleveland's victory. During the campaign, Jersey Democrats emphasized the interests of urban ethnic voters who opposed restrictions on personal freedom, while Republicans focused on promoting moral virtue and traditional values in their appeal to pietistic rural WASP voters. The Democrats ended up enhancing their control of the legislature by a wide preponderance of thirty-nine to twenty-one in the assembly and sixteen to five in the senate.[78]

Track managers worked during the election to elect protrack legislators. They raised a lot of money for the party, including twenty-five thousand dollars from Thompson. These funds relieved the Democratic National Committee from sending a lot of money into the state on behalf of Cleveland and Werts. The price for the aid was passage of proracing and gambling legislation.[79]

Racetrack operators in the 1893 legislative session made their strongest effort ever to legalize racetracks and on-course gambling. They were in a great position because of their role in the election campaign and the Democratic domination of what was known as the "Jockey Legislature." The newly elected Democrats were not of the highest moral fiber. According to one contemporary expert, "Almost every Democrat who floated to a seat in either house of the Legislature in 1893 represented a ring, or one of the disreputable bosses or a job, or had been tempted to his candidacy by the hope of illegitimate gain." The assembly now included Thompson, bookmaker Teddy Carroll, and Speaker Thomas Flynn, the former starter at Gloucester.[80]

Horse racing dominated the start of the legislative session. The Democrats backed the racetracks and the gamblers, while the Republicans opposed the wagering, the crooked racetracks, and the political corruption of the Democratic machines. Monmouth's new management helped get the racing interests to finally unite in their mutual struggle to legalize racing, putting up forty thousand dollars for lobbying and the buying of votes, although Mike Dwyer was not willing to "contribute" to the effort.[81]

On 21 February 1893, Republican assemblyman William T. Parker, who represented Monmouth, introduced three controversial bills on behalf of the racetracks. His main proposal would grant local governmental agencies, such as city councils or county boards of freeholders, authority to license racecourses. Existing courses would need approval only by a simple majority, but new facilities needed a two-thirds vote. Parker's second bill called for the legalization of bookmaking and pool selling at licensed tracks, and the third exempted poolrooms belonging to owners of licensed racetracks from being categorized as disorderly houses, as previously happened in Elizabeth and Linden.[82]

No public hearings were held, and these bills were rushed through the assembly as strictly partisan measures. They were immediately favorably reviewed by Thompson's Committee on Municipal Corporations, and the assembly approved them by identical votes of thirty-four to twenty-three. Parker was one of only two Republicans who backed the bill. The other was a former Democrat who had switched parties when he moved into a Republican district. Political favors and money helped secure the necessary votes. Assemblyman Reuben Strahan of Monmouth supported the racing bills at the request of local Democratic chief David Crater, who promised him the nomination for county sheriff. The next day was Washington's Birthday, but the Senate met anyhow to hurry the bill along. It passed by a narrower vote of twelve to nine, with just one Republican voting with the majority.[83]

The bill was swiftly passed through, supposedly to help finish the legislative calendar, but actually to prevent the emergence of organized opposition. Governor Werts had five days to consider the Parker acts, but vetoed the bills the next day, ostensibly to prevent them from getting through by default. Actually, the Democratic leadership initiated this astute parliamentary move to protect Werts from the wrath of the electorate and to facilitate a certain override that required only a simple majority before the track's foes mobilized. On 24 February, the day after the veto, the assembly repassed the measures by a vote of thirty-three to twenty-five. The senate required a one-day wait before voting and then met on Saturday, which was almost never done, to approve the Parker Acts by a vote of eleven to nine.[84]

The legislature also considered the thorny issue of winter racing. In mid-February, Democratic assembly floor leader Lane of Union County proposed ending racing from December through March and authorizing the governor to use the state police or militia to stop it. Lane had originally been in line to become Speaker, but his antiracing views cost him the post. The bill went to Thompson's committee, where it died.[85]

The Public Response to the Parker Acts

The reaction to the legitimization of racetracks and the legalization of racetrack gambling was stinging. Most newspapers in metropolitan New York were livid in their criticism and called for a reform movement to undo the harmful laws. The *Times*, for instance, decried the action:

> It is plain that these bills were devised by the race-track owners for their own benefit, and driven through the Legislature by them, with the knowledge that they were in defiance of public opinion and of the wishes of the people of the State. Together they constitute an infamous surrender of the lawmaking power into the hands of a gambling fraternity, and are intended not to promote or encourage the cultivation of speed in horses or to regulate legitimate competition upon race tracks, but simply and solely to make the New-Jersey race track serve the purposes of gambling in one of its most demoralizing and pernicious forms, and to keep the business in the hands of the ring which now controls it and which has gone into politics for the very purpose of accomplishing this object.[86]

The *Times* ranked the sitting government "as one of the most disgraceful, reckless, and brazen Legislatures that ever sat in the State of New Jersey."[87]

An antiracing coalition immediately mobilized against the new legislation. About five thousand racing opponents quickly descended to the state capitol and invaded the assembly hall to express their views and deliver petitions to the legislature. Evangelical ministers throughout the state delivered ringing Sunday sermons full of outrage and organized meetings and rallies to fight the tracks and mobilize sentiment against gambling. By mid-April, local Citizens' Leagues were formed to organize a movement to defeat legislators who had supported horse racing and elect new men pledged to repeal the odious laws.[88]

The antiracetrack coalition was primarily composed of pietistic Protestants, particularly Methodists and Presbyterians, who sought to use their political influence to regulate social behavior. They believed the state was obliged to supervise individual morality in conformity with traditional American values. There was, on the other hand, very little support for repeal among Catholics, Jews, and other religious ritualists who did not believe the state should regulate personal conduct. Historian Samuel McSeveney, the leading student of late-nineteenth-century New Jersey politics, found that the reaction to the racetrack issue had strong overtones of a cultural conflict symbolized by the moral issue of gambling. An individual voter's perspectives toward racing and gambling transcended his attitudes toward sport, or even toward betting, epitomizing his entire worldview. This position made the fight against racing particularly important, since it represented the pietists' struggle to protect their country, culture, and way of life against urbanization, immigration, and other forces of social change.[89]

The considerable adverse reaction, especially in the press, worried state and national Democratic leaders. President-elect Cleveland saw the negative drift in public opinion against the party. He met with Senator Smith, which led to a decision to counter the criticism by supporting the end of winter racing. Party leaders responded by making an about-face on the issue, and Assemblyman Byrne of Essex, a Thompson associate, submitted a bill barring contests from 1 December to 1 March with a maximum penalty of a ten-thousand-dollar fine and two years in jail. As one observer explained, "It is really Thompson's bill to hit the Guttenberg fellows for their meanness and stinginess, by cutting off their Winter racing business," even if it harmed his own track. Assemblyman Timothy J. Carroll of Hudson, a Jersey City bookmaker and devoted supporter of McLaughlin and Guttenberg, sprang up to fight it but could not prevail against the unusual coalition of Gloucesterites and antiracing forces. Republicans in the assembly did not support it because they thought the proposal was a trick, but Republican senators went along since the act did reform the racing scene. The antiracing measure sped through the legislature on 11 March in less than an hour.[90]

Thompson backed the winter ban, not only because the president and Senator Smith promoted it but also because he believed the HCJC had not borne its share of the cost of securing proracing measures or worked for any of his own bills. The Duke decided he could afford to give up midwinter profits for the sweet taste of revenge. The *Times* reported he was looking to turn over a new leaf in his quest for social acceptance for himself and his family: "He holds himself above the gang whose money has made him rich. He has nothing but contempt for the low-grade gamblers and disreputable sports and blacklegs that swarm his grounds. He lives in magnificent style, but his princely home with its stately mansion and broad lawns and game preserves, seems like an idle mockery to him when neighbors who haven't the thousandth part of his wealth, snub him, and refuse even to enter his doors. . . . He is . . . quite ready to make a sacrifice of business to escape the ostracism of his neighbors by making his occupation as reputable as it can be made."[91]

Such considerations prompted him to freely spend money in the legislature to cover his track with the mantle of legality. According to the *Times*, "Thompson committed his jockeys of both houses to the passage of the act, and [former sheriff] Davis persuaded the Essex men, by way of repaying McLaughlin's opposition to the election of Smith to the United State Senate, to fall in with the procession." Davis had been the sheriff in Hudson County, but did not get along well with Boss McLaughlin, who had appointed him, and periodically threatened to send the grand jury after Guttenberg if the boss took a position Davis opposed. Guttenberg was the boss's special pet, and it had helped make him one of the richest men in the county. McLaughlin had used his control over the grand juries to protect touts, gamblers, and bookmakers.[92]

McLaughlin did not reslate Davis in 1890 but let him choose his own successor, John J. McPhillips, who basically let the former sheriff run the department and collect the fees. However, when McPhillips died in office, Governor Abbett chose Dennis McLaughlin's nominee for sheriff, Mayor Edwin Stanton of Hoboken, to keep the boss's support in his drive for the U.S. Senate. Then in 1893 when a bill came up to halt winter racing, Davis ardently supported it out of revenge against McLaughlin and his faction of the Hudson County Democracy.[93]

McLaughlin was relatively indifferent to the question of legalized racetrack gambling. His primary concern was to maintain control over the Hudson County Grand Jury so he could protect his machine from prosecution. However, Thompson's situation in Camden was becoming more vulnerable, and he had less control over the grand jury than ever before. The Duke of Gloucester was actually indicted for gambling that winter and pleaded guilty to keeping a disorderly house. He was fined $50, plus $47 in court costs.[94]

Racing Is Back in Business

Monmouth Park was the first shuttered track to reopen. On 2 March, the Eaton-town Board of Freeholders issued Monmouth a license almost immediately after the enactment of the Parker laws was approved. The MPRA was so confident of the legislative process that it had filed a license application even before the bill passed. The directors figured there was a lot of local support because of the track's enormous economic influence in the mostly rural township of 2,953. The board originally set a nominal $1 fee, but public opposition to a "giveaway" resulted one week later in a new license fee of $5,000, intended to improve local roads, including the ones that ran to the track. By comparison, Guttenberg's license was merely $100 a year for five years and Gloucester's $250 a year, which it never bothered to pay.[95]

Monmouth's cocky management was rather inept and right from the start made unwise decisions. They fired 200 local men who did security work and other duties at the track, which created a lot of ill well, especially when they were replaced by New Yorkers who had campaigned for candidates favorable to the racing association.[96]

Monmouth, under its old regime, had been the most prestigious track in the state and one of the great American racecourses. However, Monmouth's reopening drew considerable negative press reports that it was falling to the level of the Guttenbergs and the Gloucesters. The *Times,* the *Tribune,* and even the county's own Democratic newspapers printed derogatory articles decrying the declining integrity of the races. The *Tribune* criticized the track for knowingly running injured horses without informing the public, for having its president send his agent to make bets on races over which he might have to rule, and for having Lucius Appleby, the operator of a notorious faro bank, run the betting ring.[97] The track was also criticized for a falloff in the quality and size of crowds to about 3,500, without the usual high-class horse fanciers and well-known celebrities. Instead, the spectators included a lot of young men who used to bet in New York poolrooms before Boss Croker began his drive to close the poolrooms, as well as many Tenderloin women who came with passes and complimentary tickets for the refreshment stands given to them by bookmakers.[98]

The MPRA reacted strongly to the critical press and tried to muzzle or buy off critics. In mid-July, Tracey Bronson of the *Times* and a *Tribune* reporter were refused admission to the track in retribution for unfavorable comments. The reform-minded *Chicago Daily News* reacted very critically: "The vilest crap-shooter, tout, disreputables of either sex, could be admitted to Monmouth, but a racing reporter who does his duty and exposes fraud must go." Monmouth not only tried to restrain trenchant journalists but also sought to ingratiate itself with the press by paying two New York reporters nearly $100 to serve as racing judges, which likely colored their commentary.[99]

The track's efforts at censorship only heightened the *Times*'s critical commentary, which claimed that large numbers of prostitutes and other disreputables were roaming the grandstand and the rest of the park looking for business. Decent people were crowded off the promenade behind the first tier of grandstand seats by lowlifes who associated with trainers, jockeys, and touts, "and freely patronized the 'ladies' restaurant, where late in the afternoon empty champagne bottles gave silent evidence to their drinking habits." The *Times* further complained that racing was becoming more like the Louisiana Lottery, "where the public has no chance. . . . Big stakes and everyday racing have killed whatever sport there was in it, and it is now nothing more nor less than a gambling game." Such reprehensible conditions required the suppression of horse racing, even if it hurt the breeding industry.[100]

The *Tribune* was also very derogatory, remembering that under Withers, "the betting ring and the ladies-in-waiting were not so offensively conspicuous. . . . They were kept in discreet restraint, but this year they have been permitted to flaunt themselves so prominently in public view and the standards of the sport has been so seriously lowered as to alienate and repel the better class of admirers of the turf. . . . Already a large proportion of the better class of people who like to see high class racing . . . has been driven away from the place."[101]

Management was accused of swindling the public, since every day, just before post time, several horses would be scratched and new horses added. This scheme worked out well for Michael Dwyer, a new stockholder, who used his clout to enter events at the last moment in which his horses would be favored. According to the *Chicago Daily News*, "He saw the entries and the weights and then put in the entries of horses belonging to him if he thought they could win."[102] The *Times* also heavily criticized the bookmakers, some of whom hired women as touts to promote betting. Certain bookmakers were described as "undertakers," who bet against horses whose owners had warned them that they were losers.[103]

Horsemen and bettors soon became increasingly disenchanted with Monmouth because of the adverse press coverage, their own bad experiences there, the poor quality of the crowds, and even a murder at the track by a fired drunken trainer. Attendance declined markedly during the summer meet, and the number of bookmakers dropped from eighty-six to forty-one. Management tried to bolster the crowds by liberally doling out passes, but by mid-August, the situation was so dismal that about two-thirds of spectators got in free. These promotions, which worked well at low-class tracks by encouraging potential bettors who normally gambled at poolrooms or with handbooks to wager at the track, indicated that Monmouth had fallen close to the level of the outlaw courses. On 15 August, when the ten-thousand-dollar added Omnibus Stakes was raced, the track lost at least six thousand dollars, an amount equaled twice again over a seven-day period. Losses for the week amounted to fifteen thousand. Monmouth ended its meet in severe financial disarray, with its third straight year of losses and a three-hundred-thousand-dollar debt coming due.[104]

In mid-August, the Citizens' League, with branches in all the townships, began in earnest its fight to halt gambling in Monmouth County. The reformers distributed a flyer titled "Shall the Gamblers Rule New-Jersey?" that compared Jersey to New York, which had recently passed the Saxton Act, prohibiting pool selling in poolrooms, and to Connecticut, which had passed an antipool law barring gambling at racetracks. As the *Times* pointed out, "New-Jersey . . . at the dictation of a convicted criminal, has chosen to become the Mecca for all the gamblers, the blacklegs, the criminals and vicious elements of the great cities lying near us, who sweep down upon us in carloads and boatloads and overflow our towns and cities. The effect of these laws has also been to place the Town and County Governments, in some instances, under the control of the gamblers."[105]

Reopening the Proprietary Tracks

The passage of the Parker bills enabled the state's other closed tracks to also reopen. The Elizabeth track reopened under the leadership of its new president, David Gideon, a former New York assemblyman, member of the MPRA's executive committee, big Gravesend stockholder, and well-known heavy plunger. The NJJC spent heavily in the 1893 election to secure proracing politicians, which paid off when Elizabeth officials narrowly voted the track a five-year license at an annual fee of five thousand dollars, permitting thirty days of racing in the spring and fall.[106]

The Clifton Racetrack also sought to resume following pardons of management for their convictions for running a disorderly house. However, in March, the Passaic Board of Chosen Freeholders rejected their bid for a permit by a vote of ten to seven. The board reversed itself on 1 August by a vote of eleven to one because of anticipated patronage from the Engemans and granted a three-year license for one thousand dollars a year.[107]

The local Citizens' League decried this action, fearful that the racing game would bring disreputable and undesirable types into town who would contaminate its youth and destroy private property. The *Orange Herald* criticized the granting of licenses as marking "the full fruition of the hopes of the cabal of political gamblers who have for four years been engaged in the desperate attempt to bring the State of New Jersey under complete subjection to their depraved will." The paper further noted that Passaic County was "the breeding-place of the most continuous and flagrant scandals that have disgraced the public life of New Jersey for thirty years." However, the *Passaic Herald* supported the decision, arguing that the racecourse would create many new jobs, serve as an important source of revenue, and attract law-abiding crowds.[108]

The *Brooklyn Eagle* also strongly supported the Clifton Racetrack, proud of its Brooklyn management, and anticipated that Brooklynites would flock to the course, which was more accessible for them than Guttenberg. The *Eagle* lauded its accommodations, describing the grandstand, paddock, and refurbished betting ring (now electrically illuminated and completely enclosed) as far more commodious than Engeman's Brighton Beach Racetrack. The *Eagle* was not so naive as to miss the importance of politics in New Jersey racing: "Politicians and especially racetrack politicians are a yard wide and a foot deep in Jersey. Wine and Greenbacks have to be as the leaves of the trees at the start and then the whole families of the town board have to be given sinecures at the finish. The small politicians trusted and believed when they allowed Mr. Engeman to reopen his own track that all the male population of Passaic County should be given a job and three free passes into the enclosure. Eighty men . . . were employed the first day and the local politicians got angry at once because the number was not three times eighty."[109]

Clifton's successful reopening encouraged Linden to resume. However, securing a license was problematic in a Republican town in Union County. The Republicans held a caucus in March for prospective committee members, selecting men who favored licensing and supplanting committeemen who had previously voted against a license. Proracing men packed the meeting, many reputedly ineligible to vote in the caucus. On the following day, racing supporters gained control of the Democratic slate, which seemed to ensure victory for the track in the general election. However, an independent law-and-order ticket also ran candidates for the town's committee and swept the election, surpassing the combined vote of the established parties. Despite this setback, the LBHA still negotiated a deal with the committeemen on 16 August and secured its license by a surprising vote of seven to one. The board established an annual five-thousand-dollar fee, which did not go to the township but instead went directly to the Roselle Land Improvement Company, a construction company owned by a township commissioner who had voted for the license. The firm then got a contract to build a sewer, part of which went through the track. Reformers condemned the deal as pure bribery. One local church was so disgusted that it suspended the membership of two committeemen.

The racetrack opened with a very successful ten-day fall meet that reportedly netted fifty thousand dollars.[110]

Racing and the Election of 1893

Horse racing and gambling overshadowed the depression in the fall legislative elections. The *Times* interpreted the substantial opposition to racetrack gambling and the widespread hopes for repeal of the Parker laws as symbols of discontent with Democratic misrule. Their bad leadership encompassed gerrymandering the state legislature, destroying home rule, multiplying government jobs for patronage purposes, and legitimizing horse racing.[111]

The press, law-and-order organizations, and evangelical Protestant societies led the fight to oust proracing legislators. The *Newark Evening News* ran such editorials as "The End of the Race Track Gambling Law" and "Who Should Vote for Lobsters?" (the latter a popular term for "fools"). The *Times* ran full-page stories about Jersey racing in two Sunday issues just before the election, examining the racetracks' corruption and political machinations.[112]

Antiracing associations sought to prevent the renomination of incumbents, virtually all of whom were Democrats who had supported the gambling interests. They endorsed Republicans and the few Democrats who had supported repeal of the Parker Acts, encouraged certain candidates to withdraw on behalf of aspirants more supportive of cleaning up horse racing, and even ran independent candidates pledged to reform. Several intraparty conflicts emerged, particularly among Democrats, when dominant protrack factions were challenged for party leadership.[113]

Reformers in racetrack counties also got very involved in sheriffs' contests. Friendly sheriffs were invaluable to racing and gambling interests because they could provide advance information about raids, prevent arrests by poorly enforcing the law, and protect perpetrators by packing grand juries with friends of horse race wagering. Law-and-order organizations backed nominees pledged to fight gambling and publicized the records of candidates beholden to track managers and bookmakers.[114]

William Thompson was very concerned about keeping control of the sheriff's office in Camden County. The *Philadelphia Inquirer* claimed that Thompson ordered the purchase of votes and that election judges secretly marked ballots cast by Republicans and then tossed them out. Assessments on party officials to pay for the campaign were said to surpass the money raised for presidential campaigns.[115]

Thompson and his cronies realized they were in for a very tough fight, but they expected to prevail with financial support from the railroads and the use of such traditional machine tactics as stuffing ballots, importing thugs, and "colonization" (importing out-of-towners to vote for five dollars, plus food, clothing, and shelter) to ensure a large Democratic turnout. According to the *Times*, Thompson was colonizing Camden County with "the riffraff of the negro, Italian, and Hungarian vote of Philadelphia, which he has had placed on the registry lists, with the connivance of his servile tools on the police force." He had 260 colonists register as living at his stables and had men in Camden recorded as residents of saloons and even a deserted canal boat.[116]

Colonization occurred in nearly all heavily populated counties, especially the ones with racetracks. Newark's saloon keepers and Italian boardinghouses lodged many illegal voters, while in Atlantic City, African Americans from Baltimore and Washington claimed residence because they were hotel waiters.[117]

During the campaign, it became apparent that the state assembly was probably going to be taken over by antiracing interests, regardless of party affiliation. Consequently, Thompson revised his campaign plans just before election day, focusing on the senate, where only seven seats were up, making the Democrats almost certain to have enough representation to block any antiracing measures. Furthermore, Thompson was hoping to move into the U.S. Senate in 1896 and needed control of the upper house for that bid. The *Times* speculated that Thompson could count on eighteen proracing votes in 1894 from the senators he personally controlled and those under the influence of racing lobbyists.[118]

The election results shocked all prognosticators, as the Democrats suffered a resounding defeat, losing both the assembly and the senate. Not even the most optimistic Republicans would have anticipated a net gain of nineteen seats in the lower house and six in the senate, where they lost just one seat. Furthermore, antitrack candidates for sheriff were victorious in Hudson and Camden counties, home of the outlaw tracks.[119]

Samuel McSeveney's sophisticated analysis of the 1893 state election returns found that the antiracing and antigambling crusades were the most important factors in the election, particularly among rural and nonindustrial small-town voters. He found that the turf's opposition mainly came from pietistic Methodists and Presbyterians for whom moral values were of utmost significance. Their stand on racing and gambling was consistent with their views on other ethnocultural issues like Prohibition and Sabbatarianism.[120]

The greatest shift in voting patterns occurred in heavily Methodist southern counties, especially Cape May, a region swept by a moral revolution. The voters' ire was aimed at racing supporters, regardless of party. For instance, the Atlantic County Republican assemblyman who voted for the racetrack bills was defeated by an antiturf Democrat who made notable inroads among antigambling

Germans. German voters opposed crusades against drinking and the Continental Sabbath that threatened their cultural and moral standards but sided with pietists on the gambling issue and moral respectability.[121]

Antiracing sentiment was even stronger in Monmouth and Camden counties. Monmouth's Democratic senator was defeated, and Republican assemblyman Parker, who had introduced the racing bills, was not even renominated. His seat was captured by a Democrat, and a Republican–Citizens' League coalition won the other Monmouth seats. In Camden County, Assemblyman Thompson repulsed a Republican–Citizens' League–Independent Democratic coalition, but the Republicans took a normally Democratic assembly seat and retained their own senate and assembly seats.[122]

In the heavily populated Northeast, a traditional Democratic stronghold, the combination of the depression, the moral revolt against gambling, and factional fighting within the party resulted in some Democratic defeats. McSeveney found that the Socialist Labor Party used the prevailing economic problems to siphon off enough Democratic votes in certain districts to tip the election for the Republicans, whose victories there were impressive, if less dramatic than in rural New Jersey. Republicans gained eleven assembly seats in Essex, Bergen, Union, and Hudson counties; lost one in Hudson County; and took two senate sets in Essex and Union.[123]

The moral issue, symbolized by racetrack gambling, produced a spectacular triumph for the Republican Party. The Republicans successfully sold themselves as the representative of traditional values, morality, and social control. The ethnocultural and economic issues contributed to a national realignment of the electorate outside the solid South. However, the gains made on the gambling question were short-lived, because those Jersey counties that swung most radically in 1893 returned to traditional voting patterns one year later.[124]

The Impact of the Election on Racing

The Republican victory signaled the end of racing in New Jersey. Everyone anticipated that the incoming legislature would abrogate the laws permitting on-track gambling and that new local officials, like the independent sheriff in Camden County, would, unlike their predecessors, block any horse race betting.[125] The *Times* applauded the outcome: "Jersey justice asserted itself at the ballot boxes . . . and administered a rebuke to the arrogant ringsters that have brought the State into disrepute by the most audacious legislation for the benefit of as corrupt a ring as ever got control of the affairs of a State. Democrats and citizens of all political faiths joined hands to wipe out of power the gang of miscreants that have saddled themselves on the State." The result was a through housecleaning in favor of candidates pledged to the number-one issue in New Jersey: wiping out the Thompson-McLaughlin ring. The victory by the people over the rings meant the reorganization of the state Democratic Party. Particularly important was the election of reform candidates for sheriffs in three racetrack counties. The *Times* considered it the worst possible blow to the gamblers because future grand juries would be able to do their duty free of political pressure.[126]

The 1893 racing season ended on 1 December because of the new ban on winter racing. No one could predict when, or if, racing would ever resume. The sport's future became particularly bleak at the end of the year when Eatontown announced it had secretly revoked Monmouth Park's license on 7 August, virtually guaranteeing that the state's most prestigious course would be closed in 1894. The death of racing purportedly cost the community $1 million a year.[127]

Thompson and his cronies made one final effort to save horse racing. They tried to prevent certain newly elected Republicans from taking their seats when the senate reconvened in 1894, thereby preserving a Democratic majority. Racing supporters argued that only the nine Democrats and four Republicans whose terms had not expired should judge the credentials of new members. The plan was to seat four of the new Republicans and one new Democrat while blocking three Republicans, including Monmouth's new senator, and a reelected Camden senator who was Thompson's arch foe.[128]

The uncertainty ended on 8 January 1894, when the judiciary effectively killed racetrack gambling in New Jersey. The state supreme court ruled unanimously in *City of Elizabeth v. New Jersey Jockey Club* that the 1893 racing laws were unconstitutional. Justice Lippincott asserted in a seminal ruling that the legislature had unlawfully sought to regulate the internal affairs of towns and counties, illegally granting corporations, associations, and individuals exclusive privileges, immunities, or franchises. The tracks had spent an estimated $150,000 to pass the Parker laws and then secure their licenses, and now they were out of business.[129]

The *Tribune* lauded the ruling, believing the racing crowd had earned their due: "Never was legislation enacted in NJ with a bolder disregard of decent opinion and with a more reckless defiance of the sentiments of respectable people." If the track managers had run their operations as smartly as the CIJC, and with respect for honest folk, they would probably still be open. "The whole racing element in the state was practically responsible for the infamies which were practiced at Trenton," noted the *Tribune,* namely, "the briberies, the bullying and browbeating, the frauds and crimes which were committed there."[130]

Even though the courts had finished off the tracks, the new antiracing legislature went ahead to overturn the racing laws. As soon as the elected representatives convened, the assembly initiated the necessary steps to repeal the Parker Acts and on 10 January forwarded it to the senate for its concurrence. That afternoon the new senators took their seats and passed the antiracing bill, which then went on to Governor Werts, who signed the measure into law.[131]

Insult was added to injury three days later when indictments were delivered against the Guttenberg syndicate and its police allies, stemming from a raid on 16 January 1892. Reform League officials tried to arrest the track managers and certain bookmakers for running a disorderly house, and off-duty policemen working as track guards assaulted Pinkerton agents trying to make arrests. No arrests were made that day despite overwhelming evidence. But the recent election of a Republican sheriff changed Hudson County's political climate, and the new sheriff put together a grand jury more receptive to enforcing the antigambling laws. The Big Four—Carr, Crusius, McLaughlin, and Walbaum—all pleaded guilty to charges of running a disorderly house and received a year in prison and a $500 fine, which upon appeal was remitted to just the fine.[132] The convictions were long in coming, according to the *Tribune:* "The audacity and insolence of the Guttenburg [*sic*] gang were unapproachable. They owned the greater part of the police force in the various communities in Hudson County; they owned a number of trial justices; they owned the Democratic Sheriff, and the Democratic Governor . . . was their amiable and complaisant friend. They spat upon the law, they jeered at decent public opinion, they robbed and fleeced and swindled great numbers of victims, and they amassed fortunes from the proceeds of fraud and lawmaking."[133]

After the repeal was passed, the legislature gave Guttenberg three months' reprieve before the law barring racing went into effect. Walbaum recommended to his partners that they race in the interim, figuring he could make about $300,000 in that time. They disagreed and closed up: "Next year we'll get a new law and we can re-open." Walbaum responded optimistically, "The new law you are going to get you can put in your pipe and smoke it." However, he was wrong, and the property was eventually sold for 40 percent of its value.[134]

Conclusion

The state of the turf in New Jersey had important ramifications for thoroughbred racing throughout the United States. When the social elite ran Monmouth Park, it was a national model for the sport and encouraged the creation of prestigious racetracks throughout the country. On the other hand, the notorious outlaw tracks of Guttenberg and Gloucester promoted a negative image of the turf, encouraged the creation of other low-class proprietary tracks (like Chicago's Garfield Park), and enflamed reformers to do away with the sport and its gambling. The state's elite and proprietary tracks were operated by men with powerful political and economic connections that enabled them to operate despite laws that did not support racing and considerable public opposition. New Jersey's machine politicians, who controlled the illegal off-track betting and the outlaw tracks, allied with more respectable businessmen and politicians to control the state government in 1893 and pass laws protecting racing interests. However, they overstepped, and a groundswell of opposition rose up against them. A populist revolt kicked their allies out of the state legislature and overturned the legalization of on-track gambling. The situation in New Jersey had an immediate negative impact on the turf in Chicago, where Washington Park closed up, and in New York, where racing was nearly banned.

The speedy and sudden demise of horse racing in New Jersey had a very long-term effect on the sport in the Garden State, where there was no racing for nearly fifty years. Even during the Great Depression, when state after state legalized racing to gain badly needed revenues, there was no thoroughbred racing in New Jersey, although there was dog racing in 1934 and 1935. Finally, in 1940, economic exigencies resulted in the legalization of pari-mutuel racing under a state racing commission, leading to the opening of Garden State Race Track in 1942 and Monmouth Park four years later.[135]

6

From the Board of Control
to The Jockey Club, 1891–94

Racing at present in this country is hostile to anything savoring of government. But it is certain that unless we have government the gentlemen who race for sport will soon sell out and abandon the turf. In that case racing will decline. It will be confined to proprietary tracks run on the principle of a theater or other public amusement. The great stakes races will be abandoned. . . . Gradually nobody but toughs and thugs will go to the races.
—*Spirit of the Times*, 23 September 1893

In 1890, thoroughbred racing was so popular in New York that President C. F. Prince of baseball's third major league, the newly established Players' League, complained to his colleagues, "Horse racing, to all intents and purposes, has superceded the national game in popular favor in this city."[1] Although this statement might have been an exaggeration, New York remained the national center of racing, with huge crowds attending prestigious and lucrative events and extensive press coverage of the sport. The high-status tracks were prominent resorts for the social, economic, and political elites; their wives and lady friends; and other sports fans who enjoyed wagering on the races. Up to one hundred bookmakers worked the big races, servicing the gambling hunger of racing fans. The already heavily politicized sport became even more political. Tammanyites, most notably Boss Richard Croker, became more prominent than ever, not just as gamblers but also as breeders and owners. The turf retained some of its raffish character, particularly at the proprietary tracks, yet local jockey clubs prided themselves with the increased presence of women at their tracks, who provided an aura of respectability, although there was growing concern about their penchant to gamble.

Eminent track operators and horsemen tried to bring order to the sport by establishing in 1891 an organization to oversee it in metropolitan New York, the Board of Control. The turf flourished in the early 1890s, but there was soon widespread dissatisfaction with the board's work, particularly in protecting the sport's integrity. In the critical 1894 season, when the state government in neighboring New Jersey closed the tracks, The Jockey Club, a small group of racetrack directors who made up the crème de la crème of New York society, took it upon themselves to supplant the feckless Board of Control. TJC took upon itself the task of protecting the sport by setting rules and licensing participants to promote the search for order, not just for the metropolitan turf but also for thoroughbred racing across the country.

The 1891 Racing Season

The New York Jockey Club

The much anticipated opening day on 1 June at Morris Park marked a changing of the guard as it took over the social position of Jerome Park in its prime: "The butterflies of fashion, male and female, were out in their glory, the boxes being occupied by people whose faces are familiar in the season at Tuxedo, Lenox, Newport, and other ultra-fashionable resorts." Their presence was seen as providing "life and color to the scene, that was a pleasant offset to the intensely business side of racing which alone interests the speculators who are the regulars at every race track." The feature race was the inaugurations of the Metropolitan Stakes, one of the richest events in the United States. There were about a hundred bookmakers in the betting ring. James E. Kelly managed the pari-mutuels, electrically powered for the first time. The machines recorded every bet instantly, automatically adjusting the odds. Three-fourths of the bets were from two to ten dollars, and mainly on place rather than win. Betting was light on the $5 French pools, which was the most popular way to bet at Sheepshead Bay. One expert recommended the track initiate $2 French pools on win, place, or show, which would take business from the bookmakers.[2]

The day also marked the formal unveiling of Morris Park's $240,000 elegant six-story elevator-serviced, brick-and-iron clubhouse with sixty-six rooms, built on the highest point in Westchester County. Elite club members enjoyed the clubhouse year-round, which combined the best features of the suburban country club and the downtown city club. The *Spirit of the Times* admired the "luxurious playground," whose "comfort, completeness and beauty of interior surpass our most extravagant anticipations." It set a new standard for clubhouses, with its large hall leading to a handsome ninety-by-sixty-foot ballroom, "a feast for the eye," with fireplaces and carvings, a polished oak floor, and a $28,000 orchestrion (a machine designed to play music and sound like an orchestra), the largest in the United States. The main floor included "charmingly furnished" ladies' reception rooms and a "broad and spacious piazza, from which a perfect view of the races can be had." The piazza seated one thousand people. The second floor had a billiard room, ten private dining rooms that had excellent views of the track, and forty-two beautifully furnished second-floor bedrooms, with steam heat and electric and gas lighting. The airy bedrooms were cooled by refreshing breezes off Long Island Sound. The clubhouse even provided facilities for women athletes, including locker parlors and the promise of tennis courts in the future.[3]

The *Spirit* expected Morris Park Racetrack would become the leading jockey club in the world and predicted the clubhouse "will be the most attractive rendezvous in America, and under its inspiration new men of wealth and position will be drawn upon the theater of racing and its influence upon the sport and its tone cannot be estimated." The *Spirit* further predicted that "the social feature of racing, which began at Jerome Park and which contributes so greatly to the prestige and influence of the sport, will assume greater power at Westchester and render it what Ascot is to England, and invest racing with a social and financial power that will protect it from harm."[4]

Tammany was out in force a few days later for the first Saturday of the meet to see one of the biggest races of the year, the $25,000 Eclipse Stakes for two-year-olds. Among the individuals present were Boss Croker, Mayor Hugh J. Grant, former register John Reilly, and "a couple of hundred of the lesser toads in the political puddle at the track, who represented all shades and faction in politics except the extreme Prohibitionists and the intensely hayseed Alliance men. Tammany men predominated, and that being the case, it was fitting that a colt named Tammany should have won the richest prize . . . of the meeting." Self-made Montana copper magnate Marcus Daly, an Irish immigrant and a prominent Democratic politician, owned the horse. Before the race, Daly's trainer, Matthew Byrnes, tipped off his friend Mayor Grant, a big racing fan, to bet on another one of their horses, the favorite, Sir Matthew, to win, with Tammany to place. The mayor said, "I'm much obliged to Mr. Byrnes for his tip, but I can't see why Tammany shouldn't win. Tammany takes about everything in its reach so far as my observation goes, and there doesn't seem to be any good reason why Tammany shouldn't take the richest plum of a racing meeting." He bet $20 on Tammany, half to win at forty to one and half to place at twenty to one. Boss Croker was not as shrewd as Mayor Grant was. As the *Times* reported, "He simply argued that Tammany always gets a place, and so he only played the horse for a place." The Stecklers, a well-known family of reformers, were contrarians who "would not have Tammany at any price, and all of them played Delusion when they found the politicians backing Tammany, because they had found Tammany's promises a delusion. As usual, the Tammany boys got all the money, for Tammany won the race." Daley was the second-biggest

10. The Morris Park Clubhouse was not merely an adjunct to the racing course but a hotel open year-round for its elite members. Drawn by Charles Graham. *Source:* "The Club-House of the New York Jockey Club," *Harper's Weekly* 35 (20 June 1891): 465.

winner at the spring meet, surpassed only by the stable owned by John A. Morris and son Alfred Heenan Morris, the track's general manager.[5]

The Morris family and the Democrats had a lot of political clout in the Fifteenth Senatorial District, remapped in 1892 from a heavily Republican area that included Rockland County to an overwhelmingly Democratic district that included Westchester and Putnam counties and New York City's Twenty-fourth Ward. Alfred H., a Harvard man, started out in politics in 1890 when appointed to the newly formed Westchester Park Commission. He won election in the spring of 1892 as supervisor of the town of Westchester in the county's hottest campaign in history, heavily supported by his father's money and former Westchester sheriff John Duffy. According to the *Times*, "His only interest on the board was to improve the roads leading from Westchester and improving his and his father's property," although he also wanted to reduce the assessment on the track from $275,000 to $200,000. Shortly thereafter, Alfred won an assembly seat. He was a lethargic legislator who took his cues from Lieutenant Governor Sheehan and "was a most subservient attaché of the machine."[6]

In 1893, Alfred did very little, "except when the Saxton pool bill came up, or any matter dealing with racing" or gambling, and was expected to support the legalization of prizefighting. Otherwise, he "displayed an indifference and an ignorance surprising in a man of his appearance and apparent intelligence." He did get a bill passed to assess Westchester taxpayers $1 million to create a sewerage system that would significantly benefit the racetrack. Morris gave a modest speech to the county meeting when running for the state senate in 1893 that demonstrated to the *Times* reporter that "on national and State topics he was as dumb as any horse in his father's stable." He was defeated in the Republican landslide of 1893, in large part, according to the *Times*, because the constituents resented the bosses imposing him on them.[7]

The Monmouth Racing Association Moves to New York

At the last moment in late June, the Monmouth Racing Association gave up any hopes of holding its meet in Long Branch without interference by the authorities. It had already reorganized itself under New York State laws as the Monmouth Park Racing Association and announced it was switching to New York from 8 July through 25 August. The MPRA raced thirteen days at Morris Park, featuring its major stakes events, and then seventeen dates at Jerome Park. Withers did not expect to make money at Jerome Park, estimating his daily costs would be about $12,000, but the *Tribune* expected a daily profit of at least $1,350. The paper figured he would make $8,000 a day from bookmakers fees, $3,500 from the gate, $800 from bar and restaurant privileges, $250 from the program privileges, and $800 from the Harlem Railroad for the carrying privilege.[8]

When the summer meet began, Withers got the New York railroads, which provided excellent service, to drop the old round-trip rate of $0.60 to $0.40. In the past, the railroads paid the AJC the difference. It was not an act of charity, but a response to competition from the Brighton track, where the carfare from New York was $0.55. Management also introduced the free field, copying Morris Park and Brighton, figuring it would take away business from city poolrooms that the jockey clubs hoped to close.[9]

A boycott by owners of mid- and low-quality horses that usually raced at Brighton Beach hurt business at the track. They should have jumped at the chance to race for the MPRA's purses. The crowd that controlled the Brighton Beach, Buffalo, Boston, and Clifton tracks set up the boycott. They considered Monmouth "an interloper" on their turf.[10]

Morris Park's facilities then surpassed Sheepshead Bay's, although it never equaled it in the size of attendance or the quality of the racing. The CIJC opened its 1891 season with a new two-tiered eleven-thousand-seat grandstand that was 640 feet long and provided an unobstructed view of the whole course. The open basement provided free passage under the building from the lawn to the betting ring, and the roof was used for standing room. However, the *Spirit of the Times* thought these improvements were insufficient: "The clubhouse is a farce compared to Morris Park [and Monmouth]. . . . Race-goers have a right to demand first-class accommodations from an association which has had such a great share of their good dollars as has the Coney Island Jockey Club." The grandstand was described as "a dreadfully patched-up affair," while the concession stands were hard to reach and required walking through malodorous passageways. The *Spirit* criticized Sheepshead Bay's fine-looking paddock as impractical, because its top was a light-metal latticework leaving everything visible, which tended to upset nervous horses. In addition, the walk from the paddock to the betting ring was so long that "if anyone is so foolish as to attempt to make his way through the passage under the stand on a crowded day, the race is likely to be over before he reaches his destination." Finally, the *Spirit* considered the railway facilities to be abominable: "A man has to be an athlete to get a seat on a train. How then about the ladies?"[11]

In the fall season, the New York Jockey Club shifted nine days of its thirteen-day meet to Jerome Park because the Monmouth Park Racing Association had used up so many of its available thirty days. Morris allowed Western Union to collect information and send it to city poolrooms for a daily fee of $1,600, equal to what the telegraph company got from the poolrooms. He was under pressure from Peter De Lacy, who threatened to retaliate against Morris's lottery and policy business unless the NYJC cooperated with the wire service. The club saved money by doing away with musical entertainment performed by a military band.[12]

Women at the Tracks

Track officials and racing journalists delighted in the presence of respectable women at the racetracks, but thought that jockey clubs still had a ways to go in providing them with adequate accommodations similar to the finest European tracks. As the *Spirit* explained, "The tone given to a race-course by the attendance of ladies is something to be coveted, but it will always be found impossible to get a goodly gathering of the fair sex where there is discomfort. Crowding above all, means discomfort to them. . . . Ladies will be given suitable facilities so they can see the horses through a kiosk like [at] Longchamps."[13]

Management tried to protect all customers on the course, but especially women. The tracks relied on Pinkerton agents to watch for gate jumpers, counterfeit betting slips, and known pickpockets and sneak thieves who took advantage of the jostling crowds and careless winners to pilfer the unsuspecting. Thomas F. Eagen, who printed the betting slips, himself supplied Pinkertons to the Brooklyn tracks to prevent losses he would have to make up. On 13 June 1890, Pinkertons arrested Harry Cohen, a tout who preyed on female gamblers, for trying to cash an altered bookmaker's ticket. He had some fifty tickets in his pockets that skilled artists could modify with a good pencil. When Cohen steered women bettors to a winning horse, he would alter an old ticket and give it to them. Cohen would take tickets for his "clients" to the cashier and cash in the bets before anyone detected any fraud.[14]

Many male racing fans were uncomfortable with women at the tracks, especially the ones who seemed ill bred. The renowned chief inspector Thomas F. Byrnes, who headed the Detective Bureau (1880–88) and authored *Professional Criminals of America* (1886), while simultaneously enriching himself with payoffs and financial tips from Wall Street contacts, wondered about the behavior of many female racing fans:

What respectable man who knows the racetracks for what they are will today take his wife or his daughter to a racetrack to see the races for the pleasure of seeing them? He must sit among a lot of overly dressed women who yell and shout like men and who act as decent men would be ashamed to act. To seat a good woman or a good girl among the hordes of hardened, gambling-crazed females who are found in the grandstands on every racing day is an insult to the entire sex. Respectable women do not go; but among the crowd of bad women and worse men, they look sadly out of place.[15]

Byrnes, who became police superintendent in 1892, was a critic of horse racing and off-track gambling. He thought that tracks were a disgrace that "have infested this city with harpies, confidence men and thieves. . . . If racing continues around this city as it is conducted now for another decade, the criminal percentage of the population will increase almost beyond estimate. Racecourses, such as are around New York, and I except none, are the most fruitful kindergartens of crime."[16]

The betting rings were off-limits to women, who often bet vicariously through their husbands or dates, which enhanced the exciting atmosphere of the tracks. Women often went one step further and found a way to bet on their own. It was a bit risqué for Victorian women, but at the racecourse people felt freer than in most social settings, like bathers at Coney Island beaches. The jockey clubs, especially Gravesend, catered to women's interest in betting by furnishing messenger boys supervised by T. F. Eagen, the ticket printer, to take their wagers to the betting ring on behalf of their clients. He enlisted youths who paid him eight dollars for the opportunity to be messenger boys. They typically worked with bookmakers, usually ones who offered the lowest odds and swindled their clients, who paid the youths two dollars to direct business their way. At the end of the 1891 season, when the Pinkertons tried to break up this business, the boys came up with a new scheme, collecting betting stubs as old as a year. When the boys received a commission, they got the best possible odds but kept the receipts for themselves and wrote lower odds on the old tickets. If the horse won, they cashed their stubs and paid clients at the lower odds, keeping the difference. The scheme unraveled because some lads got too greedy, and customers discovered the fraud. Three boys were arrested with about five hundred old tickets in their possession.[17]

The BJC in September developed a new way to facilitate women's betting. The track set up a pari-mutuel stand just for women as well as space for bookmaking right in the grandstand, misleadingly described as a "betting office" for "ladies," where women could hire commissioners to take their bets to the betting ring. Fans interviewed by the press found this reprehensible, although many spectators walked over to watch the activity in the gambling corner "to see the painted women go up and make their bets." The innovation was vigorously opposed by the *Times*:

> There is nothing that will so quickly and properly set public opinion against racing as the placing of books in the grandstand and driving women to bet there. It is a temptation that the average woman cannot resist, and there is no good reason

why it should be thrown in their way. It is bad enough for women to bet as they do, "on the quiet," but it is a thousand times worse to put these books in the stand, where they are constantly in reach if they wish to go to them. Worst of all, the book is apparently one run by the Jockey Club itself. . . . The club cannot afford to be known as backing a book and publicly inviting women to bet there. That is going a bit too far in the mad scramble for money.

The public agreed with the *Times,* and within a week, public pressure led to the closing of the bookmaking facilities, but women continued to bet with the pari-mutuels.[18]

The *Brooklyn Eagle* ran a feature story in 1893 titled "Gamblers in Petticoats: A Study of the Women of the Race Track," by a journalist who respected women's ability to make bets and have a good time at the track. He pointed out that in early spring, the "betting sisterhood begins to bestir itself" and did a lot of things that would shock the average woman. "A singular and withal interesting creature is the racing woman," continued the writer. "She is an outgrowth of the modern craze for horse racing, a byproduct of the freedom vouchsafed to American femininity, an object lesson on the misuse of her sex's disenfranchisement from old fetters and old forms." She came from all ages and social levels.[19]

The *Eagle* further reported that although sportsmen did not encourage women to study racing forms, they did not oppose it either, and admired how women researched and listened, avoided big risks, and were willing to win small amounts. Women attending the races who were not upper class rode to the tracks by train or ferry and discussed with each other odds, scratches, jockeys, and horses. Female racing fans were mostly "not drawn from that class that one would imagine would be likely to evolve the famed 'sport.'" They included "widows with small competencies, women with friends in the racing business . . . , women with a belief in the money making possibility of the track as compared with other means of livelihood, and the female scions of sporting families." Then there were the women described as "sham sports," who "[wear] ultra sporting garb, talk loudly of their bets, give cheap information for the benefit of those about them, and in other ways seek to make themselves as conspicuous as possible. Women of this type, for the most part, simply use the track as a blind to their actual profession."[20]

In the summer of 1894, renowned journalist Nellie Bly, whose previous accomplishments included traveling around the world and sparring heavyweight champion Jim Corbett, visited Saratoga to expose the local gambling scene. She visited the betting parlors operated by Richard A. Canfield and Caleb Mitchell and went to the track, where she found women from all backgrounds. They included "the woman who has a house of her own, carriages galore . . . ; there is a poor woman hushing a babe in long clothes on her shoulder as she waits to bet the bit of silver she clutches in her hand . . . a fat, jolly looking creature with a half-dozen gaily dressed girls with her . . . , and nearby is a woman who certainly looked as if her sins were scarlet."[21]

Bly reported that bookmakers used different-colored paper and printing designs for each race. They used indelible ink to print their business names and a number on the tickets. The bookmakers who catered to women did not operate in the main betting stand but were in a separate ring at the top landing in the rear of the grandstand. The *New York World* called it "the only race-track betting ring in America for women." The bets, like at Gravesend, were carried by messenger boys, who received a ten-cent fee from women gamblers that doubled if the horse won.[22]

Bly went to the women's ring, connected to the main ring by a telephone. She found a blackboard with entries and odds and a counter behind a wire screen at one end where three bookmakers worked. In one race when a long shot won, the main ring paid off at about two hundred to one, but the two women who had bet on the victorious horse were paid off only at forty to one.[23]

Bly preferred that women bet for themselves but was no fan of the women's betting ring, which she found totally decadent: "If one enjoys a democratic crowd then one would love this woman's pool-room. If woman's suffrage would produce such a scene, then God prevent suffrage. I claim to be liberal in my views; I believe in liberty and the right to do as one pleases, but I don't think I should like to see such an assemblage . . . , even at the Day of Judgment." She pointed to "a Negro woman, with paint upon her yellow checks, diamonds as large as peas in her ears, her breast ablaze with costly pins and her gown straight from Paris and never worn before," to a "big fat white woman in black and gold silk," and "dozens of children . . . in the room." Bly encountered a girl with a two-dollar bill who explained, "Mama told me to bet it on Ducat." Thereafter, Nellie went to the clubhouse: "At the tables upon the veranda sit a number of women, actresses and society women but all women whose names appear frequently in print. They are betting and drinking, but with the exception of one woman, who is rapidly and surely becoming intoxicated, they are orderly. If women must bet, I supposed this is the least objectionable way."[24]

However, not just the demimonde went to the tracks. Respectable women went to the tracks, notably upper-class wives whose names appeared in the papers following opening day and other big events. They attended for the enjoyment of a carriage ride from home, the excitement of the races, the opportunity to show off their newest outfits and to conspicuously display their husband's wealth, and the social aspects of the day, when they met their peers at the clubhouse to dine and party. They could afford to bet a few dollars on a whim, such as the color of the horse's silks or its name. These women were also beautiful adornments and temporary visitors in a masculine world. However, women who were serious gamblers and studied the racing charts seemed to be stepping out of their stereotyped gender role as the cautious nester and into the role of aggressive, risk-taking males. It was unacceptable.

The Board of Control

By 1886, if not earlier, the press was calling for a regional or national supervisory authority for the track similar to Great Britain's Jockey Club that licensed jockeys and trainers. There owners and riders who participated in races for prizes under one hundred pounds were forbidden from competing on the prestigious tracks, which, according to the *Tribune*, discouraged the opening up of "little thieving racecourses like those with which the neighborhood of New York is infested," such as Brighton Beach, Guttenberg, and Clifton.[25]

The BJC tried to arrange a conference in early 1887 to form an association to limit the sport to reputable courses that excluded owners, jockeys, and horses that competed at disreputable tracks. The older clubs ignored the call, but in September, the BJC and the CIJC united in adopting rules similar to those of the English Jockey Club. They agreed to bar from their grounds owners, trainers, and jockeys who took part in races of under one mile and for purses below five hundred dollars to push the Brighton Beach Racetrack to "step out of the gutter, cleanse her bedraggled skirts and live a clean and wholesome life."[26]

Early in 1890, trainers and jockeys formed an organization to counter injurious comments about them and fight arbitrary rulings from racing judges or officials. The *Tribune* said the public needed an association to protect itself against dishonest trainers and jockeys, judges blind to fraud, and jockey clubs concerned only with big profits rather than honest racing: "The great jockey clubs of the East . . . have no licensing system, and any ruffian, any blackguard, any criminal, no matter how black his career, no matter how recent his crimes, can train horses and ride horses on American race-tracks."[27]

The *Tribune* averred that the only reason for racing was to improve the breed, "but that excuse is getting very stale. Horses have been sufficiently improved already for all practical purposes." It recommended repealing Ives and shutting the tracks unless the jockey clubs made racing less vicious and degrading, kept out the disorderly and dishonest, and gave spectators clean and honest sport. The *Times* was concerned that the Big Four clubs (the NYJC, BJC, CIJC, and MPRA) had lost control of the men who raced at their tracks.[28]

There was, of course, the problem of fixed races. New York tracks then were probably among the most honest in the country, although Brighton's trainers had a reputation for running horses to exhaustion the evening before a race. Jockeys were known to pull horses to lose, and there were occasions when starters and judges had their integrity questioned. There was also a lot of suspicion about bookmakers' involvement in fraudulent races.[29]

These problems led to the establishment of the Board of Control in 1891 to supervise the sport. The scheme, which originated at a famous dinner of the city's elite, was drawn up by August Belmont II and Pierre Lorillard, who recognized the need for jockey clubs to cooperate and halt their squabbling. Belmont had just taken over the family's international banking house following his father's death one year earlier. He became a major figure in New York Democratic politics, who helped finance the construction of the city's first subway, the Independent Rapid Transit Company, in 1904. The junior Belmont first went heavily into racing in 1882 when he began running the Nursery, his father's breeding farm, sold eight years later for $639,500. Belmont reestablished the stud farm in 1892 and spared little expense in rebuilding his stock. In 1895, he spent $72,000 for two former Belmont Stakes champions, Henry of Navarre and Hastings.[30]

Belmont and Lorillard threatened to drop out of racing unless the jockey club leaders gained control of the sport. They wanted an organization comparable to the English Jockey Club, with its judicial role, and the French Jockey Club, with its social functions. However, the time was not yet ripe for this idea, and instead they created the Board of Control, which was supposed to be run on behalf of both track operators and horsemen, but in reality, the tracks dominated. The original seven members included chairman David D. Withers (Monmouth Park), J. G. K. Lawrence (Sheepshead Bay), P. J. Dwyer (Gravesend), and John A. Morris (Morris Park), and horse owners A. J. Cassatt, John Hunter, and James Galway. Hunter was a former president of the AJC, while Cassatt and Galway were closely tied to the MPRA. The "Big Four" tracks represented a combined investment of nearly $5 million.[31]

The board was empowered to grant and withhold licenses to officials and jockeys, fix dates for all meets, investigate any matters relating to racing, and rule out anyone who violated the organization's codes. Unlicensed jockeys were barred from riding or even entering the jockeys' quarters. The *Tribune* believed the licensing system would encourage jockeys to ride to win and make it a lot easier to keep bad jockeys off the courses.[32]

When Withers died in 1892, the heir apparent was Lawrence because of his experience with the CIJC. Yet the *Times* was worried about his political connections with Tammany Hall, particularly through John M. Bowers, attorney for the

11. Financier August Belmont II (1853–1924) was founding head of The Jockey Club in 1894 and first chairman of the New York State Racing Commission in 1895. He also organized the Westchester Racing Association in 1895 and built Belmont Park in 1905. *Source:* Josiah Flynt, "The Pool-Room Vampire and Its Money Mad Victims," *Cosmopolitan* 42 (Feb. 1907): 369.

CIJC, the BJC, and the NYJC and racing's chief lobbyist, who fought objectionable bills in Albany. Bowers, who had a $20,000 practice, was politically ambitious and sometimes relied on influence to secure votes for the tracks, the efforts of lobbyists he hired, and at other times simply money. How much, no one knew. Bowers annually billed the three tracks $500 to $1,000 each for his own services and expenses (which did not include the costs of payoffs) as well as for other lobbyists he hired. In addition, the tracks had Al Orr on retainer as their eyes and ears at Albany for $1,500 a year.[33]

The track owners did not want to publicize the connection between racing and Tammany Hall, a connection that worried the *Times:*

> Tammany should not be allowed to get its clutches on the racetracks. That would as certainly kill racing as the control of the turf by politicians has killed it in New Jersey where there is now no chance of honest and decent sport for years to come thanks to the operations of the political gang of Hudson County, which operates the track at Guttenberg for the benefit of the ring. Racing men want nothing of

that kind in this State. Even the suspicion that the Tammany gang might get control would drive from the turf the men of affairs and of reputation.[34]

In 1892, the Board of Control tracks promoted pari-mutuel betting, employing twenty-two new American Mutual machines, including ten adding machines to record the straight bets, ten to record individual place betting, and a compound adder (totalizer) for each set to record the total number of tickets sold straight and place. The selling stands were conveniently located directly under the platform holding the machines and were connected electrically with each of the machines and the totalizers so that the sales were recorded and added instantly. A mechanical counter on the ringing-up machine recorded sales on each horse from that stand, and another device, which was electrically connected with the ringing-up machine, showed the total sales from that stand. The machines sat on an eight- to ten-foot platform, making the numbers on their indicators very visible throughout the betting ring. These machines provided greater accuracy than the bookmakers, paid off 10 percent more than the books, and seemingly removed all incentives for fraud. They remained open until the horses took off, and results were posted immediately.[35]

The Board of Control did some creditable work, especially trying to counter the demoralizing and degrading influence of the outlaw Jersey tracks. In late 1891, the board barred members' horses from Guttenberg and Gloucester. Then in 1892, the board cast out trainer Frank van Ness for suspicious riding of his horse Indian Rubber at Morris Park (though his Elkton Stables was reinstated in 1893) and set down noted jockey Snapper Garrison for several months for betting. The board organized a boycott of winter racing that year but had no influence with Guttenberg or with bookmakers who took winter bets. In 1893, the board clarified for everyone the term *starter*, which had been a common problem for bettors. Previously, a horse was legally a "starter" once the horses were in the hands of the starter. Hereafter, the horse was a "starter" once the telegraph board posted its name as a participant.[36]

The board got involved in the issue of racing platters, which was a practice of entering high-quality horses in low-class selling races just to win large wagers. In 1893, the board ordered that all horses beaten in nonstakes races should be liable to be "claimed." The purpose was to halt wealthy owners, especially Mike Dwyer, from abusing selling races. Dwyer entered his horses in events far below their value and won many bets on them. In 1896, for example, when Dwyer won forty-eight races, they were mostly selling races in which he would outbid anyone trying to buy his winning horse. However, the problem continued for several years. As racing expert Walter S. Vosburgh explained, "A tacit agreement seemed to prevail not to bid upon or claim each others horses. As a result, stake horses swept the selling races and alienated the poorer owners, compelling them to seek the outlaw tracks where they had a chance to win. It also operated to ruin the market for horses of the poorer class." The answer in the future was to make some cheap selling races into claiming races. Then the winner could be claimed for his selling price by the owner of any other horse in the race instead of being sold by auction. This system prevented an owner from entering a horse in a claiming race below his value.[37]

Aside from some small concrete achievements, the board was insufficiently vigilant to make a big impact. It did little investigation of questionable riding, mainly ending up as a board of appeal for the rulings of local club officers; did not stand up against Guttenberg and Gloucester; and granted licenses to trainers and jockeys of bad reputation. By May 1893, the racing community as well as the press were ready to see it go.[38]

That summer, with the country in the midst of a deepening depression, the Board of Control decided that the BJC, CIJC, and NYJC should drop their purses by 40 percent. These three tracks, together with Monmouth, were widely seen as a "trust" that controlled 80 percent of capital investment in eastern tracks and more than half the value of all American tracks. This decision represented the board's judgment that racing as then constituted was a failure.[39]

The *Eagle* criticized this proposal as unwise, pointing out that in the prior five years, no other investment was as inflated as horse racing because of the huge purses made available: "The sums asked and paid for absolutely untried horses sufficed ten years ago to equip a whole racing stable." There were more than twenty breeding American farms worth more than $200,000. This was not limited to the United States. In England, Ormonde, the winner of the United Kingdom's Triple Crown, was sold in 1893 for $150,000. Big purses were essential to justify such expenditures. Furthermore, the prestigious racetracks were suffering from competition from less-well-regarded proprietary tracks. Monmouth Park's trade was hurt by racing at the same time at Brighton Beach, while Guttenberg cut into the revenues of the CIJC and NYJC.[40]

The board got into hot water when its tracks challenged the freedom of the press. In July, Monmouth threw two journalists who management thought was excessively critical off the track and then asked the CIJC to honor its action and exclude those writers as well. When the CIJC refused, Monmouth took the matter to the board, which backed it up, implicitly censuring the CIJC. The CIJC responded by quitting the board in September, reflecting the growing lack of confidence and loss of respect in the board.[41]

At that point, financier August Belmont II joined the Board of Control, which hoped his presence would enhance its stature. As the *Spirit* reported, "It will encourage many gentlemen of private fortune to enter the field, encouraged by the presence of a man of his character at the head of affairs, and will revive the prestige of racing among a class of people whose support is necessary to its popularity and confidence with the public. A few more of the type of Mr. Belmont at the head of affairs, and shaping racing policy, will save racing from falling into disrepute as a sport."[42] The *Spirit* was worried that without sound supervision, sporting gentlemen would abandon the turf, leaving racing to "proprietary tracks run on the principle of a theater or other public amusement," caring only about making money.[43]

The Turf Season of 1893

Boss Croker Joins the Horsey Set

Early in 1893, Boss Richard Croker of Tammany Hall threw himself heavily into thoroughbred racing under the mentorship of Michael Dwyer, who advised him in his betting and purchasing of horses. Born in Blackrock, County Cork, Ireland, in 1841 of English and Scottish stock, Croker, the son of the village blacksmith, and his family migrated to New York when he was three years old. He went to work at age thirteen as a machinist and by nineteen was a prizefighter. He became the head of the politically active Fourth Avenue Tunnel Gang and promoted illegal boxing matches. In 1863, Richard joined the volunteer fire department as an engine-company engineer, which marked his entry into politics. In 1865, the state established the Metropolitan Fire Department, and he became an engineer on a fire department steamer. Croker was elected alderman in 1868 on the "Young Democracy," an anti-Tweed ticket, though he soon became a Tammany loyalist. Two years later, he was appointed superintendent of markets, rents, and fees, a post with many opportunities for graft. In 1872, after the fall of Tweed, he joined up with "Honest John" Kelly, the new Tammany boss, and one year later was elected coroner. Then, in 1874, Croker was indicted for the fatal election-day murder of John McKenna, an associate of political rival and former sheriff Jimmy O'Brien, but was acquitted. He was reelected coroner in 1876. Croker was elected alderman in 1883 but resigned one year later to become fire commissioner. He became Tammany boss one year later, following the death of John Kelly, and also head of its Finance Committee. He supervised a machine composed of ninety thousand party workers. His last civic position was as city chamberlain in 1889–90 at a salary of $25,000.[44]

Croker became very wealthy by taking advantage of his clout as boss for honest graft, defined by his Tammany colleague George Washington Plunkitt as "I seen my opportunities and took 'em." Businesses seeking government contracts, especially construction companies, would make Croker a partner and sell him stock at deflated prices or buy surety bonds from insurance companies affiliated with the boss. Croker also used inside information to buy real estate cheaply before word came out of city plans to buy the site or news that a transit company planned to lay tracks nearby. One of his closest friends was real estate agent Andrew Freedman, a prominent Tammanyite who owned the New York Giants from 1895 to 1902 and was Croker's best man at his second marriage. Freedman provided Croker with a lot of inside information about hot deals. Croker's business acumen enabled him to live in an $80,000 brownstone on East Seventy-fourth Street and spend $100,000 renovating it. He also owned a Palm Beach estate; a second estate at Glencairn, Ireland; and a $500,000 stock farm near Utica. His estate at his death in 1922 was estimated at $5–$10 million.[45]

In 1893, Croker paid $250,000 for a half-share in Tennessee's Belle Meade stud (8 stallions and 125 brood mares and colts), which the previous year had won 340 races worth more than $300,000. Croker also spent more than $100,000 for untested thoroughbreds, including $20,000 for the Dobbins yearling at the dispersal sale of Frank A. Ehret's stable, the best in the nation that year, and $24,000 for Yankee Belle.[46]

Croker's entrance into the turf got a lot of attention, particularly from the *Brooklyn Eagle*, which covered the Coney Island tracks in depth. The *Eagle* recognized his considerable wealth from politics and business but warned that by getting into racing, he risked losing it all:

> Richard Croker . . . is out to amuse himself with horse races. This fact should be interesting to several classes of people. The professional sporting men, because his entrance upon the racetrack will increase their profits; to the politicians, because they will have an opportunity of winning back some of the money which they contributed to his support, and to the friends of government because the attention of the boss of Tammany Hall will be divided between the business of apportioning the spoil and the sport of cutting his losses. . . .
>
> Racing should be either an amusement for the rich or a vocation for the professional sporting man who knows all about horses. It is a costly pleasure for the inexperienced and a precarious business for the men who know all about it. Races nowadays are not decided on the track by the speed of the horses. It is in the pool box and the stall of the bookmaker that the winner is named. Then he goes to the course and crosses the lines first whether his condition is good or not for the simple reason that it has been decreed that he shall win. . . . [Racing] is a game, which has not the element of fairness which there is in poker. It rather resembles three-card monte, where the chances are well with the thrower.[47]

Croker's wide-ranging interests in the turf led him to consider taking over a racecourse or two. In February 1893, he and Mike Dwyer led a syndicate that tried to lease the Ivy City Track in Washington, DC, the former site of the National Jockey Club, and Baltimore's Pimlico track. One month later, his syndicate offered $900,000 for the Jerome Park track site, but attorney William A. Duer, the primary stockholder of the Jerome Park Villa Site and Improvement Association, refused to take less than $1 million.[48]

The crusading *Chicago Daily News,* which was leading the fight to end racing in Chicago, keenly followed the New York turf and its relationship to local politics. Unlike the New York press, it was very critically interested in Croker's role in the sport, tying him, for no apparent reason, to the expulsion of sportswriters from Monmouth Park in the summer of 1893. The *Daily News* asserted, "It has been proved that to write honest, fearless criticism upon racing means expulsion from the racetrack. This did not occur until Richard Croker became a factor in racing circles. As far as Croker is concerned, he has done little to elevate racing. His horses have come to the post and run and little attention was paid to the fact whether they were fit to race or not."[49]

Croker's leadership of Tammany Hall was badly hurt by the 1894 Lexow Committee investigation of the police department, which led to Tammany's defeat at the polls. Croker left New York for England, establishing an estate and stud at Wantage, but he had little success on the track and a hard time getting accepted by the racing set. In 1897, he sold the Belle Meade stud to Gen. W. H. Jackson and returned home to help elect Robert A. Van Wyck as the first mayor of Greater New York and then divide up patronage. Four years later, there was a second major investigation of police corruption by the state legislature. The so-called Mazet Committee's findings resulted in a huge debacle in the subsequent election. After that fiasco, Croker retired in 1902 and moved to Glencairn, Ireland, where he raced thoroughbreds. The racing stewards barred his horses from training at Newmarket Heath, the great semipublic training ground of the English turf owned by the English Jockey Club, so instead Croker leased an expensive private stable. He moved his stock to Baldoyle, Ireland, and bred several winners.[50]

Croker's racing career peaked in 1907 at the Epsom Derby, watching from a box with August Belmont II as his stallion Orby, son of an American dame and a British sire, won the $32,500 Epsom Derby, the most prestigious race in the world. Tim Sullivan, the number-two man in Tammany Hall, was also a big winner, having wagered $250 with English bookies at fifteen-to-one odds on Orby, supposedly more for sentiment than any expectation of winning. The *Times* applauded the triumph that showed Croker had learned how to breed, train, and run racehorses. Furthermore, "Mr. Croker's victory is all the more amazing to turfmen

12. Richard Croker, following tradition, leads his three-year-old stallion Orby, winner of the Epsom Derby in 1907, back to the paddock, passing in front of King Edward VII's royal box. *Source:* "Richard Croker, Derby Winner," *Harper's Weekly* 51 (29 June 1907): 946.

on account of the difficulties against which he had to contend and the attitude of the English Jockey Club toward American turfmen in general and Mr. Croker in particular." The victory made him a hero in New York. One week later, the *Times*'s Sunday edition published nearly a full-page story titled "Richard Croker: The Story of His Ancestry."[51]

Croker was just the third American after Pierre Lorillard and William C. Whitney to win the classic English race. This triumph was poorly received by local sportsmen, who resented an American, much less a political boss, impinging on their turf. They were further irked because the winning jockey was an American, Johnny Reiff. English political editorials were very unfriendly to Croker, although their sportswriters were more praiseworthy. His Majesty, King Edward VII, a huge racing fan, snubbed Croker by not inviting him to his Derby Day dinner, which was reported in banner headlines in the United States.[52]

Racing in the Depression

At the start of 1893, American thoroughbred racing was flourishing, with great racetracks all across the country, and especially in metropolitan New York, plus more than twenty breeding farms worth between $200,000 and $300,000. Important new money came into the sport through wealthy men like Richard Croker and copper king Marcus Daly, who invested nearly $1 million to stock his stable. Among the major tracks, Monmouth had a forty-six-day meet, and Gravesend, Sheepshead Bay, and Morris Park each had thirty days. The most lucrative races were the Suburban ($25,000), Realization ($35,000), and Futurity ($49,715) stakes, all at Sheepshead Bay, surpassed only by the $50,000 purse for the American Derby at Chicago's Washington Park, heavily subsidized to coincide with the Columbian Exposition.[53]

The *Brooklyn Chronicle* compared racing favorably to baseball, rating thoroughbred racing ahead of the national pastime as the number-one spectator sport because of fan popularity and economic considerations. In metropolitan New York alone, flat racing was a $12 million enterprise:

> Probably no sport to-day comes nearer to enjoying a universal popularity than the racing of horses. The rapidly growing establishment of free fields, where the public can go and watch the races, makes the sport open to all. But base ball [*sic*] in its palmiest days never had the devotees the racetracks have to-day. Never did base ball [*sic*] or any other sport draw so heavily on the Yankee purse, and it is not surprising that the question is asked so frequently, "Will racing be dropped too?"
>
> The American turf has a far stronger side to it than base ball [*sic*] ever had, for it caters to the love of outdoor sport as well as to the indoor passion for gambling. It is the best and most scientific means of gambling known, and, surrounded with the romance that has always been attached to a racetrack, there seems little necessity for taking a pessimistic view of the sport, for the present at least.[54]

One of the biggest events of the season was the $25,000 Brooklyn Handicap at Gravesend in May. Despite the onset of the depression, it drew a record crowd of some thirty thousand, about eight thousand more than usual, thanks to the beautiful weather, the closing of local poolrooms prior to the meet, and reduced ticket prices. However, the gate was only about $20,000 because tickets cost as little as $0.50. There were 108 bookmakers in attendance, each charged $100 to rent a stand, and fifty bars and lunch counters to service the thirsty and hungry. Spectators included the sporting fraternity, men from all occupations, family groups, nearly all the elite horsemen of the day (notably August Belmont II and William K. Vanderbilt), prominent politicians such as former mayor Hugh Grant and Boss Croker, and celebrities such as DeWolf Hopper, renowned for his interpretation of "Casey at the Bat." Female attendees were mostly characterized "by complexions so delicate as to suggest artifice; by a display of jewelry, especially of diamonds . . . by costly and showy gowns, wraps, and hats, and by a general air of assertiveness."[55]

The Brooklyn Handicap drew such a large field that it was difficult to run the race, "especially with rough riders, since it is an old-fashioned narrow oval, with painfully sharp turns." The long-shot winner was Diablo, ridden by the great Fred Taral, who won $18,000. His owners, A. F. Walcott and John Campbell, also captured about $100,000 in bets made at odds ranging from fifty to one to twenty-five to one. Experts blamed the upset of Lamplighter on renowned jockey Willie Sims getting caught in a pocket on the rail.[56]

The transportation to the track was very crowded, and the return home was hectic. The last train home did not leave until 9:00 p.m. and could barely carry its heavy load. Chaos reigned when riders transferred to elevated trains (at Fifth Avenue and Thirty-sixth Street), while passengers taking the Culver Line route to New York barely averted a disaster when the connecting ferry from Bay Ridge listed and nearly capsized.[57]

At the Sheepshead Bay meet in June, there was a rare dispute at the track prior to the running of the Suburban Stakes. President John Hunter of the Board of Control, and a member of the CIJC's Board of Stewards, objected when the starter moved Banquet, a horse known for its viciousness, from the outer rail to the inner rail. The other board members supported starter James Rowe, because the rules permitted him to change starting positions of unruly or vicious animals, although starters normally did not assign nasty-tempered horses to the rail. Rowe's decision was apparently made in behalf of Mike Dwyer, owner of Raceland, a popular choice with the bettors, though Dwyer himself plunged on Bill Daley's Count. Hunter, considered the "soul of honor," and one of the most respected and honorable of eastern turfmen, reacted by resigning from both boards. The *Chicago Daily News* was very critical of the episode because it exemplified how certain owners no longer ran to win but raced merely to facilitate winning bets. The winner in an upset was Lowlander, owned by bookmaker Fred Lowe, who was so broke he had not made book for the past several weeks. He let it all ride on Lowlander, and his horse came in.[58]

The Business of Racing in the Depression

In 1893, despite high expectations, the metropolitan meetings all had below-average financial returns, and some even lost money. This was largely attributed to the depression. The CIJC made a profit, but not the NYJC, whose average attendance during the week was less than two thousand, insufficient to pay for its substantial overhead. The BJC probably made money with its better attendance and smaller expenses and the advantage of no competition during its spring meet.[59]

Gravesend took in the most gate money with $132,521 in 1893 ($4,417 a day), up from $97,208 in 1892 when it had the third-highest box office sales, followed by Sheepshead Bay at $113,936 ($3,798 a day) and Morris Park with $81,493 ($2,716 a day). By comparison, Chicago's Washington Park Jockey Club in twenty-five days, with the advantage of drawing upon the huge crowds attending the World's Fair, equaled the receipts of ninety days' racing at those three New York tracks. Its average daily purse was a national-leading $11,172, followed by the CIJC with $9,330.[60]

Most big stables did poorly, and it was a bad year for leading bookmakers and heavy plungers. Pierre Lorillard won nothing that season, and Pittsburgh Phil, the greatest bettor of the era, had the worst year of his career. The decline in betting, according to the *Chicago Daily News,* caused 20 percent to 50 percent of the bookies to close up. Ninety percent of the sheet writers who lasted the season lost money, which for a few ran into hundreds of thousands of dollars.[61]

The metropolitan tracks regularly attracted about fifty bookmakers, with eighty to one hundred at the big races. A bookmaker's overhead was about $150 a day ($22,050 for the year), and he needed $10,000 in cash to cover bets. Overhead expenses included a daily fee of $100 to operate at the track; $10 each to his cashier, sheet writer, and ticket writer; and $20 for tickets, stationery, and staff to watch the stables to provide inside information to help set odds or watch rival bookmakers and big bettors. On an average day, a bookmaker would pull in about $570 from losing gamblers.[62]

The top eastern sportswriters saw the turf in serious decline in 1893, particularly the renowned Charles Trevelyan, who complained that Americans should not be emphasizing running over trotting, which he attributed to the "insane desire to be English." He also criticized the widespread adoption of the English betting system, "a system tainted with a century of fraud." He blamed the betting ring, not the off-track poolrooms, for the decline in attendance. Trevelyan reported that men of poor reputations controlled tracks, few highly regarded men owned stables, and honest jockeys were very scarce, "but not as scarce as honest owners."[63]

Trevelyan dated the beginning of the downfall of eastern racing to the moment the AJC was forced to go to the wall by the NYJC. He blamed John A. Morris for not taking forceful-enough actions against fraud for fear of generating a public scandal. Patrons were cheated by horse owners whose animals were not always raced at their fittest, by racing officials who did not protect them from jockeys who lost racing favorites, and by "owners and trainers who were too intimately associated with the betting ring." The *Chicago Daily News* further pointed out that "the great wealth of the owners of Morris Park, emboldened unscrupulous owners to race their horses as they saw fit. In-and-out racing became the rule, not the exception." The crusading paper also noted that those track owners who owned large stables raced their horses daily, regardless of their condition, to fill up the races and attract crowds. Consequently, when favorites lost to a rank outsider, the owner "would say that his race was not such a startling reversal of form as Mr. So and So's horse showed, and he runs the race-track."[64]

The New York press, including the *Herald* and the *Times,* compared thoroughbred racing unfavorably to trotting. The latter lamented that despite the disproportionate number of New Yorkers who owned and drove fast horses, "running races, being more picturesque, and, to the ordinary looker-on, more attractive than trotting races, have become both more fashionable and more popular." The consensus was that metropolitan trotting men had less suitable places for exercising and speeding than anyone else did. As the antiracing *Chicago Daily News* pointed out, "Trotting races are for the improvement of the breed of horse; racing is for the profit of the betting-ring."[65]

In September, the turf suffered a great loss when Pierre Lorillard quit racing on the advice of his physician because he worried too much and needed peace and quiet. Lorillard had nearly one hundred broodmares at his fabled Rancocas breeding farm but noted:

> It is becoming too much of a business rather than a sport. It is depending too much upon the professional betting element for its attendance and support. That means that it is not making the same popularity with the masses that come for sport and casual betting. Now the history of all sports shows that when they lose the support of men of character and standing in a community, they decline. The public have confidence in anything which is under the direction of its representative citizens and which attracts people of standing. Remember how popular trotting once was and how it declined.

Lorillard suggested ending bookmaking and substituting the French mutuel system, which he had recommended as far back as 1884, and was "roundly abused" for it in racing circles. He believed the mutuel system would ensure racing's integrity because it was not suited to heavy bettors and blamed the big bookmakers for most of the criticism to the mutuels:

> I am opposed to bookmaking because I think it is a standing menace to a fair race. It offers an inducement to stop the favorite and win a large sum. To do this, the jockey and trainers must be influenced, and there is an inducement to

bookmakers to corrupt jockeys and trainers. Many of them rely upon trainers for information already, and it is reasonable to suppose they reward them. The fault of bookmaking is that it encourages attempts to prevent a horse winning. Betting should, on the other hand, stimulate each one to look for his horse to win. In the French mutual [sic] betting the inducement to stop a favorite does not exist.

Every man stands upon the same footing. It would not suit purely professional owners, but that's the trouble. There are too many professional owners. If you don't encourage amateurs to come in and keep race-horses, the sport will lose caste and confidence with the public. An amateur should be content to win the stake or purse, not to raid the bookmakers and those are the kind you want.

Finally, Lorillard pointed out how well the pari-mutuels did in France, where the government was in charge and shared in the profits. Bookmaking at the French tracks about six years before nearly killed the sport, but the pari-mutuel system promoted the turf by building up confidence in racing. Lorillard expected pari-mutuels would do the same in the United States. The revenue from betting might decline, but it would be made up by higher gate receipts: "The public should be made to feel that they are not getting the worse end of it. For one man who bets now there would be ten. See how it took hold in France! Why, the business was so enormous that they cut down the percentage—they were making so much money."[66]

Lorillard's point of view, and the perspective of most experts, was supported in an unsigned article in *Harper's Weekly* titled "The Profits of Book-Makers" claiming that bookmakers probably had more influence in managing racing than anyone since they owned horses and tracks, made the laws, and broke the laws when it suited them. The author blamed many turf scandals or bankruptcies on bookies betting on their own account. Legitimate bookmakers could expect to make ample profits if they did a mathematically sound job setting odds, but nearly all bookmakers looked for sure things: "The chances of making a large sum out of one race, by means rightly considered to be disreputable are so great that it is a most exceptional book maker who will not go into a combination of conspiracy to deceive and rob the public." The banning of faro banks, lotteries, policy shops, and other gambling institutions left bookmaking alone as a way to fleece the public: "There has never been a scheme devised by which large amounts of money can be taken from the public without rending any consideration in return more certain and ingenious than book making as at present conducted on American tracks." The writer argued that racing's flaws far surpassed any good it did. He asserted that if the breed could not be improved without racing, and there could be no racing without bookmaking, then let the breed decline.[67]

The End of the Board of Control

By late 1893, a significant number of racehorse owners were ardently opposed to the Board of Control, disparagingly known as the "Racing Trust." They believed the board operated too loosely, granted too many licenses, and had done nothing but benefit the clout-heavy stables controlled by the ring of Croker, Phil Dwyer, John A. Morris, and Daly and the tracks run by the combine of John A. Morris, bookmaker "Luce" Appleby of the MPRA, and Mike Dwyer, who had investments in at least three tracks. After the new year, there were rumors of a big scandal brewing involving Croker and the sources of his wealth. A longtime head of a leading eastern stable alleged that certain manipulations involving Croker's stable helped him win ninety thousand dollars in purses in 1893.[68]

Notable scandals occurred at some of the board's tracks, while the thriving Sheepshead Bay track was the best-conducted course in the United States, free of the "Grab-All Clique." A prime example of the board's ineffectiveness was Mike Dwyer's Elizabeth track, whose racing secretary, Colonel McIntyre, was described by a noted trainer as merely Dwyer's clerk, employed to fit racing conditions specifically for Dwyer's horses. Trainers would make up entries for events they considered winnable with the necessary weights and give them to the colonel, which Dwyer then checked out. Horsemen believed similar conditions prevailed at Monmouth, Morris Park, and Gravesend.[69]

In early 1894, the *Tribune* described the ruling panel as the "Board of Misrule," which damaged everything it touched. The board was described as "arrogant, exclusive, [and] secretive," setting itself above the mass of racing supporters of racing. The members' "social aspirations are so lofty that they look down with haughty contempt upon the common run of turf men. They can hardly condescend to speak to their fellow-creatures, they feel so far above them." The board was also chastised for entangling itself "in the nets of the Tammany and Brooklyn rings" and for making poor appointments. One board member was castigated because he "is extremely hot-headed . . . narrow-minded, petulant, and peevish," constantly trying to get himself a salaried position on the turf. A second board member was rated a backstabber, chastised for having "a quivering cast of currant jelly in place of a spinal column," and a third was rebuked for "the eagerness with which he risks his future on the hazard of a die, and for the stubbornness with which he hangs up his creditors."[70]

According to the *Tribune,* the group who arranged races at the major area tracks (excluding Sheepshead Bay) on behalf of Dwyer and his friends were "in almost every instance allies and associates of the leaders of Tammany Hall or of the leaders of the Brooklyn ring."

The Grab-All Clique attempted to run racing in the East, and to rule it in just a way as Tammany Hall has grabbed everything in the city government of New-York, and got the whole municipal administration, the entire public treasury, all the functions of government and all the public funds within its clutches.

The methods of the Grab-All-Clique of the turf were exactly similar to those of Tammany Hall in local politics. All sorts of schemes, all sorts of combinations, all sorts of arrangements, were made by the members of this clique in order that racing in the East might be made to yield the largest possible revenue for the filing of their individual pockets. Every member of the clique was determined to get all the money that he possibly could get out of racing without consideration for the reputation, the advantage and the benefit of the turf for public opinion and the requirements of public spirit. The members of this clique raced on every day that they could grab on their three racecourses. In every detail of the sport they ransacked all things in order to lay hold of the largest profits for themselves. It is not all surprising that the general public became weary and disgusted of racing conducted in this style and with these methods, just as the respectable and decent people of New-York are thoroughly tired and disgusted with Tammany methods in this city and with the methods of the Brooklyn ring in Kings County.

The *Tribune* asserted that beyond the arrangements and conditions of races, the clique also weighted handicaps at their tracks to their advantage and made sure their horses got the best starts and their jockeys had the most leeway from the stewards. They consistently won most close decisions because these men hired the handicappers and starters, judges, and other racing officials. The paper recommended that racing had to changes its ways and end ring methods for racing to flourish and gain public confidence.[71]

At the end of 1893, when James R. Keene learned about the tracks' plans to cut purses, he initiated the supplanting of the ineffective Board of Control. Keene that year owned the most profitable stable in the world, led by two-year-old Domino, winner of the lucrative Futurity. He proposed a new organization modeled after the English Jockey Club made up of men more interested in the turf than in particular meets. Persons attending that meeting included sportsman and brewery heir Jacob Ruppert, a prominent member of Tammany Hall, senior aide to Governor Roswell P. Flower, and future congressman and owner of the New York Yankees; Boss Croker; and Board of Control members James Galway and A. F. Walcott. Keene proposed a racing club that would select a few stewards with expertise in horses, jockeys, and betting procedures and empower them to punish bookies, gamblers, owners, trainers, and jockeys. The stewards would ensure the integrity of track handicappers and base their decisions on performance, not the whims of owners or trainers.[72]

The board saw the new movement for reform as a graceful way out and accepted Keene's proposals. On 2 January 1894, the Board of Control was dismantled after a team composed of Belmont, Hunter, and Galway was appointed to confer with a committee appointed by horse owners to choose men to form a jockey club to represent all racing associations that agreed to conform to the club's rules. The new organization would protect the sport from the sharks of the track and betting ring and have the power to license trainers, jockeys, and bookmakers and make all rules governing racing and betting.[73]

The Jockey Club

The Jockey Club had its first meeting on 10 February 1894 when it formally elected its stewards and other members, just before the legislature began considering proposals to repeal or amend the Ives Act. TJC was an organization of racetracks, not horsemen, and its leadership was nearly identical to the old Board of Control. The Board of Stewards chairman was John Hunter, former chair of the Board of Control, who received a salary of ten thousand dollars. The other stewards were James R. Keene, August Belmont II, J. O. Donner, Dr. G. L. Knapp, Col. W. P. Thompson, and Frank K. Sturgis, who doubled as TJC secretary. Hunter was replaced as chairman in 1895 by Belmont, who served until his death in 1924 as a hands-on leader. August was deeply involved in Democratic Party politics, supporting a cross-class coalition to advance his traction interests and also protect racing from antigambling reformers.[74]

The Jockey Club initially had fifty members, soon raised to nearly one hundred, nearly all New Yorkers or turfmen involved in New York racing. They paid a two-hundred-dollar initiation fee and one hundred dollars in dues, which entitled them to free admission at tracks it supervised and a few minor privileges. They were a veritable who's who of New York's WASP elite and included such blue bloods as businessman J. J. Astor IV, investment banker J. P. Morgan, and Cornelius Vanderbilt II, head of the New York Central.[75]

TJC was also financed by license fees for jockeys (five dollars) and trainers (fifteen dollars), forfeits and fines for misdeeds at the track, and the sale of the *American Stud Book,* the bible of breeding, which since 1868 was the recognized listing of thoroughbred horses. TJC adopted the Board of Control's racing schedule and rules but implemented them more effectively; allotted racing dates; published the *Racing Calendar,* which was its official record; appointed officials; and banned anyone caught cheating. TJC set limits on the distance horses could race, barred foreign books, and, like its English model, took no cognizance of bets. Tracks that did not accept its authority were considered outlaws, and any person or horse involved with them could be barred from member tracks. As many as twelve hundred horses were on the outlaw list at one time.[76]

Racing experts backed the formation of The Jockey Club. The *Brooklyn Eagle,* for instance, supported TJC and its intent of halting the free field at Morris Park that "persuades people, who otherwise, would not do so, to go to the tracks and lose their money with the bookmakers." However, it did not want TJC to suppress popular modes of bookmaking. The *Spirit of the Times* gave a lot of the credit to TJC when it applauded the 1894 racing season in New York: "There was no division of authority, as under the old regime, when judges one day punished offenders but the following day, the stewards the following day remitted the punishment."[77]

As TJC's prestige grew, out-of-town tracks began aligning with it, including upstate Saratoga and Chicago's Washington Park and Hawthorne Park. However, smaller stable owners found its decisions unfair; opposed the agreement between TJC and the Turf Congress, which controlled western racing; and protested a section of the charter that banned owners from participating in tracks that neither board licensed. Bookmakers were unhappy with TJC's support of pari-mutuel betting, of which the tracks kept 5 percent, because it took business away from them. In addition, many racing fans opposed the ending of free admissions.[78]

Contesting the Ives Law

The fight against the Ives Law gained momentum on 28 December 1893 when Syracuse justice of the peace P. B. McLennan decided that racing pools were lotteries, a form of wagering decided on pure chance. He delivered his opinion in a civil case instigated by an underworld attorney on behalf of Milton C. Reilly, who lost $1,150 at Saratoga's pari-mutuels and auction pools and sued to regain his wagers. Abe Hummel, junior partner in Howe and Hummel, a law firm renowned for its criminal trial work, said this decision implied that Ives was unconstitutional since it allowed betting (that is, lotteries) inside racetracks, which was explicitly barred by the state constitution. Of course, as the *Times* noted, the decision was untenable because races were not lotteries but contests decided on merit. A racing expert could intelligently evaluate the likely outcome of a race based on the entrants' prior form.[79]

A more significant test of the Ives Law was decided on 7 May 1894, involving a $1,085 wager lost by Joseph B. Britton to bookmaker Robert G. Irving at Morris Park on 19 February 1890. Britton gave Irving three notes for the debt and then refused to pay up, contending a gambling debt could not be collected because bookmaking and pool selling were illegal since the state constitution banned lotteries. The bookmaker sued Britton for one of the promissory notes, and Judge

Fitzsimmons ruled for the plaintiff in city court. However, on 7 May 1894, the decision was unanimously overturned in the court of common pleas. Judge Roger A. Pryor ruled for the court that a gambling debt was not collectable and the Ives Law that authorized pool selling was unconstitutional because a pool on a horse race was a lottery, which the state constitution prohibited. The *Times* thought it was wrong to use the courts to recover a bet and said that, as in the *Reilly* case, the court erred in finding Ives unconstitutional because the constitution did not ban gambling. The *Times* anticipated the ruling would kill racing unless the constitution was changed. But two weeks later, Judge Milton H. Merwin, in upstate Utica, issued a contrary opinion in a gambling case, ruling that betting on horse races was not a lottery.[80]

Spokesmen for the major racetracks considered the Pryor ruling a minor setback. John Bowers claimed the ruling would have no impact, since the courts had long ruled against enforcing bets, and further pointed out that the Ives Law was limited to permitting bookmaking at racetracks during certain specified periods. However, the general feeling was that the ruling would be a serious obstacle in the 1894 season.[81]

An important trial similar to the *Irving* case took place in upstate Utica. Thomas D. Reilly bought $600 in French pools and $550 in auction pools at Saratoga on 1 August 1892. After his horse lost, he demanded, unsuccessfully, a refund. Reilly claimed the Ives Pool Law was unconstitutional since betting on a race was like participating in a lottery and won the initial trial. However, on 22 May 1894, Judge Merwin ruled that the Ives Act was constitutional because betting on horse races required judgment, not mere chance. The *Times* agreed, pointing out that no one ever imagined betting on races to be a lottery until poolroom keepers came up with the notion. However, the paper still believed that gambling on horses was demoralizing and should be restricted, if not completely suppressed. The *Eagle* opposed repealing Ives, but sought a quick and reasonable compromise since the public wanted to bet on horse racing.[82]

A new legal problem emerged at the start of the 1894 racing season as the result of poolroom kingpin Peter De Lacy's clash with Mike Dwyer, whose fight to close up the poolrooms culminated in the Saxton Act (see chapter 7). De Lacy unabashedly admitted harassing Dwyer for revenge. On 15 May, De Lacy had Dwyer, three racing judges, and twelve bookies arrested for their involvement in gambling at Gravesend. Rival attorneys worked out a compromise by which De Lacy agreed to stop interfering with the races, suspend most of the litigation, and concentrate on Dwyer's arrest as a test case.[83]

Judge William Gaynor, a future mayor and an ardent advocate of personal freedom and liberty who decided several cases dealing with the restriction of boxing clubs and amateur Sunday baseball, decided the Dwyer case in late May.[84] Gaynor ruled, like Merwin, that stakes races were not lotteries and matters of pure chance but involved a lot of skillful riding, endurance, and speed, which bettors could evaluate, based on prior form. He recognized that state statutes regarding horse race stakes dated back to 1802 when they were first made illegal. However, the 1887 Ives statute suspended that proscription at racetracks for thirty-day periods. De Lacy was upset that Gaynor's ruling supported the Ives Law and did not enable poolroom men to follow their trade as legitimate businessmen. The *Eagle* supported Gaynor and chastised De Lacy, who "is about as much interested in public morals as a Fiji Indian is in the rotation of the planets."[85]

Amending the Ives Act

In February 1894, just as TJC was being established, Republican assemblyman John H. Clark of Niagara proposed repealing the Ives Act, but his measure had no realistic change of passing. The Republican *Tribune* backed the concept, however: "There is no reason why a Republican Legislature should give aid and comfort to Tammany and the Brooklyn Ring" whose members, directly and indirectly, made a lot of money from the tracks. The article compared racing a generation earlier at Jerome Park, when elite New Yorkers dominated it and the track had limited and inoffensive pool selling, to the contemporary scene, with its betting rings and bookmakers trying to bribe jockeys and trainers and convince owners to run fraudulent races. The editor criticized the current emphasis on making money, which meant more bookmakers, often drawn from the criminal classes, and recommended the legislature curtail the power and influence of the bookmakers.[86]

The *Tribune* supported Republican assemblyman Hamilton Fish's plan to amend the Ives Act, which set the tax at tracks to 5 percent of the gate. He proposed that all racing associations submit their financial records to the state comptroller and pay 5 percent of *total receipts*, which would be distributed to county agricultural societies for their various functions. The *Tribune* recommended going even further, calling for a 10 percent tax of the gross. Some tracks had grossed more than $250,000, with the betting rings alone bringing a track as much as $200,000 a season. Ticket sales, members' dues, concession sales, and the $0.10 charged for programs brought in as much as $75,000 a year.[87]

The Fish bill passed the legislature, and on 31 March, Republican governor Levi Morton signed it. TJC considered the legislation a setback because of the higher taxes. However, the dispersion of revenues to agricultural societies was seen as a way to create a more favorable sentiment toward racing among rural legislators that would help prevent substantive antiracing legislation. The state received about $30,000 from racing in 1893 but anticipated revenues from the new tax of nearly $100,000 a year.[88]

Racing in the Pivotal 1894 Season

The 1894 racing season started auspiciously despite the various off-track problems and the ongoing depression. Gravesend's opening was well attended, albeit with a somewhat tougher crowd than usual, in part because of the closing of New York's poolrooms and the banning of racing in New Jersey. There were 110 bookmakers present, each paying $100, and the track took in nearly $20,000 that day, a record. The *Eagle* reminded readers that there could be no racing without betting and that the lawmakers were astute to confine such wagering to racetracks: "Between going to a track primarily to see the races and incidentally to bet, and going into a poolroom primarily to bet and with no interest in the racing other than the results announced on the ticker, there is a wide difference, and the law recognizes the fact. To proceed further and forbid track betting would in effect be to abolish horse racing, and this the public certainly does not want."[89]

Despite the BJC's successful inaugural, the spring meet was a disappointment. Jockeys were now supervised not by the track starter but by stewards they did not respect. The *Eagle* expressed dissatisfaction with the track's limiting "1, 2, 3," (win, place, show) betting to the French mutuels that the BJC controlled. This setup cut off one-third of the bookmakers' business, and so fewer worked the track, resulting in less competition and lower odds. The *Eagle* blamed the Anglophonic Jockey Club for the turf's current problems but did not consider the impact of the depression:

> There is to be sure a thin scattering of the substantial business and professional men of the two cities, but that number is much smaller than ever before on the big tracks. The crowd down at Gravesend is the normal attendance at Guttenberg with their nondescript raiment and their two-dollar bets. The great tracks cannot live on this sort of patronage, and in fact, this sort of patronage cannot survive long enough to begin to support the expensive methods of the larger sport. The practical managers of the large racetracks know this as well as anybody; and when their interests have been so severely injured by the new jockey club and its antiquated and foolish rules they will throw the whole thing over and run racing as the public wants it and not as a few ultra-fashionable Anglomaniacs desire the thing to be done. There seems to be no virtue in the present system except that it is English.[90]

De Lacy and the Outlaw Queens Tracks

The Jockey Club dealt with a number of thorny issues in its inaugural season, beginning with the licensing of racetracks. The Jockey Club did not grant licenses to three newly opened Queens County tracks of dubious integrity. The *Spirit* concurred with the decision, because otherwise "the suburbs of Brooklyn would be presently honeycombed with half-mile tracks having formed book appendages, and a public sentiment would be created against racing that in the course of a year or two would be almost certain to cause the appeal for the Ives bill in this State."[91]

On 4 July 1894, a modest, unlicensed fifteen-hundred-seat racetrack opened at the site of the old Flushing Driving Club, within the village of Flushing (at Flushing and Whitestone) in Queens County. The facility, backed by Peter De Lacy, was managed by President Charles Weeks of the Flushing Jockey Club (FJC) to promote pool selling and provide a substitute for the recently shuttered Guttenberg Track. New Yorkers reached the track via a twenty-three-minute LIRR ride and then a stagecoach for the remaining three-quarters of a mile. The round-trip ticket cost $0.70. The FJC's purses were in the range of $150–$200 and drew about twenty-five hundred spectators. Three-fifths of the spectators came from New York to bet on foreign (non-FJC) races, while the rest were locals who looked like they were out at the county fair. Two bookmakers took bets on the on-site races and four on races at Brighton and Sheepshead Bay for as little as $0.50 or $1.00.[92]

Flushing residents objected to the enterprise, especially the open-air poolroom, the track's chief attraction. Village trustees failed to get an injunction to block the track but refused to permit telegraph wires to run from their town to the track and fined management, which raced without a permit, $30 per race, or $150 a day. However, local businessmen, who anticipated a rise in property values, supported the project, and neighboring Whitestone allowed the erection of telegraph poles. The meet lasted only a few weeks until a raid broke up the foreign pool selling.[93]

On 11 September, De Lacy and his associates opened the Newtown Jockey Club in Maspeth under club president Max Frank, a former Long Island City (LIC) poolroom owner. A steamboat connecting the track to Harlem was a veritable floating gambling hall backed by Johnny Green, a Bowery gambler with considerable political clout. The inaugural thirty-day meet scheduled 310 events and offered $63,600 in purses, which amounted to a meager $205 per race. The typical crowd was a few thousand but one night drew seven thousand fans, and thirty bookmakers, who took wagers as small as $0.50.[94]

The *Times* compared the track to a similar operation in Madison, Illinois, near St. Louis, a resort of "the very lowest and most degraded people that form the dregs of a great city." The outlaw course opened with 5 races in the afternoon and then, after an intermission, a second session of 5 races in the evening, illuminated by electric lights. There were about a thousand people there who the *Times* averred came to gamble on anything running the track, be it horses, dogs, cats, mice, or goats. The visitors included "a choice collection of thugs, sneak thieves, pickpockets, touts of the very worst sort, and Bowery loafers, who are kept out of respectable racing inclosures," who were there to take advantage of factory workers, laborers, and clerks who could not attend daytime races and often frequented poolrooms, though they could not afford to lose their money. There were also "a couple of hundred . . . of the worst-type of race-track women."[95]

Queen's third outlaw racetrack opened on 27 September at Aqueduct, a suburb of Jamaica's Woodhaven neighborhood and site of the old Union Race Course built in 1821. The land belonged to the Brooklyn Water Works, where a conduit brought water from Hempstead Plain to New York. The sponsor was the Queens County Jockey Club (QCJC), the same people who ran the Flushing course. It was more accessible than the FJC, with a station on the New York and Rockaway Beach Railroad, twenty minutes from Long Island City, which helped it draw a good-size audience. The QCJC had the advantage of being in an unincorporated area, which resulted in less government interference, making law-abiding Jamaicans unhappy.[96]

Aqueduct, which had a three-quarter-mile track, scheduled a thirty-day meet, six days a week, employing low-quality horses ridden for purses that rarely exceeded $125. Admission was merely $0.50, and there was an ample supply of complimentary passes. A new grandstand was erected to seat one thousand alongside the old stand that seated fifteen hundred. Racing historian William Vosburgh described it as "a shanty held up by stilts." Aqueduct's most prominent feature was the space in the tent roof for bookmakers designed like an old-time poolroom. The track reportedly lost about $20,000 in its first season.[97]

Brighton and Jerome Park

Turf experts rated Brighton Beach's racing in 1894 as more dubious than prior meets in its already questionable past, with a lot of the blame placed on bookmakers and thoroughbred owners who too often instructed jockeys not to go full-out unless in a race with long odds. In addition, the *Eagle* claimed that owners of favorites seemed to be ordering their jockeys to pull back on their mounts and then made agreements with bookmakers to split their gaming profits. "The manner of running horses at the track is dreadful," complained James Keene, "but how are you going to help it? No sooner are one or two men punished for crookedness than a half dozen others come to the surface with methods far worse than those who have been punished do. There seems no end to it." The *Eagle* praised TJC's inner circle and the racing stewards for trying to keep the sport honest in the face of such problems.[98]

Jerome Park, last used in 1891, reopened for one last year before the city took over the site for a reservoir. M. F. Dwyer and his NJJC associates secured control of the old American Jockey Club, with Mike elected president. The summer meeting was just for "overnight" races (contests arranged at the last minute), with daily added money ranging from $5,000 to $6,000. Opening day drew about five thousand spectators and nearly fifty bookmakers. A last hurrah in August was seen as ideal for local turf fans who could not get away for a long vacation.[99]

The Sheepshead Bay Racetrack

The only track that produced an outstanding meet was Sheepshead Bay, the track most closely tied to TJC. The feature event was the 1.625-mile Realization Stakes in which Croker's Dobbins upset Lucky Baldwin's California colt El Rey Santa Anita, winner of the recent American Derby. Croker's winning share was worth $33,850, plus a $5,000 bet at two-to-one odds. Even the *Chicago Daily News*, no great friend of racing, had only the highest regard for this elite racetrack. After Washington Park, Chicago's elite racetrack, decided to close in 1894, the *Daily News* announced that the CIJC was the only "great race course in America which is not a racing machine—one run by a track owner." It noted that even it "would have fallen into the hands of the race track 'dukes' but for the fact that a Vanderbilt owns the stock. Indeed, Coney Island is about the only track that makes a pretense to honest racing. And this was due to Mr. Vanderbilt's threat that unless jobbery was stopped, he would close the track. . . . [I]n fact, it is Coney Island that has given racing just a taint of responsibility in New York."[100]

The *Daily News* also applauded the track's excellent location, the perfect condition of its running surface, which was "almost as hard and springy as the dirt course," and its ambience: "It is believed there is no track in the country so popular as that of the Coney Island Jockey club, which lies almost in hearing distance of the ever-sounding seas. Here the millionaire rubs elbows with the man who walked from Brooklyn to see the race and ladies who are leaders in the ultra-fashionable set occupy seats next to those occupied by leaders of another set. Love of the sport temporarily removes social barriers and for the time all are actuated by the same desire to see the horse carrying their money land a winner." Furthermore, the drive to the track through Prospect Park and Ocean Parkway "in itself is sufficient to put any one in good humor with himself and the world passing as it goes through tree-embowered glades and along lake-fringed paths and then past country villages and low-eaved farm-houses surrounded by evidences of plentiful comfort."[101]

The CIJC hosted exciting races with large fields of high-class horses and nearly perfect handicapping. Attendance was very large, and capacity was taxed on holidays and getaway day. As the *Spirit* pointed out, "More ladies were present than at any other meeting of the year, and anyone who mixed at all with the crowds could easily discern that the well-to-do occasional pleasure seeker was far in the ascendant over the professional follower of the sport usually so strongly in evidence at all our race-tracks." The typical spectators were not racing experts, and they had a grand time even if "their investments were guided rather by sentiment than by careful observances of form."[102]

It is difficult to determine the CIJC's, or other tracks', bottom line. In 1892, the club's gate was $129,480, significantly more than the NYJC ($104,380), the BJC ($97,209), and the BBRA ($54,322). Two years later, the CIJC's gate nearly doubled to $245,610, and it grossed $552,148, mainly from gambling fees, but also concessions. The BJC's gate also nearly doubled ($184,524) in 1894, but its gross quadrupled ($438,920). Yet they were both surpassed by Brighton's gate of $330,933, a year in which it reportedly netted $180,000. However, the faltering economy that lingered into 1895 and the problems with maintaining racing in the face of a revised state constitution that nearly caused the tracks to close resulted in dismal returns. The BBRA had just a $12,000 profit, which was far better than the other New York tracks.[103]

CIJC attorney John M. Bowers reported to the state assembly's Committee on Codes that the track in 1894 took in $240,000 from bookmaking and pool-selling privileges, while expenses for prizes, premiums, purses, and operating the track amounted to $236,625. Bowers claimed this figure amounted to a tiny profit of $3,375, negated by the $27,000 (actually $27,608) paid to the state in taxes, leaving a final deficit of $23,625. But he failed to account for such vital revenue sources as ticket sales and concessions. The Society for the Suppression of Vice offered an alternate accounting and then subtracted the track's reported expenses. The SSV estimated a net profit of $276,375. The press claimed the tracks netted $40,000 (it is unclear if this amount is after taxes). The CIJC's gross included $151,713 from gambling fees ($5,619 a day) and $245,610 ($9,097 a day) from gate receipts. This analysis left unaccounted $154,824 ($5,734 a day) that came from other sources, including restaurant, bar, and program privileges; payments from Western Union ($67,500, computed at the rate of $2,500 a day); and paddock fees.[104]

Peter De Lacy, not the most reliable or unbiased source, claimed the five metropolitan tracks took in $3,315,000 in 1894. He estimated they got an average of

TABLE 2. FINANCIAL REPORT OF THE CONEY ISLAND
AND BROOKLYN JOCKEY CLUBS, 1894

	Coney Island Jockey Club	Brooklyn Jockey Club
Days raced	27	27
Gross receipts	$552,147.80	$438,920.00
Amount from books and pools	$151,713.38	$227,594.58
Gate receipts	$245,610.00	$184,523.50
Amount raced for	$400,000.00	$251,550.00
Taxes to state	$27,607.80	$21,946.00

Source: Spirit of the Times 131 (22 Feb. 1896): 153–54.

$7,000 a day from their bookmakers (at $100 a day apiece), which was alone sufficient to cover expenses, and $2,200 a day from mutuel pools (which included
$200 for the odd cents on mutuel pools that the tracks kept). Telegraph privi-
leges to out-of-town poolrooms brought in $1,100, programs $1,000, gate receipts
$10,000, bar privileges $500, and fruit and other concessions $30, for a grand total
of $21,830 a day.[105]

By my accounting, if the CIJC made $552,147.80, and had expenses of $236,625.00,
with state taxes of $27,607.80, then the net was $287,915.00, a more than tidy sum.

Saratoga Racing

Another focal point of summer racing in 1894 was Saratoga. The upstate track in
the 1880s was a haven from the turf's problems in the metropolitan area. When
Morrissey died, Charles Reed and Albert Spencer, partners in a New York City
gambling hall, took over the track. Reed sold out to his partner in 1887, tired of
harassment by reformers and his snubbing by high society. By 1889, Spencer was
under pressure to sell out from Wall Street broker Spencer Trask, who sought to
halt the resort's open gambling, but local businessmen backed the racecourse
because they thought the town needed gambling as a tourist attraction. Spencer
tried to stave off the opposition by bribing two village commissioners each with
$1,500 and donating money to the Episcopal parish house.[106]

In the fall of 1890, there were false rumors of Saratoga's sale to a syndicate
that included Belmont and Lorillard. Then two years later, the racing community
was shocked when "Dutch" Fred Walbaum, who became racing secretary in late
1891, purchased the track for $375,000 and became president. Walbaum had previ-
ously run the outlaw Guttenberg Track in Hudson County, New Jersey, chastised
in one publication as "a synonym for all the crookedness . . . in the horse-racing

business," where he allegedly used electric prods and drugs on his horses. Journalist Nellie Bly described Guttenberg in a headline in the *New York World* as "Our Wickedest Summer Resort." This acquisition put the prestigious track at one of the elite's favorite summer retreats into the hands of a lowlife who formerly operated one of the most corrupt tracks in North America. According to the *Sporting World*, Saratogans were worried that "their peace and perhaps their very lives would be in danger as soon as the horde of outlawed official and horsemen were prepared for their attack on the village."[107]

Walbaum was not the most astute businessman. According to Edward Hotaling, the historian of Saratoga racing, Walbaum, an experienced bookmaker, took bets even after a race had started, often with his own staff. They cheated him by having one person watch the race and then signal confederates to bet when one horse was far ahead. The "Dutch Book," a poorly planned arrangement of odds that guaranteed the client a profit if he bet every horse, was named for Walbaum.[108]

Hotaling credited Walbaum with at least one positive action. On 25 July 1892, Walbaum opened Saratoga's handsome new five-thousand-seat multisteepled Victorian-roofed grandstand, an adjoining clubhouse, a betting pavilion, and beautifully designed lawns and flora. It was, according to the *Spirit*, "the prettiest race course in the country." The grandstand is today the longest currently operating one in American professional sports.[109]

Otherwise, Walbaum's tenure was a disaster. One day in July 1894, his horses won the first four races, and there were no entrants for the next two events. He tried increasing betting options at Saratoga by bringing back auction pools and pari-mutuels to compete with the bookmakers. Relations with bookmakers, not good to begin with, worsened after Riley Grannon, a betting bookmaker, offered to take virtually any size bets on horses he did not favor. Some of Walbaum's partners, who were among the smaller bookmakers, became irate, so the president asked Grannon to leave. However, Grannon was extremely popular with his colleagues, who successfully petitioned for his reinstatement. Another big problem was the abandonment of most of Saratoga's prestigious stakes races. The esteemed Travers Stakes was continued, but the purse dropped in 1895 to merely $1,125. Walbaum tried to drum up interest among New York City residents by changing the starting time of races from 11:30 a.m. to 2:30 p.m., enabling fans to leave the city in the morning and get to Saratoga in time for the first race. However, few New Yorkers opted for the commute. Meanwhile, the time revision upset hotel guests, accustomed to going to the track after a late breakfast. The *Times* concluded that Walbaum was "getting himself generally disliked by his dictatorial acts." The situation became so bad that in 1896, the course shut down. When reopened the following season, Walbaum was out as president, replaced by Tammanyite Edward

Kearney, a close friend of Boss Croker who was in the auction business. Kearney belonged to several New York clubs, including the CIJC.[110]

Conclusion

Metropolitan New York was the national center of racing in the early 1890s with its prestigious Sheepshead Bay and Morris Park racecourses and its prominent profit-oriented tracks at Coney Island. The men who ran these tracks all had important political clout, primarily through the Democratic Party and Tammany Hall, whose boss, Richard Croker, was himself heavily involved in the sport. State laws supported the local turf, which had the most important races in the country and the largest purses and drew most of the largest crowds. Yet even in New York, the sport was under severe attack from the daily press, moral reformers, and politically connected off-track poolroom operators. The racing elite tried to bring order to the sport with the Board of Control, but it was ineffective, and they replaced it with the highly respected Jockey Club that made an earnest effort to regulate the sport with the most rigorous standards. However, the sport in the United States was in great distress after the closing of the New Jersey tracks, followed by the shuttering of the prestigious Washington Park Racetrack in Chicago, which had just staged a great meet one year before, during the Columbian Exposition. The future of New York racing was soon itself in doubt at the upcoming state constitutional convention.

7

The Poolroom Business in Metropolitan New York, 1863–98

Pool-selling has become a great evil. The pool-sellers, even when they carry on their business in a "square" way, are engaged in a demoralizing work, and must be ranked among the foes of society. It is believed that some of them do not refuse to make with jockeys "arrangements" that are as fraudulent as any of the tricks and schemes of a wire-taper. Under the present system . . . the young clerk who earns scarcely enough to pay his board, and even the errand boy, can take a chance by the side of the "plunger" and the man who has made betting his business for twenty years. It . . . makes thousands of new gamblers very year . . . who may at any time be tempted by losses or by hope of large gains to risk money that is not their own. It brings them into contact with demoralizing companions and leads them to gambling of a more disreputable and ruinous kind.

—"Gamblers' Losses," *New York Times,* 15 October 1883

All opponents of sports betting agreed that their biggest enemy was illegal off-track betting parlors, known as poolrooms.[1] Poolrooms originated as betting rooms set up to take wagers on races at nearby tracks, often the night before the race, starting in 1863 when Dr. Robert Underwood established the first "poolroom" in the basement of the United States Hotel. The term first appeared in the *New York Times* in 1866 in reference to an operation run by Underwood and James McGowan. By 1872, Marshall and Johnson maintained a New York City poolroom at Twenty-eighth and Broadway, and three years later, at least three rooms ran auction pools and pari-mutuels on elections as well as horse races anywhere in the country. The busiest was probably the New York Turf Exchange, owned or operated by Kelly and Bliss, that even ran auction pools on major English races.[2]

Advocates of on-track betting joined moral reformers opposed to all gambling in criticizing the poolrooms. They despised poolroom operators as parasites who took advantage of public interest in gambling on racing without contributing to the turf, hurting the sport's public image, and taking business away from the race-tracks. The media decried their clients as gambling fiends just interested in making bets and not true racing fans who went out to the tracks.

The influential *Spirit of the Times* joined reformers in criticizing poolrooms because they were illegal and hurt the racing business, both financially and reputationwise, and because the off-track betting rooms lured and ruined youths who did not know better. The weekly claimed the public accepted horse race betting only at regular meets of legitimate jockey clubs and nowhere else. The editor believed that horse race betting should not be a business at the expense of public morals: "It is a monstrous invasion upon the rights of society to set up stands in public places and tempt, by adroit advertisements, the disposition of boys and young men to hang about and invest their earnings in ventures of the most alluring and inviting character, but which are generally followed by disastrous losses. These losses rather stimulate than discourage their appetite for gain, and step by step, as in all other species of gambling, they plunge into the vortex of ruin, and often into disgrace in infamy."[3]

Despite all the disparagement of poolrooms by journalists, sportsmen, and reformers, the illegal enterprises were enormously successful, fulfilling a substantial public demand. Gambling was a popular working-class hobby, and horse race betting became increasingly attractive through accessible poolrooms and on-street betting with handbooks. Playing the horses was not just a matter of luck like the lottery but called for rational decision making based on expertise. It was for many the working-class equivalent of the stock market. In the late nineteenth century, there were many sources of information in newspapers and the sporting press for literate bettors about the form of horses, their breeding, the weights they carried, their jockey, track conditions, and odds available. Bettors who had less confidence in their knowledge relied on touts or tipster sheets. As English historians, notably Mike Huggins, Mark Clapson, and Ross McKibbin, have already recognized, betting fitted into the economics of working-class life, with its boom-and-bust cycles and failure to save for the future. It was also socially functional, providing excitement for men stuck in boring, repetitive jobs.[4]

The betting parlors secured protection from police interference by payoffs, alliances with machine politicians who looked after their interests, and affiliations to organized crime syndicates. These growing criminal enterprises focused on victimless crimes, particularly such vices as gambling and prostitution that did not generate the public outrage given to victim crimes or create as much pressure on the police. The underworld provided such important services as ready cash, means to limit entry into the business, fast racetrack news, ways for poolroom operators to lay off risky bets (by betting the opposite way with another professional gambler and thereby lessening their exposure), and the muscle to ensure debt payment. The betting parlors were a central element in the rise of organized crime in metropolitan New York.

Poolrooms and the 1877 Antipool Law

The Jersey Scene

New York's antipool law of 1877 aimed primarily at halting betting at gambling parlors on horses and any other competitive contests, including other sports and elections. The new law encouraged many New York gamblers to flee to Jersey City in northern New Jersey, where pool selling was already popular and closely connected to the metropolitan sporting scene. However, in June, corporation counsel Leon Abbett, under orders from Republican mayor Charles Seidler, proclaimed that pool selling in New Jersey was an indictable offense. His pronouncement encouraged the pool sellers to move on to wide-open Hoboken.[5]

Hoboken's gamblers had a very shady reputation, reflected by Charles E. Courtney and James E. Riley's rowing race in July 1877 at Greenwood Lake, canceled after Courtney was drugged with arsenic, presumably at the behest of heavy bettors. The *Times* claimed that poolroom gamblers, mainly former New Yorkers, knew about the plot since they had bet so heavily against Courtney. The *Times* condemned the harmful impact that gambling had on pretty much all publicly conducted sports, particularly baseball.[6]

Hoboken's three poolrooms were busy night and day in June, selling pools on American sporting events. In response, Justice Hoffman of the county court of sessions sent officers to collect evidence against poolroom proprietors. On 4 June, he issued bench warrants for the arrest of several gamblers, including Kelly and Bliss, William Lovell, T. B. Johnson, and John T. McDougall. They put up five hundred dollars' bail and returned to work. However, the grand jury at first failed to bring in a true bill against the pool sellers.[7]

A few months later, on 19 October, the authorities again moved against the pool sellers, arresting everyone they could catch. Constables and deputy sheriffs arrested twenty-two men, including proprietors, auctioneers, clerks, markers, and many boys. The police charged them with keeping disorderly houses and selling lottery tickets. Their punishment was the inconvenience of a night in jail, and the rooms soon reopened.[8]

According to the *New York Clipper*, "General sympathy in favor of the pool sellers prevailed among the citizens of Hoboken on account of the increased circulation of money which their presence there has created, and it was openly boasted that no Grand Jury could be found to find an indictment against them." Judge Knapp rebuked the jury for its inaction, and then the grand jury came back with twelve indictments, mainly against Kelly, Bliss, McDougall, Johnson, and their chief workers. Yet even when the men were convicted, punishments were usually very lenient, usually a slap on the wrist and not the prescribed five-hundred-dollar fine, one year in jail, or both. Lovell, for instance, pleaded guilty to criminal misconduct and received a ten-dollar fine.[9]

Pool sellers became adroit at circumventing antibetting laws. For instance, in Boston in 1878, a veteran pool seller appeared at Beacon Park as an "auctioneer" for an art sale. He brought several pictures of horses, labeled with the names of trotters scheduled for a particular race. He "sold" them for first, second, and third choices (places). Afterward, he announced that the owners of the winning horses wished to purchase and frame the pictures, so he set up a time and place to buy them back. The prices paid amounted to the winnings of the pool, less the usual commission.[10]

The New York City Poolrooms

The New York police may have enforced the antipool law right after enactment, but by July 1878, poolrooms were back in business. Some rooms listed horses on a blackboard along with the number of tickets sold on each horse, similar to a track pari-mutuel. Certain betting parlors claimed they were simply taking orders for the purchase of pari-mutuels at tracks where their sale was legal and paid off the bets at track odds. At the end of the month, an uptown police captain in whose precinct turf exchanges abounded visited a poolroom and saw a man drop five dollars and get a slip with some writing. The officer procured a piece of paper with a ticket number from Kelly and Bliss for a five-dollar pari-mutuel ticket at Saratoga and made an arrest. However, the corporation counsel ruled that a blank receipt for a pool ticket was insufficient evidence because the law required proof of an actual ticket sale on a contest of skill, speed, or power or on an election.[11]

The antipoolroom law was soon largely a dead letter in Manhattan, although, according to the *Times*, it was "most harshly enforced where the pool selling was least objectionable," namely, Jerome Park, the site of racing. One result was that "under cover of . . . [a] test case the petty pool sellers who had journeyed to Hoboken and other foreign cities, returned to New York," and returned to their old business. It was ironic that each night, "the police could be seen enforcing order among the throngs assembled to break the law" by betting at poolrooms.[12]

The *Spirit* was very concerned about the popularity of poolrooms and its negative impact on the turf:

13. This downtown New York betting parlor in 1892 drew a well-off clientele, reflected by the clothing and the features of the gentlemen present. There are a couple of ethnic-looking youths in the forefront who are smoking and trying to look "tough." Drawn by W. A. Rogers. *Source:* "A New York Pool-Room," *Harper's Weekly* 31 (2 Apr. 1892): 324.

It is a lamentable fact that in every city of any size in the country there are from one to a half dozen rooms in existence where pools are sold on racing, boating, base-ball, yachting, elections, and every class of events that can provoke a wager. They are necessarily very demoralizing, particularly to young men, and sooner or later other States will follow in the footsteps of New York, and make war upon the system, and, unfortunately, will not stop with a prohibition against these establishments, conducted to make money for the proprietors, but will make the provisions of the law extend to race-courses.[13]

The cooperation of the authorities with gamblers who brazenly flaunted the law disturbed the *Times:* "The Police so far from interfering with the illegal traffic of the men who live upon their wits and the want of wit in others, actually throw around them the mantle of official protection, keeping back the crowds from pressing too closely on the 'cashiers,' precisely as they do in the streets on the occasion of a grand parade or a review." Once the racing season began, the poolrooms opened without concealment or disguise, like faro and keno halls, and were no more secretive than ordinary saloons. The rooms openly advertised in certain newspapers to help clients find them. "If the business were the most legitimate in the City," the *Times* noted with chagrin, "more thorough publicity could not be given it, or more thorough immunity from all unpleasant embarrassments granted to it."[14]

On 23 June 1880, the *Times* ran a major story on the poolroom menace titled "Police and the Pool-Box: The Public Fleeced and the Gamblers Protected." It discussed how rooms operated full blast to take bets on Saratoga, seemingly "under the special protection of the Police." The trade was centered in "Gamblers' Paradise" (West Twenty-eighth Street, between Fifth Avenue and Broadway), as well as on Barclay Street in Lower Manhattan (site of 9/11) and at Hunter's Point, a neighborhood in Long Island City, a town of 15,600, near the East River, opposite Midtown Manhattan. There, "crowds of young boys mingle with hoary-headed gamblers, and invest their little savings, or the money of their employers, upon the doubtful results of a horse-race." The Barclay Street rooms sold cheap pools and were "so thronged with people that the crowd overflows into the street and blocks the sidewalk." An officer stood guard outside one betting parlor "to keep a path clear for pedestrians; but no member of the Police force seems to consider it any part of his duty to see that the law against pool-selling is enforced."[15]

The *Times* also complained about the swindling of young, low-income men trying to make fast, easy money. Since the authorities were not doing their job, the paper felt responsible for educating these foolish youths and opening "their eyes to the fact that they are in the hands of swindlers, and that every dollar that they invest in the illegal business of buying pools is placed in the control of men who are bound to victimize them by every device known to the gambling fraternity."[16]

During the late spring, when the authorities tried to halt bookmaking at Jerome Park, there were some raids at Gamblers' Paradise. Several arrests ensued, including poolroom operators William Lovell, John Tully, and Joseph McDonough. Their cases were dismissed, but pool sellers John Van Buskirk of T. B. Johnson's rooms and Edward Smith of Kelly and Bliss were held for five hundred dollars' bail. Antigambling folk saw these arrests as an indication that open violations of gambling laws would be stopped, but the poolrooms at Barclay and West Twenty-eighth streets were still going strong. As the *Times* pointed out, "The Police, for some mysterious reason, made only spasmodic attempts to enforce the law, the gamblers became bolder, and to-day their offices are open and in full blast, apparently under the protection, and certainly under the eyes of the Police, who are supposed to protect the public from their snares."[17]

The *Times* was not very keen on working-class gambling at racetracks where the democratic pari-mutuels enabled anyone with five dollars to bet, unlike the old auction pools in which only the well-heeled participated. The paper was nearly as critical of bookmakers, who offered better odds than the poolrooms, especially on combination pools (such as picking winners in three straight races), because such wagering schemes encouraged men to bet more than they could afford: "These systems form a part of the business of the firms who suck the blood of the poor man," pointed out the *Times*. "In both systems the percentage in favor of the seller is tremendous, and he grows steadily and certainly rich, while his victims certainly grow poor."[18]

The poolroom clientele were reportedly mechanics, clerks, and petty gamblers who did not have the time and money to go to the tracks, while "the heavy gamblers and sporting men go to the race-course and do their betting on the ground." The *Times* had a low regard for the uptown off-track betting crowd: "The class of people who patronize these up town places is composed principally of men who live by their wits—bunco players, steerers for faro banks, petty gamblers, and disreputable creatures who live and gamble on the earnings of unfortunate. Very few that can boast of even the appearance of gentlemen frequent these 'exchanges' and the spectacle of the 'finest Police in the world' protecting this class in the open violation of law is an edifying one."[19]

Uptown rooms in Gamblers' Paradise operated wide-open, with no pretense of concealment. Any police officer could easily walk in and made arrests, but none did. The rooms did a lively business selling mutuel and combination pools until almost three in the afternoon, one-half hour before post time for the first races. The crowd then dispersed, with winners returning at eight o'clock for their payoffs.[20]

Similar scenes occurred downtown on Barclay Street, where the bettors were more usually young men, some scarcely out of their teens. They included young clerks, "who spend their lunch money in gaming, and men who live in Jersey City and Brooklyn, and have neither the time nor the money to go to the race-track."[21] The main poolrooms there included Kelly and Bliss, the largest and most heavily patronized, and its neighbors, Cridge and Murray, Tully and Simmonds, and T. B. Johnson, with W. Lovell's poolrooms located upstairs. Stakes ranged from fifty cents to five dollars. The downtown rooms opened at ten and were busy until three thirty, when the first race began. A *Times* reporter went to the popular Hackett and De Lacy poolroom one block away (1½ Barclay Street), pushed in a screen door that opened directly from the street, and "found himself in the midst of a throng of about 20 men and boys, most of them of respectable appearance and all consulting a large black-board on which 'combinations' were being rapidly made. Many of them look young enough to be at their studies in school, instead of making up books at a horse race." Combinations were cheaper there than uptown, as low as fifty cents, and mutuel pool tickets were sold for one dollar. The room also offered pools on the Democratic presidential convention in Cincinnati, "but the subject was not so engrossing as the races, and but little stock was taken in them."[22]

In late June, John Hackett was taken into custody after a detective bought a pari-mutuel pool ticket at his poolroom. However, the presiding magistrate discharged him because the arresting officer had not seen the horse named on his ticket actually run. Hackett might have been singled out for soliciting bets on Democratic candidates. One sporting man complained, "The police are willing to wink at us as long as we only bet on horse races, but the moment we begin to invade politics again, there will be more trouble." Hackett and his partner, Peter De Lacy, learned their lesson and stopped taking pools on party nominations.[23]

At the start of August, the police raided pool sellers en masse. Inspector Thomas F. Byrnes instructed Detective William Adams to make bets at various poolrooms, including Hackett and De Lacy's, Lambrecht's, and T. B. Johnson's, and then visit the track to see if the horses named on the tickets actually started. Adams subsequently arrested eight clerks and cashiers, who at their arraignment were readily identified as poolroom workers by their clothing and accessories. They were all "in fashionable attire, and nearly all sported diamonds and heavy gold watch-chains." Police Justice Smith originally called for one thousand dollars' bail, but when he saw James Kelly, the powerful gambler, present, he remanded them all to his custody. "It has come to this," Byrnes complained to the press, "that a gambler's word is worth as much as a merchant's bond."[24]

The Long Island Poolrooms

Wide-open Long Island City (LIC) was created in 1870 by the merger of several villages. The city became well known for the strong ties between local machine politicians and the sporting crowd. In 1879, three poolrooms opened in Long Island City, operated by famed New York saloon keeper Harry Hill and bookmakers Kelly and Bliss and William Lovell, that catered to New Yorkers who arrived by the Thirty-fourth Street Ferry. Lovell's one-hundred-seat room, a refurbished stable that adjoined a low-class hotel, was the most popular. He sold French pools on three sides of his room, while the fourth had a blackboard and platform occupied by an auctioneer and three clerks. A Long Island City police captain told the press, "I think the pool-rooms are a good thing for this place. They make business lively, and their New York patrons drop a lot of money over here. I haven't heard any complaint against them yet, and I don't suppose they'll be interfered with."[25]

William Lovell was among the most notorious poolroom men in America yet operated with impunity. As one of his clerks told a reporter in 1887, "We are only arrested occasionally by our protectors to keep up their reputations. They will now have to make less arrests, and when they do make them, seize upon some outsider who is not connected with the establishment." The clerk said Lovell made a lot of money but had to "give away so much of it for protection that he is continually grumbling." He was so wealthy that in 1886, he built a fifty-thousand-dollar stable at Fifty-eighth Street near Broadway and one year later bought a fifty-five-thousand-dollar house on Thirty-second Street, near Fifth Avenue.[26]

A fourth poolroom, the Hunter's Point Turf Exchange, opened in Long Island City in 1881. Like Lovell's facility, it not only ran pools and made book but also had *rouge et noir* tables where players bet on the color of the cards dealt. The exchange usually had about two to three hundred boys and men crowded into its "reading-room." Efforts by the authorities to break up these rooms were ineffective. An unnamed city official claimed that one of the poolroom operators paid hush money to ten government officials.[27]

The efforts of the "better sorts in town" and the Law and Order Society, disappointed with the inaction of the LIC police, resulted in a secret raid on 26 August 1882 by Sheriff Alonzo B. Wright, employing twenty-five out-of-town deputies to keep the foray clandestine. Mayor Henry S. De Bevoise met that morning with Coroner Robinson and William Huzzey, a well-known gambler who ran a *rouge et noir* table, warning local poolrooms and gambling dens of the upcoming raids, staged midday when the rooms were at their busiest. However, when the authorities got to the rooms of Kelly and Bliss (whose room was in the rear of Coroner Robinson's saloon), Lovell and White, and Johnson, they were completely empty. As Sheriff Wright pointed out, "At least two-thirds of the people are in sympathy with the pool-sellers, and in consequence the police commissioners are hampered in every way." Besides, the police were poorly motivated, since for the past twenty months they were paid only by certificates discounted at 12 percent.[28]

Cleaning Up the Poolroom Evil

Anthony Comstock and the War on Poolrooms

One of the reformers trying to clean up the city's poolrooms was Anthony Comstock, who considered gamblers as agents of Satan, and he left few stones unturned in his efforts to clean up that vice. He argued that betting on pools "is conscienceless, heartless, and infamous. It makes embezzlers, defaulters, and thieves in every grade of society. It is more fatal to the morals of youth than faro, roulette, or other banking-games, because it seems to offer greater inducements for comparatively small sums, promising a prompt return."[29]

In August, Comstock led raids against poolrooms on Barclay Street, and then the Long Island Law and Order League invited him to help them out. One of Long Island City's police commissioners had just ordered a raid, and the mayor reacted by asking for his resignation. Comstock was convinced the Queens district attorney was tied to the sporting crowd and that the police protected the gambling establishments. He secured warrants based on his colleagues' investigations and on 9 October led a surprise raid on LIC's four poolrooms with twenty deputized associates unknown to the gamblers, riding carriages supposedly bound for a funeral. Comstock's men captured about twenty-five thousand dollars in paraphernalia.[30]

No Honor among Thieves

Sharpsters considered pool operators fair game. Kelly and Bliss were stung in 1880 by crooks who sent them a fraudulent message over the racing wires. Ripple captured the one-and-three-quarter-mile Shrewsbury Handicap at Monmouth Park on 4 July, but instead of the correct information, the message "Krupp Gun First" was delivered, verified by a second dispatch signed "O.K. K & B." Their Hunter's Point room manager authorized a payoff on the wrong horse, and Kelly and Bliss were out three thousand dollars.[31]

A far bigger fraud occurred on 13 October 1883 when pool sellers across the country were fleeced for the third time in four years, this time for one hundred thousand dollars. Eole won the fourth race at Jerome Park, but the wire reported that General Monroe won. By the time the error was discovered, poolrooms in Chicago, Coney Island, Baltimore, and elsewhere had already paid off on the wrong horse. Western Union's chief operator later discovered a wiretap located between Fordham and the track.[32]

Reformers pressed the police that summer to close New York's poolrooms. Police captain Alexander "Clubber" Williams turned the heat up so much that even Lovell opened only to people he personally knew. Lovell told the *Times* that "Capt. Williams has practically ruined our business for us." Williams was one of the toughest and most famous police officers in America, who reputedly coined the term *tenderloin* to describe his corrupt Midtown Twenty-ninth Precinct. The Lexow Commission (discussed below) in 1894 revealed that Williams took bribes from poolrooms and brothel keepers, and Clubber retired under fire to an estate in Connecticut.[33]

Pool Selling on Sundays

A new poolroom problem emerged on 3 February 1885 when they opened on Sundays for the first time. This move shocked devout Protestants, who observed a quiet American Sabbath reserved for religious activity. Pietistic native-born Americans tried to clamp down on Sabbath infractions like drinking, the opening of museums, or professional baseball, fearing they could be entering wedges for a Continental Sabbath, a day of recreation after church. Such Sundays were customary among Catholic German and Irish folk and the new immigrants from eastern and southern Europe. Old-stock Americans saw strict blue laws as a means to exercise social control over immigrants and protect their own traditional way of life. Sunday racing began in the 1870s in wide-open New Orleans, the only city where it existed. A poolroom opened on Sunday at West Brighton's Jumbo Hotel, a facility formerly occupied by poolroom keeper John J. Flynn, while pool maker Fred Walbaum and his partners set up business at Paul Bauer's nearby pavilion. According to the *Times,* "Several hundred sports from this city and Brooklyn, who had heard of this move, went to Coney Island, and a lively business was transacted during the afternoon."[34]

When several Gravesend constables arrived at the rooms with arrest warrants, an alarm went off and the crowds rushed out. As one reporter noted, "The constables fired a few shots to frighten the sports, who thereupon became excited and prepared to resist. The constables fearing to capture the pool sellers or buyers lest a general fight should take place concluded it best to wait a while. The sports were allowed to depart in peace." The next day, the constables got warrants for the arrest of Gottfried Walbaum, identified as a "commission merchant." He resisted and fought the constables until they drew their revolvers. Other gamblers arrested included Paul Bauer, Bill Corrigan, and Ed Crosby.[35]

Bauer was charged with keeping a Coney Island clubhouse where pools were sold. He pleaded guilty, admitting he owned the site, but said he was not in the betting business. Bauer expected a token punishment but got a stiff $750 fine and three months in jail. It was a rare instance when DA Ridgeway got a conviction. However, Bauer served only a few days in jail. By 17 June, Walbaum and other pool sellers operating in the vicinity of the Brooklyn Bridge closed up. Walbaum advised his clients to take their business to Hoboken. This move marked the end of the short-lived experiment of Sunday pools in Brooklyn and New York.[36]

The Ives Act and the Poolrooms

Efforts to clean up the poolroom menace in the early 1880s made limited headway. In 1885, for instance, the *Brooklyn Eagle* found that virtually everyone bet on races and that the hard work of discouraging and abolishing horse race betting was futile. Betting on races was commonplace at Wall Street, the Tenderloin, and in the dry-goods area of mid-Manhattan. Tickers at saloons and other centers of the male bachelor subculture between four and five o'clock were all busily reporting results of local racetracks.[37]

Two years later, the Ives Act was passed with the intent of closing the pool-rooms while preserving gambling at the racetracks. As far as the *Times* was concerned, there was not a big distinction between betting on or off the tracks. It attributed swindling in the sport to both poolrooms and racetrack bookmakers: "Fraud is practiced to-day on every race-course where pools are sold, and in every pool-room in this City. If men will place their money in the keeping of thieves, they must expect to have it stolen." The editors also criticized professional gamblers for deceiving their clients, beginning with a 5 percent commission for little work. The paper noted, somewhat humorously, "The debt of the United States bears a less interest for one year than these men demand for holding their victims' money for a few minutes." The pool sellers squeezed out every penny they could, retaining the odd cents on bets, so that a winning ticket with a payoff of $20.29 received $20.20.[38]

The *Times* also pointed to the deceptions caused by the engagement of pool sellers in complementary businesses like bookmaking and gambling halls and to the frequent conflicts of interest among pool sellers who owned racehorses and operated racetracks. In 1887, for instance, poolroom operators Kelly and Bliss held the bookmaking privilege at Saratoga, while A. H. Cridge made book at Gravesend. Charles Reed and his partners, Spencer and McCormack, former Morrissey associates, had gambling houses in New York City and at Saratoga, owned a large stud of horses, and controlled the majority of stock at Saratoga.[39]

The Ives Pool Law did not drastically alter poolroom conditions. Poolrooms remained very accessible, flourished openly, and operated with impunity. In addition, the nearby Jersey shore became an increasingly important site for off-track horse race betting. By June, barges were set up near Weehawken by New York gamblers. They were fastened to shore by a gangplank, placing them under Jersey jurisdiction. Some gamblers tried to sell pools for the Monmouth races on a steamboat between New York and Sandy Hook. A raid resulted in arrests and the seizure of materials and $300 in cash.[40]

The *New York World* found at least eight poolrooms in business right after the law went into effect and published names and locations. The *World* claimed there was more betting at the poolrooms than at the track: "The poolroom keepers themselves admit that they have no intention of observing the Ives law and make this statement, and prove it by actual fact, right under the nose of the police, or for that matter, right under the shadow of Anthony Comstock's society." The rooms were mainly located behind barricaded doors with a tiny peephole. They were simply furnished, but within a few years, the best rooms had mahogany furniture, expensive mirrors, and beautiful carpets.[41]

Poolrooms used the commission system to dodge the law. In one notable case, Detective Curtis tried to place a bet with Holmes and Company clerk William Tappen, who told him that Holmes did not take bets but would deliver wagers to the track for a fee. Curtis then signed a document commissioning the house to act as his agent and place a bet for him at Jerome Park. Detective Curtis subsequently arrested Tappen. The clerk was defended by Howe and Hummel, on retainer for the Pool Sellers Association. They argued their client had made a legal transaction, and Tappen was acquitted because there was no evidence of books, registry, or betting paraphernalia.[42]

Cridge and Murray's poolrooms (13 West Twenty-eighth Street and 75 University Place, the latter a few blocks north of Greenwich Village) were among the most successful in 1887, doing a daily business of at least $1,000, half of which was clean profit, with an estimated annual return of $112,000. A clerk told a reporter that Cridge and Murray was secure "because we are fully protected and have no reason to expect any interference with our business. Our protection is three-fold. We are under the special protecting wing of an agent of Comstock's society, of the 'fly cop' of the Captain of the precinct, and of the marble building in Mulberry Street [Police Headquarters]." There were occasional arrests "by the very persons who are paid to protect us, but they never produce any evidence against their prisoners so there is nothing for the Police Justice to do but to discharge them. Then the police get a 'puff' in the newspapers, which is good for them and does no harm to us." Their customers "are generally poor devils who cannot afford the time or money to go to the race track. We generally give about half the odds that they could get at the track and half of every dollar that we take in we either win or keep."[43]

Pools continued to be openly bought and sold in Long Island City. A journalist reported, "The pool sellers have boasted that they could carry on their business with impunity as the city magistrates could not be induced to interfere with them." One particularly popular operation was on the second floor of Michael Kearney's lager beer saloon opposite Calvary Cemetery. Mayor Patrick G. Gleason (1887–92, 1896–97), a close associate of the sporting crowd, ordered Police Board president Henry C. Johnson to close the poolroom or resign. This demand was out of character for Paddy Gleason, who ran the city like Boss Tweed had run New York. While mayor, he rented a lot of property to the city, including the site of city hall and land for schools, and leased his horses to the fire department. Paddy was a boxer in Ireland before migrating to America and promoted matches in Long Island City before they were legalized by the state in 1896.[44]

Alderman Winans, who had previously complained about the room, approached Johnson about taking action. Johnson told him he was going to the Catskills to visit his wife and soon boarded a boat for New York, where he got on the railroad, watched all the time by one of Kearney's men. Instead of heading out to Sullivan County, Johnson got off at Fifty-ninth Street and went to a nearby court, where he wired the corporation counsel, instructing him to detail some officers for his immediate return. Johnson returned to LIC and by midnight had prepared the necessary paperwork for a one o'clock raid. The foray resulted in several arrests, including Alderman Winans, found with Kearney in the telegraph operator's room. Mayor Gleason, acting as magistrate, fined Winans $51. Many of the arrested men, who had no more than $1.50 on them, swore they had not bought pool tickets and were discharged.[45]

In early May 1888, the New York police made "a farcical raid" against some rooms, which all reopened a week later. As a reporter discovered, "the crowd going in and out of Cridge & Co.'s, George Lovell's, and the Windermere Hotel, on West Twenty-eighth street were so numerous as to be not only visible to all except the conveniently blind police officers and detectives of Capt. Reilly's precinct, but a nuisance to people whose business required them to pass through the street." The gamblers were selling pools on races at Baltimore, Lexington, and Clifton. The *Times* chastised the police: "It wouldn't require a fine-tooth comb to discover some 30 of these dives around town if Police Superintendent Murray's men really wished to locate and close them." Overall, from 1886 to 1890, the police annually made about sixty arrests for poolroom violations. The police blamed their poor success on conflicting court rulings, especially the ones permitting commission betting, and numerous lawsuits and called for more definitive crime statutes.[46]

On 17 April 1889, Judge Henry A. Gildersleeve ruled in a pool-selling case dating back to July 1888 that the commission system in which poolrooms charged $0.05 to $0.25 to execute bets at racetracks was legal. This decision contradicted the ruling of Judge Fish of the state supreme court in an identical case, *People v. Barber*, who found the commissioner system illegal. Officer Robert W. Clark bought a pool ticket from William Spencer at a poolroom at 80 Park Row for $5.00 on Cruiser at odds of five to two for a fee of $0.25. Clark received a card, which he signed, that the wager would be delivered to the Brighton Beach track and the bet would be placed there. The *Tribune* criticized Gildersleeve for violating the letter of the Ives Pool Law that allowed betting only at the track and for making it easier to open a poolroom: "The pool-sellers are bubbling over with joy at what they consider a great victory for them." Of course, "the 'commission' trick is the baldest of frauds" because the pool sellers never sent any of the money bet with them on to the tracks.[47]

Following Gildersleeve's ruling, several recently closed rooms reopened. Poolrooms on several streets, including Park Row, Barclay Street, and Twenty-seventh Street, resumed with a lively business on Clifton and Memphis races. Business went on in the old style with odds posted in the twenty-minute intervals between races. The reopening resulted in lower attendance at Clifton and a drop in bookmakers there from forty-five to twenty-three. Many of them avoided the daily $75 fee at the track and did their business in New York City.[48]

The Poolroom Clients

Rev. Dr. Howard Crosby of the Society for the Prevention of Crime reported in 1889 that conditions had improved a great deal in the twelve years since the passage of the antipool law. Nonetheless, gambling was still destroying hardworking men: "There are many instances of persons losing everything and being compelled to pawn the clothing on their backs in order to obtain food. The frequenters of such places are often men of respectability and standing. Bookkeepers, clerks, elevated railroad employees, and firemen . . . are numerous." Clarence Greeley, general agent of the International Law and Order League, claimed that poolroom customers also included businessmen, women of wealth, and college students. The SPC received forty-seven complaints from parents "whose sons have been ruined in poolrooms that are merely dens of thieves." According to its investigation, "The profits of such places at noon, when young men drop in to bet on favorite horses, are extraordinary." It found a poolroom in Midtown made a profit of $25,000 in a few months before it closed, and some rooms had daily receipts of $5,000–$6,000. Certain poolrooms sold 2,506 tickets, and there were some 31,500 persons present in just a few hours. Crosby informed captains in four precincts where poolrooms were concentrated, but no action was taken.[49]

The press was less impressed by the quality of the "office boys, young clerks and persons of narrow means" who bet at poolrooms. These men were not ruined by betting at the tracks because they did not have the time or money to travel out to the racecourses. It was the more convenient poolroom wagering that harmed them and often led to thievery: "Men . . . earning their bread laboriously by the sweat of their brow, cannot generally get half-holidays oftener than once a week," when they might go to the track. However, the accessible poolrooms, open six days a week, provided a venue for working men. The paper worried that the poolroom problem was reaching beyond these groups. Businessman Henry Villard's butler confessed he had lost so much money at the poolrooms that he considered stealing his employer's silver, while Yale's faculty was concerned that students were spending too much time and money at New Haven poolrooms. The *Tribune* worried that because of the Gildersleeve decision, "a city pool-room may be opened on every corner . . . in every liquor-saloon in New York," and called for the legislature to respond accordingly.[50]

Other newspapers echoed the *Tribune*. The *Eagle* described the poolroom crowd as "butcher boys with their hair aprons on" and office boys, probably young loafers who stole time from their other duties, who bet $1 unless some chipped in for a $2 bet. Well-dressed clerks were a couple of steps up, earning about $15 a week: "They think they are experts, and would bet $2–5." They mainly bet at the downtown rooms. The SPC blamed them for many thefts, embezzlements, and defalcations. Other customers were workingmen; small bettors, considered among the least numerous among poolroom clients; and, finally, the sad, broken-down sports. Another category found at poolrooms was the shabbily dressed, tough older boy with disreputable morals. He was a "loafer, pure and simple, just hangs around rooms if closed—does odd jobs around saloon, etc." He patronized the poolroom not to bet but to pick up small change. The paper quoted a stable owner who disparaged poolroom customers as people "who could only afford two dollar bets that they managed to scrap together and who look as if they hadn't had a new suit of clothes for years. Go and see what sort of people they are. A broken down lot."[51]

Women also patronized poolrooms, though not as widely as they would a decade later. In June 1889, a gambler in Captain Reilly's precinct advertised a poolroom that catered to women bettors by placing cards under apartment doors and in mailboxes: "Ladies unable to attend the races can do their betting at the Ladies Club, 109 West Thirty-third Street, Room 5, and one flight up. All the latest information appertaining to starters, jockeys, scratchers; also first, second and third getting. Charges, tickets purchased for 10 cents cashed for 15 cents. Open all day." The club was a barely furnished three-room flat that was an annex of a notorious poolroom across the street. By 1892, there were a dozen women's poolrooms attached to men's betting parlors.[52]

The Poolrooms Close

Shortly after the new year in 1890, the city's poolrooms were tipped off by a "mysterious" source about a large raid. Afterward, forty-three poolrooms taking bets on Clifton and Guttenberg tracks closed down. The word on the street was that newly appointed judge James Fitzgerald of the court of general sessions or his close friends were behind the raids, in retaliation for poolroom men supposedly raising $30,000 for Judge Gildersleeve's unsuccessful campaign against Fitzgerald, who was backed by the city's liquor dealers. Poolroom operators were irate that as a result, a lot of people were going to the Jersey tracks to bet or else to gambling saloons in localities like the Bowery, Park Place, or Ann Street.[53]

A well-known bookmaker claimed that the real cause of the raid was Western Union, whose year-old Racing Bureau was levying exorbitant rates for its service, requiring each poolroom to pay $10 per day for its correspondent at the New Orleans track and $75 a month for each operator at its New York offices. The racing wire also imposed an extra-word rate for "expedited service," and poolrooms with multiple facilities lost the privilege of retransmitting telegrams to their branches.[54]

A number of poolrooms were back in business by April, although the press claimed that only one room was operational in late May when the New York racing season began. The *Times* wavered between crediting the closings to Anthony Comstock, Western Union, or the police who raided De Lacy's poolroom on 17 May, which resulted in an important test case of the commission system. One prominent bookmaker attributed the distress of the poolrooms to Chairman David J. Whitney of the SPC's Committee on Enforcement of the Law. Whitney, a commission merchant by profession, was determined to close poolrooms because they were a source of revenue for the police and other well-connected groups. His agents began visiting prominent businessmen in March, seeking signatures for a petition urging the legislature to abolish the current fashion of gambling. Whitney even claimed that poolroom landlords were supporting his drive, which is unlikely, since they charged poolrooms twice as much for rent as any other business. A small poolroom near city hall rented for $3,000–$5,000 a year.[55]

The poolroom business apparently picked up dramatically with the new racing season because several rooms were in full swing. A letter writer to the *Times* visited Peter De Lacy's at 33 Park Row and then "The" Allen's, at Bleecker Street and South Fifth Avenue. He found white and black prostitutes in the saloon sending money downstairs to the poolroom, which was crowded with a hundred men and boys from all classes, "nearly all of whom bore the stamp of the criminal class," and saw odds written on the board. A man stationed behind the screen called the race from the wire information coming off a ticker.[56]

A big poolroom raid occurred in June in Long Island City when District Attorney John Fleming secured indictments against Patrick J. Murphy, Mayor Gleason's right-hand man, who was king of the local poolrooms. Murphy was a partner in a building constructed by Gleason that housed the Puritan Athletic Club, a club with a lot of political pull that ran large poolrooms in sight of the county courthouse and would soon be the site of illegal boxing shows. Some of its leading members were indicted for gambling violations in July, but since so many

Long Island City officials and sheriff's employees were on the club's payroll, it was nigh impossible to arrest, much less convict, them. In September, the grand jury indicted the principal managers of the club and compelled the sheriff to carry out arrests. The poolroom was back in business the next day.[57]

The Racetrack War Against the Poolrooms

The Wynn Case

The poolroom commission business got a big boost at the beginning of 1891 from Judge C. H. Van Brunt's decision in the case of Thomas F. Wynn, an alleged betting commissioner at Peter De Lacy's poolroom. Back on 17 May 1890, an officer went to the room at 5 Barclay Street to bet five dollars on Fordham, running at Gravesend. Wynn said he could not take the bet but would deliver it for twenty-five cents to the track, where it could be wagered, and gave the policeman a receipt. A contract was printed on tickets indicating that all purchases were commissions to be taken to the track and bet for a percentage fee. The officer then arrested Wynn in what became a test case to determine the legality of the commission system. Judge Van Brunt ruled that it was legal for poolrooms to serve as commission agents if they actually took their clients' money to the track and bet it there. Thereafter, all pool sellers identified themselves as betting commissioners, whether they were or were not.[58]

Off-track betting flourished that winter, doing a lively business on the races at Guttenberg and Gloucester because of the Van Brunt decision and the poolroom operators' powerful political connections. As many as fifty-eight rooms were open in mid-March, even though uniformed police walked right in front of the doors. As one policeman explained, "They're fixed at headquarters and the room keepers are solid through Tammany. The current rumor was that the rooms were protected through payoffs of $500 to the right man." One-fourth of the protection payoffs went to Tammany, half to two ranking police officials, and the rest to wherever it would do the most good. The most secure room in the city may have been one at Fourteenth Street managed by former deputy sheriff Julius Kaufman, a Tammanyite and friend of Mayor Hugh Grant.[59]

The poolroom situation was so out of hand that a major meeting was held in early spring by representatives from the four New York tracks, as well as Monmouth, Linden, Elizabeth, and an attorney from the City Reform Club, to consider ways to fight the city poolrooms. The tracks worried they stood to lose heavily from the off-course competition. They purportedly raised a legal fund of thirty-one thousand dollars to fight the rooms and hired Robert Pinkerton, who ran the security at several metropolitan tracks, to go after the poolrooms. He got warrants

694 **NIP & TUCK**

3 & 5 FIRST PLACE

PATENTED, 1887.

When countersigned by me or my agent at point

of issue I agree to transmit the sum of $_____

to_____Race Track and

follow the instructions of sender.

In the event of delay or accident, not due to my negli-

gence, I shall be responsible for amount deposited only.

COMMISSION CHARGE, TEN CENTS.

14. Betting receipt. When a gambler bet at a poolroom that identified itself as a "commission house," the clerk gave him a stamped receipt indicating payment, and the customer would indicate the horse selected, the position he would come in, and the odds. He would pay his wager and get a receipt. The bet supposedly went by courier to the track, where an agent made the wager. *Source:* Flavel Scott Mines, "The Study of a Pool-Room," *Harper's Weekly* 36 (17 Dec. 1892): 1210.

from the sheriff's office and shuttered five rooms. In the meantime, the state appealed the *Wynn* decision, and this time he was convicted.[60]

Reform to the Forefront

Public criticisms, bolstered by negative press publicity, especially from the *Times,* which informed the police commissioners as to which poolrooms were open, and lobbying by social improvement groups like the City Reform Club led to several raids in late March directed by Inspector Byrnes. Long Island City's officials also seemed serious about fighting the pool sellers. Queens district attorney John Fleming secured indictments and convictions resulting in two-thousand-dollar fines against poolroom men working at the Gleason-protected Puritan Athletic Club.[61]

There were also pending indictments against Western Union, which was apparently convinced to get out of the racing business, although the race wire was its most profitable service. Directors Jay Gould, the infamous robber baron, and banker and railroad executive Russell Sage announced their conscience could not permit them to have anything to do with gambling. Local revenue supposedly ran eighteen thousand dollars a week, or fifty dollars a day, six days a week, for each of the estimated sixty poolrooms in New York that received data from the New Jersey tracks. Nationally, Western Union reportedly made from one to two million dollars a year from its racetrack service. However, Western Union's exit from the racing-wire service was mainly for publicity. The firm actually established a dummy corporation, under Henry Clay Ditmas, a member of its staff, known as the Ditmas News Association that continued sending track results to poolrooms and other facilities. Seventy-five members of the Western Union staff put in four hours a day working for the DNA at Western Union facilities, paid by Western Union.[62]

New York district attorney De Lancey Nicoll ordered one of the first major raids on 23 March, a surprise foray at Mike Minden's poolroom at the busy intersection of Twenty-ninth and Broadway in the heart of Uptown. Minden's, the pride of the pool sellers, was presumed immune from police interference. The entrance on Broadway was under "Minden's," a large sign in gilt letters that led into a well-kept saloon with pictures of horses in gilt frames. His magnificent facility included a reading room warmed by an open fireplace, with cedar walls decorated with oil paintings. His clerks took about a hundred bets an hour. The raid by detectives from the central office occurred after the staff announced the winner of the first race at Guttenberg. The officers arrested the sheet writers.[63]

The Minden's closing had a minimal immediate impact, coming at the end of the winter racing season at Guttenberg and Gloucester, but gave the impression that the police were enforcing the laws. District Attorney Nicoll announced he would let the courts test the legality of the Minden raid before harassing other gamblers. The pool sellers expected that Nicoll and Mayor Grant would continue to look the other way, but the *Times* hoped they would enforce the law, since they "can't afford to be regarded as protectors of the most dangerous class of lawbreakers."[64]

The *Times* lacked confidence in the criminal justice system. It did not trust police inspectors against "a class of malefactors that are so important in local politics as the pool seller." The *Times* complained in early April that the inaction of the authorities was evidence that "the men whom [the public] elect to govern them are governed by powers behind their respective chairs of administration" and blamed the mayor, the district attorney, and the police department.[65]

The seven poolroom workers arrested at the Minden's raid were defended by a star-studded team that included former Republican district attorneys Daniel G. Rollins and John R. Fellows, who was headed to Congress, and the notorious

Howe and Hummel. They were very confident of the outcome, figuring they had the support of Democratic jurors. More than one hundred bookmakers attended the trial and were shocked when guilty verdicts were returned. The Minden's manager got three months and a one-thousand-dollar fine. The outcome showed that the commission-business dodge was a flimsy defense. Inspector Byrnes ordered all poolrooms closed for the near future, and for the next few days, virtually every local poolroom except De Lacy's shut down. However, several reopened in early April.[66]

De Lacy's goal was to monopolize off-track betting. He was a Tammany power broker whose clout protected him. He had recently supported New Jersey reformers in their fight against racing in revenge against the Clifton Racetrack, which the prior summer prevented poolroom operators from getting its results. De Lacy was credited with shutting down Jersey racing outside of Guttenberg and Gloucester in early 1891. He blackmailed the politically powerful Guttenberg Track management into working on his behalf by having them refuse to pay off the Elizabeth and Linden tracks affiliated with Coney Island tracks when they gave up racing dates that benefited Guttenberg. De Lacy blamed the conflict on greedy track operators, especially the Dwyers, and warned, "If they don't let me alone I'll have them planting corn on their track at Gravesend. . . . As for John A. Morris, I will turn his $2,000,000 track into a cornfield too. And I'll do worse for him. I'll see that not a single Louisiana Lottery ticket is sold in this city." De Lacy told a reporter that the Coney Island racing crowd has "got sense enough to see that if they close up the pool-rooms the pool-rooms will close them up."[67]

The Legislature and the Poolrooms

The poolroom operators were under governmental attack on three fronts: the police, the courts, and the state legislature, where antipoolroom bills were being introduced. The poolrooms recognized the growing crisis and hired some of the most aggressive lobbyists in Albany. They demanded protection from Governor David B. Hill in return for their substantial contributions to his recent campaign and for promises of more funds for the Democratic Party for the upcoming fall elections. Their chief representative was Assemblyman Timothy D. "Dry Dollar" Sullivan of the Lower East Side (1886–94), who in 1892 became the party's second assembly district leader and went on to become the number-two man in Tammany Hall. "Big Tim" reportedly had twenty-five to thirty-five thousand dollars at his disposal to influence legislative votes. He later served in the state senate (1894–1903, 1909–12), where he introduced the Sullivan Act (1911) that required gun owners to have permits, and also in the U.S. Congress (1906–9). Historian

Daniel Citron credits him with creating a new big-city political style by combining traditional machine politics (a lot of patronage for his Irish followers, although his ward was increasingly Jewish), commercialized leisure (the equivalent of "bread and circuses," according to historian Steven Erie), and underworld connections with such gangsters as Paul Kelly, Monk Eastman, and Kid Twist, who helped his political campaigns. He was an early proponent of urban machine liberalism, supporting labor reforms and women's suffrage.[68]

Sullivan was a prominent sportsmen who in the early 1890s backed the banned sport of professional boxing, which had found a home at Coney Island. He then played a big role in getting the legislature to pass the Horton Act in 1896 that legalized prizefighting. Thereafter, Sullivan and his partners monopolized the promotion of boxing matches in Manhattan, which reportedly was worth fifty thousand dollars a year. However, the Horton Act was repealed in 1900, and thereafter pro boxing was limited to so-called membership clubs. Sullivan was also heavily involved in off-track gambling. His Centre Street saloon had a second-floor poolroom, but more important, he was the head of the Gambling Trust that determined who could enter the business.[69]

15. Big Tim Sullivan (1862–1913) was one of the major Tammany leaders at the turn of the century. *Source:* Josiah Flynt, "The Pool-Room Vampire and Its Money Mad Victims," *Cosmopolitan* 42 (Feb. 1907): 362.

That spring Senator Charles T. Saxton (R–Wayne County) introduced a bill in Albany to restrict pool selling to racetracks. The BJC and the NYJC supported the bill, but not the CIJC, possibly a result of the political ambitions of certain Coney Island racing officials. The senate approved the Saxton bill, but it died in committee in the assembly. However, Saxton would not give up, and he became a problem for the poolroom operators.[70]

The Poolrooms Reopen

The Poolroom Keepers' Association (PKA) kept its rooms closed from mid-April until 15 May, when, led by about a dozen operators, including De Lacy, "The" Allen, "Shang" Draper, Ridge Levein, and Barney Michaels, they reopened. However, this move might have been bluster, because a day later, only five were in operation, all identified as "commission houses." On advice of counsel, signs were posted all over their rooms, indicating that no bets would be accepted on the premises. They charged ten cents to send wagers directly to the tracks, with winners paid off at the poolroom after the race. De Lacy's clients filled out a form indicating their choices and received a receipt that indicated the firm was acting only as a common carrier to transfer money to the track. However, the money was never taken to the tracks. De Lacy made up his own, less favorable, betting odds compared to the tracks and took wagers right up to post time, making it impossible to make bets at the tracks, even if instructions were wired to waiting agents.[71]

The Tracks Fight Back

The racetrack managers were disheartened at the return of the poolrooms. Phil Dwyer had them agree to take the fight to the poolrooms when the BJC opened on 15 May. He had a particularly strong grievance against De Lacy, whose fight against New Jersey track betting forced Dwyer's Elizabeth course to close. When Gravesend opened the 1891 racing season, Phil Dwyer ordered Western Union's office there closed and refused to allow any dispatches from poolrooms or their agents to the track. This maneuver cost him twenty-five dollars a day that the poolrooms were paying him for information. Western Union formally moved out but continued to send simple messages, using the wire the BJC leased, on the Kiernan News ticker. Dwyer provided wire service for newspapers only after each day's final race and barred transmissions of results to poolrooms. He also instructed Pinkerton guards to prevent known poolroom agents from entering the track.[72]

The poolrooms and the ticker services hatched several schemes to get the results from Gravesend while simultaneously claiming to transmit commissioned bets to the track. De Lacy claimed he sent his commissions to his awaiting agents at Western Union's Sheepshead Bay office, three-fourths of a mile from Gravesend. Meanwhile, Western Union clerks at the BJC sent information after each race by messengers to telephone operators stationed outside the track, who then passed on the data. The Pinkertons soon recognized the dodge. They did not prevent people from leaving the track but compelled anyone who left early to depart from an exit far from where closing odds were posted.[73]

Dwyer quickly decided to be more proactive and on 19 May announced a lock-in once races began, so no one could leave early and send messages to the poolrooms. Some of his 130 Pinkertons clubbed anyone who challenged the order. The press, including the *World* and the *Sun,* largely responded negatively to "jailing racegoers," but not the *Times,* which argued that spectators exiting early were mainly poolrooms' Western Union confederates. The criticism convinced management to retract immediately its decision, and it resumed its policy of making early leavers take a roundabout exit, which the *Tribune* thought was still wrong. The fight against the pools paid off at the box office, though, as the BJC drew its largest spring-meet attendance to date, which was subsequently surpassed by the late-summer meet.[74]

Poolroom agents came up with another scheme to report track results. They laid a telephone wire from Sheepshead Bay to a roadhouse nearly opposite Gravesend, stationed a man on the roof of the building, and smuggled other men into the track. Once inside, an operative reported each race's outcome to his colleague on the roof by hand gestures. The results were then signaled to a confederate, who phoned the results to Sheepshead Bay. From there, the names of winners were wired to poolrooms all over the city.[75]

Western Union tried to circumvent the limitations on early departers by supplying their agents at the track with wooden balls similar to the ones used by ticker services to send messages through pneumatic tubes. The clerks wrote the names of winning horses and track odds inside the balls and then hurled them over the fence to colleagues waiting along a highway. However, the clerks were not the best tossers, and few balls reached their destination; some were even intercepted by vigilant Pinkertons. In another scheme, telegraph workers inside the track designated to represent each horse in a particular race lined themselves up in a row at a location visible to confederates outside the course to simulate the official order of finishers. When Dwyer discovered this ploy, he kicked out the perpetrators. By the end of the meet, Dwyer built a fifty-foot fence around the track to limit visibility from outside. Western Union got around this maneuver by having a worker sit and watch the races from the tower of a nearby hotel.[76]

The poolrooms' difficulty in getting the necessary information left clients in the few open poolrooms extremely dissatisfied. Men sitting at the poolrooms heard very slow race reports that were often so inaccurate that the wrong horse reportedly won. Sometimes the race descriptions included the efforts of scratched horses. Most important, the clients typically got lower payoffs than at the tracks.[77]

While Dwyer ardently fought the poolrooms, other track operators caved in and cooperated with Western Union, which paid them fifteen dollars per poolroom serviced. The poolrooms' substantial political clout threatened most track managers, but not Dwyer, the only Brooklyn operator without business or political alliances that could entangle him with the poolroom men. His struggle with the betting parlors was not morally motivated but financially so, since the rooms drew off potential spectators. The NYJC was afraid to fight the poolrooms because of threatened retaliatory raids on John Morris's policy shops and agents of his Louisiana Lottery. In addition, the *Times* pointed out that the CIJC's managers "happen to be in sympathy with Tammany Hall and deep into politics, and they dare not, therefore, antagonize the poolroom keepers, all of whom are good, loyal Tammany men" who contribute liberally each month to the Hall's "legislative fund." Business at Sheepshead Bay was down, and the bookmakers who paid one hundred dollars a day to operate were angry. The *Times* concluded, "The Coney Island Club is simply reaping the fruit of consorting politically with the Tammany crowd."[78]

The poolrooms became much more active after the end of the BJC's spring meet, boosted by the court of appeals decision in the *Wynn* case on 22 June that overturned his conviction. This ruling put pool sellers in their strongest position ever by apparently legitimizing their current method of doing business. By the end of the month, the press estimated there were seventy-five to one hundred poolrooms in operation.[79]

The racing clubs decided they could compete more effectively against the poolrooms by reducing clients' expenses. It cost about three dollars to take the train and buy a ticket to the Westchester tracks, so the NYJC opened its infield for free in the spring, reducing the cost of attending to fifty-five cents, which paid for a round-trip ticket and a ten-cent program. In addition, Morris Park offered pari-mutuel machines that allowed bettors to wager two dollars on win, place, or show. The plan worked there by getting more people to the track, which produced more revenue for the pari-mutuel machines and concessions. The spring meet took in about twenty-five hundred to three thousand dollars daily just from its 5 percent cut of pari-mutuels. Consequently, when Sheepshead Bay held its June meet without a free field, many racegoers acclimated to the other tracks' free admission policy (including access to the betting ring) chose to stay at home. Jerome Park, along with Brighton Beach, followed with free fields in the early summer. This move made Brighton Beach a bargain for gamblers, who then paid fifty to sixty cents for round-trip travel (depending on the route) and a program.[80]

The *Times* reported in September that the poolrooms were finished and that for the first time in years, there was racing in metropolitan New York without off-track betting: "What the law and the police under the direction of Tammany Hall have found it impossible to do has been perfectly accomplished by the owners of a single racing association, enforcing their own unquestionable legal rights of property. Nothing could be more gratifying in its way and nothing could be more beneficial to horse racing than the showing that pool selling away from track is by no means a necessary accompaniment of the sport."[81]

However, the *Times* was wrong. The poolrooms were not dead, though they were struggling. Western Union sought a rapprochement with Phil Dwyer in late September, offering him sixteen hundred dollars for the privilege of sending Gravesend racing results all over the country, the same as it paid the CIJC and the NYJC. Dwyer countered, asking four thousand dollars, figuring that since Western Union was serving 84 poolrooms in New York, and another 120 around the country, he deserved a bigger share. Dwyer was negotiating from a position of strength because Gloucester was the only other local track operating that did business with Western Union. Many poolrooms promoted business by simulating the Gravesend races in their rooms. However, without the racing wire, they did not even have a complete list of entrants for each race. Some reported results from the Associated Press that were inaccurate and incomplete.[82]

In the meantime, Western Union went to even greater lengths to transmit information on the Gravesend races. One woman signaled information from a window in the ladies' room to a colleague. She waved a handkerchief from an open window, employing Morse code to send the names of competing horses. The company built a crow's nest 120 feet up in the air, a half mile from the track, where an employee tried to watch the races with field glasses without success. (High-quality binoculars became available three years later.) Another complicated scheme involved associates who left the track early, ostensibly to catch a train back to New York. They got on the train and then wrote down the results of the prior race, placed them in a bottle, and tossed the bottle out the window after going about a mile. Telegraph agents retrieved the bottle and forwarded the information.[83]

An imaginative method to transmit data was to employ a coachman to signal off-track associates by concealing a battery-powered telegraph instrument in his hat that set off flashes of light as the current went on and off. This flashing produced a visual code, seen and interpreted at a distance by a Western Union operator. But even more audacious was the employment of women wearing large dresses under which they hid carrier pigeons. After a race was over, they would put notes in a capsule attached to a bird's leg and send it off to its roost. However, track security uncovered this plot. The pigeons were confiscated and later released with false results.[84]

The Poolrooms in 1892

Despite some setbacks in 1891, the poolrooms were operational in 1892, encountering little effective opposition. Philip Dwyer could not single-handedly defeat the rooms, and the racing Board of Control did not marshal racing interests against the poolrooms. In early March, Police Commissioner Charles F. MacLean assailed the Tammany-protected poolrooms at a meeting of the Baptist Social Union, claiming they caused more trouble than the once-monthly sale of lottery tickets.[85]

The *Tribune* continued vigorously fighting the poolrooms, each of which supposedly paid Tammany seventy-five dollars a week to stay in business. The *Tribune* castigated the poolroom menaces who "rob and plunder more people daily than are despoiled by all the pickpockets, burglars, bunco-steerers and thieves of every sort in this city." Their clients "are as completely under the spell of the vilest and most debated form of gambling as the opium eater is enthralled by the fascination of the maleficent drug which holds him captive." It particularly noted that bettors "were fleeced and swindled" and driven to destitution during the winter when they bet on the races at Guttenberg and Gloucester, "which are so clearly prearranged swindles and frauds as are the tricks of the thimble-rigger and the bunco-steerer." The *Tribune* believed it was possible to halt off-track betting, noting the closure of Brooklyn's poolrooms. It chastised the New York district attorney and the New York Police Department for not doing their jobs and recommended the Police Board put all captains and their superiors on trial unless the poolrooms were immediately closed.[86]

The Brighton Beach racecourse provided some help against the poolrooms. Its management informed recently promoted Police Superintendent Byrnes on July 6 that it would not accept poolroom commissions, which meant that any poolroom claiming to transmit bets there was lying. The course also halted business with Western Union, unable to agree on the fee. The result that day was that Brighton Beach drew eight thousand people, its largest crowd of the season.[87]

The popular middlebrow *Harper's Weekly* brought the poolroom evil to national attention with two articles in 1892. The magazine reported that the "poolroom evil" far surpassed gambling at tracks or stock exchanges because the rooms were wide-open and "nearly as accessible as the corner bar." District Attorney

Nicoll admitted to its reporter that he could do nothing, even though mothers had told him how gambling ruined their children and employers told him how their workers embezzled to cover their losses. *Harper's* identified bellhops, whose jobs put them in with bad crowds, as especially tempted by the poolroom evil. They often acted as betting agents for friends, notably inexperienced clerks, artisans, and other small-wager earners.[88]

The 1893 Antipoolroom Crusade

The antipoolroom movement came to a head in 1893, at which time there were an estimated 60 to 175 poolrooms in New York. An agent of the International Law and Order League claimed the annual local gambling income was about ten million dollars. The *Tribune* in early March published an editorial, "To Close the City Poolrooms," that decried the poolrooms as among the most "thoroughly efficacious" vice institutions in the city, driving losers to financial ruin, leading to criminality. The editors estimated that at least six hundred thousand dollars a week, "drawn mostly from the pockets of men who do not earn more than $20 a week, change hands in these poolrooms." A few days later, the *Tribune* called the poolroom menace "a worse pestilence than cholera, smallpox, or yellow fever."[89]

Michael F. Dwyer, like his brother, who had pushed the poolrooms out of Brooklyn, also sought to close New York poolrooms. Dwyer had recently moved to Manhattan, following his wife's death, leaving his neighborhood known as "Sportsmen's Row," where he and his brother had lived. The move was reportedly because of his close ties to Boss Croker.[90]

Observers might have expected Croker to back the poolrooms with their clout and their lucrative payoffs. Instead, he became Dwyer's ally in the antipoolroom fight, befitting his own interests as a breeder and thoroughbred owner. The *Brooklyn Eagle* indicated that "the coalition . . . between the Brooklyn turf man and the New York politician promises many things of good import of legitimate racing so far as rightly directly political influence can bring them out." Cleaning up the poolrooms topped their agenda.[91]

New York's police started a concentrated effort to close up the poolrooms, which Superintendent Byrnes attributed to Croker's involvement, notably the pressure he put on Mayor Thomas F. Gilroy. Thereafter, police magistrates were told to do their duty and convict alleged poolroom men.[92]

Byrnes began the crackdown on 13 March with a rare attack on fourteen flourishing poolrooms, seeking sufficient evidence to upset the commission subterfuge. He sent undercover detectives to make wagers at different poolrooms at the last possible moment on the second race at Guttenberg, while other officers went to the track to note the event's exact starting time of 3:03 p.m. Some operatives actually bought their tickets shortly after the races were over, making it physically impossible for their wagers to have been sent to the track and bet there. The district attorney pursued three cases involving five arrested poolroom operators to test the law. The major rooms all closed down under advice of their counsel until the matter was resolved.[93]

The *Times* applauded the raids, urging the police and judges to deal roughly with poolroom workers: "The poolroom evil should be absolutely suppressed" because it was just as "demoralizing and mischievous as the maintenance of lotteries." The editors called for the closing of all loopholes and encouraged restricting horse wagering as much as possible.[94]

The *Tribune* commended Byrnes who had demonstrated that no organized vice operation could exist in New York without the practical consent of the police department. However, even with good police work, Tammany still protected its criminal friends through its control of the district attorney's office, the police courts, and other lesser courts.[95]

The gamblers amassed a $300,000 fund to fight back and hired Benjamin Steinhardt of Howe and Hummel to defend the arrested poolroom men. He blamed the harassment as retaliation by jockey clubs against off-track parlors for taking away business and for hurting racing's prestige, injured in 1892 by rumors of fixed races.[96]

The Saxton Poolroom Bill

While the police were busily going after the poolrooms, a movement was underfoot in Albany to toughen off-track betting laws, especially loopholes that permitted poolrooms to evade the law through the commission system. In early March, Republican state senator Saxton and Democratic assemblyman Urban Prescott of the small western town of Machias (Cattaraugus County) introduced a new antipoolroom bill prepared by the Society for the Suppression of Vice that made keeping a poolroom and serving as a commission agent for off-track clients a felony, penalized by a one- to five-year prison sentence. The Saxton bill was widely praised by the press, especially since making the crime a felony took prosecution taken away from the lower courts, where Tammany was the most influential. The poolroom interests bitterly opposed the bill, which sought to close them down. Howe and Hummel reportedly offered the SSV $10,000 to drop the bill and instead try to repeal the Ives Act.[97]

The Saxton bill passed handily, with a lot of credit going to the Dwyer-Croker alliance. The only opposition in the senate was from Tammany district leader

George Washington Plunkitt and Brooklyn's Democratic leader, Pat McCarren, a renowned turf plunger. In the assembly, Republicans held their first caucus in three years and agreed to vote for the Saxton bill exactly as it came from the senate. "Dry Dollar" Sullivan tried to kill the bill with various amendments, but it won easy passage, 112–7, despite rumors of payoffs of $250–$500 a vote. Sullivan, the poolroom's chief supporter in Albany, then tried to get the legislature to overturn the Ives Law and bar all gambling. His pandering proposal to improve public morality was a smoke screen to save the poolrooms, because without legal gambling, the police would cooperate with the pool men and continue to look the other way. On 25 April, Republican governor Roswell P. Flower signed the Saxton bill, making off-track betting a felony.[98]

The passage of the Saxton Act encouraged many poolroom operators to move across the Hudson River to New Jersey. Even Assemblyman Tim Sullivan, the poolroom's best friend in Albany, admitted that "now they have the poolrooms hard and fast." De Lacy opened a big room in Fort Lee, just opposite Manhattan, that focused on Morris Park and the Jersey winter tracks. Guttenberg tried to bar him from getting their results so they could keep up their own attendance. Morris Park also fought De Lacy by keeping him out of the information circuit, allowing only wire services that transmitted results to the West and South.[99]

In 1893, the police, under Superintendent Thomas F. Byrnes, confiscated 24,900 pool tickets, about the same as in 1889 (23,615), and a big increase from 1887, the first year of the Ives Act, when they garnered 9,380 pool tickets. In addition, the police also confiscated two betting slates and eight record books, not a very impressive haul. The department did not maintain separate records for poolroom arrests, aggregating them among all arrests for gambling.[100]

The Poolrooms Come Back

Passing the Saxton Act turned out a lot easier than enforcing it against the more than one hundred poolrooms in Manhattan alone, including one in Mrs. Adeline Eichorn's home at Thirty-eighth Street that catered to women. Each new poolroom reportedly paid a $500 initiation fee to the Poolroom Keepers' Association, which controlled most of New York's poolrooms.[101] According to "The" Allen, one of the most infamous connected poolroom men, in the business since at least 1878, the PKA's two hundred members spent about $1.5 million on payoffs to Tammany. They each contributed $6,000 to the fund, except one who put up $3,000. Allen claimed the PKA contributed more to Tammany than any other organization in the city.[102]

That summer, the gambling resort of "Little Monte Carlo" opened, two hundred yards north of New York City, connected to "some of the corrupt Democratic officials of the Democratic ring of Westchester County." The poolroom took bets on several tracks close up to post time. Its establishment dramatically increased traffic along the West Farm trolley line, whose stockholders, not coincidentally, included many of the county's Democratic power brokers as well as members of Tammany Hall. The room drew more than four thousand patrons a day and eight thousand on a busy afternoon. Sheriff Duffy of Westchester, who saw nothing wrong was going on, was subsequently brought up on charges before Governor Flower by the League for the Enforcement of the Law for failure to close a poolroom in his jurisdiction.[103]

The Lexow Investigation

In September 1894, the Republican-dominated state senate initiated a major inquiry, known as the Lexow Investigation, which was one of the widest-ranging government studies ever of police matters, ranging from crime detection to relationships with local politicians. Republican senator Clarence Lexow's committee demonstrated how Tammany and the police department collected bribes from the underworld involved in such illegal enterprises as prostitution and gambling. The committee subpoenaed more than three hundred people and heard testimony from more than six hundred. The statements were often reported verbatim in the *Times,* and the published report was more than ten thousand pages long.[104]

One area of inquiry was the relationship between Tammany, the police, and poolrooms. Several prominent police leaders testified, including Police Commissioner John C. Sheehan, who was asked why the department did not make a major effort to close the poolrooms from 1887, when the Ives Law was passed, until April 1893, when requested by Boss Croker. This segment was highlighted by the testimony of Capt. Max F. Schmittberger of the Tenderloin precinct, who admitted that his ward men (detectives) collected $200 a month in payoffs from two poolrooms on Canal Street, some of which ended up at police headquarters on the desk of Inspector Thomas F. McAvoy. Schmittberger claimed poolrooms could not exist without his or McAvoy's knowledge. The captain previously worked on the Upper East Side, where he made monthly collections from three poolrooms that he shared with Inspector "Clubber" Williams. After the hearings, Schmittberger was transferred to Kingsbridge, in the Bronx, which had the "leanest in pickings of any in the city." The hearings contributed to a Republican sweep of state offices in 1894, the passage of a referendum on the revised state constitution, and the election of Republican William L. Strong as head of a fusion ticket as mayor of New York.[105]

Peter De Lacy and the Defense of the Poolrooms

In 1895, the revised state constitution all but banned horse racing (see chapter 8), but the turf managed to keep the sport operating through the Percy-Gray Act that created a state racing commission to supervise the sport. The legislature also passed the Wilds Act, which reasserted the illegality of poolrooms. Nonetheless, poolrooms remained open in freestanding downtown betting parlors, back rooms, or second floors of Tenderloin saloons and across the Hudson River in Harrison and Hoboken, New Jersey. One Manhattan room was run under the guise of a bucket shop, with the blackboards full of stock prices. The rooms operated under political protection, providing advance warnings of police raids and help in bailing out and defending any arrested workers.[106]

Peter De Lacy, the driving force behind the poolrooms, soon tried to get Percy-Gray declared unconstitutional through two test cases he arranged with Howe and Hummel that focused on an article of the new law concerning sweepstakes (races for which the stakes were put up by the competing horse owners) and races at his unlicensed Flushing Jockey Club. He had a race staged there on 15 May 1895, with a sweepstakes offered in place of traditional wagering, but the winners were not paid off. John C. Dudley sued the FJC to recover $175, the value of a sweepstakes won by his horse, Brown Dick. He contended that the four horses entered put up $100 and the Flushing Jockey Club another $100. Dudley got back only his $25 entrance fee. In the other test case, Harry C. Judson claimed the FJC swindled him and sued for $225 in winnings. Dudley's attorney, Benjamin Steinhardt, argued that the sweepstakes was a fund created by the horse owners who raced for a prize of their own creation, tantamount to a lottery. On 28 August, Judge Henry Bischoff in the court of common pleas ruled for the plaintiff, agreeing with Steinhardt's position that the race was a lottery. Then he asserted that Percy-Gray was unconstitutional because it permitted the operation of a sweepstakes, but the constitution banned any gambling. However, in the *Judson* case, Justice Leonard A. Giegerich ruled just the opposite, that Percy-Gray was constitutional.[107]

The Dudley ruling surprised the racing elite, who worried it might hinder the upcoming meet at Morris Park. The CIJC, where every race that season was a "sweepstakes," ordered their attorneys to take up the matter, which they believed was a trumped-up affair, orchestrated by De Lacy to retaliate against TJC's efforts to close his poolrooms. The court called for a reargument to resolve the contrasting decisions before former judge Van Hose. Former district attorney De Lancey

Nicoll and attorney Joseph Auerbach represented the State Racing Commission, facing off against Steinhardt and Joel Marx, who represented the FJC as well as the two complainants. The SRC's attorneys claimed that De Lacy was both plaintiff and a defendant in these cases and was trying to trick the court into making a decision so he could get his revenge on the tracks. Witnesses testified that De Lacy orchestrated this sham event, ordering Steinhardt to set up the races on the morning of 15 May, without prior public advertisement, as normally employed before a race. Steinhardt served as judge, timer, and starter. Almost no spectators were present to watch four livery and stable horses meander over a half-mile course. Most important, for the case at hand, the litigants were De Lacy's puppets. Dudley was a porter at De Lacy's poolroom, where Judson's father was the doorman. The referee threw the cases out as collusion, making Judge Bischoff's ruling on Percy-Gray moot.[108]

The Jockey Club and other prominent racing men expected De Lacy and his poolroom friends to seek revenge because the SRC closed down De Lacy's Newtown Jockey Club that operated the crime-riddled Maspeth racetrack. De Lacy was also angry with the newly established Westchester Racing Association that took over the Morris Park Racetrack because of its close ties to TJC and the State Racing Commission.[109]

The WRA decided to act rather than wait for a diabolical De Lacy plot. District Attorney John R. Fellows hosted a meeting that included Police Commissioners Andrew Parker and Theodore Roosevelt, Acting Police Inspector John McCullagh, SRC chairman Belmont, TJC counsel Joseph Auerbach, Secretary John Boden of TJC, President Col. Samuel R. Lawrence of the WRA, and its renowned corporate attorney, Elihu Root, a future secretary of war and secretary of state. They arranged their own test case in which Lawrence would be arrested for advertising a meet contrary to Judge Bischoff's recent legal ruling. Belmont also wrote a letter to James Gordon Bennett, the wealthy owner of the *Herald,* criticizing him for letting his paper allow Howe and Hummel to influence racing attitudes and thereby hinder turf reform.[110]

The test case originated when the WRA offered a prize to the owner of the winning horse in a stakes race on 12 October, in which a portion of the purse came from entrance fees. Lawrence was arrested for contriving a lottery, pool selling, and maintaining a nuisance. The case went to trial two days later, with Lawrence defended by Auerbach and Root. The next day, Justice George L. Ingraham in the New York Court of Oyer and Terminer, the criminal branch of the state supreme court and the highest court of original jurisdiction in the state, ruled that racing for prizes was legal and did not constitute a lottery. Most of the press applauded his decision.[111]

In the meantime, De Lacy, together with the Anti-Gambling League, represented by Steinhardt, orchestrated a raid on Morris Park on 24 October to test Percy-Gray. Thirteen men were charged with gambling or recording bets, and the judges and the clerk of the scale were arrested for assisting in maintaining a lottery. Lawrence himself was arrested the following day. August Belmont disclosed that De Lacy had offered to stop interfering with the WRA for a $200,000 bribe. He intended to use the money to pay for lobbyists, organize lawsuits, and obtain police protection. At this time, poolroom operators were paying De Lacy $100 a week to secure police protection.[112]

Orlando Jones, the well-known bookmaker, was selected from among the arrested men to stand trial and test the legality of Percy-Gray. Jones said he had taken bets from people he personally knew and that his clerk, Joseph Sturgis, had recorded their names in a book. All financial exchanges were by check, and no betting paraphernalia was discovered. Jones denied he was a bookmaker, that is, a public poster of odds who took bets from anyone and received cash from clients. The court released Jones but held over Sturgis and Lawrence for trial. On 18 December, Justice Ingraham dismissed their cases, upholding the legality of Percy-Gray. He ruled that Sturgis's recording of bets did not make him a bookmaker, released Lawrence because the WRA was not conducting a lottery, and claimed that private betting was legitimate. Ingraham argued that since the outcome of a race depended on speed, endurance, and strength, a bettor was wagering not on chance (like in a lottery) but on his ability to evaluate the merits of different horses to select a probable winner.[113]

Anthony Comstock and the Poolroom Raids

Anthony Comstock had his hands in many matters but still actively fought the poolrooms, particularly in Long Island City. In May 1896, he assigned agents to gather evidence on the poolrooms there and in July invaded Mayor Patrick J. Gleason's domain with the begrudging support of Sheriff Doht of Queens County. Doht supported the venture only after Republican governor Levi P. Morton, who was very familiar with the gambling situation in Long Island City, wrote him to do his duty. Comstock organized a raid against a gambling house in a building owned by Gleason and two poolrooms in the Blissville area. One room, reportedly financed by Murphy, was in Alderman Richard E. Kane's roadhouse. The other room was in Michael Tuite's roadhouse, backed by Gleason's Front Street Clique. A mob of more than one hundred sports and toughs, including firemen from Engine Company No. 2, repeatedly threatened Comstock and his cohorts as they took the arrested men to court.[114]

Comstock did not rest on his laurels, convinced that prominent bookmakers had found a scheme whereby they could still operate under cover. After Percy-Gray passed, a number of well-known professional gamblers were spotted in New York, including Joe Ullman, president of the notorious East St. Louis Jockey Club, rated by the *Times* as the greatest bookmaker in America. Ullman reputedly made about $160,000 at his track and in nearby St. Louis, where he ran the foreign book. Ullman bet as much as $20,000 with other bookmakers and took bets on his own at Sheepshead Bay, including some from a Comstock agent. In the early fall of 1896, Comstock secured the arrest of Ullman, his brother Alexander, and two other men at a poolroom on West Twenty-sixth Street in Manhattan, simultaneous with the arrest of three of their sheet writers at Gravesend. The Ullmans claimed they were operating a brokerage company that provided a betting service to clients, taking wagers placed with them to the track where they were bet, but the Ullmans were simply operating as bookmakers.[115]

Comstock's raids received considerable publicity but had little impact. Poolrooms remained wide-open in Queens County in 1897, especially in Long Island City. The *Brooklyn Eagle* was not surprised, since the county could rely only on sheriff's deputies and town constables. It decried Long Island City as a wide-open paradise governed by a free and easy mayor who seemed to represent local poolroom proprietors who were rarely interrupted. Elsewhere in Queens that summer, scores of residents complained to District Attorney William J. Youngs about poolrooms, dance houses, and houses of ill repute that abounded in Ridgewood, a community one mile from Brooklyn, especially on Saturdays, which was payday. A poolroom at John Homeyer's park there often had about twelve to fifteen hundred patrons. The room was raided in early July, and the proprietor and his staff were fined about $3,000. However, business immediately resumed, taking in $3,000 to $4,000 a day and netting a profit of $400 to $500.[116]

TR

At this time, probably no police official was as committed to cleaning up the poolrooms as Theodore Roosevelt, who became president of the Police Board in May 1895, a position he held for two years. The future president had a strong sense of civic duty and responsibility and had already served three terms in the state assembly, run unsuccessfully for mayor in 1886, and chaired the U.S. Civil Service Commission. He was committed to reforming the police department and was especially concerned with suppressing vice. Roosevelt pushed for greater efforts against gambling that resulted in more raids, arrests, and seizures of property, along with greater scrutiny of organized gambling, than ever before.

TABLE 3. NEW YORK CITY POLICE AND GAMBLING ARRESTS, 1888–99

Year	Arrests	Convictions (%)	Dismissals (%)	Pending (%)	Fines ($)	Cash seized ($)
1888	276	27 (9.8)	135 (48.9)	114 (41.3)	3,940	3,428.09
1889	292	63 (21.6)	143 (49.0)	86 (29.4)	4,103	2,377.18
1890	409	103 (25.2)	195 (47.7)	111 (27.1)	6,688	7,732.63
1891	358	78 (21.8)	146 (40.8)	134 (37.4)	1,482	2,093.49
1892	497	186 (37.4)	244 (49.1)	67 (13.5)	1,144	380.58
1893	605	197 (32.6)	342 (56.5)	66 (10.9)	1,250	13,918.59
1894	776	322 (42.8)	323 (41.6)	131 (16.9)	4,106	1,530.96
1895	1,443	336 (23.3)	883 (61.2)	224 (15.5)	3,360	754.51
1896	1,570	455 (28.9)	865 (55.1)	250 (15.9)	3,199	3,383.14
1897	816	55 (6.7)	538 (66.0)	223 (27.3)	610	601.47
1898	1,076	342 (31.8)	590 (54.8)	144 (13.4)	1,317	1,000.87
1899	1,333	591 (44.3)	663 (49.7)	79 (5.9)	1,077	1,242.75

Source: New York City Police Department, *Annual Report of the Police Department of the City of New York* (New York: Martin B. Brown, 1889–1900).

Vice squads repeatedly inspected private clubs with uniformed men outside to discourage business.

There was a big increase in police activity under Roosevelt, as gambling arrests nearly doubled from 776 in 1894 to 1,443 in 1895, with a smaller increase in 1896 to 1,570. There were more arrests in those two years than any other in the decade. However, the conviction rate of 42.8 percent in 1894 fell to 23.3 percent in 1895 and 28.9 percent in 1896. The rate bottomed out in 1897, at merely 6.7 percent, but jumped up to 44.3 percent in 1899, a record up to then. In regards to horse race gambling materials, the police had little to show for their efforts. In 1894, the police seized no gambling paraphernalia. Two years later, despite Roosevelt's vigorous leadership, the police confiscated all of 10 racing cards, 3 receipt books, 17 racing tickets, and 107 racing programs. However, they did recover 124 books of records, which was a potentially invaluable haul. Overall, from 1888 to 1899, only 29.2 percent of cases resulted in convictions, compared to a 53.6 percent rate of dismissals.[117]

The State of Poolrooms at the End of the Century

In September 1897, President Frank Moss of the Board of Police Commissioners, a prominent Republican lawyer and president and counsel of the SPC, claimed that his men had nearly killed off the poolrooms. Moss investigated poolrooms upon taking over as president and found them largely operating freely, with significant police collusion, that went up from the men on the beat to headquarters. Moss discovered that poolroom men were being warned about raids by messages sent from police headquarters by an unknown party signed "Falk." The tips were sent to the central office of the Gleason poolroom syndicate, which used to be at 197 Bowery Street, with branches in six cities, that for some years had been sending out sporting news to at least twelve cities. The syndicate also had another major office at 2068 Fifth Avenue, from which it sent results to affiliated poolrooms throughout New York. Moss claimed his men closed Gleason's operation, though it still had a Midtown office (Forty-second and Sixth). James Mahoney ran another big syndicate, headquartered in the Knickerbocker Building (Thirty-eighth and Broadway), which was then supposedly moribund.[118]

Poolrooms received little mention in the press for more than a year, but they had not disappeared. In 1898, however, there was an important article in *Harper's Weekly* in conjunction with Richard Croker's return from Europe, titled "Wide-Open New York." Author Franklin Mathews, who had written a similar article about Chicago one year earlier, reported that the one hundred poolrooms in New York were charged three hundred dollars to open and one to three hundred dollars a month for protection. Franklin claimed that a man close to Croker (presumably Big Tim Sullivan) was in charge, and the rooms were back in business. They printed odds on a paper card on races at four different tracks.[119]

The State Racing Commission criticized the policy of benign neglect. The SRC hired its own detectives, who confirmed the activity of poolrooms at record levels, and forwarded the data to the police. Police Chief John McCullagh, hired in 1897 with the backing of the Police Board to suppress gambling, led fifteen policemen in the only major raid in 1898. The officers broke into "The" Allen's club, a three-story brick building at 80 Sixth Avenue, reputedly the worst poolroom in the city. They arrested Allen, "an undersized man with a stoop, with lank, dark hair growing too thinly to cover the baldness of the top of his head, with a high, bold forehead, and small, humid, grayish eyes, a short mustache, which would be white if it was not dyed a dense black and a face wrinkled and seamed." His rooms had been raided more than a hundred times. He himself had been accused of many crimes, including murder. "The" Allen claimed he was just a sporting man who owned the West Side Club in the back of the building and despised gamblers.[120]

The police used axes and "jimmies" to break in the hall door and then broke through the vestibule door inside that was secured by bolt and chain. By then, employees had cut the telegraph wires and removed the apparatus. The clientele "were in various stags of shabbiness and looked like a gathering of broken-down followers of the races and gambles of the lower orders." Bettors wagered by putting their money with slips containing their names, amounts bet, and horses selected under screens. Winners presented duplicate slips for their payoffs.[121]

16. "The" Allen's Poolroom at 80 Sixth Avenue, on the second floor of the building. Allen was one of the most notorious gamblers in New York, with more than two hundred arrests. He was reportedly worth five hundred thousand dollars at the time of his death. *Source:* Josiah Flynt, "The Men Behind the Pool-Rooms," *Cosmopolitan* 42 (Apr. 1907): 642.

McCullagh's relations with the two Democratic members of the Police Board, President Bernard J. York, a protégé of Brooklyn boss Hugh McLaughlin, and John B. Sexton, a Tammany district leader and undersheriff in New York County, soon fell apart, especially after Sexton ordered him to transfer a number of officers and he refused. Sexton sought to transfer Patrolman Mathew McConnell after he raided one of gambler Frank Farrell's poolrooms that was protected by Big Tim Sullivan. In response, Mayor Van Wick fired the two Republican commissioners and then pushed McCullagh into retirement, replaced by the crooked William Devery, who ran the department for his own and Tammany Hall's profit.[122]

Conclusion

The poolroom business prospered in New York City and the surrounding metropolitan area despite the earnest efforts of reformers and racing men to curtail it. Raids by reformers such as Anthony Comstock; laws such as the Anti-Pool Room Act of 1877, the Ives Act, and the Saxton Act; and efforts by track operators to kick out the poolrooms' agents from the racetracks failed to halt organized crime and the gambling menace, protected by their allies in Tammany Hall, city hall, the police department, and the local courts.

As the century came to an end, the poolrooms were still flourishing, and the heads of a powerful gambling syndicate "licensed" new poolrooms that paid an initiation fee and additional monthly fees in return for permission to operate and protection from municipal interference. The city's poolroom connection to Tammany was featured in the state legislature's 1899 investigation of police corruption in New York City. Soon thereafter, the public learned of a notorious multimillion-dollar poolroom trust masterminded by Big Tim Sullivan that included Frank Farrell (owner of New York's most luxurious casino), Police Chief Devery, and Mayor Robert Van Wyck that controlled about four hundred poolrooms.[123]

8

New York Racing
under Attack, 1894–96

Persons who want to race horses should not be hindered from doing so, provided that they can have their sport without doing too much harm to the community. The Gray bill and the measures supplementary to it represent an attempt to make legitimate racing practicable in New York State, and to minimize all the evils that have been used to accompany it.

—"New Hopes for Horse Racing," *Harper's Weekly,* 18 May 1895

B y late 1894, there was a lot of momentum behind the efforts of reformers to end horse race gambling in New York State, especially since neighboring New Jersey had just closed its racetracks and Chicago's prestigious Washington Park also halted operations. The antigambling coalition focused its attention on the meeting in September of the fifth state constitution convention, and the first since 1867, where they hoped to place specific wording in the document to bar such wagering. Their voices found a lot of support among the predominantly Republican, rural, and upstate delegates who drew up a document that seemingly meant the termination of the racing game in New York, especially after the voters ratified the revised constitution. However, the racing crowd employed its own political clout to get new laws passed that saved the turf despite the proscriptions in the state's fundamental legal code. New York became the first state to establish a state racing commission to supervise the sport, operating in conjunction with the elite, self-appointed Jockey Club. Thoroughbred racing survived in the Empire State for another fifteen years despite the glaring disconnect between the new state law and the constitution.

Racing and the State Constitution

The new state constitution had a number of innovations, mostly aimed at weakening the power of metropolitan New York's Democratic machines. The number of

214

assemblymen rose from 128 to 150 and senators from 32 to 50, to give upstate New York more representation in the legislature. No more than half the seats could go to New York and Brooklyn. In addition, future state elections would be in alternate years from municipal elections, also to weaken machine influence.[1] The convention also dealt with social issues, including the fate of horse race gambling. Social reformers, clergymen, and other turf critics seized the moment to amend the constitution to totally ban gambling, particularly wagering on horses. Sentiment in the state had been growing against the gambling evil, particularly poolrooms where young men, especially low-paid clerks and blue-collar workers, and even women, would steal a few moments from their jobs to bet their hard-earned funds or, worse, stolen money. Even betting at tracks had lost considerable public support following years of publicity about the negative impact of horse race gambling. Reformer Anthony Comstock, the leader of antigambling moralists, lobbied hard against horse race betting, often reciting tales of poor youths becoming criminals because of gambling debts. His supporters included some unusual allies, such as Morris Tekulsky of the Liquor Dealers' Association, whose complaint against racing was that the sport diverted money from saloons. The turf had some outstanding leaders like Belmont, Lorillard, and Keene, but thoroughbred racing had really fallen in public esteem because of proprietary owners like the Dwyers and Engemans, more interested in lining their purses than in improving the breed, and frequent reports about fixed races.[2]

The debate on gambling was closely followed by social reformers and the racing community outside New York because the outcome was expected to influence the racing scene elsewhere, as in Illinois, where a measure to kill racing had already nearly passed. The debate over horse betting began when Fred Storms of Bay Shore, Long Island, presented an amendment to Section 9, Article 1, of the Constitution with the new phrase: "Nor the sale of lottery tickets, pool selling, bookmaking or any other kind of gambling hereafter be authorized or allowed within this state, and the Legislature shall pass appropriate laws to prevent offences against any of the provisions of this section." Storms had been petitioned by the Flushing Village Association, a neighborhood improvement group, to do something about the poorly regarded Aqueduct Racetrack that blighted their locality. The FVA complained that under the Ives Law, the authorities could not prevent low-class racing in their neighborhood.[3]

Several newspapers in New York City and elsewhere saw the amendment as a Republican, or anti-Tammany, measure backed by small-town WASPs trying to exercise social control over the urban masses. It was also seen as politically motivated because track operators and horsemen were disproportionately Democratic and often Tammanyites. Furthermore, as the *Tribune* noted, "The bookmakers at most eastern tracks were controlled by Democratic bosses, Democratic rings and the Democratic Party in general."[4]

The *Spirit of the Times* followed developments because it recognized that Storms's amendment would end all trotting and race meetings since they could not survive without bookmaking, and that outcome would be unfair to racing fans and detrimental to the breeding industry. The weekly estimated that there were more than one hundred stock and breeding farms in the United States, constituting a $300 million industry. New York was second only to Kentucky as a racing state, with around a hundred tracks and sixty-five agricultural societies closely connected to racing. More than $50 million was invested in trotting tracks and stock farms alone. The state had trotting meets in Syracuse, Binghamton, Elmira, Albany, and Buffalo, all important stops in the Grand Circuit, which, the *Spirit* claimed, promoted tourism. Buffalo's two-week meet had a total purse of $75,000, and Rochester's was $50,000. The *Spirit* also pointed out that in 1893, thoroughbred tracks had paid $113,000 in taxes that went to county fairs for prizes to encourage animal breeding and agricultural operations. Then, in 1894, with a new law that taxed gross receipts instead of net, the state collected $180,345 from the racecourses, a one-year increase of about 160 percent. The *Spirit* thought that halting racing would mostly hurt the "little people." Local fairs would lose an important source of revenue, and small breeders would have to close, while the bigger breeders would relocate their farms and ship their horses to other markets.[5]

The *Chicago Daily News* countered the *Spirit*, arguing that the turf's financial contribution was overestimated. Racing's main financial value, particularly in major population centers, was the real estate. The *Daily News* estimated that the metropolitan racetracks were worth $6.5 million, led by Morris Park, at more than $2.5 million, Sheepshead Bay $2 million, Gravesend $1 million, and Brighton $500,000. The lesser Long Island tracks were worth a combined $500,000.[6]

The *Times* expected the pool-selling amendment would be the second most contentious issue at the convention after a section on apportionment, because it meant the end of racing. It expected the combined forces of breeders, racing associations, and track patrons would make a big fight. Also alarmed by the proposed amendment were members of stock and grain exchanges, worried the law might be construed to bar the sale of futures, options, and short stocks. The *Times* warned that passage of the amendment still left enforcement contingent upon legislative action, never a sure thing, especially if public sentiment did not demand new laws to bar pool selling and bookmaking. Otherwise, the Ives Pool Law would still be in effect, permitting betting at the tracks.[7]

The working-class *Herald* opposed the amendment because it embodied a "narrow, puritanical prohibition which is not in keeping with the liberal public sentiment of the day and has no proper place in the fundamental law of the first State in the Union." The *Herald* pointed out that the civilized world accepted horse racing as a legitimate sport. It reiterated the economic argument and criticized the proposal for taking away power from the legislature to consider in any way permitting racing. The *Herald* wanted the state to face the real problem: "The pools selling is the source of demoralizing abuses that must be suppressed in the interest of public morality. . . . Suppress the evil. But to attain this end it is not only unnecessary, but reckless, to go to an extreme which will do more harm than good."[8]

The debate was largely window dressing because passage of the antiracing codicil was nearly certain from the start, since the Republican majority at the convention overwhelmingly favored the amendment. It passed by a vote of 109–4. After the convention approved the revised constitution, the legislature approved it and sent it to the voters for their consent. A few weeks before the referendum, Peter De Lacy, one of the antigambling amendment's self-proclaimed strongest advocates, put out an open letter pointing out that the big names of racing feared that there would be no attendance at the tracks without betting. "The plain fact," he noted, "is that the pools sold and the books made on the races at the track form the greater part of the large receipts of the [horse racing] trust and hence contribute the principle part of the money realized by the members of the trust."[9]

De Lacy claimed the gambling trust had spent $350,000 to pass the Ives bill, whose "sole object was to compel the bookmakers to yield to the greedy demands of the trust and to drive them to the tracks." He criticized track managers who were "indifferent to the fact their enormous gains are wrung from the slaves of the gambling passion; a vice worse than the passion for drink, dragging thousands and tens of thousands of men and women down to poverty, and even death." Finally, De Lacy noted the degrading scenes in the stands, including women gambling: "Is it an unusual sight to see women on the grand stands, with their hands filled with bills, yelling, cursing, and swearing at the jockeys in a close finish? . . . Can anything be conceived more vile than to hold out inducements to weak women, afflicted with the gambling mania, to steal their husband's money, set aside probably for the rent, and to squander it on the race track?"[10]

As the election neared, New Yorkers saw the Chicago gambling situation as portentous for the future of racing, especially since the Windy City's antigambling crusade had made such great headway. As the *Tribune* pointed out, "Even in Chicago the true metropolis of the country for faro, keno, roulette and pools, the gambling hells have been invaded by the police and the votaries of chance have been routed." The reality, of course, was far different, since Chicago remained a wide-open town.[11]

Surprisingly, the reform- and independent-minded *Times* criticized the convention for going too far in its fight against gambling and potentially harming the breeding industry. The paper thought that pool selling was the principal problem and that the Ives Law already empowered the authorities to fight it, while TJC effectively disciplined pool sellers who took bets on out-of-town races. The editors wondered, "Is it worthwhile to take these facilities away from the tracks at the cost of destroying the turf, wiping out the capital invested in blooded horses, and arresting so far as this state is concerned, the improvement in horse breeding that is undoubtedly the consequences, as it is the public justification, of horse racing? In Continental Europe, this improvement in the breed of horses is the concern of the State, and the fostering of racing for this purpose is also a Government matter."[12]

The *Times* wanted to salvage racing, which financed agricultural fairs. The sport enabled breeders to raise top colts, for otherwise breeding might be reduced to the production of ordinary commercial horses, a declining business with the displacement of horse-drawn streetcars by electrified trolley cars and the replacement of private horses by bicycles. "Is it worth while [*sic*] to make an end of horse racing, and of the unquestionable public benefits that come from horse racing, now that the abuses that were justly complained of have been removed by the existing and stringent law?"[13]

The *Spirit of the Times* joined the *Times* in justifying racing because of the need to build up the breed. The *Spirit* also argued that the track was not merely a place for gambling but a means to an end, unlike baseball, which was just a pastime:

> Horse racing is a sport, the greatest of all out-door sports; but it is more than that, it is the pleasurable end of the greatest breeding industries in the world. The race-track and the trotting track has developed the two most valuable breeds of horses in the world, and it is only in contests of speed that the best of those breed can be discovered, and it is only by breeding the best to the best that the superiority of these breeds can be maintained. It is true that the vast majority of the thousands who go to the race or trotting tracks, go simply to be amused, but they are indirectly assisting in the development and prosperity of the great breeding industry which is a vast source of wealth to the State.[14]

In contrast, the conservative *Tribune* vigorously supported the antigambling amendment: "Why should gambling be permitted on the turf any more than on baseball grounds? Baseball contests, football contests and other forms of innocent, healthful, enjoyable sport do not need any protected gambling attachment." It argued that racing had been extremely prosperous and that tracks could live with smaller profits. They did not need gambling or huge stakes to carry on, since $5,000 stakes were sufficient for great races and $1,000 for excellent events. It claimed racing had fallen to a lower level than in the early days of the AJC, when most owners were influential men of substance and betting was inconspicuous and inoffensive, without huge, crowded betting rings. However, by 1894, many owners had achieved their wealth "by conducting lotteries, by keeping faro-banks, by running roulette-wheels and by other forms of professional gambling."[15]

The *Tribune* further pointed out that "the disreputable elements in American life have flocked to the racetracks; they have lowered and degraded the standard of sport, and have exercised an evil influence. It is no exaggeration to say that at least two-fifths of the owners, trainers and jockeys of America are essentially dishonest . . . ; ready to practise trickery and to fleece the frequenters of the racetracks whenever they feel confident that they can do this without fear of punishment." They were interested not in the quality of horses but just in making money. The *Tribune* complained that the current style of racing that emphasized short races harmed the breed, since those events did not test endurance, speed, or courage.[16]

Most major racing figures other than John Morris and Richard Croker kept a low profile during the public debate, but did work hard behind the scenes and spent heavily to protect their investments. In 1894, for instance, Croker's Manhattan Stables had earned $77,098, third highest of any eastern stable. The racing crowd formed a literary bureau to educate rural voters about the dire impact of the revised constitution upon the breeding industry and the impending loss of funds for agricultural societies. The racing lobby reminded voters that the state had distributed an average of $25,763 a year to agricultural groups since passage of the Ives Act. The sport's supporters also distributed circulars that claimed the end of racing would cost $200 million and pointed out to farmers that their market for blooded stock would soon completely disappear. Trolley and cable cars were replacing the twenty thousand horses used in New York in 1893 for pulling streetcars, and livery-stable business was down by 50 percent.[17]

On 7 November, the electorate approved the new state constitution by a vote of 410,697 to 327,402. This approval was understood as meaning the total ban of horse race betting. In New York County, two-thirds of the electorate voted *against* the new constitution, but it passed handily elsewhere. The *Times* reported that the least-favored section of the new document was the revised gambling article, which would have been defeated if voted upon by itself. Another paper indicated that out of thirty-one revised sections, the gambling article generated the most public criticism.[18]

The crusading *Chicago Daily News* considered the election the most important ever for the turf. Its reporter believed that only a small percentage of voters were really concerned about the turf, though many were glad at the outcome, if for no other reason than it went against Tammany and track owners like the Dwyers, Morrises, and Walbaums, who "were not of a class to compel respect." The *Daily News* anticipated that the impact would be far greater nationally than the closing of the outlaw New Jersey tracks and likely to shake up racing in the West.[19]

The *Times* thought the vote meant the end of racing in the state, although it believed there was no practical way to stop the public from betting. In England, where betting had no more legal authority than in New York, there was probably more betting than anywhere else in the world. English bookmakers operated independently of the tracks and had no financial connections with them. The *Times* further pointed out that "neither the Legislature nor the racing associations can prevent people from risking their money in wagers on horse races. Pool selling and bookmaking as they are now allowed have this advantage from the point of view of the bettor, that they furnish a betting market in which the odds against every horse are nearly as well defined by 'quotations' as the price of stocks in Wall Street. . . . Of course, it is quite impossible to prevent men from betting if they choose to bet."[20]

The *Tribune* was much more optimistic about halting off-track betting. It pointed out that with reformers like Charles Parkhurst and Senator Charles Lexow taking the lead, and the (supposed) ending of "the days of barter and sale" in the police department, where appointments were sold for up to fifteen to twenty-five thousand dollars, the poolrooms were doomed—unless "the city is once more turned over to a political boss."[21]

The *Brooklyn Eagle* anticipated the vote meant the end of racing, since without gambling, attendance would be small and tracks would no longer get revenue from bookmakers.[22] Yet it was relatively optimistic that somehow racing would be saved by the heavy lobbying of racing men. Then racing would return to the pristine era before political hacks had taken it over:

> There will be racing. There will, however, be more of it as it was before the political gangsters of Brooklyn and Tammany Hall monopolized the sport. More of it as it was when the Belmonts, the Lorillards, the Jeromes and the Lawrences controlled it, and less of it as the Crokers, Nolans, Dalys and others of that kind have perverted it. The politics of crime became too hot for sundry folk who found even more iniquitous profit and less legal danger in racing as affected by bookmaking

rather than by horses. Now the people propose to make that kind of "racing" which is probably the crookedest thing in the world too hot for these politicians and their dupes.[23]

The *Eagle* hoped for the best but feared the worst, a future when horse racing "will be considered just as disreputable as prize fighting." Nonetheless, the editors pontificated, "we have no sympathy with the senseless crusade against a form of sport, which is as healthy and wholesome as any in the world if properly conducted. Horse racing in itself should be encouraged, but it should not be made the medium of ventilating the gambling instincts of the community. Some day human nature will undergo a change. Then it will be possible to witness a horse race without wanting to bet on it."[24]

Finally, the *Spirit* hoped the passage of the constitution did not mean the end of racing and recommended that major tracks reduce purses, increase entrance and nomination fees, and stay in operation. However, it was not optimistic about racing surviving without gambling: "Racing . . . on a large scale, without any betting whatever, is an anomaly not likely to ever exist either here or in any other country." It recommended, as a last resort, conducting meets with betting on the English credit system, in which bets were made by nods. Debtors settled up on a weekly basis. Such a system would not work well in New York, where a larger proportion of the bettors had insufficient funds to set up accounts they could draw upon.[25]

The Percy-Gray Bill and Racing under the New Constitution

Supporters and foes of racing all anticipated that racing interests would stage an all-out fight in early 1895 to salvage their sport. Before the legislature convened in February, Assemblymen A. B. Gray of St. Lawrence (R–Dutchess County) and Welton Percy (R–New York County) consulted with operators of the most prestigious turf stables, breeding farms, and tracks and secured the support of upstanding social and business leaders. They then prepared a bill ostensibly aimed at securing turf sports without bookmaking, pool selling, or protected gambling. The tracks would be encouraged to operate profitably without betting by maintaining spectator interest by offering large stakes to attract high-quality horses and then making money from the gate and concessions.[26]

The Percy-Gray proposal called for racing associations to operate under the supervision of The Jockey Club, making a nongovernmental organization a semi-official body. The established racing clubs would receive automatic approval, but new thoroughbred and trotting courses would need a license from TJC. The racing season would run from 1 April to 31 October, with a maximum of forty days at any one course. Thoroughbred tracks had to be at least a mile in length, purposely excluding smaller tracks to prevent the rise of disreputable facilities like New Jersey's outlaw tracks. Winter and evening racing was banned, and signs had to be posted reminding spectators that gambling was forbidden. The linchpin of the bill was that it criminalized off-track pool selling, bookmaking, and lotteries but not betting at the tracks. The only penalty for making a bet at the track was that the wagerer could regain his bet through a civil suit. The first draft freed track owners from any responsibility should (the inevitable) gambling occur, thereby preventing harassment and prosecution of track management and their employees, as De Lacy had recently done against Gravesend and several New Jersey tracks. Finally, to make the measure more palatable for rural legislators, each track would be assessed a 5 percent tax on net earnings, with the revenue earmarked for agricultural societies.[27] Assemblyman Howard P. Wilds (R–New York County) simultaneously proposed accompanying legislation that would forbid all kinds of off-track gambling, pool selling, and bookmaking, setting the penalty for bookmaking or gambling at two hundred dollars plus up to five years in jail.[28]

On 21 February, the assembly's Codes Committee held hearings on the racing bills. Anthony Comstock, the principal opposition spokesperson, called it an insult to the committee's intelligence because its secret purpose was to enable gamblers to fleece the public. Comstock argued that the gambling situation was so bad that even bank presidents were embezzling funds to pay betting debts, and he named six prominent men who either had blown out their brains or were languishing in prisons because of gambling. Comstock pointed out that the bill's proponents had opposed the new constitution, including the "so called respectable men" who were "whacked up" with the professional gamblers. He decried it as an entering wedge for unrestricted future racing. Comstock also claimed the proposal was unconstitutional because it would permit forty days of racing without punishment, although racing was illegal the rest of the year. He did not recognize there were precedents, such as hunting seasons, which established limited periods when hunters could kill specified game. The old curmudgeon finally argued that poolroom operators wanted new legislation passed that would repeal the antipoolroom law and provide only minimal penalties and insufficient deterrents against off-track gambling.[29]

August Belmont II and representatives of racing associations spoke out in support of Percy-Gray. Belmont denied Comstock's allegations and indicated the authors had honestly framed the law to deal with those abuses about which Comstock complained. Belmont did not believe the constitutional convention intended to pass a measure prohibiting betting but wanted to prevent the exploitation of the turf. He asserted that TJC intended to clean up the sport and maintain it properly. Attorney Joseph S. Auerbach, of Davies, Stone, and Auerbach, spoke for TJC, asserting that Percy-Gray would prohibit pool selling and the betting ring. James Keene spoke on behalf of breeders, horse owners, and advocates of respectable racing. He pointed out that Belmont had lost forty-one thousand dollars in racing in 1894 and Marcus Daly nearly fifty thousand dollars, losses willingly incurred because they believed in the value of thoroughbred racing as much as other elite sports like yachting.[30]

The Codes Committee amended the bill, partly to satisfy certain smaller tracks who opposed granting TJC too much power over racecourses. The committee suggested setting up a three-man unpaid Racing Commission, appointed by the governor for five years, who would regulate the licensing of tracks and supervise the sport in cooperation with TJC. In response to criticism that the poolroom proscription was too weak, an amendment made the taking of betting commissions a felony. The committee also changed the basis of the levy from a share of the net to a percentage of the gross. The final bill established a racing season from 15 April to 15 November with a maximum forty-day meet, required running tracks to have a mile-long course, and allowed the primarily rural trotting tracks to operate without a license.[31]

The *Sun*, *Times*, and *Tribune* as well as sporting periodicals such as the *Spirit* and the *Police Gazette* endorsed the amended bill. The *Gazette* said that the best proof of the value of the bill was the poolroom opposition, noting that De Lacy was so frightened of the new law that he was allying with church groups against Percy-Gray. He sent a circular letter to fifty-eight hundred New York clergymen appealing for a new crusade against the racetracks. The dispatch asserted that the bill's goal was to create a gigantic racetrack trust and that there was an unlimited corruption fund available to secure passage.[32]

The proposition impressed the *Times*, because it would "permit . . . racing and trotting as a sport pure and simple, and will tend to elevate and encourage one of the grandest sports in the world, as well as to encourage the breeder of the high-class horse." The plan also wiped out despicable methods previously used by unscrupulous entrepreneurs, especially at smaller tracks, that were centers of scandal and "nothing but gambling hells complicated with cruelty to animals." The editors pointed out that the new constitution had not dealt with racing abuses other than gambling, such as winter racing, "a cruel and scandalous sport, in which no man who had a real fondness for horses or a real respect for men would consent to engage [in]."[33]

The *Times* was confident that TJC could maintain high standards and bar "objectionable practices that are incidental and not essential to the sport." It lauded TJC as "an association of gentlemen of wealth and standing, who are . . . opposed to everything that has tended to bring racing into disrepute . . . while maintaining and increasing its attractiveness as a popular pastime and its real and unquestionable usefulness as an agency for improving the breed of horses."[34]

The *Tribune* also supported the bill as a practical method to remove the abuses and evils of racing. The paper chastised racing critics allied with De Lacy and the poolroom crowd and blamed most of the hostility to the bill on selfish or dishonest motives. The editors thought that Percy-Gray would be as good a bill as the legislature and governor would approve, and without it, the turf had no future in New York.[35]

Despite the efforts of Comstock, De Lacy, and their allies, the assembly approved the Percy-Gray bill on 2 April by a resounding vote of eighty-nine to ten.[36] When Percy-Gray came up for a vote in the senate on 1 May, only eighteen members were present. The men present favored the bill by a two-to-one margin (twelve to six), but thirteen senators were absent, and the measure needed sixteen votes, a majority of the senate, to pass. The missing senators were either blackmailing the racetrack interests in return for their votes or acting on behalf of certain gamblers and representatives of disreputable tracks who feared Percy-Gray would leave them out in the cold. A second ballot took place the next day with the missing legislators present, and it passed, twenty-two to three. The Wilds anti–pool selling bill also passed by a nearly identical vote, twenty-two to four, with Senator Tim Sullivan in the minority. The filibusterers returned because they got either a payoff or political favors. Some returned after recognizing that their tactics were not going to succeed and wanted to record their votes on the winning side.[37]

Eight days later, Republican governor Levi Morton signed the Percy-Gray and Wilds bills. He argued that the constitutional convention had not intended to completely prohibit horse racing but just halt pool selling and bookmaking. The new laws would save the sport, he claimed, and afford all reasonable safeguards against gambling at the races. Morton expected that the laws would successfully prevent the transmission of betting orders by telegraph or telephone and proscribe individuals from betting with bookmakers who gave them a receipt or certificate of their bet. The possible punishments for violating the racing laws were fines, imprisonment, and loss of license. Morton appointed August Belmont II to the new State Racing Commission, along with former Republican congressman John Sanford of Amsterdam, a well-known breeder and racer, and sportsman Edwin D. Morgan, commodore of the New York Yacht Club.[38]

The Impact of Percy-Gray

The passage of Percy-Gray boded well for the future of horse racing in New York. The *Brooklyn Eagle* optimistically anticipated that the new system would put the local turf on the same level as in England. It hoped for a betting scheme like in England, with private wagers paid up the next day, usually at the tracks or in Midtown Manhattan. The State Racing Commission took charge of the 1895 season, setting up the racing calendar to prevent any competition, and licensed the Brighton Beach Racing Association, Brooklyn Jockey Club, Coney Island Jockey Club, New York Steeplechase Association, Queens County Jockey Club, Saratoga Racing Association, and the newly established Westchester Racing Association.[39]

The *Eagle* did not expect betting to end under the new law but rather reemerge in a less profitable format. It thought that the bookmakers had grown too powerful, making tracks financially dependent on them, frequently consulting bookies when drawing up fields. Bookmakers invariably insisted on staging races with large fields, especially five- and six-furlong races for two-year-olds, because those events were full of uncertainty, which encouraged speculation.[40]

In early May, the new Westchester Racing Association, capitalized at three hundred thousand dollars, leased Morris Park from John A. Morris for two years at twenty-five thousand dollars a year, with an eight-year option. He was under great stress from the struggles of his new Honduras-Florida lottery business and reports of widespread bribery. The WRA's leadership included August Belmont II, James R. Keene, and Dr. Gideon L. Knapp; was mainly composed of the same people who ran the NYJC; and added people such as J. P. Morgan and Cornelius Vanderbilt. The WRA also took over the Bennings track in Washington, DC. The shareholders agreed to take no more than 5 percent earnings on their stock, with the rest going back to the track. Shortly thereafter, Morris suffered a stroke and died at age fifty-nine. His obituary appeared on the front page of the *Times*.[41]

The new syndicate tried to make Morris Park more exclusive, improve its accessibility, and remodel the plant. Workers redesigned the paddocks, replacing a perch where stable boys congregated with a path to a new coach stand for four-in-hand vehicles so their elite owners could avoid the motley crowd of racegoers and have easier access to an exclusive section of the grandstand. Transportation was improved by the New York, New Haven, and Hartford Railroad, and the WRA used its clout to get the city and county to macadamize the 9.4-mile road to the track from northern Central Park, providing a more delightful ride for wealthy coach riders.[42]

The first event under Percy-Gray was the National Steeplechase meet on 11 May at Morris Park, attended by thirty-five hundred people. The ambience was a lot calmer than most opening days, which was not surprising since steeplechasing drew a mainly upper-crust crowd. The *Tribune* found the atmosphere in the grandstand perceptively improved: "The hurrying messengers who placed bets for women of no particular standing had vanished, as well as their patrons." There was betting, but "it was done so quietly and with such rapidity that it did not offend anybody." It was pleased to report that "the two-dollar betters will soon become memories of the past."[43]

Four days later, Gravesend opened with about fifteen thousand attending the prestigious Brooklyn Handicap. This event marked the beginning of flat racing under Percy-Gray. According to the *Eagle*, the crowd ranged "from the swell clubman with his drag to the humble citizen who had walked to the track and crept past the doorkeepers in the early hours of the morning." Betting was at its typical level for opening day, although bookmakers did not occupy boxes or booths or call out or post their odds. Instead, they penciled their odds on cards they pulled out for prospective bettors. The bookmakers would then write a false name of the client into a book together with the amount bet. There were no receipts, but the bookmakers paid off winning wagers. The authorities notified the BJC that the bookmakers' actions violated the spirit of the law, and President Dwyer issued strict orders to bar ready money betting. Robert Pinkerton individually cautioned the bookies, and the police were very active in preventing cash betting. However, the *Times* warned that the authorities were tilting at windmills because betting was not preventable. The betting occurred unobtrusively, decorously, and out of the view of the grandstand so that it hardly subverted public morals.[44]

Conspicuously absent on opening day were "the professional politicians and officeholders who have hitherto claimed a monopoly of the sport." The *Times* found that absence a promising development: "If Mayor Strong in New York and Mayor Schieren in Brooklyn can succeed in holding the officeholders down to their desks during the current racing season they will have inaugurated a reform for which the better class of turf patrons no less than the public generally will have profound cause for gratitude."[45]

The *Eagle* had trouble making its mind up about the credit betting system. During the spring season, the *Eagle* opposed credit betting, arguing that it would promote recklessness, agreeing with *Turf, Field, and Farm,* a popular national periodical focusing on rural sport. The *Eagle* thought, like TJC, that the system was fine for the wealthy, but humbler bettors needed protection. The newspaper was concerned that credit betting would injure and ruin more people than under the old system.[46]

The *Eagle*'s judgment changed by late August, concluding that the new format worked quite well because bookmakers avoided betting with impecunious and irresponsible men and boys: "Whatever betting is done is done upon honor. The man makes his wager and if he loses, he sends a check the next day to the man who accommodated him on the track. If he wins the gentleman at the track sends him a check. The new law has raised racing in dignity and in interest while it has protected youths from temptation to which they should not yield. . . . The law has not discouraged legitimate racing, but it has driven out of business a lot of unscrupulous speculators."[47]

However, the credit system resulted in disappointing audiences because small bettors who could not place a bet stayed away. Concern arose that only tracks supported by wealthy sportsmen could manage under the new system. The tracks tried to maintain a high level of purses and stakes races but struggled without fees from bookmakers. The tracks also suffered from a decline in confidence among horse owners, which led to an unusual number of scratches at Sheepshead Bay. The return of the poolrooms in New York and nearby Harrison, New Jersey, also hurt racing.[48]

The Constitutionality of Percy-Gray

De Lacy's fight against racetracks heated up in the fall of 1895. He offered to halt his efforts to close them for $200,000, which would supposedly compensate him for lost business at his poolroom at 33 Park Avenue, since reduced to headquarters for a handbook. In addition, there were his expenses for organizing and running several law-and-order leagues in New Jersey and the cost of his fight against the New York tracks that refused to furnish his poolroom with racing news at his price.[49]

The next step in the conflict was to arrange test cases to determine the legality of Percy-Gray. Representatives of the CIJC met De Lacy, the Anti-Gambling League, and Joseph Sturgis, a clerk for bookmaker Orlando Jones. They agreed to set up a test case following the Withers Stakes on 17 October so the courts could assess the legitimacy of Percy-Gray. The police arrested former CIJC president Lawrence for contriving a lottery by organizing the Withers Stakes, registering a bet, unlawful conduct of a horse race, and maintaining a nuisance of Morris Park and took Sturgis into custody a week later.[50]

The Business of Racing

Financial returns in 1895 were very disappointing. Nearly all thoroughbred and trotting tracks lost money. Buffalo, formerly a very profitable stop on the harness circuit, where the betting privilege was worth $20,000–$30,000 annually, lost a lot of money without that revenue. Buffalo lost so much money it canceled the 1896 meet, as did Rochester. The Brighton Beach Racing Association dropped from $180,000 in profits in 1894 to just $12,000 in 1895, still considerably better than the other New York tracks, which all lost money. The BJC's spring meet barely broke even, attributed to poor weather, expensive stakes, and the new system of betting. Saratoga was $42,000 in the red, and the CIJC lost nearly as much. The days of 20 percent dividends seemed gone. Breeders were also badly hurt but were not sure if they should blame Percy-Gray or the economy, still reeling from the depression of 1893.[51]

Racing at Sheepshead Bay, the most popular track among both the elite and the masses, was an artistic success, with very generous purses, but a financial disaster. The Realization was worth $34,000, of which $30,150 went to the winner, Bright Phoebus, owned by W. S. Hobart, a Harvard student. The Futurity was attended by twenty thousand people, the largest crowd of the year. The winner, Requital, owned by former New York alderman David Gideon, won $53,750 out of a total of $69,250, the second richest prize in nineteenth-century North American racing. Gideon's horse won three of the first eight Futurities.[52]

The Coney Island Jockey Club paid "enormous dividends" for several years, but in 1895 the track ran a $30,000 deficit compared to a profit of nearly $40,000 the year before. Gross receipts in 1895 dropped by two-thirds, from $552,147 to $183,190, which constituted one-third (33.6 percent) of all the local tracks' receipts. What especially hurt the CIJC was lower attendance and an accompanying loss of more than $150,000 in gambling revenues from bookmakers. In 1894, with twenty-seven days of racing, the CIJC netted $243,000 from the gate (an average daily gate of $9,000), but one year later, twenty-six racing dates brought in $142,000 ($5,462 a day) as attendance dropped by more than 40 percent. The main reason for the decline was the new $2 price for general admission and the introduction of the unpopular oral betting. The lower attendance contributed to a huge decline in revenue from the betting, restaurant, bar, and program privileges. The track not only lost money but also paid a tax of $9,159 for the privilege of losing money. The *Spirit* thought the old level of business would resume once the public became accustomed to the current betting system and as prosperity returned to the economy.[53]

The declining racing business compelled the Brooklyn Jockey Club, whose valuable plant cost more than $300,000, to drop twelve stakes events and lower the purses of several others. The BJC lost money when the Dwyers first established it in 1886, but profits from 1888 through 1894 were worth ten times the original investment. Daily fees from bookmakers, which exceeded $6,500 and up, plus concessions and programs, more than paid for the purses, and after deducting the

TABLE 4. FINANCIAL REPORT OF THE CONEY ISLAND AND BROOKLYN
JOCKEY CLUBS, 1895

	Coney Island Jockey Club	Brooklyn Jockey Club
Days raced	26	25
Gross receipts	$183,190	$148,700
Amount from books and pools	0	0
Gate receipts	$142,045	$124,336
Amount raced for	$308,540	$216,336
Taxes to state	$9,159	$7,435

Source: Spirit of the Times 131 (22 Feb. 1896): 153–54.

overhead, everything else was clear profit. However, without bookmaking, the
BJC suffered a huge drop in gross receipts, from $438,920 in 1894 to $148,700 in
1895. The track lost $227,594 for the season by going without betting fees ($8,429
per day), and the gate dropped by two-thirds, from $184,524 to $124,336 (or a daily
falloff from $6,824 to $4,973). Like the CIJC, the amount the BJC paid in state tax
dropped by two-thirds to $7,435, but seemed like a lot when the track was so deep
in the red.[54]

In early 1896, the State Racing Commission presented its first annual report.
The document pointed out that in 1895, the racing associations paid out $792,453
in purses, with about 80 percent of winnings going to horses bred within one
hundred miles of New York City. The purses of some of the major stakes races
remained stable, but there was an overall decline in all stakes events and overnight purses. Sales of elite horses at public auctions were still high, but the average
value was dropping. In 1894, 1,515 yearlings sold for $809,795 compared to 1,137
for $385,359 in 1895. The average price dropped by nearly 42 percent, from $535
to $312, and several yearlings went unbid. The major tracks asked the SRC for
relief, pointing out the 5 percent tax on gross profits originated as a license fee or
a fine for betting privileges (which no longer existed). The tracks were reduced
to paying the levy out of capital funds, and moreover, each facility was assessed
$5,000 toward the commission's expenses. The SRC recognized that the tracks
needed relief and recommended a new tax, either a 5 percent tax on net profits or
a reduced percentage on gross earnings. The commission was also concerned that
the new $2 price for general admission had lowered attendance but was willing to
allow the tracks to charge higher fees for special seating areas.[55]

The racing season of 1895 was a financial setback, but considering how the
year had begun under the new state constitution, New Yorkers were fortunate

that they still had racing. Before the year ended, though, the turf suffered another setback. On the evening of 12 December, Brighton Beach caught on fire. The fierce blaze, sustained by strong winds blowing from the sea, hampered the firemen, who had access to just three fire hydrants. The conflagration began in a small stove used by a night watchman in the main office. The entire grandstand, mainly built of pine, was in flames before firemen could get a strong stream going.[56]

Despite the disaster, the Brighton Beach Racing Association had sufficient confidence to invest $100,000 to rebuild the grandstand and paddock and make other improvements. The new fireproof steel structure was in the same spot as the old grandstand but set back 115 feet instead of 65 feet and sloped to give everyone standing a perfect view. Management thought about moving the stands to the opposite side of the track, but the nature of the soil and the impossibility of rearranging the railroad terminal killed that notion. The new 250-foot, three-thousand-seat grandstand was 75 feet high. The building was supported by steel columns resting on granite decks and piles driven deep into the sandy soil. It had a cantilevered overhang protecting fans against sun and rain. The seats had plenty of room and provided largely unobstructed views. The grandstand had very good air circulation, since all the risers between stages were composed of open lattice girders. This change was a big improvement over the old stand that was closed in the back, which cut off cooling sea breezes.[57]

On New Year's Day, 1896, Judge George L. Ingraham discharged Lawrence and Sturgis. Lawrence's advocates, Auerbach, Bowers, and Root, argued successfully that racing was not a lottery since pure chance did not determine the outcome. In Sturgis's case, the arresting officer saw him make an entry in a book: "Forty to fifty on Navarre." The defense successfully claimed that this action did not constitute the exchange of any token or wager or any form of bookmaking since no money exchanged hands, there was no betting ring, and the track did not permit betting. Orlando Jones testified that all his bets were with acquaintances and not any comers. The *Spirit* also applauded the ruling, noting, "Its moral effect upon the legislatures of other States where the sport has been brought under a cloud through hostile legislation must in the end be great, and all interested in the sport of kings, breeders in particular, must now feel that it is assured a glorious future."[58]

The racing men were elated, expecting that magistrates would no longer issue warrants against men taking private bets on races, and the local press expected that the turf would thenceforth flourish under the SRC and TJC. The *Times* pointed out that the main opposition to Gray-Percy had come "because there was danger that under it horse racing would become too clean and honest a sport to suit the purposes of the assailants . . . men who had prospered by the abuses of horse racing."[59]

The decision was appealed and not resolved until 2 March 1897, when the appellate division of the state supreme court unanimously upheld Ingraham's decisions. The appellate judges agreed with him that racing was not a lottery, because "the event is determined by the superior speed and endurance of one of the horses under the conditions of the race. This superiority is the quality for which horses are bred and trained, and it is secured, not by chance, but by the superior skill and judgment of breeders and trainers and owners." The court also ruled in the *Sturgis* case that the exclusive penalty provision of a civil action to recover a wager was legitimate.[60]

The 1896 Racing Season

The press was very optimistic about the 1896 racing season. The *Times,* for instance, was sanguine because of the leadership exercised by TJC's Belmont, Morgan, and Sanford. On 4 May, racing resumed at the greatly renovated Aqueduct Racetrack. Management enlarged and relocated the grandstand and opened a new enclosed betting ring. Eight days later, the WRA opened Morris Park, featuring the Metropolitan Handicap, won by Counter Tenor, owned by Jacob Ruppert, the heir to the Knickerbocker Brewery, a future Tammany congressman, and owner of the New York Yankees.[61]

August Belmont II, on advice of counsel, asked the police to arrest a bookmaker to test the laws against wagering. The police arrested Nathan Frank, a well-known figure at the track, for taking a five-dollar bet. Frank's attorney, De Lancey Nicoll, asserted that the *Sturgis* ruling governed the case and that his client was liable only to the forfeiture penalty. Justice Truax released Frank, confirming TJC's opinion that the passage of money did not constitute a crime.[62]

As the racing season unfolded, the daily press continued to write favorably about thoroughbred racing. The *Brooklyn Eagle,* for instance, applauded the direction of local racing:

> The turf is being treated to a process of purification. The time is not far distant when it will be added to the lists of sports the most scrupulous can afford to patronize. Its false foundations are decaying. It promises to become a perfectly wholesome pastime instead of a somewhat doubtful means of livelihood, and the *Eagle* is more than a willing contributor to its higher density. There was a

time when to a great extent sinister influences dominated it, regulating its pro-grammes governed its starts and finishes, and made what was not altogether clear the wisdom of being seen upon a grandstand.[63]

Gravesend was set for a great meet. It was more accessible than ever because of the Brooklyn Union Elevated Railroad's new thirty-minute route from the Brooklyn Bridge. On opening day, bettors wagered hundreds of thousands of dollars on the Brooklyn Handicap. As the *Brooklyn Eagle* pointed out in an editorial, prior to passage of Percy-Gray, racing was an incidental feature of poolrooms and had been run into the ground. So many workers had their careers ruined and were becoming thieves that companies had to draw up blacklists of habitual gamblers. Racing regained some of its lost luster with the closing of many poolrooms and the closing of the vile tracks at Guttenberg and Gloucester in New Jersey. The editor was concerned about reports of welshing at the BJC and pointed out that "in England welchers do get stoned and mobbed. A little of the same vigorous treatment might not be without benefit on this side of the ocean."[64]

Sheepshead Bay in 1896 ran one of the outstanding meets of the nineteenth century, though it began under a cloud because management raised admission prices while doing away with the popular Lavender Orchestra that entertained the crowds. It had been the only Brooklyn track in the 1890s with musical accompaniment. The *Times* criticized the decision as "penny-wise and pound foolish," since it heavily detracted from the ambience and cut down on the crowd. The CIJC drew its main audience from "the classes and not of the masses and they must be catered to or it will lose all the prestige it has taken so many years to acquire."[65] The CIJC grossed $320,847, nearly one-third (31.7 percent) of the gross of all New York tracks, slightly below its share of the area's total gross in 1895 (33.6 percent). However, the CIJC's yield was still just 58.1 percent of its record gross of $552,147 in 1894.[66]

The *Times* gave front-page coverage to the thirteenth running of the one-and-a-quarter-mile Suburban Handicap, taking note of the presence of many pretty women, including actress Lillian Russell. One novel feature was that two hundred fans arrived on bicycles, for which the track was completely unprepared, even though cycling was at the height of a popular fad because of the invention of the safety bicycle. The closely contested $7,500 event was won by the great Henry of Navarre, owned by August Belmont II.[67]

The big race that closed the twelve-day meet was the Realization Stakes on 11 July. It was the longest race of the year on dirt, one mile and five furlongs, and worth $17,665 to the winner. The victory went to Requital, winner of the previous year's Futurity, ridden by the renowned Snapper Garrison, the top jockey in the United States. Requital set an event record of 2:49.6, beating the old mark by a second.

The CIJC second summer meet ran for eight days. The highlight was the Futurity, won by Montana copper magnate Marcus Daly's Ogden, earning $44,290 out of a bonanza purse of $57,290. Daly reportedly won $1 million in bets that day and became known as "Marc the Bookmaker Killer."[68]

The tracks did not make money in 1896, but conditions were moving in a positive direction. The *Times* saw a concrete improvement in racing that it attributed to the good work of the State Racing Commission that put speculators under control. As a result, "men of wealth and social position have once more taken up the sport."[69]

The next year was a financial success for the track operators. Attendance picked up, and tracks received fees from the members of the Metropolitan Turf Association, who paid for the privilege of making book. One of the year's biggest events was the $20,000 Realization at Sheepshead Bay, won by the Friar, whose owners, A. H. and D. H. Morris, won $26,435 during the twelve-day meet. This amount was again surpassed by the Futurity, captured by L'Alouette, who returned $40,000 to his proprietors, the Thompson brothers.[70]

Conclusion

At the start of 1895, the future of New York racing was extremely shaky, following the revision of the state constitution that barred horse race betting. However, the racing interests succeeded in saving the sport through the passage of the creative Percy-Gray Act that allowed the tracks to operate, ostensibly without betting, under an experimental three-man State Racing Commission to supervise the sport in cooperation with TJC. Opinon makers and racing men were optimistic that the new system would preserve racing and that it would continue to flourish in New York State. The sport resumed with high hopes, abetted by cashless betting that helped bring out the racing fans. The old tracks continued to operate, but crowds were down, as bettors were uncomfortable with the new betting scheme. The decline in attendance and the loss of revenue from bookmakers who no longer had to pay a fee to operate hurt the turf, and nearly all the tracks lost money until 1897.

The future of New York State racing was measurably helped by the ruling in April by the state court of appeals in the *Lawrence-Sturgis* case that declared Percy-Gray constitutional.[71] Once the spring meets were under way, New York's status as the racing capital of America was saved through the political clout of its leaders, who successfully protected their interests, unlike turfmen in other states, such as neighboring New Jersey. New York was one of the few states where racing was a major sport to survive the efforts of reformers to close their operations. New York racing continued to thrive for several years, but the reformers refused to go away, and in 1910, under the leadership of Republican governor Charles Evans Hughes, the state halted thoroughbred racing. However, unlike Chicago, where racing was banned in 1905 for two decades, the hiatus in New York was brief, and in 1913 racing returned to the Empire State.

9

A Glorious Decade of Racing

The New York Turf, 1897–1907

It is clear that never was legitimate racing in such a prosperous condition. This is shown in the great increase of public patronage and public confidence, which has enabled the various associations to offer premiums of greater value than in the past and to plan stakes for the future which eventually will have no parallel in the world in value, and which are the mainstay of the breeding industry.
—*Spirit of the Times*, 8 February 1902

Metropolitan New York continued to be the dominant site of American racing at the turn of the nineteenth century. Between 1896 and 1905, the total gross receipts of the licensed New York tracks rose from about $500,000 to nearly $4 million, with total purses of $1.5 million.[1] The city had two of the most prestigious tracks in Sheepshead Bay and Morris Park, the latter replaced in 1905 by the superlative new Belmont Park, and successful proprietary courses. There was also the celebrated upstate track at Saratoga that was part of the New York circuit. The metropolitan jockey clubs sponsored some of the richest and most prestigious races in the world, like the Futurity, the Realization Stakes, and the Belmont Stakes, which drew the largest crowds in the United States. Racing prospered for around ten years despite major problems with the thriving illegal off-track gambling business and constant pressure from moral reformers who opposed all horse race betting. At a time when racing was halted across the country, including such racing centers as Chicago and St. Louis, and in nearly every state in the Union, the sport was flourishing in New York. Racing aficionados expected continued prosperity for the New York turf, but the election of progressive governor Charles Evans Hughes in 1907 led to the temporary demise of their beloved sport.

The Proprietary Racetracks

Aqueduct Racetrack

The racing seasons began each spring at Aqueduct on Long Island, just off Jamaica Bay, and ended there in November. Attendees spent $0.50 on transportation, $0.10

cents for a program, and $2.00 for admission. Aqueduct featured the credit system of betting previously employed at Gravesend and Morris Park. It mainly appealed to serious wagerers and betting addicts, not to casual fans who preferred the ambience of the more established elite tracks that showcased the star thoroughbreds, like Morris Park, which opened a few weeks later.[2]

The press had modest expectations for the track. As the *Times* explained in 1899, "A meeting under the auspices of the Queens County Jockey Club at the little Aqueduct racecourse does not bring very high-class racing, but it serves very well the purpose for which it is intended—to arouse an interest in the doings of the thoroughbred horse after a winter's rest."[3] The *Tribune* was far more critical, complaining that the racing stewards "were so apathetic and inefficient that scandals were frequent, and there is reason to believe that several of the races were flagrant jobs."[4]

Management made significant improvements in the Queens County Jockey Club's shoddy physical plant for opening day, 27 April 1897, but the ambience was still far behind the feel of other metropolitan facilities. On that bleak and blustery day, Aqueduct attracted five thousand spectators who watched competitive contests with high-quality fields. The course had several failings, particularly a long homestretch that was not visible to most spectators. Aqueduct had a reputation for doing things on the cheap, as spectators discovered on opening day, 1902, when poorly manufactured programs fell apart. Another problem was that until 1905, betting commissioners who worked the grandstand serviced women bettors. These agents, sometimes mere boys working for bookmakers, gave women terrible odds and often absconded with winning bets.[5]

Aqueduct was the lowest-grossing track in metropolitan New York and in 1898 made just about half of the second lowest. The track subsequently grew in public esteem. On opening day, six years later, fifteen thousand people attended, despite the frigid weather, to watch the $8,000 Carter Handicap. The only thing missing was the presence of society. The track that year grossed nearly $400,000.[6]

Jamaica Racetrack

The press in the late 1890s speculated about Tammany Hall bosses setting up their own track. The *Tribune* in 1898 recommended that Boss Croker, who had five years' experience in thoroughbred racing, head the executive committee and the board of stewards of such a track because of his executive ability, leadership, and clout:

> Mr. Croker has the intelligence to see that certain owners, trainers, jockeys and bookmakers are scheming frequently to fleece the public, which supports the

turf, and he has the energy and force to throw those rascals outside the gates when a Tammany track is opened on Long Island next season. Tammany Hall could raise the necessary capital in a few days. No difficulty would be encountered in getting suitable grounds. Tammany has sufficient political and other resources to carry on a triumphant campaign, both at Albany and in New York against Sheepshead Bay, Morris Park, Gravesend, Brighton, and Aqueduct, were those tracks to try a fight. On the new course, competent starters, chosen from the membership of Tammany Hall . . . might handle the flag efficiently and acceptably. . . . [Croker could] secure the support of the honest masses who want honest sport. Mr. Croker could purify, revolutionize and reform the turf in this State, and obtain new honors and distinction for Tammany Hall.[7]

Croker considered establishing a track at Coney Island, but that project never came to fruition. In 1901, Tammanyites did organize a new turf association, the $300,000 Metropolitan Jockey Club (MJC). Its incorporators included Big Tim Sullivan, while other important men affiliated with the track were former senator W. H. Reynolds (R–Kings County), the thirty-three-year-old club president, and reportedly the principal stockholder; Senator P. H. McCarren; and gambler Frank Farrell. The track hoped to open in 1902, but TJC did not consider its application for recognition in time. The *Times* reported that once Tammany lost the recent election, the MJC lost its chance to have its application expedited.[8]

The politically connected Metropolitan Jockey Club bought a 107-acre site for $89,353, located about a mile and a half southeast of Jamaica, Queens, by the LIRR's Locust Station. The track opened on 26 April 1903, featuring the $7,000 Excelsior Handicap. Trains reached the track from Long Island City in seventeen minutes, and it was accessible from the Brooklyn Bridge by elevated trains and trolley connections. The course had a well-drained (sandy loam, like at Aqueduct) mile-long elliptical track, with a hundred-foot chute for a straightway course of five and a half furlongs. Fans enjoyed a spacious clubhouse with space for five hundred people, a five-hundred-foot sixty-five-hundred-seat grandstand, thirty-five hundred seats in the field stand, and a betting room twice the size of Sheepshead Bay's. Jamaica did have one notable flaw because the finish line was on a slant, making it difficult for spectators watching for their horse to finish. It became known as the "people's track."[9]

Purses at Jamaica in its first season averaged $941, which ranked very high nationally, but it lagged well behind the top New York tracks. Jamaica outgrossed Aqueduct in three of its first five years, and in 1907 the MJC's gross of $389,235 enabled it to surpass Saratoga for the first time.[10]

TABLE 5. TAXES PAID BY NEW YORK THOROUGHBRED RACING
ASSOCIATIONS, 5 PERCENT OF GROSS, 1895–1909

Year	WRA	CIJC	BJC	BBRA	QCJC
1895	$2,084.25	$9,159.51	$7,347.33	$4,831.15	$2,262.05
1896	11,709.84	16,042.37	12,443.57	8,660.34	1,751.98
1897	13,260.70	19,340.87	14,190.26		
1898	15,742.38	20,014.56	18,716.99	14,467.89	7,388.05
1899	14,859.46	23,386.02	23,133.72	14,386.70	7,319.91
1900	16,152.06	24,744.75	23,747.39	15,365.57	6,802.41
1901	21,609.39	32,609.32	29,673.64	20,380.59	11,270.88
1902	28,558.94	42,009.20	38,069.73	25,147.01	16,208.89
1903	31,156.56	45,156.44	39,527.35	27,967.40	14,145.04
1904	28,307.21	42,721.06	36,577.96	31,341.86	19,677.50
1905	29,617.38	42,448.70	32,432.24	29,846.76	15,625.87
1906	29,932.77	45,389.40	34,863.07	32,773.51	15,742.12
1907	32,899.36	54,001.36	41,312.23	40,623.73	20,111.73
1908	19,084.23	11,050.07	15,900.52	4,098.43	10,590.88
1909	9,765.00	14,562.53	9,334.58		2,418.71

Source: New York, State Racing Commission, Annual Report of the State Racing Commission [1907–1909]
(New York: W. H. H. Hull).

Note: BBRA = Brighton Beach Racing Association; BJC = Brooklyn Jockey Club; Buff. R.A. = Buffalo
Racing Association; CIJC = Coney Island Racing Association; ECTC = Empire City Track Club;
MJC = Jamaica Racetrack; QCJC = Queens County Jockey Club; UHA = United Hunts Association; WRA = Westchester Racing Association.

The Gravesend Racetrack and Brighton Beach Racetrack

The two established proprietary tracks were very successful at the turn of the century, each running twenty-eight to thirty days a year, with purses that by 1905 averaged more than $1,900, among the highest in the United States. Gravesend's meet began every spring with the prestigious Brooklyn Handicap that drew from twenty-five to forty thousand fans and drew so many bookmakers that the track took in $10,000 just from their fees. Gravesend's gross rose from $462,674 in 1899 to more than $826,000 by 1907. Its income surpassed the profits of Morris Park and nearly equaled Sheepshead Bay track in 1899 and 1900.[11]

Brighton Beach had one of the fastest courses in the country, especially after a resurfacing in 1897. Yet three years later, when Voter set a world record of 1:38 for one mile, there was widespread suspicion that the track was actually shorter than a mile. The BBRA's president took umbrage at the charges and offered a donation to charity if the allegation was true. An evening paper hired a city surveyor, who

TABLE 5 (continued)

MJC	Saratoga	ECTC	UHA	BUFF. R.A.	Total
	$1,536.45				$27,220.74
					50,608.10
	3,665.50				64,034.64
	4,453.98				80,483.85
	7,714.93				90,791.74
	8,227.76	3,571.59			103,385.00
	13,630.61				128,581.50
	17,967.12			3,124.99	170,085.88
17,763.53	21,982.47			3,042.88	200,741.67
15,369.80	19,677.50			5,324.45	190,256.30
17,391.00	21,508.36		539.00	4,334.00	193,744.43
16,456.43	20,282.63			5,613.83	193,201.00
19,461.75	17,876.93	280.70	12,435.48	7,426.52	246,429.16
8,926.21	5,077.82	367.30	2,371.29		77,486.85
2,309.52	8,670.12	22.29	5,420.02		65,166.00

measured the track three feet from the inner rail and found it was nine feet and a few inches longer than a mile.[12]

Both tracks underwent important improvements for the 1902 season and enjoyed banner seasons with substantially increased grosses. Gravesend's gross rose 30.6 percent compared to the prior year, while Brighton increased by 23.4 percent. Yet they were both below the metropolitan track average increase of 32 percent. Gravesend built more space to alleviate overcrowding at major stakes events, tripling the size of the field stand, and adding nearly three thousand grandstand seats. Management also constructed new stables and kitchens. The BJC enhanced spectator comfort by enclosing the new grandstand's back with storm glass, hinged by an ingenious device to provide fresh air in pleasant weather, and also put in new counters for refreshments that ran the entire length of the grandstand.[13]

Brighton Beach spent $100,000 on renovations, producing, the *Spirit* crowed, "one of the handsomest, best appointed and most commodious club-houses between the Atlantic and the Pacific." The new three-story clubhouse was one hundred feet long and reached by an elevated walk from the grandstand. Facilities included a large café, a reception room for five hundred people, and well-appointed parlors and dining rooms on the third floor "with the numerous comforts which will go to make an afternoon's outing enjoyable for the wives, sisters, and daughters" of club members.[14]

The Elite Racetracks

Sheepshead Bay Race Track

The pearl of New York racing was Sheepshead Bay, running the most outstanding meets that drew the largest crowds and outgrossing every other New York track from 1895 through 1907. Wealthy fans at classic events like the Futurity and the Realization congregated at the clubhouse, where they drank mint juleps or other beverages, dined at an excellent restaurant, and placed their wagers in the betting ring via messengers. Bookmakers in the betting ring were beneath the main grandstand, where tickets cost $3, the highest in the country, and took single bets as high as $25,000. Working-class fans who stood watched the races from the $1 field stand and usually bet $1 or $2 and rarely more than $5.[15]

In 1900, the track grossed nearly $495,000 and then $650,000 the following year. Two years later, when American tracks distributed more money to horse owners than ever before, the CIJC was the most successful, grossing $840,184, nearly a 60 percent increase in just two years. Fifty thousand spectators attended the 1902 Suburban Handicap. About three hundred bookmakers took bets, including around ninety members of the Bookmakers' Association, who arrived at the track with about $1 million in cash. Two years later, some forty thousand attended the Suburban Handicap and thirty thousand in 1905 when the filly Beldame won a $20,000 purse. Sheepshead Bay's gross remained stable through 1906 and then in 1907 jumped up to $1,080,027, the first American track to gross more than $1 million.[16]

The Futurity from 1904 to 1906 typically drew about forty thousand or more spectators and total purses of at least $45,000. On those days, the track stood to make about $100,000 just from the gate (30,000 tickets at $3 and 10,000 at $1), as well as $2,700 from the sale of twenty-seven thousand programs at $0.10 each. The $3 million facility had significant overhead expenses that included $300 a day for officials (including the starter at $50, two judges at $50, clerk of the scales at $25, and various assistants), $167 for the handicapper (paid $5,000 for the season), $100 a week for a physician, and an additional outlay for a veterinarian. In addition, the track spent $700 a day for labor, as much as $750 for 150 Pinkertons at big stakes races, and $150,000 a year (or $5,000 a day for a thirty-day meet) for maintenance.

The largest single expense was $150,000 for purses. By my estimation, these costs came to about $320,000, resulting in a minimal annual profit since 1901 of $175,000 before taxes.[17]

Saratoga Race Course

The Saratoga Race Course underwent important developments at the turn of the century, which enabled it to recover the status it had until the early 1890s when it fell under the control of the notorious bookmaker Gottfried Walbaum. Walbaum bought the track in 1892, did well at first, but encountered problems in the mid-1890s when business fell off, and the track closed in 1896. One year later, socially liberal Democrats captured the village election, and the new trustees picked A. P. Knapp as mayor. The broad-minded mayor granted permission to Richard A. Canfield, the most famous professional gambler of the era, to reopen his gambling hall, originally established by John Morrissey. However, Canfield's chief rival, Cale Mitchell, who had recently received enormous negative publicity because of his love affair with journalist Nellie Bly, was not relicensed.[18]

The track reopened shortly afterward. Walbaum used his political pull to force the SRC to grant him a large number of racing dates that helped the track finish in the black in 1898 and 1899. He then stepped down as track president, replaced by Tammanyite Edward Kearney, a former butcher and auctioneer and close friend of Boss Croker. Kearney continued Walbaum's policy of admitting children to the track, which management claimed promoted a family atmosphere there.[19]

17. Upper-class racing fans enjoyed a gracious ambience at the Saratoga Racetrack on 5 August 1905. The day's highlight was the Saratoga Special for two-year-olds, won by Mohawk II, owned by state racing commissioner John Sanford. *Source:* "The Racing Season at Saratoga: The Running of the 'Saratoga Special,'" *Harper's Weekly* 49 (19 Aug. 1905): 1191.

The moneymaking track drew the attention of several syndicates who wanted to buy out Walbaum, but he drove a hard bargain, demanding $50,000 more than anyone offered. He got his price at the end of 1901, selling the track for $300,000 to the Saratoga Association for the Improvement of the Breed, which promised to take no more than a 5 percent profit and plow any excess earnings back into the physical plant. The Jockey Club's leaders included President John Collins Whitney, P. J. Dwyer, J. H. Alexander, F. R. and T. Hitchcock, R. T. Wilson, and John Sanford, who brought back the prestige of the old Saratoga track.[20]

President Whitney was a prominent New York lawyer and city corporation counsel who in 1885 was appointed secretary of the navy by President Grover Cleveland. Originally an anti-Tammanyite, he joined the organization in 1890. Two years later, he managed Cleveland's second successful presidential campaign but turned down an offer to become secretary of state to remain in the private sector, partnering with Thomas Fortune Ryan in the Metropolitan Street Railway Company. By 1900, the Metropolitan controlled nearly all Manhattan and Bronx surface transit lines.[21]

Whitney got into racing in the autumn of 1897, although he had a long-standing interest in equine sports. He owned trotters that he drove, was a director of the National Horse Show, an original incorporator of TJC, and a founding member of the Turf and Field Club. He spent a fortune on his new hobby, establishing the Westbury Stable at his Long Island country estate. Just one year later, Whitney's horses won twenty-five events worth $38,461 and thirty in 1899 ($61,550), including the Belmont with Jean Beraud, purchased the year before for an unheard-of price of $40,000. Whitney's stable took thirty-one races in 1900 ($92,545), plus another seven in England, most notably the Epsom Derby in 1901 with Volodyovski, a horse he had leased. He won $108,440 in the United States in 1901 and $102,569 in 1903, leading the nation in money winnings both years. Whitney's oldest son, Harry Payne Whitney, also became a great horseman, with twelve Triple Crown victories.[22]

The elite Saratoga Association spent $1 million redesigning the course, which included resurfacing the track and enlarging it by an eighth of a mile. The five-thousand-seat grandstand was expanded by 20 percent and moved closer to the track, at an angle that put the sun behind the spectators. Unfortunately, the new design made it almost impossible to see the finish line. Whitney raised general admission from $2.00 to $3.00 but kept the field stands at $0.75, which he justified by noting that Saratoga's crowds were only half as large as the throngs at the top New York City tracks, and it needed the extra capital to offer larger purses to attract the best horses and bring back the fans. During the summers, when racing shifted to Saratoga, there was a noticeable increase in poolroom business and the rise of new handbooks. Whereas hundreds could scrape up $0.75 for a field stand, few working-class gamblers could afford the time and cost of travel to Saratoga Springs.[23]

TABLE 6. AMERICAN RACETRACKS, PURSES, AND RACING DATES, 1905

Racetrack	Purses ($)	Average purse ($)	Races	Dates
CIJC	571,300	3,174	180	30
New Calif. JC	450,145	496	907	150
WRA	375,930	2,089	180	30
BJC	349,165	1,918	182	30
BBRA	325,495	1,915	170	28
Latonia JC	300,925	452	666	109
Crescent City JC	300,170	566	530	67
Saratoga Assoc.	283,840	2,150	132	22
City Park JC	256,270	498	515	82
Los Angeles JC	216,665	463	468	105
New Memphis JC	136,415	568	240	40
Delmar JC	135,590	385	352	58
Metropolitan JC	129,800	941	138	23
QCJC	126,952	1,041	122	20
New Louisville JC	125,540	519	242	40
Washington JC	118,530	567	209	34
Kansas City JC	114,090	512	223	37
American RA	112,250	328	342	34
Fort Erie JC	110,150	342	322	50
Buffalo RA	85,850	462	186	31
Hot Springs JC	81,910	525	156	26
Ontario JC	80,065	602	133	20
Oakland JC	75,370	462	163	27
St. Louis FA	72,715	547	133	19
Tennessee BA	70,425	405	174	39
Highland Park	57,000	380	150	25
Narragansett BA	49,400	537	92	18
New Louisiana JC	46,750	557	84	12
Maryland JC	46,090	397	116	19
Kinlock JC	34,340	464	74	12
Windsor JC	21,700	314	69	11
Kentucky RA	21,400	594	36	6
Country Club	17,965	1,198	15	3
Arkansas JC	16,330	454	36	6
United Hunts RA	13,860	770	18	3
Miscellaneous	146,400	. . .	. . .	. . .
Total	$5,476,792	$788[a]	7,755	1,266

Source: New York Times, 4 Mar. 1906, 11.

Note: BA = Breeding Association; BBRA = Brighton Beach Racing Association; BJC = Brooklyn Jockey Club; CIJC = Coney Island Racing Association; JC = Jockey Club; Metropolitan JC = Jamaica Racetrack; QCJC = Queens County Jockey Club; RA = Racing Association; St. Louis FA = Fairmount Park; WRA = Westchester Racing Association

[a]Average of 35 racetracks.

Whitney did not allow the approximately one hundred bookmakers at Saratoga to run affairs as they had under Walbaum, although they remained extremely powerful until the coming of pari-mutuels in 1939. Bookmakers did business with both the occasional bettor and the nearly four hundred professional bettors at Saratoga, fewer than the number who frequented the more conveniently located Sheepshead Bay or Morris Park tracks. Writer Julian Ralph described the professional gamblers as typically young African American, Irish, or Hebrew, who dressed simply in business suits, with straw hats, and little or no jewelry: "It is true that they do no good by their mode of life, but it is equally certain that they do little harm. They get along without what we call work, but no one who studies them with intelligent observation would exchange a working life for theirs."[24]

Saratoga shined in the early 1900s, as it had in the pre-Walbaum era, regaining its elite status. By 1905, its average purse of more than $2,000 a race was among the highest in the United States, surpassed only by Sheepshead Bay. However, because of its shorter August meet that lasted about twenty-two days, and its distance from New York City, it was usually no better than fifth among New York tracks in gross profits.

The Demise of Morris Park and the Rise of Belmont Park

The Westchester Racing Association, which operated Morris Park, struggled in its first year in the abbreviated 1895 season, when it grossed only $40,805, less than Aqueduct. However, it improved to $234,197 a year later and helped make Morris Park one of the most successful operations in America. From 1895 through 1904, it grossed a total of $3,668,816. Yet although Morris Park ranked very high nationally, it only made about two-thirds its peer, Sheepshead Bay, and less than the popular Gravesend course. It did pull in more revenue than Aqueduct, Jamaica, and Saratoga and more than Brighton Beach until 1903 (see table 5).

Morris Park staged some of the finest events in North America, including the Metropolitan Handicap on opening day, and the Withers Stakes, which went back to 1874. In 1902, the track did well at the box office, beginning with the $8,950 Metropolitan Handicap that drew thirty thousand fans, including many who arrived by motor carriage. The Withers, one week later, drew fifteen thousand spectators, and twenty-five thousand attended the closing day of the meet. When the Metropolitan Handicap in 1903 drew thirty thousand fans, the *Times* concluded it had reached parity with the great spring handicaps at Coney Island. An outstanding array of carriages brought elite spectators to the grounds, and there was also an overflow of automobiles.[25]

Yet as the course became more popular, developers and other interested parties in the Bronx were clamoring for the track to go because it seemed to be blocking access to promising new neighborhoods. Property values near Morris Park were rapidly escalating and expected to rise even higher with the coming of the subway. There were calls for condemnation of the site, and city maps were beginning to show the track subdivided with streets running through it. By 1902, the WRA seriously considered moving elsewhere because its lease with the Morris estate was expiring in two years, and the leaders looked into potential locations in Queens County where they could own a site instead of renting. These develop- ments convinced the Morris estate in late 1902 to grant the Port Chester Rail Road a right-of-way through the property and sell the site to a syndicate that intended to divide the land into twelve hundred lots for houses selling for more than $6,000.[26]

In the fall of 1902, the WRA found a 666-acre site for a new track in the hamlet of Elmont (town of Hempstead), 14.5 miles from Manhattan, just outside the city limits, at the old Mananice Place in Nassau County. It was near a Long Island Railroad station, twenty-seven minutes from Long Island City, and the coming of rapid transit cut traveling time from LIC to eighteen minutes. The plan called for a lavish course, expected to become the American Newmarket, the equivalent of Great Britain's leading track. The WRA increased its capital stock to $1.2 million to help pay for the new track. The SRC applauded the project as fitting its own plan to stabilize the turf by making racing associations, facilities, and programs per- manent. The SRC did not want new tracks built in locations likely to see real estate booms that would encourage owners to close and sell the sites.[27]

The facilities at the $2.5 million twelve-thousand-seat Belmont track were beyond anything ever seen in the United States. The stables alone covered 200 acres. The complex had five courses, including a mile path for yearlings, another mile track for horses in training, and three separate tracks for competition: a mile- and-three-furlong turf course, a one-and-a-quarter-mile steeplechase track, and the outer one-and-a-half-mile oval. The races were run clockwise in the English style, a format used nowhere else in the United States, a tradition that lasted until 1921. The back lot was connected by tunnels to the main track, enabling horse walkers to lead their horses to the paddock without going through the public. The only criticism by journalists was that the track was mainly geared for the comfort and convenience of the clubhouse crowd.[28]

On 4 May 1905, forty thousand fans went to the track's opening to view the grand new course and attend the fourteenth running of the Metropolitan Handicap. The best general admission seats were at the foot of the grandstand and cost $5 on top of the regular admission fee. Society turned out en masse and filled five acres of parking lots with their automobiles. According to the *Times*, "There has never been a more brilliant assemblage at any race meet." The papers gave a lot of coverage to upper-class couples and their parties, reporting who attended and if they arrived by car or carriage. Opening day was marred only by an unusually large number of pickpockets—at least twelve on every train arriving from Long Island City. One man lost $1,000, another $500, and dozens others lost more than $400.[29]

The Metropolitan ended in a remarkable dead heat between four-year-old Race King, owned by O. L. Richards, and three-year-old Sysonby, owned by James Keene, who had not raced in seven months and carried ten pounds more than his rival. Sysonby, largely forgotten today, was the leading money winner in 1905 and one of the greatest horses of all time. His only defeat came in a race in which he had been drugged.[30]

In 1906, the Memorial Day races at Belmont, highlighted by the fortieth renewal of the Belmont Stakes, drew nearly fifty thousand fans, the largest verifiable crowd up to then in American horse racing history. Unfortunately, the transit companies made no special preparations for the holiday crowd, and it took more than an hour before extra trains were prepared. Belmont Park was so crowded that conditions were uncomfortable, if not dangerous, and some people fainted from the heat and the foul atmosphere in the tunnel leading to the grandstand. The field stands with twenty thousand spectators were severely overcrowded. Seats were so hard to find in the grandstand that by early afternoon, many people sat on top of the stands.[31]

Despite Belmont's ballyhooed opening, it took a few years before it approached the returns of the Brooklyn racetracks. It grossed nearly $600,000 in 1905 and 1906 and then $657,987 in 1907, leaving it behind the three old Brooklyn courses. However, by 1908 Belmont was the top-grossing track in the metropolitan area and second to the CIJC in 1909 (see table 5).

In 1905, when the WRA left Morris Park, car racing replaced the thoroughbreds. David Heenen Morris, who was selling the land on behalf of his family, was an avid car fancier and president of the Automobile Club of America. However, development of the site struck a snag because the new owners went bankrupt. In 1908, it became an important site of aeronautic testing as well as the first public air show, attended by twenty thousand people. The landlord auctioned off plots in 1913 to more than fifteen hundred people, including the Astors and other prominent New York families. Yet development occurred at a snail's pace, and as late as the 1930s, the neighborhood was still characterized as "wilderness."[32]

A New Course: The Empire City Race Track

The final track to open up in the New York area was the Empire City Race Track in Mount Vernon, one mile from the city limits, just outside the city of Yonkers. It was at the former site of the Fleetwood Driving Park, whose last Grand Circuit meet was in 1897. The main person behind the project was W. H. Clark, a copper

magnate and former Tammany city corporation counsel, a high roller who reportedly lost nearly $100,000 playing faro at Canfield's Casino. Clark in 1899 revived
harness racing at Yonkers, New York, with the Empire City Trotting Club (ECTC),
together with his main partner, grocery tycoon James Butler.[33]

Clark believed that a palatial, modern mile-long track with a beautiful clubhouse and excellent stables would draw racing fans. The club spent about $780,000
to renovate the track, much of which came from Clark himself. The ECTC built a
six-thousand-seat steel grandstand for $218,000 on the highest point of the area,
providing a great view of Long Island Sound and the countryside. The project cost
triple the original projection, partly because the contractor had to level a hill.[34]

Despite the planning and money spent, the finished product had serious flaws.
First, the track was too fast, with turns banked like a cycle track, which made the
horses' legs sore. Then Clark did not purchase enough land along the backstretch
because it was too expensive. Third, the grandstand was built facing the sun, no
pleasure for the spectators watching the races. Finally, the track did not have good
access. Ideally, carriage riders from Central Park could get there via the newly
macadamized Jerome Avenue in less than forty minutes. The train ride from New
York on the New Haven Railroad line to Mount Vernon or the New York Central
to nearby Yonkers was fine, but there was just a single-line trolley from the station to the track that did not keep a regular schedule, failed to double service as
promised, and terminated far from the grandstand. The *Spirit* described the trip
from the city north to the course as an "awful journey" with which no New Yorker
would put up. Empire City opened on 4 September 1899, drawing twelve thousand. The track made money in its first meet when it was a novelty but lost money
at the next meet.[35]

Soon after Empire City opened, thoroughbred men began eyeing it, recognizing that Morris Park's future was short. Empire City offered to lease the course
to the WRA. However, the *New York Morning Telegraph,* the most expensive daily
paper in America (costing $0.05 an issue) that specialized in sport, theatrical, and
vaudevillian news, expected TJC to take over Empire City. The transportation
problem looked like it would be soon alleviated because the New York Central
was going to put in a line of double track and other improvements to make Empire
City very convenient.[36]

Clark passed away early in 1900, but the ECTC went ahead with plans to run an
experimental thoroughbred meet in the fall under the direction of Philip Dwyer.
The trial was not a success. The track grossed just $71,432 (computed from data in
table 5), though it had one memorable race, the Empire City Handicap, in which
Charentus set a world record of 2:04 for one and a quarter miles. Racing experts
found the course unsatisfactory, noting that the constant galloping brought many

pieces of rock to the hard racing surface that endangered the horses. The SRC complained about the track's inaccessibility and deficient accommodations, particularly the sun-facing grandstand. The ECTC decided to sell the course and cut its losses. Senator Patrick McCarren considered purchasing Empire City that fall for $300,000 and turning it into a racing track but backed off because of the transportation problems and a need for new stables. In the end, the track was foreclosed and sold on 26 December 1901 to gambling kingpin Frank Farrell and his syndicate for the bargain price of $218,000. Former congressman John J. Adams, acting for Clark's widow, secured a temporary stay at the last minute, hopeful that other bidders would raise the price. Adams claimed that collusion between Farrell and sales agents had resulted in a rip-off price, since the property alone was worth $500,000. He also pointed out that businessman Nathan Straus had previously offered at least $300,000 and possibly $500,000. One month later, Justice Keogh set aside the sale.[37]

Shortly thereafter, a syndicate composed of eleven members of the New York Driving Club, a prestigious organization of men who competed in amateur trotting races, led by ECTC president James Butler and ECTC vice president Frederick Gerken, bought the track for $300,000. Their syndicate included former parks commissioner Nathan Straus, the owner of R. H. Macy's; C. K. G. Billings, the recently retired president of Chicago's Peoples Gas, Light, and Coke Company who was moving into the New York social scene; and the commissioner of highways, T. J. Brady. They planned to get a railroad spur to the park and move the grandstand to the opposite side of the track.[38]

In 1903, the stockholders raised the association's capitalization from $5,000 to $550,000 but disagreed about how to apportion it. Former mayor Hugh Grant, Gerken, and Billings wanted to create a land corporation worth $545,000 but were outvoted. Then they and businessman Henry Morgenthau sold their stock to the majority shareholders.[39]

In 1906, James Butler, a staunch Republican, sought a license from the SRC for Empire City to run as a thoroughbred track, but his application was ignored.[40] The SRC remembered the track's disappointing thoroughbred meet in 1900 with its poor attendance, unsatisfactory sight lines, and inadequate transportation. It was also concerned that licensing the ECTC would threaten Saratoga because the only time slot available was in the summer when the upstate course held its meet.[41]

Butler reapplied one year later after the SRC had been reorganized and was controlled by Republicans, who he thought would be friendlier to his request. In February, Rear Adm. J. Russell Soley, a former assistant secretary of the navy, represented Empire City before the racing commission. The attorney explained that the problem of glare in the face of spectators could be resolved by erecting an umbrella-like extension to the roof, like the one employed at Brighton Beach and Belmont Park, and a planned railroad spur to the track would resolve the travel issue. Soley made a fairly aggressive presentation, warning the commissioners that Empire City would sue the board if it did not get a license.[42]

The SRC turned down Empire City on 5 March, explaining that the state's seven licensed tracks each had from twenty-two to thirty days of racing, available dates in August were set aside for Saratoga, and they did not consider it in the public interest to have a competing New York track open then. The SRC also pointed out that in 1900, it had allocated Empire City racing dates in October and November that went largely unused. The committee disregarded the impact of Clark's death one month after the allotment of dates and that his friends had carried out the meeting in his place. Finally, the SRC criticized the ECTC for waiting six years to reapply for a license, but during those years, the club had not been in a position to resume operation.[43]

Butler did not accept the SRC's ruling and ratcheted up his efforts. On 14 March, Soley sought a peremptory writ of mandamus from supreme court justice Isaac N. Mills of White Plains, directing the SRC to give Empire City a license. Soley complained about gross favoritism and partiality on behalf of established tracks and asserted that TJC had a sinister influence on New York racing. He concluded by stressing that the law required the SRC to grant Empire City a license and racing dates. However, Judge Mills ruled against Empire City, indicating that the SRC did not have to grant a license if it so chose.[44]

The ECTC appealed Mills's judgment to the appellate division of the supreme court and won a reversal. The court granted a peremptory writ of mandamus against the SRC, compelling it to issue the ECTC a license for 1907, which was awarded on 6 July. The ruling did not go over well with TJC, which indicated it would not recognize the ECTC and would disqualify men who worked there and horses who raced there.[45]

The *Times* blasted TJC in an editorial titled "The Horse Octopus" for trying to restrain trade and making the ECTC a metaphor for "the sufferings of a people borne down by the plutocrats." It supported Butler's effort to move from trotting to the more exciting horse racing: "Mr. Butler's August meeting would not only give great pleasure to himself, his friends, and his patrons, but it would impart an otherwise unattainable vivacity to the tranquil life of the near-by city of Yonkers. Unmoved by these considerations, disregarding the law, and flouting commercial morality, The Jockey Club sets in motion against the Empire city concern those restraining devices of intimidation and boycotting which have so profoundly shocked the people when employed by the Beef Trust." The Jockey Club made a tactical retreat and, on 24 July, accepted the new club.[46]

Butler and his associates went right to work and hired contractors who put up a new two-thousand-seat grandstand in less than three weeks in preparation for the 10 August opening, attended by nearly fifteen thousand spectators. Unfortunately, there was a thirty-minute delay before the first race because the inadequate trolley service completely broke down. Electric power failed, and about 150 heavily laden cars were stalled along a nearly four-mile stretch of Jerome Avenue. Many spectators had to walk most of the way to the course. The return trip home was not much better.[47]

Despite the travel woes, the press rated the opening as a remarkable success, comparable to a Brooklyn Handicap or Suburban Day, as "perfect order and real horse racing ruled within the club grounds." People prominent in club life and social circles were present. According to the *Times*, "While the crowd lacked the class of Belmont Park, it was a thoroughly representative gathering. Men from all walks of life were on hand. Staid businessmen rubbed elbows with lawyers, doctors and actors with the utmost good nature and decorum." The clubhouse was nearly full, with many women seated in the balcony. There were seventy-six busy books in the betting ring and eighty more in the open field. A big delegation came down from the meet upstate in Saratoga in two special twenty-car trains.[48]

Empire City had a daily attendance of about fourteen thousand over thirteen dates, demonstrating the popularity of August racing in metropolitan New York. Transportation improved, management was praised by TJC for its work, and races were competitive, with a high proportion of favorites winning.[49] Consequently, at the start of the next season, the established jockey clubs made room for Empire City. Saratoga took a smaller season but regained its August monopoly. In return, Empire City got a brief, exclusive early-October meet for which it seemed better suited than either Jamaica or Aqueduct, both buffeted in the fall by cold ocean winds.[50]

The Business of Racing

Thoroughbred racing operated at a deficit in 1895 and 1896, when it was under enormous pressure from reformers who nearly killed the sport and when the economy was still struggling from the depression of 1893. However, the 1897 season was a financial success, with gross returns nearly double 1895's, and nearly 20 percent better than 1896, and it was an artistic success to boot. Attendance picked up, the tracks pulled in revenue from bookmakers, and there was an increase in the number of horses nominated for future stakes races. The *Times* attributed the improvement to the good work of the State Racing Commission, which took more control over the gambling at the track. The result was that "men of wealth and social position have once more . . . taken up the sport."[51] However, the benefits did not yet reach breeders and horse owners. The typical thoroughbred cost $200 to breed, but ordinary yearlings were often sold for just $100. Even foals of stakes winners went for $750 to $1,000 compared to the early 1890s when the son of a stakes winner could sell for between $3,000 and $5,000.[52]

The tracks' gross increased by another 20 percent in 1898, and 10 percent in 1899, which the *New York Morning Telegraph* rated as an excellent year. The tracks grossed $1.8 million in 1899 and drew their largest crowds in several years. Gravesend and Sheepshead Bay were the largest-grossing tracks, while Brighton had its most prosperous meet since the early 1880s. The prestigious Morris Park outgrossed Brighton, but its heavy overhead reduced its profits below the three Brooklyn tracks.[53]

Just about every year saw bigger purses, bigger gates, and bigger profits. All the associations made more money in 1901 than ever before, especially Saratoga, which doubled its profits in just two years. The state's share of the gross rose to $128,582, 30 percent more than the year before. Racing was so popular that many clubs were patronized beyond their capacity on holidays and major stakes races. According to the *Spirit*, "It is clear that never was legitimate racing in such a prosperous condition. This is shown in the great increase of public patronage and public confidence, which has enabled the various associations to offer premiums of greater value than in the past and to plan stakes for the future which eventually will have no parallel in the world in value."[54]

The State Racing Commission's report for 1901 was very positive and vigorously supported the major stakes events that attracted big crowds and had a positive influence on the price of racing stock. However, the SRC warned against overexpansion and cautioned against building new tracks where they would be crowded out by urban development or rising property values. The SRC also criticized "fly-by-night" tracks that specialized in overnight races (events for which entries closed ninety-six hours before the race) and jockey clubs that went into the business just to make money and not aid the breeding industry.[55]

It is extremely difficult to determine the profitability of American racetracks, especially since press reports rarely explained how results were derived. For instance, in 1902–4, the last years of racing in Chicago, net profits were simply reportedly more than $400,000, without accompanying data. The New York State Racing Commission's *Annual Reports* provided data only on gross returns and not net profits. The *Los Angeles Times* reported the Ascot Association's expenses and receipts for its 93-day meet in 1905 but was incomplete and did not even estimate profits. The article reported expenditures of $275,000, including purses worth about $250,000, and $25,000 for advertising, laborers, and officials. However, money for stakes events also included entry fees and money donated by sponsors, which reduced the track's costs. In addition, such major expenses as maintenance, security, and mortgage payments went unmentioned. The receipts included $167,400 from bookmakers' fees (typically eighteen bookmakers who paid $100 a day), about $25,000 from field books and the combination book, and an unspecified amount from the sale of privileges like the bar and cigar and fruit stands. There was no mention of revenue from admissions and fees from poolrooms that paid for access to each day's results.[56]

Horse racing flourished over the next several years in metropolitan New York, even as it was being halted in Illinois, Missouri, and Indiana in 1905. Four of the five American tracks that awarded the largest total purses were in metropolitan New York, and the eighth was Saratoga. New York tracks combined for one-third of the total national purse of $5,477,952 in 1905, even though they hosted just 12.7 percent of American racing dates (972) and 12.5 percent of all the races (7,763). The best horses competed in the New York races because they offered the biggest purses, led by the CIJC, the top track by a wide margin, distributing $571,300 in 30 days (180 races). The New California Jockey Club was second, well behind with $450,145, even though it had five times as many race dates (150) and nearly as many dates as all the New York City tracks combined (161) (see table 6). The CIJC average purse was $3,174 compared to $496 for the New California JC or $452 for the Latonia JC in Covington, Kentucky. By comparison, the United Kingdom held 2,021 races (including 337 steeplechases), with a combined value of $2,638,120, which most observers considered evidence of mass interest in the sport. This figure barely exceeded the eight New York State tracks, which distributed $2,284,000 in purses.[57]

Racing continued to be extremely successful the next two years. In 1906, even Aqueduct, the smallest track in the metropolitan area, grossed more than $314,000, while Sheepshead Bay took in more than $900,000 (see table 5). The *Times*, hardly a friend of racetrack gambling, recognized how well the tracks were doing. In an editorial titled "The Prosperous Race Tracks," it noted that the June races at the CIJC distributed more than $300,000 in premiums, surpassing anything in England or France. Coney Island staged an early version of the Triple Crown for three-year-olds, composed of the Jockey Club Stakes ($25,000 purse), the Tidal ($20,000), and the Lawrence Realization ($22,000), with a $10,000 bonus if the winner captured all three races.[58]

In 1907, the tracks pulled in $4,928,858 at the gate, a 16 percent increase over 1906 ($4,203,790). They all set new records except Saratoga, which had its poorest meet in years, competing that summer with Empire City, which grossed $248,710. The *Times* reported the new racing course netted about $100,000, a very respectable return, especially considering it had to put its meet together very rapidly. The *Times* estimated that the CIJC made $400,000, which amounted to 40 percent of its gross for 30 days of racing. Gravesend made nearly as much, and Belmont Park supposedly made more than the CIJC. However, another source reported that the CIJC and Brighton each made $150,000, followed by Gravesend ($140,000), Belmont ($130,000), Jamaica and Aqueduct (each $110,000), Empire ($100,000), Saratoga ($80,000), and Buffalo's Kenilworth Park (1902–7), owned by August Belmont, which made $50,000.[59]

The increased returns reflected a 20 percent rise in attendance for New York racing, which approached a daily average of about 10,000, with a single-day high of 46,000 at Belmont. By comparison, the New York Highlanders of the American League averaged 4,606, the Brooklyn Dodgers 4,085, and the New York Giants a National League–leading 6,946. The *Times* estimated that the average patron spent $1 for incidental expenses (which amounted to $1,740,000 for the 174-day season). The large crowds attracted some two hundred bookmakers each day (and up four hundred for a major stakes race). The daily cost of supporting the betting ring was $20,000, or $3,480,000 for the season. Overall, the *Times* estimated that racing cost New Yorkers $10,220,000 (combining the gate, incidentals spent at the track, and gambling).[60]

Bookmakers and Gambling at the Tracks

Journalists had no idea how bookmakers made out. Sometimes they offered wild estimates of profit making, while other times they pointed out the high rate of bankruptcies. A typical bookie was said to handle $2,000 a day and might collectively handle about $400,000 in wagers. Between 1895 and 1902, an estimated five thousand men worked as bookmakers, on and off the tracks, most ending up without their bankrolls. In 1904, a bookmaker usually paid $67.50 to the track to operate. There were typically about seventy-five bookmakers at each track, producing $5,062.50 for the jockey club. The *Times* estimated in 1907 that the average bookmaker spent about $50 to pay his staff and netted $50 a day.[61]

Their occupation purportedly underwent significant changes by the turn of the century, becoming very competitive. Journalists described it as a very seductive occupation, and former bookmakers never seemed to get "reformed": "The allurements of a trade which promises the chance to hold a fat percentage for the light work of holding other persons' bets for a period of twenty minutes to half an hour, perhaps are too strong for the men who once engage in the business of 'laying the odds.'" Failed bookies seemed to have dropped off the earth, while the successful "wear so many signs of prosperity that they shut out all behind them." J. E. McDonald, a Tammany man and the richest local bookie, was an exception.[62]

The cornerstone of the betting business remained the Metropolitan Turf Association, established back in 1887. The MTA, also known as the "Big Ring," had about eighty members and sought to monopolize bookmaking at the tracks. Beginning in 1899, new members paid a $1,000 fee, double the original levy. The MTA had a board of managers to settle disputes and represent the association with the jockey clubs. Members tried to offer identical odds, generally set by MTA president George Wheelock, a renowned handicapper, or one or two other bookmakers, so their clients could not benefit from internecine competition.[63]

Relations between the tracks and the MTA were never cordial. When Aqueduct opened for its summer meet in 1897, Thomas D. Reilly, a prominent Tammanyite who was the QCJC's main stockholder and president, announced a $50 fee for bookmakers to do business there. They countered with a proposal of $35, claiming that since Aqueduct lacked first-class horses and did not get big bettors, the suggested fee was too high. The MTA organized a boycott, marking the first time American bookies combined against a racing association. They were accustomed to paying $50 a day to make book, a "voluntary contribution" since the tracks had no right to charge a bookmaking fee since gambling was "illegal."[64]

On 26 July, the first day of Aqueduct's summer meet, thirty independent bookmakers took the places of the MTA inside the betting ring, paying the track $25 for the privilege. They offered much shorter odds than usual, but were more willing to take bets under $2, and did a fair business. The independents organized themselves the next day into the Metropolitan Turf Alliance, with Peter Worth as temporary chairman. However, within a few days, the MTA was back in business, and the alliance collapsed.[65] The MTA later renamed itself the Metropolitan Turf Alliance.

New York meets drew not only local bookmakers but also preeminent odds layers from across the country. In 1902, for instance, Chicago's gambling kingpin Jim O'Leary came to New York, but he was blackballed by three votes when he tried to join the MTA. Instead, he backed Joe Ullman and Barney "Kid" Weller's "Big Store," the single largest bookmaking enterprise of the day, which operated at Sheepshead Bay and Saratoga and reportedly cleared $500,000 for the season. The Big Store got its nickname for taking single bets as large as $75,000 and $155,000. One season, they handled $3 million at Saratoga, pocketing 10 percent of the action. One-fifth of the profits went to Ullman and Weller and the rest to O'Leary and his bankrollers, who included two of the nation's biggest "plungers" (extremely heavy bettors), Wall Street financier John A. Drake and John Warne "Bet-a-Million" Gates, who made his fortune in oil and by establishing American

Steel and Wire, a barbed-wire monopoly that he sold to US Steel in 1901. Gates got his nickname in 1900 by winning $600,000 in England on a $70,000 bet. In 1905, he won $350,000 at Brighton Beach, though from his perspective, he was simply recouping the $200,000 he had lost there two years earlier.[66]

Other well-known plungers included horseman James R. Keene, who in the 1907 season was purportedly up $400,000, and Big Tim Sullivan, who that year lost $130,000. Sullivan was a partner in a racing stable with Frank Farrell and David C. Johnson, known as the "Big Three." Sullivan decided after the season to get out of racing horses, having bet too heavily on his favorite jockey, Walter Miller, and listening to his misguided friends, who made a living by betting on the horses.[67]

The greatest and most astute horse player was George E. "Pittsburgh Phil" Smith, who died in 1905 at the age of forty-three with at least $2 million in the bank or in real estate. He was born in Pittsburgh, where he trained as a cork cutter as a youth, making $10 a week. Young George frequented poolrooms and found he had the ability to evaluate races. Smith moved to Chicago in 1884, the year that Washington Park opened, to operate poolrooms. In 1887, having made about $200,000, he moved to New York, the national center of racing. Pittsburgh Phil became the leading gambler in New York because of his understanding of racing sheets and knowledge of private training sessions. His biggest betting coup came in 1891 when he won $87,000 on his horse King Cadmus, trained by his brother, but Phil made most of his profits on other owners' horses. His big win was an unofficial record in New York until 1905 when a two hundred–to-one filly won a race for nonwinners at Sheepshead Bay. He was a brilliant student of the turf whose judgment was unparalleled, stuck to betting on form, and never allowed feelings to muddle his rational analysis. Pittsburgh Phil became well known for such aphorisms as "Cut your bets when in a losing streak and increase them when running in a spasm of good luck," "Double your wages when you have the bookmakers' money in hand," "Winners repeat frequently while the defeated are apt to be defeated almost continuously," and "A good jockey, a good horse, a good bet. A poor jockey, a good horse, a moderate bet. A good horse, a moderate jockey, a moderate bet." He is credited with discovering the great jockey Tod Sloan.[68]

In 1905, there was a big dispute in Queens over the management of the betting rings. On 25 April, opening day at Jamaica, fifteen thousand were in attendance, with 152 bookmakers in the betting ring, including 62 of the MTA, plus about another 50 bookies working on the infield. The MTA tried to compel the owners of Jamaica and Aqueduct, which had opened eleven days earlier, to employ a friendly face as ring manager who would help the connected gamblers get the choice locations to take bets and put nonmembers in the back lines. The MTA wanted to replace the respected ten-year veteran John Cavanaugh, but Jamaica's president, W. H. Reynolds, refused, explaining that the track did not recognize the MTA, which was the essence of the conflict.[69]

When Belmont Park opened up for the first time on 5 May, the track, led by August Belmont II, went to battle with the MTA to establish an open betting ring. The owners of the new course wanted to show the MTA who was boss and publicly demonstrate that the tracks were not beholden to bookmakers, so they would not be attacked by reformers or sued by any foes of on-track betting, including the poolrooms. The racing associations announced "the absolute severance of all business relations, directly and indirectly, with the Metropolitan Turf Association and all other organizations, or individual bookmakers," and promised that the betting area would be "free of all restrictions, with free admission to anyone buying a ticket, known to the track police as personally reputable and financially stable." The Associated Press considered this idea one of the most important steps in racing since the passage of Percy-Gray.[70]

The WRA announced that unless the MTA could guarantee that 80 members would operate daily at each metropolitan track, outsiders would have a shot at the highly sought-after betting-ring booths. Its goal was to end the MTA's monopoly over choice betting locations. On opening day, when 77 MTA members appeared, 3 outside men were allowed to make book in the prime betting location for the first time since 1895. Each bookmaker paid about $57 to do business, compared to the $100 a day before the passage of the Percy-Gray Act.[71]

On the second day, when 76 MTA men appeared, no outsiders were allowed into the big ring. The 3 outsiders who had worked opening day were politely asked to go back to their old positions. The MTA thought they had won a partial victory upon resuming control of the front row on the big ring with fewer than the 80 layers in line and paid the fee for the missing 4 slots.[72] Then, on 11 May, when there were 72 MTA bookmakers present, Cavanaugh stepped in to fill the rest of the places but found only 5 back liners interested. The back liners were charged only $37, and the so-called hurdlers, who worked without stools and were situated one row farther back, paid $17.[73]

A few days later, on 20 May, Belmont Race Course dramatically changed its arrangement with the MTA. Ring manager Cavanaugh announced that the bookmakers would no longer be charged to operate in the betting ring and that instead, bookmakers, like everyone else, would have to buy admission tickets to get into the track. Bookmakers would have to buy fifty-seven $2 admission tickets from Robert Pinkerton to lessen the appearance of any direct connection with track management. Nonetheless, Timothy Sullivan made his rounds of the ring as usual and collected fees from his members and also from the back-line bookies and the hurdlers, which came to around $6,000. However, Cavanaugh did not accept the money and let only the men he knew had previously worked the track into the betting ring. The MTA was still in the first line, with 62 members, and Cavanaugh moved 6 men from the back line to the front. The change in betting arrangements resulted in a sharp drop in the value of an MTA membership from $4,800 in the past winter to just $3,500.[74]

The decision to not charge bookmakers any longer cost New York tracks $1.2 million over two hundred racing dates. Consequently, sportswriters expected admission prices would have to be raised, or else racegoers would have to pay for the privilege of betting by buying an extra ticket to the betting ring. Ticket prices rose 50 percent starting with the Gravesend meet, to $3.00 for men and $1.50 for women for grandstand seats, and $1.00 for general admission to the field stand. The $0.50 fee for paddock badges remained. The *Times* editors thought the tracks were playing with fire. An editorial titled "Racing Suicide?" warned, "The sportive individual who longs for the shady luxury of a grand stand seat from which to pick the winner may conclude that it is cheaper to join the Stock Exchange and gamble there. The impecunious 'piker' may prefer to stay in town with PETER." The tracks learned their lesson; by 1907, they were again charging bookmakers to operate at their facilities.[75]

Racing and the Press

Although New York was the national center of thoroughbred racing, and the state was reaping its share of the revenue with taxes, the sport remained under enormous pressure from the press, moral reformers, and Republican politicians. Journalists covered horse racing in as much depth as any sport, giving particular attention to opening-day festivities and major stakes events, but with a much more critical eye than any major sport except for boxing. Newspapers consistently reported on the problems of racing, primarily the gambling issue, but also occasional stories of mistreated horses, improperly run matches, and even fixed races. Faultfinding commentary appeared in the upper-middle-class *Times* and *Tribune*, but also in the more plebeian *Sun, Journal, Herald,* and the crusading *World.* The press kept the public on top of government investigations and poolroom raids and reported on how gambling ruined working people driven to embezzlement and other crimes to pay off their debts, and editors penned censorious editorials about the gambling menace.

In addition to the daily press, popular periodicals were increasingly attentive to the problem of horse race gambling. They were following in the footsteps of muckraking journalists like Lincoln Steffens, Ida Tarbell, and Ray Stannard Baker and novelists Frank Norris and Upton Sinclair, who examined political corruption, monopolies, and the dangers of slum life. There was also a significant critical literature on sports, most notably Henry B. Needham's inquiry of intercollegiate football in *McClure's* that brought to light some of the problems of the game, notably that college stars did not attend classes, jumped from school to school, and were compensated to play.[76]

In the early 1900s, there was a plethora of critical reports about horse racing in such periodicals as *McClure's, Collier's, Scribner's, Cosmopolitan,* the *Independent,* and *Outlook,* and even Thomas Kennedy's lengthy poem *The Racing Swindle: A Satire.* They were not always breaking new ground, since the daily and weekly press covered racing very thoroughly, but the muckrakers were a highly respected source of information for middle-class Americans, and their essays carried more weight than newspaper stories that were read and soon forgotten. The most important magazine articles focusing on racing and gambling included Mark Sullivan's "Pool Room Evil" in *Outlook* (1904), which gave a lot of attention to racing because of the illegal gambling nexus; David Graham Phillips's article "The Delusion of the Race-Track," in *Cosmopolitan* (1905); and especially the well-known journalist Josiah Flynt's three-part exposé of the poolroom business, also in *Cosmopolitan* (1907).[77]

Phillips, a novelist and journalist, was best known for his 1906 exposé, "The Treason of the Senate," published in William Randolph Hearst's *Cosmopolitan,* a family magazine that the press mogul had bought a year earlier for four hundred thousand dollars and turned into an investigative monthly. The article revealed that US senators were receiving large payments to support the interests of major corporations. In "The Delusion of the Race-Track," Phillips identified racing as a seventy-five-million-dollar business that "in results, in dividends, no other activity, not even the liquor traffic, compares with racing." He decried racing as "the largest agent, and the most successful, in recruiting for the criminal class. It makes more thieves, more murderers, more moral wrecks than any other does. And to deprave and debauch is its chief object." He claimed that the turf's manifest function was to improve the breed, but it was just an incidental, if not accidental, part of the sport, because racing's real purposes were to gain status for the idle rich and promote gambling. Phillips described racehorse owners as rich men without character: "How can it be otherwise when they market their livelihood and their career by creating and by trafficking with profligates and thieves? How could it be otherwise then they are engaged in a business whose most respectable patrons are of necessity law-breakers and law-defiers, bribers of police and legislators?" They were despicable people who pushed horses into "premature decrepitude." Phillips decried the track owners, bookmakers, touts, tipsters, and even jockeys, whom he considered "rascals" or criminals.[78]

The relationship between horse race gambling and the press was examined by John D. Workes in "The Race-Track Evil and the Press" in *Arena* (1908). First, he criticized gambling as one of the most subtle and degrading of evils, not limited by class or gender. Horse race gambling made public officials betray their trust, businessmen negligent, trusted employees embezzlers, privileged individuals thieves and deceivers, and workers inefficient and dishonest. Betting husbands forgot their duties and vows, and gaming wives had forsaken their families. Workes argued that the main difference between track gambling and other betting formats, like poker, was publicity. Gambling at the tracks was glamorous and exciting and had a tone of respectability because of the presence of the rich.[79]

Workes, like many racing critics, placed a lot of blame for current racing conditions on the press because it publicized the sport. Sports sections were often printed on colored paper that added glamour and excitement to the sports pages, while the less flamboyant sections pushed morality and religious services. The daily press printed records of competitors, tips from sportswriters, advertisements for tipsters, information about coming events, and results of concluded races:

> Grasping avarice and consuming greed sap the honesty, morals, and integrity of the newspaper and make it the sponsor and aide and abettor of the race-track evil just as these evil propensities take men and women to the race tracks and make gamblers and felons out of them and they should be held strictly responsible for the large part they are taking in the spread of the evil. If the newspapers only had the moral courage to exclude from their columns and all mention of race tracks or their performance, in the form of paid advertising or otherwise, the crushing out of the vile would not be difficult.

Workes recommended prohibiting papers from publishing or advertising racing information or providing notices about horse race gamblers. Furthermore, he urged good Christians, especially ministers, to stop subscribing to papers that supported vice. All of New York's dailies except the *Times* and the *Evening Post* posted racing odds.[80]

Seeking Repeal of Percy-Gray

The ongoing efforts of conservative moral reformers to fight horse race gambling continued in the early 1900s. In 1906, there was considerable optimism that the Cassidy-Lansing Anti-Pool Selling Bill had a good chance to pass and clean up the betting problem. The proposed legislation sought to make on-track betting a crime by amending the last sentence of the Percy-Gray Act that had made gambling inside racetracks legal. The bill sought to alter the penalty for gambling to be a minimum of one year and a maximum of two, plus a fine instead of the current two-year maximum (no minimum) and a two-thousand-dollar fine. Anthony Comstock reputedly drew up the legislation at the behest of Rev. Wilbur Crafts, head of the International Reform Bureau, who was described by the *Times* as a "confused fanatic." The plan received a lot of support from clergymen of all creeds, but primarily evangelical Protestants and their organizations like the Society for the Suppression of Vice, the Christian Endeavor, and the IRB, which claimed a strong connection between gambling at tracks and stealing, presumably to cover lost bets.[81] Despite the *Times*'s less than laudatory evaluation of the Reverend Crafts, it did support Cassidy-Lansing because it would bar the posting of odds in the betting ring, ending the bookmakers' use of slates, and thereby dramatically alter betting procedures. Bookmakers would have to use verbal quotations and not have to quote prices to all customers. Furthermore, poolrooms would be hampered in getting information.[82]

Horse race gambling was a highly partisan issue in Albany, mainly opposed by Republicans, whose upstate conservative base considered gambling immoral. Party leaders also thought that too many of the 740 jobs connected to racetrack management in the state were filled by Democrats and their allies, instead of good Republicans. Several of New York's top racing men were Democrats, particularly August Belmont II, chairman of the State Racing Commission, who had just completed his second five-year term. The Republicans wanted Belmont out, ostensibly because of a conflict of interest in his other duties as chairman of TJC and its Board of Stewards since their decisions ultimately went on to the Belmont-chaired SRC for final approval.[83]

The Cassidy-Lansing bill became the object of heavy lobbying. Some representatives of agricultural societies who were getting about two hundred thousand dollars a year in tax revenue from licensed tracks claimed that without racing revenues, county fairs would have to close unless they found new sources of funds. Joseph Auerbach, counsel to TJC and the turf's main lobbyist, told the Joint Committee on Codes that Percy-Gray, which the courts had ruled constitutional, limited gambling and kept the wagering where it could be watched. He asserted that betting at tracks was merely incidental to the industry, that stopping bookmaking would not halt gambling, and that the present racing laws had stimulated large investments in thoroughbred racing. The lobbyist further claimed that the state had no business interfering with vested rights it had fostered and discussed the reported collusion of poolroom men who supported antiracing actions. Auerbach pointed out that the influential Rev. Thomas Slicer of New York City's All Souls' Unitarian Church, the chief member of the Legislative Committee of the interfaith

State Conference of Religions (SCR), a longtime foe of the turf, had changed his antiracing views once he learned that poolroom men were behind the drive to restrict on-track horse racing.[84]

Slicer told the committee that since stopping betting was impossible, the next best thing was to get the cooperation of responsible turf leaders. He opposed Cassidy's bill for a number of reasons: "It would put Belmont on the same grounds as a poolroom keeper; if track men were forced out, the poolroom guys will come in and return racing to the day of the Gloucesters; and, it would be to the advantage of poolrooms which contribute nothing to racing." The SCR joined TJC in opposing the bill, having gotten its promise to "sterilize" track betting by initiating oral betting in which bookmakers would not maintain slates with written odds visible to all comers but offer odds orally and pay off the next day.[85]

Slicer's defection from the antiracing forces drew a lot of negative comment. Crafts claimed Slicer switched because Belmont and other turf leaders had signed a contract granting him control over future betting methods at the track, agreeing to bar bookmakers from ostentatiously displacing odds on their slates, and blocking the transmission of betting-ring odds to poolrooms.[86]

The *Times* was also amazed by Slicer's change of mind. It was not troubled that the poolroom crowd or other nefarious sorts were behind Cassidy's bill, because it was good legislation, nor did it buy Slicer's arguments that the betting would be restricted to where it could be controlled (and exploited) by responsible persons. He was criticized for falling into company with cynical rustics who said they must have their money for their annual fairs, his view that doing away with local racing would not stop poolrooms, and for delaying the triumph of decency. The *Times* assumed that the public was less excited by out-of-state races than local contests, which resulted in fewer poolrooms and less business. More important, if New York would emulate the states that had already ended racetrack gambling, it would hasten the end of the problem altogether.[87]

On 18 March, Republican governor Frank W. Higgins, who had promised to keep his personal position on the racing bill private until it reached his desk, came out in favor of the Cassidy-Lansing proposal. Higgins's support was no surprise, since as a state senator, he had opposed Percy-Gray as unconstitutional and also immoral because it permitted an action (gambling) that was not allowed outside the track.[88]

The next day, Crafts got several pietistic organizations, including the Presbyterian Ministers' Association (PMA), the Baptist Ministers' Conference, and the Methodist Ministers' Meeting, to unanimously endorse the Cassidy-Lansing bill. Comstock spoke to two hundred Methodist ministers in Manhattan and bitterly attacked Slicer, who, he implied, was in the pay of track interests. Crafts told a

PMA meeting that the opponents of reform had bribed the framers with more than two hundred thousand dollars for their state fairs.[89]

The Jockey Club fought back with its own bill on 20 March sponsored by Senator Henry J. Coggeshall of Waterville (R–Oneida County), who in responding to a committee representing the agricultural fairs' call for additional revenue proposed raising the tax on track receipts by 3 percent to provide an additional sixty thousand dollars for the expositions. The bill succeeded in bolstering rural support for racing because a few days later, the senate Committee on Codes killed the Cassidy-Lansing bill owing to weakened public demand for action and an understanding legislators had reached over track receipts.[90]

Coggeshall's bill passed the legislature, but the governor vetoed it on 23 April. Higgins roundly condemned the tracks for giving hush money to county fairs to facilitate an evasion of the state constitution. He explained, "Race track gambling, while technically prohibited, is in fact fostered and encouraged and made a monopoly by law. If the present tax were expended for general purposes, the moral sense of the community would scarcely tolerate racetrack gambling but the largesse of a quarter of a million dollars, distributed actually among agricultural fairs throughout the State has created a selfish and unnatural community of interest, which is to be deplored." The *Times* applauded Higgins's veto message, which it thought should shame supporters of the bill, and recommended he call a special meeting of the legislature to reconsider the Cassidy bill.[91]

Shortly thereafter, Governor Higgins dropped Belmont and E. D. Morgan, whose terms had expired in 1905, from the State Racing Commission. It was the first personnel change in the SRC since it was established in 1895. Belmont's firing was long expected given his partisanship, having worked for Democratic presidential candidate Alton Parker in 1904 and against Higgins when he ran for governor, and because of his views on Cassidy-Lansing. Higgins kept only former Republican congressman John Sanford, a carpet manufacturer from Amsterdam whose father owned the famous Hurrican Farm, one of America's great stables, and added two more Republicans, former congressman James W. Wadsworth of Geneseo, an amateur horseman whose son was Speaker of the state assembly, and Harry K. Knapp, a New York banker and member of the Board of Stewards of TJC. Knapp and his brother owned Kiamesha, who had tied the world's record for the mile the prior season at Belmont Park.[92]

New York racing men were relieved that racing had survived but were so concerned that "Bet-a-Million" Gates, Andrew Miller, and John Drake formed the New England Breeders Club, a racing syndicate that built the one-million-dollar Rockingham Track in Salem, New Hampshire, so they would be sure racing would continue in the East. More than ten thousand people attended the opening on 28 June. However, local citizens, including the former owner of the track site, protested, and on the third day of racing, the authorities arrested all the bookmakers. The meet continued with betting done on the quiet, but the track closed after the conclusion of the twenty-one-day program. There was no more thoroughbred racing at the New Hampshire site until 1931 when new owners rebuilt the track. However, the meet had no gambling, and Rockingham closed down a week later. The state legalized horse race gambling in 1933, and Rockingham reopened with betting.[93]

Conclusion

New York racing was properly acclaimed as the center of American racing in the early 1900s. Its elite racetracks were sponsored by the crème de la crème of society, who belonged to the most exclusive metropolitan clubs and owned the finest stables in North America. Opening day at the Coney Island Jockey Club, the Morris Park Racetrack, and Belmont Park and the afternoons of the classic stakes events were among the great social events of the calendar. These tracks contested the richest events on the continent and drew the largest crowds. Even the city's proprietary tracks supported outstanding meets that attracted some of the finest thoroughbreds in the world, attracted huge audiences, and made a lot of money.

Nonetheless, the metropolitan turf did not escape the criticisms that racing encountered throughout the country, which mainly centered on the gambling (though there was relatively little negative comment about the integrity of the contests). The New York racing scene seemed vulnerable, particularly as tracks across the country were closed by local governments in response to the demands of moral reformers. It seemed at first blush that the New York tracks had sufficient political clout, mainly through their connections with Tammany Hall and the state Democratic Party, to protect racing, having defeated efforts in the legislature to overturn the Percy-Gray Act. However, the big push to halt racetrack gambling was only beginning, and even the exalted position of the turf in New York State could not block the coming storm.

10

The Gambling Trust and the Poolrooms, 1899–1913

We climbed some stairs leading to the parlor floor.... On reaching the first landing we met a second guard.... This fellow was heavy, red-faced, and brutal looking,... but he knew my friend by sight, and nodded. He looked me over carefully
... and I was freely passed into the spider's den....

There were about a hundred men in the room....

After fifteen or twenty minutes of betting, a person in the employ of the
house ... sang out, "They're off at Bennings!" ... As the calls came over the wire
and were sung out into the room, there was the silence that tells of an uncon-
trolled passion and the foolishness of a racing-mad crowd.

—JOSIAH FLYNT, "The Pool-Room Spider and the Gambling Fly,"
Cosmopolitan, March 1907

P ublic opinion makers, ranging from muckrakers to capitalists and theologians,
from progressives to conservatives, all reviled off-track gambling. As much as
critics took racetracks to task for their flaws, the turf did have its advocates for the
positive contributions the sport made to promote the breed, provide employment,
raise money for the state, and entertain fans, and even the on-track gambling that
made the sport possible. However, there was not much of a debate when it came
to off-track betting. The poolroom operators and their political allies tried to avoid
the public limelight. However, off-track bettors spoke out stridently through their
patronage of poolrooms and handbooks.

Businessmen complained about off-track betting's negative impact on their
employees' fiscal responsibility and honesty, religious leaders about its immorality, and progressives about its criminality and corrupting influence on customers,
the police, and urban politicians. Supposedly, at least 60 percent of the poolroom
employees got their jobs through political connections. Journalist Clarence Cul-
lin claimed that many regular track bettors first got the betting bug by going to
poolrooms, especially clerks, small businessmen, waiters, coachmen, and eleva-
tor boys. The great bettor Pittsburgh Phil Smith, for instance, graduated from a

poolroom to become a regular, and then a plunger. Even worse, critics envisioned the poolrooms as corrupting their clients, pushing some into a life of crime to pay for their gambling debts.[1]

New York City struggled to eliminate, or at least curtail, the poolroom problem. The authorities had limited success, even though thoroughbred racing across the country was in disarray, and the New York turf itself feared termination. This chapter examines how the poolroom and handbook businesses survived and often thrived in the early 1900s, despite widespread opposition, by using payoffs and political connections. The key factors were the enormous public interest in accessible horse race betting and the close alliance among organized crime, Tammany Hall, and the police, who worked together to protect a profitable and popular, albeit illegal, form of amusement.

Clean Up the Poolrooms

New York department stores, including Saks, Macy's, Siegel Cooper, and other large businesses, were concerned about the negative results of their employees' gambling, such as going into debt, losing their work ethic by trying to get rich quick, and destroying their character. Consequently, they forbade workers from betting on races or made it known that dallying with gaming could mean dismissal. Employers similarly discouraged their staff from borrowing money from loan sharks because they worried workers would steal or embezzle to repay their debts.[2]

Close supervision supposedly made it easy to ward off bookies seeking clients from department store clerks. When merchant F. Norton Goddard, a leader in the nonpartisan Civic Club, a reform group established in 1892 to promote efficient and honest government, found a nice young man in his employ betting on the horses, he fired him. Goddard could not trust a staff member once he got the betting fever. However, there was less close control in financial offices, which were supposedly productive sites for professional gamblers.[3]

Poolroom foes, except for gambling's most ardent critics who believed that all wagering was vile, distinguished between legal gambling at tracks and illegal off-course betting. They also differentiated between racing fans who took the time and trouble to go to the tracks to bet and gambling addicts who bet at poolrooms or with handbook men. Critics also emphasized the importance of social class when it came to laying wagers. The well-to-do gambled at tracks, not poolrooms. Goddard differentiated between betting at suburban tracks by men of leisure who could afford their losses and "the poolrooms [that] are an invasion of neighborhoods in which wage-workers, salaried men, and boys are likely to be tempted. The small businessman, the clerk, the laborer, or the office boy, who cannot find the time to go to a racetrack, can spare a few minutes in place a bet on the horses in a pool-room."[4]

Despite the nearly universal criticism of poolrooms and handbooks, New York City remained the national center of off-track betting at the turn of the century, and its large betting community avidly supported the illicit gambling. A 1909 congressional investigation held in conjunction with a proposed bill to bar the transmittal of racetrack betting odds over telegraph or phone lines heard Henry Brolaski, a California gambler, bookmaker, and racetrack owner, estimate there were one hundred thousand handbook and poolroom players in New York, serviced by fifty poolrooms and five hundred handbooks. He further (under-) estimated that there were ten to twenty poolrooms and a thousand handbooks located elsewhere in the United States.[5]

The metropolitan press in the early twentieth century blasted poolrooms, as did the national media, which saw the problem mainly limited to New York and Chicago. The most thorough exposé of the poolroom menace outside the daily press came from a three-part piece in 1907 by journalist Josiah Flynt in *Cosmopolitan* that tried to blow the lid off the problem in those two cities. Flynt, a nephew of social reformer Francis Willard, was a former tramp and a student at the University of Berlin, who had previously written *Tramping with Tramps: Studies and Sketches of Vagabond Life* (1899), *Notes of an Itinerant Policeman* (1900), and *The World of Graft* (1901). The first article, "The Pool-Room Vampire and Its Money Mad Victims," set the tone of the series. *Cosmopolitan* editor Ernest Crosby introduced the trilogy by describing poolrooms "as a canker on our national life" and "a traffic that has destroyed more homes than Wall Street, that counts more victims than the bucket-shop, that is conducted by a series of trusts more rapacious, more absolute, than the Standard Oil Company."[6]

Flynt described the entire poolroom operations, including "the big gambling spiders and the little human flies that get enmeshed in the pool-room web." He discussed in depth the Gambling Trust that controlled the business, the system of police protection, and the "men of culture and refinement" who allowed the system to operate and benefited financially from it. He depicted the betting world of horse racing as a "dopeland," where horses were "doped"; gamblers were doped by hunger to bet, anesthetizing their brains, just like drugs (dope); and the "dope" or racing information was fed through the press and by "dope" sheets sold by "dopesters" for a dollar or two to their clients ("dopes"). Flynt quoted an expert who estimated that $110 million was annually bet at tracks in the United States, and an equal amount illegally off the tracks. His friend also said that legal on-track bookmakers grossed about $15.5 million, but the illegal gamblers made around $20 million.[7]

Virtually no one outside the poolroom business or their political allies spoke favorably of poolrooms except for the sports-oriented *New York Morning Telegraph*, where Bat Masterson manned the sports desk. It had no special quarrel with either poolrooms or bookmakers: "Conducted properly [poolrooms] . . . may be regarded as legitimate as enterprises carried on by many who inveigh and crusade against them." As to the bookmakers, they "serve their purpose. . . . They are gentlemen adventurers who hold themselves out to lay against the information, the hunches, the mathematics of all comers and will take chances against the inspiration furnished by all the dream books ever printed."[8]

The Mazet Investigation

In spring 1899, Governor Theodore Roosevelt and other leading Republicans, including U.S. Senator Thomas C. Platt, state party chairman Benjamin B. Odell, a U.S. congressman and future governor (1900–1904), and New York Assembly Speaker Samuel F. Nixon, prodded the state assembly to conduct a thoroughgoing investigation of Tammany Hall's corruption and the alleged wasteful mismanagement of New York City's government. Roosevelt claimed to have received some two hundred letters claiming that Tammany officials had contributed money to a fund to influence legislation and had levied $500 "donations" from police captains. The special investigative committee intended to focus on governmental operations, primarily the police department, and an alleged corruption fund raised by policemen, saloon keepers, and resort owners to influence government officials. Republicans saw this inquiry as a great opportunity to destroy Tammany by publicizing the nexus between organized crime and machine politics, thereby discrediting the Democratic Party, and to promote their plan to establish a single police commissioner for New York City who would take politics out of law enforcement. The investigation's motivation was overtly partisan, according to the independent *New York Times* and the Democrat-leaning *Brooklyn Eagle*. However, there *was* a lot of corruption to unravel, and the investigation helped blow the lid off the poolroom business.[9]

Attorney Robert Mazet (R–New York County), a second-term assemblyman and chairman of the Committee on Cities, led the investigation. His inquiry was widely recognized as a follow-up to the 1894 Lexow Investigation, the first thorough examination by a government agency of the relationship among police, the underworld, and politicians. Mazet and chief investigator Frank Moss, associate counsel of the Lexow committee, called nearly every prominent Tammany leader to testify and devoted considerable attention to suspected malfeasance related to gambling.[10]

On 6 April, the day before the committee convened, journalists visited dozens of New York City poolrooms. The *Times* found 38 rooms operating and suggested that there were probably another dozen in business. The *Journal* claimed there were 250 poolrooms just in Manhattan and another 50 elsewhere in the city. A *Times* reporter investigated one of the city's largest poolrooms, Joe Young's Arcade in the East Village of Lower Manhattan, a favorite with the police, and counted as many as two thousand customers present, including eight uniformed or plain-clothes officers.[11]

The *Times* reported little or no evidence that the police had tried to close the gambling establishments. Most rooms took bets as small as $1, though Levein's pretentious second-floor facility (20 Dey Street) took only $5 bets, as did Charley Reilly's parlor on the third floor of the old Downing Building (108 Fulton Street). Gamblers recorded their bets on a slip of paper and gave them to a sheet writer seated behind an enclosure. The bettor got no receipt, but if he won, he made an exact duplicate of his original slip. The bookie paid off if the handwriting matched.[12]

Many resorts remained open the next day but were very cautious about admitting strangers. Some operated as private clubs that required membership cards for admittance. Others carefully scrutinized potential customers before admitting them. As one cashier noted, "As long as the 'knock' is confined to the newspapers, we are in no danger of going out of business. . . . I imagine, however, that we will go on until we get the tip to stop."[13]

The *Times* described the poolroom crowd as "the raggedest, most forlorn looking, tattered and battered set that it is possible to imagine." Their reporter encountered many touts, especially in the dollar rooms: "He knows the symptoms of doubt on the face of the bettor when the latter views the board and he lights on his victim like a hawk on a sparrow. There is no escaping him. Many of the rooms employ these touts to give victims false information. Should the victims win by any possibility, the tout comes in for his share of the proceeds. If the victim loses then the tout looks to the room keeper for his reward."[14]

New York's poolrooms at the turn of the century had a daily overhead of $75–$100, which included $37–$42 for the staff (manager, cashier, sheet writer, telegraph operator, lookout, and guard), $5–$10 for rent (typically double the normal cost of legitimate businesses), $30 for telegraph services, and $7 for incidentals, which included payoffs. One poolroom operator who had a modest facility at Third Avenue near Thirty-seventh Street, and spent $100 a month in rent, paid the police, politicians, and even people from the antivice societies $1,200 a month to leave him alone. He cleared more than $54,000 after expenses in just seven months.[15]

When the Mazet Committee convened on 7 April, one of the first witnesses was Police Chief William Devery. Two years earlier, the courts convicted Captain

Devery of bribery and extortion, resulting in his dismissal. However, he appealed, won his case, and gained reinstatement. Then in less than six months, he jumped to inspector, deputy chief, and then chief, thanks to his connections to Tammany and Mayor Robert A. Van Wyck.[16]

The committee grilled Devery on various topics, including police transfers and the poolroom problem. He denied all knowledge of poolrooms and was skeptical of their existence, even though two days earlier, reporters gave him a list of nearly 100 poolrooms they had visited. The committee also questioned him on his close ties to certain notorious New Yorkers, including gambling king-pin Frank Farrell, who owned Devery's home and had bailed him out of jail in 1897. Farrell, the city's second most famous gambling entrepreneur after Richard Canfield, operated lavish Midtown casinos that offered a wide variety of gaming options, as well as a poolroom at 54 West Twenty-eighth Street, which he claimed belonged to Big Tim Sullivan. Farrell and Devery belonged to Sullivan's Lower East Side political club. In 1903, they used their political clout to become co-owners of the city's new American League baseball team, the Highlanders (later known as the Yankees).[17]

The Mazet Committee interrogated several police officers who said they knew nothing about poolrooms in their districts and several prominent political leaders, including Mayor Van Wyck, Police Commissioner John B. Sexton, and Police Board president Bernard York. Van Wyck, a former judge, was a combative witness, denying any involvement in poolrooms. He admitted knowing pool-room king James A. Mahoney, whom he saw every few days at the Democratic Club, and said that they had been partners in an unprofitable Texas poolroom a decade earlier but was unaware of his current off-track dealings. Van Wyck was followed by an angry, "well dressed, squared jawed and square shouldered" Sexton, who (along with York) acknowledged gambling was probably going on but claimed that police captains had cleaned it up. He admitted knowing both Mahoney and Farrell for at least fifteen years but said that he had not followed up on reports that the poolrooms were syndicate controlled because he thought they were idle rumors.[18]

James A. Mahoney, a racetrack gambler, and the number-one poolroom operator in the city, with interests in building and real estate and reportedly worth $7 million, was the most prominent gambler called to testify. Mahoney started out as a downtown Chicago bookmaker and poolroom owner in 1885 when its downtown betting parlors operated openly. He was an extremely hostile witness, questioning the committee's right to investigate him because he was a private citizen. Mahoney admitted membership in the Democratic Club and said that his friends included Van Wyck, Sexton, and city clerk John F. Carroll, one of Boss Croker's chief deputies.

The witness tried to avoid answering questions about poolrooms but conceded having operated a poolroom in Lower Manhattan (12 Centre Street) as recently as 1893. Mahoney did not respond to a query asking if he had at least fifty telephones at his business at Forty-second Street. However, one year later, Mahoney admitted to a journalist that he had 64 poolrooms in Greater New York, plus more in New Jersey and elsewhere, with each room netting $125 a day. Mahoney reportedly made more than $1 million from 1900 to 1905 from his poolrooms.[19]

Mazet Committee detective John R. Wood investigated some 125 poolrooms between 7 April and mid-May, including all the rooms cited in a recent *Times* investigation, and found the police had taken no actions to halt the poolrooms. Wood interviewed some patrons, including clothing manufacturer Philip Cohen, who told him that the police took their time responding to his complaint about a poolroom cheating him out of a $200 bet, and Hans J. Widness, who claimed to have lost more than $4,000 at a poolroom. Widness never had any trouble finding an open poolroom, since he "just followed the crowd."[20]

The newspaper disclosures about the poolroom problems, along with the Mazet Committee's revelations that about eight to ten thousand people were regular poolroom clients, brought renewed public attention to the poolroom problem. Uptown rooms, concerned about greater scrutiny, began using several lookouts instead of a single person, and strangers entering poolrooms had to either flash a "membership" card or run a security gauntlet to gain admission.[21]

On 20 May, Chief Devery, who had long denied the existence of poolrooms, finally reported the problem of poolrooms to his precinct commanders. Three days later, headquarters told ward men to put out the "word" that poolrooms had to close up or their workers would face arrest. Thereafter, only De Lacy dared admit unfamiliar people into his hall. The rooms stopped posting odds and refused bets at second-rate Aqueduct and on out-of-town events. Bettors could write the names of their horses on their ticket but nothing else, and they had to return the following day to cash in at track odds. Bettors who wagered on events at Aqueduct or out of state took their business to curbstone bookmakers who got their information from saloon tickers.[22]

When Gravesend opened on 27 May, some poolrooms reopened to make book on the Brooklyn Handicap, because, one room keeper explained, it was worth the risk: "It was too good a thing to let go by. All the people who think they know everything about a horse race and who don't know anything at all, are brought out by big events like the Brooklyn Handicap, and we want their money." By mid-June, poolrooms were pretty much back in operation.[23]

In late October, just before the upcoming election, Boss Croker spoke out in support of his Democratic slate and proclaimed that no poolrooms were operating because Chief Devery "told me so." However, Moss's detectives told Croker a couple of days later that seventy-two rooms were going full blast, many becoming full-blown gambling parlors in the evening. The detectives claimed that recent mandatory large campaign contributions to Tammany had secured the rooms' greater immunity than ever before.[24]

The Mazet investigation produced a lot of negative publicity for Tammany but did not immediately shake things up. No one ever went to prison because of the revelations, and Tammany even did well in the upcoming election. The Democrats defeated Assemblyman Mazet, upped their representation from New York in the lower house from forty-five to forty-six, and increased their presence on the sixty-man Board of Aldermen from forty-seven to forty-nine. The police "war" on the poolrooms was very brief, and mainly for public relations, falling apart once the local racing season was going full swing. The *Times* attributed the police inattention to Devery's connections to the gamblers and the malfeasance of Police Commissioners Abell, Sexton, York, and Jacob Hess. In March 1900, in the midst of a new exposé, the *Times* called on Mayor Van Wyck to dismiss the lot of them, which he did not do. Nonetheless, the exposure was bad publicity for Tammany, and contributed to a major defeat for Tammany and the Democrats in the 1901 mayoral election.[25]

There were adequate laws on the books to go after the poolrooms, but the problem was enforcement. It was hard to make arrests stand up, even with corroborating evidence. Police Commissioner Henry E. Abell passed the buck to magistrates, whom he blamed for making it nearly impossible to imprison violators because they required evidence of registered bets. Board president Bernard York admitted that in cosmopolitan Manhattan, "It is one of those sores that cannot quite be eradicated."[26]

The publicity generated by the Mazet Committee and the press convinced many state legislators that the innovative technology employed by off-track gamblers, particularly telephones, generated a need for innovative legislation to fight back. On 2 March 1900, Assemblyman Leon Sanders (D–New York County) resubmitted a bill introduced the year before, prohibiting the furnishing of betting odds or results by any mechanical device on any contest of skill, speed, power, or endurance, of man or beast. A first offense would receive just a $50 fine or thirty days in jail, but the second offense would be a felony carrying a minimum $2,000 fine and at least two years in jail. On 29 March, his bill passed the assembly by a resounding vote of seventy-nine to twelve. However, it never got to a vote in the senate because of the formidable lobbying by telegraph and phone companies and ardent canvassing by poolroom operators. A prominent senator, presumably Tim Sullivan, reportedly assessed more than four hundred poolrooms $350 to build up a fund to block the Sanders bill. On the same day, Sullivan's boxing business suffered a major setback when the legislature repealed the Horton Act that had legalized prizefighting in 1896. Sanders reintroduced his bill a year later, but again it went nowhere.[27]

The Poolroom Trust

At the turn of the century, the more than four hundred poolrooms in New York City each serviced more than one hundred customers a day, or some forty thousand players. Unbeknownst to the public, a notorious poolroom trust controlled this business. The first poolroom trust probably began in the mid-1890s in wide-open Long Island City, where illegal gambling flourished under Mayor Gleason. James Mahoney, who was already operating rooms all over New York, played a big role when he joined the syndicate. He originally paid Western Union $5 for a telegraph report of each race and a salary for one operator per room, plus $10 per room for expenses. Mahoney was Western Union's single largest customer and consequently sought a rate reduction. After the wire service rejected his request, Mahoney retaliated by announcing a plan to set up his own wire service. This threat convinced Western Union to lower his fee to $1 a race. Mahoney had three hundred workers at his Forty-second Street central exchange, where he also had a printing plant producing cards, tickets, and other betting paraphernalia.[28]

The syndicate's main figure was Big Tim Sullivan, the boss of the Lower East Side and the number-two man in Tammany Hall. Journalists often saw him at a poolroom located over a saloon at Fortieth Street and Sixth Avenue, supposedly operated by protégé George Considine, the Broadway AC boxing matchmaker, though it was widely believed that Sullivan was the actual owner. He and Considine were also partners in a vaudeville booking agency and ran about forty theaters in the western United States.[29]

The poolroom men and their political allies supported the concept of a trust, emulating the structure of major corporations that dominated basic American industries. The syndicate facilitated the acquisition of racing information at the cheapest possible prices and the circumvention of legal restrictions. It provided protection from the authorities, maintained control over subordinates, and rationalized the industry to save money through such schemes as establishing four central stations to reduce telegraph tolls and then resending the data over phone lines.[30]

The public was unaware of the Gambling Trust until the press, particularly the *Times* and the *World*, revealed its presence in early March 1900. Reporters alleged that the organization annually collected more than $3 million to keep its resorts free of interference by bribing police captains and certain Democratic and

Republican politicians. The five men in charge, whose names went unmentioned, reportedly included two state senators, a city commissioner, and the "dictator of the poolroom syndicate."[31]

Nearly two years later, when William Travers Jerome was running for district attorney under a reform fusion ticket composed of Republicans and the Citizens' Union, he named as the trust's leaders the police commissioner, Joseph Sexton; the city clerk, John F. Carroll; gambler Frank Farrell; former police chief William Devery; and former mayor Van Wyck, with Boss Croker in charge. Jerome's list was accurate except for Croker, who was averse to off-track gambling, and his omission of the real man in charge, Senator Big Tim Sullivan. In addition, James A. Mahoney and Peter De Lacy had permission from Sullivan and the Gambling Trust to run their own syndicates.[32]

The trust's leadership comprised a "gambling commission" that met weekly at a member's apartment to apportion profits and "license" gambling operations. They permitted rooms to expand gambling options because of all the competition, to include craps, faro, and roulette. License applicants paid the local police captain a $300 initiation fee, and then had to pass a reliability check. Once approved, operators paid regular fees to authorized collectors ("bagmen"), usually a policeman who was the ward man for a captain or inspector. The poolrooms were assessed $300 a month, amounting to $1,440,000 a year, the single largest source of revenue for the gambling commission. The trust also made big money by licensing five hundred craps games at $150 a month ($900,000), two hundred small gambling houses at $150 a month ($360,000), twenty large gambling houses at $1,000 a month ($240,000), and fifty envelope games (in which people "bought" envelopes supposedly full of money) at $50 a month ($30,000). Finally, there was policy, where the city's two bankers contributed a lump sum ($125,000). In policy, bettors had to pick three numbers randomly selected by the game operator, usually from the last three digits of that day's stock transactions. These fees all amounted to $3,095,000 a year.[33]

The trust limited entry into the business, protected members from police harassment, and negotiated with Western Union. Its racing bureau charged poolrooms $5 for information on each race that included a list of entries and weights, riders, scratches, first and second betting, and a description of the race and its outcome. Poolroom managers also had to pay $5 to their own operator and clerk at the track that sent the data. Rooms received information on races six days a week, year-round.[34]

The *Times* estimated that Western Union received $65 a day from each of the city's poolrooms in the late 1890s, or $26,000 a day. These charges came to $8.14 million a year for 313 days, with no racing on Sundays. The syndicate cut these fees by establishing four central receiving stations in Manhattan that received dispatches directly from the tracks and relayed the information to their clients. Consequently, wire-service fees in 1900 dropped to less than $1,000 a day. Poolrooms paid the combine $1 per race for telephone services (typically $15 a day), plus a fee to rent the phones.[35]

The trust actually was less of a monopoly than the press realized. Besides the well-known Mahoney and De Lacy operations, there was at least one other independent syndicate run by Robert H. Davis and Charles J. Reilly, with the support of Michael J. Reardon and J. P. Robison under the protection of Senator Thomas F. Grady and other Tammanyites. The ring began in 1897 but was uncovered only when a police raid at the end of March 1907 at 112 Fulton Street uncovered its records. The police found about two thousand checks at one of the syndicate's six banks, which in one year amounted to $1,752,428, reflecting an annual turnover of more than $8 million in losses and winnings. From 1899 until late in 1901, the organization made about $20,000 a month, with about 16 percent going to Grady. While the raid was in progress, an investigator picked up a ringing phone and spoke to Grady, who was on the line, making a $200 bet. Grady became the butt of cartoonists for the next several months.[36]

The revelations of the poolroom trust led to renewed criticism of off-track gambling. On 9 March, the day the *Times* broke the story about the trust, it informed Deputy District Attorney McIntyre that one of the city's largest poolrooms was directly across the street from the county courthouse, regularly visited by District Attorney Asa B. Gardiner's staff. The *Times* published a list with more than one hundred poolrooms that could not be operating without police involvement. An editorial derisively attacked the Police Board, calling on Mayor Van Wyck to fire them for "criminal negligence."[37]

Right after the *Times* exposé, the Police Board had a stormy four-hour meeting that led to Gardiner's announcing that he would go over the head of the police, if necessary, to halt the poolrooms. In response, headquarters ordered police districts to halt neighborhood poolrooms and sent news simultaneously to the betting parlors, which closed up by noon. The *Times* concluded, "If the police of New York can close up the gambling houses in twenty-four hours, it follows that the gambling houses cannot open at any time, without their knowledge and consent."[38]

The closures were reminiscent of events following an earlier *Times* exposé of poolrooms in 1893. Then, Boss Croker, who backed the racetracks, ordered them immediately shuttered. However, poolroom men knew that after a brief reform respite, trade would return to normal. The *Times* claimed that the big gamblers, particularly Mahoney, saw the temporary closings as an opportunity to push small betting shops out of business. Mahoney reportedly lost $6,000 a day because of the closings, but he planned to offset those losses by opening handbooks at his poolrooms.[39]

On 13 March, some poolroom betting occurred on the New Orleans races using track odds, but otherwise the betting parlors had little action for more than a month. However, this absence did not mark the end of off-track betting, because bettors opted for handbooks, even though they could not get track odds and other essential information. At Wall Street, bettors looking for action placed wagers through messenger boys, bartenders, and waiters in big cafés or at one of two open poolrooms. Bartenders who passed bets to bookmakers employed a code with their clients in which each drink represented a horse's name. Hence, "Whiskey Sling regular" meant a $2 bet on Blue Girl to win, while "water on the side" indicated a place bet. If the wager was higher, the bettor told the bartender to "put 10 on the ice."[40]

The poolrooms started to reopen in mid-April with the coming of the local racing season. One well-known bookie sent out cards to his old clients: "The Winter is over; the police have been fixed. Business resumed at No.—Sixth Avenue."[41] By 5 May, when Morris Park opened, the poolrooms were pretty much wide open. They had watchers at all doors, but anyone looking like a betting man could get in. A *Times* reporter went to De Lacy's, where the crowd did not seem well-to-do, walked right in, and won a dollar bet. The poolroom displayed cards with the names of horses, jockeys, and betting odds behind a glass partition. The reporter then visited a room owned by the gambling syndicate over Foley's Saloon (Centre and Franklin streets), where newspaper clippings with the records of horses and various tips were posted on a blackboard, along with a book full of charts of prior races. The room received its information by telephone.[42]

The poolroom situation harmed the Democratic Party's reputation, and consequently Boss Croker, who had opposed the poolroom for years, established the Tammany Committee for the Suppression of Vice (also known as the Tammany Vice Committee of Five) in late fall to investigate the situation. Croker recruited Lewis Nixon, a noted naval architect and manufacturer who used to work for him, to lead the task force to publicize the fact that the boss had never benefited from the poolroom business. Croker warned that any Tammany man who had taken money from the poolrooms should resign because he disgraced the organization. Nixon's colleagues on the committee were Fire Commissioner John J. Scannell, President Michael C. Murphy of the Health Board, Commissioner of Charities John W. Keller, and Parks Department President George C. Clausen. Nixon did a conscientious job and at the end of 1900 sent police headquarters a list of more than sixty-one gambling resorts and poolrooms. Nixon chastised Chief Devery for not closing up the rooms earlier and accused fifteen other Tammanyites of obstructing the fight.[43]

William Travers Jerome's Crusade Against the Poolrooms

The poolrooms fared well in the winter of 1900–1901, even though just a few southern tracks were operating. The *Eagle* indicated that from "December to April the rooms were thronged with men, eager to speculate, and willing to take all the worst of the prices." The rooms offered mediocre odds to hungry bettors, generally 5 percent to 50 percent of track odds, paying off on either ticker or morning-paper odds and never paying more than twenty to one. Their clients lacked a lot of the information people had at racecourses, such as the conditions of the horses, the weather, and the track.[44]

The police department reorganization in 1901 had little impact on the poolrooms. The Republican-controlled government in Albany passed a law restructuring the force to weaken Tammany's control by replacing the board of commissioners and the police chief with a single police commissioner. Mayor Van Wyck appointed the president of the board of health, Michael C. Murphy (who, ironically, was not in good health), as police commissioner. Former chief Devery, still protected by Croker, became chief inspector, the highest-ranking uniformed officer. Murphy subsequently promoted him to first deputy chief and largely left him in charge of the department. Historian James Richardson found that Devery's behavior "became more outrageous than ever."[45]

Early in 1901, New York's district attorney, Eugene A. Philbin, with the cooperation of Justice William Travers Jerome, made a big effort to fight the poolroom menace. Governor Roosevelt appointed Philbin, a Democrat, in December 1900, after firing Tammanyite Asa Gardiner for misfeasance, malfeasance, and neglect of duty after he failed to conduct proper investigations of election fraud and protected Chief Devery against indictments for encouraging mob violence.[46] Justice Jerome, a nephew of Leonard Jerome, had served on the Lexow Investigation and managed reformer William Strong's successful run for the mayoralty in 1894 before gaining appointment to the court of special sessions in 1895.[47]

On 18 February, Philbin, accompanied by two assistant district attorneys and detectives, raided the Parole Turf Club (20 Dey Street), one of the trust's largest poolrooms, a few blocks from city hall. Old-time bookmakers Ridge Levein and Henry Stedeker, a prominent member of the Democratic Club, owned the club. Jerome went along as a precautionary measure to maintain the raid's secrecy. Philbin was worried about possible tip-offs if detectives sought a warrant from a magistrate's court. The raid's aim was less to break up an illegal resort than to contest the politicians' protection of the poolrooms. Philbin intended to arrest the proprietors, hold the customers as witnesses, and pressure them to give sufficient evidence to convict the room keepers. He then intended to get Levein or

Stedeker to turn state's evidence and reveal their protector. The *Tribune* warned, "The collector is a politician high up in the councils of Tammany Hall . . . , but he covers the tracks so skillfully that the hunt for him will be both difficult and exciting."[48]

Philbin's foray relied on information supplied by detectives hired by Nixon's Committee for the Suppression of Vice, including J. R. Wood, who had worked for the Mazet investigation. When Stedeker stopped Wood at the entrance, the detective told him he was a former member of the Parole Turf Club and paid one dollar to reregister. Wood went into the building and entered a crowded room where there was betting. He passed a two-dollar wager through a partition to a betting clerk.[49]

The raiders encountered a barricaded door on the first floor and battered it down. They went up to the second-floor poolroom and rushed in while lively betting was taking place on races in San Francisco and New Orleans. A wild scramble ensued, and there were nearly eighty arrests, including Maurice F. Holahan, president of the Board of Public Improvements, and eight police officers. Jerome subsequently interviewed the poolroom's clerks and patrons right on the spot.[50]

The raid split Tammany between Croker and the Carroll-Sullivan-Farrell-Devery crowd. Several Tammanyites were mad that Nixon's study, protected by the Fire Commissioner Scannell, had put their organization in a bad light, since the poolroom employees, including sheet writers, cashiers, and doormen, were generally political appointees. Tim Sullivan's new political organization, "The Eagles," was reportedly entirely composed of poolroom and gambling-house employees. Tammany district leaders were jealous that poolroom profits were going not to them but to the Gambling Trust and about a dozen other leading Tammanyites.[51]

The Heat Is On

Pressure on the gamblers increased when the racing season commenced in April at Aqueduct, coming mainly from Judge Jerome and the Committee of Fifteen, a prestigious citizens' group organized in late 1900 to help rid the city of prostitution and gambling. Their attorney told Police Commissioner Murphy that any captain unaware of gambling in his precinct was incompetent, that captains were tipping off poolrooms, and that Detective Hughes of the West Twentieth Street station delayed sending his men on a raid so the alleged perpetrators could escape. The brass scoffed at these charges, claiming that station houses had men posted at the doors to prevent messengers from getting the word out to the poolrooms. Murphy recognized that the committee could stage raids without police cooperation, which they did in mid-April. The *Eagle* claimed this threat "instilled a dread among . . . [the poolrooms] which even police protection is not wholly able to allay."[52]

Jerome, together with Frank Moss, resumed the raids on April 25. Jerome told the press, "It is nonsense to say that gambling can't be stopped in this city. No man real white and 21 years of age would believe that 7,500 uniformed men in the Police Department could not suppress gambling if they wanted to." He interviewed captains, who all told him that no poolroom or gambling houses could exist in a precinct for two days without the captain knowing about it. Jerome wondered how that could be, since he recently found ten poolrooms in the Tenderloin district within four hundred yards of the station house.[53]

On 6 June, Jerome, former police chief John G. McCullagh (now state superintendent of elections and superintendent of the Committee of Fifteen), committee counsel Col. Robert Grier Monroe, and a staff of detectives paid an informal visit to a Frank Farrell–backed poolroom at 109 West Thirty-seventh Street in a two-story brick building that looked like a private home. They found some two hundred betting customers on the second floor. One day later, Jerome and Moss led a raid sponsored by the Society for the Prevention of Crime on the Germania Assembly Rooms and Dance Hall (291–93 Bowery), without local police because the SPC thought that its prior raids in Captain Moynihan's precinct were often tipped off. They came prepared with armed detectives carrying hammers, sledges, and hatchets. The raiders found three hundred customers present, but the owner was tipped off and had a stove ready with a can of kerosene to destroy the evidence.[54]

Three months later, the police raided Frank Farrell's Amsterdam Club (29 West Thirty-fourth Street), a four-story converted dwelling adjoining respectable homes. It was one of the city's best-known and most pretentious poolrooms, taking no bets less than $5. Fifty well-dressed people were found in the room. The club was equipped with ornate furnish and fittings, polished oak desks, chairs with soft leather cushions, and a buffet. The poolroom covered the entire third floor, and a fancy gambling room was upstairs.[55]

In August, the SPC ran a test to determine if its staff tipped off targeted poolrooms by misinforming its operatives about planned raids and then waiting for the response. The police warned twenty-five poolrooms, including De Lacy's, about forthcoming raids, and the rooms responded accordingly. The SPC found that a former agent, Edgar A. Whitney, was the primary tipster and had the police arrest him for aiding and abetting gambling. Whitney confessed, explaining he had been hired by ward man Edward Glennon of the Tenderloin Station, one of Devery's closest associates. Glennon had a checkered police career, having been dismissed on fifty-six charges after the Lexow Investigation, including neglect of duty and bribery. However, a court order reinstated him.[56]

Glennon knew Whitney had worked for the SPC and offered him a large fee for information about future SPC raids. A few days later, Whitney gave SPC agent Charles F. Dillon a list of twenty-eight protected poolrooms he had received from Glennon and dropped about $100 into Dillon's letter box. Whitney told Dillon that he was employed by people in the bookmaking business and offered him $250 a month if he would provide information about planned poolroom raids against the sheltered rooms. Dillon agreed, but it turned out he was a double agent gathering evidence for the SPC. The protected rooms paid SPC operatives $700 a month for advance information on raids, in addition to the $280 a month they regularly paid the police and another $2,800 to the police and other parties as special assessments.[57]

The Poolrooms Go to Court

Benjamin Steinhardt, Howe and Hummel's point man when it came to defending alleged bookmakers and poolroom operators, claimed that he was at heart a long-time critic of horse race betting. Steinhardt believed all citizens should be treated equally: "But so long as the opulent are permitted to gamble at Morris Park, I don't see why other citizens should not be permitted to lay odds on Manhattan Island." Steinhardt chastised the Ives Law race for criminalizing bookmaking and attacked the Committee of Fifteen for playing into the hands of the "so-called" Gamblers Trust.[58]

Poolroom men at the end of July arranged a test case involving Charles Bennett, a former employee of The Allen, indicted back on 16 April for operating a poolroom. Howe and Hummel brought in a heavy hitter to defend Bennett, John R. Dos Passos, father of the novelist, a renowned corporate and financial lawyer, and a constitutional expert. The firm wanted him to take the case straight to federal court to ascertain the constitutionality of Percy-Gray and the right of the district attorney to indict poolroom men for felonies. Dos Passos got the case shifted from the court of general sessions to the court of appeals for the Second Circuit based on his claim that Percy-Gray violated the Fourteenth Amendment, which prohibited the imposition of different penalties for the same offense.[59]

People of the State of New York v. Charles Bennett became a major legal contest. Dos Passos asserted that Bennett merited immediate release because the alleged events did not constitute a crime. He noted that since 1831, betting was punishable by a criminal penalty or forfeiture of wager but not imprisonment. Dos Passos then asserted that the 1887 Ives Act made gambling on tracks or in poolrooms equally punishable. He reviewed the theory that Percy-Gray was class legislation, giving people who could afford to visit the tracks and bet there a special privilege over gamblers who wanted to invest money on tests of speed but lacked the time or money to attend a race. It was unfair that "a man who goes in with a $5 bill in a privileged place should be exempt from arrest, when the man who has only $1 to invest, and seeks one of these secluded nooks, may be arrested by the police for doing so." Dos Passos also claimed that Percy-Gray was discriminatory because it authorized gambling only at racetracks and that the statute provided unequal and different punishments for the same offense, creating class legislation.[60]

Assistant DA Charles E. Le Barbier, representing the state, claimed the indictment was legal and said that there was no call for federal intervention. Joseph S. Auerbach of TJC filed an amicus curiae brief, supporting the state, claiming the distinction between bookmaking on the course and off the track was proper and legal. On 14 January 1902, federal judge Emile H. Lacombe upheld the Percy-Gray law.[61]

The Impact of the 1901 Election

Croker and the machine were in real trouble as the 1901 election loomed, especially because of all the adverse publicity about police corruption. Reformer Seth Low, the former mayor of Brooklyn and current president of Columbia University, ran for mayor on a fusion ticket, promising to clean up city hall. Also on the ticket was William T. Jerome, who ran for New York County district attorney, campaigning on a platform that included a promise to clean out the poolrooms if possible. Tammany responded by chastising Jerome and his raids as a threat to personal freedom. Tammany suffered a debacle in the November 1901 election, with Low elected mayor and Jerome district attorney. The defeat marked the end of Croker's regime as boss, and he soon moved to Ireland to race horses. Nixon replaced him as boss and remained in charge until May 1902, when Charles Francis Murphy took over. The results dismayed poolroom keepers. According to the *Eagle*, "The passing of Tammany Hall with its protection to these rooms—for a consideration, and no small consideration either—was a body blow to the backers of the rooms. Fear of raiding and prosecution force them to obey the law."[62]

The expected reform wave began almost immediately, beginning in Harlem, where popular poolrooms in the "Leadville" neighborhood (125th Street between Park and Third avenues) were suddenly deserted. An old poolroom in the rear of the Golden Oar, formerly owned by street-cleaning commissioner Percival E. Nagle, the local Tammany district leader, became a billiards parlor. Nagle had offered one thousand dollars before the election to anyone who could show him a poolroom or gambling house in the area, a bit cheeky, since himself ran a gambling hall that serviced some two to three hundred customers at any time. Despite the crackdown, Harlemites continued betting on the horses, relying on several handbooks who openly took bets on the streets without police interference.[63]

At the end of November, Acting Captain Churchill of the Fifth Street Station led a big raid in the Bowery against a poolroom in the Germania Assembly Rooms, run by Harry D. Burbridge for Frank Farrell, a facility Jerome raided back in June. This time the police found a front door six times as thick as the average, which required men with axes and crowbars to smash through the entry. The raiders had to bust through four more doors until they got into the poolroom, by which time its nearly three hundred customers had escaped.[64]

The police staged a major raid on Christmas Day, focusing on the Tenderloin, the heart of the gambling trade. Then the next day, all of Farrell's and Mahoney's Tenderloin rooms were shut down after the first race at New Orleans, along with "Honest John" Kelly's, who had operated without interruption since the end of 1898, even though he never paid off the police. Kelly was a former baseball player, major league umpire, and boxing referee. He got his nickname for turning down a ten-thousand-dollar bribe offer in 1888 to shade decisions in favor of the Boston nine. Kelly became a stockbroker and succeeded Richard Canfield as the city's leading gambling proprietor, with a famous club at Forty-fourth Street. The police "besieged" the building from 1918 through early 1922, when Kelly got out of the gambling business.[65]

Jerome's pressure pushed a lot of the winter gambling business to the handbooks, scores of which had sprung up all over. They had virtually no overhead and handled smaller sums than poolrooms, but like the poolrooms, they did not offer odds higher than twenty to one. Bettors worried about their welshing, although they rarely did.[66]

In early 1902, Seth Low and the reformers moved into city hall. They seemed to be making headway against the gamblers, and when the racing season began at Aqueduct on 15 April, the poolrooms were still quiet. The police seemed more vigilant than in the past. Deputy Police Commissioner Frederick H. Ebstein, in charge of Brooklyn and Queens, increased police attention against off-course gambling, assigning fifty police to harass the busy handbooks.[67]

Increased attention did not equate to stricter enforcement because of payoffs and the guile of poolroom operators and handbook men. Poolrooms came up with innovations to confound the authorities, such as outfitting themselves as coffee and cake restaurants. Patrons sat at tables as if waiting to give an order until a "waiter" appeared with a "menu" that posted betting odds in the margins. The patrons ordered their bet, paid their tab, and if they won, they received the profits from the waiter. In one case, Brooklyn police arrested two men for betting at an eatery after an officer made a bet with them and got a receipt. However, despite the airtight case, Magistrate James G. Tighe released the defendants. Ebstein decried Tighe's decision as "demoralizing." He was irate that the press did not chastise the courts for lax enforcement but always held the police responsible. The police thought their best and only response was to constantly harass the handbooks, drive them from place to place, and push them out of business.[68]

Women and the Poolrooms

The press recognized that women were ardent racing fans who enjoyed going to the track and betting on the horses. However, there is little data on women's attendance, and few women can be seen in photographs of crowd scenes. They do appear in pictures of clubhouses, restaurants, and other expensive seating areas. In 1904, the *World* estimated that fifty thousand women annually went to local tracks, and seven years later, the *Times* claimed that women constituted one-fourth of regular attendees, which seems far too high.[69]

Certain women were so addicted to the excitement of betting on racing that they went into saloon back rooms to bet. Women would not patronize poolrooms open to the general public but frequented rooms operated just for them. Journalist Josiah Flynt estimated that 2.5 percent of all New York's poolrooms catered exclusively to women, who presumably had learned to bet at the tracks. The public considered off-track betting by women to be reprehensible, and the press covered nearly every raid made on women's poolrooms. Men still held women up on a pedestal for their superior moral virtues, and it made news when they did not approach expectations. These stories were bad publicity for off-track betting.[70]

Josiah Flynt in his important investigation of poolrooms found women's rooms typically disguised themselves as honest shops where women of different classes who shared a common interest in betting could enjoy moments of excitement that provided an escape from humdrum lives: "In these rooms social caste was unknown. . . . The woman of wealth and social standing mingles with women of the half-world and with shop-girls." These rooms often advertised themselves as legitimate businesses, such as "'button-factories,' 'Millinery-shops,' 'Dressmaking-parlors,' and other establishments—but in reality pool-rooms."[71]

The police in 1900 raided a number of women's poolrooms. On 5 June, for instance, there was a big raid at a poolroom at 264 Eighth Avenue, where seventy women were present. The room was on top of the Greenroom, a concert hall and saloon. Neighbors became suspicious because an unusual number of women were seen coming in and out of the saloon, often a tip-off. There was also an incursion at another site following a husband's complaint to the police about his wife's gambling. The enterprise had been operating for six weeks and was adapted to "the wants of women who were anxious to increase their pin money." Chief Devery, not known for his alacrity in fighting poolrooms, directed the raid, probably for the publicity. The alleged proprietor, Mrs. Edward H. Martin, a.k.a. Grace Ryan, a.k.a. Gussie McKee, was previously arrested on 16 October 1899 for running a poolroom. Her husband was an army officer, court-martialed for mismanagement of the post exchange and canteen at Fort Hancock, New Jersey. The police arrested thirty-four women, including wives of well-to-do businessmen and merchants, for disorderly conduct, while others escaped. The presiding magistrate ruled, "These women had a perfect right to bet on the races. There is no law that makes it an offense for them to be found in a poolroom. . . . I discharge them all."[72]

Another raid occurred six days later at the second floor of the Colonial Hotel (243 West Seventeenth Street), a Raines Law facility where the sale of alcoholic beverages on Sundays was restricted to serving guests dining or reposing in their bedrooms. The incursion began at four o'clock, with the police dressed like long-shoremen to avert suspicion. Some detectives went through an alleyway, found a shed level with the second floor, and climbed up. They broke a door, which alarmed women inside in two small betting rooms. The invaders arrested twenty-eight women and four men, including the building's owner, and John Martin, the poolroom operator. The police found a phone, racing cards, and other betting paraphernalia. Nearly half of the women arrested fainted when they saw there was no escape. These alleged housewives were poorly dressed, and many were middle-aged and gray-haired. When the women bailed out left court, "almost every woman carried a newspaper or fan with which to shield her face from the curious glances of the people in the courtroom."[73]

Even after the discontinuance of racing in New York, in 1910 certain poolrooms and handbooks still catered to avid female bettors. Some ladies bet with other women who worked as agents of poolroom and handbook men at department stores, taking bets from female salesclerks. In 1911, a reporter saw fifty women on park benches reading newspapers containing past performances at Cincinnati's Latonia Race Track. He also found several poolrooms where between races, women bet at chuck-a-luck wheels at ten to fifteen cents a game and one poolroom in the shopping district that had three to four hundred regular players. Another favorite spot was the southwest corner of Central Park, where poolroom runners brought tips and carried bets to a nearby saloon that had a full service on races.[74]

One reporter found two poolrooms catering to women operating just ten minutes from the Times Building. One was a dairy restaurant on Sixth Avenue, where many women were seen reading the racing pages. They often split the cost of a bet, each putting in a dollar, or several would collect change for a two-dollar bet. A female reporter visited another nearby restaurant and café that served as a poolroom, which took no bets less than five dollars. It looked small and inconspicuous to pedestrians. However, inside the room were carpeted floors and walls covered by pictures of racehorses. Waiters' took notes from customers and exchanged currency in actions that appeared unrelated to the restaurant business. The regular customers came from all social classes, including a wealthy widow, a schoolteacher, a buyer for a local shop, and one poor woman who pooled funds from shop clerks to wager at the restaurant. These women lacked expertise and were "playing blind," though women elsewhere played more scientifically.[75]

One woman explained the sad situation to a reporter: "You cannot realize the awful temptation to which the woman bettor is exposed. She is frequently concealing the fact that she is betting on the races from her husband and friends. When she loses, she must make excuses. A great many times she borrows money. The people with whom she associates during racing hours are of a class to take quick advantage of a woman's need and extremity, and many a respectable woman does things in desperation which eventually lead to her disappearance in the Tenderloin."[76]

Reformers and the Poolroom Scene, 1903–4

The fusion regime came into office with great expectations, but won only a two-year term owing to recent changes in the city charter. Low promoted civil service and brought in competent and efficient administrators, cut graft in the police department, expanded city services, lowered taxes, and employed underrepresented ethnic groups. However, the regime had little success in fighting the poolroom business. By the fall of 1902, Jerome admitted that there were many more rooms operating than when he campaigned to become district attorney. He claimed his office lacked the financial resources to do the job and blamed the police for insufficient cooperation.[77]

The Regime of Mayor George B. McClellan Jr.

In 1903, Tammany resolved to kick out Seth Low and his crew of reformers and return to power. Tammany's new leader was Charles Francis Murphy, a liberal machine boss, who came up with his own reform candidate to head the Democratic ticket and clean up the machine's poor public image. Democratic mayoral nominee George B. McClellan Jr., a thirty-seven-year-old lawyer and son of the famous Civil War general and presidential candidate, had already compiled an impressive career in public service as a Tammany Democrat and was receiving attention as a potential candidate for national office. McClellan was completing his fourth term in Congress after having served as president of the Board of Aldermen (1892–94). Many voters hoped he would run a clean regime, though Tammanyites anticipated his victory would enable them to resume their old ways with a veneer of integrity. The poolroom syndicate was not happy with McClellan's nomination, concerned that he would break up their protection system, which was all right with Murphy.[78]

McClellan was elected by a wide margin over Mayor Seth Low (53.4 percent to 42.7 percent). He turned out to be an honorable and independent mayor who concentrated on internal improvements. A biographer described him as "a nineteenth-century aristocratic gentleman who sought to contribute to the common good." He opposed the poolrooms and in 1904 backed Assemblyman Jacob D. Remsen's (R–Kings County) unsuccessful bill making it a misdemeanor for a phone or telegraph company to furnish entries, odds, results, or other details of racing. The mayor had a tough reelection campaign in 1905 when the office reverted to a four-year term, winning with just 38.7 percent of the total vote. McClellan had a 3,485-vote plurality out of 604,673 ballots cast over publisher and Democratic U.S. congressman William R. Hearst (37.2 percent), who ran on the independent Municipal Ownership League ticket, with Republican William M. Ivins (22.7 percent) a distant third. During McClellan's second term (1906–9), he vigorously fought against gambling, prostitution, corruption, and other vices, which resulted in a falling out with Murphy. After his term expired, he returned to private life, and in 1912, he became a professor of economics at Princeton. McClellan was among the finest mayors of his era, but historians have largely neglected him.[79]

During McClellan's first term, he and Boss Murphy stood behind his new police commissioner, William McAdoo, a former U.S. congressman and assistant secretary of the navy who opposed a wide-open city and promised to suppress poolrooms and other gambling houses. The *World* thought the new administration did a great job in its first two weeks in pushing the police to close up the rooms and noted that "practically every pool-room in town was closed. . . . The Town is closed tighter than it has been for many years."[80]

There were reportedly seventy-four poolrooms operating when McClellan became mayor, and they soon complained that the authorities were harassing them. Some machine leaders tied to the gamblers issued an ultimatum to certain Tammany officials to go on record against police interference with poolrooms, especially since the gamblers had given them a lot of money for the last election campaign. The poolroom syndicate warned that unless the machine agreed to let them operate quietly, their rooms would open anyhow and announce they had gotten permission.[81]

Tammany's leadership reached a compromise, although no one expected the police commissioner to support it. However, as an insider pointed out, "Well, Mr. McAdoo is only a Police Commissioner. The Police Department is going to be run by a Police Sergeant who will have more say in police affairs than any Captain, Inspector, or other official in the City of New York. Wait and See."[82]

The gambling syndicate agreed to set a new fee schedule for protection and required poolrooms to reapply for permission to operate. A rate schedule was set up with a maximum assessment of $400 for the 32 largest rooms, sliding down to $350 for 67 rooms, $250 for 90 rooms, and $100 for the smallest 112 rooms. Only half of the places applying to resume business were accepted. They pledged to operate inconspicuously and have a responsible man at the door to check potential clients. They were also required to hire an inside guard ($4 a day), a blackboard writer ($6), and two sheet writers ($10), who got their jobs based on the local Tammany leader's recommendations.[83]

The most popular poolrooms then were wired rooms connected to a syndicate, but there were also unconnected wire rooms and telephone rooms. Wire rooms got their news directly from the track by wire or from a nearby central distributing station. Phone rooms got their news from a wire room, were usually a branch of a main wire room, and were the cheapest to operate. Virtually all syndicate rooms had telephone service, carpeted floors, and free liquor. Bets were rarely less than $2 and ranged from $1 to thousands of dollars. The consortium expected managers to report immediately to their central office any bets on a favorite of more than $50 and any large bets on a long shot so the syndicate could lay off those wagers at the track or place the bets with another group to protect against a big loss.[84]

The Harlem Poolrooms

Early in 1904, the *New York World* ran a series of articles about gambling in Harlem, a neighborhood rapidly becoming one of the largest Jewish neighborhoods in the world. Harlem was mainly inhabited by first- and second-generation Jews moving up and out of the Lower East Side. Community leaders made a big push to clean up the area, which encouraged several rooms to move north to the Bronx. The *World* blamed the gambling in Harlem on the police's connections to Tammany, particularly the third deputy police commissioner, John F. Cowan, a Tammany ward leader who was accused of being friendly with certain folk who kept the lid off the Harlem gamblers. The *World*'s criticisms led to his resignation.[85]

The *World* was especially incensed at the first deputy commissioner, Thomas F. McAvoy, a twenty-five-year veteran of the force who was a West Side Tammany district leader. He was in the construction business and in 1903 got a $200,000 contract to excavate the Hilltop site at 165th Street for owners Bill Devery and Frank Farrell to build the ballpark. The *World* claimed he was unfit to hold an executive position in the police department because of his "tainted record," as revealed back in 1894 in the Lexow Hearings, and because his political lieutenant was involved in Harlem poolrooms. The paper accused him of neglect of duty for failing to close poolrooms secretly operated by political associates. In 1905, McAvoy sued the paper for $250,000 for damaging his reputation. The jury concluded that the poolrooms were open, but not "wide open," and doubted that it was McAvoy's job to investigate and close the rooms. The jury ruled that the *World* wrongly singled him out but awarded him just $1,000 for compensatory damages and $3,000 in punitive damages.[86]

Western Union and the Racing Wire

Western Union at the turn of the century grossed $5 million or more a year just from the poolroom trade. The business was so lucrative that for several years, Western Union paid $25,000 to the Postal Telegraph and Cable Company just to stay out of the sporting news business! Western Union's daily revenues nationwide were reportedly $13,000. New York's one hundred independent poolrooms each paid $20 a day, while the city's four syndicates that controlled twenty-five or more rooms paid $250, and outside of New York, two hundred poolrooms paid an average of $50. The company, in turn, paid $3,000 a day to the tracks for permission to send the racing news but kept overhead low by requiring poolrooms to pay for their own operators. Such expenses as wire installation and maintenance were more than balanced by net receipts just during the winter racing season when the New York tracks were closed. Revenue for the fiscal year ending on 30 June 1903 was $8,214,472, of which $2,268,722 was profit.[87]

On 10 January 1904, Western Union increased its prices for each poolroom to $25 for the first track's report and $5 more for each additional track, while paying tracks $10 for every poolroom that received its results ($1,500 a day). The company anticipated the new fee schedule would produce $30,000 a day in revenue. Gamblers passed on the higher rates to clients, partly by offering them poorer odds than before. The *Chicago Record-Herald* believed this sharp increase would be a disaster for off-track gambling and cause 75 percent of the poolrooms to close. The new fees would do more to hinder poolrooms than any police raid.[88]

Western Union was under enormous criticism from reformers for transmitting racing news to its clients, which the company's executives pointed out was a legal obligation. The firm was indicted three years earlier in Louisville, Kentucky, for maintaining a nuisance in furnishing track news to "the Kingston," a local gambling house. The Kentucky Court of Appeals ruled the company was duty bound to transmit all messages tendered to it if written in decent language.[89]

On 27 April, Capt. F. Norton Goddard, chairman of a City Club investigative committee, concluded in a major report that Western Union was "a Fountain Head of Poolrooms" that deliberately aided and abetted the gambling evil. Born in 1861, Goddard was a man of enormous character, whose merchant father left him and his brother each $6 million. Goddard attended Harvard and then moved into an East Thirty-third Street tenement, where he formed a self-help group among his neighbors that evolved into the progressive City Club. He got involved in reform politics and became an East Side Republican district leader. Goddard gained considerable fame for his fight against policy gambling that resulted in sending Al Adams, king of the policy racket, to jail.[90]

Goddard procured data on Western Union's poolroom business by assigning three operatives to purchase racing information. Two met with David H. Mitchell, manager of Western Union's Special Wire Bureau. They told him of their intent to open a poolroom in time for the Aqueduct meet and their need for a special wire. He sent them to meet Superintendent J. W. Dealy of the Commercial News Department, where the third investigator joined them, identifying himself as the poolroom's backer. He told Dealy he wanted to be careful in "squaring the police and public authorities" and needed a "fly" (clever) operator who knew the right people. Mitchell promised to provide an experienced man who "knows enough to climb out of the window when trouble comes."[91]

Western Union's response to Goddard's report was that its job was merely transmitting information and had no legal responsibility for the use of the data. District Attorney Jerome rejoined that the company's directors might not be legally guilty of compounding a felony, but they did bear moral responsibility for the continuance of the poolrooms. Jerome recognized that the company had the right to sell their news to anyone but asserted the directors could stop it if they chose, which would immediately close the gambling houses.[92]

Western Union was also criticized by the labor movement, mad that members of the Commercial Telegraphers' Union in America were losing jobs. On 1 May, New York's Central Federated Union adopted resolutions against the company, based on Goddard's revelations that the company was in league with poolroom gamblers, touts, and vice supporters.[93]

Three days later, Col. Robert C. Clowry, president and general manager of Western Union, told the Associated Press that the company would cooperate with the authorities in suppressing poolrooms, though he reiterated that the company was required by law to transmit all decently worded messages. Clowry pointed out that the company had been transmitting sporting news for forty years, including results of cycling, car races, baseball, football, and other sports.[94]

Clowry's announcement led the *Times* to postulate that the perfect moment had arrived to suppress poolrooms because they were most vulnerable at the point where they got their information. The paper believed that even if reformers, including Commissioner McAdoo, could not convince the company to drop the business, there was a good chance the legislature would take action against Western Union and also the New York Telephone Company (NYTC) because of their gambling connections. The *Times* recommended both firms immediately exit the racing business and thereby make up for past indiscretions and improve their public image.[95]

Despite Western Union's promised cooperation, it tried to forestall action by demanding the authorities first hand over a list of alleged poolrooms for whom it should discontinue service. McAdoo, Jerome, and the press denounced these stalling tactics, and the firm soon acceded to pressure, particularly Jerome's threat to take action against the company for its gambling connections. On 17 May, Western Union halted service to New York racing news distributors and poolrooms but maintained service to other clients. Telegraphers at the tracks still sent racing news to Western Union headquarters, from which it was relayed to out-of-town customers. The city's poolrooms responded by securing race results from distant poolrooms by telegraph or phone. Tenderloin rooms reported only ten-minute delays in reporting information, with no serious interruption in paying out bets.[96]

The next day, Clowry ordered his workers to not collect racing results and withhold data from all clients in the United States. This decision seemed to mean the end of a very profitable business. Jerome applauded the Western Union's public-spirited corporate mentality, giving up large profits for the welfare of the community. The *Tribune* believed this move was the biggest jolt to the poolrooms in more than a decade: "The Western Union's sweeping order was the worst blow the poolrooms have felt since twelve years ago, when a certain member [Croker] of Tammany Hall sent word to the poolroom kings to shut up shop and stay closed until further orders."[97]

The New York Telephone Company responded to Western Union's actions with a promise to take its wires and instruments out of Mahoney's headquarters at East Forty-second Street and cooperate fully with Commissioner McAdoo. It also pledged not to provide service to any place where extension wires connected a room to the alleged exchange.[98]

The city's poolrooms opened anyhow and struggled to get the necessary information. They got no results from Gravesend but did from Morris Park, fed from phones to the poolroom exchanges. At least twenty men sat atop houses near the track with their eyes glued to ponderous field glasses. From 2:00 p.m. until long after dusk, every phone in the neighborhood was engaged in sending racing news. However, service was slow, and some rooms faked reports of the races in progress. Certain Tenderloin rooms got their returns about ten minutes late by phone and were afraid to take late bets. They closed betting at 2:30 for a 3:00 p.m. race to prevent anyone from getting the results and then placing bets. Syndicate rooms held back news on several races when the favorites did poorly so they could get more action.[99]

Poolrooms that relied solely on telephone service got the names of jockeys and scratches, but not track odds, and could not provide full descriptions of races, an important feature of the poolroom ambience. A lot of the poolrooms paid off the next day, employing newspaper odds. One expert believed there was just as much money bet as before, but the poolrooms were losing business to the growing numbers of conveniently located handbooks that offered credit and accepted bets as small as a quarter.[100]

Almost immediately after Western Union's pronouncement, Commissioner McAdoo instituted a concerted effort to close up the betting parlors. On 20 May, the police made a record coordinated raid at 4:00 p.m., simultaneously breaking into seven exchanges and fifteen poolrooms, including rooms owned by "The" Allen and "Honest John" Kelly. There were seventy arrests, and 15 telegraph installations and 152 phones were confiscated.[101]

McAdoo estimated that the raids forced more than a hundred rooms out of business or deprived them of access to racing news. McAdoo kept up the pressure over the next few days, with raids at some three hundred facilities in Manhattan, in what he hoped would be a deathblow to the poolrooms. The raids found no one or any gambling apparatus in dozens of places. In all, only sixteen prisoners were taken and 124 phones confiscated, which New York Telephone promised not to reinstall.[102]

Western Union's actions turned out to be less deleterious to the poolroom business than originally expected, and plenty of gambling went on. The syndicates' information bureaus relocated to the banking district and secured racing data sent over wires independent from Western Union, which operatives forwarded by phone to affiliated poolrooms. The syndicates provided customers with track odds five minutes before post time but not much other information, such as the call of a race. One phone operator at a Harlem room amused the audience by "describing" a race with the horses Dr. Parkhurst, Captain Goddard, Judge Gaynor, and Jerome.[103]

At the end of May, Capt. Max F. Schmittberger raided the headquarters of the New York and New Jersey Distributing and Circulating Company, an information firm that distributed sports and stock information. Its phone service, which had cost $48,000 over the prior four years, was suspended. However, the company secured a writ of mandamus that compelled resumption of the phone service.[104]

Schmittberger's incursion resulted in an important test case. In July, Judge Gaynor ruled in *Charles Hammond et al.* that the police had acted without a warrant and censured the police for their "criminal lawlessness." Gaynor further noted that the business of collecting and distributing sporting news was legal, a decision that protected betting syndicates seeking racing information.[105]

The NYTC dragged its heels for months despite substantial pressure from reformers. The phone company, at the end of the year, promised not to furnish telephones to metropolitan poolrooms, which should have compelled poolroom operators to find alternative sources for their racing data. Some rooms secured the needed information from news tickers that also carried stock market reports or paid a neighborhood shopkeeper $10–$15 to use his phone. In the winter of 1905, one syndicate manager contracted for a direct wire to New Orleans for the winter season. However, such efforts were soon unnecessary, because most poolrooms had little trouble getting their own phones.[106]

Western Union Exits the Poolroom Hustle

Western Union's pledge to close up its horse racing business in 1904 was apparently just that, a promise, because when the spring 1905 racing season began, it resumed the business of distributing racing information. The City Club thereupon solicited the company's board of directors to take Western Union completely out of the racing business and especially out of the poolrooms, and there was talk of criminal action against the directors. On 12 July, the board (including U.S. Senator Chauncey Depew, the longtime railroad president, and Frank and George J. Gould, sons of robber baron Jay Gould, who had a controlling interest in Western Union in the 1880s) adopted a resolution drawn up by their colleague Jacob H. Schiff, the renowned banker and Jewish philanthropist, to leave racing. An important contributor behind the scenes was Helen Gould, a major stockholder and philanthropist who spent much of her life trying to amend for her father's misdeeds. She strongly supported the decision to dissociate from racing because of the moral question.[107]

Western Union announced the closing of the Racing Bureau in September 1905. Employees would no longer collect racing news, but the company would still transmit messages passed to it through normal business operations. Hence, a customer could wire information amassed on his own, including data about horse races. Thus, racing news could be sent by a client to a Western Union office in New

York and then distributed by messenger boys in the ordinary commercial way. The closing of the Racing Bureau proved costly to Western Union. Overall profits for the 1904–5 fiscal year dropped by $215,755, which President Clowry attributed to the discontinuance of racing reports.[108]

Replacing Western Union

The exiting of Western Union from the racing business created a vacuum that several groups tried to fill. According to the *Tribune,* once Western Union got out of the business of distributing racing news, "it virtually handed to the racetrack news syndicates a business more valuable, if properly managed, than many a Klondike gold mine." The *Tribune* expected the closing of its racing bureau would not hurt the betting business because of the mania of bettors who "will put up with all sorts of inconveniences to gamble away his money."[109]

By autumn, six poolroom syndicates, reportedly on good terms with each other, began collecting racing news themselves, employing men unconnected to Western Union. Syndicate men at Gravesend filed reports to a Western Union station where their colleagues took messages from the operator. They then went to a nearby building where phones were set up and called the data into the syndicate's distribution station, from which it was resent to associated poolrooms. This organization's daily phone expenses were about $250. The most glaring problem with this new system was that it became very hard to lay off bets because messages that had once taken minutes now took hours.[110]

Most poolrooms outside the city got news reports from the Metropolitan Turf News Company, owned by Enright and Saunders of Louisville, which distributed racing information on events at Fort Erie, a Canadian racetrack established in 1897, and Gravesend, for about $25 a day. Service at first was very slow, but within days, the poolrooms were up to speed, quickly securing accurate and essential information, except for race descriptions. However, the quality of service did not keep up. In late November, a journalist found that reports were very inaccurate, since almost daily the racing wire reported certain horses playing a big role in races even if they had started poorly and were never in the race.[111]

The poolrooms that fall came up with a new tactic to foil interference. They began securing injunctions against police meddling, which gave officers, not that eager to fight the poolrooms anyhow, a pretext to leave them alone. In some cases, totally fake raids were staged just to give rooms a chance to get injunctions against further intrusion. Judge William Gaynor, well known as a supporter of personal freedom, particularly for sportsmen seeking to play their favorite game on Sundays, abetted this plan. Gaynor denounced the police for usurping power and declared that the police had no right to forcibly enter social clubs (including pool-rooms), except with a search warrant, unless pursuing a fleeing criminal or in response to a distress call.[112]

By the end of 1905, there were just about forty poolrooms in Manhattan and another twenty in the rest of the city. This low number did not necessarily mean a big drop in off-track gambling, since many bettors, especially in working-class neighborhoods, were wagering with handbooks. The *Times* gave a lot of credit to the City Club for pressuring the authorities, mainly the police, to fight the pool-room evil and to Commissioner McAdoo. However, the mayor, who was very seri-ous about fighting gambling, thought the commissioner was a failure, unable to control a force that was really run by the inspectors. McAdoo resigned at the end of the year when McClellan's first term expired.[113]

Many new poolrooms soon opened up, and in 1906, there were more open than at the start of McClellan's administration.[114] The new police commissioner, Gen. Theodore Bingham, a West Pointer who was a stickler for the law, was brought in to clean up crime. Bingham's tenure was very turbulent because, as promised, he raised hell, fighting graft and corruption with military precision and transferring many untrustworthy officers from their old haunts. Bingham's plan to combat poolrooms was not to raid established rooms but to prevent them from even opening. Hence, whenever a new clubroom opened, Bingham sent over an officer in civilian clothing to inspect the interior. The officer would then sit down and stay until two in the morning, when another officer replaced him. This sce-nario went on for weeks, until uniformed officers took over the chair. This policy was an irritant but had little impact, at least until mid-1908.[115]

The prime provider of racing information was National News, also known as the Payne Telegraph Service of Cincinnati. Its chief executive, John H. Payne of Covington, Kentucky, was a former Western Union telegraph operator, and for-mer Western Union executive David Mitchell was general manager. Payne hired spotters at various racetracks who used a mirror to flash a coded race result to a telegrapher at a nearby building who wired the results to poolrooms and hand-books in major cities. Payne's company leased Western Union's wires to transmit the information.[116]

National News was the primary supplier of racing information throughout the United States until 1911, when Mont Tennes's General News Bureau sup-planted it. Tennes was a major Chicago gambler, who in 1907 secured a monopoly from Payne to distribute racing information in Illinois. Two years later, Tennes gained total control over off-track gambling in the Windy City by employing his control of the racing wire and by employing strong-arm tactics, including bomb-ing his rivals. Tennes supplied racing data to seventy poolrooms in New York for four thousand dollars a week, ninety in Chicago for thirty-six hundred, and others around the country. The Interstate Commerce Commission investigated his operations but found nothing illegal about the transmission of horse race results and related information.[117]

When the 1906 racing season opened at Aqueduct, poolrooms could not guarantee their information's accuracy because they had no direct access to tracks that had no phones. There was a telegraph office at the foot of Aqueduct's betting ring where a sign that formerly read "Western Union" was now marked "Bureau of Information and Investigation." The BII was a news service controlled by The Jockey Club. Western Union leased certain lines to TJC, which sent racing news only to legitimate enterprises. The BII reported scratches just for the first race and names of jockeys only twenty-five minutes before post time. There was no distribution of results, even to the press, until twenty minutes after the races. The poolrooms then were posting on their boards what seemed to be official odds, scratches, and other information, but their data were so unreliable that each room put up signs indicating that reporting conditions were not favorable and that management could not guarantee accuracy. The staff offered newspaper odds to their clients who agreed to settle up the next day.[118]

Pinkerton agents on the second day of the Aqueduct meet intercepted poolroom agents at the entrances and all afternoon kept an eye out for anyone giving signals to confederates. Two afternoon papers rented a house that had two phones located behind the paddock to make their reports, while a third sent a messenger a half mile away to use a phone.[119]

Some days later, the poolrooms tried to get race results by sending bicycle riders from the track to the nearest phone in Ozone Park, the community where the track was located. The police guessed that some patrons on the promenade overlooking the LIRR station signaled the riders with a secret code, so management covered part of the numbers block that designated the official finish to prevent people from outside viewing the results with a telescope or field glasses.[120]

The supplying of racing information was no better when Jamaica opened at the end of April. A very bad mix-up occurred on 1 May when several uptown poolrooms reported Accountant, who won the fifth race, as a scratch. One poolroom nearly had a riot.[121]

Nonetheless, as the season progressed, the racing information became more thorough and timely, and there were even race descriptions. Poolrooms did not close betting until after post time, confident they were getting quicker and more accurate results than their customers. By the time the racing season shifted to Belmont, TJC thought that some of its BII workers were cooperating with the poolrooms. Observers also noticed that men dressed in gray and black, some with numbers on their backs, seemed to be sending signals to confederates.[122]

When the Brighton Beach season started, poolroom agents rented a house near the backstretch where they had a good view of the course from a second-story window. The track police rigged up a canvas screen to block their view. Then when the poolroom men began watching from the roof, the track's security responded with a still higher screen. By the last week of the meet, the poolroom operatives built a scaffold on the roof, and then the track police gave up.[123]

Jerome and Groundbreaking Investigative Methods

Off-track betting continued to flourish, and in 1907 the *Times* estimated there were around five hundred poolrooms and handbooks. Lt. John H. Ayers in the *Police Review* estimated that there were about two hundred poolrooms in the city, mainly between Twenty-third and Forty-second streets, especially clustered around Twenty-eighth and Twenty-ninth and Sixth Avenue, with another bunch south of Chambers Street in Lower Manhattan.[124]

The district attorney continuously tried innovative schemes to counter the gambling menace. In 1905, Jerome first employed the new Dowling Act, which empowered him to subpoena individuals involved in a suspected criminal activity. They were guaranteed immunity, if willing to testify, but otherwise were charged with contempt of court. Jerome hoped that pressure on the small fry would help him catch the big fish, particularly James Mahoney, but he was unsuccessful.[125]

Jerome found more success with wiretaps, which the police employed in 1907 to locate key poolroom exchanges. This activity led to major raids on 11 June against William J. Hannigan and John H. McCormick's New York and New Jersey Distributing and Circulating Company, considered an outlaw information service, and David H. Mitchell and Bob Davis's Inter-State News Bureau that had more than sixty-four phones servicing syndicate rooms. The next day, officers raided seventeen poolrooms simultaneously, including the ones run by De Lacy, Joe Reagan, and Gene Comiskey that were also news-distributing centers. Assistant DA Almuth C. Vandiver estimated that the phone company was making $100,000 a month from illegal poolrooms. De Lacy subsequently announced he was quitting the business, claiming, "Gambling don't pay!" Although most observers took that declaration with a grain of salt, he was thereafter out of the public limelight, except when sued in 1909 for not paying $50,000 to a lobbyist at Albany. When De Lacy died eight years later, he left an estate worth $862,890, mainly in real estate.[126]

The Poolrooms Go On and On and On

Despite the best efforts of reformers like District Attorney William Travers Jerome, the poolroom business just kept on going. Even the racing blackout in New York from 1910 through 1912 failed to put them out of business. Business seemed to pick up with the resumption of racing in 1913.

The enduring problem of poolrooms was examined on 7 February 1913 by the Curran Investigating Committee of the New York City Board of Aldermen, which had been researching police corruption. James Purcell of the Society for the Prevention of Crime, a longtime poolroom operator, who had been a professional gambler from 1896 to 1911, provided rare insider testimony about the payoffs poolroom operators made to the police. Purcell admitted that from 1901 through 1911 he had paid about $50,000 for protection, mainly to the police in Manhattan and Queens, and that business had suffered when he had not paid off. He named several policemen he had bribed, prior to 1908, when the five-year statute of limitations protected the alleged recipients of the bribes.[127]

Purcell operated several different poolrooms in the early 1900s, including one at East Thirty-sixth Street. But first he met local Tammany boss Mike Cruise, who asked him, "How much do I get out of it?" After they negotiated, Purcell was told to see Cruise's man Murtha when he was ready to open:

> When I got ready I saw Murtha and he asked me what I was going to give up. I said I thought about $120 a week. Fifty for the leader, fifty for the Inspector, and $10 apiece for Stevens and Lee, the ward men. Stevens . . . said it would be $125 or nothing, and it was $125. After I had opened a short time, Lee was kicked to another precinct and I kicked against paying so much. It didn't do any good. Five weeks later I got a 'phone message telling me to close up. Murtha said the word came from Sevens and I closed up.[128]

The poolroom business continued unabated, which resulted in the two largest poolroom raids ever made in New York. In 1914, newly elected progressive mayor John Purroy Mitchel appointed former reform-minded deputy chief commissioner of police Arthur Woods to run his department, and he tried to close up the poolrooms. Wood initiated a new policy, ordering his staff to arrest every man they found and humiliate them with a ride to the station in a patrol wagon. Previously, the police concentrated only on arresting poolroom operators (whom they seldom nabbed) and their henchmen. On the afternoon of 29 July 1914 the commissioner ordered a raid at 242 Canal Street in Lower Manhattan. Before the officers reached the third-floor gambling den, the operators had ripped up the telephones and removed them from the premises. The officers arrested sixty-nine men on disorderly conduct charges, which required eleven patrol wagons to bring them in. Later that afternoon a "floating" poolroom at 290 West Broadway, near Canal Street, was also raided. Ninety-four men were arrested in that raid. Unfortunately, the poolroom business just rolled on.[129]

The Handbooks

Many bettors in the early 1900s patronized handbooks in their neighborhoods, especially from noon until three. They were extremely accessible, found in saloons, candy stores, and cigar shops, and right on the streets, taking bets of $0.25 and up and even offering credit. These bookmakers were mostly independent operators who employed agents known as "cappers" to recruit customers. They did not write up prices, fearing arrest, and paid off the next day, using newspaper odds.[130]

Herman Michaels: A Case Study

Handbook operators were part of a subterranean subculture, about which we know very little. They were men from working-class backgrounds who sought to remain in the shadows. They did not keep extensive records or write diaries about their experiences, unlike pickpocket George W. Appo, a late-nineteenth-century New Yorker.[131] One of the few handbook men who told his own story was Herman Michaels, the "Handbook King" of Harlem, who in 1913 discussed some of his experiences with the *Morning Telegraph*. Like most others in his line, he paid protection for the privilege of running games of chance that included handbook making, poolroom betting, craps, poker, and roulette. As Michaels told the *Telegraph*:

> I've been a gambler ever since I can remember, but I started to operate in Harlem about 1907 as a handbook maker, working entirely on the street. My beat was on Eighth Avenue, from 124th to 145th streets. Inspector Thompson was then in the district. The police wouldn't let me alone. I was arrested time and again and finally driven from corner to corner, until finally I realized that I'd either have to come across or quit the district. I paid. During 1907 to 1909 I paid to [Sgt.] Peter Duffy. During 1909 to 1911 I paid to [Officer James] Wrenn. After June 1911, Duffy was the collector again and I paid Duffy up until last October.[132]

Periodically, when Inspector Thompson stopped by, the betting games ceased, but no one put away the paraphernalia, and announcers reported the races as usual. The typical handbook paid the police $50 a month to look the other way. When business was poor, Michaels did not always make payments and got arrested and taken to magistrate court. After he paid up, or made satisfactory promises to pay later, his case would be thrown out.

Along with operating a handbook, Michaels in 1907 opened up pool and craps rooms at 136th Street and Eighth Avenue, paying $75 a month for protection. The first time he refused to pay, the police promptly raided him. Thereafter, whenever he was recalcitrant and held back the payoffs, another raid occurred. Michaels got tired of this cycle and gave up the poolroom, returning to the handbook trade. However, he resumed his poolroom business in 1910 with a room at 145th Street and Eighth Avenue, where Inspectors Hussey and Murtha charged $200 a month for protection. Two years later, his high overhead, including $150 for rent and $240 for protection, forced him out of business.[133]

The Rosenthal Murder

Crimes of violence against bookmakers seldom made the pages of major New York newspapers. However, the assassination of Herman Rosenthal in 1912 became one of the biggest crime stories of the early twentieth century because of its brazen nature and because Lt. Charles Becker was indicted for ordering the hit. He became the first New York police officer executed in the electric chair.[134]

Rosenthal came to America as a five-year-old from Russia, and as a fourteen-year-old newsboy, he drew the attention of local Tammany district leader Big Tim Sullivan, who got him a job as a poolroom runner. Rosenthal graduated to become a handbook operator in Far Rockaway and later ran some Second Avenue poolrooms and bookmaking at local tracks. He subsequently ran the gambling at the Hesper Club on Second Avenue, a popular hangout for Tammanyites, run by Patrick Sullivan, Big Tim's brother.[135]

Rosenthal's rooms were raided a number of times despite his connections to Sullivan because he would not pay off the police. Instead, he chose to keep out undercover investigators with thick doors and attentive doormen and tried to bribe city officials to inform him of upcoming raids. He also employed Spanish Louie (John Lewis), a Sephardic Jew, and his Humpty Jackson gang to protect his poolrooms. Rosenthal managed the Red Raven Club at 123 Second Avenue, raided on 15 August 1903. The police caught Herman trying to burn the day's records. The police closed the club again on 23 December 1910, and when it reopened on 19 March 1911, District Attorney Charles Whitman led another raid on the Red Raven Club. Some of these problems came from rival gamblers who disliked his tactics and sent anonymous letters to Mayor McClellan's office.[136]

The police in June 1911 established three strong-arm squads, two to fight vice and a third to deal with street toughs. Chief Rhinelander Waldo appointed Lt. Charles Becker to run a "special squad" to fight hoodlums. Becker, a former bag-man for his precinct captain, used his twenty-man crew to shake down gamblers and madams for more than one hundred thousand dollars. They also made some raids, especially on poolrooms that were not paying off the police.[137]

In 1911, Rosenthal teamed up with Beansey Rosenfeld in a gambling hall at 116th Street. They had a falling out, and Herman hired a thug to beat up his partner. This attack resulted in a police raid and the closing of the club. When it reopened, associates of his old partner bombed the hall. Rosenthal then turned back to Sullivan to help him set up late in the year a new thirty-five-thousand-dol-lar casino at Forty-fifth Street in Midtown. Rosenthal refused to pay a thousand dollars a week in graft when the club opened, and the authorities promptly closed it. The club reopened on 20 March 1912.[138]

Becker then sought a five-hundred-dollar payoff from Rosenthal to help defend the officer's press agent, Charles Plitt, indicted for killing a man during a police raid on a dice game. Rosenthal balked at first, but Becker persevered in quest of a payoff, since Big Tim Sullivan, their mutual mentor, was ill and could no longer protect Rosenthal against his thugs. Yet Rosenthal persisted in standing up to Becker's threats. Becker, meanwhile, was under pressure from Waldo to close the club. Chief Waldo ordered Inspector Cornelius Hayes, head of the local pre-cinct, to post a guard outside the casino to close it down and another guard inside to make sure it remained closed.[139]

Rosenthal was irate and threatened to tell the district attorney about protec-tion and the gambling business. He went to the West Side Police Court to protest the department's oppressive action in stationing a uniformed officer in front of his place. Herman had a sworn affidavit published in the *World* on 14 July assert-ing that Lieutenant Becker had been his partner in the gambling house and had raided him for personal reasons. Rosenthal personally told his story to District Attorney Charles S. Whitman the next evening, and the DA promised to convene a grand jury to look into the charges. Rosenthal then went to the Hotel Metropole at Forty-third Street, a famous gangster hangout, to socialize. At two in the morning, a waiter told him someone was looking for him in front of the building, and when Rosenthal went out to look, he was murdered.[140]

The use of violence directed at poolroom operators and bookmakers occurred, but it was rare compared to other criminal activities like arson or extortion. Rivals employed threats of police raids or actually had raids staged against competi-tors, but they did not bomb their rivals, as occurred in Chicago between gambler

Mont Tennes and his rivals. Unlike poolrooms, handbooks were more likely to extend credit. Bookies cut off nonpaying clients but did not have their arms and legs broken for withholding payment, as they would in the future. Clients would be embarrassed into paying up for fear their gambling habit would inform their employer, who would fire them. This threat was how loan sharks then guaranteed that their customers paid up, although that policy changed by the 1930s when their bodies became their collateral.[141]

The police did not rush in to find the culprits. Whitman was certain Becker was involved, but he had an airtight alibi. Whitman ran his own investigation outside the police department, found the getaway driver, and granted him immunity for his testimony. The driver's statement led the police to arrest several alleged perpetrators who worked for "Big Jack" Zelig, a longtime associate of Becker, who had taken over Monk Eastman's notorious Lenox Avenue gang. Zelig was indicted for arranging the murder. When Zelig was called to testify, rumors swirled that he would turn state's evidence in return for lenient treatment. On 5 October, the day before Big Jack was to testify, Zelig was assassinated on a trolley car by "Red" Phil Davidson. Afterward, Becker was indicted for murder.[142]

The Becker trial received extensive press coverage that exceeded the first "murder of the century" back in 1906 when socialite Henry K. Thaw murdered his wife's lover, Stanford White, the renowned architect of Madison Square Garden, which he had designed in 1890 and where he kept an apartment. Becker was quickly found guilty of first-degree murder but won an appeal on the ground that presiding judge John Goff was biased. Becker was retried, again found guilty, and in 1915 was executed.[143]

Conclusion

The biggest menace of horse race gambling was not the wagering on the tracks but the illegal betting off the tracks with poolrooms and handbooks. New York was the national center of the poolroom business, which existed mainly in Lower and Midtown Manhattan, but also existed in Brooklyn, Harlem, Long Island City, and the Bronx. Reformers of all stripes agreed that it was a vile crime, but despite the best efforts of city reformers, law-and-order organizations, state investigations, investigative journalists, and political progressives, poolrooms and handbooks remained open, even after Western Union removed itself from the business.

The poolrooms mostly operated as a part of politically connected gambling syndicates that provided security from police interference and changing laws, protection from interlopers, access to racing news, and financial protection against betting coups through a simplified layoff system. New York's gambling structure and its ties to Tammany Hall promoted cooperation in the early 1900s, unlike in Chicago, where rivalries led to bomb-throwing wars between crime syndicates. Customers included the working class and petit bourgeois men and some women, more interested in betting than in going to the races, or else they simply preferred the convenience of off-track betting. They saw this betting as a opportunity to put some excitement into their lives and as a rational means to enhance their bankroll. Average New Yorkers did not worry a lot about illegal enterprises and victimless crimes but focused their outrage on crimes with victims. The outcome of the general public's lukewarm concern about gambling, and the benefits that Tammany Hall and government officials reaped for nonenforcement of the penal codes, contributed to the failure to put the clamps on off-track betting.

11

The Demise and Resurrection of Racing in New York, 1907–13

When we consider the oral bookmaking bill we feel that the asininity of legislators could not go further. . . . What is behind all these dark legal enactments, this virulent confusion, this palpable hatred? The effect of the laws, if they could be carried out in the sense and intention of their framers, would be, some say, to close the racetracks forever. . . . There are forces at work at Albany hostile to racing itself, or, at any rate, for reasons of their own, determined to destroy it.

—*New York Morning Telegraph*, 10 May 1910

The future of American racing in 1907 was bleak outside of a few states. Only twenty-seven racetracks remained, of which eight were in New York. The other courses were in Arkansas (one), California (two), Kentucky (three), Louisiana (four), Maryland (one), Massachusetts (three), Pennsylvania (three), Washington, DC (one), and an outlaw track in Norfolk, Virginia. In addition, Canada had six tracks.[1] Even in the Empire State, where the racecourses promoted high-class honest racing, drew huge audiences, and operated in the black, reformers, energized by antiracing successes elsewhere, hoped to kill racing, perceived as a panacea for many social ills. Their hopes brightened one year later, when New York's progressive governor, Charles Evans Hughes, came out foursquare in favor of halting racetrack gambling and promised to do everything in his power to make that aim possible. It was a struggle, but Hughes got a law passed that seemed to do the trick, and antiracing crusaders across the country lauded him for his achievement. However, the tracks remained open for two more years until another law shut them down, seemingly for good, by making track operators responsible for any illegal gambling on their property. When the New York racecourses closed for 1911 and 1912, it left Maryland and Kentucky as the only states with significant thoroughbred racing. Then, in 1913, a court decision in a betting case provided an unexpected entering wedge to allow the reopening of New York's tracks, although Brooklyn's three tracks and Buffalo's Kenilworth Park Race Track never reopened.

302

Charles Evans Hughes and the Fight to Halt Racing

At the start of 1907, District Attorney William T. Jerome continued to lead the anti-racetrack gambling fight. Jerome blamed the Percy-Gray Act for urban gambling and considered it "a gross scandal to the jurisprudence of this state." He complained that there had been "created a sentiment in the community that these offenses are comparatively of no importance." He promised to rigidly prosecute anyone arrested during gambling raids but also turned his attention to trying to repeal the current racing law.[2]

Jerome sought new laws to end loopholes in the penal codes that protected management from liability if gambling occurred at their tracks and to rationalize the penal codes on bookmaking. A felonious bookmaking conviction carried two years in prison or a fine of $2,000 (and the loss of citizenship), but judges typically applied more lenient laws. Jerome had a bill drawn up to make all racetrack gambling a misdemeanor, punishable by a $500 fine, imprisonment for a year, or both, that would make gamblers, clients, and track operators all liable for violations. He anticipated a lesser penalty that would result in more convictions. Jerome also sought to sway rural voters against horse race betting by recommending a $210,000 stipend for agricultural societies, thereby freeing them from reliance on the state tax on track receipts.[3]

Senator George Bliss Agnew (R–New York County), a former Wall Street businessman and assemblyman, first elected to the senate in 1906, presented Jerome's bills to the legislature. On 20 March, members of the assembly's and senate's Codes Committees attended a public hearing on the horse race gambling issue. Just like in 1906, clergymen representing every part of the state protested the evils of racetrack betting. Rev. Dr. E. B. Sanford, secretary of the National Federation of Churches, asserted that nearly every college president favored the measure, while Dr. Walter Laidlaw of the New York Federation of Churches read a petition from the New York Board of Jewish Ministers: "Danger to the commonwealth lies in the anarchy of high society rather than in the anarchy of the poor. If you permit the rich man to enjoy pleasures which are made a crime to the poor you are encouraging injustice for which society must pay the price." Canon William Sheafe Chase, rector of Brooklyn's Christ Church, a longtime fighter against bookmaking, chastised the tracks as "legalized colleges of gambling." On the other side, the agricultural societies opposed any changes unless they got a $200,000 appropriation to replace the racing taxes they received.[4]

Jerome never had the votes, but his effort struck a chord with Governor Charles Evans Hughes, whose administration had previously focused on other reform issues. Hughes, a prominent Republican lawyer, first gained political fame in 1905 as special counsel for state legislative committees investigating chicanery in the gas, electric, and life insurance industries. Hughes narrowly won the governorship a year later over publishing mogul William Randolph Hearst, by 57,897 votes out of 1,452,467 cast. Racing was not a major issue in the gubernatorial campaign, though it did come up. At a meeting of the Presbyterian Ministers' Association of New York, Arthur Brisbane, Hearst's chief editorial writer, was asked how Hearst could justify giving so much coverage in his papers to degrading sports like boxing and horse racing. Brisbane explained that Hearst was opposed to the turf and fought it whenever he could: "Racing men know this and have contributed thousands of dollars to the campaign against him." However, the publisher had many customers who wanted access to racing results. Perhaps they could be "reclaimed by the other features of the newspapers they read."[5]

Hughes was the only Republican who had won a statewide contest back in 1906. He saw himself as the people's tribune and evolved into a progressive supporter of such programs as workmen's compensation and commission government. The governor was attracted to Jerome's crusade because of his strong interest in constitutional matters. On 15 June, Hughes promised Chase that he would root out all illegal gambling and told legal counsel Edwin W. Sanford to study the legality of Percy-Gray.[6]

The Governor Takes Charge

On 1 January 1908, Governor Charles Evans Hughes addressed the state legislature, setting the program for his second year in office. He called for new banking laws, direct primaries, conservation, and a pure food act. He particularly stressed the need to halt racetrack gambling by repealing Percy-Gray, which he decried as unconstitutional, and by making bookmaking at tracks punishable by incarceration. The governor's attack on gambling created the biggest stir of his entire address. Hughes noted that the subtle wording of the present gambling law relieved on-course bookmakers from any liability except for the recovery of the amount bet by the other party, though other states punished them by a fine, imprisonment, or both. He pointed out that those prior efforts to repeal Percy-Gray because it was a discriminatory law, or because the act stimulated the gambling evil instead of correcting it, failed because of the influence of the racetracks and agricultural societies. Hughes recommended securing the latter's support by direct subsidies. The address set up a key stage in the battle to end racing in New York, which attorney and political scientist Benjamin Parke De Witt regarded as one of Hughes's biggest fights, along with the creation of public service commissions and the failure to secure the direct primary. Hughes's biographer Dexter Perkins went even further, rating the antiracing struggle as the most dramatic battle of his governorship.[7]

Robert Wesser, author of the definitive study of Hughes's governorship, did not find much enthusiasm in Albany at the start of the year in fighting horse race gambling. Legislators backed by influential agricultural societies beholden to racing had recently turned down similar proposals to curtail the widely popular horse race gambling. Furthermore, the racing crowd had considerable political clout and almost unlimited financial resources to hire lobbyists and buy votes.[8]

Racing advocates incorrectly argued that betting at racetracks could not be suppressed (it had been recently banned in Missouri and Illinois). They also claimed that efforts to stifle it would foster secret gambling and wholesale violations since human nature encouraged thrill seeking. Furthermore, the proracing crowd pointed out that if the constitutional argument against wagering was as strong as Hughes claimed it was, then the state should bar all betting, including gambling on elections and wagering among friends.[9]

Most legislators believed that unless public sentiment became more forceful, the governor needed more than his prestige to bar horse race betting. Senator Martin Saxe, one of Hughes's chief supporters and a member of the Codes Committee that had considered the Jerome bills in 1907, opposing halting betting because it would destroy the investment New Yorkers had made in the turf. Assembly Speaker James W. Wadsworth, son of the SRC's chairman, was understandably silent on the issue. However, Senator Harvey D. Hinman believed that Hughes would push public feelings against racing and carry the day, while Senate Majority Leader John Raines, formerly pessimistic about changing Percy-Gray, now became very optimistic. According to historian Geoffrey Blodgett, Hughes sacrificed partisan support to achieve his goals, which alienated many party regulars.[10]

Hughes's crusade created a big stir in political and horse racing circles. Attorney Welton C. Percy, designer of the Percy-Gray Act and the SRC's counsel, strongly disagreed with the governor's analysis. Percy remained foursquare behind his carefully designed law that resulted in the SRC's excellent regulation of the turf. Percy believed that racing interests had worked hard to safeguard public interests and conform to the law. Racing's spokesmen worried that sending bookies to jail would wipe out the odds layers the tracks needed to survive. The jockey clubs expected to raise a fund of three hundred thousand dollars to lobby the legislature and keep the sport going. On the other hand, poolroom men supported Hughes for opposing discrimination against outside betting.[11]

Public Opinion on Agnew-Hart

Hughes received considerable press support for his initiative, especially from upstate, except from Saratoga and Buffalo, which protected their local racetracks.[12] The *Times* largely agreed with the governor and hoped that ending racetrack gambling would save foolish clerks from their own "aleatory passions." The editors believed Hughes had raised the crucial question: did equivocal legislation circumvent the constitution's intent? The *Times* thought that horse race gambling, ipso facto, violated the constitution and occurred only by evasion and pervasion of the law. Furthermore, the course of civilization depended on restraining malevolent passions like wagering. The betting evil should cease because it gratified and stimulated greed, encouraging people to get something for nothing. Gambling benefited no one morally and hurt many people: "Thousands of young men have been ruined by the always accessible facilities of race-track gambling. The people who thrive by it are generally objectionable citizens. The money secured through it is the mainstay of evil resorts."[13]

The *Times* was optimistic that Hughes could win, although the gambling crowd was experienced in the secret ways of influencing legislators and had the early support of farmers who benefited from the current situation. The *Times* urged churches, farmer organizations, boards of trade, businessmen, and bankers to join the fight against gambling, although it opposed singling out agricultural fairs for special financing.[14]

In New York City, other papers as disparate in their political and social views as the elitist *Tribune* and the working-class *New York American,* the *Evening Journal,* and the *World* all favored halting racetrack gambling, along with the *Brooklyn Eagle.* The other Brooklyn papers and the *Sun* wanted to maintain racing. Hearst's *American* was in the forefront of the fight against corrupt Tammany Hall and sought to protect working men and their families from the curse of gambling. Hearst's *Journal* considered "public gambling, on the racetrack or anywhere else . . . an insult to the Constitution, an offence against morals and common decency." The evening paper supported Hughes for interfering "with the vice of tens of thousands of harassed, worried gamblers, and with the moneymaking amusements of a few rich lawbreakers." The *World* hoped it was the first step to stop all gambling, including the speculation on Wall Street. The *Eagle* added that Percy-Gray promoted and protected pool selling on the tracks by making the penalty nominal and proof of its violation nearly impossible.[15]

The plebeian newspapers relied heavily on cartoons to educate their readership. Renowned political cartoonist Homer Davenport drew many sketches in the *Evening Mail* depicting the vile impact of racing. In one drawing, he drew a scene of families ruined by horse race gambling, and in another, fast-talking horsemen misled earnest farmers who supported racing for its funding of agricultural fairs. Hearst cartoonists in the *American* and the *Evening Journal* skewered Tammany politicians and their racing allies like August Belmont. In one particularly remarkable sketch in the *New York American,* titled "In the Shadow of Justice," conniving racetrack gamblers conspire behind a statue of "Justice" with her eyes blindfolded.[16]

In the Shadow of Justice

18. "In the Shadow of Justice." The cartoonist depicts to his working-class audience the perversion of the American justice system by racetrack gamblers. *Source: New York American,* 14 Oct. 1909.

Hughes selected Senator George Agnew, who had introduced antiracing bills in 1907, and Assemblyman Merwin K. Hart (R–Oneida County) to introduce his legislative package. On 6 January, Agnew submitted several bills in the senate that called for imprisonment for gambling, set the same penalty for gambling on and off the tracks, and proposed an annual $250,000 appropriation to agricultural societies. Hart brought up the same bills in the assembly nine days later.[17]

The administration encouraged reform groups to back up the governor. The International Reform Bureau was the first to jump on board on 10 January. Three days later, President Wilbur F. Crafts of the IRB met with Hughes to discuss his plans and joined leaders of six other groups, including the City Club of New York and the Women's Municipal League, to consult with Agnew and Hart.[18]

The reformers created the broad-based Citizens' Anti–Race Track Gambling League to back the governor, directed by Republican attorney Joseph Choate and Secretary Walter Laidlaw of the Federation of Churches. The committee planned a lot of grassroots organizing in key senate districts. Church and civic organizations led the fight in New York City, and the IRB took the lead elsewhere. Rural church groups and agrarian societies, most notably the seventy-thousand-member state Grange, passed resolutions backing the governor.[19]

The official jumping-off point for the antigambling fight was a mass meeting on 2 February at New York's Midtown Majestic Theater. Hughes told the audience that he favored an antiracing law because of constitutional grounds, the bad aspects of gambling, and the pernicious influence of having a dead law on the books. Choate, Crafts, and Rabbi Stephen Wise all spoke out in support, criticizing the current gambling laws as anarchic and providing unequal rights to racecourse spectators.[20]

The Jockey Club responded with a thirty-one-page pamphlet titled *The Truth about Racing* that claimed betting was inevitable and that the state's best choice was to regulate wagering and restrict it to licensed racetracks. The leaflet stuck to the old proracing arguments, explaining that racing was the only venue to test different strains and the sole means of improving the breed, and it provided sport, recreation, and aid to farmers and breeders, who spent heavily in support of the sport. The booklet ingenuously claimed that 90 percent of spectators did not care about the betting but simply wanted to escape the city for pure fresh air, a chance to commune with nature, and the pleasure of watching horses gallop. Finally, it identified poolroom operators as key supporters of the plans to shutter the racetracks.[21]

The Hughes plans received considerable attention across the country. Horsemen and other sportsmen were often negative, while progressive periodicals supported him. Horsemen from as far away as Kentucky, Tennessee, and Virginia sent memorials to legislators urging them to vote against any changes. Seventy percent of Kentucky's state legislators signed a petition against reform, while railroad directors, businessmen, and breeders whose racing interests would be hurt by halting racing compiled anti-Hughes resolutions.[22]

Caspar Whitney, editor and part owner of the prestigious *Outing Magazine,* a periodical that covered uplifting middle-class sports, like cycling and football, and all field sports, was one of the most prominent sports authorities to discuss Hughes's reforms. Whitney was an ardent supporter of Theodore Roosevelt's "Strenuous Life" theory and, with Walter Camp, had selected the first All-American football teams (1889–97) for the *Week's Sport.* He was very involved in the Olympic movement as an American representative to the International Olympic Committee and later as president of the American Olympic Committee. His wife, Florence Canfield, was a founder of the League of Women Voters.[23]

Whitney did not expect Agnew-Hart to pass. He recognized that all "right-minded citizens" opposed gambling, including playing the stock market, but thought coercive tactics were unfeasible and likely to fail, "however praiseworthy the intention." Whitney blamed "the impractical, publicity-seeking reformer of the Parkhurst type" for hurting the human condition and genuine reform by driving the gambling problem underground. He saw it not as a moral question but as a matter of economics and practicality: "It is not a crime—it is a weakness." There was no way to abolish betting, any more than other vices, and he recommended regulation: "Because unscrupulous men rob their employers of money to 'play the races' is no reason why honest citizens may not wager a few dollars on the outcome of a horse race." Whitney believed that if Agnew-Hart passed, the outcome would be "scandalous race track condition[s] and increased prosperity for the corrupting pool room." Betting would shift from controlled track gambling "to the outlawed pool room of debauching influence and evil association." He wanted TJC to gain greater power over the gambling, abolish the field stands that attracted smaller gamblers, possibly introduce the English system that operated cash free at the tracks, and work harder to suppress poolrooms.[24]

The powerful Senator Tim Sullivan notified Democratic legislators that they were free to support their constituents' desires. However, commentators presumed he would line up urban Democrats against the antiracing bill, especially since he headed up the poolroom crowd and operated a well-known racing stable. Sullivan claimed he would not personally suffer too badly if the Agnew bills passed, since his $125,000 investment in the Jamaica Racetrack would remain valuable even if racing ended and the site was cut into building lots.[25]

Progressive periodicals across the nation strongly backed Hughes. Rev. Lyman Abbott's *Outlook,* a highly regarded liberal Christian periodical, criticized TJC's weak response, pointing out that if nearly all spectators came just for the sport, then why was there a need for gambling? The *Independent* claimed the state constitution already forbade all gambling and asserted that the state should enforce its basic laws. The periodical noted that racing associations mostly profited from racing, and it criticized the tax paid to support agricultural fairs as a bribe of the righteous. The *Independent* pointed out that just as breeders could raise birds without testing them in cockfights, they could breed horses without racing. Furthermore, even if racing actually was necessary for breeding, the sport could occur without wagering. The *Independent* criticized racing's supporters for trying to convince the public that breeding was more important than laws and warned that gambling threatened the breed of American men.[26]

The Turf Crowd Fights Back

Racing supporters met at Delmonico's Restaurant to discuss tactics and raise money for a secret fund to foil the antiracing legislation. Attendees included August Belmont and New York City chamberlain Charles H. Hyde, brother-in-law of Brighton Beach's William Engeman, for whom he had lobbied legislators since 1902. Eight jockey clubs each put up $33,000, and ninety-three bookies in the Metropolitan Turf Association put up $3,000 apiece for a fund that reached $543,000.[27]

There are no records documenting how the money was spent. Two Republicans senators each reportedly demanded $25,000 for their votes. Tammany senator James Gaffney allegedly got $125,000 "to take care of three or four members of the Legislature—Tammany men," which he denied. Gaffney, a New York contractor connected to Little Tim Sullivan (majority leader of the New York City Board of Aldermen) and Boss Charles F. Murphy, was prominent in the sporting world. In 1911, Gaffney bought the Boston Rustlers of the National League and renamed them the Braves in honor of Tammany Hall. Senator Thomas F. Grady, a close friend and spokesman for Murphy, Tammany's chief orator, and a poolroom backer, admitted years later that he was given $4,000 to support the turf. However, he claimed the "gift" was irrelevant: "There wasn't a Democratic Senator who voted against the bill who would have dared to vote otherwise. If he had, he would have been hung when he returned home. He couldn't take the attitude that it was all right to bet on Wall St. and not on the race track."[28]

Brooklyn Democratic boss Patrick H. McCarren was irate that he was not put in charge of the fund since he was a big supporter of racing, owned his own stable, and had wagered as much as $30,000 on a single race. Nonetheless, McCarren worked hard to block the antiracing legislation. He put a lot of pressure on

Brooklyn Republican senator Foelker, who represented a normally Democratic district whose prior occupant had been a big racing fan, to vote against the bill. McCarren told Foelker, "You need not fear the indignation of your constituents. If you are afraid of possible reelection or have any doubts about election time, I think I can fix it up for you so you can name your own opponent at the coming election." Foelker admitted two years later in the trial of former senator Frank Gardner, who was accused of bribing him, that he had been offered as much as $50,000 to vote against the bill.[29]

The racetrack magnates originally claimed spending about $43,000 to fight the proposed legislation and not the huge amounts reported in the press. They admitted paying $7,500 to former governor Frank S. Black, the Agricultural Fair Association's lobbyist, to represent them at Agnew bill hearings. They subsequently confessed to having spent $126,817 on "legal services" and "publicity." Two years later, the Legislative Graft Investigating Committee (LGIC) heard from former senator William H. Reynolds, president of the Metropolitan Jockey Club, who admitted spending $32,936 on behalf of racing, mostly for TJC treasurer F. K. Sturgis. The CIJC's books carried a charge of $2,216 to secretary C. J. Fitzgerald of the BBRA for legal expenses, although he was not a lawyer. The CIJC also paid $3,000 to Assemblyman Frank H. Houston of the Independence League for testing the constitutionality of Agnew-Hart, while TJC paid former judge Edward P. Coyne $40,290 to lobby in its behalf in 1906–7. Belmont claimed that TJC's expenditures were not for bribes but to pay attorneys for legitimate services, particularly expensive litigation, as well as to promote friendly feelings for racing among the state's clergy. Lobbyists focused on the state senate, where the Republicans had a smaller majority than in the assembly, and where it was easier to work with 51 senators rather than the 150-member assembly.[30]

Nearly 1,000 New Yorkers went to Albany for the first of three hearings on 19 February, including such eminent racing men and breeders as Harry Payne Whitney, James B. Haggis, James R. Keene, Hugh J. Grant, August Belmont II, W. P. Thompson, P. J. Dwyer, and Jacob Ruppert Jr. Counsel Joseph Auerbach of TJC led the fight, criticizing legislators for allowing the governor to dictate to them and going against public sentiment. James Keene, the renowned stable owner and self-proclaimed nonbettor, testified that passage of antitrack legislation would only transfer betting to the poolrooms, where wagering was less orderly and respectable. He claimed that, contrary to Senator Agnew's views, at least a hundred poolrooms were currently operating in New York. Keene warned that $50–$60 million worth of property would become valueless if Agnew-Hart passed. He claimed, disingenuously, that racing's purpose was to improve the breed, and any betting was just incidental. August Belmont II agreed that racing were essential to enhance the racing stock, that good breeding prepared younger trotters for work, and that betting was unfortunate but indispensable for the turf.[31]

Hughes originally emphasized constitutional errors in his critique of Percy-Gray, but during the legislative debate on Agnew-Hart, he mainly focused on moral reform. His foes were "those who would sacrifice the morals of our youth by extending the area of unnecessary temptation; who would inflict needless suffering upon helpless women and children . . . and who would imperil the welfare of thousands of our people simply because of their selfish desire to make money." Hughes pointed out that he was not going after the sport or racetracks but "at public gambling, prohibited by the constitution, condemned by the moral sense of the people, irrespective of creed, and conceded to be the prolific source of poverty and crime."[32]

The governor tried to make Agnew-Hart a party issue to help get it passed. Hughes proclaimed at a meeting in Poughkeepsie of the Dutchess County Republican Club: "The Republican Party is . . . the party to which clearly is entrusted the safeguarding of our institutions and the protection of all that we hold most dear. . . . We have always been a party of moral purposes. If the party does not practice that, it will go steadily into a decline. Here is one of those questions where you are not trying to execute some impossible moral reform by visionary legislation. The abolition of this evil will be the saving of thousands of men who are now going to their ruin. The Republican Party cannot afford to dodge this issue."[33]

However, not all Republicans supported Hughes. President Theodore Roosevelt, for instance, apparently favored the continuance of racing, although he opposed all gambling on moral grounds, be it on horses, playing cards, lotteries, or the stock market. He backed the Brackett (R–Saratoga County) Bill that proposed to ban the interstate transmission of racing news.[34]

Despite a few Republican defections, Agnew-Hart seemed destined to pass the assembly, where the Republicans had a strong majority, especially once the Codes Committee unanimously endorsed it. Wesser found that the reform movement's ability to flood the governor's mansion with supporting letters helped convince moderate assemblymen to support the bill. The trend was so strong that even Democratic state chairman William Connors supported the bill, and Tammany opposition in the assembly collapsed. On 26 March, a bill removing the Percy-Gray limits on penalties for race wagering passed by a resounding 129–9, and an accompanying bill to stiffen penalties was approved 129–7. However, the near unanimity did not reflect the sentiment of Tammany Democrats, who were still ready to fight, knowing the real contest would come up in the senate.[35]

On 1 April, Agnew-Hart came up for an important preliminary vote in the senate before a packed gallery, with Grady and McCarren leading the opposition.

Grady said passage would only interfere with betting in its least-hurtful forms, while doing nothing about gambling on Wall Street. McCarren told his colleagues that horse race gambling had been popular since time immemorial: "You cannot suppress gambling. You can only drive it under the skin where you will corrupt the entire body politic. Tests of endurance and speed appeal to all human beings. We learn that Plato once adjourned a philosophical discussion in order that he and his pupils might attend a horse race. I wish they would make betting a capital offense punishable by electrocution; because then they would never find a jury to convict." A test vote to postpone consideration was defeated, 26–23, largely on party lines.[36]

On 7 April, the day before the final ballot, McCarren counted his votes and came up just one shy of blocking the ordinance. He met Albany County Republican boss William Barnes Jr., editor of the *Albany Journal,* who regularly met secretly with Democratic leaders to discuss legislative matters. McCarren convinced him to get his senator, William Grattan, to vote no. Grattan had already promised his pastor and his mother that he was voting for the Agnew-Hart bills but obeyed his boss. Barnes originally claimed his intent to stay out of the fight but got involved because he bitterly opposed many of the governor's policies and was worried that racetrack reforms would hurt nearby Saratoga. Furthermore, Barnes had no interest in helping Hughes's political ambitions and preferred William Howard Taft for his party's presidential nomination.[37]

Racing men, unaware of Barnes's decision, were certain the day they had dreaded was at hand. On 8 April, a bitter four-hour debate preceded the final vote, said to be the harshest discussion in anyone's memory, while behind the scenes, proracing lobbyists furiously worked the senate halls looking for votes. Grady again led the attack, claiming the governor had tried to coerce legislators and create public sentiment against the sport. The proponents of Agnew-Hart mainly argued that the government needed to end inconsistencies between the constitutional ban on gambling and racing's special situation.[38]

Opponents of Agnew-Hart did everything they could to defeat the bill. Some unknown parties, presumably closely tied to the turf, "detained" Senator Albert T. Fancher of Chautauqua, a strong supporter of Agnew-Hart, at his home just before the crucial vote. The senate's sergeant at arms and Albany detectives discovered Fancher around noon, with his watch turned back to 9:00 a.m. He then made it to the senate and cast his vote. Fancher later told reporters that he had received a phone call to go there because some friends had a surprise for him, presumably a long night of poker.[39]

The vote was a stunning surprise, a tie (25–25). Democratic lieutenant governor Lewis Stuyvesant Chanler was not empowered to cast a vote and break the tie, and so the proposal was defeated. Eight Republicans sided with 17 Democrats in voting no. Immediately afterward, Senator Grady proposed a resolution to prevent reconsideration by the same sitting senate, which would have buried the bills. However, the motion was tabled with the backing of Chanler, a parliamentary procedure making it possible to revive the Agnew-Hart bills at a later date. Racing men all over the state were ecstatic, while reform organizations, like the Citizens' Union, saw the outcome as a public disgrace. The *Brooklyn Eagle* published a cartoon titled "Representation!" that mocked the senate for stepping over the governor's purpose and the will of the people and tossing the state constitution into the wastebasket. The vote was generally seen as a shattering blow to Hughes's prestige and a serious setback to his presidential aspirations.[40]

The press attributed the defeat to the shifting positions of Senators Cassidy, Knapp, and Grattan, who had previously voted to advance the bills. Cassidy had introduced legislation similar to Agnew-Hart back in 1906, and when the clerk called his name in the roll call, his voice was barely audible. Cassidy begged to explain his position, complaining the bills were inadequate to prevent racetrack gambling. It turned out he voted incorrectly because of miscommunication from Congressman Jacob S. Fassett, who had telegrammed Cassidy to remind him to vote "yes," but a clerk incorrectly transmitted the message as recommending a "no" vote. Senator Grattan had previously announced he was for the bills but changed his mind on Barnes's orders. Knapp voted against the bill because his constituents, except for local ministers who had never done anything for him, favored racing and gambling.[41]

A fourth vote originally pledged to back Agnew-Hart that went the other way came from Senator John T. McCall (D–New York County), whom the Citizens' Union had rated "unfit for public office" when he was elected two years earlier. He represented a very prosperous, heavily Catholic East Side Manhattan district whose local priests supported Archbishop John Farley's recommendation that Catholic societies support reform. McCall claimed that Murphy and Big Tim Sullivan originally urged him to vote his conscience, so when he changed his mind, it was widely assumed the leaders put pressure on him to support the party line.[42]

Robert Wesser argued that President Roosevelt's noninvolvement might have been the key factor in the outcome. TR was backing Taft over Hughes, who he thought was too independent, for the presidential nomination and did not want Hughes doing anything that could jeopardize Taft's chances to carry the state in the presidential election. Still, Roosevelt respected Hughes for becoming an activist who originally promised to have nothing to do with legislation. He wrote Lyman Abbott that Hughes "abandoned and reversed this attitude and deliberately fought thru the legislature an anti–race gambling bill."[43]

REPRESENTATION!

19. "Representation!" This cartoon illustrates the New York State Senate running roughshod over Governor Charles E. Hughes and the will of the people who wanted to end horse race gambling. The senators thereby relegated the state constitution to the wastebasket. *Source: Brooklyn Eagle,* 9 Apr. 1908.

However, Roosevelt may not have been totally neutral. August Belmont sought TR's support against the bill because he expected the end of racing would hinder the breeding of cavalry horses. Seven years later, Barnes testified in an unsuccessful suit against Roosevelt for libel that the president, based on Belmont's advice, had urged the Republican boss to work against the Agnew act.[44]

A Second Chance

Hughes was disappointed with the outcome but vowed to continue his crusade. He reiterated his position that racetrack gambling was demoralizing, promoted vice, and was a source of unnecessary temptation, especially for clerical workers. Furthermore, respect for the legal system had to triumph: "This is a state where law and order prevail and where no interest is powerful to keep on the statute books deceitful provisions whereby prohibition becomes profitable license and a favored class of law-breakers are afforded substantial immunity." Hughes promised to renew the fight by calling a special election to fill the vacant seat of the late Republican senator Stanislaus Franchot of Orleans-Niagara and then initiate a special legislative session to reconsider the racing bills. The governor assured his supporters that if he failed to secure passage, he would make racetrack gambling the main issue in the next election.[45]

Vacant seats in the legislature typically went unfilled until the next general election, so the call for a special election was unusual. However, Hughes was looking for one more vote to pass his legislation. Republican nominee William C. Wallace supported Hughes's position on racing, while Democrat Henry A. McMahon took no firm stand on the issue, but presumably opposed it. Hughes campaigned on behalf of Wallace, who on 12 May won the election by the narrowest margin in the district's history, 248 votes out of 14,954 ballots cast.[46]

Hughes anticipated Wallace's victory and called the legislature back into session the day before the election. Racing supporters immediately went to work to protect their victory and tried to convince a few antigambling senators to change their votes. They received thousands of letters, even Agnew, who got nearly 1,000 messages from alleged constituents. His office sampled 177 letters and found that only 29 were legitimate. Senator Page of Harlem, who represented a district that was turning black, also received many letters on the racing issue, 31 percent of which were forgeries and 28 percent from names unknown at their recorded addresses.[47]

Agnew-Hart did not come up for a vote until 10 June, the day before adjournment. The administration was in no hurry because Wallace was seated only two weeks after the election, and Senator Foelker had an appendectomy in late May and was too ill to travel. The measure breezed though the assembly, ninety-eight to twenty-six, and then the drama switched to the senate, where the racing interests concentrated their lobbying. Agnew convinced the rehabilitating Foelker to rise out of his sickbed, against doctor's orders, and come up to Albany from New York to vote. Foelker was so weak that he collapsed on the train ride. The senate was considering an amendment to the bill when Foelker dramatically entered the chambers on the arms of Canon Chase and Assemblyman Thomas J. Surpless

(R–Kings County) and was half carried to his seat, barely conscious. The bill passed by a vote of twenty-six to twenty-five, as Foelker cast the deciding vote. Two men from each party switched their votes from the previous month. Hughes was gratified by the outcome and promptly signed the bill, declaring, "It is a victory for law and order, the importance of which cannot be overestimated." He applauded Foelker's courage, equal to "distinguished service on the battle field." The law went into effect on 12 June.[48]

Reformers in New York and across the country lauded Hughes for his achievement. The praise helped propel him into contention for the Republican vice presidential nomination. District Attorney William Travers Jerome praised the governor for single-handedly getting the laws changed. Jerome said the main dilemma was not racetrack gambling per se but the lack of respect for laws. The *Evening Mail* thought that Hughes's triumph demonstrated that "public opinion when rightly interpreted and courageously expressed, will assert itself and dominate every situation. . . . The house of politics is cleaner than it was thanks to the 'animated feather duster.'" The *Tribune* captured the popular feeling that "the victory in the anti-gambling fight will only serve to intensity the public unwillingness to see him retire." Not so thrilled with the outcome was his old foe William Barnes, who considered the outcome an "absurd blunder." He was worried about the political impact of the new law and its consequences for Saratoga's economy.[49]

Newspapers and periodicals that opposed racetrack gambling applauded its apparent end in New York. *Outlook* praised Foelker for voting at the risk of his life, while criticizing the sordid work of the nineteen Democrats led by Grady and McCarren and six Republicans, most notably Cassidy, who opposed reform. Journalists criticized proracing senators for their loyalty to bosses and gamblers rather than to their oaths to protect the constitution.[50]

The *Chicago Record-Herald* was thrilled to see the end of New York racing, blaming not just the gambling problem but also "the brutal arrogance of the Tammany faction that has killed the game in New York. . . . Bitter complaints have been made continuously of treatment of patrons at tracks like Jamaica and Aqueduct. It has often been charged that the employees of these concerns are appointed strictly through political 'pull,' and it is said that even the judges appointed by the jockey club are powerless to stop inconsistent racing if the offending horse or jockey happens to be connected with the Tammany ring." The *Record-Herald* compared the ambience at New York racetracks unfavorably to other commercialized entertainment:

> In baseball, at the theaters—in fact, at every other public form of amusement or sport, patronage are treated civilly and an effort is made to please them. On the

contrary, the race tracks have been run on the Tweed idea of "What are you going to do about it?" There is no redress here for a patron who wishes to complain of uncivil treatment or of worse usage.

Probably the worst impression has been created by the very element which has direct profit by the game. The men employed as clerks of the bookmakers have so frequently offended bettors who have to come in contact with them, that even the patrons of race courses have turned against the game. Considering that these men often draw down $10 for about two and one-half hours of work in the afternoon, it is difficult to see why they should insult the bettors.[51]

Financial Ramifications

The press estimated that some $50 million was invested nationally in breeding farms, $25 million in racehorses, and $6 million in New York racetracks. Racing in New York alone employed forty thousand people directly or indirectly, including five thousand on breeding farms and fifteen thousand at its fifteen hundred stables. The *Morning Telegraph,* a great backer of racing, anticipated that the legislation would result in "the virtual confiscation of racing property and reduce the value of horseflesh in New York State and elsewhere by 50 per cent."[52]

The local racing industry was expected to lose $26.1 million, which included $6 million in salaries, $6 million in track admissions, $10 million in concessions, $1 million in trade for stores located near tracks, $750,000 in feed, $200,000 in fares for the Long Island Railroad and $150,000 for the Brooklyn Rapid Transit Company, and $2 million in yearling sales. The town of Saratoga was expected to be the biggest loser of all because of its heavy dependence on the turf. Across the nation, the racing industry feared the worst. Californian James B. Haggin, who owned more than two thousand thoroughbreds, the largest stud in the world, estimated his stable's value had dropped by 75 percent and was expected to sell his Kentucky stock farm.[53]

Heavy losses were also foreseen in related industries. Besides the rail lines and trolley lines losing fares from riders bound for the tracks, the Thirty-fourth Street Ferry, which carried thousands bound for the three Queens County tracks, was expected to be hit especially hard, as were the bootblacks working at its depot. As one Italian shoe shiner noted, "We make a da mon when da horse race is run. In da race time we getta from twelve's to fifteen dol' more a day. Every boy we can get is on da job shini' da shoes of da sports." Midtown restaurants that served tourists and other racing fans as well as bookmakers and their staffs figured to lose a lot of business.[54]

Racing, Agnew-Hart, and Bribery

Rumors about possible bribes to block Agnew-Hart did not fade away, and in 1910, the Legislative Graft Investigating Committee convened to look into it. The hearings centered on lobbyist and former Republican senator E. L. Gardner, leader of Brooklyn's Twelfth Assembly District, a reputed follower of Timothy Woodruff, Republican leader of Kings County, and also a close friend of Democratic boss P. H. McCarren. Gardner spent ten weeks in Albany in 1908, working to kill the Agnew-Hart bills, where he reputedly handled racing's $500,000 lobbying fund. He allegedly gave Foelker $10,000 for his vote, with the promise of another $15,000.[55]

New York Assistant DA Robert Elder told the committee that Gardner admitted to him that he had tried to block the antigambling laws by using funds raised by stable owners James Keene and H. P. Whitney and current city chamberlain C. H. Hyde, who contributed money on behalf of Engeman of the BBRA. Gardner told Elder that the proracing forces had met at Delmonico's with a Mr. Parsons representing bookmakers, lobbyist Eugene D. Wood, and David Mitchell, the former head of Western Union's Racing News Bureau, and that he had accompanied Hyde to Albany to arrange their efforts to win votes.[56]

Senator Foelker testified that at least six politicians had approached him seeking a no vote on the legislation. Foelker claimed that Sheriff Alfred T. Hobley, a Republican district leader in Brooklyn, warned he would not be renominated if the senator voted for the bill, while Senator McCarren told him that if he voted against the bill, he could name his own opponent for the fall election, and Gardner promised him help with his Democratic friends. Foelker further claimed that New York City's quarantine commissioner, Frederick Schroeder, offered him $45,000 for his vote and later upped the offer to $50,000. Foelker told the committee that Hyde informed him that another senator had gotten $225,000 for his vote. As Foelker recalled, Hyde told him, "Otto, we need your vote against the Race Track bill. I want you to vote against it, and I will take care of you from a financial standpoint if you do. In fact, I will treat you better than some of the other Senators. If you will stand and vote against the bill, I will give you $2,000 more."[57]

Senator Gaffney was named as a briber by Senator Eugene M. Travis (R–Kings County), who held Gardner's old senate seat. Travis claimed that when the racing advocates were looking for just one or two votes, Gaffney offered him $100,000 to vote against the antigambling bill. Travis also claimed that Senators Carpenter of Westchester, Gates of Madison County, and Fuller of Brooklyn were also offered bribes.[58]

The committee examined, in addition, the role of bookmakers lobbying the legislators. Orlando Jones, former treasurer of the MTA, denied that on-track bookmakers had been tapped to fight the bill, although the executive board did hire lawyers and assessed members for the costs. Current MTA treasurer John J. Evans claimed he could not find the MTA's missing financial records when he was grilled for nearly an hour. He denied that bookmakers had raised a bribe fund but admitted paying $12,500 to De Lancey Nicoll and the law firm of Davies, Stone, and Auerbach for "legal services" but not specifically to fight racing bills.[59]

The investigation had little impact. Gardner was indicted for bribing state legislators, most notably Senator Foelker, who cast the deciding vote in the 1908 special legislative session. The case was front-page news for several days until a jury acquitted Gardner in just seventy minutes.[60]

The 1908 Racing Season

The Jockey Club, before the 1908 racing campaign started, revised the betting system to make it less anathema to its critics. The Jockey Club required tracks to prevent bookmakers from walking around, barred bookies from perching on tall stools because it gave them too much recognition, and banned unaccompanied minors from the tracks. The Jockey Club also tried to curb public betting by forbidding layers in the grandstand from accepting wagers under $5, conforming to the rule that prevented bets under $2 in the field stand.[61]

The racing season began with Buffalo's Kenilworth track closed for the year. Aqueduct led off the metropolitan season in April with a huge opening-day crowd of twenty thousand, along with nearly three hundred bookmakers and their staffs. Stallion Jack Akin won the $10,000 Carter Handicap. The round-trip train fare on the LIRR was raised a nickel to $0.55. The racing reforms led to the absence of visible betting and made bets too expensive for "pikers." Bookmakers arrived with satchels instead of money boxes and stood on the betting-room floor instead of perching on stools. Clubhouse betting was all by commission, mainly on credit, and there was virtually no cash betting with bookmakers. Despite the huge crowd, the amount of betting was the lowest in memory for an opening day.[62]

Belmont opened with the $13,000 Metropolitan Stakes and thirty-five thousand in attendance, as fashionable as ever, with a large female presence. Jake Akin won the race, carrying the highest weight ever (128 pounds) and setting an event record. Bookmakers operated without any betting paraphernalia but a tablet to record bets. Belmont dropped TJC's betting reforms because many $3 grandstand patrons moved to the $1 field seats, where they could make bets of less than $5.[63]

Despite the new law, the tracks did the best they could to continue their scheduled stakes events. Newspapers other than the *Times* or the *Evening Post* still printed racing charts with past performances, and journalists provided readers with full reports. Still, most observers predicted a bleak future and expected no racing without gambling.

Management insisted there be no betting until the legal issues were resolved, and betting manager John Cavanaugh was instructed not to assign bookmakers places in the betting ring. Consequently, the rings were bare of the usual long lines of bookies. About thirty MTA members were present, making bets with people they knew and committing them to memory until they could secretly inscribe them in their books. There were just enough efforts by bookies to conduct public betting to throw the old betting enclosures into turmoil. Police Commissioner Theodore Bingham sent a large force to the track to crush the betting, and they made fourteen arrests.[64]

The next day, Saturday, drew the typical half-holiday crowd of fifteen thousand, with an unusually large percentage of women. The lawns were very crowded, but without public gambling, the course was bereft of the usual excitement. Nearly three hundred policemen, forty Kings County deputies, and the track's security staff were present. A line of uniformed officers surrounded the betting ring to prevent betting. Only three amateur gamblers were arrested for taking oral bets, yet there was sufficient secret and private betting among professional bettors and horsemen to provide a basis for quoting starting prices for newspaper reports and form charts. Over the next few days, the gate and the number of bookmakers both declined. The police were instructed to prevent no more than three people from congregating and to arrest anyone making notes that looked like recorded bets. Gravesend opened on 1 June, and its attendance dropped substantially after Agnew-Hart went into effect. However, the meeting made so much over the first ten days that it made a profit.[65]

Sheepshead Bay followed the BJC, having spent $200,000 in refurbishments. On 19 June, opening day, Justice Bischoff of the state supreme court granted the CIJC an ex parte injunction restraining Commissioner Bingham and his officers from interfering with "lawful use" of their premises and meddling with individuals who were not disorderly or committing a crime. Bingham still assigned three hundred men to the track.[66]

A crowd estimated at eighteen to twenty thousand attended the Friday opening, well below the usual crowd for the $25,000 Suburban, but still very respectable considering the new gambling laws. James R. Keene's Ballot, the betting favorite, won the one-and-a-quarter-mile race in an event record 2:03. The *Times* gushed in its report of the beautifully dressed holiday-making crowd arriving in coaches, carriages, and automobiles. A few bookies immediately began surreptitiously taking wagers, with widely varied betting odds. Ballot, for instance, went off at odds that ranged from two to one to even money. Attendance the following day was nearly as high for the $20,000 Tidal Stakes, captured by Keene's undefeated three-year-old Colin, with his fifteenth straight victory in an event record of 2:04 for the one-and-a-quarter-mile distance.[67]

Bookmakers arranged a test case on opening day to evaluate the breadth of the Agnew-Hart Act. Melville Collins, a new MTA member, was arrested after the last race, by Robert Pinkerton, on an affidavit from fellow MTA member James Moran, who claimed Collins had accepted $5 from him in payment of a verbal bet. Two weeks later, Judge Bischoff ruled Collins innocent since the Agnew-Hart Act did not prohibit private and individual betting on races, even if made at the track, because the law covered only professional gambling. This important ruling led to the implementation of oral betting later that summer at Saratoga.[68]

The CIJC's closing event was the prestigious $22,000 Realization for two-year-olds, won by August Belmont's Fair Play, the future sire of Man O'War. The track managed to keep its stakes events going during the meet, but there was a precipitous 50 percent drop in attendance because of the gambling situation. The jockey club cut costs, reducing up to 50 percent of added money for lesser events. The worst day of the meet occurred on 27 June, when the CIJC held three major races with nearly $50,000 in purses, including the $25,000 Coney Island Jockey Club Stakes, but took in just $2,000 at the box office, causing a staggering $40,000 loss that day. The track relied almost totally on gate receipts and concessions to cover expenditures, since it could not charge bookmakers for operating there, and lost between $150,000 and $250,000.[69]

An unintended result of Agnew-Hart was a boost in the handbook business. According to the *New York Times*, "The handbook maker has been in evidence as never before. Customers who used to visit the track now remain in the cities, and the bookmaker moves about mysteriously, visits offices and other public and semi-public places and does a 'land office business.'" This activity was seen as a greater menace to the public than the racetrack bookmakers were. However, the *Times* offered a positive spin, since the authorities in Washington, DC, had cleaned up a similar problem the year before.[70]

The racing season shifted on 7 July to the Brighton Beach Racetrack, which canceled sixteen of the most lucrative stakes races, including the $25,000 Brighton Handicap, because of the ban on gambling. The average purse was merely $467, the smallest in twenty years. The BBRA drew small crowds because there was no prospect for gambling. Nonetheless, Brighton managed a small profit.[71]

The BBRA's management was hard-pressed by the new laws. On 21 July, the police arrested its primary stockholder, William Engeman, track president C. J. Fitzgerald, and John Cavanaugh, former superintendent of betting rings for the metropolitan tracks, for conspiring to allow Joseph Vendig, Orlando Jones, and other bookmakers to operate, providing advance information to bookmakers, and possessing call sheets on which information was given that enabled bookmakers to calculate and quote odds. Cavanaugh's Bureau of Advance Information sold tips at the tracks fifteen minutes before the official notice boards posted the data for $2 on slips of tissue paper with the names of horses and their riders. This procedure enabled clients (bookmakers and bettors) a better chance to evaluate the upcoming race. When the police complained that these slips could be considered a gambling device, the bureau distributed them for free.[72]

The BBRA's attorneys filed a demurrer on the charges of providing advance or inside information at the tracks, questioning the complainants' legal sufficiency because the actions did not constitute a crime. The court upheld their petition, ruling that paper was not a gambling device. Then, in November, they were tried for allowing betting by a four-judge panel in Brooklyn Supreme Court. The jurists ruled unanimously on 31 December that oral betting by nonprofessional bookmakers did not violate the Agnew-Hart law because the state aimed its penalties at stakeholders, bookies, and pool sellers. The gamblers were ecstatic at the ruling, although the *Times* warned that the "gamblers rejoice too soon."[73]

In August, the racing scene switched to Saratoga, where opening day attracted fewer than half its typical ten thousand fans. Saratoga bettors adopted an oral betting plan, following Judge Bischoff's ruling in the *Collins* case. Sheriff John Bradley Jr. operated under the advice of the county's Republican political boss, former senator Edgar T. Brackett, and did not rigorously enforce the law. There were upwards of a hundred bookmakers working the track, openly taking bets from 80 percent of the crowd.[74]

Walter Laidlaw of the Citizens' Anti–Race Track Gambling League charged Bradley with not fulfilling his duties. Governor Hughes impaneled a special commission to consider the allegation. Laidlaw's agent, Robert H. Scott of Brooklyn, testified that he saw a lot of open gambling at Saratoga, with money openly passed ten feet from the police and deputy sheriff, who did nothing about it. Scott said that prior to each race, there were more than twenty groups of about ten to twelve people on the course, all gathered around bookmakers quoting odds, while their clerks recorded bets on a program. These bookmakers even took future bets at a local hotel, employing bellboys to bring them clients. Despite the incriminating testimony, Bradley kept his job.[75]

Saratoga Race Track reportedly lost $30,000 in its fifteen-day meet. Nonetheless, the spa apparently did much better over the next few years than the state's other tracks, which historian Edward Hotaling attributed to the closer connection there between bettors and bookmakers. As Hugh Bradley, historian of Saratoga Springs, pointed out, "Bookies and big betters, living for a month in the same hotels, found it fairly convenient to bet in advance and collect at leisure." In addition, the resort's economy was intimately tied to the success of the track, and local politicians bent over backward to protect their jewel.[76]

Agnew-Hart's impact became much stronger in the fall, when racing struggled. Brighton Beach, which made money in the summer, canceled its fall meet, replaced by races at Aqueduct. Losses were especially high at Sheepshead Bay, which by late September was attracting only about a thousand spectators. Belmont had some stellar racing, particularly Fair Play's American record for a mile and five-sixteenths in the Jerome Stakes, followed three days later by his winning the Municipal Handicap, but at most fifteen hundred showed up one Saturday. The fall season ended at Jamaica, which cut expenses to the bone yet still lost about $2,000 a day. As a result, a *Times* headline on November 5 proclaimed, "'Taps' Is Sounded on Racing Here."[77]

The tracks had made about $1 million in 1907, but in 1908 had a $525,000 deficit, despite operating as cheaply as possible, with purses cut by $1 million. The tracks' gross dropped from $4,928,583 to $1,549,336. The CIJC's two meets alone ran a $350,000 deficit, compared to the track's usual $400,000 profit, and its payout to the state dropped by 80 percent. The other tracks lost a combined $175,000. Aqueduct, Jamaica, and Belmont Park all had profitable spring meetings before Agnew-Hart went into effect and ended up slightly in the black, despite losing money in their fall meets. The BJC had ten racing days before the law was enacted, followed by six more days, and closed the spring meeting with a slight profit. However, the fall meet lost about $60,000. Empire City, Coney Island, and Saratoga staged their meets under the new law and suffered big losses. After Brighton Beach repudiated its stakes obligations, winning horsemen sued to secure payment of their purses. The BBRA broke even for the year, but paid only $4,098 to the state in taxes, 10 percent of the prior year. The state's overall take dropped from $246,429 to $77,487, a 68.6 decline. The bottom line for 1908 did not bode well for the next season.[78]

Thoroughbred racing's shaky future convinced several breeders to send their stock to England. American owners first sent horses to England in the 1850s, led by Richard Ten Broeck, and in the late 1890s, there was a veritable invasion by American owners and jockeys. The English resented the success of the foreign riders and in the early 1900s barred several of them. American owners continued to race in Great Britain, and the number increased in 1908 with the uncertain future of New York racing. James R. Keene, for instance, shipped ten of his finest horses overseas, including Colin, the undefeated three-year-old champion, and also the outstanding four-year-old Ballot. H. P. Whitney and Belmont both sent some of their finest horses to Europe, including the latter's Fair Play.[79]

In September, Richard Croker was interviewed in Dublin about the New York racing situation and was very critical about the efforts to clamp down on betting. He believed it was in man's nature to gamble—even buying insurance was a gamble—and thought that gambling laws should apply equally to the stock market as well as to the racetrack. If someone wagered more than he can afford, "This is his own affair. If he didn't put his money on a horse he would probably get rid of it some other way." Croker compared the American turf scene unfavorably to England's:

> They [Hughes and the Republicans] are ruining the country; ruining the racetracks, in which a get deal of money is invested; ruining the breeders of horses, many of whom are breaking up their studs, and that in a free country! It is a free country no longer. You have more freedom over here. I go to race meetings here and I see a fine crowd of people, ladies and gentlemen, enjoying themselves, and King Edward himself at their head.
>
> King Edward is the finest sportsman in the world. If there was anything wrong in it, do you think he would be at the head of all kinds of sport in this country? In London you have a national sporting club. They encourage all kinds of sport and are allowed to make a certain amount of money; the rest goes to hospitals and charities.[80]

Croker forgot to mention how Edward snubbed him when he captured the Epsom Derby back in 1907.

Croker returned to the United States in April 1909 and visited the White House. While there, he asserted, "You cannot have horse racing without the accompaniment of betting. . . . I regret the growing disposition in this country to force the so-called 'wave of reform.' Every man who can afford it should be allowed to spend his money as he sees fit. In my opinion bookmaking should be legalized. There should be some way of restricting wagers to fit the bettor's means."[81]

Racing and the 1908 Gubernatorial Election

Hughes ran for reelection in 1908 against Lieutenant Governor Lewis Chanler. Hughes won easily, 804,651 (49.08 percent) to his Democratic foe's 735,189 (44.84 percent), with the rest going to third parties, but he ran behind the entire statewide Republican ticket. The racing men did what they could to support Chanler, including sending up 540 men ("colonizers") from Baltimore's Pimlico Racetrack just to vote for him.[82]

Horse racing was not a top issue in the campaign, but it did come up. William R. Hearst, chairman of the Independence League Party, stumped for his candidate, Clarence J. Shearn. In a lecture at Cooper Union in mid-October, Hearst told his audience that Chanler was running on behalf of track gamblers: "The platform upon which the demoralized grand old Democracy of the State of New York insolently stands is that anybody, from the Standard Oil Company to an illegal bookmaker, is at liberty to plunder the people if he will pay for the privilege with a campaign contribution." Furthermore, "every race-track tout and tipster, every Standard Oil tool and every Standard Oil attorney, will vote the grand old demoralized democratic ticket. . . . How inspiring it must be for the citizenship of this great Nation to see the race-track Democracy of New York jockeying and starting, and finally running its forlorn race." Hearst claimed that the Democratic platform called for "Graft and gambling. Loot and license. Immorality and immunity. Hurrah for the racetrack and to Hades with the home! Give us a wide-open town and a wide-open till. Let the boys pilfer from their employers and spend it on the ponies. . . . There are too many churches and schools and not enough poolrooms." His lecture concluded with a mock horse race of Democratic bosses "Fingey" Connors, Charles F. Murphy, Big Tim Sullivan, and Little Tim Sullivan, respectively mounted on "Boodler, Grafter, Colonizer, and Repeater."[83]

A few days later, Chanler asserted that he would enforce all the laws on the books, including gambling laws, and denied any intent to repeal Agnew-Hart. A New York correspondent for the *Louisville Courier-Journal* reported, without confirmation, that the racing crowd had raised a $500,000 fund to support Chanler. Supposedly ten prominent racing men, including August Belmont, Henry P. Whitney, "Bet-a-Million" Gates, James B. Sanford, Phil Dwyer, James B. Reynolds, Tim Sullivan, Patrick McCarren, and George Considine, had promised to raise $30,000 apiece, with the latter three raising their pledges from among gambling friends. In addition, five leading bookmakers, Sol Lichtenstein, Orlando Jones, George Rose, Tom Shaw, and Joe Vendig, were going to come up with another $40,000 each to make a total fund of $500,000.[84]

The National Impact of Agnew-Hart

Two weeks after New York passed the Agnew-Hart Act, the Louisiana legislature passed the Locke Anti-Gambling Law that resulted in the ending of racing in early 1909. Then in February 1909, California passed the Walker-Otis Act that banned pool selling and bookmaking, which killed thoroughbred racing there. The *Times* did not revel in the news, interpreting it as "Puritanism claiming new victims." It noted that no state had actually barred the sport of horse racing and hoped racing could continue and thereby protect the property rights of racing associations and breeding interests. However, the editors thought that thoroughbred racing was doomed unless viable without gambling, which seemed impossible.[85]

The Future of Agnew-Hart

The SRC report in March 1909 strongly chastised the Agnew Act and warned that if it remained in force, the law "will seriously cripple if not absolutely destroy thoroughbred racing of high class in this State." This criticism did not bother Agnew, who had even more ideas about halting racing and gambling. He proposed a law barring newspapers or wire services from publishing tips or racing odds, which he borrowed from a plan drawn up the year before by Louis Marshall, the noted Jewish jurist and reformer. District Attorney Jerome backed the concept because it would place greater obstacles in the way of poolrooms and handbooks that used press odds to settle debts. However, the *Times,* which did not print racing odds, opposed the proposal as censorship and a dangerous and reprehensible example of legislative meddling with the freedom of the press that would only slightly inconvenience gamblers. On 13 March, the bill passed the senate by a vote of thirty-one to thirteen, but it never got out of the assembly.[86]

Owners and breeders met at TJC on 14 April to plan more sophisticated schemes to salvage the sport than the trial-and-error methods employed in 1908. Harry Knapp, an SRC member and CIJC steward, chaired a new committee that included J. B. Haggin, the largest breeder in the world, and Schuyler Parson of the CIJC, to raise money for certain stake events. Owner and breeder associations provided $20,000 to help fund ten stakes races. Professional gamblers and bookies offered to subscribe, but their generous offer was rejected.[87]

The Jockey Club decided that all future revenues must come from admission fees: "Racing must live on its own merits as a sport and survive or perish as public patronage may decide." The turnstiles would test public support. General admission was kept at $3.00 for men and $1.50 for women, and passes were eliminated. The Jockey Club also determined that Brighton, Aqueduct, and Jamaica would not open in 1909. However, during the summer, the decision was reconsidered, and the Queens tracks got the go-ahead to open in the fall.[88] Brighton never reopened.

Appellate division justice William J. Gaynor decided an important test case regarding racetrack betting just before the racing season began. This case involved George R. "Sol" Lichtenstein and Orlando Jones, two of the most preeminent New York bookmakers, who with twenty of their colleagues were arrested at Brighton

Beach Racetrack on 10 July 1908 when they took wagers they heard but without writing any memos. Gaynor ruled that oral bets did not constitute bookmaking because a conviction required a written record (such as a book, sheets of paper, or a bulletin board) and acquitted Lichtenstein and Jones. The *Times* was not surprised at Gaynor's ruling, though it considered a bookmaker as the man who took bets and arranged, or tried to arrange, the odds in his favor, even if done in his head without paper. Gaynor's ruling seemed to practically nullify the state constitution's antigambling provisions.[89]

The 1909 Racing Season

The owners and breeders put together a $110,000 fund to prop up the New York racetracks. Racing began on 13 May at Belmont with just three days of racing a week. Opening day drew eight thousand, considered surprisingly large given the conditions. Fans adapted to the new oral betting format, which had no advertising, posting of odds, or paraphernalia in sight, backing their choices within the limits of the law. Bookies dared not take big wagers since they could not lay them off, while bettors worried about the fairness of the odds they got. Consequently, hundreds of bookies, and many big bettors, stayed on the sidelines. Crowds grew as the public became more familiar with oral betting, and more dates were scheduled. Empire City took a bold position by racing eighteen straight days.[90]

The Jockey Club viewed the situation cautiously, claiming the public had the right to bet. It believed that many racegoers were "timid and furtive" about "making their harmless wagers as if they feared raids and arrests," blaming the police's "reckless abuse of authority" the year before. The Jockey Club asserted that "there is absolutely no grounds for the timidity, for betting under the restrictions which eliminated bookmaking is entirely within the law, and the racing associations stand ready to protect patrons in the exercise of their privileges and liberty under the law."[91]

The summer racing season got a boost at Saratoga, which drew a prominent national audience and where women made up about half of the grandstand and clubhouse crowd. Saratoga, encouraged by Empire City's success, scheduled twenty-four days instead of the planned fifteen. There were seven thousand present on opening day (2 August), about 50 percent larger than the year before, though weekday attendance was about the same. The managers opened a field stand, the first at any New York course that season. However, the cheap seats drew poorly, possibly because there was only credit betting.[92]

On 4 September, Governor Hughes wired Assistant DA Robert H. Elder and Sheriff Alfred T. Hobley, informing them he had heard the antigambling law was being violated at Sheepshead Bay and ordered them to investigate. Elder swore in twenty-five well-groomed, smart-appearing young men as special detectives and gave them money to bet. As they moved around and made wagers, the operatives spotted a clerk standing near his bookmaker jotting down on a tiny pad in his palm or attached to his coat lining their initials, the horse bet, and the amount wagered. Any winning bettors went to a third man for the payoff.[93]

When racing moved to Gravesend at the end of the summer, detective squads from Brooklyn district attorney John F. Clarke's office made nineteen arrests at the track for aiding and abetting bookmaking. There were about sixty "layers" (the new term used for bookmakers) present, sufficient to service the crowds that averaged about three thousand people. Clarke reported that the bookies were having a hard time with the oral betting system and were again recording bets.[94]

These raids occurred without the help or foreknowledge of Brooklyn sheriff Hobley. He did not interfere with bookmaking, worried about lawsuits for false arrests, claiming that no one was ever convicted under the Agnew-Hart Act. Rumors developed that he would be accused of neglect of duty, but it did not happen. There was also buzz about a Gravesend police official getting $1,000 a day from men seeking to gamble there. One month later, the grand jury probed conditions at the Brooklyn tracks and indicted twenty-four alleged bookmakers for making and recording bets. Inspector J. J. O'Brien and two of his staff were indicted for failure to suppress gambling, and John Cavanaugh, the CIJC, the BJC, and four Pinkertons were accused of knowingly permitting bookmaking.[95]

There were 139 days of racing in 1909, down by 26 from the year before. Purses totaled more than $1 million, and daily operating expenses were about $5,000. Belmont Park, which sponsored some high-priced stakes, lost $25,000 in its fall meet, while Sheepshead Bay, Gravesend, and Jamaica broke even. Jamaica lost a "trifling," but Empire City canceled its fall meet because of opposition by the local authorities. Belmont paid the state barely half of the taxes it did in 1908, while Aqueduct and Jamaica, with abbreviated seasons, paid only about 25 percent. In Brooklyn, Gravesend dropped by 41.3 percent, but Sheepshead Bay actually increased by nearly 25 percent. Saratoga produced 58.5 percent more revenue, but the biggest gainer was Empire City, whose tax payments increased by 128 percent! The authorities did not interfere with oral betting until September, when they made some three hundred arrests, but not a single case ever went to trial.[96]

Once the season was over, the MTA broke up. Historian Michael Alexander claims that the decline of the MTA, along with the closure of the elegant gambling halls, like Canfield's Club House, pushed by progressive reformers, created opportunities for second-tier bookmakers, like young Arnold Rothstein, who used oral betting, to flourish. Operating a book using oral betting was a difficult skill to master since the odds were always changing. Many of these marginal bookmakers were Jewish, including Bill Cowan, Leo Mayer, Maxie Blumenthal, and Sam Adler. Old-timer Sol Lichtenstein, a renowned bibliophile and "king of the ring," adapted well to the new system. He reputedly made $50,000 a year during his career. Alexander points out that the bookmakers could not make enough on summer racing and in the fall got involved in underground card and casino games. These "smart Jew boys," many of whom were protected and mentored by Big Tim Sullivan, including Rothstein and Sam Paul, "Bridgey" Webber, and Herman "Beansy" Rosenthal, built their own casinos. They catered not to gentlemen, like Canfield, but to the new rich and the middle class. However, other than Rothstein, who became the prince of gamblers with whom other gamblers laid off their bets, a stable owner, and a fixer of races, their tenure at the top was very brief. Rothstein reportedly won $850,000 on a single race at Aqueduct.[97]

Racing and the Mayoralty Election

Racetrack gambling became an issue in the nasty 1909 mayoralty election between Democrat W. J. Gaynor, the civil libertarian judge, Republican-Fusionist Otto T. Bannard, a banker, and the Civic Alliance's William Randolph Hearst, making his second bid at the mayoralty. Gaynor, an unpopular choice among the Tammany faithful, won with about 257,000 votes, but the Fusion slate took the rest of the ticket. Bannard was second with about 175,000, followed by Hearst with 150,000. William M. Ivins, the 1905 Republican mayoralty candidate, who supported Hearst, spoke at a rally when Hearst was nominated for the mayoralty. He accused the judge of a midnight deal on 11 June 1908 (the day after Agnew-Hart passed) with Boss McCarren, Eugene Wood, a "notorious" lobbyist, and Randolph Block, a businessmen involved in the construction of the subway, to help nullify the new law, which Gaynor reportedly thought was unconstitutional. Ivins decried Gaynor as "a friend and adjutant of the race-track ring."[98]

Gaynor and McCarren denied the accusations, but the allegations were corroborated and amplified by Assistant DA Robert H. Elder, who claimed reliable sources informed him that Gaynor had advised Democratic politicians how to nullify Agnew-Hart. Elder pointed out that Gaynor's ruling in the golf betting case of *People ex rel. George Stirling* benefited racing men indicted as common gamblers. The defendant in that case allegedly bet with another golfer and recorded the bet on a card. Gaynor ruled that "an ordinary bet is not a crime whether made in your parlor, or a race track, nor is the making of a note or memorandum thereof." Elder was also suspicious of Gaynor's racetrack rulings because he reportedly wrote some opinions before hearing the case. These serious charges impugned the honor and integrity of the bench but were never proven.[99]

Shortly before the election, the press discovered that Gaynor, as executor for the BBRA, had held Coney Island land worth $6,250 from January 1906 until August 1909. The judge claimed that his duties were more of a burden and an honor than a means to make money. Still, the revelations were awkward because Gaynor's campaign chairman was his former law student Charles H. Hyde, counsel to the BBRA, lobbyist for the racing industry, and brother-in-law of William Engeman, the main owner of the Brighton Beach track.[100]

One week after the election, the court of appeals upheld Gaynor's ruling in the Lichtenstein oral betting case, *People ex rel. Lichtenstein v. Langan* (132 AD 937), by a two-to-one decision. Judge Alfred Haight ruled that the law barred ordinary bookmakers from the tracks. He defined a bookmaker as an odds layer who prepared lists of horses entered in races and set the probabilities of the outcome by a percentage that guaranteed him a profit regardless of the outcome. The bookie's vice was mainly in soliciting and inducing the public to take chances in a carefully figured and planned scheme. Judge Haight's view was that oral betting was never a crime. His colleague Chief Judge Edgar M. Cullen voted with Haight. Cullen argued that the law made gambling a crime only when accompanied by a record, registry, or paraphernalia, except for pool selling, where no record was needed to constitute a crime. Cullen questioned the possibility of enforcing the laws against every wager given the present morals and community tastes. Judge Irving G. Vann dissented, noting the law was aimed at blocking an insidious activity, not the making of a record of the wager. The ruling meant that the oral system of betting could continue. The *Times* attacked the ruling as injurious to many and beneficial to none and criticized the court's narrow interpretation of the intent of the lawmakers who drew up the antigambling laws.[101]

The State Legislature and Racing in 1910

The Jones-Lichtenstein case had a big impact in Albany because it seemed that the racetracks had found a way to circumvent the Agnew-Hart Acts and were about to resume operating full throttle. Governor Hughes in his State of the State speech recommended amending Agnew-Hart to penalize bookmaking, whether records were kept or not. Harry C. Perkins of Binghamton (R–Broome County) introduced three bills in the assembly to strengthen the gambling laws in line with Hughes's suggestions. One proposal intended to meet the court's recent ruling by making bookmaking, "with or without writing," a misdemeanor, which would end oral betting. A second bill tightened up Agnew-Hart by applying the law to all betting establishments, and a third, and ultimately most important, made directors of racing associations liable for violations on their grounds. Since track executives would risk imprisonment if gambling occurred at their facilities, they would almost certainly close down. Agnew introduced similar bills in the senate in mid-March.[102]

In April, the senate's Codes Committee held hearings on these bills. The consensus among committee members was that they only wanted to halt professional bookies and not interfere with people betting with friends. TJC representatives claimed such laws would be a death blow to breeding and put every private wagerer at the mercy of the public prosecutor. J. S. Auerbach told the senators that Agnew-Hart had been passed by a senate based on an unconstitutional apportionment and put through on the vote of an "intruder" (Wallace) who had replaced the late senator Stanislaus Franchot. Auerbach further pointed out that Percy-Gray was sufficient to regulate the sport and that there was no public outcry for reform. E. A. Tipton, a major breeder, also spoke against the bill, arguing it would kill his industry. He pointed out that his business had sharply declined from $1.5 million in 1901 to $450,000 in 1909. The antigambling forces were represented by Canon William S. Chase, head of the IRB, and Rev. O. R. Miller, state superintendent of the New York Civic League, who pointed out that the problems of gambling still needed to be cleaned up. Betting, Chase asserted, "fosters the worst anti-social spirit there is to-day. It demoralized business and creates crime."[103]

On 20 April, the Agnew-Perkins anti–oral betting bill passed the assembly, ninety-one to thirty-six, after a stormy hour of filibustering. A companion bill, holding directors and trustees of racing associations personally liable for gambling at their facilities, passed by a similar margin, ninety-four to thirty.[104] The legislation then went to the senate, where the racing crowd lobbied hard for an amendment striking out the prohibition on the laying or publishing of odds, orally or otherwise, to permit friendly wagers. However, the senate voted it down, twenty-six to twenty-one, setting the stage for the final vote on 4 May. This time the senate, unlike 1908, went along with the assembly, passing the anti–oral betting bill by a vote of thirty-one to fifteen. The vote was on party lines, with only two Democrats in support and three Republicans against. The senate also agreed by a vote of thirty-eight to eight to repeal the section of Percy-Gray that exempted trustees or directors of racetracks that posted signs indicating the prohibition of gambling on the premises from personal liability, effective as of 1 September. Henceforth, racing association officers keeping a room, an enclosure, or anyplace where gambling was conducted committed a misdemeanor. A third antiracing bill passed, prohibiting the publication or advertising of race-betting odds if that data facilitated bookmaking or poolrooms, except in newspapers when they were a matter of news. In addition, Senator John F. Schlosser's (R–Dutchess County) bill also passed, repealing the 5 percent tax on tracks' gross receipts for agricultural societies. In 1909, it amounted to only $65,166, about two-thirds of the tax in 1900. Of course, if racing was dead, the tax question became moot.[105]

In a last-ditch move, TJC asked the governor for an opportunity to convince him that the new laws were ambiguous and dangerous to racetracks, breeders, horse owners, and the general public, and Hughes scheduled a public forum on gambling before he signed off on the new laws. J. S. Auerbach argued at the meeting that the new laws were so loosely drawn up that they would invite prosecution of railroad directors for allowing card playing for stakes on commuter trains and hotel proprietors whose guests played cards. He further pointed out that there had never been a successful prosecution under Agnew-Hart and that the courts had quashed scores of indictments under that law. Not surprisingly, Hughes was unmoved by the discussion and on 15 June signed four antigambling bills.[106]

Progressives and moral reformers were elated. *Outlook* considered Hughes's fight against horse race gambling one of his most important achievements. He was applauded for using public sentiment "to defeat the powerful and insidious interests which opposed in the legislature his campaign for decency and loyalty to the Constitution." The magazine disagreed with the sport's advocates who expected the breeding industry to decline without racing, but even if the breeders were hurt, it was not worth saving the sport just to elevate horse breeding and denigrate the human breed. On the other hand, the *Brooklyn Eagle*, which had supported repeal of Percy-Gray in 1908, was very critical of this outcome. The editors warned that the antibetting laws were unenforceable, just as it was impossible to prevent the departure or return of Halley's comet. They also chastised the legislature for their real purpose, which was not to stop wagers but to end racing.[107]

The End of Racing

The passage of the Perkins-Agnew Acts was the death knell of New York racing. The tracks in mid-February had planned 184 days of racing, but the new law making track administrators accountable for betting at their facilities put everything in a new light. None relished the notion of prosecution under the Directors' Liability Act.[108]

The tracks made a faint effort to operate but soon had to give up. The racing season started at Aqueduct on 15 April with considerable trepidation while the Agnew-Perkins bills were under consideration. The Carter Handicap on opening day drew eight to ten thousand, with some betting, but nothing that merited the attention of the sheriff or special policemen. The racing scene moved to Belmont Park on 13 May for the nineteenth running of the Metropolitan. Opening day drew a much smaller attendance than normal, but it did draw the social set. By then, the reform bills had passed the legislature, and the writing was on the wall. Belmont closed on 30 May, with the $10,000 Belmont Stakes that drew a motley group of horses.[109]

Thoroughbred racing moved on to Gravesend for the $6,000 Brooklyn Handicap, and then to Sheepshead Bay in mid-June, where the Suburban Handicap on opening day drew twelve thousand. Numerous special police mingled with the crowd to prevent gambling, and there was no betting ring or betting commissioners. The biggest crowd of the season came on 4 July, when J. R. Keene's Sweep took the Realization and the first-place purse of $9,555. However, it was the final day of racing ever at the fabled track. Perhaps reflecting the decline of the turf, the *Times* report appeared on page 10, whereas in earlier years, it would have been a front-page story.[110]

The racing scene switched to Empire City, which had picked up the unopened Brighton Beach's dates, for two weeks, and subsequently held its own 12-day meet in August. Several speed records were set at the ECTC, which had the most profitable season of any New York track. Brighton Beach, on the other hand, soon became the site of international aviation contests.[111]

The last track to operate in 1910 was Saratoga, whose 21-day meet in August had a style absent elsewhere in the state. Saratoga had a distinct advantage over the other tracks because so many wealthy people were there to vacation, as well as see the races. Furthermore, as Saratoga historian Hugh Bradley explained, "Bookies and big bettors, living for a month in the same hotels, found it fairly convenient to bet in advance and collect at leisure." There were thirty-two stakes events, including new races, and the value of several older races actually rose, thanks to individuals who subscribed funds to make the meet a rousing success. The biggest event was the nearly $20,000 Hope Stakes for two-year-olds, the richest event in the United States. The session began with the Saratoga Handicap that drew a large attendance despite a heavy rain. A few days later, a highly fashionable crowd of twelve thousand, about the largest of the entire racing season, attended the Travers Stakes.[112]

When the Directors' Liability Act went into effect on 1 September, the tracks were all shuttered and the fall meets canceled, surprising many racing men who expected at least abbreviated meets. The racing laws seemed to leave no loopholes, and several poolrooms and handbook men also shut down, worried that they could no longer even offer a wager by word of mouth. New York's jockey clubs later decided not to apply for future racing dates as long as the liability law existed, having already hemorrhaged money since 1908 when the first antiracing law was enacted.[113]

The closing of the tracks harmed racing in New York, injured related businesses, and cost thousands their jobs. Agricultural societies had received $1.87 million in taxes since Percy-Gray was enacted in 1895 but now lost a major source of their revenue. The ending of racing damaged tourism in Brooklyn and contributed to the 1911 decision to raze the Manhattan Beach Hotel.[114]

The impending closing of New York racing in 1908, and its actual halting two years later, had negative ramifications nationally. In early 1911, TJC reported its registry of horses had declined by 2,300 in three years, two-thirds of American stallions were exported, and the number of broodmares and foals dropped by more than 50 percent. Yearlings in 1911 sold for a record average low of $230, and the number sold fell a year later to an all-time low of 243, compared to 550 in 1910. There were still more than 1,000 thoroughbred races in 1910 and 1911 (the most ever between 1907, when data were first kept, until 1921), but the average purse in 1911 was a historic low $371.75, and the total purses won by Worth, the champion two-year-old ($12,524), and Meridian, the three-year-old champion ($12,840), were record lows. Samuel C. Hildreth, the leading owner in 1911 (for the third straight year), amassed just $47,473, one-third of what he made in 1910. He became so discouraged that he sold his entire stable to New York piano manufacturer Charles D. Kohler.[115]

The *Morning Telegraph* estimated that owners shipped $3 million in horseflesh out of the United States. Gen. Leonard Wood, the army chief of staff, reported to Congress that so many thoroughbred studs were being exported that it created a potential national calamity, threatening the army's supply of horses. August Belmont II was a particularly important contributor to the military's cavalry, donating several outstanding stallions, including Henry of Navarre and Octagon, each worth $30,000, and others collectively valued at $64,000. The English, previously concerned about the invasion of American jockeys, now became so worried about the influx of American horses that the Jockey Club passed the Jersey Act in 1913, making horses ineligible for its stud book unless they traced all ancestors to already registered equines. These standards made most American horses half-breeds and disqualified from racing in Great Britain.[116]

The end of New York racing encouraged the passage of proscriptive legislation elsewhere, leaving only Kentucky and Maryland and the Dominion of Canada as North American racing centers. The upcoming blackout helped Louisville's Churchill Downs and Baltimore's Pimlico move to the top of US racing, while Woodbine in Toronto was first in daily purses for eight straight years. In 1902, Matt Winn and his syndicate took over Churchill Downs, then a second-rate course, and built it up through excellent marketing and innovative policies. He reintroduced $5 pari-mutuels at the track on Derby Day in 1908, for the first time since 1889, and bettors wagered $67,850 with the machines. Three years later, Winn reduced the minimum bet to $2. The Derby began to attract wider attention in 1913, with a huge upset by Donerail, who went off at ninety-one to one. One year later, the Derby's total purse reached $10,000, and then in 1915 it rose by 50 percent, when Regret, owned by Harry Payne Whitney, became the first filly to capture the Derby. Her victory helped popularize the event among the eastern racing establishment.[117]

Racing in Maryland also benefited from the demise of the New York turf. Its greatest event, the Preakness, originated at Baltimore's Pimlico in 1873 and continued there through 1889, when flat racing was halted there. The race moved to New York's Morris Park in 1890, but then was suspended until 1894, when it resumed at Gravesend. The race did not return to the Maryland Jockey Club's Pimlico until 1909, when many New York owners and trainers moved their operations there, with purses and betting on the rise. A racing boom soon followed, and in 1911, Laurel Race Track opened, followed by Havre de Grace in 1912, and Bowie in 1914. These mile courses were abetted in 1913 with the introduction of pari-mutuel wagering. In 1918, the Preakness purse was raised to $18,000, the same as the Kentucky Derby.[118]

The Future of the New York Tracks

The *Times* had no empathy for the New York jockey clubs and their tracks because of the harm gambling had caused, management's opportunities to convert the racecourses to more profitable and productive uses, and the better alternative spectator sports, particularly baseball, available to racing fans:

> The expensive race establishments do not in any sense, minister to the needs of the people. Money spent for the maintenance . . . represents a loss in wealth to the State. . . . The tracks will represent economic gain when converted to some productive purpose such as of agriculture or of residence. The money now invested in racing will be directed to more useful channels. . . . Clerks in business establishments will not be tempted to rob their employers' tills of money that would go to increasing the profits of the keepers of poolrooms, the bookmakers, or the turfmen.
>
> Gambling is one of the most expensive and perilous forms of public luxury. For the average man safer and quite as diverting forms of relief are at hand. Baseball, for instance, is a great popular amusement which can be supported without the charging of exorbitant fees of admission.[119]

The *Times* estimated that the tracks were worth $12.5 million. The Belmont and Sheepshead Bay were evaluated at $2.5 million, Brighton Beach $2 million, Gravesend $1.5 million, and Jamaica, Empire City, Aqueduct, and Saratoga each $1 million. The three Brooklyn tracks never again had thoroughbred racing. Beginning in 1910, Sheepshead Bay and Brighton were employed for motorcar racing, while Gravesend was used for training horses. Brighton was sold in 1922 to William E. Harmon for $675,000. He divided the property for building lots for small single-family homes, which had become much more accessible since the completion of a single-fare rapid transit system from Manhattan to Brooklyn. The 430-acre CIJC, 90 percent owned by William K. Vanderbilt, was sold in 1915 for $3.5 million to the Sheepshead Bay Speedway Corporation, a syndicate of car manufacturers and Wall Street men, who constructed a multimillion-dollar thirty-five-thousand-seat grandstand for car racing. Eight years later, it was sold for $20 million to developer Max N. Natanson as a site for single-family homes.[120]

The Democrats Take Over

In the 1910 election, the Democrats gained control of the state government, capturing the governor's mansion for the first time since 1894, and both houses of the state legislature for the first time since 1893, with a plurality of twenty-two seats in the assembly and seven in the senate. The new governor was John A. Dix, chairman of the New York Democratic Party, who had run unsuccessfully for lieutenant governor two years earlier with Lewis S. Chanler. Dix defeated Wall Street lawyer Henry Lewis Stimson, the former US attorney for the Southern District of New York (1906–9) and a future secretary of war (1911–13, 1940–45) and secretary of state (1929–33), 689,700 (48.0 percent) to 622,299 (43.3 percent), with the remainder divided among four independents. Stimson tried to make horse racing a campaign issue, especially following the Legislative Graft Investigating Committee's examination of the alleged corruption fund set up by Democrats and the racing crowd to fight passage of Agnew-Hart. Dix responded by asserting he had no intention of trying to change the laws, but said that it was up to the electorate. Nonetheless, the Democratic sweep encouraged the racing crowd to redouble efforts to legitimize gambling on the turf.[121]

Richard Croker and the State of Racing

In early April 1911, the *Morning Telegraph* interviewed Richard Croker about the current sad state of racing. He pointed out that Americans were going abroad to escape the puritanical racing laws that "do not express the opinions of the majority.

I am in favor of option in racing matters. If Saratoga could have her own way there would be racing there. As it stands, racing here is going to the dogs, and this is a great mistake. The matter should be referred to popular vote." The *Times* took umbrage with his comments, pointing out, disingenuously, that the laws were not against racing but against gambling.[122]

Croker recommended racing be conducted on the same local option like the liquor trade: "There are a great many persons interested in racing besides those who want to bet on the horses, and particularly in this country, where the people are supposed to rule themselves, they ought to be allowed to decide whether they want racing or not. Submit this question to the people and let them decide whether they want the sport in their own localities or not."[123]

The *Morning Telegraph* reported that turfmen thought that local option was the best solution to the racing situation: "In every locality where racing has been legislated out of existence the opposition to the sport has invariably come from sections remote from where the sport was carried on, and in almost every instance this successful opposition has been carried on by persons least interested and with the least knowledge of the very sport they were destroying." In Louisiana, for instance, the big opposition to the turf came from outside New Orleans, the state's primary site of racing. In New York State, Saratoga was the place most likely to get a positive vote in a referendum.[124]

The Renewed Fight for Racing in 1911

The fight to reinstate legalized gambling at the tracks began when Assemblyman William M. Martin (D-Saratoga) introduced a bill to repeal the Directors' Liability Law. Then President R. T. Wilson Jr. and Secretary Andrew Miller of the Saratoga Racing Association met with Governor Dix on 17 April to try to win him over.[125] On 8 May, Senator Robert H. Gittins (D-Niagara), with the encouragement of Wilson, introduced two bills in the senate to amend the racing laws. One proposal sought to reopen the tracks by exempting track directors from liability if betting arrests occurred. The other bill defined bookmaking without writing as applying just to the laying or publication of odds to all comers, or to the public, in a professional way, but not to friendly bets.[126]

Gittins's bills got limited publicity, since the jockey clubs did not want to create a moral uprising against them, as had sometimes happened in the past, and because his Democratic colleagues did not heavily support him. Party leaders were not strongly committed to fighting for racetrack gambling and did not want to make it a party measure. Assemblyman Al Smith, a rising Tammanyite who chaired the powerful Ways and Means Committee, did not push it, and Governor

Dix was silent on the matter. Tammany boss Charles Murphy was anxious to protect the new Democratic majority and avoided controversial policies that could create problems at the polls, especially without Dix's backing.[127]

R. T. Wilson Jr. and representatives of breeders and hoteliers testified before the senate's Codes Committee in support of the Gittins proposals. Wilson explained that the bills would protect not just racetracks but also owners of railroad lines, ballparks, and all other property not intended for gambling from liability if used for wagering. He claimed that if Saratoga reopened, there would surely be betting despite management's best efforts, and they should not be punished for events beyond their control.[128]

The status quo was supported by Henry Brolaski of the New York Civic League. The longtime gambler and bookmaker told the committee that there were fifty poolrooms and five hundred handbooks in New York, serving a hundred thousand customers, yet the police did nothing about it. Brolaski claimed, naively, that stopping betting at the tracks would wipe out the poolrooms, but poolrooms and handbooks were currently enjoying a monopoly of the betting business, relying on action from out-of-town races.[129]

Canon W. S. Chase criticized the Gittins bill in a letter to the *Times* because it would immunize anyone keeping an open-air enclosure for gambling but not indoor facilities, making the law class legislation favoring rich entrepreneurs. He pointed out that there would be no effective way to punish professional betting at tracks and would enable poolrooms to operate in connection with a restaurant, saloon, or cigar store. Chase worried that the bill would start up a new era of unprecedented professional gambling in New York, drawing professional gamblers from all over the world.[130]

The *Times* opposed the Gittins bill. It compared horse racing unfavorably to baseball, which also used to be a gambling game until fans got disgusted with dubious games and stayed away until the gambling was eradicated and confidence renewed in the national pastime's integrity. Racing, unlike baseball, was intrinsically interesting to just a few spectators. Wherever gambling on the turf was stopped, the sport went out of business.[131]

When the Gittins bill came up for a vote in the senate on 13 July, it needed twenty-six votes to pass. Nine senators were absent, and it was defeated, as expected, by a vote of twenty to twenty-two. Six days later, with the absentees in the chamber, the senate completely reversed itself and passed the bill by a vote of twenty-six to twenty-two. Five senators absent on the first ballot voted for the bill, presumably having been sufficiently "educated" by racing lobbyists. Senator A. J. Griffin (D–New York County) changed his vote to support the proposal, now convinced that the tracks should have a chance to prove they could bar gambling. Six

Republican senators, primarily from around Saratoga, including Senator Brackett, voted for the bill, which they saw as crucial for the community's financial well-being. Nearly every Tammanyite voted for the bill, except majority leader Senator Robert Wagner, who was joined by eight other Democrats, mainly from upstate. Racing folk had expected more solidarity from their traditional friends. Wagner was a liberal machine politician and humanitarian who probably believed horse race gambling harmed his constituents.[132]

The Gittins measure came up for a vote in the assembly the next day. Governor Dix, previously noncommittal, announced he would sign it if approved by the lower branch. The press presumed he was under a lot of pressure from leading Democrats who wanted passage. The proponents needed seventy-six votes to pass the assembly, and so Tammany brought in its heavy hitters to try to convince independent Republicans and upstate Democrats to support the bill. However, it was to no avail, and the Gittins Act was soundly defeated, fifty-three to sixty-three. Thirty-three members avoided going on record on the measure, because they either were absent or did not answer the roll call. Downstate Democrats were solidly behind the bill, but a majority of upstate Democrats (eighteen) voted no or did not answer the roll call, reflecting their strong commitment to local values over party solidarity. They did not want to be perceived as Tammany puppets. Only four Republicans backed the bill. The *Times* interpreted the results as evidence that the Directors' Liability Act passed not because Governor Hughes bulldozed it through but because it represented popular sentiment.[133]

The Gittins bill was reconsidered in the fall session when it seemed headed for certain passage, backed by both Republican boss Barnes of Albany and Tammany boss Murphy. Murphy had not pushed it earlier in the year, uncertain of the governor's support, but now he ordered his men to use every trick to get it approved. At first, Democrats Senator Tim Sullivan and Assemblyman Martin of Saratoga and their foe Rev. O. R. Miller of the Civic League agreed that the proponents had the necessary seventy-six votes already lined up. However, the Democratic Party pulled back once it became apparent the governor would not sign the bill because he feared that three-fourths of upstate Democratic legislators could lose their seats over the bill.[134]

The Democrats' failure to reestablish racing was particularly galling because the legislature did pass the Frawley Act, authorizing professional boxing. Pugilism had first been legalized in 1896 by the Horton Act that permitted "sparring" at facilities owned by incorporated athletic associations for a maximum of twenty rounds. New York was the second state after Louisiana to permit prizefighting. However, in 1900, the Republican-dominated legislature repealed the law, barring professional boxing, which thereafter was limited to brief "sparring" bouts, mainly at Tammany-connected "membership" clubs. These organizations evaded the ban on prizefighting by hosting bouts to entertain club members, whose dues were the price of a ticket of admission. Several bills were introduced in the early 1900s to legitimize professional boxing, primarily by Senator James J. Frawley, a Harlem Tammanyite very active in the sporting world. One bill legalizing prizefighting passed in 1906 but was pocket vetoed by Governor Higgins, and one year later, a bill permitting amateur boxing was vetoed by Governor Hughes. Then, in 1911, with the Democrats in control of the legislature, Frawley got a bill passed that Governor Dix signed, creating a state athletic commission that licensed boxing clubs and participants and levied a 5 percent fee on gross profits. The *Times* thought that legalizing pugilism was a big mistake that led to many new problems, including rioting by spectators upset by the actions of referees and by the outcomes of bouts. Governor Dix, who had signed the bill under pressure from party leaders, soon changed his mind. He now agreed with the *Times*'s analysis and called for the repeal of Frawley. This experience accounted in part for Dix's lukewarm attitude toward horse race gambling.[135]

Another Year, Another Fight

The Democrats suffered a debacle in the 1911 assembly elections, dropping from 85 Democrats to merely 48, with the Republicans growing from 63 to 101. There were 2 independents in 1911, and in 1912 there was 1, the first socialist ever elected to the chamber, Herbert M. Merrill of Schenectady. The Democratic disaster was statewide, including 20 lost seats in New York City. Pundits blamed the outcome on opposition to Tammany's efforts at changing the state charter and opposition to bossism, but also Republicans turning out in large numbers to defeat independent Democrats in swing districts. It was a bad year for bosses elsewhere, notably the Penrose-McNichol gang in Philadelphia and George B. Cox in Cincinnati.[136]

Despite the Democratic fiasco, efforts were instigated right at the start of the 1912 legislative session to revive racing, encouraged by the result of the appeal of a case involving Michael Lambrix, who was found guilty in March 1910 of receiving and recording racing bets and sentenced to six months in the penitentiary. However, the conviction was overturned on 23 January 1912 by the court of appeals that ruled that a bet between two people did not violate the Agnew-Hart antigambling law. The court ruled that a bettor giving a note to a bookmaker with betting information did not constitute a crime. However, if anyone connected to the bookmaker passed a similar memo, it would constitute a crime. The intent of the law, as in *Lichtenstein,* was against public gambling. The implication was that track patrons who made friendly wagers could attend races without fear of arrest. Racing advocates interpreted the decision as going beyond the protection of casual racing fans, "for it makes legal the personal wagers on baseball, elections, or any of the other various questions of chance that the law under a previous interpretation made illegal." However, it still left open the definition of bookmaking.[137]

In the legislature, Assemblyman Louis A. Cuvillier (D–New York County) reintroduced the Gittins bill to relieve directors of tracks and county fairs of legal responsibility for gambling on their premises without their knowledge and another amending the penal law by defining bookmaking without writing as the laying or publishing of odds to all comers or to the public at race meetings. However, given the realignment of the assembly, his proposals had no chance.[138]

The Shane Decision and the Return of Racing

While politicians were trying to revive racing, the sport's prospects continued to fade. By mid-March, nine fairgrounds had sold their properties, gone on the market, or entered into mortgage lawsuits. The only organizations that requested licenses from the State Racing Commission were two elite amateur groups, the United Hunts Racing Association for a four-day meet and the Meadow Brook Steeplechase Association for a two-day meet, both at Terminal Park, a steeplechase course operated by the UHRA located right behind Belmont Park.[139]

The UHRA was a very privileged organization whose meet drew an upper-class crowd of men and women. Club president Perry Belmont, an attorney, was a younger brother of August Belmont II and a founding member of TJC. He was a four-term Democratic congressman, former ambassador to Spain, and progressive reformer. He and other UHRA officials took special pains before their meet to make sure no gambling was allowed. In the past, several bookmakers who paid off the authorities took commissions "on the nod" at UHRA meets. Belmont hired a dozen Pinkerton agents to halt such gambling, and they forewarned gamblers that any semblance of betting would result in ejection. The Pinkertons detained bookmaker Paul Shane and certain other men, who were subsequently arrested by Deputy Sheriff Michael Williams. Shane was accused of walking around the grounds and making oral bets with people who handed him a memo they wrote after making a wager.[140]

President Perry Belmont believed that it was impossible to organized a race meet unless some gambling was allowed somewhere on the grounds and took the arrest of Shane as an opportunity to assess the legality of the liability law. Belmont was not present on the grounds that day, but given his interest in racing, his family background, and his professional training, he undoubtedly intended all along to set up a test case. Shane hired John J. Graham, an attorney for the LIRR, a member of TJC, and an owner of racing trotters, to defend him on charges of bookmaking. Graham claimed Shane was just making private bets and that his nods to alleged customers were no indications of bookmaking. Graham argued that bookmaking required publicity: the posting of odds, a stand to take wagers, a scheme of laying odds to give the layer and profit, and an actual exchange of money. The state, on the other hand, claimed that according to Agnew-Perkins, a bet was a bet. Exchanging notes, orally making a transaction, or even nodding constituted a bet, which was a misdemeanor.[141]

On 13 October, Supreme Court Justice Townsend Scudder of Nassau County made a seminal decision in *People ex rel. Shane v. Gittens.* He ruled that the information against Shane was insufficient to charge him with bookmaking and, more significantly, asserted that track directors were liable for criminal activities at their facilities only if they had foreknowledge of professional bookmaking in which odds were set to ensure a profit. Scudder cited as precedent *Lichtenstein* in which the bookmaker was acquitted because there was no written accounting of a bet. Scudder pointed out that the state constitution banned bookmaking but failed to define it. He tried to get at the legislature's intent by referring to *Lambrix,* in which Justice Cullen had interpreted Section 986 of the penal code as aimed only at public gambling, professional gamblers, and the maintenance of gambling houses. Scudder contended the Agnew-Perkins Act did not intend to make betting a crime but dealt solely with bookmaking, so ordinary wagering on horse races was no crime. The decision established the important precedent that individuals had the right to wager privately at a track as long as the betting was not a business and not carried on with paraphernalia.[142]

The ruling exhilarated racing interests, who saw it as the entering wedge needed to get back into business. It provided a loophole that the laws did not ban racing or betting but prohibited pari-mutuel betting or bookmaking. Chairman August Belmont II of TJC found the decision encouraging, especially since recent antiracing laws had not cured gambling but killed racing. Belmont recommended that the tracks adopt pari-mutuel wagering to restore horse racing and eliminate bookmaking. The Appellate Division of the Superior Court of Brooklyn unanimously upheld Scudder's opinion on 22 February 1913. Four days later, TJC's racing stewards and executives of leading tracks announced the resumption of racing on 30 May following the closing of meets in Virginia and Maryland.[143]

The Owners Fund was established in April by several prominent turfmen, including August Belmont, Joseph E. Widener, Thomas F. Ryan, H. P. Whitney, and James Butler, to support the reopening of the racetracks by helping jockey clubs fund stakes events and stables pay for entrance fees. In addition, Belmont and two other stockholders paid off Belmont Park's $120,000 debt so it could reopen. The Jockey Club drew up a schedule for 1913 without the Brooklyn tracks, with the season to start at Belmont Park with 18 racing days spread over six weeks. This calendar was followed by the MJC meet on 7 July for 12 dates, and then the reopening of Saratoga, which raced every day in August except Sundays. The season ended with fall racing at Belmont, Empire City, Jamaica, and Aqueduct.[144]

The tracks had a friend in the state's new governor, Democrat William Sulzer, the former "boy wonder," who was Speaker of the assembly in 1893 at age thirty and later served eighteen years in Congress. Governor Dix failed to win renomination, despite the backing of Boss Murphy, because of opposition from the party's anti-Tammany wing. Sulzer was slated instead. He won the general election with 664,488 votes because the Republican vote split between Job E. Hedges and Oscar Straus of Teddy Roosevelt's Progressive (Bull Moose) Party. Their combined vote was 829,817. Led by Woodrow Wilson at the top of the slate, the Democrats increased their majority in the state senate from 26 to 33 and recaptured the assembly with 104 seats to 42 for the Republicans and 4 for the Progressives.[145]

Sulzer's position on the turf and gambling was that the law did not prohibit running races or the making of wagers on races. He claimed no power or disposition to interfere with the reopening of the tracks but expected county officials to act if any prohibitions against gambling were violated. However, Sulzer did not get to fully enjoy the return of racing because he was impeached in August. He filed false campaign finance reports with the secretary of state, employed campaign contributions for personal use, and committed perjury and threatened to suppress evidence before an assembly committee. Sulzer was ignominiously removed from office and replaced by Lieutenant Governor Martin H. Glynn.[146]

The two-year racing blackout ended on Memorial Day at Belmont Park with the start of an 18-day meet. This started 67 days of racing in New York State. General admission at Belmont was $3, but one-third of the grandstand, located far from the finish line, was set aside for $1 tickets. A huge crowd of thirty thousand, entertained by a forty-piece orchestra, saw Harry Payne Whitney's six-year-old Whisk Broom II, who had raced four seasons in England, win the twentieth running of the Metropolitan Handicap. Management had anticipated a crowd of about half that size, and printed up just fifteen thousand programs. Society flocked to the track, including Mr. and Mrs. Theodore Roosevelt Jr., motoring in from their Long Island estates or city mansions. Reporters gave a lot of attention to the ladies' colorful outfits, such as the one worn by Mrs. W. K. Vanderbilt Jr. that included a white diagonal serge and lace frock, a black silk cutaway coat, and a large black hat. According to the *Times,* "The presence of women in the clubhouse precincts, in the paddock, and on the lawns lent brilliancy to the crowds." Two hundred

Pinkertons were on hand along with fifteen deputy sheriffs to discourage any gambling. Some veteran bookies attended, but the authorities made sure they did no business. There was just one arrest for gambling, although men and women spectators bet orally "among friends."[147]

The betting was all on credit; strangers had to be introduced to bookmakers before betting, with winnings paid up after the races or the following day. The bookmakers were at an important disadvantage because many bettors welshed on their bets. The "layers" (bookmakers) had no redress against the "players" (their clients) other than to offer less favorable odds to help cover losses. Welshers usually did not return to the tracks because of the embarrassment that could occur and instead bet at poolrooms, barbershops, and cigar stands, where cash exchanged hands. The *Times's* racing expert, Bryan Field, considered the whole betting format to be hypocritical, unpopular, and hard to operate.[148]

On 21 June, Whisk Broom II captured the Brooklyn Handicap and one week later, carrying 139 pounds and ridden by future Hall of Fame jockey Joe Notter, won the Suburban Handicap. He shattered the American record for one and a quarter miles of 2:02.8 in the Suburban with a clocking of 2:00 flat. However, press accounts were certain the official timer was wrong, given the splits and the times recorded by other reputable sources. The stallion was the only horse to capture the three great New York handicaps until Tom Fool in 1953, but his total purse for these victories was merely $9,625. The meet drew an average daily attendance of about five thousand, comparable to the crowds in 1910 before the halting of horse racing in New York.[149]

In the summer, the Metropolitan Jockey Club staged its 12-day meet at Belmont instead of its own Jamaica Racetrack to save money. The sport then shifted upstate to Saratoga for 26 days. Shortly after the meet opened, jockey John Wilson admitted having been bribed in some races at Belmont Park, which unsettled the scene at Saratoga. Bookmakers there were free to roam the track and offer odds to anyone who asked him for them, though they could not solicit business. Historian Hugh Bradley was very critical of the bookmakers, several of whom were insufficiently financed and could not meet their obligations.[150]

For the most part, opposition to horse racing and gambling at the tracks faded away. Assemblyman John Knight (R-Wyoming) introduced a bill in March to prohibit betting of any kind at the track, but it went nowhere, and it did no better in 1914 when he reintroduced the bill. The *Times* welcomed the return of the turf, with its excitement and pleasure, though it disingenuously claimed that racing would be enjoyed without betting. Its editors continued to deride bookmaking, which meant to them a public display of wagering but had no problem with private gambling, which presumably would not result in the systematized wagering that "had brought sham and ruin to many homes and started thousands of ignorant and weak young men on the path to perdition."[151]

In 1914, there were 100 days of racing. Aqueduct reopened for 15 days and took over the old Gravesend races, Belmont had a 30-day meet and secured the major Sheepshead Bay stakes events, and Empire City (16 days) and Saratoga (24 days) also operated. Saratoga housed some fifteen hundred horses in its stables for a particularly well-attended meet. Nearly all its hotels were full, and the boardinghouses were replete with tourists. Jamaica reopened for two weeks, the first time since 1908.[152]

The New York turf needed a few years to regain its national stature, especially because of the deleterious impact of World War I on the industry. Nationally, there were just 610 races in 1918, compared to 902 the year before. Nonetheless, by 1918, the New York tracks were operating 142 days. The five tracks (Aqueduct, Belmont, Empire City, Jamaica, and Saratoga) all had meets that ran 27 to 30 days. Purses reached $1,038,500, compared to $335,000 in 1913 when racing had resumed.[153]

However, New York racing never again dominated the sport as thoroughly as in the past because of the lost Brooklyn tracks, the establishment of the Kentucky Derby and the Preakness Stakes as two of the great classic events in racing, and the absence of pari-mutuel wagering. The SRC in 1917 recommended pari-mutuels instead of bookmaking, but that form of betting did not occur until twenty-three years later. The 1917 Derby drew a record 40,000 fans who saw Omar Khayyam capture the $16,600 purse. It was now the biggest race in America, with double the attendance at the Belmont, whose winner won just $7,500. In 1919, when Sir Barton won the three top stakes races for three-year-olds (later known as the Triple Crown), the Belmont purse was just $10,000, compared to the Preakness at $25,000 and the Derby at $20,825. One year later, 25,000 saw Man O'War set a world record for the mile and three furlongs at the Belmont (2:14.2), beating the old record by an astounding 2.6 seconds. However, the purse was under $8,000, compared to $50,000 for the Kentucky Derby. In 1922, 44,000 attended the $57,800 Derby, 30,000 went to the $50,000 Preakness, and 35,000 to the $50,000 Belmont Stakes.[154]

Overall, when measured by total attendance, purses, and betting, New York racing was back at the apex of thoroughbred racing by the early 1920s when American racing was booming. Purses in the United States more than doubled between 1918 and 1920 to $7.7 million and then nearly doubled again by 1926 to $13.9 million. In 1921, New York's tracks alone awarded $1,899,020 in purses. Several states, most notably Illinois, restored racing in the mid-1920s, as thoroughbred racing became an important feature of the "Golden Age of Sports." Nationally, the number of thoroughbreds doubled, the amount of races rose by 60 percent, and Man O'War gained heroic stature and became a part of the pantheon of sports heroes in the decade that included Babe Ruth, Red Grange, and Bobby Jones.[155]

The Agnew Acts remained on the books until 1934 when the Crawford-Bre-itenbach Law, legitimizing open betting with bookmakers, passed handily, by a margin of ninety-seven to forty-eight in the assembly and thirty-seven to ten in the senate and then was signed by Democratic governor Herbert Lehman. The new law set the penalty for bookmaking at a year and a day in prison and a $1,000 fine—unless another penalty was available, and there was, since clients could sue bookmakers for their losses. The new law also established a 15 percent tax on gross receipts of race meets. In 1934, attendance rose by 58.7 percent from 597,152 to 1,015,590, with gate receipts doubling from $1,340,189 to $2,854,712. The tracks contributed $284,875 to state coffers, compared to nothing the year before, and the federal government got $189,917. The hopes of getting such revenues encouraged states across the country, including California, Florida, Michigan, Texas, and West Virginia, to legalize horse racing in the 1930s.[156]

However, the state legislature still did not legalize pari-mutuel betting, employed by fifteen states by 1938, mainly because of Republican opposition. Florida and Massachusetts tracks, which had pari-mutuels, were paying the state double what New York tracks paid in taxes, while California courses paid four times as much ($2.6 million). In 1939, even though Republicans controlled both the assembly and the senate, the push for change got a big boost after New Jersey announced a referendum for 20 June on pari-mutuels, which was expected to pass, leading to legalized betting on racing there. The expectation was it would draw many racing fans away from the New York tracks. The opposition to pari-mutuels came partly from moral reformers opposed, in principle, to gambling, but a lot came from Tammany politicians worried about the future of their friends, the on-track bookmakers. The state legislature in May authorized a fall referendum to ask voters for their opinion on changing the antigambling provisions of the state constitution. The voters approved the proposition, and in early 1940 the legislators passed the Dunning-Penny Act to legalize pari-mutuels with bipartisan support, signed by Governor Lehman. The tracks would operate totalizator machines, tak-ing 10 percent of the betting pools, which they divided equally with the state. The belated innovation was a huge success. Racing attendance in 1940 rose by 31.7 percent to 2,054,314, who bet $103,259,359, or an average of $50 per spectator. The state's share was $5,998,953.03.[157]

Conclusion

Horse racing, all across the United States, was under severe attack in the early 1900s because of the issue of gambling. It was already barred in most states, and some of the top racing states, like Missouri, Illinois, and Louisiana, soon closed their tracks. Even in New York, the national center of the turf, gambling reformers had tried for years to halt horse race gambling for religious reasons because it was sinful, or secular reasons because the lost wagers broke men and their families, enriched the underworld, and bolstered the connections between crooked urban machine politicians and crime syndicates. The powerful coalition of racing men and Tammany Hall fought off the reformers for many years, even circumventing the amended constitution of 1894 that seemed to ban horse racing gambling. Finally, in 1908, a coalition of convenience that included progressives and conservative upstate legislators, prodded by Governor Hughes, passed the Agnew-Hart Acts that seemed like they were going to halt racetrack gambling. The three Brooklyn tracks all closed, but racing interests had fought tooth and nail, using Tammany connections and money to protect their interests. They won a reprieve in the courts, and racing continued. Two years later, Senator Agnew and his cohorts came up with an astute plan to close the tracks by making management responsible for any gambling at their courses. As a result, the tracks still in operation closed down, and there was no racing in 1911 and 1912. The turf's friends in Tammany Hall and the Saratoga area could not amass enough support in Albany to repeal the antiracing laws, even though the Democrats controlled both state houses and the governor's mansion. However, a seminal court ruling in the 1913 *Shane* case provided the entering wedge to resume racing. The Brooklyn tracks never reopened, but within a few years, racing, under oral betting, resumed, although it did not regain its former popularity until the 1920s.

12

Conclusion

Racing, Machine Politics, and Organized Crime

Horse racing was the oldest major American spectator sport, and one of the most popular, yet the turf's success often hung by a thread because of its connection to wagering. Attending races provided an extremely exhilarating afternoon for people who wagered on the events, but without betting, people were not interested in watching horses run around the course. In the late nineteenth century, racetracks were the only places in the United States where betting was legal, although there was a great deal of illegal gambling. Men with powerful political connections operated the tracks, and because of the gambling, their sport became an important nexus between urban politics and emerging criminal syndicates. Reformers, who saw gambling as sinful or socially dysfunctional, sought to ban racetracks because of the gambling. Jockey clubs needed all their political clout to fight them because without gambling, there was no horse racing.

Horse racing, along with boxing and baseball, had close ties to urban politics, reflecting the dominant role of urban machine politicians in professional sports in major American cities. These commercialized sports employed clout to secure the best possible sites for their semipublic sporting sites, protect themselves against governmental interference, and secure special treatment from local municipalities. Political machines in such cities as New York, Chicago, St. Louis, Cincinnati, and San Francisco were closely connected to the underworld, which supplied financing, graft, and votes in return for protection from police interference with illicit enterprises. At the turn of the century, professional politicians and their close associates were among the leading entrepreneurs in baseball, boxing, and horse racing. However, in Chicago and New Jersey, they were already being pressed by underworld figures, and by the 1920s, mobsters were taking over boxing across the country.[1]

Men gambled on the results of these three sports, although all betting on baseball and boxing was illegal, as was off-track wagering on horse races. Gambling was an important element in the nexus between sport, urban politics, and the

349

underworld, but especially in thoroughbred racing, where it was *the* dominant feature for fans. People went to ball games and fights even if they did not gamble, but gambling was the raison d'être for thoroughbred racing. Illegal gambling on baseball occurred surreptitiously at ballparks and outside the fields with bookmakers but was a minor issue until the Black Sox Scandal broke in 1920. Betting was also very popular among boxing fans at the fights and at neighborhood male hangouts like saloons, barbershops, and newsstands. However, the bulk of illicit sports gambling was on horse racing at poolrooms located in busy parts of town where there was a lot of street traffic, like downtown, or busy thoroughfares in the zone of emergence. In New York, this meant Midtown and Lower Manhattan. People betting with neighborhood bookmakers could meet them in the streets, bars, tonsorial parlors, pool halls, and candy stores.[2]

Large illegal enterprises emerged in the late nineteenth century to facilitate off-track gambling. In Chicago, the city's first major crime syndicate, founded by Mike McDonald in the mid-1870s, focused on gambling and relied heavily on on-track and off-track gambling as one of its first main sources of revenue. Illegal betting on the turf remained a cornerstone of the Windy City's underworld in the early twentieth century, even after racing was banned in Illinois in 1905. In New York, illegal off-track gambling was the cornerstone for the emergence of the Gambling Trust led by powerful Tammanyites, which for several years was an important source of underworld revenue. The illicit gambling operations relied heavily on political connections to protect them from police raids, secure favorable court rulings, and shield them from reformers pushing for strict law enforcement or new laws to end gambling. The reformers in the Progressive Era never did break the alliance of Tammany Hall and the gambling crowd.[3]

Thoroughbred racing in New York dated back to the colonial era, but with the coming of the Revolution, moral reformers halted the sport until the early 1820s when the metropolitan area enjoyed a rebirth of racing. This renewed interest lasted into the mid-1840s, highlighted by the great intersectional races. However, interest again faded, a product of Jacksonian moral reform, the depression of 1837, and competition from the middle-class sport of harness racing, considered a more practical sport of American origins. Thoroughbred racing was largely moribund until its introduction in upstate Saratoga in 1863, which led to a racing boom in metropolitan New York following the Civil War, beginning with the return of thoroughbred contests to the metropolitan area at the elite Jerome Park racetrack three years later. Flat racing thereafter dominated the equestrian scene in New York City and vicinity.

Racing in the Gilded Age was dominated by metropolitan elite tracks sponsored by prestigious jockey clubs, whose manifest function was to advance the sport and the breed and whose latent function was to promote and certify the social status of club members. Their success led to the establishment of business-oriented proprietary tracks in Brooklyn and New Jersey. All the racing clubs had close ties to the Democratic Party that helped them operate their enterprises and counter the moral opposition to gambling.

The development of prestigious racecourses did not put to rest concerns about the betting aspect of racing. Although jockey clubs and turf journalists may have lauded racing as a gauge of breeding that tested a horse's strength and stamina, gambling remained the reason people were interested in the sport. The public concern with betting, heightened by the wagering over the corrupt 1876 presidential election, led to the passage of a landmark anti–pool selling act in New York State one year later that was expected to seriously threaten the continuation of racetrack gambling and provide a model for antigambling forces elsewhere. However, track managers adjusted to the act by introducing bookmaking instead of auction betting or pari-mutuel betting, which the courts accepted as legitimate. Bookmaking became the main form of gambling at American tracks.

The elite ownership of racetracks may have tempered criticisms of the sport itself but not the opposition to the gambling. Moral reformers, church leaders, and Protestant organizations opposed racing because the gambling involved was perceived as sinful (encouraging greed, lusting after another's possessions, and getting money without working hard for it). Secular critics opposed gambling as criminal behavior that promoted disrespect for the law, impoverished bettors and their families, and was a stepping-stone to more serious crimes. Furthermore, horse race gambling abetted the development of organized crime because there was an extensive cash flow with huge potential profits, possibilities of fixed races, and revenue to corrupt the police and the judiciary.

The racing interests tried to protect their sport and their investments by securing the Ives Act of 1887 that legalized racetracks as unique venues that supported the sport and encouraged the advancement of the breed, with betting on the premises, but only on the races at that course. But otherwise, horse race betting was universally barred. The racing crowd successfully argued that this law would not harm poorer people who could not afford to go to the track and did not subvert the morality of the wider community. The Ives Act had important national implications as a model for other states to emulate, notably Illinois, whose legislature passed the Gibbs Act almost immediately, giving racing there its first codified protection. Six years later, the New York legislature passed the Saxton Act that tried to halt off-track betting by making it a felony instead of a misdemeanor. However, the law had little impact because of the alliance in New York City between Tammany Hall, the police, magistrates, and the poolrooms.[4]

The Ives Law, and similar laws in New Jersey, helped metropolitan thorough-bred racing flourish in the late 1880s and early 1890s, when several new tracks opened. These new courses were run by men with considerable political influence. The leaders of the elite tracks were major capitalists with a lot of clout in Tammany Hall, significantly enhanced in 1893 when Tammany boss Richard Croker bought a racing stable. The entrepreneurs who opened the new proprietary tracks were either businessmen closely tied to local machines or machine politicians themselves.

In New Jersey, the connections between urban machine politicians and the tracks, particularly the outlaw tracks of Guttenberg and Gloucester, were so strong that the racing interests actually gained control of the state legislature in the 1892 election. They passed the Parker Acts one year later, which authorized local gov-ernmental agencies to license racecourses and legalized bookmaking and pool selling at those tracks. However, the bosses were not omnipotent, and an astound-ing grassroots movement turned out the supporters of racing in 1893, just as a terrible depression occurred that severely harmed public confidence in major eco-nomic, political, and social institutions.[5] This turn of events led to the demise of thoroughbred racing in New Jersey for nearly fifty years and encouraged the anti-racing movement in Chicago, where the authorities frightened the executive board of elite Washington Park Race Track to close. Cook County's other tracks also soon closed down, albeit temporarily.

The closing of tracks in New Jersey and elsewhere encouraged New York social conservatives to redouble their efforts to curtail the gambling menace and thereby impose their values and beliefs on urban residents, primarily the working class. They saw horse race gambling as criminal, regardless of where it took place. Reformers in the summer of 1894 got the state constitution revised to criminalize all wagering, which seemed destined to end racing in New York.

However, racing in New York State was a multimillion-dollar business that encompassed breeding farms, eminent racing stables, prominent racetracks, as well as off-track poolrooms. The state's influential racing interests did not accept the inevitability of shuttering the racetracks and marshaled their powerful con-nections in the Democratic Party. The politically prominent social elite, including traction magnates William C. Whitney, August Belmont II, and Thomas Fortune Ryan, used cross-class alliances of convenience with Tammany and with Brook-lyn's Democratic machines to work for common goals, such as the protection of the turf, as well as promoting construction projects and mass transit.[6] This coali-tion of expediency worked well on the local level but less so down in Albany, where most governors were Republican and most legislative districts outside New York City were gerrymandered and firmly Republican. The protection of the city's interests in Albany was a challenge, and hardly a sure thing.

The racing crowd found a solution to their dilemma by circumventing the constitution. The state government approved the Percy-Gray Act that created the State Racing Commission to regulate the sport in cooperation with the completely private Jockey Club. The racing game was saved in what may have been the first instance in American government of such a public-private relationship.

New York's jockey clubs saved their sport while racing associations elsewhere could not, even though major racing organizations in other places, such as Chicago, New Orleans, and St. Louis, all had political connections, including machine bosses. Outside of New York, the urban machines failed to protect racing interests.

The New York City racing crowd was more cooperative than elsewhere. Managers of the city's elite courses cooperated on matters of common interest with managers of local proprietary tracks. They attended each other's meets and presented a common front when dealing with their enemies in Albany.

The New York racing elite was also much more dedicated to the turf than the upper class elsewhere. They were likely to be breeders and to own stables and racehorses, and they were committed to standing and fighting for their sport. Most jockey clubs' members were neither breeders nor racers, and not necessarily big gamblers, but the men who ran those voluntary organizations, such as August Belmont I and II, D. D. Withers, and John A. Morris, were heavily involved in the turf as an avocation. They owned several of the finest American stables and took major leadership roles supervising the sport, first through the Board of Control and then its more powerful successor, The Jockey Club.

Along with track managers, breeders, and horse owners, professional gamblers were another essential component of the racing world who helped make racing exciting. These men included legal bookmakers and operators of pari-mutuels but also men who ran illicit off-track poolrooms or handbooks. The gamblers were themselves an integral part of the nexus between politics, crime, and racing. The track odds layers were independent agents who often belonged to an organization like the Metropolitan Turf Association to help them negotiate terms with racecourses and gain protection shielding them from the reformers. In New Jersey, Illinois, and Missouri, some of the biggest bookmakers owned racetracks, like Gloucester in New Jersey or Garfield Park in Chicago. These gamblers had underworld connections and were either local politicians or closely connected to prominent urban politicians.

The jockey clubs fought to halt the poolrooms and handbooks because these illegal enterprises created ill will for the sport, which led to calls to halt the turf and because they were an unwanted source of competition that took business away from the tracks. Boss Richard Croker supported the tracks' fight against off-track gamblers after he became a prominent owner of thoroughbreds, but most

Tammanyites sided with the professional gamblers who were a valuable source of political and financial support for the machine, patronage jobs for party workers, and bribes to politicians, judges, and policemen who protected the poolrooms' illegal business. Tammany worked very closely with the poolrooms, and the Gambling Trust that dominated the business was run by Tammany leaders, most notably Big Tim Sullivan.

The conveniently located poolrooms brazenly operated in the open with little effort to camouflage themselves. The betting parlors mainly appealed to young clerks and artisans, as well as other urbanites who worked downtown. The public considered the poolrooms the most insidious venue of horse race gambling that even catered to women and drew young men to perdition. Everyone knew where they were located, except, apparently, the police, yet they survived through payoffs, political clout, and circumventions to avoid the law. The betting parlors were part of the growing alliance between the underworld and machine politicians. The crime organizations provided the gambling network with protection, financing, and speedy and accurate information. The data originated from Western Union, a legitimate and wealthy business that made millions by openly servicing a patently illegal enterprise. Poolroom operators needed capital to pay off winning bets, foreknowledge of raids, bail bondsmen to get them out of jail, attorneys to defend them, jurists to protect them, and political hacks to fend off proscriptive legislation.

Nationally, the reformers' onslaught against horse racing was very successful, though in New York, the national center of thoroughbred racing, the sport's opponents struggled for years to halt the sport, vying against the combined power and influence of Tammany Hall and its powerful upper-class allies who favored racing. The antiracing coalition, led by progressive governor Charles Evans Hughes, seemed to have achieved its goal in 1908, with the passage of the Agnew-Hart Acts, but court rulings kept the sport viable by the use of oral betting. Then, in 1910, the Directors' Liability Law resulted in the tracks' closure. It was the high point in the national war against horse racing. By then, Maryland and Kentucky were the only two important racing states whose tracks remained in operation. New York had no racing for the next two years, and it seemed the racing crowd had given up. However, they persevered in the courts and won a crucial victory in 1913, which freed track operators from gambling liability. Several tracks reopened, and the sport was saved. The New York turf suffered only a brief interruption in racing since the Civil War and fared far better than nearly all other centers of the sport, thanks in good measure to the political influence of the racing elite in the Democratic Party and their allies in Tammany Hall.

Racing did not revive nationally until after World War I. This change resulted from such factors as the popularity of gambling among the working class whose higher standard of living increased their leisure options, the political clout of inner-city Democratic politicians and their underworld allies, and state needs for new sources of revenue. The number of thoroughbreds doubled in the 1920s, and purses between 1918 and 1926 nearly quadrupled to $13.9 million. There were thirty-four tracks in operation by 1929, of which nearly 70 percent had just recently opened, including several in Illinois, where pari-mutuel racing was legalized in 1927. The trend to resume thoroughbred racing accelerated during the Great Depression when states like California and Florida legalized on-track betting to promote tourism and find badly needed money to run the government.[7]

The reformers were unsuccessful at closing off-track betting sites because of the close ties among organized crime, urban machine politicians, and their clientele. In New York, as in Chicago, where there were also major gambling syndicates, poolrooms boomed in the early 1900s. Across the country, handbooks also became very popular betting outlets. By the 1920s, New York's once tightly run Gambling Trust was supplanted by a new generation of professional gamblers, most notably Arnold Rothstein, and by ruthless crime syndicates that still bribed the police and politicians but were more reliant on violence to control their business. Although the sport of kings had its ups and downs, the kings of crime enjoyed a long run with the cooperation of their nexus with the police and urban machine politicians.

ABBREVIATIONS

NOTES

BIBLIOGRAPHY

INDEX

Abbreviations

ANB	*American National Biography*
BE	*Brooklyn Eagle*
CDN	*Chicago Daily News*
Clipper	*New York Clipper*
CT	*Chicago Tribune*
NEN	*Newark Evening News*
NYMT	*New York Morning Telegraph*
NYT	*New York Times*
NYTr	*New York Tribune*
NYW	*New York World*
Spirit	*Spirit of the Times*
TDTA	*Trenton Daily True American*
TFF	*Turf, Field, and Farm*

Notes

Newspaper page citations follow this format: NYT, 3-2. The first number is the page number; the second is the column number. A roman numeral preceding page and column numbers represents the applicable section of the newspaper.

Preface

1. Among the pioneering studies of American sport history were John R. Betts, "The Technological Revolution and the Rise of Sport, 1850–1900" and "Mind and Body in Early American Thought"; Foster Rhea Dulles, *A History of Recreation: America Learns to Play*; John A. Krout, *Annals of American Sport*; and Harold Seymour, *Baseball*. The more recent outstanding studies of American sport history include Melvin L. Adelman, *A Sporting Time: New York City and the Rise of Modern Athletics, 1820–70*; Susan K. Cahn, *Coming on Strong: Gender and Sexuality in Twentieth-Century Women's Sport*; Susan Cayleff, *Babe: The Life and Legend of Babe Didrikson Zaharias*; Elliott J. Gorn, *The Manly Art: Bare-Knuckle Prize Fighting in America*; Pamela Grundy, *Learning to Win: Sports, Education, and Social Change in Twentieth-Century North Carolina*; Stephen Hardy, *How Boston Played: Sport, Recreation, and Community, 1865–1915*; Barbara J. Keys, *Globalizing Sport: National Rivalry and International Community in the 1930s*; Peter Levine, *Ellis Island to Ebbets Field: Sport and the American Jewish Experience*; Michael Oriard, *King Football: Sport and Spectacle in the Golden Age of Radio and Newsreels, Movies and Magazines, the Weekly and the Daily Press* and *Reading Football: Sport, Popular Journalism, and American Culture, 1876–1913*; Benjamin G. Rader, *American Sports: From the Age of Folk Games to the Age of Televised Sports*; Steven A. Riess, *City Games: The Evolution of American Urban Society and the Rise of Sports* and *Touching Base: Professional Baseball and American Culture in the Progressive Era*; Randy Roberts, *Papa Jack: Jack Johnson and the Era of White Hopes*; Ronald A. Smith, *Sports and Freedom: The Rise of Big-Time College Athletics*; Jules Tygiel, *Baseball's Great Experiment: Jackie Robinson and His Legacy*; and Martha Verbrugge, *Able-Bodied Womanhood: Personal Health and Social Change in Nineteenth-Century Boston*.

2. Laura Hillenbrand, *Seabiscuit: An American Legend*. The films include Stephen Ives and Eve Morgenstern, *American Experience: Seabiscuit*; Gary Ross and Jane Sindell, *Seabiscuit*; and Nick Krantz, *Seabiscuit: America's Legendary Racehorse*.

3. The social history on horse racing in America is rather slim. A good place to start is with John Hervey, *Racing in America, 1665–1866*, 2 vols.; William S. Vosburgh, *Racing in America, 1866–1921*; and William H. P. Robertson, *The History of Thoroughbred Racing in America*. For scholarly analyses that focus on two of the major racing locations, see Adelman, *Sporting Time*, chaps. 2, 4; and Dale Somers, *The Rise of Sports in New Orleans, 1850–1900*, 2 vols., 91–114. For early Jersey racing, see Brian Danforth, "Hoboken and the Affluent New Yorker's Search for Recreation, 1820–1860"; and John T. Cunningham, "Queen of the Turf."

4. W. Robertson, *Thoroughbred Racing in America*, 196. The data is from *Goodwin's Annual Official Turf Guide for 1897*.

5. On the history of gambling, see Herbert Asbury, *Sucker's Progress: An Informal History of Gambling from the Colonies to Canfield*; Henry Chafetz, *Play the Devil: A History of Gambling in the United States from 1492 to 1955*; Ann Fabian, *Card Sharps, Dream Books, and Bucket Shops: Gambling in Nineteenth Century America*; John M. Findlay, *People of Chance: Gambling in American Society from Jamestown to Las Vegas*; T. J. Jackson Lears, *Something for Nothing: Luck in America*; Stephen Longstreet, *Win or Lose: A Social History of Gambling in America*; Virgil W. Peterson, *Barbarians in Our Midst: A History of Chicago Crime and Politics*; Richard Sasuly, *Bookies and Bettors: Two Hundred Years of Gambling*; and David G. Schwartz, *Roll the Bones: The History of Gambling*.

6. On bucket shops, see Fabian, *Card Sharps, Dream Books, and Bucket Shops*, 156–57, 188–200; Jonathan Ira Levy, "Contemplating Delivery: Futures Trading and the Problem of Commodity Exchange in the United States, 1875–1905"; and David Hochfelder, "'Where the Common People Could Speculate': The Ticker, Bucket Shops, and the Origins of Popular Participation in Financial Markets, 1880–1920."

7. Howard Chudacoff, *The Age of the Bachelor: Creating an American Subculture*, 50.

8. On the demise of racing in Chicago, see Steven A. Riess, "The Demise of Horse Racing and Boxing in Chicago in 1905"; and in St. Louis, see Charles M. Harvey, "Reform in Missouri"; and W. F. Allen, "Let's Go to the Races," 59–60.

9. Mark H. Haller, "Illegal Enterprise: A Theoretical and Historical Interpretation," 207–8, 224.

10. Ibid., 210–11; Richard Lindberg, *The Gambler King of Clark Street: Michael C. McDonald and the Rise of Chicago's Democratic Machine*; *ANB*, s.v. "Morrissey, John"; and for Morrissey's obituary, see *NYT*, 2 May 1878, 5-4. For an overview of the historiography of organized crime, see Alan A. Block, "Organized Crime: History and Historiography." On the emergence of urban crime syndicates, see Mark H. Haller, "The Rise of Urban Crime Syndicates, 1865–1905." On the relationship between sport and crime syndicates in the nineteenth century, see Lindberg, *Gambler King of Clark Street*; Steven A. Riess, "Horse Racing in Chicago: The Interplay of Class, Politics, and Organized Crime"; David R. Johnson, "Sinful Business: The Origins of Gambling Syndicates in the United States, 1840–1887" and *Policing the Urban Underworld: The Impact of Crime on the Development of the American Police, 1840–1887*, 148–81; Riess, *Touching Base*, 87–96; and Riess, *City Games*, 181–87.

11. Haller, "Illegal Enterprise," 211. On Kenna and Coughlin, see Lloyd Wendt and Herman Kogan, *Lords of the Levee: The Story of Bathhouse John and Hinky Dink*; Riess, *City Games*, 82, 174–77, 183, 185–86, 198; Steven A. Riess, "In the Ring and Out: Professional Boxing in New York, 1896–1920," 99, 102; Daniel Czitrom, "Underworld and Underdogs: Big Tim Sullivan and Metropolitan Politics in New York, 1889–1913."

12. Haller, "Illegal Enterprise," 211; Riess, *City Games*, 171–202, 257–58. The connections between sport, crime, and politics in New York City are examined in Steven A. Riess, "Sports and Machine Politics in New York City, 1890–1920."

13. Riess, *City Games*, 171–202.

14. Riess, *Touching Base*, 54–155.

15. Riess, "In the Ring and Out."

16. Mark H. Haller, "Bootleggers and American Gambling, 1920–1950," "The Changing Structure of American Gambling in the Twentieth Century," "Organized Crime in Urban Society: Chicago in the Twentieth Century," "Policy Gambling: Entertainment and the Emergence of Black Politics, Chicago, from 1900 to 1940," and "Urban Crime and Criminal Justice: The Chicago Case."

1. The Rise of Horse Racing in America

1. Hervey, *Racing in America*, 1:16. On the English background, see Dennis Brailsford, *Sport and Society: Elizabeth to Anne*; and Robert W. Malcolmson, *Popular Recreations in English Society, 1700–1850*.

2. Carl Bridenbaugh, *Cities in the Wilderness: Urban Life in America, 1625–1742*, 120.

3. Timothy Breen, "Horses and Gentlemen: The Cultural Significance of Gambling among the Gentry of Early Virginia."

4. Ibid., 240–47, 255–57; Nancy Struna, "The Cultural Significance of Sport in the Colonial Chesapeake and Massachusetts," 83–85, 89; Rhys Isaac, *The Transformation of Virginia, 1740–1790*, 98–101, 118–19; John R. Betts, *America's Sporting Heritage, 1850–1950*, 6–7; Mary N. Stanard, *Colonial Virginia: Its People and Customs*, 254.

5. For in introduction to colonial sport, see Nancy L. Struna, *People of Prowess: Sport, Leisure, and Labor in Early Anglo-America*.

6. W. Robertson, *Thoroughbred Racing*, 22; South Carolina Jockey Club, *History of the Turf in South Carolina*, 33; Randy J. Sparks, "Gentleman's Sport: Horse Racing in Antebellum Charleston," 17, 19; Bertram Wyatt-Brown, *Southern Honor: Ethics and Behavior in the Old South*, 327–61; Aubrey C. Land, *Colonial Maryland: A History*, 195–96; Elihu S. Riley, *"The Ancient City": A History of Annapolis, Maryland, 1649–1887*, 158–59; Walter B. Norris, *Annapolis: Its Colonial and Naval Story*, 55–56, 87, 96, 193–99; Nancy Struna, "Gender and Sporting Practices in Early America, 1750–1810," 25; Jennie Holliman, *American Sports (1785–1835)*, 117; Tom R. Underwood, ed., *Thoroughbred Racing and Breeding: The Story of the Sport and Background of the Horse Industry*, 141.

7. Struna, "Cultural Significance of Sport," 6–14, 17–19, 65; Bridenbaugh, *Cities in the Wilderness*, 276; Hans-Peter Wagner, *Puritan Attitudes Towards Recreation in Early Seventeenth Century New England, with Particular Consideration of Physical Recreation*, 34–35; W. Robertson, *Thoroughbred Racing*, 8.

8. Winton U. Solberg, *Redeem the Time: The Puritan Sabbath in Early America*, 229, 252; John Lucas and Ronald Smith, *The Saga of American Sport*, 33–35; Bridenbaugh, *Cities in the Wilderness*, 278, 438; Carl Bridenbaugh, *Cities in Revolt: Urban Life in America, 1743–1776*, 153, 363; J. William Frost, *The Quaker Family in Colonial America*, 207–10; J. Thomas Jable, "Pennsylvania's Early Blue Laws: A Quaker Experiment in the Suppression of Sport and Amusements, 1682–1740." On Charleston, see Walter J. Fraser Jr., *Charleston! Charleston! The History of a Southern City*, 59.

9. Bridenbaugh, *Cities in the Wilderness*, 120; J. T. Scharf and Thompson Westcott, *History of Philadelphia, 1609–1884*, 1:126.

10. Gary B. Nash, *The Urban Crucible: Social Change, Political Consciousness, and the Origins of the American Revolution*, 395.

11. Thomas J. Wertenbaker, *Father Knickerbocker Rebels: New York City During the Revolution*, 203–4. Macmillan advertised his inn "The Sign of George III" in the *New York Royal Gazette* (29 Aug. 1781). See Harry B. Weiss and Grace M. Weiss, *Early Sports and Pastimes in New Jersey*, 60; Alvin F. Harlow, *Old Bowery Days: The Chronicle of a Famous Street*, 115. There were also shooting contests as early as 1735 in conjunction with horse races. Harlow, *Old Bowery Days*, 114. See also Bridenbaugh, *Cities in Revolt*, 23, 153, 363–65; Harold D. Eberlein and Cortlandt Van Dyke Hubbard, *Portrait of a Colonial City: Philadelphia, 1670–1838*, 439; Edward Bronner, "Village into Town, 1701–1746," 55; Harry M. Tinkcom, "The Revolutionary City, 1765–1783," 120; William Milnor, *A History of the Schuylkill Fishing Company of the State in Schuylkill*; and W. Robertson, *Thoroughbred Racing*, 24. In the 1790s, there were cricket clubs in New York and Boston, a racquet club in New York (which built a court in 1800 open only to

members), golf clubs in Charleston and Savannah, and even a quoits club in Richmond. These clubs were all exclusive organizations of merchants and professionals and probably stressed conviviality as much as sports. See Holliman, *American Sports (1785–1835)*, 67–68, 71–74, 79–81; Betts, *America's Sporting Heritage*, 30–31; and Melvin L. Adelman, "The Development of Modern Athletics: Sport in New York City, 1820–1870," 613–16.

12. Tinkcom, "Revolutionary City," 120–21 (quote); Nicholas B. Wainwright, *Colonial Grandeur in Pennsylvania: The House and Furniture of General John Cadwallader*, 2; Scharf and Westcott, *History of Philadelphia*, 1:244.

13. Bridenbaugh, *Cities in the Wilderness*, 435; Bridenbaugh, *Cities in Revolt*, 364–65; Esther Singleton, *Social New York under the Georges, 1714–76*, 260, 266–70; W. Robertson, *Thoroughbred Racing*, 12.

14. Bridenbaugh, *Cities in the Wilderness*, 435; Bridenbaugh, *Cities in Revolt*, 364–65; Singleton, *Social New York*, 260, 266–67; Duncan A. Story, *The DeLanceys: A Romance of a Great Family*; Carl Becker, *History of Political Parties in the Province of New York, 1760–1776*; W. Robertson, *Thoroughbred Racing*, 12–13; David A. E. Hamilton, "Horse Racing and New York Society, 1665–1830," 35, 38, 42–44; Edwin G. Burrows and Mike Wallace, *Gotham: A History of New York City to 1898*, 179, 193.

15. Hamilton, "Horse Racing and New York Society," 27–28. Lewis Morris Jr., who won the New York Subscription Plate with his five-year-old American Childers, in June 1757, twice around Beaver Pond Track, was a signer of the Declaration of Independence. "New York Racing Returns to Its Original Home," *NYT*, 14 May 1905, X7–10. The Long Island tracks included Newmarket II, Washington, Ascot Heath, and Beaver Pond. Manhattan tracks included Harlem (near Murray Hill), Church Farm (west of Broadway near Besse), Greenwich (north of Church Farm near Greenwich Lane), and Maidenhead (near Delancey Street). The Vanderbilt Track was on Staten Island. See "New York State Racetracks."

16. Bridenbaugh, *Cities in Revolt*, 365; Sparks, "Gentleman's Sport," 19; J. Thomas Jable, "The Pennsylvania Sunday Blue Laws of 1779: A View of Pennsylvania Society and Politics During the American Revolution"; Hamilton, "Horse Racing and New York Society," 48; Burrows and Wallace, *Gotham*, 219.

17. Wertenbaker, *Early Knickerbocker Rebels*, 202–3; Hamilton, "Horse Racing and New York Society," 48; Burrows and Wallace, *Gotham*, 247, 300.

18. Betts, *America's Sporting Heritage*, 10–11; Holliman, *American Sports (1785–1835)*, 108–11; W. Robertson, *Thoroughbred Racing*, 8.

19. Hamilton, "Horse Racing and New York Society," 54–56, 66–75, 87; Burrows and Wallace, *Gotham*, 405.

20. Joseph J. Kelly Jr., *Pennsylvania: The Colonial Years, 1681–1776*, 580; Holliman, *American Sports (1785–1835)*, 111–12; Soren Steward Brynn, "Some Sports in Pittsburgh During the National Period, 1775–1860"; Leland D. Baldwin, *Pittsburgh: The Story of a City*, 170–71; Adelman, *Sporting Time*, 48.

21. George C. Rogers Jr., *Charleston in the Age of the Pinckneys*, 114; Sparks, "Gentleman's Sport," 21; W. Robertson, *Thoroughbred Racing*, 84; Holliman, *American Sports (1785–1835)*, 112–17. On turn-of-the-century Norfolk, see Thomas J. Wertenbaker, *Norfolk: History of a Southern Port*, 133–35.

22. Barbara Stern Kupfer, "A Presidential Patron of the Sport of Kings: Andrew Jackson," 244, 246–50, 253–54; John Dizikes, *Sportsmen and Gamesmen*, 23–46; Holliman, *American Sports (1785–1835)*, 117; John William Ward, *Andrew Jackson: Symbol for an Age*; H. W. Brands, *Andrew Jackson: His Life and Times*, 129–38; Edwin A. Miles, "President Adams' Billiard Table." James Madison owned a share of a racetrack, and John Q. Adams attended races at the National Race Course in Washington during his presidency. Holliman, *American Sports (1785–1835)*, 117.

23. Adelman, *Sporting Time*, 32; Burrows and Wallace, *Gotham*, 453–54.

24. Adelman, *Sporting* Time, 33; Hamilton, "Horse Racing and New York Society," 86.

25. John Eisenberg, *The Great Match Race: When North Met South in America's First Sports Spectacle*, 1–12, 17–21, 25–26; Adelman, *Sporting Time*, 33–35.

26. Adelman, *Sporting Time*, 35–36; Nancy L. Struna, "The North-South Races: American Thoroughbred Racing in Transition, 1823–1850," 31–36; Eisenberg, *Great Match Race*, 142–233; Burrows and Wallace, *Gotham*, 454.

27. Adelman, *Sporting Time*, 36.

28. Ibid., 38.

29. Ibid., 39; Wray Vamplew, *The Turf: A Social and Economic History of Horse Racing*, 38. The enclosed English tracks were trying to attract more women and, except for Sandown Park, working-class fans by charging a shilling as the minimum price and then by introducing Saturday racing. Vamplew, *Turf*, 39–42.

30. Adelman, *Sporting Time*, 39–42.

31. Struna, "North-South Races," 42–44.

32. Adelman, *Sporting Time*, 42 (quote), 50–51. See also H. Weiss and G. Weiss, *Early Sports and Pastimes*, 124; Cunningham, "Queen of the Turf," 43–48; John T. Cunningham, "Games People Played: Sport in New Jersey History"; and Danforth, "Hoboken and the Affluent New Yorker's Search." On pedestrianism at the Beacon Course, see Adelman, *Sporting Time*, 213–15.

33. Adelman, *Sporting Time*, 42–43, 45, 49.

34. Ibid., 50–51.

35. D. Johnson, "Sinful Business," 18 (quote), 20, 22.

36. "The Great U.S. Match Race: Boston v. Fashion." This is drawn from a Web site consisting of articles that appeared in *American Turf Register* from 1841 to 1842. See also *New York Herald*, 5 May 1845; Adelman, *Sporting Time*, 43; and Struna, "North-South Races," 47–48.

37. "The Fashion and Boston Match," 367, 368.

38. Ibid., 368; Adelman, *Sporting Time*, 43.

39. Adelman, *Sporting Time*, 44. By comparison, an 1826 race at Epsom supposedly attracted sixty thousand people. In the late nineteenth century, English crowds estimated at seventy to eighty thousand attended races on major bank holidays. See Vamplew, *Turf*, 136.

40. "The Fashion and Boston Match," 368–69.

41. Adelman, *Sporting Time*, 32, 44–45; James D. Anderson, *Making the American Thoroughbred, Especially in Tennessee, 1800–1845*, 208–18.

42. *New York Herald*, 15 May 1845.

43. Ibid.; "Peytona."

44. Adelman, *Sporting Time*, 32, 47–52. On antebellum southern racing, see, for example, Kenneth Cohen, "Well Calculated for the Farmer: Thoroughbreds in the Early National Chesapeake, 1790–1850"; Sparks, "Gentleman's Sport"; and Somers, *Rise of Sports in New Orleans*, 24–35.

45. Adelman, *Sporting Time*, 76.

46. Ibid., 56, 77–78, 131.

2. The American Jockey Club and the Rebirth of the New York Turf

1. Edward Hotaling, *They're Off! Horse Racing at Saratoga*, 40. On early Saratoga, see Jon Sterngass, *First Resorts: Pursuing Pleasure at Saratoga Springs, Newport, and Coney Island*, 7–39. An 1859 Long Island

Railroad schedule set the trip from South Ferry to the Union Course at forty minutes. See "Long Island Railroad Supplement to Time Table No. 2."

2. Hotaling, *They're Off!* 27–29. On the sporting interests of the baseball fraternity during the war, see George B. Kirsch, *Baseball in Blue and Gray: The National Pastime During the Civil War.*

3. Adelman, *Sporting Time,* 83–89.

4. Ibid., 84, 86.

5. See, for example, Steven A. Riess, *Sport in Industrial America,* 4–10.

6. Hotaling, *They're Off!* 45.

7. Postal, Silver, and Silver, *Encyclopedia of Jews in Sports,* 329 (quote); Hotaling, *They're Off!* 44–45. Underwood, who was born around 1824, was very familiar with the British turf. He came to New York to work as a veterinarian around 1851 or 1852 but found the market glutted, so he moved to Lexington, where he also trained trotters. He got the idea of auction pools from Price McGrath, who in New Orleans arranged a form of pool selling at his club. He placed the money bet on a race in an envelope and delivered it to the winner, but without charging a fee. Underwood made a lot of money in his career, but high living left his family improvident. For Underwood's obituary, see *NYT,* 15 Dec. 1874, 1-7.

8. Hotaling, *They're Off!* 44–45; *NYT,* 11 Feb. 1872, 3-4; *NYT,* 30 Dec. 1894, 20-3.

9. Adelman, *Sporting Time,* 80; Hotaling, *They're Off!* 45–48; Matthew Hale Smith, *Sunshine and Shadow in New York,* 402.

10. Adelman, *Sporting Time,* 80; D. Johnson, "Sinful Business," 36.

11. John C. Kofoed, *Brandy for Heroes: A Biography of the Honorable John Morrissey, Champion Heavyweight of America and State Senator;* M. H. Smith, *Sunshine and Shadow,* 398–401; William H. Harding, *John Morrissey: His Life, Battles, and Wrangles, from His Birth in Ireland until He Died a State Senator;* Sasuly, *Bookies and Bettors,* 59–60, 62–63; *ANB,* s.v. "Morrissey, John"; John Dizikes, *Yankee Doodle Dandy: The Life and Times of Tod Sloan,* 29. For a lengthy obituary, see *NYT,* 2 May 1878, 5-4.

12. Adelman, *Sporting Time,* 80, 235–37; Gorn, *Manly Art,* 108–27; Elliott Gorn, "'Good-bye Boys, I Die a True American': Homicide, Nativism, and Working-Class Culture in Antebellum New York City." Late in his life, Morrissey wanted to return to Troy, but no one would sell him a lot in the fashionable section of town. According to Sasuly, he responded by buying industrial land upwind from the elite neighborhood, where he built a soap factory that emitted awful odors. The local upper class had to buy him out. Sasuly, *Bookies and Bettors,* 62.13. Sasuly, *Bookies and Bettors,* 59–61; Hotaling, *They're Off!* 29, 31, 61; Sterngass, *First Resorts,* 147. On Murray, see his obituary in *NYT,* 15 June 1895, 9-6.

14. Seymour, *American Baseball,* 1:57; *NYT,* 28 Aug. 1877, 1-7; *NYT,* 29 Aug. 1877, 1-7.

15. Gorn, *Manly Art,* 108–27; *ANB,* s.v. "Morrissey, John"; Sterngass, *First Resorts,* 152–53. Herbert Asbury claims that Morrissey's estate was worth only seventy-five thousand dollars. See Asbury, *Sucker's Progress,* 386.

16. Hugh Bradley, *Such Was Saratoga,* 143; Hotaling, *They're Off!* 53–54, 68–70; Adelman, *Sporting Time,* 80; *New York Tribune,* 13 Aug. 1865, 1, quoted in Hotaling, *They're Off!* 70.

17. Hotaling, *They're Off!* 53–54, 68–70. On black jockeys, see the indispensable Edward Hotaling, *The Great Black Jockeys: The Lives and Times of the Men Who Dominated America's First National Sport.*

18. D. Johnson, "Sinful Business," 36–37; *CT,* 8 Aug. 1870, 3-1; *NYT,* 24 Apr. 1870, 6-2; *NYT,* 14 Mar. 1878, 8-1; *Spirit* 86 (12 Dec. 1873): 445. On McGrath and Chamberlain, see John Morris, ed., *Wanderings of a Vagabond: An Autobiography,* 197–207, 259–62; Chafetz, *Play the Devil,* 263–66. For a generally favorable obituary of Chamberlain, see *TFF* 64 (18 Aug. 1896): 273.

19. Burrows and Wallace, *Gotham,* 953; Anita Leslie, *The Remarkable Mr. Jerome,* 15–54; Adelman, *Sporting Time,* 80, 81; *NYT,* 30 Apr. 1894, 20-1. For Jerome's obituary, see *NYT,* 5 Mar. 1891, 8-1.

20. Leslie, *The Remarkable Mr. Jerome*, 15–54, 153.

21. *NYT,* 25 Sept. 1866, 8-1 (quote); *NYT,* 26 Sept. 1866, 8-1; *NYT,* 30 Apr. 1894, 20-1; Adelman, *Sporting Time,* 80; Leslie, *The Remarkable Mr. Jerome,* 78; W. Robertson, *Thoroughbred Racing,* 103–4.

22. *NYT,* 11 Sept. 1866, 2-4; *NYT,* 22 Sept. 1866, 8-1; *NYT,* 25 Sept. 1866, 8-1; *NYT,* 26 Sept. 1866, 8-1; Adelman, *Sporting Time,* 80; Leslie, *The Remarkable Mr. Jerome,* 78; David Black, *The King of Fifth Avenue: The Fortunes of August Belmont,* 283.

23. Adelman, *Sporting Time,* 80–81; *NYT,* 24 Sept. 1866, 8-1; *NYT,* 26 Sept. 1866, 8-1; Leslie, *The Remarkable Mr. Jerome,* 79; Black, *King of Fifth Avenue,* 286, 287; W. Robertson, *Thoroughbred Racing,* 103; Burrows and Wallace, *Gotham,* 954.

24. *NYT,* 16 Dec. 1866, 5-1; *Spirit* 117 (8 June 1889): 789; William S. Vosburgh, "The Passing of Jerome Park," 513.

25. *NYT,* 25 Sept. 1866, 8-1 (quote); *NYT,* 26 Sept. 1866, 8-1; Black, *King of Fifth Avenue,* 289; Vosburgh, "Passing of Jerome Park," 513.

26. *Spirit* 102 (24 Sept. 1881): 228.

27. *Spirit* 106 (29 Sept. 1883): 272.

28. "Horse-Racing," 293.

29. *TFF,* 29 Sept. 1866, quoted in Black, *King of Fifth Avenue,* 288–89.

30. "The Spring Meeting at Jerome Park" (editorial), *NYT,* 10 June 1871, 4-3.

31. Bernard Postal, Jesse Silver, and Roy Silver, *Encyclopedia of Jews in Sports,* 306–7; Irving Katz, *August Belmont: A Political Biography,* 4; Black, *King of Fifth Avenue,* 284–85, 718; *ANB,* s.v. "Belmont, August I"; and his obituary, *NYT,* 25 Nov. 1890, 1-7.

32. *NYT,* 25 Nov. 1890, 1-7.

33. Adelman, *Sporting Time,* 312n21. On the social composition of the AJC, see Adelman, "Development of Modern Athletics," chap. 4.

34. *Spirit* 19 (31 Oct. 1868): 169; *Spirit* 20 (17 Apr. 1869): 136; *Spirit* 118 (14 Dec. 1889): 748; Black, *King of Fifth Avenue,* 286; *NYT,* 30 Dec. 1894, 20-1.

35. Vosburgh, "Passing of Jerome Park," 513–14. Originally, the club was just for members and ladies in the company of members, and members were not allowed to take friends into the clubhouse on race day. *Spirit* 19 (14 Nov. 1868): 197, 201.

36. Adelman, "Development of Modern Athletics," 180–234; Adelman, *Sporting Time,* 54–56, 58, 61. In 1873, Jewish members included New Yorkers Edwin Einstein, R. W. Hyman, Montefiore Isaacs, A. Kohn, M. H. Levine, E. L. Oppenheim, Gershon A. Seixas, and S. B. Solomon. See Postal, Silver, and Silver, *Encyclopedia of Jews in Sports,* 305.

37. Adelman, *Sporting Time,* 84–85, 87. On the 1867 races, see, for example, "The Jerome Park Races" (editorial), *NYT,* 24 Oct. 1867, 4-6; *NYT,* 27 Oct. 1867, 1-5; "The Jerome Park Races."

38. *Spirit* 104 (30 Sept. 1882): 253; *Spirit* 117 (8 June 1889): 789; Adelman, *Sporting Time,* 84–85. The only major event that maintained the tradition of heat races was the Bowie Stakes at Baltimore. The CIJC tried to revive the format with the Long Island Stakes, beginning on 18 September 1880, with fifteen thousand attending.

39. *Spirit* 19 (17 Oct. 1868): 136.

40. *Spirit* 18 (6 June 1868): 273.

41. "The Spring Meeting at Jerome Park" (editorial), *NYT,* 10 June 1871, 4-3.

42. Ibid. On encouraging the interest of businessmen, see "The Fall Meeting at Jerome Park" (editorial), *NYT,* 4 Oct. 1873, 4-4.

43. "The Fall Meeting at Jerome Park," *NYT,* 4 Oct. 1873, 4-4; *NYT,* 31 Dec. 1875, 4-2 (quote).

44. *TFF* 3 (29 Sept. 1866), quoted in Black, *King of Fifth Avenue*, 289; *TFF* 13 (3 Nov. 1871): 280; *TFF* 16 (13 June 1873): 394; *TFF* 20 (11 June 1875): 424; Black, *King of Fifth Avenue*, 289 (quote).

45. *NYT*, 5 June 1870, 1-1 (quote); *NYT*, 30 Sept. 1877, 12-1. See also *TFF* 16 (13 June 1873): 394; *TFF* 20 (11 June 1875): 424; and *Spirit* 95 (20 Oct. 1877): 316. For a humorous slant on Dead Head Hill, see "Dead Head Hill on a Rainy Day," 506.

46. Adelman, *Sporting Time*, 86–88; *Spirit* 20 (24 Apr. 1869): 153; Black, *King of Fifth Avenue*, 290. See also *TFF* 12 (23 June 1871): 396. On English racing, see Mike Huggins, *Flat Racing and British Society, 1790–1914: A Social and Economic History*.

47. *TFF* 13 (27 Oct. 1871): 258.

48. "The Jerome Park Spring Meeting" (editorial), *NYT*, 29 May 1875, 4-3.

49. Vamplew, *Turf*, 130–36, 204–5.

50. *Spirit* 15 (12 Jan. 1867): 298; *Spirit* 24 (29 July 1871): 380; *NYT*, 26 Sept. 1866, 8-1.

51. *NYT*, 26 Sept. 1866, 8-2.

52. Ibid.

53. *TFF* 12 (23 June 1871): 396; *TFF* 13 (20 Oct. 1871): 248.

54. "Beauty at the Races," *Detroit Journal*, 12 June 1886, 6-1. My thanks to Howard Rosenberg for this citation.

55. Hotaling, *They're Off!* 44–45, 118–19; *NYT*, 11 Feb. 1872, 3-4; *NYT*, 30 Dec. 1894, 20-3; D. Johnson, "Sinful Business," 36–37; Dizikes, *Yankee Doodle Dandy*, 22–23; Hotaling, *They're Off!* 118–19.

56. Hotaling, *They're Off!* 95, 111 (quote); *NYT*, 23 July 1880, 8-1. In 1909, the Russian State Council considered a bill to close the totalizator but chose not to because there were riots in France and Germany when their governments had tried to ban the machine. See Louise Reynolds, *Russia at Play: Leisure Activities at the End of the Tsarist Era*, 78–82.

57. Hotaling, *They're Off!* 97, 110–11; *NYT*, 23 July 1880, 8-1; *Spirit* 25 (29 June 1872): 313; *Spirit* 126 (28 Oct. 1893): 460. There was so much interest in pools at New Jersey's new Monmouth Park that an office was opened in Manhattan to sell tickets. On the 1872 race, see Blood-Horse Publications, *Horse Racing's Top 100 Moments*, 72.

58. *Spirit* 89 (29 May 1875): 407; *Spirit* (31 July 1875): 644–45.

59. *Spirit* 86 (13 Dec. 1873): 421. Great Britain did not legalize pari-mutuels until 1927. On the history of horse race gambling in Great Britain, see Vamplew, *Turf*, 213–23; and Huggins, *Flat Racing*, 88–116.

60. *Spirit* 88 (19 Oct. 1874): 217; *NYT*, 23 July 1880, 8-1. In 1872, Saratoga under Morrissey sold 13,268 tickets for eighteen races over a six-day meet. This amounted to $66,340 at $5 a bet. The track took a 5 percent commission, or $553 a day. *Clipper* 20 (14 Sept. 1872): 186.

61. *Spirit* 99 (23 July 1880): 8-1; Hotaling, *They're Off!* 97, 110–11; *Spirit* 89 (29 May 1875): 407; *Spirit* (31 July 1875): 644–45.

62. *NYT*, 23 July 1880, 8-1.

63. *NYT*, 13 June 1880, 8-1.

64. D. Johnson, "Sinful Business," 38; Frank Menke, *The Story of Churchill Downs and the Kentucky Derby*, 12–13; Joseph B. Kelly, "At the Track: Thoroughbred Racing in Maryland, 1870–1973," 66; Hotaling, *They're Off!* 97; *NYT*, 18 May 1882, 5-3; *NYT*, 23 May 1884, 2-1.

65. D. Johnson, "Sinful Business," 38–41, 47; Sasuly, *Bookies and Bettors*, 64; Hotaling, *They're Off!* 94–95, 118; Bradley, *Such Was Saratoga*, 282; Chafetz, *Play the Devil*, 267; W. Robertson, *Thoroughbred Racing*, 93–98.

66. D. Johnson, "Sinful Business," 29; *NYT*, 20 Mar. 1887, 3-1 (quote).

67. *Spirit* 126 (28 Oct. 1893): 460.

68. Ibid.; D. Johnson, "Sinful Business," 29.

69. *Spirit* 126 (28 Oct. 1893): 460.

70. "Racing and Pool Selling" (letter to the editor), *NYT,* 2 Oct. 1877, 5-6.

71. *NYT,* 10 Dec. 1876, 1-2; *NYT,* 11 Dec. 1876, 1-4; *NYT,* 12 Dec. 1876, 1-4; *NYT,* 11 Jan. 1877, 5-1; *NYT,* 12 Jan. 1877, 4-7; *NYT,* 7 Feb. 1877, 5-4; *NYT,* 8 Mar. 1877, 1-7, 4-2; *NYT,* 15 Mar. 1877, 1-5; *NYT,* 22 Mar. 1877, 1-6; *NYT,* 10 Apr. 1877, 1-7; *NYT,* 24 June 1880, 8-1; D. Johnson, "Sinful Business," 39; Hotaling, *They're Off!* 118.

72. *NYT,* 7 Feb. 1877, 5-4; *NYT,* 2 June 1880, 8-3; *NYT,* 2 Dec. 1881, 4-6.

73. *NYT,* 7 Mar. 1877, 4-2.

74. *NYT,* 8 Mar. 1877, 1-7; *NYT,* 24 Apr. 1870, 6-2; *Clipper* 25 (24 Apr. 1877): 410.

75. *NYT,* 13 Mar. 1877, 4-1.

76. W. Robertson, *Thoroughbred Racing,* 91; *NYT,* 13 Mar. 1877, 1-5 (quote).

77. *NYT,* 10 Apr. 1877, 1-7; *NYT,* 25 Apr. 1877, 4-7; *Clipper* 25 (24 Apr. 1877): 410; *Clipper* 25 (5 May 1887): 43.

78. *NYT,* 28 May 1877, 4-1 (quote); *NYT,* 5 June 1877, 5-5; *NYT,* 23 June 1877, 8-1; *Spirit* 94 (27 Oct. 1877): 348.

79. *Spirit* 24 (29 July 1871): 380; *Spirit* 26 (5 Oct. 1872): 121; *NYT,* 21 May 1877, 8-1 (quote); *NYT,* 2 June 1877, 1-7; *CT,* 6 Aug. 1877, 7-2; *CT,* 12 Aug. 1877, 7-6. On the betting rings, see Dizikes, *Yankee Doodle Dandy,* 23–24.

80. "Racing and Pool Selling" (letter to the editor), *NYT,* 2 Oct. 1877, 5-6; *NYT,* 21 May 1877, 8-1.

81. *NYT,* 21 May 1877, 8-1.

82. Ibid.

83. *NYT,* 3 June 1877, 1-7; *NYT,* 5 June 1877, 4-2; *NYT,* 10 June 1877, 6-2 (quote); "Racing and Pool Selling" (letter to the editor), *NYT,* 2 Oct. 1877, 5-6. The extensive coverage of the Jerome Park Derby on the front page and the second page included extensive coverage of the parties in the nine four-in-hand drags lined up in front of the clubhouse and more detail about the "toilets of the ladies" than we would expect to read today about a fashion show. See *NYT,* 10 June 1877, 1-7, 2-1.

84. *NYT,* 21 May 1877, 8-1; "Racing and Pool Selling" (letter to the editor), *NYT,* 2 Oct. 1877, 5-6.

85. *NYT,* 28 Sept. 1877, 4-5 (quote); *NYT,* 30 Sept. 1877, 12-1; "Racing and Pool Selling" (letter to the editor), *NYT,* 2 Oct. 1877, 5-6; *Spirit* 94 (6 Oct. 1877): 250; *Spirit* 94 (20 Oct. 1877): 316.

86. *NYT,* 30 Sept. 1877, 12-1; *Spirit* 94 (20 Oct. 1877): 316.

87. *Spirit* 94 (6 Oct. 1877): 250; *Spirit* 95 (20 Oct. 1877): 316; *Spirit* 95 (20 July 1878): 660; *BE,* 25 Sept. 1878, 2-5; Hotaling, *They're Off!* 119.

88. *NYT,* 5 May 1878, 4-2; *NYT,* 30 May 1878, 4-2 (quote); *NYT,* 31 May 1878, 4-4; *NYT,* 1 June 1878, 12-1; *NYT,* 9 June 1878, 5-1; *BE,* 5 May 1878, 4-5; *NYT,* 9 June 1878, 4-1; *NYT,* 25 Sept. 1878, 2-5.

89. *NYT,* 6 Oct. 1878, 1-7; *BE,* 7 Oct. 1878, 4-1. For an extensive report of the ladies' finery, see *NYT,* 6 Oct. 1878, 1-7.

3. The Emergence of the Brooklyn Racetracks, 1879–86

1. *NYT,* 31 May 1879, 1-7.

2. *NYT,* 31 May 1879, 1-7; *NYT,* 1 June 1879, 1-7; *Spirit* 103 (10 June 1882): 520; *Spirit* 107 (31 May 1884): 556; *Spirit* 107 (7 June 1884): 573; Maria Kapsales, "From the Gilded Age to Progressivism: Brooklyn's Horse Race for Wealth," 22–23.

3. *Spirit* 98 (11 Oct. 1879): 241.

4. *NYT,* 12 Sept. 1879, 8-6.

5. *NYW,* 3 Mar. 1884, 2-4.

6. *NYT,* 31 May 1879, 1-7; *NYT,* 1 June 1879, 1-7; *NYT,* 30 May 1880, 9-4; *NYT,* 6 June 1881, 1-7; *Spirit* 102 (24 Sept. 1881): 256; *Spirit* 103 (10 June 1882): 520; *Spirit* 107 (7 June 1884): 573; Kapsales, "From the Gilded Age to Progressivism," 22–23.

7. *NYT,* 31 May 1885, 8-4.

8. George Juergens, *Joseph Pulitzer and the "New York World,"* 124; *NYW,* 3 Mar. 1884, 2-4; *NYW,* 2 June 1884, 7-1.

9. *NYW,* 29 Apr. 1884, 4-2; Juergens, *Joseph Pulitzer,* 124.

10. *NYT,* 25 June 1879, 2-4. See also John F. Kasson, *Amusing the Million: Coney Island at the Turn of the Century;* Oliver Ramsay Pilat and Jo Ranson, *Sodom by the Sea: An Affectionate History of Coney Island;* Kapsales, "From the Gilded Age to Progressivism," 33–34.

11. *Spirit* 106 (19 Jan. 1883): 753.

12. *BE,* 24 June 1879, 2-5; *BE,* 10 July 1879, 2-5; Kapsales, "From the Gilded Age to Progressivism," 32–33, 41.

13. Juergens, *Joseph Pulitzer,* 124; *NYW,* 2 June 1884, 7-1; *NYW,* 3 Mar. 1884, 2-4.

14. *BE,* 24 June 1879, 2-5; *BE,* 10 July 1879, 2-5; *Spirit* 97 (26 July 1879): 630; *Spirit* 98 (15 Nov. 1879): 70; *Spirit* 99 (26 June 1880): 522; *Spirit* 131 (18 Apr. 1896): 414; *NYT,* 25 June 1879, 2-4; *NYTr,* 13 Dec. 1895, 12-1.

15. Ross McKibbin, "Working-Class Gambling in Britain, 1880–1939," 162–68; Huggins, *Flat Racing,* 101–7; Mark Clapson, *A Bit of a Flutter: Popular Gambling and English Society, c. 1823–1961,* 27, 29–30, 38, 174, 176–77.

16. *BE,* 24 June 1879, 2-5; *BE,* 5 July 1879, 2-6; *BE,* 10 July 1879, 28; *NYT,* 25 June 1978, 2-4; *Spirit* 97 (26 July 1879): 630; *Spirit* 98 (15 Nov. 1879): 370; *Spirit* 99 (26 June 1880): 522; *Spirit* 106 (19 Jan. 1883): 753; *Spirit* 131 (18 Apr. 1896): 414.

17. *Spirit* 97 (26 July 1879): 630; *Spirit* 98 (15 Nov. 1879): 370; *Spirit* 99 (26 June 1880): 522; *NYT,* 25 June 1879, 2-4; *NYT,* 5 Sept. 1879, 2-1 (quote).

18. *NYT,* 1 June 1880, 3-5; *NYT,* 28 May 1885, 4-2; *NYT,* 31 May 1885, 1-7; *Spirit* 131 (18 Apr. 1896): 414. At the rate of seven thousand dollars a day, which seems very high, the annual return from the gamblers alone would amount to seven hundred thousand dollars, which is not realistic. On profit estimates, see *BE,* 12 Jan. 1884, 2-1; and Kapsales, "From the Gilded Age to Progressivism," 17.

19. See, for example, *BE,* 2 Aug. 1891, 15-5; *BE,* 26 Sept. 1891, 2-5.

20. *Spirit* 127 (17 Mar. 1894): 298; *Spirit* 131 (18 Apr. 1896): 414.

21. *NYTr,* 12 Apr. 1885, 6-3; *Spirit* 107 (10 Feb. 1883): 35; Somers, *Rise of Sports in New Orleans,* 100–101.

22. *Spirit* 131 (18 Apr. 1896): 414; *NYT,* 23 July 1896, 6-1.

23. *Detroit Journal,* 12 June 1886, 6-1. My thanks to Howard Rosenberg for the citation.

24. "Old Timer's Column," *BE,* 13 July 1952, 143, cited in Kapsales, "From the Gilded Age to Progressivism," 23.

25. *Detroit Journal,* 12 June 1886, 6-1.

26. *NYT,* 28 May 1885, 4-2.

27. *NYTr,* 12 Apr. 1885, 6-3; *NYTr,* 24 May 1885, 6-3.

28. *Spirit* 131 (18 Apr. 1896): 414; *NYTr,* 8 Aug. 1892, 10-2 (quote); *NYTr,* 13 Dec. 1895, 12-1 (quote). See also *Detroit Journal,* 12 June 1886, 6-1.

29. *Spirit* 104 (18 Nov. 1882): 456.

30. *NYT,* 1 June 1868, 5-3; *BE,* 15 June 1879, 2-4.

31. *BE,* 27 June 1879, 4-6; *Spirit* 97 (26 July 1879): 630; *Spirit* 97 (15 Nov. 1879): 370; *Spirit* 99 (26 June 1880): 522; *NYT,* 5 Sept. 1879, 5; *NYT,* 23 June 1895, 1.

32. *Spirit* 7 (15 Nov. 1879): 370; *NYT,* 25 June 1879, 2-4.

33. *NYTr,* 13 Dec. 1895, 12-1; *BE,* 7 Dec. 1879, 4-8; Michael Immerso, *Coney Island: The People's Playground,* 24–27.

34. "A Popular Amusement" (editorial), *BE,* 7 Dec. 1879, 2-2; Vosburgh, *Racing in America,* 26–28; *Spirit* 99 (6 Mar. 1880): 108; *NYT,* 27 June 1885, 8-3; *Detroit Journal,* 12 June 1886, 6-1. The average attendance for 1890 was estimated in the *Brooklyn Citizen,* 6 Sept. 1890, 2, cited in Kapsales, "From the Gilded Age to Progressivism," 63.

35. *NYW,* 27 June 1885, 6-1; *Spirit* 99 (26 June 1880): 522; *Spirit* 126 (28 Oct. 1893): 460; Hotaling, *They're Off!* 139.

36. *NYW,* 22 June 1884, 2-3.

37. *Spirit* 99 (3 July 1880): 550.

38. *Spirit* 99 (10 July 1880): 577.

39. *Spirit* 192 (26 Nov. 1881): 465.

40. *Spirit* 101 (2 July 1881): 585; *Spirit* 102 (3 Dec. 1881): 489.

41. *Spirit* 102 (26 Nov. 1881): 465; Joe Hirsch, *The First Century: "Daily Racing Form" Chronicles 100 Years of Thoroughbred Racing,* 10. Keene lost his fortune trying to corner the Chicago wheat market in 1884 and sold his horses. However, he rebuilt his fortune in the sugar trade and returned to racing in 1891. See W. Robertson, *Thoroughbred Racing,* 158.

42. *Spirit* 101 (4 June 1881): 456; Somers, *Rise of Sports in New Orleans,* 94–100.

43. Somers, *Rise of Sports in New Orleans,* 102–7.

44. *NYT,* 21 Sept. 1881, 4-5; *NYT,* 25 Sept. 1881, 6-7 (quote).

45. *Spirit* 105 (16 June 1883): 567.

46. *Spirit* 107 (14 June 1884): 605; *NYT,* 20 Mar. 1887, 8.

47. *Spirit* 107 (14 June 1884): 605; *Spirit* 126 (28 Oct. 1893): 460; *NYT,* 4 Sept. 1888, 3-1; *NYT,* 31 Aug. 1890, 2-1; *NYT,* 29 Aug. 1903, 9-1; *BE,* 30 Aug. 1890, 6-1; *BE,* 31 Aug. 1890, 3-1; Hotaling, *They're Off!* 139; W. Robertson, *Thoroughbred Racing,* 148.

48. W. Robertson, *Thoroughbred Racing,* 130–31, 133, 136–37; *BE,* 17 Dec. 1888, 2-4.

49. *Spirit* 106 (4 Apr. 1883): 14; *Spirit* 124 (26 Nov. 1892): 682 (quote); *NYTr,* 20 Apr. 1893, 10-1. For an example of Mike Dwyer's entering a prominent but unprepared horse and betting on another animal, see *BE,* 27 July 1890, 3-1.

50. *BE,* 19 Aug. 1890, 4-7; *CDN,* 29 May 1893, 10-2; *CDN,* 9 Dec. 1893, 3-1; Bradley, *Such Was Saratoga,* 250.

51. *CDN,* 29 May 1893, 10-2. On Lorillard, see *Dictionary of American Biography,* s.v. "Pierre Lorillard"; and *NYT,* 8 July 1901, 1-1.

52. *NYTr,* 20 Apr. 1893, 10-1; *BE,* 19 Aug. 1890, 4-7; W. Robertson, *Thoroughbred Racing,* 130–31, 133, 136–37.

53. *BE,* 4 Mar. 1886, 4-7; *NYT,* 21 Sept. 1891, 5-5; Kapsales, "From the Gilded Age to Progressivism," 33, 52.

54. *BE,* 4 Oct. 1886, 6-6.

55. *BE,* 26 Aug. 1886, 4-2; *BE,* 10 May 1896, 13-3; *NYTr,* 2 Aug. 1886, 8-1; *Spirit* 112 (4 Sept. 1886): 186, 192; *Spirit* 112 (18 Dec. 1886): 636; *Spirit* 112 (11 Dec. 1886): 612.

56. *NYTr,* 2 Aug. 1886, 8-1; *BE,* 25 Aug. 1886, 2; *BE,* 10 May 1896, 13-3; *Spirit* 112 (4 Sept. 1886): 186, 192; *Spirit* 112 (18 Dec. 1886): 636.

57. *NYT,* 2 June 1880, 8-3; *NYT,* 22 Dec. 1881, 4-6.

58. *NYT,* 2 June 1880, 8-3.

59. *NYT,* 3 June 1880, 8-3; *NYT,* 6 Mar. 1881, 4-5; *NYT,* 26 Mar. 1881, 14-1; *NYT,* 27 Mar. 1881, 4-3; *NYT,* 28 Mar. 1881, 4-6; *NYT,* 30 Sept. 1881, 4-2; *NYT,* 2 Oct. 1881, 8-1; *NYT,* 22 Dec. 1881, 4-6; *NYT,* 20 May 1883, 4-6; *NYT,* 29 May 1883, 4-2, 8-2; *NYT,* 30 May 1883, 2-4. In 1886 the legislature tried to impeach Judge Donohue. See *NYT,* 8 Apr. 1886, 3-1; and *NYT,* 28 Apr. 1886, 2-1.

60. *Spirit* 100 (9 Oct. 1880): 257.

61. *NYT,* 6 June 1881, 1-7.

62. *NYT,* 29 Sept. 1881, 8-1; D. Johnson, "Sinful Business," 40.

63. *NYT,* 30 Sept. 1881, 4-2 (quote); *NYT,* 2 Oct. 1881, 8-1.

64. *Spirit* 102 (18 Feb. 1882): 70.

65. D. Johnson, "Sinful Business," 40–41, 47.

66. *NYT,* 1 Oct. 1882, 2-1.

67. *NYT,* 2 Oct. 1882, 4-4 (quote); *NYT,* 8 Oct. 1882, 2-2, 4-7.

68. *NYT,* 8 Oct. 1882, 2-2, 4-7.

69. *NYT,* 20 Oct. 1882, 8-4.

70. *NYTr,* 27 May 1886, 2-1, 3-2; *Spirit* 112 (25 Sept. 1886): 287.

71. *NYT,* 2 Aug. 1886, 4-4.

72. *NYT,* 26 Sept. 1886, 3-3; *NYT,* 29 Sept. 1886, 2-6; *NYT,* 1 Oct. 1886, 2-7; *NYT,* 3 Oct. 1886, 3-3.

73. *NYT,* 3 Oct. 1886, 3-3; *NYT,* 4 Oct. 1886, 8-3; *NYT,* 3 Nov. 1886, 3-3; New York Police Department, *Annual Report of the Police Department of the City of New York for the Year Ending December 31, 1886,* 30.

74. *Spirit* 112 (9 Oct. 1886): 353.

75. *BE,* 30 Oct. 1886, 4; Harold C. Syrett, *The City of Brooklyn, 1865–1898: A Political History,* 182–83; *NYT,* 6 Mar. 1881, 4-5; *NYT,* 26 Mar. 1881, 14-1; *NYT,* 27 Mar. 1881, 4-3; *NYT,* 28 Mar. 1881, 4-6; *NYT,* 29 Sept. 1881, 8-1; *NYT,* 2 Oct. 1881, 2; *NYT,* 3 June 1880, 8-3 (quote).

76. *NYT,* 3 June 1880, 8-3; *NYT,* 22 Mar. 1881, 3-1; *NYT,* 22 Mar. 1887, 3-1. Kelly paid a fee to work as a betting commissioner at the Brighton Beach track in 1886. *NYT,* 15 Sept. 1886, 8-3.

77. *Spirit* 104 (24 June 1882): 602.

78. For biographies of Comstock, see Heywood Broun and Margaret Leech, *Anthony Comstock: Roundsman of the Lord;* Anna Bates, *Weeder in the Garden of the Lord: Anthony Comstock's Life and Career;* Elizabeth Bainum Hovey, "Stamping Out Smut: The Enforcement of Obscenity Laws, 1872–1915," 4–5. Comstock was also secretary of the Society for the Prevention of Vice. The SPV's third annual meeting in 1878 admitted no women. There were many complaints from female seminaries about the distribution of "pernicious circulars" at the meeting. Perhaps the subject matter of the meeting was "inappropriate" for their sensibilities. See *NYT,* 6 Feb. 1878, 2-6.

79. Anthony Comstock, *Traps for the Young,* xiv, 99 (quote); Broun and Leech, *Anthony Comstock,* 13–15, 219, 222. On SSV arrests, see Bates, *Weeder in the Garden of the Lord,* 108–9. For Comstock's fight against the underworld, see Comstock, *Traps for the Young,* which gave twice as much space to gambling compared to sex (Hovey, "Stamping Out Smut," 186); and Anthony Comstock, *Gambling Outrages; or, Improving the Breed of Horses at the Expense of Public Morals.* See also Richard C. Johnson, "Anthony Comstock: Reform, Vice, and the American Way," 134–35.

80. *ANB*, s.v. "Comstock, Anthony"; Bates, *Weeder in the Garden of the Lord*, 110–11; Comstock, *Traps for the Young*, xxvii; Charles H. Parkhurst, *Forty Years in New York* and *Our Fight with Tammany*. For Parkhurst's obituary, see *NYT*, 9 Sept. 1933, 13-1.

81. *NYT*, 25 Sept. 1883, 8-2; Syrett, *City of Brooklyn*, 182–83; Raymond A. Schroth, *The "Eagle" and Brooklyn: A Community Newspaper, 1841–1955*, 100. On the reform of horse race gambling in Great Britain, see Huggins, *Flat Racing*, 14–15, 110–11, 204–26.

82. Syrett, *City of Brooklyn*, 183–85; *NYT*, 12 Jan. 1884, 5-3; *NYT*, 2 Apr. 1887, 8-5; Schroth, *"Eagle" and Brooklyn*, 100; Jeffrey Standon, "Coney Island: John McKane."

83. *NYT*, 12 Jan. 1884, 5-3; *NYT*, 22 Mar. 1887, 3-1, 8-4; *NYT*, 26 Mar. 1887, 8-1; *NYT*, 2 Apr. 1887, 8-5; Syrett, *City of Brooklyn*, 182–83, 194; Schroth, *"Eagle" and Brooklyn*, 100.

84. *NYT*, 12 Sept. 1886, 3-1; *NYTr*, 30 Oct. 1886, 8-2.

85. *BE*, 30 June 1884, 4-3; *NYT*, 12 Sept. 1886, 3-1.

86. "The Persecution of Poolsellers" (editorial), *BE*, 2 July 1884, 2-2.

87. *NYT*, 6 Dec. 1884, 8-2; *NYT*, 2 Aug. 1886, 4-4 (quote).

88. *NYT*, 10 Aug. 1884, 4-4.

89. *Spirit* 108 (29 Nov. 1884): 564.

90. Ibid.; D. Johnson, "Sinful Business," 41; *NYT*, 23 Mar. 1885, 8-4.

91. *NYTr*, 19 July 1885, 6-3.

92. *NYT*, 18 Feb. 1885, 4-2.

93. *NYT*, 31 May 1885, 1-7; *NYW*, 31 May 1885, 7-5.

94. *NYW*, 31 May 1885, 7-5 (quote); *BE*, 31 May 1885, 1-1, 12; *NYT*, 4 Apr. 1887, 8-2.

95. *NYW*, 31 May 1885, 7-5; *NYT*, 6 June 1885, 2-5; Kapsales, "From the Gilded Age to Progressivism," 54–57; Pilat and Ransom, *Sodom by the Sea*, 75–80.

96. *NYT*, 6 June 1885, 2-5.

97. *NYW*, 6 June 1885, 6-3.

98. *NYW*, 7 June 1885, 2-3.

99. *NYT*, 12 June 1885, 3-4. See also *NYTr*, 12 June 1885, 4-3; *NYW*, 12 June 1885, 6-1.

100. *NYT*, 12 June 1885, 3-4; *NYT*, 14 June 1885, 5-1 (quote); *NYW*, 12 June 1885, 6-3; *NYW*, 27 June 1885, 6-1. The *Eagle* felt that common sense should administer the laws and then would not lead to such events to get around them. Its position was "so long as men neither directly nor indirectly hurt their neighbors they ought to be fee to amuse themselves in any way they see fit." The editorial tried to make a distinction between betting, which it favored as recreational and inoffensive, and gambling, which it did not support. The editorial did not define the term *gambling* but undoubtedly had in mind professional wagerers and people who speculated more than they could afford. "Betting at Sheepshead Bay" (editorial), *BE*, 27 June 1885, 2-3.

101. *BE*, 13 June 1885, 6-3; *NYW*, 14 June 1885, 2-1; *NYT*, 14 June 1885, 5-1.

102. *NYT*, 18 June 1885, 8-4.

103. "Betting on Race Tracks" (editorial), *NYTr*, 10 May 1886, 4-4.

104. *NYTr*, 17 Nov. 1885, 4-3.

105. *BE*, 23 June 1886, 4-2; *BE*, 16 Sept. 1886, 4-1; *BE*, 19 Sept. 1886, 16-1; *BE*, 24 Sept. 1886, 1-3; *NYTr*, 23 June 1886, 6-3; *NYTr*, 15 Sept. 1886, 8-2; *NYT*, 15 Sept. 1886, 8-3; *NYT*, 18 Sept. 1886, 2.

106. "A New Psychic Force" (editorial), *NYT*, 21 Sept. 1886, 4-5.

107. *NYT*, 19 Sept. 1886, 2-4; *NYT*, 21 Sept. 1886, 4-5; *BE*, 18 Sept. 1886, 6-8; *BE*, 20 Sept. 1886, 4-2.

108. *NYT*, 12 Sept. 1886, 3-1; "Mr. Comstock's Methods" (editorial), *BE*, 12 Sept. 1886, 4-4.

109. *BE*, 4 Oct. 1886, 6-3; *BE*, 5 Oct. 1886, 6-1; *BE*, 14 Oct. 1886, 6-2.

110. "Still Defying the Law," *BE*, 8 Oct. 1886, 4-1; *BE*, 9 Oct. 1886, 6-1.

111. *BE*, 13 Oct. 1886, 6-1 (quote); *BE*, 25 Oct. 1886, 4; *NYTr*, 30 Oct. 1886, 4-4.

112. *Spirit* 112 (11 Dec. 1886): 612.

113. *Spirit* 112 (6 Nov. 1886): 467.

4. The Ives Pool Law of 1887

1. *NYT*, 17 Feb. 1883, 8-3.

2. *NYT*, 12 Apr. 1884, 2-1; *NYT*, 16 May 1884, 5-2; *Spirit* 109 (21 Mar. 1885): 233; *NYW*, 5 May 1885, 5-5.

3. *NYW*, 5 May 1885, 5-5.

4. *NYW*, 6 May 1885, 4-3.

5. *NYT*, 10 May 1885, 2-3. In 1887, Lorillard's sister-in-law, Mrs. George L. Lorillard, announced she would run her late husband's stable under her own name. The only other woman who owned a racing stable was Miss Nellie Burke of Cass County, Iowa, who also managed her stable, which raced in New Orleans. *NYTr*, 14 Feb. 1887, 4-1.

6. Juergens, *Joseph Pulitzer*, 124; *NYTr*, 14 Feb. 1887, 4-1; A Friend of Jerome Park to the editor, "Betting on Race Tracks," *NYTr*, 25 Feb. 1887, 4-6.

7. Juergens, *Joseph Pulitzer*, 124; "Betting on Race Tracks," *NYTr*, 25 Feb. 1887, 4-6; *NYT*, 24 Feb. 1887, 2-6; *BE*, 24 Feb. 1887, 2-9. Ives and Foley of Saratoga both served on the Judiciary Committee, where they could use their position to protect the racing interests. *NYT*, 19 Oct. 1894, 2-3.

8. Syrett, *City of Brooklyn*, 182–83, 185 (quote); *NYT*, 22 Mar. 1887, 3-1, 8-4; *NYT*, 26 Mar. 1887, 8-1; *NYT*, 30 Mar. 1887, 8-1; *NYT*, 2 Apr. 1887, 8-5.

9. Syrett, *City of Brooklyn*, 182–83; *NYT*, 20 Mar. 1887, 3-1; "Ridgway and Comstock" (editorial), *NYT*, 22 Mar. 1887, 4-3; *NYT*, 22 Mar. 1887, 8-4; *NYT*, 2 Apr. 1887, 8-5.

10. *NYT*, 27 Mar. 1887, 3-3.

11. *NYT*, 2 Apr. 1887, 8-5.

12. *NYT*, 29 Mar. 1887, 8-1; *NYT*, 10 Apr. 1887, 3-3; *NYT*, 12 Apr. 1887, 9-7.

13. *NYT*, 22 Apr. 1887, 1-7; *NYT*, 13 May 1887, 3-2; *NYTr*, 22 Apr. 1887, 2-3; *NYTr*, 5 May 1887, 2-1; *NYTr*, 13 May 1887, 1-4.

14. *NYT*, 24 May 1887, 1-7.

15. *Spirit* 117 (23 Feb. 1889): 169; "Illinois and New York Pool Acts" (editorial), *CT*, 30 May 1887, 4-4.

16. *NYT*, 26 May 1887, 5-5 (quote); *NYTr*, 26 May 1887, 5-2.

17. *NYT*, 31 May 1887, 4-3; *NYT*, 1 June 1887, 4-1 (quote).

18. *Spirit* 114 (26 Nov. 1887): 594.

19. *Spirit* 113 (11 June 1887): 671; *Spirit* 113 (16 July 1887): 849.

20. *NYT*, 31 May 1887, 4-3; *NYTr*, 1 June 1887, 4-1 (quote); *NYT*, 22 Jan. 1888, 16-4. On efforts to test the Ives Pool Law in court, see Bennett Liebman, "Horseracing in New York in the Progressive Era," 552–53.

21. *BE*, 27 May 1887, 1-3; *BE*, 10 June 1887, 1-3.

22. *NYT*, 31 May 1887, 4-3.

23. *NYT*, 19 June 1887, 2-2; *BE*, 16 June 1887, 6-7; *BE*, 19 June 1887, 16-1.

24. *NYT*, 13 Jan. 1888, 5-3; *NYT*, 22 Jan. 1888, 16-4; *New York Sun*, 13 Jan. 1888, 5; *New York Sun*, 22 Jan. 1888, 7; *Spirit* 115 (28 Jan. 1888): 16; *Chicago Times*, 25 Jan. 1888, 3-2; Chafetz, *Play the Devil*, 267–68.

25. *NYT*, 22 Jan. 1888, 16-4.

26. *NYT*, 22 Jan. 1888, 16-4; *NYTr*, 26 Jan. 1888, 7-1.

27. *NYT*, 22 Jan. 1888, 16-4; *Spirit* 115 (28 Jan. 1888): 16; *NYTr*, 26 Jan. 1888, 7-1.

28. *NYTr*, 26 Jan. 1888, 7-1; *NYT*, 15 Jan. 1887, 3-5; *NYT*, 13 Jan. 1888, 5-3; *NYT*, 22 Jan. 1888, 16-4. For De Lacy's obituary, see *NYT*, 15 Nov. 1915, 11-5. On Scannell, who donated five thousand dollars and raised fifty thousand dollars among gamblers for the mayoralty campaign of Hugh Grant, see New York Evening Post, *Tammany Biographies*, 9–10.

29. *NYT*, 15 Jan. 1887, 3-5; *NYT*, 13 Jan. 1888, 5-3; *NYT*, 22 Jan. 1888, 16-4. Comstock quoted in Broun and Leech, *Anthony Comstock*, 219. They claimed that once there was legalized on-track betting, Comstock was reluctant to proceed against the poolrooms. This assertion was not correct, as he continued his fight for years, but he did have other priorities.

30. *NYT*, 11 Jan. 1888, 5-3; *NYT*, 22 Jan. 1888, 16-4. The Western Bookmakers Association agreed to pay $2,400 a day, or $79,200, at the Latonia (Cincinnati) meeting in 1888. See *BE*, 19 Sept. 1888, 2-7.

31. *Spirit* 115 (19 May 1888): 670; Roger Longrigg, *The History of Horse Racing*, 188.

32. *NYT*, 23 Apr. 1888, 8-1 (quote); *NYT*, 30 Apr. 1888, 8-1; *NYT*, 29 May 1888, 3-1.

33. *NYTr*, 13 May 1888, 4-3 (quote). City editor Arthur J. Bowers wrote August Belmont II in 1891 asking for advertising because of the *Tribune*'s racing coverage. Bowers to Belmont, 12 Oct. 1891, Belmont Family Papers.

34. *Spirit* 115 (19 May 1888): 670.

35. *Spirit* 115 (12 May 1888): 578.

36. *Spirit* 115 (28 Apr. 1888): 494.

37. *NYTr*, 8 May 1888, 7-3 (quote); "Pierre Lorillard on Turf Abuses" (editorial), *NYTr*, 9 May 1888, 6-4.

38. *NYTr*, 13 May 1888, 4-3 (quote). On the growing popularity of pari-mutuels, see *NYTr*, 13 May 1888, 4-3; and *Spirit* 126 (28 Oct. 1893): 460. On Louisville pari-mutuels, see Blood-Horse Publications, *Horse Racing's Top 100 Moments*, 72.

39. *NYMT*, 6 Jan. 1901, IV:1-6.

40. *NYT*, 22 Dec. 1887, 8-2; *NYT*, 5 Dec. 1888, 8-4; *NYT*, 6 Dec. 1888, 4-2; *NYT*, 3 Nov. 1889, 1-5; *NYTr*, 4 Aug. 1889, 4-4; *NYTr*, 23 Sept. 1889, 6-3; *Spirit* 117 (25 May 1889): 727; *Spirit* 117 (1 June 1889): 769; *Spirit* 117 (8 June 1889): 789. Morris offered to rent the site for the NYJC for $37,500, which would have been a 5 percent profit on the real estate company's capitalization, but was turned down. *NYT*, 3 Nov. 1889, 1-5.

41. *Spirit* 115 (2 June 1888): 699. The *Times* coverage was much briefer and had nothing to say about the crowd at all. See *NYT*, 30 May 1888, 5-4.

42. *Spirit* 115 (2 June 1888): 696.

43. *Spirit* 115 (9 June 1888): 738; *NYT*, 5 Dec. 1888, 8-4.

44. *Spirit* 115 (9 June 1888): 738.

45. *NYT*, 24 Sept. 1888, 2-2; *NYT*, 17 Nov. 1888, 5-5; *NYT*, 6 Dec. 1888, 4-2; *NYT*, 5 July 1888, 3.

46. *Spirit* 118 (14 Dec. 1889): 748.

47. *NYTr*, 17 Nov. 1888, 4-3; *NYTr*, 19 Nov. 1888, 4-3; *NYTr*, 26 Nov. 1888, 8-2.

48. *NYT*, 21 Oct. 1888, 13-3; *NYT*, 30 July 1889, 1-5; *Spirit* 118 (14 Dec. 1889): 748; Clarence Clough Buel, "The Degradation of a State; or, The Charitable Career of the Louisiana Lottery," 621, 624. For John A. Morris's obituary, see *NYT*, 27 May 1895, 1-1. On the Louisiana Lottery, see John S. Kendall, *History of New Orleans*, chap. 31. On Morris, see Nicholas Di Brino, *History of the Morris Park Racecourse and the Morris Family*, 1–11.

49. Vosburgh, "Passing of Jerome Park," 514; *Spirit* 115 (2 June 1888): 699.

50. *Spirit* 115 (9 June 1888): 738. Morris offered to lease 112 acres of Jerome Park and pay 4.5 percent on the stock for the lease if all assets of the AJC were transferred to him. These generous terms were turned down. *NYT*, 8 Nov. 1892, 9-3. On the new track, see also Scott Thompson, "The New York Jockey Club."

51. *NYT*, 12 May 1889, 3-4; *NYT*, 13 May 1889, 2-2; *NYT*, 14 May 1889, 2-3; *NYT*, 13 June 1889, 5-3.

52. *Spirit* 117 (25 May 1889): 727; *Spirit* 117 (1 June 1889): 769; *Spirit* 117 (8 June 1889): 789.

53. *Spirit* 118 (14 Dec. 1889): 748.

54. *Spirit* 115 (2 June 1888): 699; *NYT*, 12 May 1889, 9-5; *NYT*, 30 July 1889, 1-5; *NYT*, 31 July 1889, 4-1; *NYT*, 5 Aug. 1889, 8-4.

55. *Spirit* 115 (2 June 1888): 699; *Spirit* 115 (9 June 1888): 738.

56. Thompson, "New York Jockey Club"; *NYT*, 19 Aug. 1889, 2; *Spirit* 118 (24 Aug. 1889): 180; *CDN*, 14 Nov. 1894, 3-2.

57. *Spirit* 119 (24 May 1890): 792; *Spirit* 118 (17 Aug. 1889): 144; *Spirit* 118 (24 Aug. 1889): 180, 229.

58. *Spirit* 119 (24 May 1890): 792.

59. *NYT*, 2 Oct. 1889, 3-1; *Spirit* 118 (24 Aug. 1889): 180. For transportation improvements, see *Spirit* 118 (31 Aug. 1889): 229.

60. *NYT*, 22 Oct. 1889, 5-2; *NYT*, 3 Nov. 1889, 1-5; *NYT*, 5 Nov. 1889, 2-5; *NYT*, 19 Nov. 1889, 3-4; *NYT*, 21 Dec. 1889, 6-1; Black, *King of Fifth Avenue*, 715.

61. *NYT*, 10 Dec. 1889, 2-6.

62. *NYT*, 2 Oct., 1890, 8; Di Brino, *Morris Park Racecourse*, 6.

63. *Spirit* 117 (18 May 1889): 676; *BE*, 14 Aug. 1892, 14-1 (quote), 9-3.

64. *BE*, 14 June 1888, 6-8; *BE*, 19 June 1888, 8-1; *Spirit* 117 (22 June 1889): 886.

65. *CT*, 19 Apr. 1891, 43-5; "What Racing Costs" (editorial), *NYTr*, 8 Oct. 1889, 6-4.

66. "What Racing Costs" (editorial), *NYTr*, 8 Oct. 1889, 6-4. The reporter's estimated income of bookmakers seems far too high in relation to the amount of money bet.

67. *NYT*, 18 Dec. 1890, 3-6.

68. Steven A. Riess, "Horse Racing in Chicago, 1883–1894: The Interplay of Class, Politics, and Organized Crime," 120; *Chicago Journal*, 31 May 1887, 1-7; *Chicago Journal*, 30 June 1887, 2-1; *CT*, 30 May 1887, 4-4; *CT*, 4 June 1887, 4-3; *CT*, 5 June 1887, 5-4.

5. Politics and the Turf in New Jersey, 1870–94

1. George Kirsch, ed., *Sports in War, Revival, and Expansion, 1860–1880*, 171. The version of the *Spirit*'s account of the Derby is in W. Robertson, *Thoroughbred Racing*, 99–100.

2. *CT*, 8 Aug. 1870, 3-1; *NYT*, 24 Apr. 1870, 6-2; Olive Logan, "Life at Long Branch," 482.

3. *CT*, 8 Aug. 1870, 3-1; *NYT*, 24 Apr. 1870, 6-2; *NYT*, 14 Mar. 1878, 8-1; *NYT*, 22 Oct. 1893, 21; *Spirit* 86 (12 Dec. 1873): 445; Writers' Program, New Jersey, *Entertaining a Nation: Career of Long Branch*, 49.

4. *NYT*, 31 July 1870, 1-4; *NYT*, 22 Oct. 1893, 21-2; *Spirit* 85 (28 June 1873): 331; *Spirit* 86 (29 Nov. 1873): 372; *Spirit* 86 (13 Dec. 1873): 429; *Spirit* 86 (6 Aug. 1890): 387, 393; D. Johnson, "Sinful Business," 36–37; Kirsch, *Sports in War, Revival, and Expansion*, 171.

5. *NYT*, 31 July 1870, 1-4.

6. *NYT*, 22 Oct. 1893, 21-2; D. Johnson, "Sinful Business," 88. Fisk was also involved in a love triangle that ended in his murder in early 1872.

7. *NYT*, 3 July 1872, 5-1; O. Logan, "Life at Long Branch," 486.

8. O. Logan, "Life at Long Branch," 487.

9. *NYT*, Mar. 14 1878, 8-2; *NYT*, 6 Apr. 1878, 5-3; *Spirit* 79 (6 Aug. 1870): 388; *Spirit* 86 (29 Nov. 1873): 372; *Spirit* 86 (13 Dec. 1873): 429; *Spirit* 89 (7 Aug. 1875): 668. Chamberlain's past was publicized in J. Morris, *Wanderings of a Vagabond*, 197–207. See also *Spirit* 86 (27 Sept. 1873): 155–56. On McGrath, see J. Morris, *Wanderings of a Vagabond*, 259–62.

10. *Spirit* 86 (6 Sept. 1873): 85; *Spirit* 86 (13 Sept. 1873): 109; *Spirit* 86 (6 Dec. 1873): 397–98.

11. *NYT*, 22 Oct. 1893, 21-2.

12. *NYTr*, 22 Oct. 1877, 2-5; *NYTr*, 12 Nov. 1877, 2-6; *NYTr*, 6 Apr. 1878, 5-3; *NYT*, 14 Mar. 1878, 8-2; *NYT*, 6 Apr. 1878, 5-3; *NYT*, 22 Oct. 1893, 21-2; *CT*, 12 Apr. 1891, 35-3; *Spirit* 121 (28 Mar. 1891): 448; *Spirit* 123 (20 Feb. 1892): 192; *Spirit* 123 (27 Feb. 1892): 221; Ron Hale, "Historic Races in New York: The Withers Stakes." Lorillard died in 1880 at the age of forty-three following several years of ill health. On Lorillard, see *NYT*, 5 Feb. 1886, 8-2; and W. Robertson, *Thoroughbred Racing*, 129–30.

13. *NYT*, 22 Oct. 1893, 21-2; *CT*, 12 Apr. 1891, 35-3; *CT*, 15 June 1895, 9-6; *Spirit* 121 (28 Mar. 1891): 448; *Spirit* 123 (27 Feb. 1892): 221. On the poolroom migration to New Jersey, see *NYT*, 29 May 1877, 8-4; *NYT*, 5 June 1877, 5-6; *NYT*, 12 June 1877, 8-6; *NYT*, 13 June 1877, 8-2; *NYT*, 4 Nov. 1877, 5-2; *NYT*, 11 Nov. 1877, 12-2; and *NYT*, 29 July 1878, 2-2. For Murray's obituary, see *NYT*, 15 June 1895, 9-6.

14. "Detailed Report of the Racing: Fine Sport and Good Time" (editorial), *NYT*, 6 Apr. 1878, 8-1; W. Robertson, *Thoroughbred Racing*, 105–6; *Spirit* 101 (26 Nov. 1881): 465.

15. *NYT*, 15 Sept. 1893, 5-1; *NYT*, 22 Oct. 1893, 21-3.

16. *NYT*, 28 Jan. 1888, 2-6; *NYT*, 10 Jan. 1894, 1; *McClean v. the State* [1887] (20 Vroom 471); *Spirit* 121 (18 Apr. 1891): 582. See also Governor Werts's message to the state in 1894 in *Manual of the Legislature of New Jersey, 1894*, 373–74.

17. "Detailed Report of the Racing: Fine Sport and Good Time" (editorial), *NYT*, 6 Apr. 1878, 8-1; W. Robertson, *Thoroughbred Racing*, 105–6; Writers' Program, New Jersey, *Entertaining a Nation*, 89.

18. *CT*, 12 Apr. 1891, 35-3; *NYT*, 30 June 1890, 2-4; *NYT*, 4 July 1892, 2-4; *NYTr*, 4 Aug. 1889, 4-4; W. Robertson, *Thoroughbred Racing*, 105, 107, 141; *Spirit* 105 (5 May 1883): 385; *Spirit* 117 (6 July 1889): 965; *Spirit* 117 (13 July 1889): 1004; *Spirit* 119 (5 July 1890): 1057, 1060; *Spirit* 120 (16 Aug. 1890): 143; Writers' Program, New Jersey, *Entertaining a Nation*, 90.

19. *NYT*, 22 Oct. 1893, 21-4; *BE*, 7 July 1890, 6-1 (quote); *New York Sun*, 20 Apr. 1891, 5-4; *NYMT*, 19 Nov. 1899, 2-3; *Lewiston Evening Journal*, 26 Feb. 1892, 6-2.

20. NYT, 22 Oct. 1893, 21-4; *New York Sun*, 20 Apr. 1891, 5-4; *NYMT*, 19 Nov. 1899, 2-3; William E. Sackett, *Modern Battles of Trenton: Being a History of New Jersey's Politics and Legislation from the Year 1868 to the Year 1894*, 384–85; *Spirit* 122 (2 Jan. 1892): 912.

21. *NYT*, 22 Oct. 1893, 21-4; *New York Sun*, 24 Nov. 1889, 21-1; Mel Heimer, *Fabulous Bawd: The Story of Saratoga*, 101–3; Gottfried Walbaum, "Reminiscences of Gottfried Walbaum, 1920–1931," n.p.

22. *NYT*, 22 Oct. 1893, 21-4; Richard A. Hogarty, *Leon Abbett's New Jersey: The Emergence of the Modern Governor*, 16–20, 24–26; *NYTr*, 16 Feb. 1895, 16-3; *Lewiston Evening Journal*, 26 Feb. 1892, 6-2.

23. *Newark News*, 6 Feb. 1890, 1-4; *Newark News*, 26 Feb. 1890, 1-7; *Newark News*, 29 Mar. 1890, 8.

24. Walbaum, "Reminiscences of Gottfried Walbaum," n.p.

25. *NYT*, 22 Oct. 1893, 21-6.

26. *NYT*, 11 Nov. 1889, 3-3; *Lewiston Evening Journal*, 26 Feb. 1892, 6-2.

27. *NYT*, 22 Oct. 1893, 21-6.

28. *NYT*, 27 Nov. 1891, 2-2; *NYT*, 29 Sept. 1893, 3; *NYT*, 22 Oct. 1893, 21-6; D. Johnson, "Sinful Business," 88; *Spirit* 122 (2 Jan. 1892): 912; *CDN*, 16 Feb. 1893, 6-2.

29. *CDN*, 16 Feb. 1893, 6-2; *NYTr*, 3 Mar. 1890, 6-3; *BE*, 28 Dec. 1890, 8-9; *Lewiston Evening Journal*, 26 Feb. 1892, 6-2.

30. *NYT*, 27 Nov. 1891, 2-2; *NYT*, 22 Oct. 1893, 21-6; D. Johnson, "Sinful Business," 88; *Spirit* 122 (2 Jan. 1892): 912; *CDN*, 18 Sept. 1893, 2-1. Daily newspapers ranging from the *TDTA* to the *Hartford Post* freely cited the *Times* in their own reports. See, for example, *NYT*, 18 July 1893, 2-3; and *NYT*, 21 July 1893, 2-2.

31. The newspaper account reported Guttenberg was making a million dollars, which seems extremely unlikely, especially in 1886. *NYT*, 22 Oct. 1893, 21-8.

32. *NYT*, 22 Jan. 1888, 16-4; *Chicago Times*, 3 Apr. 1888, 3-4.

33. *NYTr*, 28 Jan. 1889, 10-1; John F. Reynolds, *Testing Democracy: Electoral Behavior and Progressive Reform in New Jersey, 1880–1920*, 94.

34. *NYTr*, 28 Jan. 1889, 10-1; *NYTr*, 15 Apr. 1889, 10-1; *NYTr*, 21 Oct. 1889, 10-1; *NYTr*, 24 Oct. 1889, 3-1; *NYTr*, 21 Apr. 1891, 3-1; *Spirit* 118 (18 Oct. 1889): 521; *Spirit* 118 (25 Oct. 1889): 547; *Spirit* 118 (21 Dec. 1889): 772; *Spirit* 126 (28 Oct. 1893): 473; *NYT*, 30 June 1890, 2-4; *NYT*, 29 Jan. 1891, 1-4; *NYT*, 4 Apr. 1891, 3-1; *NYT*, 28 Jan. 1893, 6-1; *NYT*, 7 Mar. 1893, 1-2; *NYT*, 22 Oct. 1893, 21-8.

35. *NYT*, 5 May 1890, 12-3; *NYTr*, 19 Mar. 1890, 6-5; *BE*, 7 July 1890, 6-1; *Spirit* 119 (19 Apr. 1890): 557; *CT*, 12 Apr. 1891, 35-3; *NEN*, 17 Sept. 1891, 2-1. The *Chicago Times* claimed that daily races in the winter of 1887 at Guttenberg and Clifton were primarily run for the benefit of illegal poolrooms in New York City. *Chicago Times*, 3 Apr. 1888, 3-4. On the connections between winter racing and metropolitan poolrooms, see editorial, *NYTr*, 15 Feb. 1893, 6-4.

36. *NYT*, 25 Aug., 1890, 8-5; *NYT*, 22 Oct. 1893, 21-4.

37. *NYT*, 29 Oct. 1893, 24-1; *NYT*, 5 Nov. 1893, 16-1, 16-3; Hogarty, *Leon Abbett's New Jersey*, 189–90.

38. *NYT*, 22 Oct. 1893, 21-4; *NYT*, 29 Oct. 1893, 24-1.

39. *NYT*, 29 Oct. 1893, 24-1; *NEN*, 27 Oct. 1893, 7-4.

40. *NYTr*, 30 July 1893, 3-1 (quote), 3-2.

41. *NYT*, 24 Mar. 1890, 2-6; *NYT*, 26 May 1890, 2-5; *NYT*, 18 June 1899, SM2-1; *NYTr*, 5 May 1890, 5-4; *NYTr*, 20 May 1890, 1-2; *TDTA*, 17 June 1890, 4-2.

42. *TDTA*, 28 Jan. 1890, 5-6; *TDTA*, 27 Feb. 1890, 5-6; *TDTA*, 17 June 1890, 4-2; *NEN*, 11 Apr. 1890, 1-1; *NEN*, 25 Apr. 1890, 3-1; *NEN*, 29 Apr. 1890, 1-1; *NEN*, 7 May 1890; *NYTr*, 5 May 1890, 5-4; *NYTr*, 20 May 1890, 1-2; *NYT*, 26 May 1890, 2-5.

43. Hogarty, *Leon Abbett's New Jersey*, 290. Hogarty did not cite any source to prove this trial-balloon hypothesis.

44. *TDTA*, 11 June 1890, 5-3; *TDTA*, 16 June 1890, 2-2, 4-2; *TDTA*, 17 June 1890, 1-4, 4-2; *TDTA*, 18 June 1890, 5-4; *NYT*, 17 June 1890, 1-7 (quote); *NYT*, 6 Mar. 1893, 8-1; *NYT*, 9 Oct. 1893, 9-1; *NYT*, 22 Oct. 1893, 21-3; Sackett, *Modern Battles of Trenton*, 386–88; *CT*, 12 Apr. 1891, 35-3.

45. *TDTA*, 17 June 1890, 4-2; *TDTA*, 18 June 1890, 4-1, 5-4.

46. *NYTr*, 5 May 1890, 5-4; *NYTr*, 20 May 1890, 1-2; *NYTr*, 23 May 1890, 2-3; *NYTr*, 29 June 1890, 6-3; *NYT*, 17 June 1890, 1-7; *NYT*, 18 June 1890, 1-5.

47. Hogarty, *Leon Abbett's New Jersey*, 291, 316, 318. On Abbett's political savvy and early career, see Richard A. Hogarty, "The Political Apprenticeship of Leon Abbett," esp. 1 (quote), 40; and J. Reynolds, *Testing Democracy*, 19.

48. *CT*, 12 Apr. 1891, 35-3; *NYT*, 17 Feb. 1891, 2-5; *NYT*, 29 Mar. 1891, 3-1.

49. *NYT*, 14 Apr. 1890, 2-3; *NYT*, 4 May 1890, 12-3; *NYT*, 7 May 1890, 2-7 (quote); *NYT*, 20 Jan. 1891, 2-5; *NYT*, 17 Feb. 1891, 2-5; *NYTr*, 20 Jan. 1891, 12-3; *Chicago Herald*, 23 Mar. 1891, 6-1.

50. *NYT,* 5 July 1890, 3-1; *NYT,* 6 July 1890, 8-1; *NYT,* 15 July 1890, 2-4; *NYT,* 20 July 1890, 2-4; *NYT,* 17 Feb. 1891, 2-5; *CT,* 12 Apr. 1891, 35-3; *BE,* 7 July 1890, 6. On the Monmouth gambling cases, see *NYT,* 6 July 1890, 8-1; *NYT,* 12 Oct. 1890, 17-6; *NYT,* 9 Dec. 1890, 8-7. On the importance of racing on Independence Day, see John Gilmer Speed, "A Holiday Crowd at the Races."

51. *CT,* 12 Apr. 1891, 35-3. On Elizabeth, see *NYT,* 21 Sept. 1890, 1-4; *NYT,* 23 Sept. 1890, 3-2; *NYT,* 17 Oct. 1890, 3-1; *NYT,* 23 Oct. 1890, 3-2; *NYT,* 24 Oct. 1890, 6-6; *NYT,* 25 Oct. 1890, 3-2; *NYT,* 15 Dec. 1890, 2-4; *NYT,* 20 Dec. 1890, 2-4; *NYT,* 8 Jan. 1891, 6-1; and *NYT,* 17 Feb. 1891, 2-5. On Linden, see *NYT,* 18 Nov. 1890, 2-4; *NYT,* 23 Nov. 1890, 6-3; and *NYT,* 19 Dec. 1890, 6-3.

52. *NYT,* 21 Sept. 1890, 1-4; *NYT,* 23 Sept. 1890, 1-5.

53. *NYT,* 1 Jan. 1891, 3-7; *NYT,* 18 Jan. 1891, 2-7; *NYT,* 20 Jan. 1891, 2-5; *NYT,* 24 Jan. 1891, 8-4; *NYT,* 29 Jan. 1891, 1-4; *NEN,* 29 Jan. 1891, 1-3; "New Jersey Courts and Racetracks" (editorial), *NYTr,* 2 Feb. 1891, 6-2.

54. *NYT,* 2 Mar. 1891, 2-5.

55. Ibid.; *NYT,* 3 Apr. 1891, 1-3.

56. *NYT,* 24 Feb. 1891, 2-7; *NYT,* 3 Mar. 1891, 2-5; *NYT,* 5 Mar. 1891, 6-2; *NYT,* 23 Mar. 1891, 2-4; *NYT,* 24 Mar. 1891, 2-6; *NYT,* 6 Apr. 1891, 2-5; *NYT,* 22 Oct. 1893, 21-3; *CT,* 12 Apr. 1891, 35-3; *Spirit* 121 (13 June 1891): 935; *NYTr,* 23 Mar. 1891, 4-1.

57. *TDTA,* 24 Feb. 1891, 4-5, 5-2; *TDTA,* 2 Mar. 1891, 5-3.

58. *NYTr,* 2 Mar. 1891, 5-1.

59. *TDTA,* 4 Mar. 1891, 4-1; *TDTA,* 5 Mar. 1891, 4-1. On criticism of the *True American*'s shifting position, and its response, see *TDTA,* 30 Mar. 1891, 4-1, 2.

60. *TDTA,* 3 Mar. 1891, 5-3; *TDTA,* 4 Apr. 1891, 4-1; *NYTr,* 23 Mar. 1891, 4-1; *CT,* 12 Apr. 1891, 35-3; *NYT,* 2 Mar. 1891, 2-5; *NYT,* 3 Mar. 1891, 2-5; *NYT,* 4 Mar. 1891, 2-7; *NYT,* 23 Mar. 1891, 2-4; *NYT,* 22 Oct. 1893, 21-6; *NYT,* 1 Nov. 1893, 9-1. During the 1893 election campaign, Senator Rogers claimed that Thompson had actually tried to legalize racetrack gambling in 1891 and had offered Rogers and two other Republicans seventy-five thousand dollars for their votes. *NYT,* 5 Nov. 1893, 16-1.

61. *CT,* 12 Apr. 1891, 35-3; *TDTA,* 10 Feb. 1891, 4-4; *TDTA,* 14 Apr. 1891, 4-1; *TDTA,* 15 Apr. 1891, 4-1. On the efforts of clergymen to fight the legislation, see *TDTA,* 15 Apr. 1891, 5-2.

62. *TDTA,* 23 Mar. 1891, 4-1; *NYT,* 9 July 1891, 8; *NYT,* 3 Aug. 1891, 2-3; *NYT,* 22 Oct. 1893, 21-7.

63. *NYT,* 3 Apr. 1891, 2-6; *TDTA,* 4 Apr. 1891, 4-1. Another estimate was that Clifton was getting seven hundred dollars a day. *Spirit* 122 (9 Jan. 1892): 965.

64. *NYT,* 5 Apr. 1891, 16-4. As in all cases, financial statistics must be treated gingerly. By the estimates reported in the *New York Times* in 1891, Western Union would have had to pay Guttenberg four thousand dollars a day, which is way out of line. In 1893, it was reported that Western Union charged a maximum of fifteen hundred dollars a day for racing results at New Jersey tracks. *NEN,* 27 Oct. 1893, 7-4.

65. *Spirit* 122 (9 Jan. 1892): 965.

66. *NYT,* 6 Apr. 1891, 2-5; *NYT,* 21 Apr. 1891, 2-6; *NYT,* 22 Apr. 1891, 2-2; *TDTA,* 6 Apr. 1891, 1-6; *NYTr,* 21 Apr. 1891, 5-3. On David and the Hudson County machine, see Hogarty, *Leon Abbett's New Jersey,* 268–70.

67. *NYT,* 6 Apr. 1891, 2-5; *TDTA,* 6 Apr. 1891, 1-6; Sackett, *Modern Battles of Trenton,* 386.

68. *NYT,* 26 Jan. 1888, 2-6; *NYT,* 27 Nov. 1891, 2-2; *NYT,* 7 Dec. 1891, 6-1; *Clipper* 39 (28 Nov. 1891): 693.

69. *NYT,* 10 Dec. 1891, 5-5; *NYT,* 22 Oct. 1891, 21-4; *NYT,* 29 Oct. 1893, 24-1.

70. *NYT,* 16 Jan. 5-5; *NYT,* 21 Jan. 1892, 5-5; *BE,* 17 Jan. 1892, 14-1; *Spirit* 123 (30 Jan. 1892): 59–60.

71. *NEN,* 5 Feb. 1892, 5-5; *NEN,* 9 Feb. 1892, 1-4.

72. *NEN,* 5 Feb. 1892, 5-5; *NEN,* 9 Feb. 1892, 1-4; *NYT,* 28 Jan. 1893, 3-5; *NYTr,* 10 Mar. 1892, 3-3.

73. *BE,* 19 Feb. 1892, 4; *Spirit* 123 (27 Feb. 1892): 221; *Spirit* 123 (2 Apr. 1892): 442.

74. *NYTr,* 6 Mar. 1893, 2-1; *NYTr,* 19 July 1893, 1-7, 2-1; *NYT,* 19 Feb. 1892, 3-4; *NYT,* 4 July 1892, 2-4; *NYT,* 4 Aug. 1893, 2-4; *NYT,* 22 Oct. 1893, 24-1. The Shanleys, Pennsylvania Railroad contractors, had 108 shares. *NYT,* 3 May 1894, 3-1. The Monmouth Park Association was also known as the Monmouth Park Racing Association at least as early as 1882. See *NYT,* 30 July 1882, 2-3.

75. *NYT,* 4 July 1892, 2-4 (quote); *NYT,* 30 July 1893, 3-1; *NYT,* 2 Oct. 1893, 1-7; Writers' Program, New Jersey, *Entertaining a Nation,* 94.

76. *NYT,* 4 July 1892, 2-4; *NYT,* 5 July 1892, 3-1.

77. *NYT,* 4 July 1892, 2-4; *NYT,* 30 July 1893, 3-1; *NYT,* 2 Oct. 1893, 1-7.

78. Samuel T. McSeveney, *The Politics of Depression: Political Behavior in the Northeast, 1893–1896,* 45–46; Sackett, *Modern Battles of Trenton,* 440–41; *NYT,* 28 Oct. 1893, 4-5.

79. *NYTr,* 23 Feb. 1893, 6-2; *NYTr,* 6 Mar. 1993, 1-6, 2-2.

80. McSeveney, *Politics of Depression,* 45–46; Sackett, *Modern Battles of Trenton,* 440–41; *NEN,* 27 Oct. 1893, 7-4; Writers' Program, New Jersey, *Entertaining a Nation,* 95.

81. *NYT,* 18 Jan. 1893, 6; *NYT,* 15 Aug. 1893, 3-5.

82. *NYT,* 22 Feb. 1893, 3; *NYTr,* 23 Feb. 1893, 6-2; *NYTr,* 6 Mar. 1893, 1-6, 2-2.

83. "New Jersey's Legalized Gambling" (editorial), *NYT,* 26 Feb. 1893, 4-3.

84. Anthony Comstock, "Pool Rooms and Pool Selling," 606–8; *NYT,* 26 Jan. 1893, 4-3; *NYT,* 28 Jan. 1893, 6-1; *NYT,* 22 Feb. 1893, 3-2; *NYT,* 24 Feb. 1893, 8-3; *NYT,* 25 Feb. 1893, 9-4; "New Jersey's Legalized Gambling" (editorial), *NYT,* 26 Feb. 1893, 4-2; *NYT,* 27 Feb. 1893, 1-7; *NYT,* 2 Mar. 1893, 4-2, 8-3; *NYT,* 3 Mar. 1893, 5-1; *NYT,* 15 Sept. 1893, 5-1; Sackett, *Modern Battles of Trenton,* 444–49; McSeveney, *Politics of Depression,* 46; *Clipper* (18 Mar. 1893): 23; *NYTr,* 22 July 1893, 1-5.

85. *NYT,* 14 Feb. 1893, 3-2.

86. *NYT,* 26 Feb. 1893, 4-3. See also "The Degradation of Horse Racing," *NYT,* 21 July 1893, 4-3.

87. *NYT,* 12 Mar. 1893, 1-7, 2-1. For the *Times'* reaction, see also *NYT,* 24 Feb. 1893, 8-3; *NYT,* 26 Feb. 1893, 4-1, 16-5; *NYT,* 27 Feb. 1893, 1-5; *NYT,* 1 Mar. 1893, l-4; *NYT,* 2 Mar. 1893, 8-3; *NYT,* 6 Mar. 1893, 8-1; *NYT,* 7 Mar. 1893, 1-3; and *NYT,* 8 Mar. 1893, 1-2.

88. Sackett, *Modern Battles of Trenton,* 448–53; McSeveney, *Politics of Depression,* 46–47; *NYT,* 17 Apr. 1893, 2-1.

89. McSeveney, *Politics of Depression,* 47–48. On the ethnocultural interpretation of political behavior, see Paul Kleppner, *The Cross of Culture: A Social Analysis of Midwestern Politics, 1850–1900;* and Richard J. Jensen, *The Winning of the Midwest: Social and Political Conflict.*

90. *NYTr,* 6 Mar. 1893, 1-6; *NYT,* 11 Mar. 1893, 3-1; *NYT,* 12 Mar. 1893, 1-7, 2-1; *NYT,* 26 Nov. 1893, 11-1; Sackett, *Modern Battles of Trenton,* 445.

91. *NYT,* 13 Mar. 1893, 8-1.

92. Ibid.

93. *NYT,* 22 Sept. 1890, 8-1; *NYT,* 13 Mar. 1893, 8-1. See also editorial comments during the election campaign. See, for example, *NEN,* 5 Oct. 1893, 1-4; *NEN,* 7 Oct. 1893, 4-1; and *Philadelphia Inquirer,* 29 Oct. 1893, 4-1.

94. *NYT,* 13 Mar. 1893, 8-1; *NYTr,* 17 Mar. 1893, 2-6.

95. *NYT,* 6 Mar. 1893, 8-1; *NYT,* 10 Mar. 1893, 5-4; *NYT,* 12 Mar. 1893, 2-1; *NYT,* 30 July 1893, 3; *NYTr,* 28 Feb. 1893, 1-4; *NYTr,* 22 July 1893, 1-5. T. M. Croft was the business manager and political manipulator for Monmouth Park and helped it evade payment of its license fee. *NYT,* 30 July 1893, 3-1.

96. *NYT,* 15 Sept. 1893, 5-1.

97. *NYTr,* 16 July 1893, 6-3. See also editorials, "Monmouth's False Position," *NYTr,* 18 July 1893, 6-3, and "Monmouth Track Must Go," *NYT,* 15 Sept. 1893, 5-1.

98. *NYTr,* 19 July 1893, 1-7, 2-1.

99. *NYT,* 15 July 1893, 3-1; *CDN,* 15 July 1893, 7-2. The track managers in an overtly political action tried to silence editor William J. Leonard of the *Monmouth Press,* an antiracing Republican nominee for the assembly. He was arrested on charges of criminal libel on the complaint of ex-sheriff Theodore Aumack, a racetrack-ring candidate for county clerk. *NYT,* 27 Oct. 1893, 2-6.

100. *NYT,* 16 July 1893, 3-4.

101. *NYTr,* 2 Aug. 1893, 3-1.

102. *NYT,* 16 July 1893, 3-4; *NYT,* 23 July 1893, 1-2; *NYT,* 26 July 1893, 3-1; *NYT,* 30 July 1893, 3-l; *NYT,* 11 Aug. 1893, 2-6; *CDN,* 16 Jan. 1894, 2-1 (quote).

103. *NYT,* 17 July 1893, 2-1. For the bookmakers' response, see *NYT,* 19 July 1893, 5-4.

104. *NYT,* 7 Aug. 1893, 2-6; *NYT,* 12 Aug. 1893, 2-6; *NYT,* 13 Aug. 1893, 2-6; *NYT,* 15 Aug. 1893, 3-5; *NYT,* 16 Aug. 1893, 6-3; *NYT,* 22 Aug. 1893, 8-1; *NYTr,* 2 Aug. 1893, 3-1.

105. *NYT,* 21 Aug. 1893, 3-5.

106. *NYTr,* 18 Aug. 1893, 4-1; *Spirit* 125 (8 Apr. 1893): 472; *NYT,* 5 Nov. 1893, 2-7.

107. *NYT,* 8 Mar. 1893, 1-2; *NYT,* 2 Aug. 1893, 3-3; *NYT,* 22 Oct. 1893, 21-7; *NEN,* 8 Aug. 1893, 2-4 (quote).

108. *NYT,* 8 Mar. 1893, 1-2; *NYT,* 2 Aug. 1893, 3-3; *NYT,* 22 Oct. 1893, 21-7; *BE,* 2 Aug. 1893, 2-3.

109. *BE,* 2 Aug. 1893, 2-3; *BE,* 11 Aug. 1893, 2-3.

110. *NEN,* 15 Mar. 1893, 4-2; *Spirit* 125 (18 Mar. 1893): 341; *Spirit* 126 (28 Oct. 1893): 473; *BE,* 16 Aug. 1893, 2-4; *NYT,* 12 Mar. 1893, 2-1; *NYT,* 1 Aug. 1893, 3-5; *NYT,* 17 Aug. 1893, 3-5; *NYT,* 22 Aug. 1893, 8-4; *NYT,* 22 Oct. 1893, 21-7; *NYT,* 18 Nov. 1893, 2-5.

111. *NYT,* 1 Nov. 1893, 9-1.

112. *NEN,* 31 Oct. 1893, 4-1; *NEN,* 2 Nov. 1893, 4-2; *NYT,* 22 Oct. 1893, 6-2; *NYT,* 29 Oct. 1893, 2-1. See also "Move on the Gamblers," *Philadelphia Inquirer,* 5 Nov. 1893, 8-1, which focused on the situation in nearby Gloucester.

113. *NYT,* 1 Nov. 1893, 9: 1-4; McSeveney, *Politics of Depression,* 57–58.

114. *Philadelphia Inquirer,* 5 Nov. 1893, 8-1.

115. Ibid. See also *NYT,* 5 Nov. 1893, 16-1.

116. *NYT,* 5 Nov. 1893, 16-2 (quote); *Philadelphia Inquirer,* 26 Oct. 1893, 4-1; *Philadelphia Inquirer,* 28 Oct. 1893, 1-4, 4-1; *Philadelphia Inquirer,* 4 Nov. 1893, 2-1; *Philadelphia Inquirer,* 6 Nov. 1893, 2-1.

117. *NYT,* 28 Oct. 1893, 4-5. On evidence of violence in the election despite precautions, see *Philadelphia Inquirer,* 7, 8 Nov. 1893.

118. *NYT,* 5 Nov. 1893, 16-1.

119. *NYT,* 8 Nov. 1893, 5-1.

120. McSeveney, *Politics of Depression,* 55–56.

121. Ibid., 56–57.

122. Ibid., 57–58.

123. Ibid., 59–61.

124. Ibid., 62, 127, 128, 159, 161, 162, 214, 226. On ethnocultural midwestern politics in the 1890s, see Kleppner, *Cross of Culture;* and Jensen, *Winning of the Midwest.*

125. *BE,* 13 Nov. 1893, 9-7; *NYT,* 8 Nov. 1893, 5-1.

126. *NYT,* 8 Nov. 1893, 5-1, 4-4.

127. *NYT,* 26 Nov. 1893, 11-1; *NYT,* 29 Nov. 1893, 1-6; *NYT,* 26 Dec. 1893, 5-3; Writers' Program, New Jersey, *Entertaining a Nation,* 97.

128. *NYT,* 24 Dec. 1893, 17-7; *Spirit* 127 (10 Feb. 1894): 127; *Spirit* 127 (24 Mar. 1894): 306; Sackett, *Modern Battles of Trenton,* 454–61.

129. *NYT,* 9 Jan. 1894, 3-5, 8-5. Nearly one year earlier, Lippincott had indicated to the Hudson County Grand Jury that the Parker laws were unconstitutional. *NYT,* 5 Apr. 1893, 2-5.

130. *NYTr,* 9 Jan. 1894, 6-4.

131. *NYTr,* 11 Jan. 1894, 1-5; *NYTr,* 13 Apr. 1894, 5-6.

132. *NYT,* 17 Jan. 1892, 3-4; *NYT,* 14 Jan. 1894, 5-5; *NYT,* 1 June 1894, 3-4; *NYT,* 17 May 1895, 1-4; *National Police Gazette* 49 (27 Oct. 1894): 11; *Spirit* 129 (23 Feb. 1895): 180.

133. *NYTr,* 16 Feb. 1895, 16-3.

134. Walbaum, "Reminiscences of Gottfried Walbaum," 8. The auctioneer was Joseph P. Day, former owner of the New York Giants. In 1897 a constitutional amendment forbade gambling or bookmaking. See Writers' Program, New Jersey, *Entertaining a Nation,* 97.

135. *NYT,* 12 Mar. 1940, 1-1; *NYT,* 19 Mar. 1940, 20-1. On dog racing, see Writers' Program, New Jersey, *Entertaining a Nation,* 138.

6. From the Board of Control to The Jockey Club, 1891–94

1. *NYT,* 16 Nov. 1890, 3-7.

2. *NYT,* 2 June 1891, 5-3 (quote).

3. *NYT,* 19 Jan. 1891, 8-4; *NYT,* 1 June 1891, 2-5; *Spirit* 121 (6 June 1891): 886 (quote); *Spirit* 121 (20 June 1891): 914–15; *NYT,* 19 Jan. 1891, 8-4; "The Club-House of the New York Jockey Club."

4. "Club-House of the New York Jockey Club"; *Spirit* 119 (24 May 1890): 792 (quote).

5. *NYTr,* 6 Jan. 1893, 3-3; *NYT,* 2 June 1891, 5-1; *NYT,* 7 June 1891, 3-1 (quote); *NYT,* 17 June 1891, 2-4. On the popularity of the track with New York politicians, see also *NYT,* 18 Sept. 1892, 11-3, which pointed out Mayor Grant, Boss Croker, Park Commissioner Straus, and Police Chief Martin among the politicians who enjoyed gambling at the tracks.

6. *NYT,* 30 Mar. 1892, 1-3; *NYT,* 2 Oct. 1893, 8 (quotes).

7. *NYT,* 1 Oct. 1893, 10-2 (quotes); *NYT,* 9 Nov. 1893, 5-3; *NYT,* 30 Mar. 1894, 5-3. There was also a lot of interest in the election in Kings County as reformers tried to halt prizefighting at Coney Island with the impending heavyweight-title bout between James J. Corbett and Charles Mitchell. See, for example, *NYT,* 28 Sept. 1893, 1-7; *NYT,* 10 Oct. 1893, 1-7; *NYT,* 21 Oct. 1893, 8-1; and "Hope for Brooklyn" (editorial), *NYT,* 2 Nov. 1893, 4-4. The *Times* reported that the heavily politicized Coney Island Athletic Club made $222,300 from sixteen matches. *NYT,* 9 Sept. 28, 1893, 8-1. See also Riess, "In the Ring and Out," 98–99.

8. *NYT,* 29 June 1891, 2-4; *NYT,* 9 July 1891, 8-1; *NYT,* 25 Aug. 1891, 8-3; *NYTr,* 23 Mar. 1891, 12-1.

9. *NYT,* 6 July 1891, 2-2; *NYT,* 1 Oct. 1891, 3-1.

10. *NYT,* 3 Aug. 1891, 2-3.

11. *Spirit* 120 (3 Jan. 1891): 933; *Spirit* 121 (20 June 1891): 914–15 (quotes). For a view of the CIJC steeplechase course, copied from the French track Autueil, see *Spirit* 128 (24 Mar. 1894): 335.

12. *NYT,* 2 Oct. 1891, 3-4. The second day of the Jewish New Year (Rosh Hashanah) was on 3 October 1891, which purportedly boosted crowds, but not among observant Jews. *NYT,* 4 Oct. 1891, 2-4.

13. *Spirit* 120 (3 Jan. 1891): 933. On women betting on racing in Great Britain, see Huggins, *Flat Racing,* 105–6, 110–11, 213–14.

14. *NYT,* 14 June 1890, 3-2; *NYT,* 3 July 1892, 14-1.

15. *NYT,* 16 Apr. 1891, 5-1. He admitted to the Lexow commission having made $350,000 from information from men like Jay Gould and was reportedly worth $1.5 million then. On Byrnes, see his obituary, *NYT,* 8 May 1910, 1-1; James F. Richardson, *The New York Police, Colonial Times to 1901,* 209–13, 237, 250; Timothy J. Gilfoyle, *A Pickpocket's Tale: The Underworld of Nineteenth-Century New York,* 249–54; and H. Paul Jeffers, *Commissioner Roosevelt: The Story of Theodore Roosevelt and the New York City Police, 1895–1897,* 83.

16. *NYT,* 16 Apr. 1891, 5-1. Byrnes was in effect already in charge of the department since he became chief inspector in 1888 when Superintendent Murphy was very ill. See *NYT,* 10 Dec. 1893, 13.

17. *NYT,* 25 May 1892, 2-1; Flavel Scott Mimes, "The Study of a Pool-Room." On social behavior that flaunted traditional norms at turn-of-the-century Coney Island, see Kasson, *Amusing the Million.*

18. *NYT,* 18 Sept. 1892, 3-1, 11-3; *NYT,* 13 Sept. 1892, 3-1 (quote); Mimes, "Study of a Pool-Room."

19. *BE,* 7 May 1893, 17-3.

20. Ibid.

21. Hotaling, *They're Off!* 154–56. Headlines inspired by Bly's exposé in the *World* included "Wild Vortex of Gambling and Betting by Men, Women, and Children" and "Sports, Touts, Criminals, and Race-Track Riff-Raff Crazed by the Mania for Gold." Cited in Hotaling, *They're Off!* 137–38, 146–47.

22. Hotaling, *They're Off!* 154–56.

23. Ibid., 154, 156.

24. Brooke Kroeger, *Nellie Bly: Daredevil, Reporter, Feminist,* 156; *NYW,* 19 Aug. 1894, 21-4; *NYW,* 26 Aug. 1894, 21-4.

25. *NYTr,* 25 Apr. 1886, 4-4. On the Jockey Club, which dates to about 1752, see Vamplew, *Turf,* 77–109; and Huggins, *Flat Racing,* 174–203.

26. *NYTr,* 16 Jan. 1887, 4-3; *NYTr,* 6 Sept. 1887, 4-3 (quote).

27. *NYTr,* 17 Mar. 1890, 6-3.

28. Ibid.; *NYT,* 11 Jan. 1892, 2-3.

29. See, for example, *NYT,* 15 July 1885, 2-1; *NYT,* 4 Aug. 1893, 2-4; and *NYT,* 11 Sept. 1896, 6-7.

30. *ANB,* s.v. "Belmont, August II."

31. W. Robertson, *Thoroughbred Racing,* 175; *Spirit* 122 (26 Dec. 1891): 868; *Spirit* 126 (23 Sept. 1893): 295; *NYT,* 18 Jan. 1892, 2-5; *NYT,* 19 Feb. 1892, 8-3.

32. *NYTr,* 19 Jan. 1891, 2-5.

33. *NYTr,* 20 Apr. 1891, 2-3; *New York Sun,* 20 Apr. 1891, 5-4; *NYT,* 29 Feb. 1892, 3-6. The *Times* claimed Bowers helped the poolrooms fight the CIJC in 1891.

34. *NYT,* 29 Feb. 1892, 3-6.

35. *Spirit* 124 (17 Sept. 1892): 296.

36. *NYT,* 26 June 1891, 2-2; *NYT,* 3 Aug. 1891, 2-3; *NYT,* 23 Dec. 1891, 8-3; *NYT,* 15 Oct. 1892, 10-1; *NYT,* 17 May 1893, 3-1; *NYT,* 20 May 1893, 9-3; *Spirit* 122 (26 Dec. 1891): 868–69; *Spirit* 122 (2 Jan. 1892): 904.

37. *Spirit* 132 (26 Dec. 1896): 703 (quote); *BE,* 28 Dec. 1896, 2-7.

38. *Spirit* 122 (9 Jan. 1892): 965 (quote); *Spirit* 126 (23 Sept. 1893): 295; *NYT,* 17 May 1893, 3-1; *NYT,* 20 May 1893, 9-3 (quote); Hotaling, *They're Off!* 146.

39. *BE,* 10 Aug. 1893, 4-2.

40. Ibid.

41. *NYT,* 23 July 1893, 1-2; *NYT,* 24 Aug. 1893, 5-3; *BE,* 8 Sept. 1893, 2-3; *NYTr,* 23 Jan. 1894, 5-1; *NYTr,* 27 Jan. 1894, 4-4.

42. *Spirit* 126 (23 Sept. 1893): 295.

43. Ibid.

44. *ANB,* s.v. "Croker, Richard"; *NYT,* 14 July 1907, V: 4-1. For Croker's obituary, see *NYT,* 30 Apr. 1922, 1-1; Gustavus Myers, *History of Tammany Hall;* M. R. Werner, *Tammany Hall;* Alfred Henry Lewis, *Richard Croker;* Lothrop Stoddard, *Master of Manhattan: The Life of Richard Croker;* and Alfred Connable and Edward Silberfarb, *Tigers of Tammany: Nine Men Who Ruled New York,* 209–10.

45. William Riordan, ed., *Plunkitt of Tammany Hall,* 3–6; *NYT,* 5 Dec. 1915, 19-1; *NYT,* 30 Apr. 1922, 1-1; "Richard Croker" (editorial), *NYT,* 1 May 1922, 14-2; *NYT,* 3 May 1922, 18-3; *NYT,* 13 May 1922, 9-3. On Croker and Freedman, see Riess, *Touching Base,* 72. Senator Plunkitt got a bill passed that appropriated funds for a racetrack (speedway) in Central Park for trotters in 1892. But then Croker and Grant came out against it, and Plunkitt had it repealed. See "A Moral of Late Events."

46. *NYT,* 8 Mar. 1893, 1-7; *BE,* 22 Mar. 1893, 5-7; *BE,* 10 Aug. 1893, 4-2; *NYTr,* 17 Mar. 1893, 5-1; *ANB,* s.v. "Croker, Richard."

47. *BE,* 1 Feb. 1893, 4-3.

48. *NYT,* 8 Nov. 1892, 9-3; *NYT,* 4 Feb. 1893, 6-1; *NYT,* 18 Mar. 1893, 1-7. The other stockholders in the Jerome Park Villa Site and Improvement Association included the bookmaker James Kelly, as well as Theodore Moss, Fred A. Lovecraft, Mrs. Lansing, Miss Catherine Jerome, and John Bloodgood. The city condemned the track in 1890 and acquired Jerome Park (which today surrounds the reservoir) in 1895. The reservoir was not completed until 1906 in the Kingsbridge Heights section of the Bronx. The reservoir was placed on the National Register of Historic Places in 2000. See New York City Department of Parks, "Jerome Park."

49. *CDN,* 27 Sept. 1893, 10-1.

50. *ANB,* s.v. "Croker, Richard"; *NYT,* 14 July 1907, V: 4-1; Myers, *History of Tammany Hall;* Werner, *Tammany Hall;* Lewis, *Richard Croker.*

51. *NYT,* 6 June 1907, 6-2; *NYT,* 14 July 1907, V: 4-1.

52. *NYT,* 6 June 1907, 1-1, 3-4; *NYT,* 30 Apr. 1922, 1-1.

53. "40 Percent Reduction in Racing Pursuits" (editorial), *BE,* 10 Aug. 1893, 4-2; *BE,* 23 Oct. 1893, 2-3; *CDN,* 21 Aug. 1893, 5-1. For Daly's obituary, see *NYT,* 13 Nov. 1900, 2-3.

54. Quoted in *NEN,* 3 Mar. 1893, 5-1.

55. *NYT,* 16 May 1893, 1-7.

56. *NYT,* 16 May 1893, 1-7, 2-1, 14-1; *NYT,* 17 May 1893, 6-1.

57. *NYT,* 16 May 1893, 2-2.

58. On the Suburban, see *BE,* 21 June 1893, 5-5; *NYT,* 21 June 1893, 8-1; and *CDN,* 22 June 1893, 8-1. On the Realization, see *BE,* 16 June 1893, 9-1; and *BE,* 2 July 1893, 3-3.

59. *Spirit* 127 (14 Apr. 1894): 458. The *Tribune* claimed that only the BJC made money. See *NYTr,* 3 Jan. 1894, 4-4.

60. *NYT,* 13 Dec. 1892, 6-2; *NYT,* 24 Nov. 1893, 3-5; *CT,* 27 Nov. 1893, 4-1; *Spirit* 126 (7 Oct. 1893): 366; W. Robertson, *Thoroughbred Racing,* 160.

61. *CDN,* 9 Dec. 1893, 3-1; *CT,* 27 Nov. 1893, 4-1.

62. "The Profits of Book-Makers"; *BE,* 23 Oct. 1893, 2-3.

63. *CDN,* 9 Aug. 1893, 2-1.

64. Ibid. It is not surprising that such a critical commentary appeared in the *Chicago Daily News,* which was ardently crusading to halt racetrack gambling.

65. *CDN,* 2 Sept. 1893, 3-1; *CDN,* 20 Sept. 1893, 2-2.

66. *Spirit* 126 (16 Sept. 1893): 262. Lorillard did have his own impecadillos and had a reputation as the sorest loser on the racing circuit. *NYT,* 20 May 1893, 2-7.

67. "Profits of Book-Makers." According to the author, "Clerks, small wage-earners, cashiers, tradesmen of various kinds, professional men, blacklegs, pickpockets, and criminals of various kinds jostle and elbow each other in the betting-ring, excited with the hope of winning money without working for it." Ibid., 1131.

68. *NYT,* 8 Sept. 1893, 8-4; *NYT,* 29 Dec. 1893, 6-1; *CDN,* 16 Jan. 1894, 2-1.

69. *NYT,* 29 Dec. 1893, 6-2; *CDN,* 16 Jan. 1894, 2-2; *NYTr,* 13 Feb. 1894, 9-1; *NYTr,* 16 Mar. 1894, 4-3.

70. *NYTr,* 22 Jan. 1894, 8-1.

71. *NYTr,* 16 Mar. 1894, 4-3.

72. *NYT,* 30 Aug. 1893, 3; *NYT,* 29 Dec. 1893, 6-2; *NYT,* 3 Jan. 1894, 3-5; *NYT,* 20 June 1897, SM4; *NYTr,* 16 Mar. 1894, 4-3. The only tracks thriving were the independent Sheepshead Bay and upstate Saratoga. On the poor situation of Board of Control tracks, see also *CDN,* 26 Feb. 1894, 2-1.

73. *NYT,* 29 Dec. 1893, 6-2; *NYT,* 3 Jan. 1894, 3-5; *NYTr,* 3 Jan. 1894, 4-4; Edward L. Bowen, *The Jockey Club's Illustrated History of Thoroughbred Racing in America,* 96.

74. *NYTr,* 3 Feb. 1894, 2-3; *NYTr,* 11 Feb. 1894, 3-5; "The Need of Turf Reforms" (editorial), *NYT,* 12 Feb. 1894, 6-3; *ANB,* s.v. "Belmont, August II."

75. *NYT,* 5 May 1894, 3-1. Membership list in Box 27, Folder 38, Belmont Family Papers.

76. *NYT,* 5 May 1894, 3-1; *NYT,* 29 May 1894, 2-5; *NYT,* 30 Nov. 1910, 1-7; W. Robertson, *Thoroughbred Racing,* 175; Bowen, *Jockey Club's Illustrated History,* 96.

77. *BE,* 4 May 1894, 9-7 (quote); *BE,* 11 May 1894, 9-3; *Spirit* 128 (27 Oct. 1894): 516.

78. *NYT,* 29 May 1894, 2-5; *NYT,* 11 May 1894, 3-1. Men from Louisville, Cincinnati, Nashville, and Lexington founded the American Turf Congress in 1866 in Cincinnati. See J. Hirsch, *First Century,* 5.

79. *NYT,* 28 Dec. 1893, 9-7; *NYT,* 31 Dec. 1893, 4-5.

80. *NYT,* 22 Nov. 1893, 2-5; *NYT,* 8 May 1894, 3-1, 4-4; *NYT,* 23 May 1894, 2-5, 3-1; *Spirit* 126 (2 Dec. 1893): 642; *Spirit* 127 (12 May 1894): 618; *NYTr,* 8 May 1894, 11-1; *BE,* 7 May 1894, 1-5; *BE,* 8 May 1894, 4-4, 12-4. Judge Daniels ruled in *Brennan v. BBRA,* 56 Hun. 188 (1890), that in the fifty years before the enactment of Section 351 of the penal code, which prohibited bookmaking in 1877, bets could not be collected in court and it was illegal to make books anywhere. See *BE,* 13 May 1894, 13-6; and *NYTr,* 13 May 1894, 20-1.

81. *NYT,* 8 May 1894, 3-1, 4-4; *NYTr,* 8 May 1894, 11-2.

82. *Thomas D. Reilly v. Milton C. Gray* (28 NYS 811); *NYT,* 23 May 1894, 2-5, 4-4; *BE,* 24 May 1894, 6-5; *NYTr,* 13 May 1894, 20-1; *NYTr,* 23 May 1894, 5-2; Liebman, "Horseracing in New York," 553.

83. *NYT,* 15 May 1894, 1-5; *NYT,* 16 May 1894, 2-4; *NYTr,* 15 May 1894, 4-1; *BE,* 17 May 1894, 9-3.

84. *BE,* 25 May 1894, 9-4; Riess, *Touching Base,* 87, 142–43; Louis Heaton Pink, *Gaynor, the Tammany Mayor Who Swallowed the Tiger: Lawyer, Judge, Philosopher,* 95; Lately Thomas, *The Mayor Who Mastered New York: The Life and Opinions of William J. Gaynor,* 91, 115–16, 467–68.

85. *NYTr,* 29 May 1894, 3-3; *NYT,* 9-5; *In re Dwyer,* 14 Misc. 204 (N.Y. Sup. Ct., 1894); Liebman, "Horseracing in New York," 553; *BE,* 29 May 1894, 6-3.

86. *NYTr,* 12 Feb. 1894, 3-1; *NYTr,* 13 Feb. 1894, 9-1; "The Need of Turf Reforms" (editorial), *NYTr,* 12 Feb. 1894, 6-3.

87. *NYTr,* 12 Feb. 1894, 3-1; "Taking the Receipts of Racing," *NYTr,* 27 Feb. 1894, 6-4. The NYJC, which originally had nearly three thousand members, raised its annual dues from twenty-five to fifty dollars.

88. *CDN,* 3 Mar. 1894, 5-2; *NYTr,* 1 Apr. 1894, 8-2; *Spirit* 127 (7 Apr. 1894): 422; *Spirit* 127 (14 Apr. 1894): 458. The CIJC hardly made expenses in 1893, while the NYJC did not do much better. The BJC did make money with large crowds and more modest expenses. *Spirit* 127 (14 Apr. 1894): 458.

89. *NYTr*, 21 May 1894, 2-1; *BE*, 16 May 1894, 4-3.

90. *BE*, 25 May 1894, 5-3.

91. *BE*, 29 June 1894, 1-6; *BE*, 3 July 1894, 5-5; *BE*, 24 Sept. 1894, 5-6. A lease for a new track cost one thousand dollars. *BE*, 12 Aug. 1894, 16-5.

92. *BE*, 3 July 1894, 5-5; *BE*, 5 July 1894, 5-5.

93. *BE*, 1 Aug. 1894, 1-3; *BE*, 3 July 1895, 5-5; *Spirit* 127 (14 July 1894): 16; *NYT*, 4 July 1894, 6-1; *NYT*, 24 Sept. 1894, 8-2.

94. *BE*, 2 Sept. 1894, 3-5; *BE*, 5 Sept. 1894, 4-2; *BE*, 12 Sept. 1894, 4-7; *BE*, 13 Sept. 1894, 4-7; *BE*, 17 Oct. 1895, 5-4.

95. *NYT*, 17 Sept. 1894, 3-3. Belmont was in correspondence with Judge Gaynor regarding the Maspeth course. See August Belmont II to William Gaynor, 5 Oct. 1895, Box 27, Folder 37, Belmont Family Papers. The track was sold at a sheriff's sale for $4,280 to meet a judgment, though valued at $50,000. *BE*, 17 Jan. 1896, 10-4.

96. *BE*, 5 Aug. 1894, 7-5; *NYT*, 26 Sept. 1894, 3-7; *NYT*, 27 Sept. 1894, 12-1.

97. *BE*, 3 July 1894, 5-5; *Spirit* 128 (21 July 1894): 9; New York Racing Association, "Media Guide, 2009," 9; W. Robertson, *Thoroughbred Racing*, 151.

98. *BE*, 31 July 1894, 2-3; *BE*, 1 Aug. 1894, 2-3.

99. *Spirit* 128 (21 July 1894): 12; *Spirit* 128 (18 Aug. 1894): 258; *NYT*, 30 Dec. 1894, 20-1.

100. *NYT*, 8 July 1894, 13; *Spirit* 127 (7 July 1894): 982; *CDN*, 15 Oct. 1894, 6-1.

101. *CDN*, 21 June 1894, 2-1.

102. *NYTr*, 14 Jan. 1894, 22-1; *Spirit* 128 (15 Sept. 1894): 302.

103. *NYT*, 6 Dec. 1892, 3-5; Kapsales, "From the Gilded Age to Progressivism," 17, 62; Charles Trevelyan, "Our Turf's Transition," 225. The *Chicago Daily News* reported, without corroboration, that despite the faltering economy, New York's principal tracks all cleared at least two hundred thousand dollars (presumably their gross). See *CDN*, 24 Sept. 1894, 7-2.

104. *New York Sun*, 22 Feb. 1895, 9-2; Anthony Comstock, *Race Track Infamy; or, Do Gamblers Own New York State? A Scathing Exposure of How the Constitution of New York State Is Flagrantly Violated by Common Gamblers*, 19–20; *Spirit* 131 (22 Feb. 1896): 153–54. As difficult as it is to determine income, it is even more difficult, if not impossible, to determine the track's expenses. There were usually five or six races each day. At six races a day, the average purse was $2,469.14; at five, the average purses was $2,962.96. However, most races had only a $600 purse. At the rate of one stake event a day, the feature races would average $11,814.81 to $12,681.48. The purses of stakes races would include entrance fees and other sources, making it unclear how much of the purses came from the track. The state report included the $400,000 spent on purses but not the other costs of running a racetrack

105. *CDN*, 16 Oct. 1894, 2-1. This estimate is not too far off the mark but sets the number of racing dates at 152. At 27 days, this would put the CIJC at $589,410, which is less than 7 percent off from the actual gross income.

106. Hotaling, *They're Off!* 136–38; Asbury, *Sucker's Progress*, 388.

107. *NYW*, 19 Aug. 1894, 29, cited in Hotaling, *They're Off!* 147; Bradley, *Such Was Saratoga*, 208; *Sporting World*, 6 Sept. 1892, 1, cited in Hotaling, *They're Off!* 147 (see also 146–47).

108. Bradley, *Such Was Saratoga*, 238; *Spirit* 128 (28 July 1894): 38; Hotaling, *They're Off!* 150.

109. Hotaling, *They're Off!* 147–48; *Spirit* 128 (28 July 1894): 38.

110. Hotaling, *They're Off!* 148–49, 156, 158–59. Kearney served as president of Saratoga until his death in 1900. For Kearney's obituary, see *NYT*, 26 Feb. 1900, 2-5.

7. The Poolroom Business in Metropolitan New York, 1863–98

1. The term *poolroom* is often confused with *pool halls,* the site of billiard games.

2. Hotaling, *They're Off!* 44–45; D. Johnson, "Sinful Business," 36; *NYT,* 27 July 1866, 5-2; *NYT,* 4 June 1867, 8-3; *NYT,* 21 May 1872, 1-5; *NYT,* 25 Apr. 1875, 12-1; *NYT,* 3 July 1875, 2-3. On election wagering, see *NYT,* 31 Oct. 1875, 1-1; *NYT,* 25 June 1876, 1-1; *NYT,* 13 Dec. 1876, 1-4. The term *poolroom* did not appear in the *Brooklyn Eagle* until 1878, in reference to baseball games fixed by the Louisville Grays in 1877. *BE,* 27 Jan. 1878, 3-3.

3. *Spirit* 94 (27 Oct. 1877): 348.

4. Huggins, *Flat Racing,* 106–8. See also Clapson, *Bit of a Flutter;* and McKibbin, "Working-Class Gambling."

5. *NYT,* 5 May 1877, 8; *NYT,* 5 June 1877, 5-4; *Clipper* 25 (24 Nov. 1877): 275.

6. *NYT,* 16 July 1877, 4-3, 8-1; *NYT,* 19 July 1877, 8-1.

7. *NYT,* 5 June 1877, 5-4; *NYT,* 7 June 1877, 8-2; *NYT,* 13 June 1877, 8-2.

8. *NYT,* 20 Oct. 1877, 5-3; *Spirit* 94 (27 Oct. 1877): 348.

9. *NYT,* 4 Nov. 1877, 5-2; *Clipper* 25 (24 Nov. 1877): 275 (quote).

10. *NYT,* 22 June 1878, 2-6.

11. *Spirit* 96 (26 Oct. 1878): 321.

12. *NYT,* 22 Aug. 1879, 8-2; *NYT,* 3 June 1880, 8-3; 23 June 1880, *NYT,* 8-1; *NYT,* 2 Aug. 1886, 4-4 (quote).

13. *Spirit* 98 (11 Oct. 1879): 241.

14. *NYT,* 3 June 1880, 8-3.

15. *NYT,* 23 July 1880, 8-1; "Long Island City Pool Rooms," 555.

16. *NYT,* 23 July 1880, 8-1.

17. *NYT,* 3 June 1880, 8-3; *NYT,* 23 June 1880, 8-1 (quote).

18. *NYT,* 23 June 1880, 8-1. A combination bet could be as simple as selecting winners in three straight races or picking the win, place (second), and show (third) horses. There were also other permutations, depending on the willingness of an entrepreneur to accept different wagers. In these bets, all horses received a number for identification purposes. In some cases, a race might include some horses that no one wanted to bet on. This group of horses constituted "the field." Bettors could wager on them as a single unit. See *NYT,* 13 June 1877, 8-2.

19. *NYT,* 13 June 1877, 8-2.

20. Ibid.

21. Ibid.

22. Ibid.

23. *NYT,* 24 June 1880, 8-1.

24. *NYT,* 4 Aug. 1880, 8-1. The men were later acquitted. *NYT,* 17 Aug. 1880, 8-3.

25. *NYT,* 4 June 1879, 8-3. Long Island City did not have the best national reputation. See, for example, "Long Island City Poolrooms," 555; and "Long Island City," 627. On boxing at Long Island City, see Riess, "In the Ring and Out," 98–99.

26. *NYT,* 1 June 1887, 8-3.

27. *NYT,* 2 Oct. 1881, 2-2.

28. "The War on Law-Breakers," *NYTr,* 27 Aug. 1882, 7-5; *NYT,* 7 Oct. 1882, 8-5.

29. Comstock, *Traps for the Young,* cited in R. Johnson, "Anthony Comstock," 134–35.

30. *NYT*, 23 Aug. 1882, 3-1; *NYT*, 7 Oct. 1882, 8-5; *NYT*, 10 Oct. 1882, 2-4; *NYT*, 7 Jan. 1883, 5-4, for another raid in New York City. On SPV arrests, see Bates, *Weeder in the Garden of the Lord*, 108–9. For Anthony Comstock's fight against the underworld, see Comstock, *Gambling Outrages.*

31. *NYT*, 5 July 1881, 3-1; *NYT*, 6 July 1881, 8-3; *NYT*, 2 June 1890, 5-3.

32. *NYT*, 15 Oct. 1883, 1-1.

33. Ibid.

34. *NYT*, 4 Feb. 1885, 3-5; Somers, *Rise of Sports in New Orleans*, 100. On Sunday baseball in the late nineteenth century, see Riess, *Touching Base*, 134–55.

35. *NYT*, 4 Feb. 1885, 3-5.

36. *NYT*, 7 Mar. 1885, 5-5; *NYT*, 18 June 1885, 8-4; *NYT*, 22 Mar. 1887, 8-4.

37. Juergens, *Joseph Pulitzer*, 124.

38. *NYT*, 2 June 1887, 5-6.

39. Ibid.

40. *NYT*, 31 May 1887, 4-3; *NYT*, 1 June 1887, 4-1; *NYT*, 18 June 1887, 8-6; *NYT*, 22 Jan. 1888, 16-4; New York City, Department of Police, *Annual Report of the Police Department of the City of New York* (1887), 37.

41. "The Quasi-Anti-Pool Bill," *CT*, 4 June 1887, 4-3; Rufus Jarman, "The Great Race Track Caper."

42. *NYT*, 9 June 1887, 2-5. On Howe and Hummel, see Richard H. Rovere, *Howe and Hummel: Their True and Scandalous History*, 6.

43. *NYT*, 1 June 1887, 8-3; *NYT*, 2 June 1887, 5-6 (quote); *NYT*, 13 Jan. 1888, 5-3. Other open pool-rooms included Shipsy and Co., 70 Bowery; Walters and Levin, 162 Fulton; De Lacy's 33 Park Row; Tully's, 14 Beekman Street; and Mahoney and Co., 86 Broad Street. See *NYT*, 1 June 1887, 8-3.

44. *NYT*, 28 Aug. 1887, 2-2; *NYT*, 21 May 1901, 9-1; Riess, "In the Ring and Out," 98.

45. *NYT*, 28 Aug. 1887, 2-2.

46. *NYT*, 10 May 1888, 8-5; New York City Police Department, *Annual Report* (1886–1891).

47. *NYT*, 18 Apr. 1889, 8-5; *NYT*, 30 Oct. 1889, 8-3; *NYTr*, 24 Apr. 1889, 6-3.

48. *NYT*, 18 Apr. 1889, 8-5; *NYT*, 23 Apr. 1889, 5-3.

49. *NYT*, 3 Mar. 1889, 8-3 (quote); "Pool Selling a National Question" (letter to the editor), *NYT*, 18 Dec. 1893, 9-4.

50. *NYTr*, 22 Apr. 1889, 10-1; "Close the City Poolrooms," (editorial), *NYTr*, 10 May 1889, 6-2; *NYTr*, 15 Mar. 1893, 6-4.

51. *BE*, 22 Mar. 1893, 5-7 (quote); *BE*, 14 Aug. 1892, 9-3 (quote), 14-1; *NYT*, 29 Mar. 1891, 3-2.

52. *NYT*, 20 June 1889, 8-4; *BE*, 22 Mar. 1893, 5-7.

53. *NYT*, 19, Feb. 1890, 8-2.

54. *NYT*, 5 Jan. 1890, 6-2; *NYTr*, 4 Jan. 1890, 3-5.

55. *NYT*, 5 Jan. 1889, 6-2; *NYT*, 11 July 1889, 6-7; *NYT*, 5 Jan. 1890, 6-2; *NYT*, 16 Mar. 1891, 5-1; "The Office Boy Takes His Employer to the Poolrooms," by "One of the Victims" (letter to the editor), *NYT*, 25 May 1890, 11-5.

56. "Office Boy Takes His Employer to the Poolrooms," by "One of the Victims" (letter to the editor), *NYT*, 25 May 1890, 11-5. De Lacy's partners there were Andrew Boyd and Samuel C. Seely. When the room closed in 1894, Boyd backed a handbook in partnership with Seely. In late 1894, Seely, the bookkeeper for the National Shoe and Leather Bank, absconded with about $250,000 of the bank's money. *NYT*, 30 Nov. 1894, 1-1.

57. *BE*, 21 Aug. 1897, 1-7. On the boxing connections of Mayor Gleason, see Riess, "In the Ring and Out," 98.

58. *NYT*, 30 Dec. 1890, 8-4; *NYT*, 6 Jan. 1891, 8-6; *NYT*, 16 Mar. 1891, 5-1; *BE*, 10 Jan. 1891, 4.

59. *NYT*, 15 Mar. 1891, 5-3 (quote); *NYT*, 7 Mar. 1891, 2-2.

60. *NYTr*, 20 Apr. 1891, 2-3; *NYT*, 6 Jan. 1891, 8-6; *NYT*, 16 Mar. 1891, 5-1. The *Tribune* reported that each track contributed three thousand dollars, so there was uncertainty about the exact amount raised to fight the poolrooms. See *NYTr*, 20 Apr. 1891, 3-3.

61. *NYT*, 29 Mar. 1891, 3-1; "Deserves Great Credit: The *Times'* Successful Warfare on Pools Commended" (from *The Christian at Work*), *NYT*, 24 Apr. 1891, 4-7; *NYT*, 23 Mar. 1891, 5-3.

62. *NYT*, 24 Mar. 1891, 1-7; *NYT*, 25 Mar. 1891, 2-2, 5-5; *NYT*, 29 May 1891, 1-5; *NYT*, 30 May 1891, 1-1.

63. *NYT*, 16 Mar. 1891, 5-1; *NYT*, 18 Mar. 1891, 5-1; *NYT*, 24 Mar. 1891, 1-7.

64. *NYT*, 28 Mar. 1891, 2-1; *NYT*, 29 Mar. 1891, 3-1; *NYT*, 1 Apr. 1891, 3-1 (quote).

65. *NYT*, 6 Apr. 1891, 2-6. See also "Winter Racing and City Pool Rooms" (editorial), *NYT*, 15 Feb. 1893, 6-4.

66. *NYT*, 29 Mar. 1891, 3-1; *NYT*, 6 Apr. 1891, 2-5; *NYT*, 9 Apr. 1891, 3-1; *NYT*, 10 Apr. 1891, 1-7; *NYT*, 14 Apr. 1891, 4-3; *NYT*, 15 Apr. 1891, 4-1; *NYTr*, 21 Apr. 1891, 3-1; Rovere, *Howe and Hummel*, 6.

67. *NYT*, 29 Mar. 1891, 3-1; *NYT*, 4 Apr. 1891, 2-3. On Morris and the lottery, see *NYT*, 6 Mar. 1891, 8.

68. On Sullivan, see Czitrom, "Underworlds and Underdogs," 542–44; Steven P. Erie, *Rainbow's End: Irish Americans and the Dilemmas of Urban Machine Politics, 1840–1885,* 100–102; and Richard F. Welch, *King of the Bowery: Big Tim Sullivan, Tammany Hall, and New York City from the Gilded Age to the Progressive Era.*

69. *NYT*, 24 Mar. 1891, 2-2; *NYT*, 25 Mar. 1891, 5-4; *NYT*, 6 Apr. 1891, 2-6; *NYTr*, 14 Mar. 1893, 2-1. According to another source, the city's sixty poolrooms had a fund of $150,000 to kill the Ives Law and aid pool seller Fisher who had been convicted of gambling. *CT*, 19 Apr. 1891, 43-5. On Sullivan's boxing career, see Riess, "In the Ring and Out," 99, 102–3.

70. *NYT*, 24 Mar. 1891, 2-2; *NYT*, 25 Mar. 1891, 5-4; *NYT*, 6 Apr. 1891, 2-6.

71. *NYT*, 11 May 1891, 2-4; *NYT*, 16 May 1891, 1-5; *NYT*, 17 May 1891, 2; *NYTr*, 16 May 1891, 3-4. For an example of a printed "Memorandum of Contract to be executed at the Race Track," see *NYTr*, 22 Apr. 1891, 3-1.

72. *NYT*, 11 May 1891, 2-4; *NYT*, 16 May 1891, 1-5; *NYTr*, 16 May 1891, 3-4; *NYTr*, 25 June 1891, 2-4.

73. *NYT*, 16 May 1891, 1-5.

74. *BE*, 22 May 1891, 1-4; *BE*, 23 May 1891, 4-2; *BE*, 24 May 1891, 6-2; *NYTr*, 23 May 1891, 6-4; *NYTr*, 21 Sept. 1891, 2-1; Jarman, "Great Race Track Caper," 92.

75. *NYT*, 17 May 1891, 2-3.

76. *NYT*, 17 May 1891, 2-3; *NYT*, 19 May 1891, 2-1; *NYT*, 22 May 1891, 5-5; *NYT*, 28 May 1891, 8-1; *NYT*, 29 May 1891, 1-5; *NYT*, 25 June 1891, 2; *BE*, 15 Sept. 1891, 4-3.

77. *NYT*, 23 May 1891, 2-5.

78. *NYT*, 24 June 1891, 8-6; *NYT*, 25 June 1891, 5-2 (quote). See also *NYT*, 20 June 1892, 6-2. Such connections between elite Democrats and Tammanyites were pointed out in David Hammack, *Power and Society: Greater New York at the Turn of the Century,* esp. 101, 315.

79. *NYT*, 24 June 1891, 8-6; *NYT*, 3 July 1891, 5-3.

80. *NYT*, 3 July 1891, 5-3.

81. *NYT*, 16 Sept. 1891, 4-1.

82. *NYT*, 16 Sept. 1891, 5-4; *NYT*, 18 Sept. 1891, 5-6; *NYT*, 20 Sept. 1891, 8-6; *NYT*, 2 Oct. 1891, 3-4.

83. *NYT*, 17 Sept. 1891, 2-5; "History of the Telescope-Binocular."

84. *NYT*, 14 Sept. 1891, 2-5; *NYT*, 15 Sept. 1891, 2-4; *NYT*, 16 Sept. 1891, 5-4; *NYT*, 17 Sept. 1891, 2-5; *NYT*, 19 Sept. 1891, 5-6; *NYT*, 20 Sept. 1891, 8-6; *NYT*, 25 Sept. 1891, 3-3; *NYT*, 26 Sept. 1891, 1-5; *NYT*, 27 Sept. 1891, 8-5.

85. *NYTr*, 7 Mar. 1892, 6-4.

86. Ibid. (quote); *NYTr*, 16 Jan. 1893, 3-3; *NYTr*, 8 Apr. 1893, 6-3; *NYTr*, 17 Apr. 1892, 6-5. One year later, poolroom keepers claimed that an organized gang of "Guttenberg buccaneers and South Jersey pirates" was swindling them by fixing the races and sending trusted agents to New York to bet with the pool sellers. See *NYTr*, 17 Mar. 1893, 5-2.

87. *NYT*, 7 July 1892, 3-1.

88. John Gilmer Speed, "The Pool-Room Evil"; Mimes, "Study of a Pool-Room."

89. *NYTr*, 9 Jan. 1893, 5-4; *NYTr*, 9 Mar. 1893, 6-2 (quote); *NYTr*, 13 Mar. 1893, 6-5; *NYT*, 14 Mar. 1893, 8-1. The *Tribune* set the number at the start of the year at 175, but the *Times* estimated 100 then and about 60 in March.

90. *NYTr*, 20 Apr. 1893, 10-1.

91. *BE*, 22 Mar. 1893, 5-5. See also *NYTr*, 17 Mar. 1893, 5-1; *NYTr*, 14 Dec. 1903, 8-2.

92. *NYT*, 27 Oct. 1894, 9-1; *NYT*, 30 Dec. 1894, 1-5.

93. *NYT*, 14 Mar. 1893, 8-1; *NYT*, 15 Mar. 1893, 8-4, 9-1; *NYT*, 15 Mar. 1893, 4-2; *NYT*, 18 Dec. 1893, 9-4; *NYTr*, 14 Mar. 1893, 1-7; *NYTr*, 15 Mar. 1893, 1-7; *Clipper* 40 (25 Mar. 1893): 41.

94. *NYT*, 15 Mar. 1893, 4-2 (quote); *NYT*, 17 Mar. 1893, 5-2; *NYT*, 25 Mar. 1893, 9-1; *NYT*, 8 Apr. 1893, 6-3.

95. *NYTr*, 15 Mar. 1893, 6-2.

96. *NYT*, 15 Mar. 1893, 4-2; *NYT*, 17 Mar. 1893, 5-2; *NYT*, 25 Mar. 1893, 9-1; *NYT*, 8 Apr. 1893, 6-3.

97. *NYTr*, 9 Mar. 1893, 6-2; *NYTr*, 13 Mar. 1893, 6-5; *NYTr*, 14 Mar. 1893, 2-1; *NYTr*, 23 Mar. 1893, 3-9, 6-2; *NYTr*, 20 Apr. 1893, 6-6.

98. *NYTr*, 20 Apr. 1893, 6-6; *NYT*, 25 Mar. 1893, 4-3, 9-1; *NYT*, 1 Apr. 1893, 4-1; *NYT*, 15 Apr. 1893, 1-7; *NYT*, 28 May 1893, 1-5; *NYT*, 3 June 1893, 3-4; *NYT*, 24 Apr. 1901, 7-2.

99. *NYT*, 16 Apr. 1893, 16-7; *NYT*, 28 May 1893, 1-5; *NYT*, 3 June 1893, 3-4. A similar law passed in Connecticut. The poolroom men there were concerned about what happened to the fund of fifty thousand dollars they had given to lobbyists. See *NYT*, 14 Apr. 1893, 10-7.

100. New York City Police Department, *Annual Report* (1888–1895).

101. *NYTr*, 14 July 1894, 8-1; *NYTr*, 26 July 1894, 3-2; *NYTr*, 28 July 1894, 3-4; *NYTr*, 22 Aug. 1894, 3-4; *NYT*, 7 Feb. 1894, 5; *NYT*, 11 Aug. 1894, 8-5; *NYT*, 15 Oct. 1894, 5-3.

102. *NYT*, 15 Oct. 1894, 5-3.

103. *NYTr*, 14 July 1894, 8-1; *NYTr*, 26 July 1894, 3-2; *NYTr*, 28 July 1894, 3-4; *NYTr*, 22 Aug. 1894, 3-4; *NYT*, 7 Feb. 1894, 5-2; *NYT*, 11 Aug. 1894, 8-5; *NYT*, 15 Oct. 1894, 5-3.

104. See, for example, Richardson, *New York Police*, 238–40; Isabelle K. Savell, *Politics in the Gilded Age in New York State and Rockland County: A Biography of Senator Clarence Lexow*; and New York Legislature, Senate, *Report and Proceedings of the Senate Committee Appointed to Investigate the Police Department of the City of New York*.

105. *NYT*, 27 Oct. 1894, 9-4; *NYT*, 22 Dec. 1894, 1-5; *BE*, 9 Jan. 1895, 12-3.

106. *NYT*, 10 May 1895, 3-4; *NYT*, 24 Aug. 1895, 16-3. For examples of raids, see *NYT*, 14 June 1895, 1-5; *NYT*, 22 June 1895, 3-5; *NYT*, 8 Aug. 1895, 1-2; *NYT*, 11 Aug. 1895, 5-2; *NYT*, 25 Aug. 1895, 9-7; and *NYT*, 26 Aug. 1895, 9-4. For a raid on a women's poolroom, see *NYT*, 31 Aug. 1895, 8-3.

107. *NYT*, 29 Aug. 1895, 10-6; *NYT*, 23 Nov. 1895, 1-1.

108. *NYT*, 29 June 1895, 6-4; *NYT*, 29 Aug. 1895, 10-6; *NYT*, 20 Nov. 1895, 8; *NYT*, 22 Nov. 1895, 6-1; *NYT*, 23 Nov. 1895, 1-3; *BE*, 28 Aug. 1895, 2-4; *BE*, 29 Aug. 1895, 5-7; *Clipper* 43 (7 Dec. 1895): 636; Liebman, "Horseracing in New York," 554.

109. *BE*, 5 Sept. 1894, 4-2; *BE*, 13 Sept. 1894, 4-7.

110. *NYT*, 29 Aug. 1895, 10-6; *NYTr*, 1 Jan. 1896, 16-1; August Belmont II to James G. Bennett, 24 Sept. 1895, Box 27, Folder 37, Belmont Family Papers.

111. *NYT*, 29 Aug. 1895, 10-6; *NYT*, 13 Oct. 1895, 6-4; *NYT*, 14 Oct. 1895, 4-3; *NYT*, 15 Oct. 1895, 8-1; *BE*, 14 Oct. 1895, 4-3; *BE*, 15 Oct. 1895, 10-5; *BE*, 25 Oct. 1895, 10-3; *BE*, 19 Dec. 1895, 10-3; *NYTr*, 1 Jan. 1896, 16-1.

112. *NYT*, 25 Oct. 1895, 1-1; *NYT*, 26 Oct. 1895, 6-3; *NYT*, 28 Oct. 1895, 3-1; "Persecuting the Racing Men" (editorial), *NYT*, 28 Oct. 1895, 4-4.

113. *NYT*, 19 Dec. 1895, 7-5; *NYT*, 1 Jan. 1896, 4-4, 6-7.

114. *NYT*, 9 July 1896, 8-4.

115. *NYT*, 2 Oct. 1896, 1-3.

116. *BE*, 24 July 1897, 6-5; *BE*, 22 July 1897, 1-7; *BE*, 23 July 1897, 14-4.

117. Jay Stuart Berman, *Police Administration and Progressive Reform: Theodore Roosevelt as Police Commissioner of New York*, 100–101; New York Police Department, *Annual Report of Department of the City of New York for the Year Ending Dec. 31, 1896*, 19, 47, 52, 56; ibid., for the years 1884–99.

118. *NYTr*, 11 Sept. 1897, 3-2; *NYTr*, 12 Sept. 1897, II: 1-4; *NYT*, 11 Sept. 1897, 12-7; *NYT*, 6 June 1920, 24-1.

119. Franklin Mathews, "'Wide-Open' New York."

120. *NYT*, 9 Mar. 1898, 5-1; *NYT*, 12 Aug. 1903, 1-3; *NYT*, 13 May 1908, 1-7. On the Gambling Trust, see *NYT*, 20 Oct. 1901, 1-7, 2-3; *NYT*, 28 Oct. 1901, 2-1, 2-5; *NYT*, 31 Aug. 1902, 29-1; Josiah Flynt, "The Men Behind the Pool-Rooms"; Maxwell F. Marcuse, *This Was New York: A Nostalgic Picture of Gotham in the Gas Light Era*, 170–71; Lloyd Morris, *Incredible New York: High Life and Low Life of the Last One Hundred Years*, 226; and Asbury, *Sucker's Progress*, 451–57.

121. *NYT*, 9 Mar. 1898, 5-1.

122. Richardson, *New York Police*, 269–71.

123. *Spirit* 131 (22 Feb. 1896): 153–54; *Spirit* 133 (1 May 1897): 461; *TFF* 62 (21 Feb. 1896): 274; *NYTr*, 18 Feb. 1896, 15-5; *NYTr*, 11 Sept. 1897, 3-2; *NYTr*, 12 Sept. 1897, II: 1-4; *NYTr*, 16 June 1899, II: 3-3; *NYT*, 7 Apr. 1899, 1-4; *NYT*, 8 Apr. 1899, 7-1; Gerald Astor, *The New York Cops: An Informal History*, 89.

8. New York Racing under Attack, 1894–96

1. "Historical Timeline of the New York State Legislature."

2. *NYT*, 24 Sept. 1894, 8-2; *Spirit* 128 (8 Sept. 1894): 372.

3. *Spirit* 128 (8 Sept. 1894): 372; *Spirit* 128 (22 Dec. 1894): 778; *NYT*, 15 Oct. 1894, 5-4; "The Fourth Constitution of New York, 1894."

4. *Spirit* 128 (6 Oct. 1894): 408; *CDN*, 9 Nov. 1894, 9-1; *NYTr*, 24 Oct. 1894, 11-4; *NYTr*, 12 Nov. 1894, 3-3.

5. *Spirit* 128 (8 Sept. 1894): 372; *Spirit* 128 (22 Dec. 1894): 778; *NYT*, 10 Nov. 1894, 7-1. The Buffalo Association under President C. J. Hamlin had tried racing without betting with little success. President George Archer of the Rochester Association used pools to meet expenses. The New York Driving Club, an upper-class social club formed to promote trotting and improve the breed, often operated at a deficit, although its 1894 Grand Circuit meeting made a profit of twenty-five hundred dollars. See *Spirit* 128 (17 Nov. 1894): 620.

6. *CDN*, 7 Nov. 1894, 13-1. The press did not rate the Brooklyn tracks' real estate highly because they were far from city hall and too far back from the seashore. Morris Park, on the other hand, was a likely site for future construction. *CDN*, 14 Nov. 1894, 3-2.

7. "The Pool Selling Amendment," *NYT*, 15 Oct. 1894, 4-3; "Enemies of the Amendments," *NYT*, 16 Oct. 1894, 4-4.

8. *Spirit* 128 (8 Sept. 1894): 372.

9. *CDN*, 16 Oct. 1894, 2-1.

10. Ibid.

11. *NYTr*, 16 Oct. 1894, 3-1. On Chicago crime, see, for example, William T. Stead, *If Christ Came to Chicago*; and Herbert Asbury, *Gem of the Prairie: An Informal History of the Chicago Underworld*.

12. "Gambling and the Turf" (editorial), *NYT*, 21 Oct. 1894, 4-6.

13. Ibid.

14. *Spirit* 128 (3 Nov. 1894): 550.

15. *NYTr*, 24 Oct. 1894, 11-4; *NYTr*, 29 Oct. 1894, 6-4.

16. *NYTr*, 29 Oct. 1894, 6-3. See also *NYTr*, 5 Nov. 1894, 6-3. For a summary of the arguments against racing and gambling, see *NYTr*, 17 Dec. 1894, 3-3.

17. *CDN*, 7 Nov. 1894, 13-1; *NYTr*, 16 Oct. 1894, 3-2; *NYTr*, 31 Oct. 1894, 2-5; *NYTr*, 10 Nov. 1894, 1-4; *NYTr*, 17 Dec. 1894, 3-3; *NYTr*, 3 Jan. 1894, 4-4.

18. *Spirit* 128 (10 Nov. 1894): 586; *NYT*, 9 Dec. 1894, 4-3; *CDN*, 9 Nov. 1894, 9-1.

19. *CDN*, 9 Nov. 1894, 9-1. Morris in 1894 reportedly made $150,000 from his track operations. *NYT*, 29 Oct. 1894, 2-3.

20. *NYT*, 9 Dec. 1894, 4-3.

21. *NYTr*, 17 Dec. 1894, 3-3.

22. *BE*, 8 Nov. 1894, 1-3.

23. *BE*, 9 Nov. 1894, 4-1.

24. *BE*, 15 Dec. 1894, 6-3.

25. *Spirit* 128 (10 Nov. 1894): 586.

26. *NYT*, 12 Feb. 1895, 6-1; *NYT*, 23 Mar. 1895, 6-1; *NYTr*, 13 Feb. 1895, 6-4; *NYTr*, 7 Mar. 1895, 5-2; *NYTr*, 9 Mar. 1895, 6-3.

27. *NYT*, 12 Feb. 1895, 6-1; *NYT*, 23 Mar. 1895, 6-1; *NYTr*, 23 Mar. 1895, 2-4; Liebman, "Horseracing in New York," 554.

28. *NYT*, 12 Feb. 1895, 6-1; *NYT*, 23 Mar. 1895, 6-1; *NYTr*, 13 Feb. 1895, 6-4; *NYTr*, 7 Mar. 1895, 5-2; *NYTr*, 9 Mar. 1895, 6-3.

29. *NYT*, 22 Feb. 1895, 9-3; *NYT*, 1 Mar. 1895, 13-5; *BE*, 1 Mar. 1895.

30. *NYT*, 22 Feb. 1895, 9-3; *NYTr*, 1 Mar. 1895, 3-3; *NYTr*, 8 Mar. 1895, 3-4. Auerbach worked for Belmont and the tracks into the 1920s, although they often wrangled over fees and payments, with some bills exceeding twenty thousand dollars. As late as 1921, he was still getting a retainer of five thousand dollars from Belmont. See August Belmont II to J. S. Auerbach, 7 Oct. 1908, Box 35, Folder 102, Belmont to J. S. Auerbach, 1 Feb. 1915, Box 42, Folder 142, Belmont to Auerbach, 3 Feb. 1922, Box 49, Folder 171, and Auerbach to Belmont, 7 Jan. 1915, Box 42, Folder 142, Belmont Family Papers.

31. *NYT*, 14 Mar. 1895, 6-2; *NYT*, 22 Mar. 1895, 3-4; *NYTr*, 22 Mar. 1895, 2-3; *NYTr*, 23 Mar. 1895, 2-4; *NYTr*, 1 Apr. 1895, 4-1.

32. *New York Sun*, 19 Apr. 1895, 8-1; *NYT*, 22 Mar. 1895, 3-4; *NYT*, 23 Mar. 1895, 4-4, 6-1; *NYT*, 1 Apr. 1895, 12-1; *NYT*, 3 Apr. 1895, 9-3; *National Police Gazette* 66 (23 Mar. 1895): 10-3; *NYTr*, 3 Apr. 1895.

33. *NYT*, 12 Feb. 1895, 4-2, 6-1 (quotes); *NYT*, 22 Mar. 1895, 3-4 (quote); 23 Mar. 1895, 4-4, 6-1; *NYT*, 1 Apr. 1895, 12-1; 3 Apr. 1895, *NYT*, 9-3.

34. *NYT*, 15 Feb. 1895, 4-5.

35. *NYTr*, 13 Feb. 1895, 6-4; *NYT*, 7 Mar. 1895, 5-2; *NYT*, 9 Mar. 1895, 6-3.

36. *NYT,* 22 Mar. 1895, 3-4; *NYT,* 23 Mar. 1895, 4-4, 6-1; *NYT,* 1 Apr. 1895, 12-1; *NYT,* 3 Apr. 1895, 9-3; *National Police Gazette* 66 (23 Mar. 1895): 10-3; *NYTr,* 3 Apr. 1895.

37. *NYTr,* 12 Apr. 1995, 2-2; *NYTr,* 18 Apr. 1895, 5-2; *NYTr,* 2 May 1895, 3-5; *NYTr,* 3 May 1895, 1-6; *NYT,* 2 May 1895, 4-4, 5-4; *NYT,* 3 May 1895, 4-3; *BE,* 3 May 1895, 6-1; *BE,* 4 May 1895, 6-2; *New York Sun,* 3 May 1895, 1-7. The *Philadelphia Press* reported that the passage was abetted by Republican boss Tom Platt, who wired senators to support the act. See Betts, *America's Sporting Heritage,* 146.

38. *NYT,* 10 May 1895, 3-4; *NYT,* 26 Sept. 1893, 8; *BE,* 10 May 1895, 10-4; *NYTr,* 10 May 1895, 2-2. The law seemed to make it possible to recover bets made at the tracks in a civil suit. *NYT,* 24 Apr. 1901, 7-2.

39. *BE,* 3 May 1895, 6-1. The National Steeplechase Association was founded on 15 February 1895 by August Belmont II.

40. *BE,* 3 May 1895, 6-1; *BE,* 4 May 1895, 6-2. See also *NYT,* 3 May 1895, 4-3; *NYT,* 13 May 1895, 7-1; *NYT,* 21 May 1895, 5-2; *NYT,* 10 May 1896, 14-2.

41. *NYT,* 11 May 1895, 4-3; *NYT,* 27 May 1895, 1-1; *NYT,* 26 July 1895, 6-4; *NYT,* 26 Nov. 1902, 1-3; August Belmont II to John Sanford, 11 Sept. 1895, Box 27, Folder 37, Belmont Family Papers.

42. *NYT,* 22 May 1895, 6-2; *NYT,* 14 Oct. 1895, 3-1; Di Brino, *Morris Park Racecourse,* 6.

43. *NYTr,* 12 May 1895, 5-3.

44. *NYT,* 16 May 1895, 1-7, 2-1; *BE,* 16 May 1895, 5-1, 5-2 (quote), 6-6.

45. *BE,* 16 May 1895, 6-6.

46. Ibid.; *BE,* 21 May 1895, 5-2; *TFF* 62 (21 Feb. 1896): 274.

47. "The Futurity" (editorial), *BE,* 24 Aug. 1895, 6-2.

48. *National Police Gazette* 66 (1 June 1895): 11-3; *National Police Gazette* 66 (29 June 1895): 10-3; *BE,* 14 Sept. 1895, 5-3; *NYT,* 24 Aug. 1895, 16-3.

49. *NYT,* 26 Oct. 1895, 6-3.

50. *NYT,* 25 Oct. 1895, 1-2; *NYT,* 26 Oct. 1895, 6-3; *NYT,* 29 Oct. 1895, 6-3; *NYT,* 1 Jan. 1896, 6-7.

51. *Spirit* 131 (1 Feb. 1896): 70; *Spirit* 130 (11 Jan. 1896): 860. The *Spirit* based its data on records from the state Tax Department and authoritative sources. See also *National Police Gazette* 66 (1 June 1895): 11-3; *National Police Gazette* 66 (29 June 1895): 10-3; *NYT,* 20 Feb. 1896, 4-5; *CDN,* 7 Jan. 1896, 7-1; and Trevelyan, "Our Turf's Transition," 225–26.

52. *NYT,* 5 July 1895, 6-4; *NYT,* 25 Aug. 1895, 1-5, 3-2; *NYT,* 26 Aug. 1895, 3-5.

53. *Spirit* 130 (11 Jan. 1896): 860 (quote); *Spirit* 131 (1 Feb. 1896): 70; *Spirit* 131 (22 Feb. 1896): 153–54, 166; *NYTr,* 18 Feb. 1896, 15-5; *NYT,* 24 June 1896, 1-7, 2-1. *Spirit* employed data drawn from the state Tax Department and other authoritative sources. See also *NYT,* 20 Feb. 1896, 4-5. In the period 1887–94, the racing associations paid the state only about $22,000 per year. The only year the racing associations paid a fee for pool selling was 1894. *Spirit* 131 (29 Feb. 1896): 190. A big chunk of the $308,000 spent on purses must have come from other sources because otherwise the CIJC losses would have had to be much more than $30,000. On the unpopularity of oral betting, see *Spirit* 131 (16 May 1896): 568.

54. *Spirit* 130 (11 Jan. 1896): 860; *Spirit* 131 (1 Feb. 1896): 70; *Spirit* 131 (22 Feb. 1896): 153–54, 166; *CDN,* 17 Jan. 1896, 2-3; *NYTr,* 18 Feb. 1896, 15-5; *NYT,* 20 Feb. 1896, 4-5; *NYT,* 24 June 1896, 1-7, 2-1.

55. *Spirit* 131 (22 Feb. 1896): 153–54, 166; *NYTr,* 18 Feb. 1896, 15-5; *NYT,* 17 Feb. 1896, 6-1; "Racing in New York" (editorial), *NYT,* 20 Feb. 1896, 4-4.

56. *NYTr,* 13 Dec. 1895, 12-1.

57. *Spirit* 131 (18 Apr. 1896): 414; *NYT,* 23 July 1896, 6-1.

58. *NYT,* 1 Jan. 1896, 1-7, 6-7; "The Racing Law" (editorial), *NYT,* 1 Jan. 1896, 4-4; *NYT,* 3 Mar. 1897, 3-6; "The Racing Law" (editorial), *NYT,* 6-2; *NYT,* 3 Mar. 1897, 3-6; *Spirit* 133 (6 Mar. 1897): 209–10.

59. *BE*, 18 Apr. 1896, 11-2; *NYTr*, 18 Apr. 1896, 5-1, 6-5; "The Percy-Gray Law" (editorial), *NYT*, 18 Apr. 1896, 4-4 (quote), 2-3.

60. *NYT*, 3 Mar. 1897, 6-2 (quote); *Brooklyn Eagle*, 2 Mar. 1897, 4-2; Liebman, "Horseracing in New York," 554–55; *People ex rel. Lawrence v. Fallon*, 152 N.Y. 12 (1897); *People ex rel. Sturgis v. Fallon*, 152 N.Y. 1 (1897).

61. "Racing in New York" (editorial), *NYT*, 20 Feb. 1896, 4-5; *NYT*, 4 May 1896, 6-1; *NYT*, 5 May 1896, 3-1; *BE*, 5 May 1896, 11-5.

62. *NYTr*, 14 May 1896, 6-5; *Spirit* 131 (16 May 1896): 568.

63. *NYTr*, 14 May 1896, 6-5; *NYT*, 31 May 1896, 14-1; *BE*, 10 May 1896, 6-5.

64. *BE*, 8 Feb. 1896, 1-5; "Welching at Horse Races" (editorial), *BE*, 6 June 1896, 6-6.

65. *NYT*, 24 June 1896, 1-7, 2-1.

66. Computed from data on taxes paid by racetracks in New York State. New York State Racing Commission, *Annual Report of the State Racing Commission, 1907*, 5.

67. *NYT*, 24 June 1896, 1-7, 2-1; *BE*, 24 June 1896, 5-1. On the cycling fad, see Richard Harmond, "Progress and Flight: An Interpretation of the American Cycle Craze of the 1890's."

68. *NYT*, 12 July 1896, 6-1; *NYT*, 16 Aug. 1896, 8-1. Four thousand dollars of the purse went to the breeder of the winning horse. On Daly's bet, see Chafetz, *Play the Devil*, 269.

69. "Respectable Racing" (editorial), *NYT*, 31 May 1897, 4-3; "The Revival of Racing" (editorial), *NYT*, 27 June 1897, 18-4 (quote).

70. *Spirit* 133 (6 Mar. 1897): 209–10; *NYT*, 11 July 1897, 1-7.

71. *Spirit* 133 (6 Mar. 1897): 209–10; *NYT*, 18 Apr. 1896, 2-3. However, all was not well for breeders and owners. A horse then cost $200 to breed, but only top-bred horses sold for more than $100. Colts sired by stakes winners sold for $750 to $1,000, a substantial drop from 1892, when the going rate was $3,000 to $5,000. *Chicago Journal*, 15 June 1897, 7-4.

9. A Glorious Decade of Racing: The New York Turf, 1897–1907

1. Rene Bache, "What an Average Day's Horse Racing Costs," 417.

2. *Spirit* 140 (25 Aug. 1900): 131; *New York Sun*, 7 Jan. 1900, 6-5; *NYT*, 28 Oct. 1902, 10-1.

3. *NYT*, 16 Apr. 1899, 9-1 (quote).

4. *NYTr*, 9 May 1899, 8-3.

5. *NYT*, 28 Apr. 1897, 10-1; *NY.T*, 16 Apr. 1902, 5-1; *NYT*, 16 Apr. 1904, 6; *NYT*, 11 Apr. 1905, 9-3.

6. *NYT*, 16 Apr. 1902, 5-1; *NYT*, 16 Apr. 1904, 6-3.

7. *NYTr*, 8 Sept. 1898, 4-2.

8. *NYT*, 18 Dec. 1901, 7-5; *NYT*, 25 Dec. 1901, 5-3. Reynolds later became a real estate mogul who built the Dreamland Amusement Park in Coney Island in 1903, developed the town of Long Beach in 1907, and served as its mayor and was involved in the project that culminated in the Chrysler Building. He left an estate worth ten million dollars. *NYT*, 14 Oct. 1931, 23-1; *NYT*, 20 Oct. 1931, 26-5.

9. *NYT*, 24 Aug. 1901, 3-2; *NYT*, 27 Apr. 1903, 8-5; *CT*, 19 July 1901, 4-3 (quote); *Spirit* 143 (15 Feb. 1902): 104; W. Robertson, *Thoroughbred Racing*, 182–83. The Ryder estate reportedly owned the track site in 1909. In 1903, McCarren supplanted Hugh McLaughlin as head of the Brooklyn Democratic organization. He broke with Charles F. Murphy, his former ally, and the Tammany machine a year later and ran the Brooklyn organization independently of Tammany. See George B. McClellan Jr., *The Gentleman and the Tiger: The Autobiography of George B. McClellan, Jr.*, 159n4.

10. Please note that "taxes paid" in table 5 refers to 5 percent of the gross, and so the gross is twenty times the taxes.

11. *NYT,* 24 May 1905, 2-3.

12. *NYT,* 13 July 1897, 3-1; *NYT,* 18 July 1900, 5-1; *Spirit* 140 (21 July 1900): 3C, *Spirit* 141 (10 Aug. 1901): 606; *Spirit* 141 (4 Jan. 1902): 1045.

13. *Spirit* 143 (15 Feb. 1902): 102.

14. *NYTr,* 16 Apr. 1902, 5-1.

15. Bache, "Average Day's Horse Racing," 412–13.

16. *NYT,* 15 June 1902, 1-7; *NYT,* 28 Aug. 1904, 1-7; *NYT,* 16 May 1905, 1-7; *NYT,* 27 Aug. 1905, 1-1.

17. Bache, "Average Day's Horse Racing," 413. I estimated an average weekly fee of one hundred dollars for the veterinarian and estimated that on average days, there were seventy-five Pinkertons on guard at five dollars apiece.

18. Jon Bartels, *Saratoga Stories: Gangsters, Gamblers, and Racing Legends,* 107–24; Bache, "Average Day's Horse Racing," 413. Canfield reportedly invented the club sandwich in 1894 and card game Canfield Solitaire. See "Club Sandwich: History of Club Sandwich."

19. Hotaling, *They're Off!* 159.

20. *CT,* 2 Nov. 1900; Hotaling, *They're Off!* 166–67.

21. *ANB,* s.v. "Whitney, William C."; Mark D. Hirsch, *William C. Whitney, Modern Warwick;* W. A. Swanberg, *Whitney Father, Whitney Heiress; NYT,* 3 Feb. 1904, 1-7, 8-1.

22. W. H. Rowe, "The Turf Career of Hon. W. C. Whitney"; W. Robertson, *Thoroughbred Racing,* 584; Bache, "Average Day's Horse Racing," 415; W. Robertson, *Thoroughbred Racing,* 181.

23. *Spirit* 143 (8 Mar. 1902): 163; *Spirit* 144 (2 Aug. 1902): 61; Hotaling, *They're Off!* 171–72, 174; *NYT,* 3 Aug. 1904, 7-1.

24. Hotaling, *They're Off!* 166–67; *NYT,* 12 Aug. 1902, 7-1 (quote).

25. *NYT,* 4 May 1902, 1-7; *NYT,* 11 May 1902, 13-1; *NYT,* 8 May 1903, 3-1.

26. *NYT,* 26 Nov. 1902, 1-3; *Spirit* 144 (6 Dec. 1902): 436; Di Brino, *Morris Park Racecourse,* 1–11. Di Brino argues, with little evidence, that Morris Park by 1900 was a disaster for the WRA. Morris Park was certainly not doing as well as such a superb facility should have, but it was not a disaster. Hotels sprang up around the track after train and buggy service from Manhattan began, including the Laconia Hotel and Restaurant. Mark B. Roman, "If You're Thinking of Living In: Morris Park," *NYT,* 31 July 1983, R9.

27. *Spirit* 144 (6 Dec. 1902): 436; *NYT,* 26 Nov. 1902, 1-3; *CT,* 26 Nov. 1902, 6-5; *CT,* 30 Nov. 1902, 122.

28. *NYT,* 26 Nov. 1902, 1-3.

29. *NYT,* 26 Nov. 1902, 1-3; *NYT,* 5 May 1905, 1-7.

30. *NYT,* 5 May 1905, 1-7, 3-7; *NYT,* 7 May 1905, 8-5; W. Robertson, *Thoroughbred Racing,* 186–88.

31. *NYT,* 31 May 1906, 8-2.

32. *NYT,* 26 Nov. 1902, 1-3; *Spirit* 144 (6 Dec. 1902): 436; Di Brino, *Morris Park Racecourse,* 1–11.

33. *NYT,* 17 Feb. 1900, 7-1; *Spirit* 134 (18 Sept. 1897): 234; *Spirit* 136 (5 Nov. 1898): 395; *Spirit* 137 (28 Jan. 1899): 704; *Spirit* 138 (26 Aug. 1899): 147. Trotting resumed there in 1942, and in 1950 the facility was renamed Yonkers Race Track and became one of the finest harness racing facilities in the country.

34. *NYT,* 17 Feb. 1900, 7-1; *Spirit* 136 (5 Nov. 1898): 395; *Spirit* 138 (26 Aug. 1899): 147; *Spirit* 141 (10 Aug. 1901): 606; *Spirit* 142 (4 Jan. 1902): 1045; *Spirit* 143 (1 Mar. 1902): 41.

35. *Spirit* 136 (5 Nov. 1898): 395; *Spirit* 138 (26 Aug. 1899): 147; *Spirit* 141 (10 Aug. 1901): 606; *Spirit* 142 (4 Jan. 1902): 1045; *Spirit* 143 (1 Mar. 1902): 141; "History of Yonkers Raceway."

36. *NYMT*, 29 Dec. 1899, 5-3.

37. *NYT*, 22 Oct. 1900, 5-1; *NYT*, 23 Oct. 1900, 1-7; *NYT*, 29 Feb. 1905, 10-1; *NYT*, 7 Feb. 1905, 7-3; *NYT*, 7 Jan. 1902, 14-3; *NYT*, 17 Jan. 1902, 2-3; *NYT*, 19 Jan. 1902, 4-4; *NYT*, 24 Jan. 1902, 2-6.

38. *NYT*, 7 Jan. 1902, 14-3; *NYT*, 17 Jan. 1902, 2-3; *NYT*, 19 Jan. 1902, 4-4; *NYT*, 24 Jan. 1902, 2-6; *NYT*, 26 Jan. 1902, 10-2; *NYT*, 22 June 1902, 6-1; *NYT*, 14 Sept. 1902, 15-4; *Spirit* 143 (1 Mar. 1902): 141; James Renner, "C. K. G. Billings."

39. *NYT*, 26 Mar. 1903, 6-4.

40. *NYT*, 3 May 1906, 1-3.

41. *NYT*, 1 Mar. 1907, II: 11-5.

42. Ibid.

43. *NYT*, 6 Mar. 1907, 6-1.

44. *NYT*, 15 Mar. 1907, 7-1; *NYT*, 31 Mar. 1907, 12-1; *NYT*, 14 Apr. 1907, IV: 1-1.

45. *NYT*, 16 Apr. 1907, 9-5; *NYT*, 15 June 1907, 7-3; *NYT*, 6 July 1907, 5-5; *NYT*, 17 July 1907, 7-5.

46. *NYT*, 21 July 1907, 6-2 (quote); *NYT*, 23 July 1907, 8-6.

47. *NYT*, 22 July 1907, 4-4.

48. Ibid. (quote); *NYT*, 11 Aug. 1907, 1-5.

49. *NYT*, 19 Aug. 1907, 5-1; *NYT*, 26 Aug. 1907, 5.

50. *NYT*, 5 Jan. 1908, IV: 4-4.

51. *NYT*, 31 May 1897, 4-3; *NYT*, 27 June 1897, 18-4 (quote).

52. *Chicago Journal*, 15 June 1897, 7-4.

53. *NYMT*, 8 Nov. 1899, 10-1; *NYMT*, 18 Nov. 1899, 10-1. The *Morning Telegraph* was the most expensive daily newspaper in the United States.

54. *BE*, 16 Dec. 1901, 17-7; *CT*, 2 Dec. 1901, 6-3; *Spirit* 143 (8 Feb. 1902): 88.

55. *BE*, 16 Dec. 1901, 17-7; *CT*, 2 Dec. 1901, 6-3; *Spirit* 143 (8 Feb. 1902): 88.

56. "Who Wins at Racetracks?" *Los Angeles Times*, 25 May 1906, 11-8. For a rare detailed accounting of Belmont Park in 1944, see Alexander M. Robb, "Racing as a Business," 26.

57. *NYT*, 4 Mar. 1906, 11-3.

58. *NYT*, 7 Mar. 1907, 10-5; *NYT*, 20 June 1907, 6-3.

59. "Ten Millions Every Years to the Race Tracks," *NYT*, 13 Oct. 1907, V: 3-1; New York State Racing Commission, *Annual Report of the State Racing Commission, 1907*, 5; "Millions in Racing," unnamed newspaper article, 8 Jan. 1908, in Robert Higginson Fuller, comp., *Hughes Administration Scrapbook of Newspaper Clippings, Etc.* New York sportswriter Frank W. Thorpe reported that the Ascot track in Los Angeles made $500,000, while Tom Williams's track in Oakland made $750,000 and that two New Orleans tracks made nearly $750,000 in 1906, which probably refers to gross, and certainly not net. See *NYW*, 20 Apr. 1907. Former bookmaker Harry Brolaski reported in 1909 to a Senate Judiciary Subcommittee that the Emeryville Racetrack in Oakland, home of the California Jockey Club, had a daily net gain of $5,852 ($8,948 receipts less $3,096 in expenses), which came to $585,200 for a 100-day meet (the track actually operated 120 days). Then after taxes, maintenance costs when not in use, and $50,000 in dividends (a 20 percent profit on the original $250,000 investment), profits netted $487,700. The main source of revenue was the gate (3,000 people at $1) and fees from on-track bookmakers (30 at $100) and off-track poolrooms (150 at $10). Other significant sources of revenue were the bar privilege ($350), programs (3,000 at $0.10), and field and combination books ($250). The bulk of expenses were the purses ($2,500 for five races). See U.S. Congress, Senate, Committee on the Judiciary, *By Telegraph:*

Hearings Before the United States Senate Committee on the Judiciary, Sixtieth Congress, Second Session, on Jan. 21, 1909, 21–223.

60. *NYT,* 13 Oct. 1907, V: 3-1. The *Times* estimated that fans that stood in the field spent $1.50, which included transportation, a program, and a beer and sandwich. If ten thousand fans attended each day, then the annual gross for attendance would be $2.61 million. However, the calculations are not that simple. An undetermined number of fans paid a premium for betting seating, and a lot of fans got in on passes. Also, note that 90 percent of wagers at the track ended up being recirculated among the betting public.

61. *NYT,* 6 May 1906, 20-3; *NYT,* 13 Oct. 1907, V: SM-3.

62. *NYT,* 15 July 1900, 16-5; *NYT,* 13 Oct. 1907, V: SM-3. On bookmakers, see also "Bookmaker Not Real Gambler," *Washington Post,* 28 Apr. 1907, MS3 (the article originally appeared in the *New York Post,* n.d.).

63. *NYMT,* 3 Mar. 1901, 8-1; *NYT,* 12 Aug. 1902, 7-1.

64. *NYT,* 26 July 1897, 3-4. For Reilly's obituary, see *NYT,* 24 Feb. 1904, 9-6.

65. *NYT,* 26 July 1897, 3-4; *NYT,* 27 July 1897, 3-5; *NYT,* 28 July 1897, 4-5; *BE,* 27 July 1897, 4-5; *BE,* 28 July 1897, 5-5; *BE,* 29 July 1897, 4-7; *Spirit* 134 (31 July 1897): 30.

66. *CT,* 10 Aug. 1901, 3-1; *CT,* 8 Sept. 1901, 4-3; *CT,* 8 Sept. 1902, 4-3; *CT,* 28 July 1907, 7-3; *Sporting News* (18 Oct. 1902): 8-2; Herman Kogan and Lloyd Wendt, *Bet-a-Million! The Story of John W. Gates.*

67. *NYT,* 13 Oct. 1907, V: 3-1; *NYT,* 4 Oct. 1907, 1-2.

68. *NYT,* 1 Sept. 1905, 9-3. See Pittsburgh Phil's obituary, *NYT,* 2 Feb. 1905, 7-1, and *CT,* 2 Feb. 1905, 8-2; and "Maxims of Pittsburgh Phil." See also Edward W. Cole, *Racing Maxims and Methods of "Pittsburgh Phil" (George E. Smith): Condensed Wisdom of Twenty Years Experience on the Track from the Most Successful Speculator in the History of the American Turf from the Only Personal Interviews Ever Given by the Famous Horseman.* One source estimated his fortune at $3.5 to $4 million. See Clarence L. Cullen, "The Racing Game."

69. *NYT,* 26 Apr. 1905, 9-7; *NYT,* 3 Oct. 1905, 7-1.

70. *NYT,* 6 May 1905, 7-1. The opening of the new Belmont track resulted in the postponement of the Dodgers-Phillies game, which did not want to compete. *NYTr,* 5 May 1905, 12-1.

71. *NYT,* 7 May 1905, 10-2.

72. *NYT,* 9 May 1905, 4-1; *NYT,* 10 May 1905, 1-3.

73. *NYT,* 12 May 1905, 16-4; *NYT,* 20 May 1905, 1.

74. *NYT,* 20 May 1905, 1-5; *NYT,* 22 May 1905, 14-7.

75. *NYT,* 21 May 1905, 1-3; *NYT,* 24 May 1905, 2, 4-3; *NYT,* 25 May 1905, 8-4 (quote); *NYT,* 13 Oct. 1907, V: 3-1.

76. Louis Filler, *The Muckrakers: Crusaders for American Liberalism;* Ida M. Tarbell, *All in the Day's Work: An Autobiography;* Lincoln Steffens, *The Autobiography of Lincoln Steffens.* For a major examination of the corruption of amateur athletics, see Henry Beach Needham, "The College Athlete: How Commercialism Is Making Him Professional," 123–25; and Henry Beach Needham, "The College Athlete: His Amateur Code, Its Evasion, and Administration," 271–72.

77. Thomas H. Kennedy, *The Racing Swindle: A Satire;* Mark Sullivan, "The Pool Room Evil," 212; David Graham Phillips, "The Delusion of the Race-Track"; Josiah Flynt, "The Pool-Room Vampire and Its Money Mad Victims," 359–60, "Pool-Room Spider and the Gambling Fly," and "Men Behind the Pool-Rooms."

78. David Graham Phillips, "The Treason of the Senate" and "Delusion of the Race-Track."

79. John D. Workes, "The Race-Track Evil and the Newspapers."

80. Ibid., 428; *NYT,* 13 Jan. 1908, 3-2.

81. *NYT,* 17 Feb. 1906, 1-3; *NYT,* 20 Feb. 1906, 3-2; *NYT,* 19 Mar. 1906, 1-1; *NYT,* 20 Mar. 1906, 1-1, 24-4.

82. *NYT,* 17 Mar. 1906, 1-7.

83. *NYT,* 17 Feb. 1906, 1-3; *NYT,* 19 Mar. 1906, 1-1; *NYT,* 20 June 1905, 4-5; *NYT,* 20 Mar. 1906, 2-4.

84. *NYT,* 15 Mar. 1906, 1-1.

85. *NYT,* 17 Mar. 1906, 1-7, 2-1.

86. *NYT,* 16 Mar. 1906, 1-1.

87. *NYT,* 16 Mar. 1906, 8-4; *NYT,* 17 Mar. 1906, 8-4.

88. *NYT,* 19 Mar. 1906, 1-1; Richard L. McCormick, *From Realignment to Reform: Political Change in New York State, 1893–1910,* 189–91, 193–94.

89. *NYT,* 20 Mar. 1906, 1-1, 24-4.

90. *NYT,* 2 Mar. 1906, 1-2; *NYT,* 21 Mar. 1906, 1-5, 8-1; *NYT,* 27 Mar. 1906, 1-2; *NYT,* 10 Apr. 1906, 1-6.

91. *NYT,* 24 Apr. 1906, 1-4 (quote); *NYT,* 3 May 1906, 1-3.

92. *NYT,* 3 May 1906, 1-3; W. Robertson, *Thoroughbred Racing,* 217; "Sanford, John"; *NYT,* 15 Feb. 1927, 24-8.

93. W. Robertson, *Thoroughbred Racing,* 196; *NYT,* 29 June 1906, 4-4; *NYT,* 30 June 1906, 7-4; *NYT,* 2 July 1906, 6-4; "Rockingham Park: New England's First and Finest Track."

10. The Gambling Trust and the Poolrooms, 1899–1913

1. Cullen, "The Racing Game."

2. *NYT,* 7 July 1904, 16-4; *NYT,* 8 July 1904, 7-3; *NYT,* 29 May 1905, 1-1; Sullivan, "The Pool Room Evil," 212; Mark H. Haller and John V. Alviti, "Loansharking in American Cities: Historical Analysis of a Marginal Enterprise."

3. *NYT,* 7 July 1904, 16-4; *NYT,* 8 July 1904, 7-3. For Goddard's obituary, see *NYT,* 29 May 1905, 1-1.

4. Quoted in Sullivan, "The Pool Room Evil," 212.

5. *NYT,* 15 Dec. 1909, 5-2. See also U.S. Congress, Senate, Committee on the Judiciary, *Interstate Race Gambling: Hearings Before the United States Senate Committee on the Judiciary, Sixty-first Congress, Second Session, on Dec. 14, 1909.* In Great Britain the 1906 Street Betting Act made all street betting illegal, but that did not mean the end of it. Huggins, *Flat Racing,* 109.

6. Flynt, "Pool-Room Vampire," 359–60, "Pool-Room Spider and the Gambling Fly," and "Men Behind the Poolrooms." For Flynt's life, see his posthumously published autobiography *My Life.*

7. Flynt, "Pool-Room Vampire," 361–63, 368.

8. *NYMT,* 9 July 1910, 1-4.

9. *BE,* 5 May 1899, 4-4; *NYT,* 30 Mar. 1899, 1-5; "The Hunt for Corruption" (editorial), *NYT,* 1 Apr. 1899, 6-1.

10. *NYT,* 30 Mar. 1899, 1-5; *NYT,* 1 Apr. 1899, 3-1. For Moss's obituary, see *NYT,* 6 June 1920, 24-1.

11. *NYT,* 7 Apr. 1899, 1-4; *NYT,* 17 May 1899, 1-7, 3-1.

12. *NYT,* 7 Apr. 1899, 1-4.

13. "What Does It Mean?" (editorial), *NYT,* 8 Apr. 1899, 6-1.

14. *NYT,* 8 Apr. 1899, 7-1.

15. Robert Stephens, "The Cure of New York's Greatest Evil in the Hands of Three Great Millionaires," *New York Journal,* 10 Jan. 1907, in Fuller, *Hughes Administration Scrapbook;* Chafetz, *Play the Devil,* 376.

16. *NYT,* 21 June 1899, 1-2; Richard J. Butler and Joseph Driscoll, *Dock Walloper: The Story of "Big Dick" Butler,* 487–91.

17. *NYT,* 8 Apr. 1899, 7-1; *NYT,* 16 May 1899, 2-3; *NYT,* 18 May 1899, 2-1; *NYT,* 10 Mar. 1900, 2-3; *NYT,* 14 Mar. 1900, 3-2; *NYT,* 8 May 1900, 3-3; Mathews, "'Wide-Open' New York," 1045. Devery was the brother-in-law of Michael T. Bergen, the principal assistant of Al Adams, one of the policy kings of New York City. See *NYT,* 11 Mar. 1900, 1-6; and Richardson, *New York Police,* 270–72, 275–76, 279–83. On the Highlanders, see Jim Reisler, *Before They Were the Bombers: The New York Yankees' Early Years, 1903–1915;* Riess, *Touching Base,* 80–82.

18. *CT,* 17 May 1899, 5-1; *NYT,* 17 May 1899, 1-7, 2-1, 3-1.

19. *NYT,* 17 May 1899, 1-7, 2-1, 3-1; *NYT,* 18 May 1899, 1-7; "Getting Down to Business" (editorial), *NYT,* 18 May 1899, 6-1; *Los Angeles Times,* 18 May 1899, 8; *NYW,* 23 Mar. 1900, 8-1; *NYTr,* 8 Feb. 1905, 3-4.

20. *NYT,* 18 May 1899, 1-7.

21. *NYT,* 18 May 1899, 1-7; *NYT,* 19 May 1899, 3-1; *NYT,* 27 May 1899, 7-7.

22. *NYT,* 21 May 1899, 12-1; *NYT,* 24 May 1899, 3-3; *NYTr,* 21 May 1899, 5-1; *NYT,* 12 June 1902, 1-4.

23. *NYT,* 27 May 1899, 7-7; *NYT,* 18 May 1899, 12-6 (quote).

24. *NYT,* 26 Oct. 1899, 3-3; *NYT,* 2 Nov. 1899, 3-1, 4-3.

25. *NYT,* 19 May 1899, 3-1; *NYT,* 9 Mar. 1900, 1-1, 6-1, 8-2; *NYT,* 10 Mar. 1900, 1-7; *NYTr,* 10 Mar. 1900, 4-1; "Why the Gamblers Are Probably Safe," *BE,* 9 Mar. 1900, 8-3; Czitrom, "Underworlds and Underdogs," 548. The Republicans controlled the assembly, outnumbering Democrats ninety-one to fifty-nine. *NYT,* 8 Nov. 1899, 1-5.

26. *NYT,* 30 Jan. 1900, 9-2 (quote); *BE,* 31 Jan. 1900, 1-7; *BE,* 1 Feb. 1900, 1-6.

27. *NYTr,* 3 Mar. 1900, 5-1, 9-4; *NYTr,* 16 Jan. 1901, 4-6; "Shut the Poolrooms" (editorial), *NYTr,* 16 Mar. 1900, 1-4; *NYTr,* 31 Mar. 1900, 2-2; *NYT,* 29 Mar. 1900, 8-2; *NYT,* 20 July 1900, 1-1; *NYMT,* 6 Jan. 1901, 4-6. Devery reportedly ordered patrolmen in early March not to contribute to a fund seeking $220,000 to bribe legislators to pass through bills reducing their hours of work, to defeat the Lewis bill that sought to end boxing in New York, and to knock out a bill prohibiting telegraph and telephone companies from servicing poolrooms with betting odds from the tracks. The latter portion was reputedly $100,000, raised from assessments on poolrooms ranging from $250 to $400. See *New York Sun,* 3 Mar. 1900, 3-3. A minor antipool bill introduced in 1901 never got off the ground. See *NYTr,* 10 Jan. 1901, 4-2.

28. *NYTr,* 3 Mar. 1900, 9-4; *NYTr,* 30 Mar. 1900, 2-4; *NYT,* 3 Mar. 1900, 9-4; *NYT,* 11 Mar. 1900, 1-6, 2-2; *NYW,* 23 Mar. 1900, 8-3.

29. *NYT,* 13 Mar. 1900, 1-7 (quote); *NYT,* 18 Mar. 1900, 1-7; Czitrom, "Underworlds and Underdogs," 547, 551–52.

30. *NYT,* 11 Mar. 1900, 1-6, 2-2; Haller, "Changing Structure."

31. *NYT,* 9 Mar. 1900, 1-1, 6-1, 8-2; *NYT,* 10 Mar. 1900, 1-7; *NYTr,* 10 Mar. 1900, 4-1; *NYW,* 10 Mar. 1900, 1-6.

32. *NYT,* 20 Oct. 1901, 1-7, 2-3; Flynt, "Men Behind the Poolrooms," 641.

33. *NYT,* 9 Mar. 1900, 1-1; *NYT,* 10 Mar. 1900, 1-7; *NYTr,* 10 Mar. 1900, 4-1, reported three hundred poolrooms.

34. *NYT,* 10 Mar. 1900, 2-1; *NYT,* 11 Mar. 1900, 1-7, 2-1.

35. Ibid.

36. *NYT,* 30 Mar. 1907, 2-4, 2-5; *NYT,* 31 Mar. 1907, 1-1; *NYT,* 2 Apr. 1907, 1-5; *NYT,* 5 Apr. 1907, 1-3; *NYT,* 9 Feb. 1908, 6-3; *NYT,* 4 Feb. 1912, 6-3; *New York Herald,* 30 Mar. 1907; Myers, *History of Tammany Hall,* 343–44. The press may well have exaggerated Grady's involvement, as he died five years later, with an estate worth only about a thousand dollars. *NYT,* 10 Feb. 1912, 1-2.

37. *NYT,* 10 Mar. 1900, 1-7, 8-1 (quote).

38. *NYT,* 11 Mar. 1900, 1-7, 2-1; *NYT,* 12 Mar. 1900, 6-1; *NYW,* 10 Mar. 1900, 1-7; *New York Sun,* 11 Mar. 1900, 1-7; *New York Sun,* 12 Mar. 1900, 4-1.

39. *NYT,* 11 Mar. 1900, 1-7, 1-6 (quote), 2-1; *NYT,* 12 Mar. 1900, 2-1.

40. *NYT,* 14 Mar. 1900, 2-1; *NYT,* 15 Mar. 1900, 2-1; *NYT,* 17 Mar. 1900, 2-1; *NYT,* 18 Mar. 1900, 1-7; *NYT,* 17 Apr. 1900, 3-1; *NYTr,* 11 Sept. 1901, 4-1 (quote).

41. *NYT,* 17 Apr. 1900, 3-1; *NYTr,* 11 Sept. 1901, 4-1 (quote).

42. *NYT,* 6 May 1900, 1-7, 2-6; *NYT,* 8 May 1900, 3-3.

43. *NYT,* 16 Nov. 1900, 1-7; *NYT,* 17 Nov. 1900, 2-2; *NYT,* 23 Dec. 1900, 5-3; *NYT,* 25 Dec. 1900, 3-1.

44. *BE,* 22 Jan. 1902, 11-4.

45. *NYMT,* 10 Mar. 1901, 2-6; *NYMT,* 19 Apr. 1901, 3; Richardson, *New York Police,* 281; Bernard Whalen and Jon Whalen, "The Birth of the NYPD."

46. *NYT,* 23 Dec. 1900, 1-6; *NYT,* 25 May 1919, 11. Gardiner's obituary did not mention his firing but went into great detail in describing the rescinding of his Congressional Medal of Honor earned during the Civil War in 1917.

47. Richard O'Connor, *Courtroom Warrior: The Combative Career of William Travers Jerome.* For Gardiner's obituary, see *NYT,* 29 May 1919, 11.

48. *NYTr,* 19 Feb. 1901, 1-1; *NYTr,* 20 Feb. 1901, 1-6 (quote); *NYT,* 8 June 1901, 16-1; O'Connor, *Courtroom Warrior.*

49. *NYT,* 25 Feb. 1901, 1-7; *NYTr,* 20 Feb. 1901, 1-6; *NYTr,* 24 Sept. 1940, 32.

50. *NYTr,* 20 Feb. 1901, 1-6.

51. *NYTr,* 20 Feb. 1901, 1-6, 8-1; *NYTr,* 22 Feb. 1901, 10-5; *NYTr,* 24 Feb. 1901, 2-4; *NYT,* 13 Mar. 1900, 2-1.

52. *BE,* 18 Apr. 1901, 3-3, 4-2 (quote).

53. *BE,* 26 Apr. 1901, 1-1 (quote); *NYT,* 30 Apr. 1901, 1-7.

54. *NYT,* 7 June 1901, 2-1; *NYT,* 8 June 1913, 1-3.

55. *NYT,* 5 Sept. 1901, 1-5.

56. *CT,* 10 Aug. 1901, 5-1; *NYT,* 11 Aug. 1901, 1-6; *NYT,* 21 Aug. 1901, 1-5.

57. *NYT,* 10 Aug. 1901, 1-7, 2-1; *NYT,* 11 Aug. 1901, 1-7. See also *CT,* 12 Aug 1901, 1-5; *CT,* 21 Aug. 1901, 2-7.

58. *NYT,* 19 Apr. 1901, 16-3; *NYT,* 24 Apr. 1901, 7-2; Rovere, *Howe and Hummel.*

59. *NYT,* 1 Aug. 1901, 12-5; *NYT,* 9 Nov. 1901, 2-5.

60. *NYT,* 9 Nov. 1901, 2-5; *NYT,* 21 Dec. 1901, 6-3; *NYT,* 10 Jan. 1902, 8-4; *NYT,* 15 Jan. 1902, 7-6; *NYTr,* 21 Dec. 1901, 5-4 (quote).

61. *NYT,* 10 Jan. 1902, 8-4; *NYT,* 15 Jan. 1902, 7-6; *Spirit* 142 (18 Jan. 1902): 28.

62. *NYT,* 2 Nov. 1901, 2-2; *NYT,* 3 Sept. 1902, 1-5; *BE,* 22 Jan. 1902, 11-4 (quote). On Low, see *ANB,* s.v. "Low, Seth." On the election, the machine, and the aftermath, see Gerald Kurland, *Seth Low: The Reformer in an Urban and Industrial Age;* and Nancy J. Weiss, *Charles Francis Murphy, 1858–1924: Respectability and Responsibility in Tammany Politics.*

63. *NYT,* 13 Mar. 1900, 2-1; *NYT,* 20 Mar. 1900, 1-5; *NYT,* 11 Nov. 1901, 5-4.

64. *NYT,* 23 Nov. 1901, 1-3.

65. *NYT,* 25 Dec. 1901, 1-5; *NYT,* 26 Dec. 1901, 1-2; *NYT,* 27 Dec. 1901, 2-4; *NYT,* 15 Oct. 1902, 1-3; *NYT,* 23 Apr. 1901, 3-4; *NYT,* 19 Nov. 1905, 12-3. On Kelly's life, see *NYT,* 20 Jan. 1922, 12-1; *NYT,* 28 Mar. 1926, 1-7.

66. *BE,* 22 Jan. 1902, 11-4.

67. *BE*, 16 Apr. 1902, 20-1.

68. *NYTr*, 1 Mar. 1901, 4-2; *NYTr*, 24 Apr. 1902, 6-3.

69. *NYW*, 6 June 1904; *NYT*, 16 June 1911, 5-2.

70. Flynt estimated that there were two thousand poolrooms in New York (most experts put the figure at four hundred) and that fifty were just for women. See Flynt, "Pool-Room Spider," 518–19.

71. Ibid., 519.

72. *NYT*, 6 June 1900, 3-4; *NYT*, 7 June 1900, 14-1 (quote); *NYT*, 12 June 1900, 2-4; *NYTr*, 6 June 1900, 10-1; *NYTr*, 7 June 1900, 7-5; *NYTr*, 24 June 1902, 2-4; *NYMT*, 27 Feb. 1901, 10-1. See also *New York Sun*, 23 May 1900, 1-4.

73. *NYT*, 12 June 1900, 2-4; *NYT*, 13 June 1900, 14-2. See also *NYW*, 7 Mar. 1904, 1; *NYW*, 8 Mar. 1904, 5-1; *New York Sun*, 16 Apr. 1904, 1-3.

74. *NYT*, 16 June 1911, 5-2.

75. *NYT*, 15 June 1911, 1-7.

76. *NYT*, 16 June 1911, 5-2.

77. *NYT*, 9 Mar. 1902, 1-4; *NYT*, 2 Apr. 24, 1902, 2-2; *NYT*, 24 June 1902, 7-4; *NYT*, 3 Sept. 1902, 1-5; *ANB*, s.v. "Low, Seth."

78. On Murphy, see N. Weiss, *Charles Francis Murphy*; *NYT*, 24 Dec. 1903, 2-2; and *NYTr*, 14 Dec. 1903, 8-2. On McClellan, see McClellan, *Gentleman and the Tiger*; *ANB*, s.v. "McClellan, George B."; and his obituary, *NYT*, 1 Dec. 1940, 61-1.

79. *NYT*, 24 Dec. 1903, 2-2; *NYT*, 12 Mar. 1904, 11-1; *NYT*, 1 May 1940, 61-1; *NYTr*, 14 Dec. 1903, 8-2; *NYTr*, 17 Mar. 1904, 1-3. On the 1905 election, see Ben H. Procter, *William Randolph Hearst: The Early Years, 1863–1910*, 201–11.

80. *NYT*, 26 Mar. 1904, 3-1; *NYW*, 15 Jan. 1904, 13-1; *NYW*, 16 Jan. 1904, 3-3 (quote). See also *NYW*, 25 Apr. 1906, 10-2; *NYW*, 18 Nov. 1906, V: 13-3; *NYW*, 29 Mar. 1904, 2-1; and "McAdoo, William (1853–1910)." On McAdoo's views and experiences in fighting the poolrooms, see William McAdoo, *Guarding a Great City*, 193–226.

81. *NYT*, 24 Dec. 1903, 2-2; *NYT*, 24 Jan. 1904, 1-1; *NYTr*, 14 Dec. 1903, 8-2.

82. *NYT*, 24 Jan. 1904, 1-1.

83. Ibid.

84. *NYT*, 26 Mar. 1904, 3-1; *NYW*, 15 Jan. 1904, 13-1; *NYW*, 16 Jan. 1904, 3-3; *NYW*, 29 Mar. 1904, 2-1; *NYTr*, 19 May 1904, 6-2. The goal of bookmakers was to produce a "round book" by which the bookmaker could get a good play against every horse in a race and stand to win regardless. This system is different from the "gambler's book" in which the bookmaker stands to lose money if one particular horse wins the race.

85. On Jewish life in Harlem, see Jeffrey Gurock, *When Harlem Was Jewish, 1870–1930*; *NYTr*, 11 Mar. 1904, 1-1. On Harlem and gambling, see, for example, *NYW*, 12 Mar. 1904, 1-3.

86. *NYT*, 13 Mar. 1904, 5-1; *NYT*, 5 Apr. 1905, 7-2; *NYT*, 6 Apr. 1905, 8-3; *NYT*, 8 Apr. 1905, 18-3; *NYT*, 12 Apr. 1905, 6-3.

87. *NYT*, 19 May 1904, 1-7; *NYT*, 20 May 1904, 14-1; *NYTr*, 19 May 1904, 2-1. On the history of Western Union, see Alvin F. Harlow, *Old Wires and New Waves: The History of the Telegraph, Telephone, and Wireless*.

88. *Chicago Record-Herald*, 12 Jan. 1904, 8-1; *NYT*, 20 May 1904, 3-3; "Dark Days for the Pool Rooms" (editorial), *NYT*, 22 May 1904, 6-1; *NYW*, 15 Jan. 1904, 13-1; *NYTr*, 20 May 1904, 14-1. These fees are different from the ones reported by the *Chicago Record-Herald*, 30 Apr. 1904, 2-3.

89. *NYT*, 29 Apr. 1904, 1-2, 2-5.

90. Goddard's obituary is in *NYT*, 29 May 1905, 1-1.

91. *NYTr,* 28 Apr. 1904, 1-4; *NYTr,* 8 July 1905, 4-4; *NYW,* 28 Apr. 1904, 10-1.

92. *NYTr,* 29 Apr. 1904, 1-2, 2-5; *Chicago Record-Herald,* 30 Apr. 1904, 2-3. See also "Directors and Poolrooms" (editorial), *NYTr,* 2 May 1904, 6-2.

93. *NYTr,* 2 May 1904, 12-4. On unionization and telegraphers, see Edward Gabler, *The American Telegrapher: A Social History, 1860–1900.*

94. *NYTr,* 5 May 1904, 6-1.

95. "The Poolroom Scandal" (editorial), *NYT,* 11 May 1904, 8-1.

96. "Nobody Closes the Poolrooms" (editorial), *NYT,* 14 May 1904, 8-1; "The Poolroom Farce" (editorial), *NYT,* 16 May 1904, 8-1; *NYT,* 18 May 1904, 1-7.

97. *NYT,* 19 May 1904, 1-7; *NYT,* 20 May 1904, 14-1; *NYTr,* 19 May 1904, 2-1; *NYW,* 18 May 1904, 6-2.

98. *NYT,* 19 May 1904, 1-1; *NYT,* 19 May 1904, 1-1.

99. *NYT,* 19 May 1904, 2-2; *NYT,* 20 May 1904, 1-1.

100. *NYTr,* 19 May 1904, 6-2.

101. *NYT,* 21 May 1904, 1-1; *NYTr,* 21 May 1904, 1-1, 1-2.

102. Ibid.; *NYTr,* 24 May 1904, 1-5.

103. *NYT,* 27 May 1904, 3-1. See also *NYTr,* 13 June 1904, 4-1.

104. *NYT,* 28 May 1904, 16-5; *NYT,* 6 Aug. 1904, 12-4. On other raids that year, see *NYT,* 17 Sept. 1904, 16-6; *NYT,* 25 Sept. 1904, 12-1; *NYT,* 28 Sept. 1904, 1-5; *NYT,* 19 Oct. 1904, 6-2.

105. *NYTr,* 3 July 1904, 1-4; *NYTr,* 6 July 1904, 4-2; "Against Gambling" (editorial), *NYT,* 3 July 1904, 4-1.

106. *NYT,* 19 Jan. 1905, 2-3.

107. *NYT,* 13 July 1905, 12-3; Naomi W. Cohen, *Jacob H. Schiff: A Study in American Jewish Leadership;* "Heroes: Useful Daughter," 7; Chafetz, *Play the Devil,* 381.

108. *NYT,* 13 July 1905, 12-3; *NYT,* 14 Sept. 1905, 9-1; *NYT,* 12 Oct. 1905, 5-4. On complaints, see *NYT,* 11 July 1905, 5-1; *NYT,* 14 July 1905, 6-6.

109. *NYTr,* 29 Sept. 1905, 4-3 (quote); *NYTr,* 19 Sept. 1905, 3-1; *NYTr,* 21 Sept. 1905, 11-3 (quote).

110. *NYTr,* 21 Sept. 1905, 11-3; *NYTr,* 29 Sept. 1905, 4-3; *NYTr,* 12 Oct. 1905, 9-2.

111. *NYTr,* 19 Sept. 1905, 3-1; *NYTr,* 20 Sept. 1905, 4-5; *NYTr,* 21 Sept. 1905, 11-3; *NYTr,* 29 Sept. 1905, 4-3; *NYTr,* 5 Jan. 1906, 10-5.

112. *NYT,* 1 Oct. 1905, IV: 1-1; *NYT,* 31 Dec. 1905, 10-3.

113. *NYT,* 4 Jan. 1906, 18-3; McClellan, *Gentleman and the Tiger,* 199–201. McAdoo claimed there were fewer than forty in the entire city at the end of 1905. McAdoo, *Guarding a Great City,* 209.

114. *NYT,* 4 Jan. 1906, 18-3.

115. *NYT,* 21 June 1908, 1-3.

116. *NYT,* 5 Jan. 1906, 10-5. On the racing wire, see Allan May, "The History of the Race Wire Service."

117. John Landesco, *Organized Crime in Chicago,* 46–48, 50–61; May, "History of the Race Wire Service."

118. *NYT,* 17 Apr. 1906, 1-3.

119. *NYT,* 18 Apr. 1906, 2-3.

120. *NYT,* 19 Apr. 1906, 22-1.

121. *NYT,* 29 Apr. 1906, 8-1; *NYT,* 2 May 1906, 18-1.

122. *NYT,* 6 May 1906, 20-3; *NYT,* 16 May 1906, 1-5.

123. *NYT,* 29 July 1906, 16-6; *NYT,* 25 Apr. 1906, 10-2.

124. *NYT,* 28 Jan. 1908, 2-6; *NYT,* 21 June 1908, 1-3.

125. *NYT,* 8 Feb. 1905, 16; *NYT,* 18 Nov. 1906, II, 1-3; *NYT,* 12 June 1907, 3; *NYT,* 28 Jan. 1908, 2-6; *NYTr,* 8 Feb. 1905, 3-4.

126. *NYT,* 12 June 1907, 3-2; *NYT,* 13 June 1907, 1-1; *NYT,* 14 June 1907, 3-5. For De Lacy's obituary and estate, see *NYT,* 15 Nov. 1915, 11-5; and *NYT,* 30 May 1916, 6-8.

127. *NYT,* 8 Feb. 1913, 2-2.

128. Ibid. A few days after Purcell gave his testimony, his wife taunted him for being a squealer, and he went after her with a gun. But instead, he shot and killed his twelve-year-old daughter, who was in bed alongside her. Purcell was sentenced to the electric chair, but eventually was sent to a mental asylum by Governor Charles Whitman. See *NYT,* 14 May 1914, 20-4; and *NYT,* 6 June 1915, 10-4.

129. *NYT,* 30 July 1914, 5-3.

130. *NYT,* 21 June 1908, 1-3.

131. For Appo, see Gilfoyle, *Pickpocket's Tale.*

132. *NYMT,* 13 Mar. 1913, 1-4.

133. *NYMT,* 13 Mar. 1913, 1-4, 2-1.

134. The Becker case has received considerable attention by historians, with the most recent study arguing that he was innocent. See Mike Dash, *Satan's Circus: Murder, Vice, Police Corruption, and New York's Trial of the Century.* See also Stanley Cohen, *The Execution of Officer Becker: The Murder of a Gambler, the Trial of a Cop, and the Birth of Organized Crime;* David Pietrusza, *Rothstein: The Life, Times, and Murder of the Criminal Genius Who Fixed the 1919 World Series;* Andy Logan, *Against the Evidence: The Becker-Rosenthal Affair;* and Jonathan Root, *One Night in July: The True Story of the Rosenthal-Becker Murder Case.*

135. Rose Keefe, *The Starker,* 153–55.

136. Ibid., 155–57.

137. Mark Gado, "Killer Cop." For an example of a Becker-led raid, see *NYT,* 21 June 1912, 8-4.

138. Keefe, *The Starker,* 156–57.

139. See, for example, Jenna W. Joselit, *Our Gang: Jewish Crime and the New York Jewish Community, 1900–1940,* 75–84; Albert Fried, *The Rise and Fall of the Jewish Gangster in America,* 72–76; Keefe, *The Starker,* 157–58; and Herbert Asbury, *Gangs of New York: An Informal History of the New York Underworld,* 317, 319.

140. Myers, *History of Tammany Hall,* 356–60; Asbury, *Gangs of New York,* 319; *NYT,* 12 July 1912, 1-4; *NYT,* 13 July 1912, 5-1; *NYT,* 15 July 1912, 5-1; *NYT,* 16 July 1912, 1-7.

141. Haller and Alviti, "Loansharking in American Cities." On the bombing wars in Chicago, see Landesco, *Organized Crime in Chicago,* 46–48, 50–61; and May, "History of the Race Wire Service."

142. See, for example, S. Cohen, *Execution of Officer Becker; NYT,* 30 July 1912, 1-5; *NYT,* 21 Aug. 1912, 1-7; *NYT,* 6 Oct. 1912, 1-7; and *NYT,* 7 Oct. 1912, 1-7.

143. *NYT,* 25 Oct. 1912, 1-3.

11. The Demise and Resurrection of Racing in New York, 1907–13

1. *Goodwin's Annual Official Turf Guide for 1907,* 2 vols., 1:590, 2:clxvii, 601. The Willow Brook Driving Club of Islip, Long Island, had just a three-day meet, the United Hunts Racing Association in Queens raced two days, and the Meadowbrook Steeplechase Association at Westbury, Long Island, raced one day. In Massachusetts, two of the tracks, the Lenox and South Lincoln tracks, each had just one day of steeplechases.

2. *NYT,* 14 Jan. 1907, 1-7; *NYT,* 16 Jan. 1907, 3-6.

3. *NYTr,* 1 Mar. 1901, 4-2; *NYTr,* 14 Jan. 1907, 1-7; *NYTr,* 16 Jan. 1907, 3-6; *NYTr,* 21 Mar. 1907, 3-3; Robert F. Wesser, *Charles Evans Hughes: Politics and Reform in New York, 1905–1910,* 190.

4. *NYT,* 21 Mar. 1907, 3-3 (quote); *NYT,* 13 Apr. 1907, 6-1; *NYT,* 22 June 1941, 32-3; Wesser, *Charles Evans Hughes,* 191.

5. Merlo J. Pusey, *Charles Evans Hughes,* 225; Wesser, *Charles Evans Hughes,* 190–91; *ANB,* s.v. "Hughes, Charles Evans"; *NYT,* 31 Oct. 1905, 4-5 (quote).

6. *NYT,* 16 June 1907, 5-2; *Washington Post,* 14 July 1907, 13; Wesser, *Charles Evans Hughes,* 190–91; Liebman, "Horseracing in New York," 556.

7. *NYT,* 2 Jan. 1908, 1-1, 6-1; Pusey, *Charles Evans Hughes,* 225; Benjamin Parke Dewitt, *The Progressive Movement: A Nonpartisan, Comprehensive Discussion of Current Tendencies in American Politics,* 61–63; Dexter Perkins, *Charles Evans Hughes and American Democratic Statesmanship,* 19.

8. Wesser, *Charles Evans Hughes,* 191–92; *NYT,* 3 Jan. 1908; "Memorandum of State Racing Commission," 8 Feb. 1908, George Bliss Agnew Papers.

9. *Chicago Record-Herald,* 7 Mar. 1908, 6-3.

10. *NYT,* 2 Jan. 1908, 1-1, 6-1; *NYT,* 1 Feb. 1908, 6-7.

11. *NYT,* 2 Jan. 1908, 1-1, 2-3; *NYT,* 3 Jan. 1908, 10-1; "The Governor's Recommendations" (editorial), *NYT,* 2 Jan. 1908, 8-1.

12. Among the upstate papers backing Hughes were the *Oswego Times,* 6 Mar. 1908; *Rochester Union,* 6 Mar. 1908; *Schenectady Star,* 6 Mar. 1908; *Syracuse Herald,* 12 Mar. 1908, *Syracuse Journal,* 15 Oct. 1908; *Utica Press,* 20 Mar. 1908; and *Watertown Times,* 5 Mar. 1908.

13. "The Governor's Recommendations," 8-1 (quote); *NYT,* 4 Jan. 1908, 6-2; *NYT,* 19 Feb. 1908, 6-2 (quote); *NYT,* 28 Feb. 1908, 6-2.

14. "The Governor's Recommendations" (editorial), *NYT,* 2 Jan. 1908, 8-1; *NYT,* 4 Jan. 1908, 6-2.

15. *NYTr,* 9 Apr. 1908, 6-3; *Syracuse Journal,* 15 Oct. 1908; *New York Evening Journal,* 20 Mar., 22 Apr. 1908 (quote); *NYW,* 31 Mar. 1908, 8-2; "Rescue and Rehabilitate the State Constitution First" (editorial), *BE,* 4 Apr. 1908, 4-1; "The Vote To-Morrow" (editorial), *BE,* 7 Apr. 1908. Papers that opposed him included the *Brooklyn Standard,* 5, 6 Mar. 1908; *Brooklyn Times,* 8 Mar. 1908; *Buffalo Examiner,* 6 Mar. 1908; *New York Evening Post,* 5 Mar. 1908; *New York Telegraph,* 4 Mar., 11 Mar. 1908; and *Saratoga Sun,* 4 Mar. 1908, in Fuller, *Hughes Administration Scrapbook,* vol. 37.

16. See, for example, Davenport's drawings reproduced in Wilbur F. Crafts, *The Truth about the New York Race Gambling Trust,* 1, 4, 16; *New York American,* 9 Apr. 1908, 1; *New York American,* 14 Oct. 1909, 1; *New York Evening Journal,* 2 Apr. 1908, 1; *New York Evening Journal,* 9 Apr. 1908, 5.

17. *NYT,* 6 Jan. 1908, 4-4; *NYT,* 16 Jan. 1908, 6-3; *NYT,* 6 Feb. 1908, 2-6.

18. *NYT,* 1 Feb. 1908, 7-2; *NYT,* 3 Feb. 1908, 1-1; Wesser, *Charles Evans Hughes,* 191n25.

19. *NYT,* 31 Jan. 1908, 4-4; *NYT,* 1 Feb. 1908, 6-7; *Rochester Times,* 16 Feb. 1907; Wesser, *Charles Evans Hughes,* 192–93; John A. Lapp, "Race Track Gambling." For evidence of local Protestant leaders' support for reform, see, for example, E. B. Sanford, "Race Track Gambling: This Is the Hour to Lend Support to Governor Hughes," *New York Observer and Chronicle,* 23 Jan. 1908, 124; Francis Edward Marstan, "The Paradox of Race-Track Gambling," *New York Observer and Chronicle,* 19 Mar. 1908, 361; and George Shipman Payson, "Curse of Race-Track Gambling: Governor Hughes Deserves the Support of All Good Citizens," *New York Observer and Chronicle,* 19 Mar. 1908.

20. *NYT,* 3 Feb. 1908, 1-1.

21. *NYT,* 4 Feb. 1908, 3-3. See also Crafts, *New York Race Gambling Trust,* 1–2.

22. *NYT,* 17 Feb. 1908, 6-7.

23. James West Davidson, "The New Narrative History: How Narrative?" 329; John A. Lucas, "Caspar Whitney," 30–32, 36.

24. Caspar Whitney, "Reforms That Do Not Reform."

25. *NYT*, 4 Feb. 1908, 3-3.

26. "The Truth about Race-Track Gambling"; "The Breed of Horses and the Bred of Men." See also "The Governor's Crusade."

27. Hyde was said to have made a subscription on behalf of Engeman (who failed to pay) and later put in a bill for personal expenses covering that amount. In 1912, Hyde was convicted of accepting a bribe in consideration for depositing public money in certain banks. He was sentenced to two years in prison but was released on appeal. See Myers, *History of Tammany Hall*, 348–51. August Belmont II denied bribing legislators but admitted paying large sums to attorneys for legitimate services. TJC was financed primarily from members' dues of one hundred dollars, forfeits and fines for misdeeds at the track, and the sale of the *Stud Book*, the bible of breeding. *NYT*, 1 Dec. 1910, 5-2.

28. *NYT*, 1 July 1908, 1-2; *NYT*, 20 Oct. 1910, 1-1; *NYT*, 21 Oct. 1910, 10-2; *NYT*, 22 Oct. 1910, 3-1; *NYT*, 23 Oct. 1910, II: 16-1; *NYT*, 1 Dec. 1910, 5-2; *NYT*, 18 Feb. 1911, 1-7; *NYT*, 19 Feb. 1911, 3-2 (quote); Myers, *History of Tammany Hall*, 343–44.

29. Myers, *History of Tammany Hall*, 349–51; *Chicago Record-Herald*, 10 Aug. 1908, 12-1; *NYT*, 19 Nov. 1910, 1-3.

30. *NYT*, 30 June 1908, 14-1; *NYT*, 1 July 1908, 1-2; *NYT*, 30 Nov. 1910, 1-7; *NYT*, 3 Dec. 1910, 1; *NYT*, 6 Dec. 1910, 4-2; *NYT*, 8 Dec. 1910, 1-1.

31. *NYT*, 20 Feb. 1908, 1-3, 2-6.

32. *NYTr*, 4 Mar. 1908, cited in Betts, *America's Sporting Heritage*, 224–25.

33. *NYT*, 8 Mar. 1908, 5-3.

34. Perkins, *Charles Evans Hughes*, 19; *NYT*, 1 Feb. 2008, 6-3; John Richard O'Hare, *The Socioeconomic Aspects of Horse Racing*, 89.

35. Wesser, *Charles Evans Hughes*, 196–97; *NYT*, 27 Mar. 1908, 5-2.

36. *NYT*, 2 Apr. 1908, 1-1; *NYT*, 3 Apr. 1908, 6-2; Daniel W. McGuire, "Governor Hughes and the Race Track Gambling Issue: The Special Election of 1908," 67; "Racetrack Gambling," Series III, Box 7, Agnew Papers.

37. Wesser, *Charles Evans Hughes*, 198, 201; *NYT*, 18 May 1915, 6-2; *NYT*, 31 Mar. 1940, 43-1.

38. *NYT*, 9 Apr. 1908, 1-1, 8-1.

39. *NYT*, 8, Apr. 1908, 6-5, 4-4; *NYT*, 9 Apr. 1908, 1-1, 8-1; *NYT*, 13 Apr. 1908, 1-3; *NYT*, 17 Apr. 1908, 2-4; *NYT*, 25 Apr. 1908, 1-3; *NYT*, 28 May 1908, 1-3.

40. *NYT*, 8 Apr. 1908, 6-5, 4-4; *NYT*, 9 Apr. 1908, 1-1; "The Defeat of the Racing Bills" (editorial), *NYT*, 8-1; *NYW*, 8 Apr. 1908, 1-7; *BE*, 9 Apr. 1908, 4; Wesser, *Charles Evans Hughes*, 201.

41. *NYT*, 8 Apr. 1908, 6-5, 4-4; *NYT*, 9 Apr. 1908, 1-1, 8-1; *NYT*, 13 Apr. 1908, 1-3; *NYT*, 17 Apr. 1908, 2-4; *NYT*, 25 Apr. 1908, 1-3; *NYT*, 28 May 1908, 1-3. For Agnew's own assessment of the eight Republican votes against him, see "Agnew Memorandum," n.d., Agnew Papers. Agnew did not think that Knapp represented the sentiment of his district.

42. *NYT*, 2 Nov. 1906, 6-3; *NYT*, 6 May 1908, 3-2.

43. Wesser, *Charles Evans Hughes*, 200–201; Elting B. Morison, ed., *The Letters of Theodore Roosevelt*, 1192.

44. *NYT*, 18 May 1915, 6-2.

45. *NYT*, 9 Apr. 1908, 1-1; *NYT*, 11 Apr. 1908, 3-3; *Brooklyn Eagle*, 9 Apr. 1908, 1-1 (quote).

46. *NYT*, 13 May 1908, 1-5; McGuire, "Governor Hughes," 66–72; Wesser, *Charles Evans Hughes*, 203–7.

47. *NYT*, 28 May 1908, 4-2; *NYT*, 6 June 1908, 1-5; *NYT*, 9 June 1908, 3-1. Periodicals were very supportive of the fight against racing. See, for example, "The Case for Gambling on Race-Tracks," "The Case Against Race-Track Gambling," and "Governor Hughes's Fight for Reform."

48. *NYT*, 11 June 1908, 1; *NYT*, 12 June 1908, 1-1, 1-7; *NYT*, 31 Mar. 1940, 43-1; Wesser, *Charles Evans Hughes*, 206–8; *Albany Journal*, 11 June 1908 (quote), cited in Pusey, *Charles Evans Hughes*, 232. Boss Platt's biographer Harold F. Gosnell points out that the old-line Republicans had joined the Democrats in opposition. Gosnell, *Boss Platt and His New York Machine: A Study of the Political Leadership of Thomas C. Platt*, 306. On the debate, see Box 7, Folder 6, Agnew Papers.

49. *New York Evening Mail*, 26 June 1908 (quote), cited in Pusey, *Charles Evans Hughes*, 232; *NYTr*, n.d. (quote), cited in ibid.

50. "The Governor's Victory" (editorial), *NYT*, 12 June 1908, 6; *NYT*, 13 June 1908, 3-2; *BE*, 11 June 1908, 4-1; "The End of Race Track Gambling."

51. *Chicago Record-Herald*, 10 Aug. 1908, 12-1.

52. *NYT*, 12 June 1908, 1-7, 2-4. The tracks were assessed in 1908 at $2.4 million for tax purposes. Track evaluations included $2.5 million for the Belmont ($750,000 just for the land), $1.5 million for Sheepshead Bay, $900,000 for the BJC, $700,000 for the BBRA, $500,000 for Empire City, $400,000 for the MJC, and $300,000 for the Aqueduct. The article expected that the track sites would be heavily depreciated since the buildings and any developed land had little utility other than for racing. See also *NYMT*, 1 Feb. 1911, 2-1 (quote).

53. *NYT*, 12 June 1908, 2-4; W. Robertson, *Thoroughbred Racing*, 143. See also *NYMT*, 1 Feb. 1911, 2-1; *NYMT*, 22 Mar. 1911, 1-1.

54. *NYT*, 12 June 1908, 1-7, 3-3.

55. *NYT*, 14 Oct. 1910, 1-5; *NYT*, 15 Oct. 1910, 1-3. See also Myers, *History of Tammany Hall*, 348.

56. *NYT*, 20 Oct. 1910, 1-1; *NYT*, 14 Feb. 1911, 18-1. See also New York Legislature, Senate, "Proceedings of the Senate in the Matter of the Investigation Demanded by Senator Jotham P. Allds." Hyde was away on a hunting trip during the hearing, thereby avoiding a subpoena, because he did not want to testify, and especially because he reportedly took upwards of $500,000 from city accounts. The chamberlain was in charge of all money paid to the municipality, for which he was paid $12,000, third highest on New York's payroll. He did write a letter to Mayor Gaynor, his former law partner, asserting that Elder's charge of his having raised $500,000 to oppose the gambling acts was "untraceable hearsay." *NYT*, 25 Dec. 1910, 8-2; *NYT*, 2 Jan. 1911, 1-6; *NYT*, 3 Jan. 1911, 1-2; *NYT*, 7 Jan. 1911, 2-5; *NYT*, 8 Jan. 1911, 2-4; *NYT*, 12 Jan. 1911, 1-1. Hyde eventually resigned his position. He was convicted of forcing President Robin of the Northern Bank to make a $130,000 loan to support the tottering Carnegie Trust Company or face removal of city funds from the Robins Bank. *Washington Post*, 4 May 1911; *CT*, 30 Nov. 1912, 1. However, the appeal overturned the conviction. *Washington Post*, 20 June 1913, 3.

57. *NYT*, 20 Oct. 1910, 1-1; *NYT*, 21 Oct. 1910, 10-2; *NYT*, 22 Oct. 1910, 3-1; *NYT*, 23 Oct. 1910, II: 16-1; *NYT*, 2 Jan. 1911, 1-6; *NYT*, 3 Jan. 1911, 1-2; *NYT*, 7 Jan. 1911, 2-5; *NYT*, 8 Jan. 1911, 2-4; *NYT*, 12 Jan. 1911, 1-1; *NYT*, 13 Jan. 1911, 2-5 (quote); *NYT*, 15 Jan. 1911, 1-1; *NYT*, 16 Jan. 1911, 1-7; *NYT*, 18 Jan. 1911, 1-3. Schroeder subsequently landed in Sing Sing for stealing $4,000 from the Eagle Savings and Loan, where he was an executive. Gardner claimed at his trial that he had heard that Foelker was willing to accept money. He claimed that he had heard Foelker was promised $15,000 and took $10,000. *Washington Post*, 22 Feb. 1911, 3.

58. Myers, *History of Tammany Hall*, 349–51; *Chicago Record-Herald*, 10 Aug. 1908; *NYT*, 19 Nov. 1910, 1-3.

59. *NYT*, 19 Nov. 1910, 1-3; *NYT*, 9 Dec. 1910, 9-1. The MTA is said to have 150 members, who pay $25 dues, down by about 50 since the Agnew-Hart laws were passed.

60. *NYMT*, 2 Feb. 1911, 1-1, 2-1, 4-1; *NYMT*, 4 Feb. 1911, 4-1; *NYMT*, 18 Feb. 1911, 1-7; *NYMT*, 21 Feb. 1911, 1-7; *NYMT*, 22 Feb. 1911, 1-1; *NYMT*, 24 Feb. 1911, 1-1.

61. *NYT*, 13 Apr. 1908, 8-3, 1-1; *NYT*, 15 Apr. 1908, 1-1.

62. *NYT*, 16 Apr. 1908, 7-2.

63. *NYT*, 14 May 1908, 1-7; *NYT*, 17 May 1908, 2-7.

64. *NYT*, 12 June 1908, 1-7; *NYT*, 13 June 1908, 1-1, 3-2. Bookies expected to see the English system of betting employed, with wagers registered in a notebook, but no money changed hands. The bettors had to be personally known by the bookmakers who took a bet on a nod or word of mouth. Tattersall's served in London as a clearinghouse. Settlements were made every Monday morning, but if either the bookie or the client failed to meet his obligations, he was suspended from Tattersall's. Another plan that got little support was to form a gambling club where bettors would establish a line of credit of about a hundred dollars. They could then bet up to that amount, with settlement at the end of the day. However, few patrons could deposit on account as much money as would have been needed.

65. *NYT*, 14 June 1908, 1-1, 3-6; *NYT*, 15 June 1908, 16-3; *NYT*, 16 June 1908, 7-1; *NYT*, 6 July 1908, 5-5.

66. *NYT*, 18 June 1898, 8-3; *NYT*, 20 June 1908, 4-2.

67. *NYT*, 20 June 1908, 1-1; *NYT*, 21 June 1908, S1-3.

68. *NYT*, 20 June 1908, 4-1; *NYT*, 23 July 1908, 4-5; NYT, "What Is Bookmaking?" (letter to the editor), *NYT*, 23 July 1908, 6-6; *Chicago Record-Herald*, 4 July 1908, 8-3.

69. *NYT*, 6 July 1908, 5-5; *NYT*, 7 July 1908, 8-5.

70. *Chicago Record-Herald*, 4 July 1908, 8-3. See also *NYT*, 3 July 1908, 14-1.

71. *NYT*, 6 July 1908, 5-5; *NYT*, 7 July 1908, 8-5; *NYT*, 8 July 1908, 8-5.

72. *NYT*, 22 July 1908, 1-5; *NYT*, 23 July 1908, 4-5; *NYT*, 1 Aug. 1908, 3-1; *Chicago Record-Herald*, 22 July 1908, 1-5; *Chicago Record-Herald*, 1 Aug. 1908, 3-1; *Chicago Record-Herald*, 2 June 1909, 16-4.

73. *Chicago Record-Herald*, 1 Jan. 1909, 18; *Chicago Record-Herald*, 2 June 1909, 16-4; *NYT*, 21 Nov. 1908, 12-3; *NYT*, 1 Jan. 1909, 8-4 (quote); *NYT*, 27 Jan. 1909, 5-3.

74. *NYT*, 11 Aug. 1908, 1-7; *NYT*, 12 Aug. 1908, 3-3; *NYT*, 13 Aug. 1908, 5-2.

75. *Chicago Record-Herald*, 19 Aug. 1908, 1-5; *Chicago Record-Herald*, 2 Sept. 1908, 2-4; *Chicago Record-Herald*, 5 Sept. 1908, 2-6.

76. *Chicago Record-Herald*, 31 July 1908, 6-3; *Chicago Record-Herald*, 12 Aug. 1908, 3-3; *NYT*, 1 Aug. 1908, 3-1; *NYT*, 12 Aug. 1908, 3-3; *NYT*, 15 Aug. 1908, 5-4; *NYT*, 3 Sept. 1908, 3-5; *NYT*, 18 Sept. 1909, 6-2; Hotaling, *They're Off!* 192; Bradley, *Such Was Saratoga*, 297.

77. *NYT*, 4 Sept. 1908, 5-3; *NYT*, 28 Sept. 1908, 5-3; *NYT*, 8 Oct. 1908, 7-6; *NYT*, 11 Oct. 1908, C4-1; *NYT*, 5 Nov. 1908, 6-2 (quote).

78. *NYT*, 5 Nov. 1908, 6-2; *NYT*, 8 Nov. 1908, IV: S3-5; *NYT*, 18 Mar. 1909, 10-6.

79. *NYT*, 15 Oct. 1908, 1-5; *NYT*, 16 Oct. 1908, 7-5. On the "American Invasion," see Vamplew, *Turf*, 46–61.

80. *NYT*, 10 Sept. 1908, 1-3.

81. *NYT*, 6 Apr. 1909, 1-5.

82. *NYT*, 18 Oct. 1908, 8-1; *NYT*, 4 Nov. 1908, 7-2.

83. *NYT*, 18 Oct. 1908, 8-1.

84. *NYT*, 22 Oct. 1908, 1-5; *NYT*, 4 Nov. 1908, 7-2.

85. *NYT,* 6 Feb. 1909, 8-4. On the ending of racing in Louisiana, see *NYT,* 24 June 1908, 3-2; *NYT,* 23 Jan. 1909, 3; *NYT,* 25 Jan. 1909, 7-1; and *NYT,* 10 Jan. 1915, 38-3. On the death of racing in California, see, for example, *NYT,* 25 Jan. 1909, 7-1; *NYT,* 5 Feb. 1909, 5-3; *NYT,* 20 Feb. 1909, 8-5; *New York Call,* 20 Feb. 1909, 3-20; and Franklin Hichborn, *Story of the Session of the California Legislature of 1909,* 52–67. Legal thoroughbred racing resumed in Louisiana in 1915 and in California in 1933.

86. *NYT,* 18 Mar. 1909, 10-6 (quote); *NYT,* 2 Apr. 1909, 8-4; *NYT,* 1 Apr. 1909, 6-2; *NYT,* 14 Apr. 1909, 3-4.

87. *NYT,* 6 Apr. 1909, 10-3; *NYT,* 15 Apr. 1909, 16-3.

88. *NYT,* 11 May 1909, 10-4; *NYT,* 6 Apr. 1909, 10-3; *NYT,* 9 Nov. 1909, 11-3.

89. *NYT,* 11 July 1908, 14-3; *NYT,* 8 May 1909, 4-4; *NYT,* 10 May 1909, 8-4; *NYT,* 17 May 1909, 8-4; *People ex rel. Lichtenstein vs. Langan* (1909) [190 N.Y., 260]; "Gaming—'Bookmaking'—Oral Bets."

90. *NYT,* 14 May 1909, 1-7; *New York Sun,* 12 Nov. 1909, 6-3.

91. *NYT,* 22 May 1909, 9-3.

92. *NYT,* 3 Aug. 1909, 8-3; *NYT,* 12 Aug. 1909, 9-1; *NYT,* 5 Sept. 1909, II: 2-2; *New York Sun,* 21 Nov. 1909, 6-3.

93. *NYT,* 5 Sept. 1909, II: 1-2.

94. *NYT,* 18 Sept. 1909, 6-2.

95. Ibid.; *NYT,* 19 Sept. 1909, 7-1; *NYT,* 28 Sept. 1909, 6-4; *NYT,* 29 Sept. 1909, 16-3; *NYT,* 2 Oct. 1909, 11-5; *NYT,* 5 Oct. 1909, 20-4; *NYT,* 6 Oct. 1909, 4-3.

96. See table 5, chap. 9; *New York Sun,* 21 Nov. 1909, 10-3.

97. On the end of the MTA, see Hotaling, *They're Off!* 192; and Michael Alexander, *Jazz Age Jews,* 29–30, 32–33. For Lichtenstein's obituary, see *NYT,* 6 June 1918, 24-6. From 1912 to 1917, Rothstein was a stockholder in the Havre de Grace racecourse. He established the Redstone stable in 1915 and began spending a lot of time at the tracks, racing against such blue bloods as Harry Payne Whitney, an activity few Jews could enjoy, much less a professional gambler. He also made very big bets, earning three hundred thousand dollars on one race at Havre de Grace in 1917 and consistently tried to manipulate the betting odds in his favor. As a result, in 1917 August Belmont II barred him from the clubhouse at Belmont Park and threatened to keep him off the track. Rothstein threatened to spend up to one million dollars to shut down the state's tracks. His friend Herbert Bayard Swope, editor of the *World,* put in a good word for him with Belmont, "German Jew to former German Jew," and Rothstein had his privileges restored. One day, Belmont was surprised to see Rothstein at the track. Rothstein said it was a holiday. "Why yes, Rothstein told him: 'You ought to know Mr. Belmont. It's Rosh Hashanah.'" Alexander speculates this all irritated Belmont "as a reminder of his assimilation and his invented heritage." Ibid., 38; Pietrusza, *Rothstein,* 110 (quote). On Rothstein and racing, see also Pietrusza, *Rothstein,* 109–22, esp. 109, 11–121, for reputed fixed races.

98. *NYT,* 12 Oct. 1909, 1-7 (quote), 2-5; *NYT,* 13 Oct. 1909, 1-5; *NYT,* 3 Nov. 1909, 1-7. On the 1909 election, see Procter, *William Randolph Hearst,* 256–62.

99. *NYT,* 12 Oct. 1909, 1-7, 2-5; *NYT,* 13 Oct. 1909, 1-5; *NYT,* 14 Oct. 1909, 8-2; *NYT,* 25 Oct. 1909, 3-7; *NYT,* 30 Oct. 1909, 3-3; Pink, *Gaynor, the Tammany Mayor;* Mortimer Smith, *William Jay Gaynor: Mayor of New York;* Lately Thomas, "Tammany Picked an Honest Man."

100. *NYT,* 25 Oct. 1909, 3-7; *NYT,* 30 Oct. 1909, 3-3.

101. *NYT,* 10 Nov. 1909, 4-1; *NYT,* 11 Nov. 1909, 7-3, 8-3.

102. Liebman, "Horseracing in New York," 560; *NYT,* 26 Jan. 1910, 6-4; *NYT,* 15 Mar. 1910, 1-2.

103. *NYT,* 6 Apr. 1910, 8-5; *NYT,* 7 Apr. 1910, 2-5 (quote); *NYT,* 14 Apr. 1910, 20-3; *NYT,* 21 Apr. 1910, 4-3; *NYT,* 22 Apr. 1910, 8-5.

104. *NYT,* 21 Apr. 1910, 8-5.

105. *NYT,* 27 Apr. 1910, 13-1; *NYT,* 4 May 1910, 5-1; *NYT,* 5 May 1910, 8-4, 10-4; *NYT,* 17 May 1910, 3-2; *NYT,* 20 May 1910, 3-3; *NYT,* 16 June 1910, 7-3; *NYT,* 2 Sept. 1910, 5-3; *NYMT,* 5 May 1910, 1-4; *NYMT,* 16 June 1910, 1-7; Liebman, "Horseracing in New York," 560.

106. *NYT,* 4 June 1910, 6-1; *NYMT,* 2 June 1910, 4-1; *NYMT,* 6 June 1910, 1-4.

107. "The Sport of Kings—or of Gamblers"; "Governor Triumphant and Legislature to Be Rattled," *BE,* 5 May 1910, 4-2; "Bury the Betting Bills," *BE,* 19 May 1910, 4-2.

108. *NYT,* 9 Feb. 1910, 9-2.

109. *NYT,* 15 Apr. 1910, 11-1; *NYT,* 16 Apr. 1910, 13-1; *NYT,* 14 May 1910, 11-1; *NYT,* 31 May 1910, 10-3; *NYT,* 14 Dec. 1911, 11-2.

110. *NYT,* 18 June 1910, 11-1; *NYT,* 5 July 1910, 10-1.

111. *NYT,* 6 July 1910, 8-5.

112. *NYT,* 25 July 1910, 11-1; *NYT,* 4 Aug. 1910, 6-3; *NYT,* 5 Aug. 1910, 6-5; *NYT,* 14 Aug. 1910, C7-1; Bradley, *Such Was Saratoga,* 297 (quote).

113. *NYT,* 2 Sept. 1910, 5-3; *NYT,* 4 Sept. 1910, C6-1; *NYT,* 22 Mar. 1911, 1-3. Belmont was partially dismantled for a series of international air contests, ensuring the audience an unobstructed view of the contests.

114. The Oriental Hotel went down in 1916. The Brighton Beach Hotel remained until 1924. See Kapsales, "From the Gilded Age to Progressivism," 107.

115. *NYMT,* 1 Apr. 1911; W. Robertson, *Thoroughbred Racing,* 204, 581, 583, 585, 590; Henry Sedley, "The Hard Case of the Thoroughbred," 188–89.

116. *NYMT,* 1 Apr. 1911; *NYT,* 12 Dec. 1911, 3-6; Pusey, *Charles Evans Hughes,* 232.

117. W. Robertson, *Thoroughbred Racing,* 197–200; *NYT,* 10 May 1914, S2-5; *NYT,* 7 May 1915, 10-3; Barbara Anne Helberg, "Pari-Mutuel Betting Origins Wagering on the Horses Originated in France, Not England."

118. J. B. Kelly, "At the Track," 69–71.

119. *NYT,* 23 Mar. 1911, 8-2.

120. *NYT,* 22 Mar. 1911, 1-3; *NYT,* 16 Nov. 1914, 12-1; *NYT,* 31 Mar. 1920, 12-5; *NYT,* 11 Jan. 1922, 30-5; *NYW,* 2 Oct. 1909; "Sheepshead Bay Race Track Demolished: Former Structures Will Probably Be Replaced with Dwellings." Sheepshead Bay was actually assessed later in 1911 at $2.75 million. See *NYT,* 14 Dec. 1911, 11-2. On Brighton, see *NYT,* 14 Dec. 1911, 11-2; and *NYT,* 28 June 1923, 19-8. The Gravesend site was originally bought for $75,000. *NYT,* 9 Oct. 1921, VIII: 3-2; Brooklyn Eagle, *Brooklyn by the "Brooklyn Eagle,"* 30–31. Gravesend was seemingly sold to Harmon back in 1920 for $2.5 million, but apparently the deal fell through, and he subsequently bought the site for one-third the price. *NYT,* 31 Mar. 1920, 12-5.

121. *NYT,* 21 Oct. 1910, 5-1; *NYT,* 7 Nov. 1910, 1-7; *NYT,* 8 Nov. 1910, 4-2; *NYT,* 13 Nov. 1910, 1-7.

122. *NYMT,* 6 Apr. 1911, 3-4; *NYMT,* 7 Apr. 1911, 12-4; *NYT,* 7 Apr. 1911, 12-4.

123. *NYMT,* 6 Apr. 1911, 3-4.

124. Ibid.

125. *NYMT,* 18 Apr. 1911, 1-7; *NYT,* 18 Apr. 1911, 12-2; *NYT,* 21 Apr. 1911, 8-2; *NYT,* 26 Apr. 1911, 6-2.

126. *NYT,* 10 May 1911, 5-2; *NYT,* 23 May 1911, 3-4; *NYT,* 24 May 1911, 7-3.

127. *NYT,* 23 May 1911, 3-4; *NYT,* 24 May 1911, 7-3; *NYT,* 25 May 1911, 10-3; *NYT,* 15 June 1911, 6-2; *NYT,* 16 June 1911, 8-4; *NYT,* 19 June 1911, 8-5; *NYT,* 21 June 1911, 5-2; *NYT,* 22 June 1911, 10-3; *NYT,* 20 Sept. 1911, 1-5.

128. *NYT,* 24 May 1911, 7-3.

129. Ibid. See also U.S. Congress, Senate, Committee on the Judiciary, *Interstate Race Gambling,* 13, 15; and Harry Brolaski, *Easy Money: Being the Experiences of a Reformed Gambler,* 328.

130. "The Gittins Bills" (letter to the editor), *NYT,* 7 July 1911, 8-6.

131. *NYT,* 30 May 1911, 10-4. The *Times* was apparently unaware that there was still a lot of betting on baseball. See, for example, Riess, *Touching Base,* 87–91.

132. *NYT,* 14 July 1911, 3-5; *NYT,* 15 July 1911, 6-1; *NYT,* 20 July 1911, 1-4; *Washington Post,* 20 July 1911, 9. On Wagner, see J. Joseph Hutchmacher, *Senator Robert Wagner and the Rise of Urban Liberalism;* and his obituary, *NYT,* 4 May 1953, 1-2.

133. *NYT,* 21 July 1911, 1-3; *NYT,* 22 July 1911, 6-3; *NYT,* 20 Sept. 1911, 1-5.

134. *NYT,* 20 Sept. 1911, 1-5; *NYT,* 2 Oct. 1911, 10-1.

135. Riess, "In the Ring and Out," 99–112; *NYT,* 8 June 1911, 2-4; *NYT,* 22 June 1911, 9-1; *NYT,* 20 Sept. 1911, 1-5; *NYT,* 21 Sept. 1911, 12-4; *NYT,* 1 Oct. 1911, 5-5; "The Persistent Legislature" (editorial), *NYT,* 2 Oct. 1911, 10-1.

136. *NYT,* 8 Nov. 1911, 2-3; "The Assembly" (editorial), *NYT,* 8 Nov. 1911, 12-2; "A Bad Year for Bosses," *NYT,* 10 Nov. 1911, 10-2.

137. *People v. Lambrix,* 204 N.Y. 261 (1912); "Bet Memorandum No Violation of Agnew-Hart Law"; *Washington Post,* 24 Jan. 1912, 8; *NYT,* 26 Jan. 1912, 9-6 (quote).

138. "Regulate Racing by Commission"; "Bookmaking to Be Defined by Law in a New Measure"; "The Race-Track Bills" (editorial), *NYT,* 24 Feb. 1912, 10-4; *NYT,* 9 Mar. 1912, 24-4.

139. "Gradual Disappearance of Fairs in the Empire State"; "Fair Associations Urge Passage of Racing Bills"; "Change in Racing Laws Is Urged."

140. *NYT,* 7 June 1912, 11-3; *NYT,* 11 June 1912, 20-3; "Important Move in New York Betting Case."

141. *NYT,* 30 June 1912, IV: 8-4; *NYT,* 27 Aug. 1917, 8-5; "Private Betting Within the Law."

142. *NYT,* 14 Oct. 1912, 3-4; *NYT,* 22 Feb. 1913, 3-3; *NYMT,* 22 Feb. 1913, 1-7; *People ex rel. Lichtenstein vs. Langan,* 190 N.Y. 260; "Ordinary Betting on a Horse Race No Crime."

143. *NYT,* 22 Feb. 1913, 3-3; *NYT,* 16 Oct. 1912, 14-5; *NYT,* 12 Mar. 1913, 9-5; "Pari-Mutuels to Restore Racing"; *NYMT,* 22 Feb. 1913, 1-7; *CT,* 27 Feb. 1913, 14-3.

144. *CT,* 5 Apr. 1913, 10-1; Hotaling, *They're Off!* 197; *NYT,* 5 Apr. 1913, 1-3. James Butler announced he had purchased five hundred of the four thousand shares of the QCJC (Aqueduct) from David Holland. The majority (twenty-two hundred shares) was held by the BJC, run by Philip Dwyer.

145. *NYT,* 6 Nov. 1912, 1-6; *NYT,* 7 Nov. 1912, 5-4.

146. *NYT,* 6 Apr. 1913, 1-4; *NYT,* 7 May 1913, 1-4. For Sulzer's obituary, see *NYT,* 7 Nov. 1941, 23-3.

147. The first horse races were run by two obscure amateur clubs, the year-old Rockaway Hunting Club followed by the Meadow Brook Steeplechase, both at Belmont Park Terminal at the end of April. See *NYT,* 28 Apr. 1913, 9-4; *NYT,* 31 May 1913, 1-8; W. Robertson, *Thoroughbred Racing,* 213; and New York State Racing Commission, *Annual Report of the State Racing Commission, 1913,* 1.

148. *NYT,* 18 Apr. 1934, 26-4.

149. W. Robertson, *Thoroughbred Racing,* 214–15; *NYT,* 22 June 1913, S2-1; *NYT,* 29 June 1913, 1-1. In his "record" race, Whisk Broom supposedly ran the final fraction in a seemingly impossible 23.2. See W. Robertson, *Thoroughbred Racing,* 215.

150. *NYT,* 1 Aug. 1913, 8-5; *NYT,* 8 Aug. 1913, 5-5; *NYT,* 9 Aug. 1913, 5-5; Bradley, *Such Was Saratoga,* 300–301; New York State Racing Commission, *Annual Report of the State Racing Commission, 1913,* 1.

151. *NYT,* 13 Mar. 1913, 1-6; *NYT,* 5 Mar. 1914, 8-6; "The Revival of Racing" (editorial), *NYT,* 31 May 1913, 10-2 (quote).

152. W. Robertson, *Thoroughbred Racing*, 217; *NYT*, 21 June 1914, S3-7; *NYT*, 12 July 1914, S2-1; *NYT*, 26 July 1914, 12-1; *NYT*, 1 Aug. 1914, 9-3; *NYT*, 27 Sept. 1914, S4-4; New York State Racing Commission, *Annual Report of the State Racing Commission, 1914*, 1. Outside the ECRT was "Dead Head Hill" where people briefly made fifty-cent bets with bookmakers until the police broke it up. See *NYT*, 26 July 1914, 12-1; *NYT*, 28 July 1914, 8-7.

153. New York State Racing Commission, *Annual Report of the State Racing Commission, 1918*, 1; W. Robertson, *Thoroughbred Racing*, 223, 583.

154. *NYT*, 13 May 1917, 20-5; *NYT*, 17 June 1917, S2-1; *NYT*, 26 Jan. 1917, 6-1; *NYT*, 28 Jan. 1917, S2-6; *NYT*, 12 June 1919, 13-3; *NYT*, 19 May 1920, 13-4; *NYT*, 13 June 1920, VIII: 1-1; *NYT*, 14 May 1922, 1-1; *NYT*, 11 June 1922, 27-1; "The History of Churchill Downs and the Kentucky Derby." The Derby of 1923 drew seventy-five thousand. *NYT*, 20 May 1923, S1-1. On the Preakness, see J. B. Kelly, "At the Track."

155. Betts, *America's Sporting Heritage*, 266–67; *NYT*, 2 Mar. 1922, 46-4.

156. *NYT*, 28 Mar. 1934, 29-1; *NYT*, 18 Apr. 1934, 1-7; *NYT*, 26 Nov. 1934, 22-1; Betts, *America's Sporting Heritage*, 267; Hotaling, *They're Off!* 238.

157. *NYT*, 1 May 1939, 1-2; *NYT*, 11 May 1939, 1-3; *NYT*, 25 June 1939, E10-1; *NYT*, 2 Apr. 1940, 1-6; *NYT*, 21 Apr. 1940, 66-5; *NYT*, 2 Jan. 1941, 29-1; Hotaling, *They're Off!* 251.

12. Conclusion: Racing, Machine Politics, and Organized Crime

1. Riess, "Sports and Machine Politics."

2. For a contemporary analysis of sports gambling, see Hugh Fullerton, "American Gambling and Gamblers." On baseball gambling, see Riess, *Touching Base*, 87–96; and Daniel E. Ginsburg, *The Fix Is In: A History of Baseball Gambling and Game Fixing Scandals*. On the Black Sox, see Eliot Asinof, *Eight Men Out: The Black Sox and the 1919 World Series*; Seymour, *American Baseball*, 2:294–339; Daniel A. Nathan, *Saying It's So: A Cultural History of the Black Sox Scandal*; and Gene Carney, *Burying the Black Sox: How Baseball's Cover Up of the 1919 World Series Fix Almost Succeeded.* On gambling in boxing, see Riess, *City Games*, 19–21, 172–73, 178–79; and Gorn, *Manly Art*, 139–40, 213, 214, 233, 243. On boxing fixes, see Colleen Aycock and Mark Scott, *Joe Gans: A Biography of the First African American World Boxing Champion*, 63–81; Jake LaMotta and Pete Savage, *Raging Bull: My Story*, 135–38, 143–44, 156–58, 161–63; Jeffrey T. Sammons, *Beyond the Ring: The Role of Boxing in American Society*, 87–88, 146–48; Teddy Brenner, *Only the Ring Was Square*, 17–20; and Steven A. Riess, "Only the Ring Was Square: Frankie Carbo and the Underworld Control of American Boxing." On the growing presence of the underworld in racing, see Riess, *City Games*, 191–94; and Humbert Nelli, *The Business of Crime: Italians and Syndicate Crime in the United States*, 229–34.

3. Lindberg, *Gambler King of Clark Street*, 165–74, 244–51.

4. *CT*, 2 June 1887, 3-1.

5. As in the depressions of 1837 and 1857, Americans seemed to become more religious and moralistic as they hoped to escape the bad times. See Whitney R. Cross, *The Burned Over District: The Social and Intellectual History of Enthusiastic Religion in Western New York, 1800–1850*; Judith Wellmann, *Grass Roots Reform in the Burned-Over District of Upstate New York: Religion, Abolition, and Democracy*; and Darrel M. Robertson, *The Chicago Revival, 1876: Society and Revivalism in a Nineteenth-Century City*.

6. Hammack, *Power and Society*, 101, 103, 111, 342n109.

7. Betts, *America's Sporting Heritage*, 266–67.

Bibliography

Archives

Agnew, George Bliss. Papers. Special Collections. New York Public Library.

Belmont Family Papers. Catalogued Correspondence. Rare Book and Manuscript Library, Butler Library, Columbia Univ., New York.

Fuller, Robert Higginson, comp. *Hughes Administration Scrapbook of Newspaper Clippings, Etc.* Microfilm. Manuscript and Archives Division, New York Public Library.

Walbaum, Gottfried. "Reminiscences of Gottfried Walbaum, 1920–1931." National Museum of Racing and Hall of Fame, Saratoga Springs, NY.

Government Documents

"The Fourth Constitution of New York, 1894." http://www.courts.state.ny.us/history/pdf/Library/1894_New_YorkConstitution.pdf.

Manual of the Legislature of New Jersey, 1894. Trenton: T. F. Fitzgerald, 1894.

New York City. Department of Police. *Annual Report of the Police Department of the City of New York [1885–1916].* New York: Martin B. Brown, 1886–1917.

New York State Legislature. Assembly. Special Committee to Investigate the Public Offices and Departments of the City of New York. *Report of the Special Committee of the Assembly Appointed to Investigate the Public Offices and Departments of the City of New York and of the Counties Therein Included.* New York: J. B. Lyons, 1900.

New York State Legislature. Senate. "Proceedings of the Senate in the Matter of the Investigation Demanded by Senator Jotham P. Allds." In *Senate Document No. 28, 133rd Session.* Albany: J. B. Lyon, 1910.

———. *Report and Proceedings of the Senate Committee Appointed to Investigate the Police Department of the City of New York.* Albany: J. B. Lyon, 1895.

New York State Racing Commission. *Annual Report of the State Racing Commission [1895–1919].* Albany: Wynkoop Hallenbeck Crawford, 1896–1920.

U.S. Congress. Senate. Committee on Interstate Commerce. *Prevention of Transmission of Race-Gambling Bets: Hearing Before the Subcommittee of the Committee on Interstate Commerce, Sixty-fourth Congress, Second Session.* Washington, DC: Government Printing Office, 1917.

U.S. Congress. Senate. Committee on the Judiciary. *By Telegraph: Hearings Before the United States Senate Committee on the Judiciary, Sixtieth Congress, Second Session, on Jan. 21, 1909.* Washington, DC: Government Printing Office, 1909.

————. *Interstate Race Gambling: Hearings Before the United States Senate Committee on the Judiciary, Sixty-first Congress, Second Session, on Dec. 14, 1909.* Washington, DC: Government Printing Office, 1909.

Racing Records

Goodwin's Annual Official Turf Guide for [1894–1907]. New York: Goodwin Bros., 1894–1907.

Newspapers and Sports Weeklies

Brooklyn Eagle. 1880–1910.

Chicago Daily News. 1875–1904.

Chicago Journal. 1897.

Chicago Record-Herald. 1904–12.

Chicago Times. 1888.

Chicago Tribune. 1870–1912.

Detroit Journal. 1886.

Lewiston (Maine) Evening Journal. 1892.

Los Angeles Times. 1899, 1906.

National Police Gazette. 1895.

Newark Evening News. 1891–93.

New York American. 1908.

New York Clipper. 1872–93.

New York Evening Journal. 1908.

New York Morning Telegraph. 1902–11.

New York Observer and Chronicle. 1908.

New York Sun. 1888, 1895, 1905.

New York Times. 1851–1940.

New York Tribune. 1885–1908.

New York World. 1884–85, 1900, 1904.

Philadelphia Inquirer. 1893.

Rochester Times. 1907.

Spirit of the Times. 1845–1902.

Trenton Daily True American. 1890–91.

Turf, Field, and Farm. 1865–75.

Washington Post. 1907.

Contemporary Sources

Bache, Rene. "What an Average Day's Horse Racing Costs." *Outlook* 48 (July 1906): 412–18.

"Bet Memorandum No Violation of Agnew-Hart Law." *Thoroughbred Record* 75 (27 Jan. 1912): 45.

"Bookmaking to Be Defined by Law in a New Measure." *Thoroughbred Record* 75 (2 Mar. 1912): 101.

"The Breed of Horses and the Bred of Men." *Independent* 64 (20 Feb. 1908): 428–29.

Brolaski, Harry. *Easy Money: Being the Experiences of a Reformed Gambler.* Cleveland: Searchlight, 1911.

Buel, Clarence Clough. "The Degradation of a State; or, The Charitable Career of the Louisiana Lottery." *Century* 43 (Feb. 1892): 618–32.

"The Case Against Race-Track Gambling." *Outlook* 89 (9 May 1908): 49.

"The Case for Gambling on Race-Tracks." *Outlook* 89 (9 May 1908): 49.

"Change in Racing Laws Is Urged." *Thoroughbred Record* 75 (30 Mar. 1912): 152.

"The Club-House of the New York Jockey Club." *Harper's Weekly* 35 (20 June 1891): 465.

"Coaches at Jerome Park on a Race Day." *Harper's Weekly* 30 (19 June 1886): 389.

Cole, Edward W. *Racing Maxims and Methods of "Pittsburgh Phil" (George E. Smith): Condensed Wisdom of Twenty Years Experience on the Track from the Most Successful Speculator in the History of the American Turf from the Only Personal Interviews Ever Given by the Famous Horseman.* 1908. Reprint, Las Vegas: Gamblers Book Club, 1968.

Comstock, Anthony. *Gambling Outrages; or, Improving the Breed of Horses at the Expense of Public Morals.* New York: American News, 1887.

———. "Pool Rooms and Pool Selling." *North American Review* 147 (1893): 601–10.

———. *Race Track Infamy; or, Do Gamblers Own New York State? A Scathing Exposure of How the Constitution of New York State Is Flagrantly Violated by Common Gamblers.* New York: Eddy Press, 1904.

———. *Traps for the Young.* Ed. Robert Bremner. 1883. Reprint, Cambridge: Belknap Press of Harvard Univ. Press, 1967.

Crafts, Wilbur F. *The Truth about the New York Race Gambling Trust.* Albany: Reform Bureau, 1908.

Cullen, Clarence L. "The Racing Game." *Everybody's Magazine* 18 (Spring 1908): 455–65.

Dewitt, Benjamin Parke. *The Progressive Movement: A Nonpartisan, Comprehensive Discussion of Current Tendencies in American Politics.* New York: Macmillan, 1915.

"The End of Race Track Gambling." *Outlook* 89 (20 June 1908): 354–55.

"Fair Associations Urge Passage of Racing Bills." *Thoroughbred Record* 75 (23 Mar. 1912): 135.

"The Fashion and Boston Match." *American Turf Register* 13 (May 1842): 367–80.

"A Finish on the Celebrated Saratoga Course." *Harper's Weekly* 50 (25 Aug. 1906): 1218.

Flynt, Josiah. "The Men Behind the Pool-Rooms." *Cosmopolitan* 42 (Apr. 1907): 636–45.

———. *My Life.* New York: Outing, 1908.

———. "Pool-Room Spider and the Gambling Fly." *Cosmopolitan* 42 (Mar. 1907): 513–21.

———. "The Pool-Room Vampire and Its Money Mad Victims." *Cosmopolitan* 42 (Feb. 1907): 359–71.

Fullerton, Huge. "American Gambling and Gamblers." *American Magazine* 77 (Feb. 1914): 33–38.

"Gaming—'Bookmaking'—Oral Bets." *Michigan Law Review* 87 (May 1910): 592.

"Governor Hughes's Fight for Reform." *Independent* 64 (30 Apr. 1908): 940.

"The Governor's Crusade." *Independent* 64 (12 Mar. 1908): 592–93.

"Gradual Disappearance of Fairs in the Empire State." *Thoroughbred Record* 75 (23 Mar. 1912): 134.

"Grand Stand, Monmouth Park: The Hurdles Race." *Harper's Weekly* 14 (13 Aug. 1870): 521–22.

"The Grandstand and Race-Track of the New York Jockey Club Preparing for the Opening." *Harper's Weekly* 33 (17 Aug. 1889): 656–57.

"The Great U.S. Match Race: Boston v. Fashion." Turf Hallmarks. http://www.tbheritage.com/TurfHallmarks/BostonvsFashion.html.

Harding, William H. *John Morrissey: His Life, Battles, and Wrangles, from His Birth in Ireland until He Died a State Senator.* New York: Richard K. Fox, 1881.

Harvey, Charles M. "Reform in Missouri." *World Today* 8 (June 1905): 599.

Hichborn, Franklin. *Story of the Session of the California Legislature of 1909.* San Francisco: Press of J. H. Barry, 1909.

"Horse-Racing." *Nation* 3 (11 Oct. 1866): 293.

"Important Move in New York Betting Case." *Thoroughbred Record* 76 (6 July 1912): 6.

"The Jerome Park Races." *Harper's Weekly* 11 (15 June 1867): 369–70.

Kennedy, Thomas H. *The Racing Swindle: A Satire.* San Francisco: James M. Barry, 1906.

Kirsch, George B., ed. *Sports in War, Revival, and Expansion, 1860–1880.* Vol. 4 of *Sports in North America: A Documentary History.* Gulf Breeze, FL: Academic International, 1995.

Lapp, John A. "Race Track Gambling." *American Political Science Review* 2 (5 Mar. 1908): 425.

Lewis, Alfred Henry. *Richard Croker.* New York: Life, 1901.

Logan, Olive. "Life at Long Branch." *Harper's New Monthly Magazine* 53 (Sept. 1876): 481–95.

"Long Island City." *Harper's Weekly* 26 (7 Oct. 1882): 627.

"Long Island City Pool Rooms." *Harper's Weekly* 26 (2 Sept. 1882): 555.

"Long Island Railroad Supplement to Time Table No. 2." http://arrts-arrchives.com/tunnel.html.

Mathews, Franklin. "'Wide-Open' New York." *Harper's Weekly* 42 (22 Oct. 1898): 1045–46.

"Maxims of Pittsburgh Phil." *Railbird Thoroughbred Racing News and Notes.* http://www.jessicachapel.com/railbird/archives/000610maxims_ofpittsburgh_phil.html.

McAdoo, William. *Guarding a Great City.* New York: Harper and Bros., 1906.

McClellan, George B., Jr. *The Gentleman and the Tiger: The Autobiography of George B. McClellan, Jr.* Ed. Harold C. Syrett. Philadelphia: Lippincott, 1956.

Milnor, William. *A History of the Schuylkill Fishing Company of the State in Schuylkill.* Philadelphia: Schuylkill Fishing Company, 1889.

Mines, Flavel Scott. "The Study of a Pool-Room." *Harper's Weekly* 36 (17 Dec. 1892): 1210.

"A Moral of Late Events." *Harper's Weekly* 36 (9 Apr. 1892): 338.

Morison, Elting B., ed. *The Letters of Theodore Roosevelt.* Vol. 6, *The Big Stick, 1907–1909.* Cambridge: Harvard Univ. Press, 1952.

Morris, John, ed. *Wanderings of a Vagabond: An Autobiography.* New York: John O'Connor, 1873.

Needham, Henry Beach. "The College Athlete: His Amateur Code, Its Evasion, and Administration." *McClure's* 25 (July 1904): 260–67.

———. "The College Athlete: How Commercialism Is Making Him Professional." *McClure's* 25 (June 1904): 115–28.

New York Evening Post. *Tammany Biographies.* 3rd ed. New York: New York Evening Post, 1894.

"The New York Jockey Club." *Harper's Weekly* 25 (17 Aug. 1889): 657–58.

"A New York Pool-Room." *Harper's Weekly* 36 (2 Apr. 1892): 324.

"Opening Race at the Jerome Park, Fordham, New York, June 8, 1868." *Harper's Weekly* 12 (27 June 1868): 408–9.

"Ordinary Betting on a Horse Race No Crime." *Thoroughbred Record* 76 (19 Oct. 1912): 183.

"Pari-Mutuels to Restore Racing." *Thoroughbred Record* 76 (19 Oct. 1912): 187.

Parkhurst, Charles H. *Forty Years in New York.* New York: Macmillan, 1923.

———. *Our Fight with Tammany.* New York: C. Scribner's Sons, 1895.

Phillips, David Graham. "The Delusion of the Race-Track." *Cosmopolitan* 38 (Jan. 1905): 251–66.

———. "The Treason of the Senate." *Cosmopolitan* 40 (Apr. 1906): 628–38.

"Private Betting Within the Law." *Thoroughbred Record* 76 (3 Aug. 1912): 50.

"The Profits of Book-Makers." *Harper's Weekly* 37 (25 Nov. 1893): 1130–31.

Quinn, John P. *Gambling and Gambling Devices: Being a Complete Systematic Educational Exposition Designed to Instruct the Youth of the World to Avoid All Forms of Gambling.* Canton, Ohio: John P. Quinn, 1912.

"The Racing Season at Saratoga: The Running of the 'Saratoga Special.'" *Harper's Weekly* 49 (19 Aug. 1905): 1191.

"Regulate Racing by Commission." *Thoroughbred Record* 75 (24 Feb. 1912): 87.

"Richard Croker, Derby Winner." *Harper's Weekly* 51 (29 June 1907): 946.

Riley, Elihu S. *"The Ancient City": A History of Annapolis, Maryland, 1649–1887.* Annapolis: Record Printing Office, 1887.

Riordan, William, ed. *Plunkitt of Tammany Hall.* 1905. Reprint, New York: Dutton, 1963.

Rowe, W. H. "The Turf Career of Hon. W. C. Whitney." *Outing* 36 (Sept. 1900): 453–56.

Sackett, William E. *Modern Battles of Trenton: Being a History of New Jersey's Politics and Legislation from the Year 1868 to the Year 1894.* Trenton: Murphy, 1895.

Scharf, J. T., and Thompson Westcott. *History of Philadelphia, 1609–1884.* 3 vols. Philadelphia: L. H. Everts, 1884.

Sedley, Henry. "The Hard Case of the Thoroughbred." *Outing Magazine* 62 (Apr. 1913): 188–93.

"Selling 'Auction Pools' on a Horse Race." *Harper's Weekly* 32 (11 Aug. 1888): 589.

"Sheepshead Bay Race Track Demolished: Former Structures Will Probably Be Replaced with Dwellings." *American Architect* 118 (14 July 1920): 60.

Smith, Matthew Hale. *Sunshine and Shadow in New York.* Hartford, CT: J. B. Burr, 1868.

South Carolina Jockey Club. *History of the Turf in South Carolina.* Charleston: Russell, Jones, 1857.

Speed, John Gilmer. "A Holiday Crowd at the Races." *Harper's Weekly* 36 (16 July 1892): 690.

———. "The Pool-Room Evil." *Harper's Weekly* 26 (2 Apr. 1892): 319.

"The Sport of Kings—or of Gamblers." *Outlook* 99 (9 Sept. 1911): 57–58.

Stead, William T. *If Christ Came to Chicago.* London: Review of Reviews, 1894.

Steffens, Lincoln. *The Autobiography of Lincoln Steffens.* New York: Harcourt, Brace, 1931.

"The Suburban Handicap." *Harper's Weekly* 36 (18 June 1892): 596–97.

Sullivan, Mark. "The Pool Room Evil." *Outlook* 77 (28 May 1904): 212–16.

Tarbell, Ida M. *All in the Day's Work: An Autobiography.* New York: Macmillan, 1939.

Thompson, Scott. "The New York Jockey Club." *Harper's Weekly* 33 (17 Aug. 1889): 657–58.

Trevelyan, Charles. "Our Turf's Transition." *Outing* 28 (June 1896): 221–30.

"The Truth about Race-Track Gambling." *Outlook* 51 (15 Feb. 1908): 334–35.

Vosburgh, William S. "The Passing of Jerome Park." *Outing* 38 (Aug. 1901): 513–20.

Whitney, Caspar. "Reforms That Do Not Reform." *Outlook* 52 (Apr. 1908): 124–25.

Workes, John D. "The Race-Track Evil and the Newspapers." *Arena* 39 (Apr. 1908): 427–29.

Other Sources

Adelman, Melvin L. "The Development of Modern Athletics: Sport in New York City, 1820–1870." PhD diss., Univ. of Illinois, 1980.

———. *A Sporting Time: New York City and the Rise of Modern Athletics, 1820–70.* Urbana: Univ. of Illinois Press, 1986.

Alexander, Michael. *Jazz Age Jews.* Princeton: Princeton Univ. Press, 2001.

———. "The Jewish Bookmaker: Gambling, Legitimacy, and the American Political Economy." In *Jews and the Sporting Life,* vol. 23 of *Studies in Contemporary Jewry,* ed. Ezra Mendelsohn, 54–69. New York: Oxford Univ. Press, 2008.

Allen, W. F. "Let's Go to the Races." *Missouri Historical Society Bulletin* 12 (Oct. 1955): 53–60.

Anderson, James D. *Making the American Thoroughbred, Especially in Tennessee, 1800–1845.* Norwood, MA: Plimpton, 1916.

Asbury, Herbert. *The Gangs of New York: An Informal History of the New York Underworld.* Garden City, NY: Doubleday, 1928.

———. *Gem of the Prairie: An Informal History of the Chicago Underworld.* New York: A. A. Knopf, 1940.

———. *Sucker's Progress: An Informal History of Gambling from the Colonies to Canfield.* New York: Dodd, Mead, 1938.

Asinof, Eliot. *Eight Men Out: The Black Sox and the 1919 World Series.* New York: Holt, Rinehart, and Winston, 1963.

Astor, Gerald. *The New York Cops: An Informal History.* New York: Scribner, 1971.

Aycock, Colleen, and Mark Scott. *Joe Gans: A Biography of the First African American World Boxing Champion.* Jefferson, NC: McFarland, 2008.

Baldwin, Leland D. *Pittsburgh: The Story of a City.* Pittsburgh: Univ. of Pittsburgh Press, 1937.

Bartels, Jon. *Saratoga Stories: Gangsters, Gamblers, and Racing Legends.* Lexington, KY: Blood-Horse Publications, 2007.

Bates, Anna. *Weeder in the Garden of the Lord: Anthony Comstock's Life and Career.* Lanham, MD: Univ. Press of America, 1995.

Becker, Carl. *History of Political Parties in the Province of New York, 1760–1776.* Madison: Univ. of Wisconsin Press, 1968.

Berman, Jay Stuart. *Police Administration and Progressive Reform: Theodore Roosevelt as Police Commissioner of New York.* Westport, CT: Greenwood Press, 1987.

Betts, John R. *America's Sporting Heritage, 1850–1950.* Reading, MA: Addison-Wesley, 1974.

———. "Mind and Body in Early American Thought." *Journal of American History* 54 (Mar. 1968): 787–805.

———. "The Technological Revolution and the Rise of Sport, 1850–1900." *Mississippi Valley Historical Review* 40 (Sept. 1953): 231–56.

Betts, Toney. *Across the Board.* New York: Citadel, 1956.

Black, David. *The King of Fifth Avenue: The Fortunes of August Belmont.* New York: Dial Press, 1981.

Block, Alan A. "Organized Crime: History and Historiography." In *Handbook of Organized Crime in the United States,* ed. Robert J. Kelly, Ko-Lin Chin, and Rufus Schatzberg, 39–74. Westport, CT: Greenwood Press, 1994.

Blood-Horse Publications. *Horse Racing's Top 100 Moments.* Lexington, KY: Blood-Horse Publications, 2006.

Bowen, Edward L. *The Jockey Club's Illustrated History of Thoroughbred Racing in America.* New York: Jockey Club, 1994.

Bowmar, Dan M., III. *Giants of the Turf: The Alexanders, the Belmonts, James R. Keene, and the Whitneys.* Lexington, KY: Blood-Horse Publications, 1960.

Bradley, Hugh. *Such Was Saratoga.* New York: Doubleday, Doran, 1940.

Brailsford, Dennis. *Sport and Society: Elizabeth to Anne.* Toronto: Univ. of Toronto Press, 1979.

Brands, H. W. *Andrew Jackson: His Life and Times.* New York: Doubleday, 2005.

Breen, Timothy. "Horses and Gentlemen: The Cultural Significance of Gambling among the Gentry of Early Virginia." *William and Mary Quarterly* 34, no. 2 (1977): 239–57.

Brenner, Teddy. *Only the Ring Was Square.* Englewood Cliffs, NJ: Prentice-Hall, 1981.

Bridenbaugh, Carl. *Cities in Revolt: Urban Life in America, 1743–1776.* 1955. Reprint, New York: Alfred A. Knopf, 1964.

———. *Cities in the Wilderness: Urban Life in America, 1625–1742.* New York: Ronald Press, 1938.

Bronner, Edward. "Village into Town, 1701–1746." In *Philadelphia: A 300-Year History,* ed. Russell F. Weigley, 33–67. New York: W. W. Norton, 1982.

Brooklyn Eagle. *Brooklyn by the "Brooklyn Eagle."* Brooklyn: Brooklyn Eagle, 1946.

Broun, Heywood, and Margaret Leech. *Anthony Comstock: Roundsman of the Lord.* New York: A. and C. Boni, 1927.

Brynn, Soren Steward. "Some Sports in Pittsburgh During the National Period, 1775–1860." *Western Pennsylvania Historical Magazine* 52 (Jan. 1969): 349–54.

Burrows, Edwin G., and Mike Wallace. *Gotham: A History of New York City to 1898.* New York: Oxford Univ. Press, 1999.

Butler, Richard J., and Joseph Driscoll. *Dock Walloper: The Story of "Big Dick" Butler.* New York: Putnam, 1928.

Cahn, Susan K. *Coming on Strong: Gender and Sexuality in Twentieth-Century Women's Sport.* New York: Free Press, 1994.

Carney, Gene. *Burying the Black Sox: How Baseball's Cover Up of the 1919 World Series Fix Almost Succeeded.* Washington, DC: Potomac Books, 2006.

Cayleff, Susan. *Babe: The Life and Legend of Babe Didrikson Zaharias.* Urbana: Univ. of Illinois Press, 1995.

Chafetz, Henry. *Play the Devil: A History of Gambling in the United States from 1492 to 1955.* New York: Bonanza Books, 1960.

Chudacoff, Howard P. *The Age of the Bachelor: Creating an American Subculture.* Princeton: Princeton Univ. Press, 1999.

Clapson, Mark. *A Bit of a Flutter: Popular Gambling and English Society, c. 1823–1961.* Manchester: Manchester Univ. Press, 1992.

Clarke, Donald H. *In the Reign of Rothstein.* New York: Vanguard, 1929.

"Club Sandwich: History of Club Sandwich." http://whatscookingamerica.net/History/Sandwiches/ClubSandwich.htm.

Cohen, Kenneth. "Well Calculated for the Farmer: Thoroughbreds in the Early National Chesapeake, 1790–1850." *Virginia Magazine of History and Biography* 115, no. 3 (2007): 370–411.

Cohen, Naomi W. *Jacob H. Schiff: A Study in American Jewish Leadership.* Hanover, NH: Univ. Press of New England for Brandeis Univ. Press, 1999.

Cohen, Stanley. *The Execution of Officer Becker: The Murder of a Gambler, the Trial of a Cop, and the Birth of Organized Crime.* New York: Carroll and Graf, 2006.

Connable, Alfred, and Edward Silberfarb. *Tigers of Tammany: Nine Men Who Ruled New York.* New York: Holt, Rinehart, and Winston, 1967.

Cross, Whitney R. *The Burned Over District: The Social and Intellectual History of Enthusiastic Religion in Western New York, 1800–1850.* New York: Harper and Row, 1965.

Cunningham, John T. "Games People Played: Sport in New Jersey History." *New Jersey History* 103 (Fall–Winter 1985): 1–32.

———. "Queen of the Turf." *New Jersey History* 96, nos. 1–2 (1978): 43–48.

Czitrom, Daniel. "Underworlds and Underdogs: Big Tim Sullivan and Metropolitan Politics in New York, 1889–1913." *Journal of American History* 78, no. 2 (1991): 536–58.

Danforth, Brian. "Hoboken and the Affluent New Yorker's Search for Recreation, 1820–1860." *New Jersey History* 95, no. 3 (1977): 133–44.

Dash, Mike. *Satan's Circus: Murder, Vice, Police Corruption, and New York's Trial of the Century.* New York: Crown, 2007.

Davidson, James West. "The New Narrative History: How Narrative?" *Reviews in American History* 12, no. 3 (1984): 322–34.

Di Brino, Nicholas. *History of the Morris Park Racecourse and the Morris Family.* Bronx: Andima Litho, 1977.

Dizikes, John. *Sportsmen and Gamesmen.* Boston: Houghton Mifflin, 1981.

———. *Yankee Doodle Dandy: The Life and Times of Tod Sloan.* New Haven: Yale Univ. Press, 2000.

Dulles, Foster Rhea. *A History of Recreation: America Learns to Play.* 2nd ed. Englewood Cliffs, NJ: Prentice-Hall, 1965.

Eberlein, Harold D., and Cortlandt Van Dyke Hubbard. *Portrait of a Colonial City: Philadelphia, 1670–1838.* Philadelphia: J. B. Lippincott, 1939.

Eisenberg, John. *The Great Match Race: When North Met South in America's First Sports Spectacle.* Boston: Houghton Mifflin, 2006.

Erie, Steven P. *Rainbow's End: Irish Americans and the Dilemmas of Urban Machine Politics, 1840–1885.* Berkeley and Los Angeles: Univ. of California Press, 1988.

Fabian, Ann. *Card Sharps, Dream Books, and Bucket Shops: Gambling in Nineteenth Century America.* Ithaca: Cornell Univ. Press, 1999.

Fetter, Henry D. *Taking on the Yankees: Winning and Losing in the Business of Baseball, 1903–2003.* New York: W. W. Norton, 2003.

Filler, Louis. *The Muckrakers: Crusaders for American Liberalism.* Chicago: H. Regnery, 1948.

Findlay, John M. *People of Chance: Gambling in American Society from Jamestown to Las Vegas.* New York: Oxford Univ. Press, 1986.

Fraser, Walter J., Jr. *Charleston! Charleston! The History of a Southern City.* Columbia: Univ. of South Carolina Press, 1989.

Fried, Albert. *The Rise and Fall of the Jewish Gangster in America.* New York: Holt, Rinehart, and Winston, 1980.

Fronc, Jennifer. *New York Undercover: Private Surveillance in the Progressive Era.* Chicago: Univ. of Chicago Press, 2009.

Frost, J. William. *The Quaker Family in Colonial America.* New York: St. Martin's Press, 1973.

Gabler, Edward. *The American Telegrapher: A Social History, 1860–1900.* New Brunswick: Rutgers Univ. Press, 1988.

Gado, Mark. "Killer Cop." *Crime Magazine: An Encyclopedia of Crime.* http://www.crime magazine.com/killercop.

Gilfoyle, Timothy. *A Pickpocket's Tale: The Underworld of Nineteenth-Century New York.* New York: W. W. Norton, 2006.

Ginsburg, Daniel E. *The Fix Is In: A History of Baseball Gambling and Game Fixing Scandals.* Jefferson, NC: McFarland, 1995.

Gittings, David S. *Maryland and the Thoroughbred.* Baltimore: Hoffmann Bros., 1932.

Gorn, Elliott. "'Good-bye Boys, I Die a True American': Homicide, Nativism, and Working-Class Culture in Antebellum New York City." *Journal of American History* 74, no. 2 (1987): 388–410.

———. *The Manly Art: Bare-Knuckle Prize Fighting in America.* Ithaca: Cornell Univ. Press, 1986.

Gosnell, Harold S. *Boss Platt and His New York Machine: A Study of the Political Leadership of Thomas C. Platt.* Chicago: Univ. of Chicago Press, 1971.

"The Great U.S. Match Race: Boston v. Fashion." *Turf Hallmarks.* http://www.tbheritage .com/TurfHallmarks/BostonvsFashion.html.

Grundy, Pamela. *Learning to Win: Sports, Education, and Social Change in Twentieth-Century North Carolina.* Chapel Hill: Univ. of North Carolina Press, 2001.

Gurock, Jeffrey. *When Harlem Was Jewish, 1870–1930.* New York: Columbia Univ. Press, 1979.

Hale, Ron. "Historic Races in New York." http://horseracing.about.com/library/blcarter .htm.

Haller, Mark H. "Bootleggers and American Gambling, 1920–1950." In *Gambling in America: Appendix,* ed. U.S. Commission on the Review of the National Policy Towards Gambling, 102–43. Washington, DC: Government Printing Office, 1976.

———. "The Changing Structure of American Gambling in the Twentieth Century." *Journal of Social Issues* 35, no. 3 (1979): 87–114.

———. "Illegal Enterprise: A Theoretical and Historical Interpretation." *Criminology* 28, no. 2 (1990): 207–36.

———. "Organized Crime in Urban Society: Chicago in the Twentieth Century." *Journal of Social History* 5, no. 2 (1971–72): 210–34.

———. "Policy Gambling: Entertainment and the Emergence of Black Politics, Chicago, from 1900 to 1940." *Journal of Social History* 24, no. 4 (1991): 719–39.

———. "The Rise of Urban Crime Syndicates, 1865–1905." Unpublished ms.

———. "Urban Crime and Criminal Justice: The Chicago Case." *Journal of American History* 57, no. 3 (1970): 619–35.

Haller, Mark H., and John V. Alviti. "Loansharking in American Cities: Historical Analysis of a Marginal Enterprise." *American Journal of Legal History* 21, no. 2 (1977): 125–56.

Hamilton, David A. E. "Horse Racing and New York Society, 1665–1830." Master's thesis, Queens Univ., 1990.

Hammack, David. *Power and Society: Greater New York at the Turn of the Century.* New York: Russell Sage Foundation, 1982.

Hardy, Stephen. *How Boston Played: Sport, Recreation, and Community, 1865–1915.* Boston: Northeastern Univ. Press, 1982.

Harlow, Alvin F. *Old Bowery Days: The Chronicle of a Famous Street.* New York: D. Appleton, 1931.

———. *Old Wires and New Waves: The History of the Telegraph, Telephone, and Wireless.* New York: D. Appleton, 1936.

Harmond, Richard. "Progress and Flight: An Interpretation of the American Cycle Craze of the 1890's." *Journal of Social History* 5 (1971–72): 235–57.

Heimer, Mel. *Fabulous Bawd: The Story of Saratoga.* New York: Holt, 1952.

Helberg, Barbara Anne. "Pari-Mutuel Betting Origins Wagering on the Horses Originated in France, Not England." http://horseracing.suite101.com/article.cfm/parimutuel _betting_origins.

"Heroes: Useful Daughter." *Time,* 2 Jan. 1939.

Hervey, John. *Racing in America, 1665–1865.* 2 vols. New York: Jockey Club, 1944.

———. *Racing in America, 1922–1936.* New York: Jockey Club, 1937.

Hillenbrand, Laura. *Seabiscuit: An American Legend.* New York: Random House, 2001.

Hirsch, Joe. *The First Century: "Daily Racing Form" Chronicles 100 Years of Thoroughbred Racing.* New York: Daily Racing Form Press, 1996.

Hirsch, Mark D. *William C. Whitney, Modern Warwick.* New York: Dodd, Mead, 1948.

"Historical Timeline of the New York State Legislature." http://www.senate.state.ny.us/sws/aboutsenate/timeline.html#1900.

"The History of Churchill Downs and the Kentucky Derby." http://www.derbypost.com/churchill1.html.

"History of the Telescope-Binocular." http://inventors.about.com/library/inventors/bltelescope.htm.

"History of Yonkers Raceway." http://www.yonkersraceway.com/general/history.html.

Hochfelder, David. "'Where the Common People Could Speculate': The Ticker, Bucket Shops, and the Origins of Popular Participation in Financial Markets, 1880–1920." *Journal of American History* 93 (Sept. 2006): 335–58.

Hogarty, Richard A. *Leon Abbett's New Jersey: The Emergence of the Modern Governor.* Philadelphia: American Philosophical Society, 2001.

———. "The Political Apprenticeship of Leon Abbett." *New Jersey History* 111, nos. 1–2 (1993): 1–42.

Holliman, Jennie. *American Sports (1785–1835).* Durham: Seaman's Press, 1931.

Hotaling, Edward. *The Great Black Jockeys: The Lives and Times of the Men Who Dominated America's First National Sport.* Rocklin, CA: Forum, 1999.

———. *They're Off! Horse Racing at Saratoga.* Syracuse: Syracuse Univ. Press, 1995.

Hovey, Elizabeth Bainum. "Stamping Out Smut: The Enforcement of Obscenity Laws, 1872–1915." PhD diss., Columbia Univ., 1998.

Huggins, Mike. *Flat Racing and British Society, 1790–1914: A Social and Economic History.* London: Frank Cass, 2000.

Hutchmacher, J. Joseph. *Senator Robert Wagner and the Rise of Urban Liberalism.* New York: Athenaeum, 1968.

Immerso, Michael. *Coney Island: The People's Playground.* New Brunswick: Rutgers Univ. Press, 2002.

Isaac, Rhys. *The Transformation of Virginia, 1740–1790.* Chapel Hill: Univ. of North Carolina Press, 1981.

Ives, Stephen, and Eve Morgenstern. *American Experience: Seabiscuit.* Arlington, VA: Insignia Films, 2007.

Jable, J. Thomas. "Pennsylvania's Early Blue Laws: A Quaker Experiment in the Suppression of Sport and Amusements, 1682–1740." *Journal of Sport History* 1 (Fall 1974): 107–21.

———. "The Pennsylvania Sunday Blue Laws of 1779: A View of Pennsylvania Society and Politics During the American Revolution." *Pennsylvania History* 38 (1976): 413–26.

Jarman, Rufus. "The Great Race Track Caper." *American Heritage* 19, no. 5 (1968): 24–27, 92–94.

Jeffers, H. Paul. *Commissioner Roosevelt: The Story of Theodore Roosevelt and the New York City Police, 1895–1897*. New York: John Wiley and Sons, 1994.

Jensen, Richard J. *The Winning of the Midwest: Social and Political Conflict*. Chicago: Univ. of Chicago Press, 1971.

Johnson, David R. *Policing the Urban Underworld: The Impact of Crime on the Development of the American Police, 1840–1887*. Philadelphia: Temple Univ. Press, 1979.

———. "Sinful Business: The Origins of Gambling Syndicates in the United States, 1840–1887." In *Police and Society*, ed. David H. Bayley, 17–47. Beverly Hills: Sage, 1977.

Johnson, Richard C. "Anthony Comstock: Reform, Vice, and the American Way." PhD diss., Univ. of Wisconsin, 1973.

Joselit, Jenna W. *Our Gang: Jewish Crime and the New York Jewish Community, 1900–1940*. Bloomington: Indiana Univ. Press, 1983.

Juergens, George. *Joseph Pulitzer and the "New York World."* Princeton: Princeton Univ. Press, 1966.

Kapsales, Maria. "From the Gilded Age to Progressivism: Brooklyn's Horse Race for Wealth." Master's thesis, City Univ., 1990.

Kasson, John F. *Amusing the Million: Coney Island at the Turn of the Century*. New York: Hill and Wang, 1978.

Katz, Irving. *August Belmont: A Political Biography*. New York: Columbia Univ. Press, 1968.

Keefe, Rose. *The Starker*. Nashville: Cumberland House, 2008.

Kelly, Joseph B. "At the Track: Thoroughbred Racing in Maryland, 1870–1973." *Maryland Historical Magazine* 89, no. 1 (1994): 63–87.

Kelly, Joseph J., Jr. *Pennsylvania: The Colonial Years, 1681–1776*. Garden City, NY: Doubleday, 1980.

Kendall, John S. *History of New Orleans*. Chicago: Lewis, 1922.

Keys, Barbara J. *Globalizing Sport: National Rivalry and International Community in the 1930s*. Cambridge: Harvard Univ. Press, 2006.

Kirsch, George B. *Baseball in Blue and Gray: The National Pastime During the Civil War*. Princeton: Princeton Univ. Press, 2003.

Kleppner, Paul. *The Cross of Culture: A Social Analysis of Midwestern Politics, 1850–1900*. New York: Free Press, 1970.

Kofoed, John C. *Brandy for Heroes: A Biography of the Honorable John Morrissey, Champion Heavyweight of America and State Senator*. New York: Dutton, 1938.

Kogan, Herman, and Lloyd Wendt. *Bet-a-Million! The Story of John W. Gates*. Indianapolis: Bobbs-Merrill, 1948.

Krantz, Nick. *Seabiscuit: America's Legendary Racehorse*. Los Angeles: Delta Entertainment, 2003.

Kroeger, Brooke. *Nellie Bly: Daredevil, Reporter, Feminist*. New York: Times Books, 1994.

Krout, John A. *Annals of American Sport*. New Haven: Yale Univ. Press, 1929.

Kupfer, Barbara Stern. "A Presidential Patron of the Sport of Kings: Andrew Jackson." *Tennessee Historical Quarterly* 29, no. 3 (1970): 243–55.

Kurland, Gerald. *Seth Low: The Reformer in an Urban and Industrial Age*. New York: Twayne, 1971.

LaMotta, Jake, and Pete Savage. *Raging Bull: My Story*. Englewood Cliffs, NJ: Prentice-Hall, 1970.

Land, Aubrey C. *Colonial Maryland: A History*. Millwood, NY: KTO Press, 1981.

Landesco, John. *Organized Crime in Chicago*. Pt. 3 of *Illinois Crime Survey, 1929*. 1929. Reprint, Chicago: Univ. of Chicago Press, 1968.

Lears, T. J. Jackson. *Something for Nothing: Luck in America*. New York: Viking, 2003.

Leslie, Anita. *The Remarkable Mr. Jerome*. New York: Holt, 1954.

Levine, Peter. *Ellis Island to Ebbets Field: Sport and the American Jewish Experience*. New York: Oxford Univ. Press, 1992.

Levy, Jonathan Ira. "Contemplating Delivery: Futures Trading and the Problem of Commodity Exchange in the United States, 1875–1905." *American Historical Review* 111 (Apr. 2006): 307–35.

Liebman, Bennett. "Horseracing in New York in the Progressive Era." *Gaming Law Review and Economics* 12, no. 6 (2008): 550–62.

Lindberg, Richard. *The Gambler King of Clark Street: Michael C. McDonald and the Rise of Chicago's Democratic Machine*. Carbondale: Southern Illinois Univ. Press, 2009.

Logan, Andy. *Against the Evidence: The Becker-Rosenthal Affair*. New York: McCall, 1970.

Longrigg, Roger. *The History of Horse Racing*. New York: Stein and Day, 1972.

Longstreet, Stephen. *Win or Lose: A Social History of Gambling in America*. Indianapolis: Bobbs-Merrill, 1977.

Lucas, John A. "Caspar Whitney." *Journal of Olympic History* 8, no. 2 (2000): 30–38.

Lucas, John A., and Ronald Smith. *The Saga of American Sport*. Philadelphia: Lea and Febiger, 1978.

Malcolmson, Robert W. *Popular Recreations in English Society, 1700–1850*. Cambridge: Cambridge Univ. Press, 1973.

Marcuse, Maxwell F. *This Was New York: A Nostalgic Picture of Gotham in the Gas Light Era*. Rev. ed. New York: LIM Press, 1969.

May, Allan. "The History of the Race Wire Service." Pt. 1, "Mont Tennes and the Birth of the Race Wire." *Crime Magazine: An Encyclopedia of Crime*. http://www.crimemagazine .com/history-race-wire-service.

"McAdoo, William (1853–1910)." http://www.infoplease.com/biography/us/congress/ mcadoo-william.html.

McCormick, Richard L. *From Realignment to Reform: Political Change in New York State, 1893–1910*. Ithaca: Cornell Univ. Press, 1981.

McGuire, Daniel W. "Governor Hughes and the Race Track Gambling Issue: The Special Election of 1908." *Niagara Frontier* 18, no. 4 (1971): 66–72.

McKibbin, Ross. "Working-Class Gambling in Britain, 1880–1939." *Past and Present* 82 (Feb. 1979): 147–78.

McSeveney, Samuel T. *The Politics of Depression: Political Behavior in the Northeast, 1893–1896*. New York: Oxford Univ. Press, 1972.

Menke, Frank. *The Story of Churchill Downs and the Kentucky Derby.* New York: Allied, 1940.

Miles, Edwin A. "President Adams' Billiard Table." *New England Quarterly* 45, no. 1 (1972): 31–43.

Moore, Glenn. "Pittsburgh Phil for a Day: Racetrack Gambling in the United States at the Turn of the Century." *International Journal of the History of Sport* 9, no. 1 (1992): 111–18.

Morris, Lloyd. *Incredible New York: High Life and Low Life of the Last One Hundred Years.* New York: Bonanza Books, 1951.

Myers, Gustavus. *History of Tammany Hall.* 2nd ed. New York: Boni and Liveright, 1917.

Nash, Gary B. *The Urban Crucible: Social Change, Political Consciousness, and the Origins of the American Revolution.* Cambridge: Harvard Univ. Press, 1979.

Nathan, Daniel A. *Saying It's So: A Cultural History of the Black Sox Scandal.* Urbana: Univ. of Illinois Press, 2003.

Nelli, Humbert. *The Business of Crime: Italians and Syndicate Crime in the United States.* Chicago: Univ. of Chicago Press, 1976.

New York City Department of Parks. "Jerome Park." http://www.nycgovparks.org/sub _your_park/historical_signs/hs_historical_sign.php?id=11042.

New York Racing Association. "Media Guide, 2009." http://www.nyra.com/Aqueduct/ mediaguide/09MG_History_Section.pdf.

"New York State Racetracks." http://www.nybreds.com/racing/trackhistory.html.

Norris, Walter B. *Annapolis: Its Colonial and Naval Story.* New York: Thomas Y. Crowell, 1925.

O'Connor, Richard. *Courtroom Warrior: The Combative Career of William Travers Jerome.* Boston: Little, Brown, 1963.

O'Hare, John Richard. *The Socio-economic Aspects of Horse Racing.* Washington, DC: Catholic Univ. of America Press, 1945.

Oriard, Michael. *King Football: Sport and Spectacle in the Golden Age of Radio and Newsreels, Movies and Magazines, the Weekly and the Daily Press.* Chapel Hill: Univ. of North Carolina Press, 2001.

———. *Reading Football: Sport, Popular Journalism, and American Culture, 1876–1913.* Chapel Hill: Univ. of North Carolina Press, 1993.

Perkins, Dexter. *Charles Evans Hughes and American Democratic Statesmanship.* Boston: Little, Brown, 1956.

Peterson, Virgil W. *Barbarians in Our Midst: A History of Chicago Crime and Politics.* Boston: Little, Brown, 1952.

"Peytona." http://www.tbheritage.com/Portraits/Peytona.html.

Pietrusza, David. *Rothstein: The Life, Times, and Murder of the Criminal Genius Who Fixed the 1919 World Series.* New York: Carroll and Graf, 2003.

Pilat, Oliver Ramsay, and Jo Ranson. *Sodom by the Sea: An Affectionate History of Coney Island.* Garden City, NY: Doubleday, Doran, 1941.

Pink, Louis Heaton. *Gaynor, the Tammany Mayor Who Swallowed the Tiger: Lawyer, Judge, Philosopher.* 1931. Reprint, Freeport, NY: International Press, 1970.

Postal, Bernard, Jesse Silver, and Roy Silver. *Encyclopedia of Jews in Sports.* New York: Bloch, 1965.

Procter, Ben H. *William Randolph Hearst: The Early Years, 1863–1910.* New York: Oxford Univ. Press, 1998.

Pusey, Merlo J. *Charles Evans Hughes.* New York: Macmillan, 1951.

Rader, Benjamin G. *American Sports: From the Age of Folk Games to the Age of Televised Sports.* 6th ed. Upper Saddle River, NJ: Pearson/Prentice-Hall, 2009.

Reisler, Jim. *Before They Were the Bombers: The New York Yankees' Early Years, 1903–1915.* Jefferson, NC: McFarland, 2002.

Renner, James. "C. K. G. Billings." http://hhoc.org/hist/billings.htm.

Reynolds, John F. *Testing Democracy: Electoral Behavior and Progressive Reform in New Jersey, 1880–1920.* Chapel Hill: Univ. of North Carolina Press, 1988.

Reynolds, Louise. *Russia at Play: Leisure Activities at the End of the Tsarist Era.* Ithaca: Cornell Univ. Press, 2003.

Richardson, James F. *The New York Police, Colonial Times to 1901.* New York: Oxford Univ. Press, 1970.

Riess, Steven A. *City Games: The Evolution of American Urban Society and the Rise of Sports.* Urbana: Univ. of Illinois Press, 1989.

———. "The Demise of Horse Racing and Boxing in Chicago in 1905." In *Sports in Chicago,* ed. Elliott Gorn, 43–61. Urbana: Univ. of Illinois Press, 2008.

———. "Horse Racing in Chicago: The Interplay of Class, Politics, and Organized Crime." In *The Chicago Sports Reader: 100 Years of Sports in the Windy City,* ed. Steven A. Riess and Gerald Gems, 60–81. Urbana: Univ. of Illinois Press, 2009.

———. "In the Ring and Out: Professional Boxing in New York, 1896–1920." In *Sport in America: New Historical Perspectives,* ed. Donald A. Spivey, 95–128. Westport, CT: Greenwood Press, 1985.

———. "Only the Ring Was Square: Frankie Carbo and the Underworld Control of American Boxing." *International Journal of the History of Sport* 5 (May 1988): 29–52.

———. *Sport in Industrial America.* Wheeling, IL: Harlan Davidson, 1995.

———. "Sports and Machine Politics in New York City, 1890–1920." In *The Making of Urban America,* ed. Raymond A. Mohl, 99–121. Wilmington, DE: Scholarly Resources, 1988.

———. *Touching Base: Professional Baseball and American Culture in the Progressive Era.* Rev. ed. Urbana: Univ. of Illinois Press, 1999.

Robb, Alexander M. "Racing as a Business." In *Thoroughbred Racing and Breeding: The Story of the Sport and Background of the Horse Industry,* ed. Tom R. Underwood, 21–29. New York: Coward-McCann, 1948.

Roberts, Randy. *Papa Jack: Jack Johnson and the Era of White Hopes.* New York: Free Press, 1985.

Robertson, Darrel M. *The Chicago Revival, 1876: Society and Revivalism in a Nineteenth-Century City.* Metuchen, NJ: Scarecrow, 1989.

Robertson, William H. P. *The History of Thoroughbred Racing in America.* Englewood Cliffs, NJ: Bonanza Books, 1964.

Rockaway, Robert A. *But He Was Good to His Mother: The Lives and Crimes of Jewish Gangsters.* Jerusalem: Gefen, 1993.

"Rockingham Park: New England's First and Finest Track." http://www.rockinghampark .com/history.html.

Rogers, George C., Jr. *Charleston in the Age of the Pinckneys.* Norman: Univ. of Oklahoma Press, 1969.

Root, Jonathan. *One Night in July: The True Story of the Rosenthal-Becker Murder Case.* New York: Coward-McCann, 1961.

Ross, Gary, and Jane Sindell. *Seabiscuit.* Universal City, CA: Universal Pictures/Dreamworks, 2003.

Rovere, Richard H. *Howe and Hummel: Their True and Scandalous History.* New York: Farrar, Straus, and Giroux, 1947.

Sammons, Jeffrey T. *Beyond the Ring: The Role of Boxing in American Society.* Urbana: Univ. of Illinois Press, 1988.

"Sanford, John." *Biographical Directory of the United States Congress.* http://bioguide.congress .gov/scripts/biodisplay.pl?index=S000047.

Sasuly, Richard. *Bookies and Bettors: Two Hundred Years of Gambling.* New York: Holt, Rinehart, and Winston, 1982.

Savell, Isabelle K. *Politics in the Gilded Age in New York State and Rockland County: A Biography of Senator Clarence Lexow.* New City: Historical Society of Rockland County, 1984.

Schroth, Raymond A. *The "Eagle" and Brooklyn: A Community Newspaper, 1841–1955.* Westport, CT: Greenwood Press, 1974.

Schwartz, David G. *Roll the Bones: The History of Gambling.* New York: Gotham, 2006.

Seymour, Harold. *American Baseball.* 3 vols. New York: Oxford Univ. Press, 1960–89.

Singleton, Esther. *Social New York under the Georges, 1714–76.* 1902. Reprint, Port Washington, NY: Friedman, 1969.

Smith, Mortimer. *William Jay Gaynor: Mayor of New York.* Chicago: Charles H. Regnery, 1951.

Smith, Ronald A. *Sports and Freedom: The Rise of Big-Time College Athletics.* New York: Oxford Univ. Press, 1988.

Solberg, Winton U. *Redeem the Time: The Puritan Sabbath in Early America.* Cambridge: Harvard Univ. Press, 1977.

Somers, Dale. *The Rise of Sports in New Orleans, 1850–1900.* Baton Rouge: Louisiana State Univ. Press, 1972.

Sparks, Randy J. "Gentleman's Sport: Horse Racing in Antebellum Charleston." *South Carolina Historical Magazine* 93, no. 1 (1992): 15–30.

Stanard, Mary N. *Colonial Virginia: Its People and Customs.* Philadelphia: J. B. Lippincott, 1917.

Standon, Jeffrey. "Coney Island: John McKane." http://www.westland.net/coneyisland/ articles/mckane.htm.

Sterngass, Jon. *First Resorts: Pursuing Pleasure at Saratoga Springs, Newport, and Coney Island.* Baltimore: Johns Hopkins Univ. Press, 2001.

Stoddard, Lothrop. *Master of Manhattan: The Life of Richard Croker.* New York: Longmans, Green, 1931.

Story, Duncan A. *The DeLanceys: A Romance of a Great Family.* London: T. Nelson, 1931.

Struna, Nancy L. "The Cultural Significance of Sport in the Colonial Chesapeake and Massachusetts." PhD diss., Univ. of Maryland, 1979.

———. "Gender and Sporting Practices in Early America, 1750–1810." *Journal of Sport History* 18, no. 1 (1991): 10–30.

———. "The North-South Races: American Thoroughbred Racing in Transition, 1823–1850." *Journal of Sport History* 8, no. 2 (1981): 28–57.

———. *People of Prowess: Sport, Leisure, and Labor in Early Anglo-America.* Urbana: Univ. of Illinois Press, 1996.

Swanberg, W. A. *Whitney Father, Whitney Heiress.* New York: Scribner, 1980.

Syrett, Harold C. *The City of Brooklyn, 1865–1898: A Political History.* New York: Columbia Univ. Press, 1944.

Thomas, Lately. *The Mayor Who Mastered New York: The Life and Opinions of William J. Gaynor.* New York: Morrow, 1969.

———. "Tammany Picked an Honest Man." *American Heritage* 18, no. 2 (1967): 34–39, 94–98.

Tinkcom, Harry M. "The Revolutionary City, 1765–1783." In *Philadelphia: A 300-Year History,* ed. Russell F. Weigley, 109–54. New York: W. W. Norton, 1982.

Tygiel, Jules. *Baseball's Great Experiment: Jackie Robinson and His Legacy.* New York: Oxford Univ. Press, 1983.

Underwood, Tom R., ed. *Thoroughbred Racing and Breeding: The Story of the Sport and Background of the Horse Industry.* New York: Coward-McCann, 1945.

Vamplew, Wray. *The Turf: A Social and Economic History of Horse Racing.* London: Allen Lane, 1976.

Verbrugge, Martha. *Able-Bodied Womanhood: Personal Health and Social Change in Nineteenth-Century Boston.* New York: Oxford Univ. Press, 1988.

Vosburgh, Walter S. *Racing in America, 1866–1921.* New York: Jockey Club, 1922.

Wagner, Hans-Peter. *Puritan Attitudes Towards Recreation in Early Seventeenth Century New England, with Particular Consideration of Physical Recreation.* Frankfurt, Germany: Peter Lang, 1982.

Wainwright, Nicholas B. *Colonial Grandeur in Pennsylvania: The House and Furniture of General John Cadwallader.* Philadelphia: Historical Society of Philadelphia, 1964.

Ward, John William. *Andrew Jackson: Symbol for an Age.* New York: Oxford Univ. Press, 1955.

Waters, Gregory J. "Operating on the Border: A History of the Commercial Promotion, Moral Suppression, and State Regulation of the Thoroughbred Racing Industry in Windsor, Ontario, 1884–1936." Master's thesis, Univ. of Windsor, 1992.

Weiss, Harry B., and Grace M. Weiss. *Early Sports and Pastimes in New Jersey.* Trenton: Past Times Press, 1960.

Weiss, Nancy J. *Charles Francis Murphy, 1858–1924: Respectability and Responsibility in Tammany Politics.* Northampton, MA: Smith College, 1968.

Welch, Richard F. *King of the Bowery: Big Tim Sullivan, Tammany Hall, and New York City from the Gilded Age to the Progressive Era.* Madison, NJ: Fairleigh Dickinson Univ. Press, 2008.

Wellmann, Judith. *Grass Roots Reform in the Burned-Over District of Upstate New York: Religion, Abolition, and Democracy.* New York: Garland, 2000.

Wendt, Lloyd, and Herman Kogan. *Lords of the Levee: The Story of Bathhouse John and Hinky Dink.* Indianapolis: Bobbs-Merrill, 1943.

Werner, M. R. *Tammany Hall.* New York: Doubleday, Doran, 1928.

Wertenbaker, Thomas J. *Father Knickerbocker Rebels: New York City During the Revolution.* New York: C. Scribner's Sons, 1948.

———. *Norfolk: History of a Southern Port.* Durham: Duke Univ. Press, 1931.

Wesser, Robert F. *Charles Evans Hughes: Politics and Reform in New York, 1905–1910.* Ithaca: Cornell Univ. Press, 1966.

Whalen, Bernard, and Jon Whalen. "The Birth of the NYPD." http://www.nycop.com/Aug_00/The_Birth_of_the_NYPD/body_the_birth_of_the_nypd.html.

Writers' Program, New Jersey (Federal Writers' Project). *Entertaining a Nation: Career of Long Branch.* Long Branch, NJ: City of Long Branch, 1940.

Wyatt-Brown, Bertram. *Southern Honor: Ethics and Behavior in the Old South.* New York: Oxford Univ. Press, 1982.

Index